Elaine Showalter

The Vintage Book of

AMERICAN WOMEN WRITERS

Elaine Showalter, a professor emerita at Princeton University, is the author of numerous books, including the ground-breaking *A Literature of Their Own: British Women Novelists from Brontë to Lessing* and *A Jury of Her Peers: Celebrating American Women Writers from Anne Bradstreet to Annie Proulx.* A frequent radio and TV commentator in the United Kingdom, she has chaired the Man Booker International Prize jury and judged the National Book Awards and the Orange Prize. She divides her time between Washington, D.C., and London.

ALSO BY ELAINE SHOWALTER

A Literature of Their Own:
British Women Novelists from Brontë to Lessing

The Female Malady:
Women, Madness and English Culture, 1830–1980

Sexual Anarchy:
Gender and Culture at the Fin de Siècle

Sister's Choice:
Tradition and Change in American Women's Writing

Inventing Herself:
Claiming a Feminist Intellectual Heritage

Hystories:
Hysterical Epidemics and Modern Media

Teaching Literature

Faculty Towers:
The Academic Novel and Its Discontents

A Jury of Her Peers:
Celebrating American Women Writers
from Anne Bradstreet to Annie Proulx

The Vintage Book of

AMERICAN WOMEN WRITERS

The Vintage Book of

AMERICAN
WOMEN
WRITERS

EDITED AND WITH AN INTRODUCTION BY

Elaine Showalter

Vintage Books

A DIVISION OF RANDOM HOUSE, INC.

NEW YORK

FIRST VINTAGE BOOKS EDITION, JANUARY 2011

Copyright © 2011 by Elaine Showalter

All rights reserved. Published in the United States by Vintage Books,
a division of Random House, Inc., New York, and in Canada by
Random House of Canada Limited, Toronto.

Vintage and colophon are registered trademarks of Random House, Inc.

Owing to limitations of space, all acknowledgments for
permission to reprint previously published material
may be found at the end of the collection.

Library of Congress Cataloging-in-Publication Data
The vintage book of American women writers / edited and with
an introduction by Elaine Showalter.—1st Vintage Books ed.
p. cm.
ISBN 978-1-4000-3445-1 (pbk.)
1. American literature—Women authors. I. Showalter, Elaine.
PS508.W7V56 2011
810.8'09287—dc22
2010032691

Book design by Rebecca Aidlin

www.vintagebooks.com

Printed in the United States of America
10 9 8 7 6 5 4 3 2 1

Contents

Introduction

THE MOTHERS OF US ALL

Since they first began to appear in print over 350 years ago, American women writers have publicly insisted that they did not care about literary fame or immortality. Anne Bradstreet, whose book *The Tenth Muse Newly Sprung Up in America* was published in 1650, declared that she was contented with her humble domestic niche as a Puritan housewife and mother, and denied any interest in winning the laurel wreath or other poetic awards. If men did her the honor of reading her poems, she wrote, "Give thyme or parsley wreath, I ask no bays." In other words, Bradstreet was content to be the Poet Parsleyate, rather than the Poet Laureate, and her imagery of the kitchen of Parnassus would be echoed by many American women writers who came after her.

Hoping for fame seemed unfeminine and self-aggrandizing, and they denied that such ambition inspired them to write. Rather than admitting their own ambitions, promoting their own creativity, or claiming their place in their nation's literary history, the founding mothers of American literature were more likely to avoid publicity and to deprecate their own achievements. They published anonymously or under a pseudonym, and they wrote conflicted accounts of their own longings to write. Lydia Maria Child signed her first novel, *Hobomok* (1824), "By an American"; she had been warned "that no woman could expect to be regarded as a *lady* after she had written a book." Child ruefully noted in her diary that for Christmas her husband had given her a laurel wreath, but "the leaves . . . were not very abundant."

When reviews of their works were scanty or harsh, women writers suffered in silence. But American male writers were more forthright and enterprising. When *Leaves of Grass* received only a handful of horrified reviews, Walt Whitman reviewed it himself—anonymously—as a work of genius by a true "American bard." Meanwhile, his great contemporary, Emily Dickinson, steadfastly refused to publish more than a handful of her poems during her lifetime.

Yet American women writers also believed that they were fully equal to the challenge of creating an American literature for a new nation. Women's rights and women's writing were closely allied after the Declaration of Independence. In 1792, Judith Sargent Murray wrote that women "were equally susceptible of literary acquirement," and envisaged herself "supplying the American stage with American scenes." Child and her generation of writers dedicated themselves to a literature of their "native land." They shared common themes as well as individual genius. From the beginning, they wrote with sympathy about the outcast, the slave, the Native American, the madwoman. They wrote about the trials and triumphs of the creative woman. They wrote dark fables about marriage. Over the centuries, they wrote both directly and figuratively about female experience and female sexuality, from abortion to menopause. They were fascinated by the images of the circus, the carnival, and the freak in relation to the situation of the odd woman and the artist. But they also wrote about male experience and, from a masculine perspective, about cowboys, ranchers, soldiers, boxers, and killers. The range of women's writing is much wider in subject and style than is generally supposed.

However, even when they were praised and celebrated in their own day, whether as bestsellers like Harriet Beecher Stowe or Nobel Prize–winners like Pearl Buck, American women writers have tended to disappear from literary history and national memory. I explore the multiple reasons for this phenomenon in my book, *A Jury of Her Peers: American Women Writers from Anne Bradstreet to Annie Proulx*. But the main reason women do not figure in American literary history is because they have not been the ones to write it. And in the twenty-first century, we need historical chronology, literary contexts, and the sense of continuity as steps toward doing the fullest justice to American women's writing. We need a sense of chronology to see how women writers fit on the literary timeline of American literature, to understand them as belonging to and affecting literary traditions, and not simply as isolated and exceptional women who popped up from time to time. We need to see women writers in context, placed in relation to their contemporaries and their precursors. Finally, we need a canon of outstanding women writers over the past four centuries both to organize their history and to begin the arguments that keep literary discussion alive.

I intend this anthology both as a companion to *A Jury of Her Peers*, making available works by important American women writers from 1650 to the present; and also as a portable and readable introduction to the literary mothers of us all. Obviously it cannot claim to be comprehensive. I have had to leave out many great women novelists because of limitations of space, and some contemporary writers because of the expense of copyright permission. But *The Vintage Book of American Women Writers* is a collection of wonderful stories, essays, fables, and poems by a remarkable group of writers who have shaped our literary heritage.

The Vintage Book of

AMERICAN WOMEN WRITERS

Anne Bradstreet
(ca. 1612–1672)

nne Bradstreet was the first American writer to attempt to create new words for a new world. She had been raised in a prosperous English Puritan family, tutored by her father in Greek, Latin, French, and Hebrew, and by the age of sixteen already thought of herself as a poet. The same year, she married Simon Bradstreet and set sail for the Massachusetts Bay Colony in 1628 aboard the famous flagship *Arbella*. Bradstreet kept writing; from 1638 to 1648, she wrote over six thousand lines of poetry, an astonishing rate of production, more than most English poets at the time ever composed. Noting her anomalous position as a woman writer, and using witty domestic imagery, Bradstreet's early poems were nonetheless based on classical and European sources and historical themes. Her first book, *The Tenth Muse Lately Sprung Up in America*, was published in London in 1650, with the approval and sponsorship of the men of Plymouth plantation. For the rest of her life, Bradstreet wrote much more personally about her own life in the harsh and dangerous colonial environment, and her own experiences as the mother of eight children, including pregnancy and maternity, empty-nest syndrome, the death of three of her grandchildren, and the destruction of her home by fire. The second edition of her book, published in 1678, six years after her death, contained several new poems that were intimate, honest, and direct, among them "To My Dear and Loving Husband."

The Prologue *(1650)*

I.

To sing of wars, of captains, and of kings,
Of cities founded, commonwealths begun,
For my mean pen are too superior things:
Or how they all, or each their dates have run,
Let poets and historians set these forth,
My obscure lines shall not so dim their worth.

2.

But when my wondering eyes and envious heart
Great Bartas' sugared lines do but read o'er,
Fool, I do grudge the Muses did not part
'Twixt him and me, that overfluent store;
A Bartas can do what a Bartas will,
But simple I, according to my skill.

3.

From school-boy's tongue, no Rhetoric we expect,
Nor yet a sweet consort from broken strings,
Nor perfect beauty, where's a main defect:
My foolish, broken, blemished Muse so sings;
And this to mend, alas, no art is able,
'Cause Nature made it so irreparable.

4.

Nor can I, like that fluent, sweet tongued Greek,
Who lisped at first, in future times speak plain.
By art, he gladly found what he did seek,
A full requital of his striving pain:
Art can do much, but this maxim's most sure:
A weak or wounded brain admits no cure.

5.

I am obnoxious to each carping tongue
Who says my hand a needle better fits,
A poet's pen, all scorn I should thus wrong,
For such despite they cast on female wits:
If what I do prove well, it won't advance,
They'll say it's stolen, or else it was by chance.

6.

But sure the antique Greeks were far more mild,
Else of our sex why feigned they those nine,
And poesy made Calliope's own child,
So 'mongst the rest, they placed the arts divine:

But this weak knot they will full soon untie,
The Greeks did nought but play the fool and lie.

7.

Let Greeks be Greeks, and women what they are,
Men have precedency, and still excel.
It is but vain unjustly to wage war;
Men can do best, and women know it well;
Preeminence in all and each is yours;
Yet grant some small acknowledgement of ours.

8.

And oh, ye high flown quills that soar the skies,
And ever with your prey, still catch your praise,
If e'er you deign these lowly lines your eyes,
Give thyme or parsley wreath, I ask no bays;
This mean and unrefinèd ore of mine
Will make your glistering gold but more to shine.

The Author to Her Book (1650)

Thou ill-formed offspring of my feeble brain,
Who after birth did'st by my side remain,
Till snatched from thence by friends, less wise than true,
Who thee abroad, exposed to public view,
Made thee in rags, halting to th' press to trudge,
Where errors were not lessened (all may judge).
At thy return my blushing was not small,
My rambling brat (in print) should mother call,
I cast thee by as one unfit for light,
Thy visage was so irksome in my sight;
Yet being mine own, at length affection would
Thy blemishes amend, if so I could:
I washed thy face, but more defects I saw,
And rubbing off a spot, still made a flaw.
I stretched thy joints to make thee even feet,
Yet still thou run'st more hobbling than is meet;

In better dress to trim thee was my mind,
But nought save homespun cloth, i' th' house I find.
In this array, 'mongst vulgars mayst thou roam,
In critics' hands, beware thou dost not come;
And take thy way where yet thou art not known;
If for thy Father asked, say thou hadst none:
And for thy mother, she alas is poor,
Which caused her thus to send thee out of door.

In Reference to Her Children, 23 June, 1659 (1678)

I had eight birds hatched in one nest,
Four cocks there were, and hens the rest.
I nursed them up with pain and care,
Nor cost, nor labor did I spare,
Till at the last they felt their wing,
Mounted the trees, and learned to sing;
Chief of the brood then took his flight
To regions far and left me quite.
My mournful chirps I after send,
Till he return, or I do end:
Leave not thy nest, thy dam and sire,
Fly back and sing amidst this choir.
My second bird did take her flight,
And with her mate flew out of sight;
Southward they both their course did bend,
And seasons twain they there did spend,
Till after blown by southern gales,
They norward steered with filled sails.
A prettier bird was no where seen,
Along the beach among the treen.
I have a third of color white,
On whom I placed no small delight;
Coupled with mate loving and true,
Hath also bid her dam adieu;
And where Aurora first appears,
She now hath perched to spend her years.
One to the academy flew

To chat among that learned crew;
Ambition moves still in his breast
That he might chant above the rest,
Striving for more than to do well,
That nightingales he might excel.
My fifth, whose down is yet scarce gone,
Is 'mongst the shrubs and bushes flown,
And as his wings increase in strength,
On higher boughs he'll perch at length.
My other three still with me nest,
Until they're grown, then as the rest,
Or here or there they'll take their flight,
As is ordained, so shall they light.
If birds could weep, then would my tears
Let others know what are my fears
Lest this my brood some harm should catch,
And be surprised for want of watch,
Whilst pecking corn and void of care,
They fall un'wares in fowler's snare,
Or whilst on trees they sit and sing,
Some untoward boy at them do fling,
Or whilst allured with bell and glass,
The net be spread, and caught, alas.
Or lest by lime-twigs they be foiled,
Or by some greedy hawks be spoiled.
O would my young, ye saw my breast,
And knew what thoughts there sadly rest,
Great was my pain when I you bred,
Great was my care when I you fed,
Long did I keep you soft and warm,
And with my wings kept off all harm,
My cares are more and fears than ever,
My throbs such now as 'fore were never.
Alas, my birds, you wisdom want,
Of perils you are ignorant;
Oft times in grass, on trees, in flight,
Sore accidents on you may light.
O to your safety have an eye,
So happy may you live and die.
Meanwhile my days in tunes I'll spend,

Till my weak lays with me shall end.
In shady woods I'll sit and sing,
And things that past to mind I'll bring.
Once young and pleasant, as are you,
But former toys (no joys) adieu.
My age I will not once lament,
But sing, my time so near is spent.
And from the top bough take my flight
Into a country beyond sight,
Where old ones instantly grow young,
And there with seraphims set song;
No seasons cold, nor storms they see;
But spring lasts to eternity.
When each of you shall in your nest
Among your young ones take your rest,
In chirping language, oft them tell,
You had a dam that loved you well,
That did what could be done for young,
And nursed you up till you were strong,
And 'fore she once would let you fly,
She showed you joy and misery;
Taught what was good, and what was ill,
What would save life, and what would kill.
Thus gone, amongst you I may live,
And dead, yet speak, and counsel give:
Farewell, my birds, farewell adieu,
I happy am, if well with you.

Here Follows Some Verses upon the Burning of Our House, July 10th, 1666 (1667)

In silent night when rest I took
For sorrow near I did not look
I wakened was with thund'ring noise
And piteous shrieks of dreadful voice.
That fearful sound of "Fire!" and "Fire!"
Let no man know is my Desire.
I, starting up, the light did spy,

And to my God my heart did cry
To strengthen me in my distress
And not to leave me succorless.
Then, coming out, beheld a space
The flame consume my dwelling place.
And when I could no longer look,
I blest His name that gave and took,
That laid my goods now in the dust.
Yea, so it was, and so 'twas just.
It was His own; it was not mine.
Far be it that I should repine;
He might of all justly bereft
But yet sufficient for us left.
When by the ruins oft I past
My sorrowing eyes aside did cast,
And here and there the places spy
Where oft I sat and long did lie:
Here stood that trunk, and there that chest,
There lay that store I counted best.
My pleasant things in ashes lie,
And them behold no more shall I.
Under thy roof no guest shall sit,
Nor at thy table eat a bit.
No pleasant talk shall e'er be told,
Nor things recounted done of old.
No candle e'er shall shine in thee,
Nor bridegroom's voice e'er heard shall be.
In silence ever shall thou lie.
Adieu, Adieu, all's vanity.
Then straight I 'gin my heart to chide:
And did thy wealth on earth abide?
Didst fix thy hope on mold'ring dust?
The arm of flesh didst make thy trust?
Raise up thy thoughts above the sky
That dunghill mists away may fly.
Thou hast a house on high erect,
Framed by that mighty Architect,
With glory richly furnished,
Stands permanent though this be fled.
It's purchaséd and paid for too

By Him who hath enough to do.
A price so vast as is unknown,
Yet by His gift is made thine own;
There's wealth enough, I need no more,
Farewell, my pelf, farewell, my store.
The world no longer let me love,
My hope and Treasure lies above.

To My Dear and Loving Husband (1678)

If ever two were one, then surely we.
If ever man were loved by wife, then thee;
If ever wife was happy in a man,
Compare with me, ye women, if you can.
I prize thy love more than whole mines of gold,
Or all the riches that the East doth hold.
My love is such that rivers cannot quench,
Nor ought but love from thee, give recompence.
Thy love is such I can no way repay,
The heavens reward thee manifold, I pray.
Then while we love, in love let's so persevere,
That when we live no more, we may live ever.

Mary Rowlandson
(1637–1711)

Puritan settler and the wife of a prominent pastor in western Massachusetts, Mary White Rowlandson was taken captive along with her children by Narragansett Indians in 1676. Rowlandson's account of her six-week trek across Massachusetts, first published in 1682, became a bestseller in America and England. Her captivity narrative dramatized the confrontation between races and cultures in the colonies, and was the precursor of the American novel. A writer of great natural gifts and strong descriptive powers, Rowlandson was compelled to write about her traumatic experience but never published anything else.

A Narrative of the Captivity and Restoration of Mrs. Mary Rowlandson (1682)

> *The sovereignty and goodness of GOD, together with the faithfulness of his promises displayed, being a narrative of the captivity and restoration of Mrs. Mary Rowlandson, commended by her, to all that desires to know the Lord's doings to, and dealings with her. Especially to her dear children and relations. The second Addition [sic] Corrected and amended. Written by her own hand for her private use, and now made public at the earnest desire of some friends, and for the benefit of the afflicted. Deut. 32.39.* See now that I, even I am he, and there is no god with me, I kill and I make alive, I wound and I heal, neither is there any can deliver out of my hand.

On the tenth of *February*, 1675, came the *Indians* with great numbers upon Lancaster. Their first coming was about Sun-rising. Hearing the noise of some Guns, we looked out; several Houses were burning, and the Smoke ascending to Heaven. There were five Persons taken in one House, the Father, and the Mother and a sucking Child, they knock'd on the head; the other two they took and carried away alive. There were two others, who being out of their Garrison upon some occasion were set upon; one was knock'd on the head, the other escaped. Another there was who running along was shot and wounded, and fell down; he begged of them his Life, promising them Money (as they told me); but they would not hearken to him, but knock'd him in head, stripped him naked, and split open his Bowels. Another, seeing many of the *Indians* about his Barn, ventured and went out, but was quickly shot down. There were three others belonging to the same Garrison who were killed. The *Indians* getting up upon the Roof of the Barn, had advantage to shoot down upon them over their Fortification. Thus these murderous Wretches went on, burning and destroying before them.

At length they came and beset our own House, and quickly it was the dolefullest day that ever mine eyes saw. The House stood upon the edge of a Hill; some of the *Indians* got behind the Hill, others into the Barn, and others behind anything that would shelter them: from all which Places they shot against the House, so that the Bullets seemed to fly like Hail: and quickly they wounded one Man among us, then another, and then a third. About two Hours (according to my observation in that amazing time) they had been about the House, before they could prevail to fire it (which they did with Flax and Hemp which they brought out of the Barn, and there being no Defense about the House, onely two Flankers, at two opposite Corners, and one of them not finished.) They fired it once, and one ventured out and quenched it; but they quickly fired it again, and that took. Now is the dreadful Hour come, that I have often heard of, (in time of War, as it was the Case of others) but now mine Eyes see it. Some in our House were fighting for their Lives, others wallowing in their Blood; the house on fire over our Heads, and the bloody Heathen ready to knock us on the Head if we stirred out. Now might we hear Mothers and Children crying out for themselves, and one another, *Lord, what shall we do!* Then I took my Children (and one of my Sisters, hers) to go forth and leave the House: but as soon as we came to the Door and appeared, the *Indians* shot so thick; that the Bullets ratled against the House, as if one had taken an handful of Stones and threw them; so that we were fain to give back. We had six stout Dogs belonging to our Garrison, but none of them would stir, though another time, if an *Indian* had come to the Door, they were ready to fly upon him, and tear him down. The Lord hereby would make us the more to acknowledge his Hand, and to see that our Help is always in him. But out we must go, the Fire increasing, and coming along behind us roaring, and the *Indians* gaping before us with their Guns, Spears, and Hatchets, to devour us. No sooner were we out of the House, but my Brother-in-Law (being before wounded (in defending the House) in or near the Throat) fell down dead, whereat the *Indians* scornfully shouted, and hallowed, and were presently upon him, stripping off his Clothes. The bullets flying thick, one went thorow my Side, and the same (as would seem) thorow the Bowels and Hand of my dear Child in my Arms. One of my elder Sisters Children, (named *William*) had then his Leg broken, which the *Indians* perceiving, they knock'd him on the head. Thus were we butchered by those merciless Heathen, standing amazed, with the Blood running down to our Heels. My eldest Sister being yet in the House, and seeing those woeful Sights, the Infidels haling Mothers one way, and Children another, and some wallowing in their Blood: and her elder son telling her that (her Son) *William* was dead, and my self was wounded; she said, And *Lord, let me die with them*: Which was no sooner said, but she was struck with a Bullet, and fell down dead over the Threshold. I hope she is reaping the Fruit of her good Labours, being faithful to the Service of God in her Place. In her younger years she lay under much trouble upon Spiritual accounts, till it pleased God to make that precious Scripture take hold of her Heart, 2 *Cor.* 12. 9. *And he said unto me, My grace is sufficient for thee.* More than twenty years after I have heard her tell, how sweet and comfortable that Place was to her. But to return: the *Indians* laid hold of us, pulling me one way, and the Children another, and said, *Come, go along with us*; I told them, they would kill me: They answered, *If I were willing to go along with them, they would not hurt me.*

O the doleful Sight that now was to behold at this House! *Come, behold the Works of the Lord, what desolation he has made in the Earth.* Of thirty seven Persons who were in this one House, none escaped either present Death, or a bitter Captivity, save onely one, who might say as he, *Job* 1. 15. *And I onely am escaped alone to tell the News.* There were twelve killed, some shot, some stabb'd with their Spears, some knock'd down with their Hatchets. When we are in prosperity, Oh the Little that we think of such dreadful Sights, and to see our dear Friends and Relations lie bleeding out their Heart-blood upon the Ground! There was one who was chopp'd into the Head with a Hatchet, and stripp'd naked, and yet was crawling up and down. It is a solemn Sight to see so many Christians lying in their Blood, some here, and some there, like a company of Sheep torn by Wolves. All of them stript naked by a company of hell-hounds, roaring, singing, ranting and insulting, as if they would have torn our very hearts out; yet the Lord by his Almighty power, preserved a number of us from death, for there were twenty four of us taken alive: and carried Captive.

I had often before this said, that if the *Indians* should come, I should chuse rather to be killed by them, than taken alive: but when it came to the trial my mind changed: their glittering Weapons so daunted my Spirit, that I chose rather to go along with those (as I may say) ravenous Bears, than that moment to end my daies. And that I may the better declare what happened to me during that grievous Captivity, I shall particularly speak of the several Removes we had up and down the Wilderness.

The First Remove

Now away we must go with those Barbarous Creatures, with our bodies wounded and bleeding, and our hearts no less than our bodies. About a mile we went that night, up upon a hill within sight of the Town where they intended to lodge. There was hard by a vacant house (deserted by the English before, for fear of the *Indians*). I asked them whether I might not lodge in the house that night? to which they answered, what, will you love *English-men* still? This was the dolefullest night that ever my eyes saw. Oh the roaring, and singing, and dancing, and yelling of those black creatures in the night, which made the place a lively resemblance of hell: And as miserable was the waste that was there made, of Horses, Cattle, Sheep, Swine, Calves, Lambs, Roasting Pigs, and Fowls (which they had plundered in the Town) some roasting, some lying and burning, and some boyling, to feed our merciless Enemies; who were joyful enough though we were disconsolate. To add to the dolefullness of the former day, and the dismalness of the present night, my thoughts ran upon my losses and sad bereaved condition. All was gone, my Husband gone (at least separated from me, he being in the Bay; and to add to my grief, the *Indians* told me they would kill him as he came homeward) my Children gone, my Relations and Friends gone, our house and home, and all our comforts within door, and without, all was gone (except my life) and I knew not but the next moment that might go too.

There remained nothing to me but one poor wounded Babe, and it seemed at present worse than death, that it was in such a pitiful condition, bespeaking Compassion, and I had no refreshing for it, nor suitable things to revive it. Little do many think, what is the savageness and brutishness of this barbarous Enemy! even those that seem to profess more than others among them, when the *English* have fallen into their hands.

Those seven that were killed at *Lancaster* the summer before upon a Sabbath day, and the one that was afterward killed upon a week day, were slain and mangled in a barbarous manner, by one-ey'd *John*, and *Marlber-*

ough's Praying *Indians*, which Capt. *Mosely* brought to *Boston*, as the *Indians* told me.

The Second Remove

But now (the next morning) I must turn my back upon the Town, and travel with them into the vast and desolate Wilderness, I knew not whither. It is not my tongue, or pen can express the sorrows of my heart, and bitterness of my spirit that I had at this departure: But God was with me, in a wonderful manner, carrying me along, and bearing up my Spirit, that it did not quite fail. One of the *Indians* carried my poor wounded babe upon a horse: it went moaning all along, I shall die, I shall die. I went on foot after it, with sorrow that cannot be exprest. At length I took it off the Horse, and carried it in my arms, till my strength failed, and I fell down with it. Then they set me upon a horse, with my wounded Child in my lap, and there being no Furniture upon the horse back; as we were going down a steep hill, we both fell over the horses head, at which they like inhumane creatures laught, and rejoiced to see it, though I thought we should there have ended our dayes, as overcome with so many difficulties. But the Lord renewed my strength still, and carried me along, that I might see more of his power, yea, so much that *I* could never have thought of, had *I* not experienced it.

After this it quickly began to Snow, and when night came on, they stopt: and now down I must sit in the Snow, (by a little fire, and a few boughs behind me) with my sick Child in my lap; and calling much for water, being now (thorough the wound) fallen into a violent Fever. (My own wound also growing so stiff, that I could scarce sit down or rise up) yet so it must be, that I must sit all this cold winter night, upon the cold snowy ground, with my sick Child in my arms, looking that every hour would be the last of its life; and having no Christian Friend near me, either to comfort or help me. Oh I may see the wonderful power of God, that my Spirit did not utterly sink under my affliction; still the Lord upheld me with his gracious and merciful Spirit, and we were both alive to see the light of the next morning.

The Third Remove

The morning being come, they prepared to go on their way: one of the *Indians* got up upon a horse, and they set me up behind him with my poor sick Babe in my lap. A very wearisome and tedious day I had of it;

what with my own wound, and my Childs being so exceeding sick, and in a lamentable Condition with her wound. It may easily be judged what a poor feeble condition we were in, there being not the least crumb of refreshing that came within either of our mouths, from Wednesday night to Saturday night, except only a little cold water. This day in the afternoon, about an hour by Sun, we came to the place where they intended, *viz.* an *Indian Town*, called *Wenimesset*, Northward of *Quabaug.* When we were come, Oh the number of *Pagans* (now merciless Enemies) that there came about me, that I may say as *David, Psal.* 27. 13. *I had fainted, unless I had believed, &c.* The next day was the Sabbath: I then remembered how careless I had been of Gods holy time: how many Sabbaths I had lost and mispent, and how evilly I had walked in Gods sight; which lay so close upon my spirit, that it was easie for me to see how righteous it was with God to cut off the threed of my life, and cast me out of his presence forever. Yet the Lord still shewed mercy to me, and upheld me; and as he wounded me with one hand, so he healed me with the other. This day there came to me one *Robert Pepper* (a Man belonging to *Roxbury,*) who was taken in Capt. *Beers* his fight; and had been now a considerable time with the *Indians*; and up with them almost as far as *Albany* to see King *Philip,* as he told me, and was now very lately come with them into these parts. Hearing I say that I was in this *Indian* town, he obtained leave to come and see me. He told me he himself was wounded in the Leg at Capt. *Beers* his fight; and was not able sometime to go, but as they carried him, and as he took oaken leaves and laid to his wound, and through the blessing of God, he was able to travel again. Then I took Oaken leaves and laid to my side, and with the blessing of God it cured me also; yet before the cure was wrought, I may say as it is in *Psal.* 38. 5, 6. *My wounds stink and are corrupt, I am troubled, I am bowed down greatly, I go mourning all the day long.* I sate much alone with a poor wounded Child in my lap, which moaned night and day, having nothing to revive the body, or cheer the Spirits of her: but instead of that, sometimes one *Indian* would come and tell me, one hour, and your Master will knock your Child in the head, and then a second, and then a third, your Master will quickly knock your child in the head.

This was the Comfort I had from them; miserable comforters are ye all, as he said. Thus nine days I sat upon my knees, with my Babe in my lap, till my flesh was raw again; my Child being even ready to depart this sorrowful world, they bad me carry it out, to another Wigwam: (I suppose because they would not be troubled with such spectacles.) Whither I went with a very heavy heart, and down I sate with the picture of death in my lap. About two hours in the Night, my sweet Babe like a Lamb departed this life, on *Feb.* 18, 1675. It being about six years and five months old. It was nine dayes (from the first wounding) in this Miserable condition, without any refreshing of one nature or other, except a little cold water. I cannot but take notice, how at another time I could not bear to be in the room where any dead person was, but now the case is changed: I must and could lye down by my dead Babe, side by side all the night after. I have thought since of the wonderful goodness of God to me, in preserving me in the use of my reason and senses, in that distressed time, that I did not use wicked and violent means to end my own miserable life. In the morning, when they understood that my Child was dead, they sent for me home to my Masters Wigwam: (by my Master in this writing, must be understood *Quannopin*, who was a Saggamore and married King *Philips* wives Sister; not that he first took me, but I was sold to him by another *Narrhaganset Indian*, who took me when first I came out of the Garrison) I went to take up my dead Child in my arms to carry it with me, but they bid me let it alone: there was no resisting, but go I must and leave it. When I had been a while at my Masters wigwam, I took the first opportunity I could get, to go look after my dead Child: When I came I asked them what they had done with it? they told me it was upon the hill: Then they went and shewed me where it was, where I saw the ground was newly digged, and there they told me they had buried it, there I left that child in the Wilderness, and must commit it, and my self also in this Wilderness condition, to him who is above all. God having taken away this dear Child, I went to see my daughter *Mary*, who was at this same *Indian Town*, at a Wigwam not very far off, though we had little liberty or opportunity to see one another: she was about ten years old, and taken from the door at first by a Praying *Indian*, and afterward sold for a gun. When I came in sight she would fall a weeping; at which they were provoked, and would not let me come near her, but bade me be gone: which was a heart-cutting word to me. I had one child dead, another in the wilderness, I knew not where, the third they would not let me come near to: *Me* (as he said) *have ye bereaved of my Children, Joseph is not, and Simeon is not, and ye will take Benjamin also, all these things are against me.* I could not sit still in this condition, but kept walking from one place to another. And as I was going along, my heart was even overwhelmed with the thoughts of my condition, and that I should have Children, and a Nation which I knew not ruled over them. Whereupon I earnestly intreated the Lord, that He would consider my low estate, and shew me a token for good, and if it were his blessed will, some sign and hope of some relief.

And indeed quickly the Lord answered, in some measure, my poor Prayer: For as I was going up and down mourning and lamenting my condition, my Son came to me, and asked me how *I* did? I had not seen him before, since the destruction of the Town: and *I* knew not where he was, till *I* was informed by himself, that he was amongst a smaller parcel of *Indians*, whose place was about six miles off, with tears in his eyes, he asked me whether his sister *Sarah* was dead? and told me he had seen his sister *Mary*; and prayed me, that *I* would not be troubled in reference to himself. The occasion of his coming to see me at this time was this: there was, as *I* said, about six miles from us, a small Plantation of *Indians*, where it seems he had been during his Captivity; and at this time, there were some Forces of the *Indians* gathered out of our company, and some also from them (among whom was my Sons Master) to go to assault and burn *Medfield*: in this time of the absence of his Master, his Dame brought him to see me. *I* took this to be some gracious Answer, to my earnest and unfeigned desire. The next day, *viz.* to this, the *Indians* returned from *Medfield*: (all the Company, for those that belonged to the other small company, came thorow the Town that now we were at). But before they came to us, Oh the outrageous roaring and hooping that there was! They began their din about a mile before they came to us. By their noise and hooping they signified how many they had destroyed: (which was at that time twenty three). Those that were with us at home, were gathered together as soon as they heard the hooping, and every time that the other went over their number, these at home gave a shout, that the very Earth rung again. And thus they continued till those that had been upon the expedition were come up to the Saggamores Wig wam; and then Oh, the hideous insulting and triumphing that there was over some *English-mens* Scalps, that they had taken (as their manner is) and brought with them. *I* cannot but take notice of the wonderful mercy of God to me in those afflictions, in sending me a Bible: One of the *Indians* that came from *Medfield* fight and had brought some plunder; came to me, and asked me, if I would have a Bible, he had got one in his Basket, I was glad of it, and asked him, whether he thought the *Indians* would let me read? He answered yes: so I took the Bible, and in that melancholly time, it came into my mind to read first the 28 *Chapter* of *Deuteronomie*, which I did, and when I had read it, my dark heart wrought on this manner, that there was no mercy for me, that the blessings were gone, and the curses come in their room, and that I had lost my opportunity. But the Lord helped me still to go on reading, till I came to *Chap.* 30, the seven first verses: where I found there was mercy promised again, if we would return to him by repentance: and though we were scattered from one end of the earth to the other, yet the Lord would gather us together, and turn all those curses upon our Enemies. I do not desire to live to forget this Scripture, and what comfort it was to me.

Now the *Indians* began to talk of removing from this place, some one way, and some another. There were now besides my self nine *English* captives in this place (all of them Children, except one Woman) I got an opportunity to go and take my leave of them; they being to go one way, and I another. I asked them whether they were earnest with God for deliverance; they all told me, they did as they were able; and it was some comfort to me, that the Lord stirred up Children to look to him. The woman, *viz.* Goodwife *Joslin* told me, she should never see me again, and that she could find in her heart to run away: I wished her not to run away by any means, for we were near thirty miles from any *English* town, and she very big with Child, and had but one week to reckon; and another Child, in her Arms, two years old, and bad rivers there were to go over, and we were feeble with our poor and coarse entertainment. I had my Bible with me, I pulled it out, and asked her, whether she would read; we opened the Bible, and lighted on *Psal.* 27. in which Psalm we especially took notice of that, *ver. ult. Wait on the Lord, be of good courage, and he shall strengthen thine Heart, wait I say on the Lord.*

The Fourth Remove

And now I must part with that little company I had. Here I parted from my daughter *Mary*, (whom I never saw again till I saw her in *Dorchester*, returned from Captivity), and from four little Cousins and Neighbors, some of which I never saw afterward: the Lord only knows the end of them. Amongst them also was that poor woman before mentioned, who came to a sad end, as some of the company told me in my travel: she having much grief upon her Spirit about her miserable condition, being so near her time, she would be often asking the *Indians* to let her go home; they not being willing to that, and yet vexed with her importunity, gathered a great company together about her, and stript her naked, and set her in the midst of them: and when they had sung and danced about her (in their hellish manner) as long as they pleased: they knocked her on head, and the child in her arms with her: when they had done that they made a fire and put them both into it: and told the other Children that were with them, that if they attempted to go home they would serve them in like manner: The Children said she did not shed one tear, but prayed all the while. But to return to my own Journey: we travelled about half a day or little more, and came to a desolate place in the

Wilderness; where there were no Wigwams or Inhabitants before: we came about the middle of the afternoon to this place; cold, and wet, and snowy, and hungry, and weary, and no refreshing (for man) but the cold ground to sit on, and our poor *Indian cheer.*

Heart-aching thoughts here I had about my poor children, who were scattered up and down among the wild Beasts of the Forest: My head was light and dizzy (either through hunger, or hard lodging, or trouble, or all together), my knees feeble, my body raw by sitting double night and day, that I cannot express to man the affliction that lay upon my spirit, but the Lord helped me at that time to express it to himself. I opened my Bible to read, and the Lord brought that precious Scripture to me, *Jer.* 31. 16. *Thus saith the Lord, refrain thy voice from weeping, and thine eyes from tears, for thy work shall be rewarded, and they shall come again from the land of the enemy.* This was a sweet Cordial to me when I was ready to faint; many and many a time have I sate down and wept sweetly over this Scripture. At this place we continued about four days.

The Fifth Remove

The occasion (as I thought) of their moving at this time, was, the English army, it being near and following them: For they went as if they had gone for their lives, for some considerable way; and then they made a stop, and chose out some of their stoutest men, and sent them back to hold the *English* army in play whilst the rest escaped. And then, like *Jehu,* they marched on furiously, with their old, and with their young: some carried their old decrepit Mothers, some carried one, and some another. Four of them carried a great *Indian* upon a Bier: but going through a thick Wood with him, they were hindered, and could make no haste; whereupon they took him upon their backs, and carried him, one at a time, till they came to *Bacquaug* River. Upon a Fryday a little after noon we came to this River. When all the Company was come up, and were gathered together, I thought to count the number of them, but they were so many, and being somewhat in motion, it was beyond my skill. In this Travel, because of my wound, I was somewhat favored in my load; I carried only my knitting-work and two quarts of parched meal: Being very faint I asked my Mistress to give me one spoonful of the Meal, but she would not give me a taste. They quickly fell to cutting dry trees, to make rafts to carry them over the River: and soon my turn came to go over: By the advantage of some brush which they had laid upon the Raft to sit on; I did not wet my foot, (which many of themselves at the other end were mid-leg-deep) which cannot but be acknowledged as a favor of God to my weakened body, it being a very cold time. I was not before acquainted with such kind of doings or dangers. *When thou passest through the waters I will be with thee, and through the rivers they shall not overflow thee Isai.* 43. 2. A certain number of us got over the river that night, but it was the night after the Sabbath before all the company was got over. On the Saturday they boiled an old Horses leg (which they had got) and so we drank of the broth; as soon as they thought it was ready, and when it was almost all gone, they filled it up again.

The first week of my being among them, I hardly ate any thing; the second week I found my stomach grow very faint for want of something; and yet 'twas very hard to get down their filthy trash: but the third week (though I could think how formerly my stomach would turn against this or that, and I could starve and die before I could eat such things, yet) they were pleasant and savory to my taste. I was at this time knitting a pair of white Cotton Stockins for my Mistriss: and I had not yet wrought upon the Sabbath day: when the Sabbath came they bad me go to work; I told them it was the Sabbath-day, and desired them to let me rest, and told them I would do as much more tomorrow; to which they answered me, they would break my face. And here I cannot but take notice of the strange providence of God in preserving the Heathen: They were many hundreds, old and young, some sick, and some lame; many had *Papooses* at their backs, the greatest number at this time with us were *Squaws*: and they traveled with all they had, bag and baggage, and yet they got over this River aforesaid: and on Monday they set their Wigwams on fire, and away they went: on that very day came the *English* army after them to this River, and saw the smoke of their Wigwams; and yet this River put a stop to them. God did not give them courage or activity to go over after us: we were not ready for so great a mercy as victory and deliverance: If we had been, God would have found out a way for the *English* to have passed this River, as well as for the *Indians* with their *Squaws* and *Children*, and all their *Luggage. Oh that my people had hearkened to me, and Israel had walked in my wayes, I should soon have subdued their enemies, and turned my hand against their adversaries, Psal.* 81. 13-14.

The Sixth Remove

On Monday (as I said) they set their Wigwams on fire and went away. It was a cold morning; and before us there was a great Brook with Ice on it: some waded through it, up to the knees and higher: but others went till they came to a Beaver-Dam, and I amongst them, where thorough the good providence of God, I did not wet my foot. I went along that day, mourning and lamenting, leaving farther my own Country, and travelling into a vast and howling Wilderness; and I understood something of *Lots* Wifes Temptation, when she looked back: We came that day to a great Swamp; by the side of which we took up our lodging that night. When I came to the brow of the hill, that looked toward the swamp, I thought we had been come to a great *Indian Town*, (though there were none but our own Company) the *Indians* were as thick as the Trees: it seemed as if there had been a thousand Hatchets going at once: if one looked before one, there was nothing but *Indians*, and behind one, nothing but *Indians*; and so on either hand: I my self in the midst, and no Christian Soul near me, and yet how hath the Lord preserved me in safety? Oh the experience that I have had of the goodness of God, to me and mine!

The Seventh Remove

After a restless and hungry night there, we had a wearisome time of it the next day. The Swamp by which we lay, was as it were, a deep Dungeon, and an exceeding high and steep hill before it. Before I got to the top of the hill, I thought my heart and legs, and all would have broken, and failed me. What, through faintness and soreness of Body, it was a grievous day of Travel to me. As we went along, I saw a place where *English* cattle had been: that was comfort to me, such as it was: quickly after that we came to an *English* path, which so took with me, that I thought I could have freely lyen down and died. That day, a little after noon, we came to *Squaukheag*, where the *Indians* quickly spread themselves over the deserted *English* fields, gleaning what they could find; some pickt up Ears of Wheat, that were crickled down; some found ears of *Indian Corn*; some found Ground-nuts, and others sheaves of Wheat that were frozen together in the Shock, and went to threshing of them out. My self got two Ears of *Indian Corn*, and whilst I did but turn my back, one of them was stollen from me, which much troubled me. There came an *Indian* to them at that time, with a basket of *Horse-liver*: I asked him to give me a piece: what (sayes he) can you eat Horse-liver? I told him, I would try, if he would give a piece; which he did: and I laid it on the coals to roast; but before it was half ready they got half of it away from me, so that I was fain to take the rest and eat it as it was with the blood about my mouth, and yet a savoury bit it was to me: For to the hungry Soul every bitter thing is sweet. A solemn sight methought it was, to see fields of Wheat and Indian corn forsaken and spoiled: and the remainders of them to be food for our merciless Enemies. That night we had a mess of Wheat for our supper.

The Eighth Remove

On the morrow morning we must go over the river, *i.e. Connecticut*, to meet with King *Philip*, two Cannoos full, they had carried over, the next turn I my self was to go; but as my foot was upon the Cannoo to step in, there was a sudden outcry among them, and I must step back: and instead of going over the River, I must go four or five miles up the River farther northward. Some of the *Indians* ran one way, and some another. The cause of this rout was as I thought their espying some *English* scouts, who were thereabout.

In this travel up the River about noon the Company made a stop, and sate down; some to eat, and others to rest them. As I sate amongst them, musing of things past, my son *Joseph* unexpectedly came to me: we asked of each others welfare; bemoaning our doleful condition, and the change that had come upon us: we had Husband and Father, and Children, and Sisters, and Friends and Relations, and House, and Home, and many Comforts of this life: but now we may say, as *Job, Naked came I out of my mothers womb, and naked shall I return, the Lord gave, the Lord hath taken away, blessed be the Name of the Lord.* I asked him whether he would read? He told me, he earnestly desired it. I gave him my Bible, and he lighted upon that comfortable Scripture, *Psal.* 118. 17-18. *I shall not die but live, and declare the works of the Lord: the Lord hath chastened me sore, yet he hath not given me over to death.* Look here *Mother* (sayes he) did you read this? And here I may take occasion to mention one principal ground of my setting forth these few Lines: even as the Psalmist sayes, To declare the works of the Lord, and his wonderful power in carrying us along, preserving us in the Wilderness, while under the Enemies hand, and returning of us in safety again. And his goodness in bringing to my hand so many comfortable and suitable Scriptures in my distress. But to return: We travelled on till night; and in the morning, we must go over the River to *Philips* Crew. When I was in the Cannoo, I could not but be amazed at the numerous Crew of Pagans that were on the Bank on the other side. When I came ashore, they gathered all about me, I sitting alone in the midst. I observed they asked one another Questions, and laughed, and rejoiced over their Gains and Victories. Then my heart began to fail: and I fell a weeping;

which was the first time to my remembrance, that I wept before them. Although I had met with so much Affliction, and my heart was many times ready to break, yet could I not shed one tear in their sight; but rather had been all this while in a maze, and like one astonished. But now I may say as *Psal.* 137. 1. *By the Rivers of* Babylon, *there we sate down, yea, we wept when we remembered Zion.* There one of them asked me why I wept; I could hardly tell what to say; yet I answered, they would kill me: No, said he, none will hurt you. Then came one of them, and gave me two spoonfuls of Meal (to comfort me) and another gave me half a pint of Pease; which was more worth than many Bushels at another time. Then I went to see King *Philip*; he bade me come in, and sit down, and asked me whether I would smoak it (a usual Complement now a days amongst Saints and Sinners) but this no way suited me. For though I had formerly used Tobacco, yet I had left it ever since I was first taken. *It seems to be a Bait the Devil lays to make men lose their precious time*: I remember with shame, how formerly, when I had taken two or three Pipes, I was presently ready for another, such a bewitching thing it is: But I thank God, he has now given me power over it; surely there are many who may be better employed than to lye sucking a stinking Tobacco-pipe.

Now the *Indians* gather their forces to go against *Northampton*: over night one went about yelling and hooting to give notice of the design. Whereupon they fell to boyling of Ground Nuts, and parching of Corn, (as many as had it) for their Provision: and in the morning away they went. During my abode in this place *Philip* spake to me to make a shirt for his Boy, which I did, for which he gave me a shilling; I offered the money to my Master, but he bade me keep it: and with it I bought a piece of Horse-flesh. Afterwards I made a Cap for his Boy, for which he invited me to Dinner: I went, and he gave me a Pancake, about as big as two fingers; it was made of parched Wheat, beaten and fryed in Bears-grease, but I thought I never tasted pleasanter meat in my life. There was a Squaw who spake to me to make a shirt for her Sannup, for which she gave me a piece of Bear. Another asked me to knit a pair of Stockins, for which she gave me a quart of Pease. I boyled my Pease and Bear together, and invited my Master and Mistress to Dinner: but the proud gossip, because I served them both in one Dish, would eat nothing, except one bit that he gave her upon the point of his Knife. Hearing that my Son was come to this place, I went to see him, and found him lying flat upon the ground: I asked him how he could sleep so? He answered me that he was not asleep, but at Prayer; and lay so, that they might not observe what he was doing. I pray God, he may remember these things now he is returned in safety. At this place (the Sun now getting higher) what with the beams and heat of the Sun, and the smoak of the Wigwams, I thought I should have been blind: I could scarce discern one Wigwam from another. There was here one *Mary Thurston* of *Medfield*, who seeing how it was with me, lent me a Hat to wear; but as soon as I was gone, the Squaw (who owned that *Mary Thurston*) came running after me, and got it away again. Here was the Squaw that gave me one spoonful of Meal. I put it in my Pocket to keep it safe: Yet notwithstanding, some body stole it, but put five *Indian* corns in the room of it: which Corns were the greatest Provisions I had in my travel for one day.

The *Indians* returning from North-hampton, brought with them some Horses and Sheep, and other things which they had taken; I desired them, that they would carry me to *Albany* upon one of those Horses, and sell me for Powder; for so they had sometimes discoursed. I was utterly hopeless of getting home on foot, the way that I came. I could hardly bear to think of the many weary steps I had taken, to come to this place.

The Ninth Remove

But instead of going either to *Albany* or homeward, we must go five miles up the River, and then go over it. Here we abode a while. Here lived a sorry *Indian*, who spake to me to make him a shirt, when I had done it, he would pay me nothing. But he living by the River side, where I often went to fetch water, I would often be putting him in mind, and calling for my pay: at last, he told me if I would make another shirt, for a Papoos not yet born, he would give me a knife, which he did when I had done it. I carried the knife in, and my master asked me to give it him, and I was not a little glad that I had any thing that they would accept of, and be pleased with. When we were at this place, my Masters Maid came home; she had been gone three weeks into the *Narrhagansett Country* to fetch Corn, where they had stored up some in the ground: she brought home about a peck and half of Corn. This was about the time that their great captain (*Naananto*) was killed in the Narrhagansett country.

My son being now about a mile from me, I asked liberty to go and see him, they bade me go, and away I went; but quickly lost myself, travelling over Hills and through Swamps, and could not find the way to him. And I cannot but admire at the wonderful power and goodness of God to me, in that though I was gone from home, and met with all sorts of *Indians*, and those I had no knowledge of, and there being no *Christian Soul* near me; yet not one of them offered the least imaginable miscarriage to me. I turned homeward again, and met with my Master; he shewed me the way to my Son. When I came to him I found him not well: and withal he had a Boyl on his side, which much troubled him: we bemoaned one another a while, as the Lord helped us, and then I returned again. When I was returned, I found myself as unsatisfied as I was before. I went up and down moaning and lamenting; and my spirit was ready to sink, with the thoughts of my poor Children: my Son was ill, and I could not but think of his mournful looks: and no *Christian Friend* was near him, to do any office of love for him, either for Soul or Body. And my poor Girl, I knew not where she was, nor whether she was sick, or well, or alive, or dead. I repaired under these thoughts to my Bible (my great comforter in that time) and that Scripture came to my hand, *Cast thy burden upon the Lord, and he shall sustain thee, Psal. 55. 22.*

But I was fain to go and look after something to satisfie my hunger: and going among the Wigwams, I went into one, and there found a Squaw who shewed her self very kind to me, and gave me a piece of Bear. I put it into my pocket, and came home; but could not find an opportunity to broil it, for fear they would get it from me, and there it lay all that day and night in my stinking pocket. In the morning I went to the same Squaw, who had a kettle of Ground-nuts boyling. I asked her to let me boyle my piece of Bear in her kettle, which she did, and gave me some Ground-nuts to eat with it, and I cannot but think how pleasant it was to me. I have sometime seen Bear baked very handsomly amongst the *English,* and some like it, but the thought that it was Bear, made me tremble: But now that was savoury to me that one would think was enough to turn the stomach of a bruit-Creature.

One bitter cold day I could find no room to sit down before the fire. I went out, and could not tell what to do, but I went in to another wig-wam, where they were also sitting round the fire, but the squaw laid a skin for me, and bid me sit down, and gave me some ground nuts, and bade me come again; and told me they would buy me, if they were able, and yet these were strangers to me that I never saw before.

The Tenth Remove

That day a small part of the Company removed about three quarters of a mile, intending farther the next day. When they came to the place where they intended to lodge, and had pitched their Wigwams; being hungry, I went again back to the place we were before at, to get something to eat: being encouraged by the Squaws kindness, who bade me come again;

when I was there, there came an *Indian* to look after me: who when he had found me, kickt me all along: I went home and found Venison roasting that night, but they would not give me one bit of it. Sometimes I met with Favour, and sometimes with nothing but Frowns.

The Eleventh Remove

The next day in the morning they took their Travel, intending a dayes journey up the River. I took my load at my back, and quickly we came to wade over the River; and passed over tiresome and wearisome Hills. One Hill was so steep, that I was fain to creep up, upon my knees: and to hold by the twigs and bushes to keep myself from falling backward. My head also was so light, that I usually reeled as I went, but I hope all these wearisome steps that I have taken, are but a forwarding to me of the Heavenly rest: *I know, O Lord, that thy Judgments are right, and that thou in faithfulness hast afflicted me, Psal.* 119. 75.

The Twelfth Remove

It was upon a Sabbath day morning, that they prepared for their Travel. This morning I asked my Master whether he would sell me to my Husband? He answered *Nux*: which did much rejoyce my spirit. My Mistriss, before we went, was gone to the burial of a *Papoos*; and returning, she found me sitting, and reading in my Bible: she snatched it hastily out of my hand, and threw it out of doors; I ran out and catched it up, and put it into my pocket, and never let her see it afterward. Then they packed up their things to be gone, and gave me my load, I complained it was too heavy, whereupon she gave me a slap in the face, and bade me go: I lifted up my heart to God, hoping the Redemption was not far off: and the rather because their insolency grew worse and worse.

But the thoughts of my going homeward (for so we bent our course) much cheered my Spirit, and made my burden seem light, and almost nothing at all. But (to my amazement and great perplexity) the scale was soon turned: for when we had gone a little way, on a sudden my Mistriss gives out, she would go no further, but turn back again, and said I must go back again with her, and she called her Sannup, and would have had him gone back also, but he would not, but said he would go on, and come to us again in three days. My Spirit was, upon this (I confess) very impatient and almost outrageous. I thought I could as well have died as went back. I cannot declare the trouble that I was in about it: but yet back again I must go. As soon as I had an opportunity, I took my Bible to read, and that quieting Scripture came to my hand, *Be still, and know that I am God Psal.* 46. 10. Which stilled my spirit for the present: but a sore time of trial I concluded I had to go through. My Master being gone, who seemed to me the best Friend that I had of an *Indian*, both in cold and hunger, and quickly so it proved. Down I sat, with my heart as full as it could hold, and yet so hungry that I could not sit neither; but going out to see what I could find, and walking among the trees, I found six Acorns, and two Chestnuts, which were some refreshment to me. Towards night I gathered some sticks for my own comfort, that I might not lye a Cold: but when we came to lye down they bade me to go out, and lye somewhere else, for they had company (they said) come in more than their own: I told them, I could not tell where to go, they bade me go look: I told them, if I went to another *Wigwam* they would be angry, and send me home again. Then one of the Company drew his Sword, and told me he would run me through if I did not go presently. Then was I fain to stoop to this rude fellow, and to go out in the Night, I knew not whither. Mine eyes have seen that Fellow afterwards walking up and down in *Boston*, under the appearance of a *Friend-Indian*, and several others of the like Cut. I went to one *Wigwam*, and they told me they had no room. Then I went to another, and they said the same: at last an old *Indian* bade me come to him, and his Squaw gave me some Ground-nuts: she gave me also something to lay under my Head, and a good Fire we had: and through the good Providence of God, I had a comfortable lodging that Night. In the morning, another *Indian* bade me come at night, and he would give me six Ground-nuts, which I did. We were at this place and time about two miles from *Connecticut River*. We went in the morning (to gather Ground-nuts) to the River, and went back again that Night. I went with a good load at my back (for they when they went, though but a little way, would carry all their trumpery with them) I told them the skin was off my back, but I had no other comforting answer from them than this, that it would be no matter if my Head were off too.

The Thirteenth Remove

Instead of going toward the Bay (which was that I desired) I must go with them five or six miles down the River, into a mighty Thicket of Brush: where we abode almost a fortnight. Here one asked me to make a shirt for her Papoos, for which she gave me a mess of Broth, which was thickened with meal made of the Bark of a Tree: and to make it the better she had put into it about a handful of Pease, and a few roasted Ground-nuts. I had not seen my Son a pretty while, and here was an *Indian* of whom I made inquiry after him, and asked him when he saw him? He answered me that such a time his Master roasted him; and that himself did eat a piece of him, as big as his two fingers, and that he was very good meat: but the Lord upheld my Spirit, under this discouragement; and I considered their horrible addictedness to lying, and that there is not one of them that makes the least conscience of speaking of truth. In this place, on a cold night as I lay by the fire, I removed a stick that kept the heat from me, a Squaw moved it down again, at which I lookt up, and she threw a handful of ashes in my eyes; I thought I should have been quite blinded and have never seen more: but lying down, the Water run out of my eyes, and carried the dirt with it, that by the morning, I recovered my sight again. Yet upon this, and the like occasions, I hope it is not too much to say with *Job, Have pity upon me, O ye my Friends, for the Hand of the Lord has touched me.* And here I cannot but remember how many times sitting in their Wigwams, and musing on things past, I should suddenly leap up and run out, as if I had been at home, forgetting where I was, and what my condition was: but when I was without, and saw nothing but Wilderness, and Woods, and a company of barbarous Heathen: my mind quickly returned to me, which made me think of that, spoken concerning *Sampson*, who said, *I will go out and shake myself as at other times, but he wist not that the Lord was departed from him.* About this time I began to think that all my hopes of Restoration would come to nothing. I thought of the *English* army, and hoped for their coming, and being taken by them, but that failed. I hoped to be carried to *Albany*, as the *Indians* had discoursed, but that failed also. I thought of being sold to my Husband, as my Master spake; but instead of that, my Master himself was gone, and I left behind: so that my spirit was now quite ready to sink. I asked them to let me go out, and pick up some sticks, that I might get alone, and pour out my heart unto the Lord. Then also I took my Bible to read, but I found no comfort here neither: yet I can say, that in all my sorrows and afflictions, God did not leave me to have my impatience work towards himself, as if his ways were unrighteous. But I knew that he laid upon me less than I deserved. Afterward, before this doleful time ended with me, I was turning the leaves of my Bible, and the Lord brought to me some Scriptures, which did a little revive me, as that *Isai.* 55. 8. *For my thoughts are not your thoughts, neither are your ways my ways, saith the Lord.* And also that *Ps.* 37. 5. *Commit thy way unto the Lord; trust also in him, and he shall bring it to pass.*

About this time they came yelping from *Hadly*, where they had killed three *English-men*, and brought one Captive with them, *viz. Thomas Read*. They all gathered about the poor Man, asking him many Questions. I desired also to go and see him; and when I came, he was crying bitterly: supposing they would quickly kill him. Whereupon I asked one of them, whether they intended to kill him; he answered me, they would not. He being a little cheared with that, I asked him about the welfare of my Husband. He told me he saw him such a time in the *Bay*, and he was well, but very Melancholly. By which I certainly understood (though I suspected it before) that whatsoever the *Indians* told me respecting him, was vanity and lies. Some of them told me, he was dead, and they had killed him: some said he was Married again, and that the Governour wished him to Marry; and told him he should have his choice, and that all perswaded him I was dead. So like were these barbarous creatures to him who was a liar from the beginning.

As I was sitting once in the Wigwam here, *Philips* maid came in with the Child in her arms, and asked me to give her a piece of my Apron, to make a flap for it, I told her I would not: then my Mistress bad me give it, but still I said no. The Maid told me if I would not give her a piece, she would tear a piece off it: I told her I would tear her Coat then: With that my Mistress rises up: and take up a stick big enough to have killed me, and struck at me with it, but I stept out, and she struck the stick into the Mat of the Wigwam. But while she was pulling of it out, I ran to the Maid and gave her all my Apron, and so that storm went over.

Hearing that my Son was come to this place, I went to see him, and told him his Father was well, but melancholly: he told me he was as much grieved for his Father as for himself; I wondered at his speech, for I thought I had enough upon my spirit in reference to my self, to make me mindless of my Husband and everyone else: they being safe among their Friends. He told me also, that a while before, his Master (together with other *Indians*) were going to the *French* for powder; but by the way the *Mohawks* met with them, and killed four of their Company, which made the rest turn back again, for it might have been worse with him, had he been sold to the *French*, than it proved to be in his remaining with the *Indians*.

I went to see an *English* Youth in this place, one *John Gilbert* of *Springfield*. I found him lying without doors, upon the ground; I asked him how he did? He told me he was very sick of a flux, with eating so much blood. They had turned him out of the Wigwam, and with him an *Indian Papoos*, almost dead (whose Parents had been killed) in a bitter cold day, without fire or clothes: The young man himself had nothing on, but his shirt and waistcoat: This sight was enough to melt a heart of flint. There they lay quivering in the cold, the youth round like a dog; the *Papoos* stretched out, with his eyes, and nose, and mouth full of dirt, and yet alive, and groaning. I advised *John* to go and get to some fire: He told me he could not stand, but I perswaded him still, lest he should lye there and die. And with much ado I got him to a fire, and went my self home. As soon as I was got home, his Masters Daughter came after me, to know what I had done with the *English-man*. I told her I had got him to a fire in such a place. Now had I need to pray *Pauls* prayer *That we may be delivered from unreasonable and wicked men* 2 *Thess.* 3. 2. For her satisfaction I went along with her, and brought her to him; but before I got home again, it was noised about, that I was running away and getting the *English* youth along with me: that as soon as I came in they began to rant and domineer: asking me where I had been, and what I had been doing? and saying they would knock me in the head: I told them I had been seeing the *English Youth*: and that I would not run away: they told me I lied, and taking up a Hatchet, they came to me, and said, they would knock me down if I stirred out again: and so confined me to the Wigwam. Now may I say with *David, I am in a great strait* 2 *Sam.* 24. 14. If I keep in, I must dye with hunger, and if I go out, I must be knockt in head. This distressed condition held that day, and half the next; And then the Lord remembered me, whose mercies are great. Then came an *Indian* to me, with a pair of Stockins that were too big for him; and he would have me ravel them out, and knit them fit for him. I shewed myself willing, and bid him ask my Mistress, if I might go along with him a little way: she said yes, I might, but I was not a little refresht with that news, that I had my liberty again. Then I went along with him, and he gave me some roasted Ground-nuts, which did again revive my feeble stomach.

Being got out of her sight, I had time and liberty again to look into my Bible: which was my guide by day, and my Pillow by night. Now that comfortable Scripture presented it self to me, *For a small moment have I forsaken thee, but with great mercies will I gather thee Isai.* 54. 7. Thus the Lord carried me along from one time to another: and made good to me this precious promise, and many others. Then my Son came to see me, and I asked his Master to let him stay a while with me, that I might comb his head, and look over him, for he was almost overcome with lice. He told me, when I had done, that he was very hungry, but I had nothing to relieve him; but bid him go into the Wigwams as he went along, and see if he could get any thing among them. Which he did, and (it seems) tarried a little too long; for his Master was angry with him, and beat him, and then sold him. Then he came running to tell me he had a new Master, and that he had given him some Ground-nuts already. Then I went along with him to his new Master who told me he loved him: and he should not want. So his Master carried him away, and I never saw him afterward: till I saw him at *Pascataqua* in *Portsmouth*.

That night they bade me go out of the Wigwam again: my Mistress's *Papoos* was sick, and it died that night, and there was one benefit in it, that there was more room. I went to a Wigwam, and they bad me come in, and gave me a skin to lye upon, and a mess of Venison and Ground-nuts, which was a choice Dish among them. On the morrow they buried the *Papoos*, and afterward, both morning and evening, there came a company to mourn and howl with her: though I confess, I could not much condole with them. Many sorrowful days I had in this place: often getting alone; *like a Crane, or a Swallow, so did I chatter; I did mourn as a Dove, mine eyes fail with looking upward. Oh, Lord, I am oppressed; undertake for me, Isai. 38. 14. I could tell the Lord, as Hezekiah,* ver. 3. *Remember now O Lord, I beseech thee, how I have walked before thee in truth.* Now had I time to examine all my ways: my Conscience did not accuse me of unrighteousness toward one or other; yet I saw how in my walk with God, I had been a careless creature. As David said, *Against thee, thee only have I sinned*: and I might say with the poor Publican, *God be merciful unto me a sinner*. On the Sabbath days, I could look upon the Sun and think how People were going to the house of God, to have their Souls refresht; and then home, and their Bodies also: but I was destitute of both; and might say as the poor Prodigal, *he would fain have filled his belly with the husks that the swine did eat, and no man gave unto him Luke* 15. 16. For I must say with him, *Father, I have sinned against Heaven and in thy sight,* ver. 21. I remembered how on the night before and after the Sabbath, when my family was about me, and relations and Neighbors with us, we could pray and sing, and then refresh our bodies with the good creatures of God: and then have a comfortable bed to ly down on; but instead of all this, I had only a little Swill for the body and then, like a Swine, must ly down on the ground: I cannot express to man the sorrow that lay upon my spirit; the Lord knows it. Yet that comfortable Scripture would often come to my mind, *For a small moment have I forsaken thee, but with great mercies will I gather thee.*

The Fourteenth Remove

Now must we pack up and be gone from this Thicket, bending our course toward the Bay-Towns; I having nothing to eat by the way this day, but a few crumbs of Cake, that an *Indian* gave my Girl the same day we were taken. She gave it me, and I put it in my pocket; there it lay, till it was so mouldy (for want of good baking) that one could not tell what it was made of; it fell all to crumbs, and grew so dry and hard, that it was like little flints; and this refresht me many times, when I was ready to faint. It was in my thoughts when I put it into my mouth, that if ever I returned, I would tell the world what a blessing the Lord gave to such mean food. As we went along they killed a *Deer*, with a young one in her: they gave me a piece of the *Fawn,* and it was so young and tender, that one might eat the bones as well as the flesh, and yet I thought it very good. When night came on we sate down, it rained, but they quickly got up a Bark Wigwam, where I lay dry that night. I looked out in the morning, and many of them had lain in the rain all night, I saw by their Reeking. Thus the Lord dealt mercifully with me many times: and I fared better than many of them. In the morning they took the blood of the *Deer*, and put it into the Paunch, and so boyled it. I could eat nothing of that, though they ate it sweetly. And yet they were so nice in other things, that when I had fetcht water, and had put the Dish I dipt the water with into the Kittle of water which I brought, they would say, they would knock me down; for they said, it was a sluttish trick.

The Fifteenth Remove

We went on our travel. I having got one handful of Ground-nuts, for my support that day: they gave me my load, and I went on cheerfully (with the thoughts of going homeward) having my burden more on my back than my spirit: We came to *Bacquaug* River again that day, near which we abode a few days. Sometimes one of them would give me a Pipe, another a little Tobacco, another a little Salt: which I would change for a little Victuals. I cannot but think what a Wolvish appetite persons have in a starving condition: for many times when they gave me that which was hot, I was so greedy, that I should burn my mouth, that it would trouble me hours after; and yet I should quickly do the same again. And after I was thoroughly hungry, I was never again satisfied. For though sometimes it fell out, that I got enough, and did eat till I could eat no more, yet I was as unsatisfied as I was when I began. And now could I see that Scripture verified (there being many Scriptures which we do not take notice of, or understand till we are afflicted) *Thou shalt eat and not be satisfied Mic. 6. 14.* Now might I see more than ever before, the miseries that sin hath brought upon us. Many times I should be ready to run against the Heathen, but the Scripture would quiet me again, *Shall there be evil in the City and the Lord hath not done it? Amos 3. 6.* The Lord help me to make a right improvement of his word, and that I might learn that great lesson: *He hath shewed thee, Oh Man, what is good; and what doth the Lord require of thee, but to do justly, and love mercy, and walk humbly with thy God? Hear ye the rod, and who hath appointed it Mic. 6. 8-9.*

The Sixteenth Remove

We began this Remove with wading over *Bacquaug* River. The Water was up to the knees, and the stream very swift, and so cold that I thought it would have cut me in sunder. I was so weak and feeble, that I reeled as I went along, and thought there I must end my days at last, after my bearing and getting through so many difficulties. The *Indians* stood laughing to see me staggering along, but in my distress the Lord gave me experience of the truth, and goodness of that promise, *When thou passest through the waters, I will be with thee; and through the Rivers, they shall not overflow thee Isai. 43. 2.* Then I sate down to put on my stockins and shoes, with the tears running down mine eyes, and many sorrowful thoughts in my heart, but I got up to go along with them. Quickly there came up to us an *Indian*, who informed them that I must go to *Wachusett* to my Master: for there was a Letter come from the Council to the *Sagamores*, about redeeming the Captives, and that there would be another in fourteen days, and that I must be there ready. My heart was so heavy before that I could scarce speak, or go in the path; and yet now so light, that I could run. My strength seemed to come again, and recruit my feeble knees, and aking heart: yet it pleased them to go but one mile that night, and there we stayed two days. In that time came a company of *Indians* to us, near thirty, all on Horse back. My heart skipt within me, thinking they had been *English-men* at the first sight of them: for they were dressed in *English* apparel, with Hats, white Neck-cloths, and Sashes about their waists; and Ribbons upon their shoulders: but when they came near, there was a vast difference between the lovely Faces of Christians, and foul looks of those *Heathens*: which much damped my spirit again.

The Seventeenth Remove

A comfortable Remove it was to me, because of my hopes. They gave me a pack, and along we went cheerfully: but quickly my Will proved more than my strength; having little or no refreshing, my strength failed me, and my spirits were almost quite gone. Now may I say with *David, I am poor and needy, and my heart is wounded within me. I am gone like the shadow when it declineth: I am tossed up and down like the locust; my knees are weak through fasting, and my flesh faileth of fatness Psal.* 119. 22-24. At night we came to an *Indian Town*, and the *Indians* sate down by a Wigwam discoursing, but I was almost spent, and could scarce speak. I laid down my load, and went into the Wigwam, and there sate an *Indian* boiling of *Horses feete*: (they being wont to eat the flesh first, and when the feet were old and dried, and they had nothing else, they would cut off the feet and use them) I asked him to give me a little of his Broth, or Water they were boiling in: he took a dish, and gave me one spoonful of Samp, and bid me take as much of the Broth as I would. Then I put some of the hot water to the Samp, and drank it up, and my spirit came again. He gave me also a piece of the Ruffe or Ridding of the small Guts, and I broiled it on the coals; and now may I say with *Jonathan, See, I pray you, how mine eyes have been enlightened, because I tasted a little of this honey* 1 *Sam.* 14. 29. Now is my Spirit revived again: though means be never so inconsiderable, yet if the Lord bestow his blessing upon them, they shall refresh both Soul and Body.

The Eighteenth Remove

We took up our packs, and along we went. But a wearisome day I had of it. As we went along I saw an *English-man* stript naked, and lying dead upon the ground, but knew not who it was. Then we came to another *Indian Town*, where we stayed all night. In this Town there were four *English Children*, Captives: and one of them my own Sisters. I went to see how she did, and she was well, considering her Captive condition. I would have tarried that night with her, but they that owned her would not suffer it. Then I went into another Wigwam, where they were boiling Corn and Beans, which was a lovely sight to see, but I could not get a taste thereof. Then I went to another Wigwam, where there were two of the *English Children*: the Squaw was boiling horses feet, then she cut me off a little piece, and gave one of the *English Children* a piece also. Being very hungry, I had quickly eat up mine: but the Child could not bite it, it

was so tough and sinewy, but lay sucking, gnawing, chewing and slob-
bering it in the Mouth and Hand. Then I took it of the Child, and eat it
my self; and savoury it was to my taste.

Then I may say as *Job, Chap.* 6. 7. *The things that my Soul refused to touch,
are as my sorrowful meat.* Thus the Lord made that pleasant refreshing,
which another time would have been an Abomination. Then I went
home to my Mistresss Wigwam: and they told me I disgraced My Master
with begging: and if I did so any more, they would knock me in the
Head: I told them, they had as good knock me on the Head, as starve me
to death.

The Nineteenth Remove

They said, when we went out, that we must travel to *Wachuset* this day.
But a bitter weary day I had of it; travelling now three days together,
without resting any day between. At last, after many weary steps, I saw
Wachuset hills, but many miles off. Then we came to a great Swamp,
through which we travelled, up to the knees in mud and water, which
was heavy going to one tired before. Being almost spent, I thought I
should have sunk down at last, and never got out; but I may say, as in *Psal.*
94. 18. *When my foot slipped, thy mercy, O Lord, held me up.* Going along, hav-
ing indeed my life, but little Spirit, *Philip,* (who was in the company)
came up, and took me by the hand, and said, *Two weeks more, and you shall
be Mistriss again.* I asked him if he speak true? he answered, Yes, and
quickly you shall come to your Master again: who had been gone from
us three weeks. After many weary steps we came to *Wachuset*, where he
was; and glad I was to see him. He asked me, when I washt me? I told
him not this month. Then he fetch me some water himself, and bid me
wash, and gave me the Glass to see how I lookt, and bid his Squaw give
me something to eat. So she gave me a mess of Beans and meat, and a
little Ground-nut Cake. I was wonderfully revived with this favour
showed me, *He made them also to be pitied of all those that carried them Cap-
tives Psal.* 106. 46.

My master had three Squaws: living sometimes with one, and some-
times with another. One, this old Squaw, at whose Wigwam I was, and
with whom my Master had been those three weeks. Another was *Wetti-
more,* with whom I had lived and served all this while. A severe and proud
Dame she was; bestowing every day in dressing herself neat as much
time as any of the Gentry of the land: powdering her hair and painting
her face, going with her Neck-laces, with Jewels in her ears, and bracelets

upon her hands. When she had dressed her self, her Work was to make girdles of Wampom and Beads. The third Squaw was a younger one, by whom he had two Papooses. By the time I was refresht by the old Squaw, with whom my Master was, *Wettimores* Maid came to call me home, at which I fell a weeping; Then the old Squaw told me, to encourage me, that if I wanted victuals, I should come to her, and that I should lye there in her Wigwam. Then I went with the Maid, and quickly came again and lodged there. The Squaw laid a Mat under me, and a good Rugg over me; the first time I had any such Kindness shewed me. I understood that *Wettimore* thought, that if she should let me go and serve with the old Squaw, she would be in danger to lose not only my service, but the redemption-pay also. And I was not a little glad to hear this; being by it raised in my hopes, that in Gods due time there would be an end of this sorrowful hour. Then came an *Indian*, and asked me to knit him three pair of Stockins, for which I had a Hat, and a silk Handker chief. Then another asked me to make her a shift, for which she gave me an Apron.

Then came *Tom* and *Peter*, with the second Letter from the Council, about the Captives. Though they were *Indians,* I got them by the hand, and burst out into Tears; my heart was so full that I could not speak to them: but recovering my self, I asked them how my Husband did? and all my Friends and Acquaintance? they said, they are all very well but Melancholy. They brought me two Biskets, and a pound of Tobacco. The Tobacco I quickly gave away: when it was all gone, one asked me to give him a pipe of Tobacco, I told him it was all gone; Then began he to rant and threaten; I told him when my Husband came, I would give him some: Hang him Rogue (says he) I will knock out his brains, if he comes here. And then again in the same breath, they would say, that if there should come an hundred without Guns they would do them no hurt. So unstable and like mad men they were. So that fearing the worst, I durst not send to my Husband; though there were some thoughts of his coming to Redeem and fetch me, not knowing what might follow; for there was little more trust to them than to the Master they served. When the letter was come, the Saggamores met to consult about the Captives, and called me to them to inquire how much my Husband would give to redeem me: When I came, I sate down among them, as I was wont to do, as their manner is: Then they bade me stand up, and said, they were the *General Court.* They bid me speak what I thought he would give. Now knowing that all we had was destroyed by the *Indians,* I was in a great strait. I thought if I should speak of but a little, it would be slighted, and hinder the matter; if of a great Sum, I knew not where it would be procured: Yet at a venture, I said *Twenty pounds*, yet desired them to take less: but they would not hear of that, but sent that message to *Boston*, that for *twenty pounds* I should be redeemed. It was a Praying *Indian* that wrote their letter for them. There was another Praying *Indian*, who told me, that he had a Brother, that would not eat Horse; his Conscience was so tender and scrupulous, (though as large as Hell, for the destruction of poor *Christians*). Then he said, he read that Scripture to him, *There was a famine in* Samaria, *and behold they besieged it, until an Asses head was sold for four-score pieces of silver, and the fourth part of a Kab of dove's dung for five pieces of silver* 2 *King*. 6. 25. He expounded this place to his brother, and shewed him that it was lawful to eat that in a Famine, which is not at another time. And now, says he, he will eat Horse with any *Indian* of them all. There was another Praying *Indian*, who when he had done all the Mischief that he could, betrayed his own Father into the *Englishes* hands, thereby to purchase his own Life. Another Praying *Indian* was at *Sudbury* fight, though, as he deserved, he was afterward hanged for it. There was another Praying *Indian*, so wicked and cruel, as to wear a string about his neck, strung with *Christian* fingers. Another Praying *Indian*, when they went to *Sudbury* fight, went with them, and his Squaw also with him, with her Papoos at her back: Before they went to that Fight they got a company together to *Powaw*: the manner was as followeth. There was one that kneeled upon a *Deer-skin*, with the Company round him in a Ring who kneeled, striking upon the Ground with their hands, and with sticks, and muttering or humming with their Mouths. Besides him who kneeled in the Ring, there also stood one with a Gun in his hand: Then he on the Deer-skin made a speech, and all manifested assent to it; and so they did many times together. Then they bade him with the Gun go out of the Ring, which he did; But when he was out, they called him in again; but he seemed to make a stand; then they called the more earnestly, till he returned again. Then they all sang. Then they gave him two Guns, in either hand one. And so he on the Deer-skin began again; and at the end of every Sentence in his speaking, they all assented, humming or muttering with their Mouths, and striking upon the Ground with their Hands. Then they bade him with the two Guns go out of the Ring again: which he did a little way. Then they called him in again, but he made a stand, So they called him with greater earnestness: but he stood reeling and wavering as if he knew not whither he should stand or fall, or which way to go. Then they called him with exceeding great vehemency, all of them, one and another: after a little while, he turned in, staggering as he went, with his Arms stretched out; in either hand a Gun. As soon as he came in, they all sang and rejoyced exceedingly a while. And then he upon the Deer-skin, made another speech unto which they all assented in a rejoycing manner: and so they ended their business, and forthwith went to *Sudbury* Fight. To my thinking they went without any scruple but that they should prosper and gain the Victory. And they went out not so rejoycing, but they came home with as great a Victory. For they said they had killed two Captains, and almost an hundred men. One *English-man* they brought along with them; and he said it was too true, for they had made sad work at *Sudbury*; as indeed it proved. Yet they came home without that rejoicing and triumphing over their Victory, which they were wont to show at other times: but rather like Dogs, (as they say) which have lost their Ears. Yet I could not perceive that it was for their own loss of Men: They said they had not lost above five or six: and I missed none, except in one Wigwam. When they went, they acted as if the Devil had told them that they should gain the Victory: and now they acted, as if the Devil had told them they should have a fall. Whither it were so or no, I cannot tell, but so it proved: for quickly they began to fall, and so held on that Sum-mer, till they came to utter ruine. They came home on a Sabbath day, and the Powaw that kneeled upon the Deer-skin came home (I may say, with-out abuse) as black as the Devil. When my Master came home, he came to me and bid me make a shirt for his Papoos, of a Hollandlaced Pillow-beer. About that time there came an *Indian* to me, and bade me come to his *Wigwam* at night, and he would give me some Pork and Ground-nuts. Which I did, and as I was eating, another *Indian* said to me, he seems to be your good Friend, but he killed two *English-men* at *Sudbury*, and there lye their Cloathes behind you: I looked behind me, and there I saw bloody-Cloathes, with Bullet-holes in them: yet the Lord suffered not this Wretch to do me any hurt. Yea, instead of that, he many times refresht me: five or six times did he and his Squaw refresh my feeble Carcass. If I went to their *Wigwam* at any time, they would always give me some-thing, and yet they were strangers that I never saw before. Another *Squaw* gave me a piece of fresh Pork, and a little Salt with it: and lent me her Frying pan to fry it in: and I cannot but remember what a sweet, pleasant and delightful relish that bit had to me, to this day. So little do we prize common mercies, when we have them to the full.

The Twentieth Remove

It was their usual manner to remove, when they had done any mischief, lest they should be found out; and so they did at this time. We went about three or four miles, and there they built a great *Wigwam*, big enough to hold an hundred *Indians*, which they did in preparation to a great day of dancing. They would say now amongst themselves, that the *Governoor* would be so angry for his loss at *Sudbury*, that he would send no more about the Captives, which made me grieve and tremble. My Sister being not far from the place where we now were, and hearing that I was here, desired her Master to let her come and see me, and he was willing to it, and would go with her; but she being ready before him, told him she would go before, and was come within a Mile or two of the place: Then he overtook her, and began to rant as if he had been mad, and made her go back again in the Rain; so that I never saw her till I saw her in *Charlestown*. But the Lord requited many of their ill-doings, for this *Indian*, her Master, was hanged afterward at *Boston*. The *Indians* now began to come from all quarters, against the merry dancing day. Among some of them came one Goodwife *Kettle*: I told her my Heart was so heavy that it was ready to break: so is mine too, said she, but yet said, I hope we shall hear some good news shortly. I could hear how earnestly my Sister desired to see me, and I as earnestly desired to see her; and yet neither of us could get an opportunity. My Daughter was also now about a Mile off: and I had not seen her in nine or ten Weeks, as I had not seen my Sister since our first taking. I earnestly desired them to let me go and see them: yea, I entreated, begged, and perswaded them, but to let me see my Daughter: and yet so hard-hearted were they, that they would not suffer it. They made use of their Tyrannical Power whilst they had it: but through the Lord's wonderful mercy, their time was now but short.

On a Sabbath-day, the sun being about an hour high, in the Afternoon, came Mr. *John Hoar*, (the council permitting him, and his own foreward spirit inclining him), together with the two forementioned *Indians*, *Tom* and *Peter*, with the third Letter from the Council. When they came near, I was abroad; Though I saw them not, they presently called me in, and bade me sit down and not stir. Then they catched up their Guns, and away they ran, as if an Enemy had been at hand, and the Guns went off apace. I manifested some great trouble, and they asked me what was the matter? I told them I thought they had killed the *English-man* (for they had in the meantime informed me that an *English-man* was come). They said No; they shot over his Horse, and under, and before his horse, and they pusht him this way and that way, at their pleasure: shewing what they could do. Then they let them come to their *Wigwams*. I begged of them to let me see the *English-man*, but they would not. But there was I fain to sit their pleasure. When they had talked their fill with him, they suffered me to go to him. We asked each other of our welfare, and how my Husband did? and all my Friends? He told me they were all well, and would be glad to see me. Amongst other things which my Husband sent me, there came a pound of *Tobacco*: which I sold for nine shillings in Money: for many of the *Indians* for want of *Tobacco*, smoked *Hemlock*, and *Ground-ivy*. It was a great mistake in any, who thought I sent for *Tobacco*: for through the favour of God, that desire was overcome. I now asked them whether I should go home with Mr. *Hoar*? They answered No, one and another of them: and it being Night, we lay down with that Answer: In the morning Mr. *Hoar* invited the *Saggamores* to Dinner: but when we went to get it ready we found that they had stollen the greatest part of the Provision Mr. *Hoar* had brought out of his Bags in the Night. And we may see the wonderful power of God, in that one passage, in that when there was such a great number of the *Indians* together, and so greedy of a little good Food; and no *English* there, but Mr. *Hoar*, and myself: that there they did not knock us in the Head, and take what we had; there being not only some Provision, but also Trading Cloth, a part of the twenty pounds agreed upon: But instead of doing us any mischief, they seemed to be ashamed of the Fact, and said, it were some *Matchit Indians* that did it. O that we could believe that there is nothing too hard for God! God shewed His power over the Heathen in this, as he did over the hungry lions when *Daniel* was cast into the den. Mr. *Hoar* called them betime to Dinner; but they ate very little, they being so busie in dressing themselves, and getting ready for their Dance: which was carried on by eight of them, four Men and four Squaws: my Master and Mistriss being two. He was dressed in his Holland Shirt, with great Laces sewed at the tail of it; he had his silver Buttons, his white Stockins, his Garters were hung round with Shillings, and he had Girdles of Wampom upon his Head and Shoulders. She had a Kersey Coat, and covered with Girdles of Wampom from the Loins and upward. Her arms from her Elbows to her Hands were covered with Bracelets; there were handfuls of Neck-laces about her Neck, and several sorts of Jewels in her Ears. She had fine red Stockins, and white Shoos, her Hair powdered and Face painted Red, that was always before Black. And all the Dancers were after the same manner. There were two others singing and knocking on a Kettle for their Musick. They kept hopping up and down one after another, with a Kettle of Water in the midst, standing warm upon some Embers, to drink of when they were dry. They held on, till it was almost night, throwing out Wampom to the standers by. At night I asked them again, if I should go home? They all as one said no, except my Husband would come for me. When we were lain down, my Master went out of the *Wigwam*, and by and by sent in an *Indian*, called *James*, the PRINTER, who told Mr. *Hoar*, that my Master would let me go home to morrow, if he would let him have one pint of *Liquors*. Then Mr. *Hoar* called his own *Indians*, *Tom* and *Peter*: and bid them go, and see whether he would promise it before them three: and if he would, he should have it; which he did, and he had it. Then *Philip* smelling the business called me to him, and asked me what I would give him, to tell me some good news, and to speak a good word for me, that I might go home to morrow? I told him I could not tell what to give him. I would give any thing I had, and asked him what he would have? He said two Coats and twenty shillings in Money, and half a bushel of Seed-corn, and some *Tobacco*. I thanked him for his love: but I knew the good news as well as that crafty Fox. My Master after he had had his Drink, quickly came ranting into the *Wigwam* again, and called for Mr. *Hoar*, drinking to him, and saying he was a good man; and then again he would say, Hang him Rogue. Being almost drunk, he would drink to him, and yet presently say he should be hanged. Then he called for me; I trembled to hear him, yet I was fain to go to him; and he drunk to me, showing no incivility. He was the first *Indian*, I saw drunk all the while that I was amongst them. At last his Squaw ran out, and he after her, round the *Wigwam*, with his money jingling at his knees: but she escaped him; but having an old Squaw, he ran to her: and so through the Lords mercy, we were no more troubled that night. Yet I had not a comfortable nights rest: for I think I can say, I did not sleep for three nights together. The night before the Letter came from the Council, I could not rest, I was so full of fears and troubles (God many times leaving us most in the dark, when deliverance is nearest) yea at this time I could not rest night nor day. The next night I was over-joyed, Mr. *Hoar* being come, and that with such good Tydings. The third night I was even swallowed up with the thoughts of things; *viz.* that ever I should go home again: and that I must go, leaving my Children behind me in the Wilderness; so that sleep was now almost departed from mine eyes.

On *Tuesday* morning they called their General Court (as they stiled it) to consult and determine, whether I should go home or no: And they all as one man did seemingly consent to it, that I should go home: except *Philip*, who would not come among them.

But before I go any further, I would take leave to mention a few remarkable passages of Providence; which I took special notice of in my afflicted time.

1. Of the fair opportunity lost in the long March, a little after the Fort-

fight, when our *English* army was so numerous, and in pursuit of the Enemy; and so near as to overtake several and destroy them: and the Enemy in such distress for Food, that our men might track them by their rooting in the earth for Ground-nuts, whilst they were flying for their lives: I say, that then our Army should want Provision, and be forced to leave their pursuit, and return homeward: and the very next week the Enemy came upon our Town, like Bears bereft of their whelps, or so many ravenous Wolves, rending us and our Lambs to death. But what shall I say? God seemed to leave his People to themselves; and order all things for his own holy ends. *Shall there be evil in the City and the Lord hath not done it? They are not grieved for the affliction of Joseph, therefore shall they go Captive, with the first that go Captive. It is the Lord's doing, and it should be marvellous in our Eyes.*

2. I cannot but remember how the *Indians* derided the slowness, and dullness of the *English* army, in its setting out. For after the desolations at *Lancaster* and *Medfield*, as I went along with them, they asked me when I thought the *English* army would come after them? I told them I could not tell: it may be they will come in *May*, said they. Thus did they scoffe at us, as if the *English* would be a quarter of a Year getting ready.

3. Which also I have hinted before; when the *English* army with new supplies were sent forth to pursue after the Enemy, and they understanding it; fled before them till they came to *Bacquaug River*, where they forthwith went over safely: that that River should be impassable to the *English*, I can but admire to see the wonderful providence of God in preserving the Heathen for further affliction to our poor Country. They could go in great numbers over, but the *English* must stop: God had an over-ruling hand in all those things.

4. It was thought, if their Corn were cut down, they would starve and die with hunger: and all their Corn that could be found, was destroyed, and they driven from that little they had in store, into the Woods, in the midst of Winter; and yet how to admiration did the Lord preserve them for his holy ends, and the destruction of many still amongst the *English!* strangely did the Lord provide for them: that I did not see (all the time I was among them) one Man, or Woman, or Child, die with Hunger.

Though many times they would eat that, that a Hog or a Dog would hardly touch: yet by that God strengthened them to be a scourge to his People.

The chief and commonest food was Ground-nuts: they eat also Nuts, and Acorns, Hartychoaks, Lilly-roots, Ground-beans, and several other weeds and roots that I know not.

They would pick up old bones, and cut them in pieces at the joynts, and if they were full of worms and maggots, they would scald them over the fire to make the vermine come out; and then boyle them, and drink up the Liquor, and then beat the great ends of them in a Morter, and so eat them. They would eat Horses guts and ears, and all sorts of wild birds which they could catch: also Bear, Venison, Beavers, Tortois, Frogs, Squirils, Dogs, Skunks, Rattle-snakes: yea, the very Barks of Trees; besides all sorts of Creatures, and provision which they plundered from the *English*. I cannot but stand in admiration to see the wonderful power of God, in providing for such a vast number of our Enemies in the Wilderness, where there was nothing to be seen, but from hand to mouth. Many times in a morning, the generality of them, would eat up all they had, and yet have some further supply against they wanted. It is said, *Oh, that my People had hearkened to me, and Israel had walked in my wayes; I should soon have subdued their Enemies, and turned my hand against their adversaries. Psal.* 81. 13-14. But now our perverse and evil carriages in the sight of the Lord, have so offended him; that instead of turning his hand against them, the Lord feeds and nourishes them up to be a scourge to the whole Land.

5. Another thing that I would observe is, the strange providence of God, in turning things about when the *Indians were at the highest*, and the *English at the lowest*. I was with the Enemy eleven weeks and five days; and not one Week passed without the fury of the Enemy, and some desolation by fire and sword upon one place or other. They mourned (with their black faces) for their own losses: yet triumphed and rejoyced in their inhumane (and many times devilish cruelty) to the *English*. They would boast much of their Victories; saying, that in two hours time, they had destroyed such a Captain and his Company, in such a place; and such a Captain, and his Company, in such a place; and such a Captain, and his Company, in such a place: and boast how many Towns they had destroyed, and then scoffe, and say, they had done them a good turn, to send them to Heaven so soon. Again, they would say, this Summer that they would knock all the Rogues in the head, or drive them into the Sea, or make them flie the country: thinking surely, *Agag-like, The bitterness of Death is past.* Now the *Heathen* begin to think all is their own, and the poor *Christians* hopes to fail (as to man) and now their eyes are more to God, and their hearts sigh heaven-ward: and to say in good earnest, *Help Lord, or we perish;* when the Lord had brought his People to this, that they saw no help in anything but himself; then He takes the quarrel into his own hand: and though they had made a pit (in their own imaginations) as

deep as hell for the *Christians* that Summer; yet the Lord hurll'd themselves into it. And the Lord had not so many ways before, to preserve them, but now he hath as many to destroy them.

But to return again to my going home; where we may see a remarkable change of providence: at first they were all against it, except my Husband would come for me; but afterwards they assented to it, and seemed much to rejoyce in it: some asked me to send them some Bread, others some Tobacco, others shaking me by the hand, offering me a Hood and Scarf to ride in; not one moving hand or tongue against it. Thus hath the Lord answered my poor desires, and the many earnest requests of others put up unto God for me. In my Travels an *Indian* came to me, and told me, if I were willing, he and his Squaw would run away, and go home along with me. I told him, No, I was not willing to run away, but desired to wait Gods time, that I might go home quietly, and without fear. And now God hath granted me my desire. O the wonderful power of God that I have seen, and the experiences that I have had. I have been in the midst of those roaring Lions, and Salvage Bears, that feared neither God, nor Man, nor the Devil, by night and day, alone and in company, sleeping all sorts together; and yet not one of them ever offered the least abuse of unchastity to me, in word or action. Though some are ready to say, I speak it for my own credit; but I speak it in the presence of God, and to his Glory. Gods power is as great now, and as sufficient to save, as when he preserved *Daniel* in the Lions Den, or the three Children in the Fiery Furnace. I may well say, as he, *Psal.* 107. 1, 2. *Oh give thanks unto the Lord, for he is good, for his mercy endureth for ever. Let the redeemed of the Lord say so, whom he hath redeemed from the hand of the Enemy;* especially that I should come away in the midst of so many hundreds of Enemies, quietly and peaceably, and not a Dog moving his tongue. So I took my leave of them, and in coming along my heart melted into Tears, more than all the while I was with them, and I was almost swallowed up with the thoughts that ever I should go home again. About the sun going down, Mr. *Hoar*, and my self, and the two *Indians* came to *Lancaster*, and a solemn sight it was to me. There had I lived many comfortable years amongst my Relations and Neighbours, and now not one *Christian* to be seen, nor one House left standing. We went on to a Farm-house that was yet standing, where we lay all night, and a comfortable lodging we had, though nothing but straw to lye on. The Lord preserved us in safety that night, and raised us up again in the morning, and carried us along, that before noon, we came to *Concord*. Now was I full of joy, and yet not without sorrow: joy, to see such a lovely sight, so many *Christians* together, and some of them my Neighbours. There I met with my Brother, and my Brother in Law, who asked me, if I knew where his Wife was? poor heart! he had helped to bury her, and knew it not; she being shot down by the house, was partly burnt, so that those who were at *Boston* at the desolation of the Town, and came back afterward, and buried the dead, did not know her. Yet I was not without sorrow, to think how many were looking and longing, and my own Children amongst the rest, to enjoy that deliverance that I had now received; and I did not know whether ever I should see them again. Being recruited with Food and Raiment, we went to *Boston* that day, where I met with my dear Husband, but the thoughts of our dear Children, one being dead, and the other we could not tell where, abated our comfort each to other. I was not before so much hem'd in with the merciless and cruel *Heathen*, but now as much with pitiful, tender-hearted and compassionate *Christians*. In that poor, and distressed, and beggarly condition, I was received in, I was kindly entertained in several houses: so much love I received from several, (some of whom I knew, and others I knew not) that I am not capable to declare it. But the Lord knows them all by name: The Lord reward them seven-fold into their bosoms of his spirituals, for their temporals. The twenty pounds, the price of my Redemption, was raised by some *Boston* Gentlewomen, and M. *Usher*, whose bounty and religious charity I would not forget to make mention of. Then Mr. *Thomas Shepherd* of *Charlstown* received us into his House, where we continued eleven weeks; and a Father and Mother they were to us. And many more tender-hearted Friends we met with in that place. We were now in the midst of love, yet not without much and frequent heaviness of heart, for our poor Children, and other Relations, who were still in affliction.

The week following, after my comming in, the Governour and Council sent forth to the *Indians* again; and that not without success: for they brought in my Sister, and Goodwife *Kettle*. Then not knowing where our Children were, was a sore trial to us still, and yet we were not without secret hopes that we should see them again. That which was dead lay heavier upon my spirit than those which were alive amongst the *Heathen*: thinking how it suffered with its wounds, and I was no way able to relieve it: and how it was buried by the *Heathen* in the Wilderness, from among all *Christians*. We were hurried up and down in our thoughts; sometime we should hear a report that they were gone this way, and sometimes that: and that they were come in, in this place or that: we kept inquiring and listening to hear concerning them, but no certain news as yet. About this time the Council had ordered a day of publick *Thanks-giving*: though

I thought I had still cause of mourning; and being unsettled in our minds, we thought we would ride toward the eastward, to see if we could hear any thing concerning our Children. And as we were riding along (God is the wise disposer of all things) between *Ipswich* and *Rowly* we met with Mr. *William Hubbard,* who told us our son *Joseph* was come in to Major *Waldrens,* and another with him, which was my Sisters son. I asked him how he knew it? He said the Major himself told him so. So along we went till we came to *Newbury*; and their Minister being absent, they desired my Husband to preach the *Thanks-giving* for them; but he was not willing to stay there that night, but would go over to *Salisbury,* to hear farther, and come again in the morning; which he did, and preached there that day. At night, when he had done, one came and told him that his Daughter was come in at *Providence*: here was mercy on both hands. Now hath God fulfilled that precious Scripture, which was such a comfort to me in my distressed condition. When my heart was ready to sink into the Earth (my Children being gone I could not tell whither) and my knees trembled under me, and I was walking through the valley of the shadow of death: then the Lord brought, and now has fulfilled that reviving word unto me: *Thus saith the Lord, Refrain thy voice from weeping, and thine eyes from tears, for thy work shall be rewarded, saith the Lord, and they shall come again from the Land of the Enemy.* Now we were between them, the one on the East, and the other on the West: our Son being nearest, we went to him first, to *Portsmouth,* where we met with him, and with the Major also: who told us he had done what he could, but could not redeem him under seven pounds, which the good People thereabouts were pleased to pay. The Lord reward the Major, and all the rest, though unknown to me, for their labour of love. My Sisters Son was redeemed for four pounds, which the Council gave order for the payment of. Having now received one of our Children, we hastened toward the other: going back through *Newbury,* my husband preached there on the Sabbath day: for which they rewarded him many fold.

On Monday we came to *Charlstown*; where we heard that the Governour of *Road-Island* had sent over for our Daughter, to take care of her, being now within his Jurisdiction: which should not pass without our acknowledgments. But she being nearer *Rehoboth* than *Road-Island,* Mr. *Newman* went over, and took care of her, and brought her to his own house. And the goodness of God was admirable to us in our low estate, in that he raised up compassionate friends on every side to us; when we had nothing to recompense any for their love. The *Indians* were now gone that way, that it was apprehended dangerous to go to her: but the

Carts which carried Provision to the *English* army, being guarded, brought her with them to *Dorchester*, where we received her safe: blessed be the Lord for it, *for great is his power, and he can do whatsoever seemeth him good.* Her coming in was after this manner: she was travelling one day with the *Indians*, with her basket at her back: the company of *Indians* were got before her, and gone out of sight, all except one Squaw: she followed the Squaw till night, and then both of them lay down: having nothing over them but the Heavens; and under them but the Earth. Thus she travelled three days together, not knowing whither she was going: having nothing to eat or drink but water, and green *Hirtleberries.* At last they came into *Providence,* where she was kindly entertained by several of that Town. The *Indians* often said, that I should never have her under twenty pounds: but now the Lord hath brought her in upon free cost, and given her to me the second time. The Lord make us a blessing indeed, each to others. Now have I seen that Scripture also fulfilled, *If any of thine be driven out to the outmost parts of heaven, from thence will the Lord thy God gather thee, and from thence will he fetch thee. And the Lord thy God will put all these curses upon thine enemies, and on them which hate thee, which persecuted thee. Deut.* 30. 4-7. Thus hath the Lord brought me and mine out of that horrible pit, and hath set us in the midst of tender-hearted and compassionate *Christians.* 'Tis the desire of my soul that we may walk worthy of the mercies received, and which we are receiving.

Our Family being now gathered together (those of us that were living) the South Church in *Boston* hired an house for us: then we Removed from Mr. *Shepards* (those cordial friends) and went to *Boston,* where we continued about three quarters of a year. Still the Lord went along with us, and provided graciously for us. I thought it somewhat strange to set up House-keeping with bare walls, but, as Solomon says, *Money answers all things*: and that we had through the benevolence of *Christian* friends, some in this Town, and some in that, and others, and some from *England,* that in a little time we might look, and see the house furnished with love. The Lord hath been exceeding good to us in our low estate, in that when we had neither house nor home, nor other necessaries, the Lord so moved the hearts of these and those towards us; that we wanted neither food, nor rayment, for our selves or ours, *There is a Friend which sticketh closer than a Brother. Prov.* 18. 24. And how many such friends have we found, and now living amongst! and truly such a Friend have we found him to be unto us, in whose house we lived, *viz.* Mr. *James Whitcomb,* a Friend unto us near hand, and afar off.

I can remember the time, when I used to sleep quietly without workings in my thoughts, whole nights together: but now it is otherwise with me. When all are fast about me, and no eye open, but his who ever waketh, my thoughts are upon things past, upon the awful dispensations of the Lord towards us: upon his wonderful power and might, in carrying of us through so many difficulties, in returning us in safety, and suffering none to hurt us. I remember in the night season, how the other day I was in the midst of thousands of enemies, and nothing but death before me: it is then hard work to perswade my self that ever I should be satisfied with bread again. But now we are fed with the finest of the Wheat, and (as I may so say) with honey out of the rock: instead of the husks, we have the fatted Calf: the thoughts of these things in the particulars of them, and of the love and goodness of God towards us, make it true of me, what *David* said of himself *Psal. 6. 6. I water my Couch with my tears.* Oh the wonderful power of God that mine eyes have seen, affording matter enough for my thoughts to run in, that when others are sleeping mine eyes are weeping.

I have seen the extreme vanity of this World: One hour I have been in health, and wealth, wanting nothing: But the next hour in sickness and wounds, and death, having nothing but sorrow and affliction.

Before I knew what affliction meant, I was ready sometimes to wish for it. When I lived in prosperity; having the comforts of the World about me, my Relations by me, my heart chearful, and taking little care for anything, and yet seeing many (whom I preferred before my self) under many trials and afflictions, in sickness, weakness, poverty, losses, crosses, and cares of the World, I should be sometimes jealous least I should have my portion in this life; and that Scripture would come to my mind, *Heb. 12. 6. For whom the Lord loveth he chasteneth, and scourgeth every Son whom he receiveth:* but now I see the Lord had his time to scourge and chasten me. The portion of some is to have their Affliction by drops, now one drop and then another: but the dregs of the Cup, the wine of astonishment, like a sweeping rain that leaveth no food, did the Lord prepare to be my portion. Affliction I wanted, and Affliction I had, full measure (I thought) pressed down and running over: yet I see when God calls a person to any thing, and through never so many difficulties, yet he is fully able to carry them through, and make them see and say they have been gainers thereby. And I hope I can say in some measure, as *David* did, *It is good for me that I have been afflicted.* The Lord hath showed me the vanity of these outward things, that they are the *Vanity of vanities, and vexation of spirit*; that they are but a shadow, a blast, a bubble, and things of no continuance; that we must rely on God himself, and our whole dependance must be upon Him. If trouble from smaller matters begin to arise in me, I have something at hand to check my self with, and say why am I troubled, It was but the other day, that if I had had the world, I would have given it for my Freedom, or to have been a servant to a *Christian*. I have learned to look beyond present and smaller troubles, and to be quieted under them. As *Moses* said, *Exod.* 14. 13. *Stand still and see the salvation of the Lord.*

Judith Sargent Murray
(1751–1820)

T he first woman of letters in America, Judith Sargent Murray, wrote poetry, fiction, and drama, but was most famous as an essayist who spoke for women's rights after the Revolution. Her first publication in 1784, under the pen name "Constantia," was titled "Desultory Thoughts upon the Utility of Encouraging a Degree of Self-Complacency, especially in Female Bosoms," but despite its cautious and diffident presentation, the poem and accompanying essay were actually a bold and original call for women to develop intellectual confidence, high self-esteem, and self-respect—qualities her contemporaries would have regarded as dangerous feminine vanities. Murray followed up with "On the Equality of the Sexes," which appeared in the *Massachusetts Magazine* in 1790, two years before Mary Wollstonecraft's *Vindication of the Rights of Woman*. Her introductory poem to the essay is included here. Murray was born in Gloucester, Massachusetts, and spent most of her life in Boston, where she was also an ardent advocate of women's education and American literary arts, including the novel and the drama.

Desultory Thoughts upon the Utility of Encouraging a Degree of Self-Complacency, especially in Female Bosoms (1784)

> Self-estimation, kept within due bounds,
> However oddly the assertion sounds,
> May, of the fairest efforts be the root,
> May yield the embow'ring shade—the mellow fruit;
> May stimulate to most exalted deeds,
> Direct the soul where blooming honor leads;
> May give her there, to act a noble part,
> To virtuous pleasures yield the willing heart.
> Self-estimation will debasement shun,
> And, in the path of wisdom, joy to run;
> An unbecoming act in fears to do,

And still, its exaltation keeps in view.
"To rev'rence self," a Bard long since directed,
And, on each moral truth he well reflected;
But, lost to conscious worth, to decent pride,
Compass nor helm there is, our course to guide:
Nor may we anchor cast, for rudely tost
In an unfathom'd sea, each motive's lost,
Wildly amid contending waves we're beat,
And rocks and quick sands, shoals and depths we meet;
'Till, dash'd in pieces, or, till found'ring, we
One common wreck of all our prospects see!
Nor, do we mourn, for we were lost to fame,
And never hap'd to reach a tow'ring name;
Ne'er taught to "rev'rence self," or to aspire,
Our bosoms never caught ambition's fire;
An indolence of virtue still prevail'd,
Nor the sweet gale of praise was e'er inhal'd;
Rous'd by a new stimulus, no kindling glow.
No soothing emulations gentle flow,
We judg'd that nature, not to us inclin'd,
In narrow bounds our progress had confin'd,
And, that our forms, to say the very best,
Only, not frightful, were by all confest.

I think, to teach young minds to aspire, ought to be the ground work of education: many a laudable achievement is lost, from a persuasion that our efforts are unequal to the arduous attainment. Ambition is a noble principle, which properly directed, may be productive of the most valuable consequences. It is amazing to what heights the mind by exertion may tow'r: I would, therefore, have my pupils believe, that every thing in the compass of mortality, was placed within their grasp, and that, the avidity of application, the intenseness of study, were only requisite to endow them with every external grace, and mental accomplishment. Thus I should impel them to progress on, if I could not lead them to the heights I would wish them to attain. It is too common with parents to expatiate in their hearing, upon all the foibles of their children, and to let their virtues pass, in appearance, unregarded: this they do, least they should, (were they to commend) swell their little hearts to pride, and implant in their tender minds, undue conceptions of their own importance. Those, for example, who have the care of a beautiful female, they assiduously guard every avenue, they arrest the stream of due admiration, and endeavour to divest her of all idea of the bounties of nature: what is the consequence? She grows up, and of course mixes with those who are less interested: strangers will be sincere; she encounters the tongue of the flatterer, he will exaggerate, she finds herself possessed of accomplishments which have been studiously concealed from her, she throws the reins upon the neck of fancy, and gives every encomiast full credit for his most extravagant eulogy. Her natural connexions, her home is rendered disagreeable, and she hastes to the scenes, whence arise the sweet perfume of adulation, and when she can obtain the regard due to a merit, which she supposes altogether uncommon. Those who have made her acquainted with the dear secret, she considers as her best friends; and it is more than probable, that she will soon fall a sacrifice to some worthless character, whose interest may lead him to the most hyperbolical lengths in the round of flattery. Now, I should be solicitous that my daughter should possess for me the fondest love, as well as that respect which gives birth to duty; in order to promote this wish of my soul, from my lips she should be accustomed to hear the most pleasing truths, and, as in the course of my instructions, I should doubtless find myself but too often impelled to wound the delicacy of youthful sensibility. I would therefore, be careful to avail myself of this exuberating balance: I would, from the early dawn of reason, address her as a rational being; hence, I apprehend, the most valuable consequences would result: in some such language as this, she might from time to time be accosted. A pleasing form is undoubtedly advantageous, nature, my dear, hath furnished you with an agreeable person, your glass, was I to be silent, would inform you that you are pretty, your appearance will sufficiently recommend you to a stranger, the flatterer will give a more than mortal finishing to every feature; but, it must be your part, my sweet girl, to render yourself worthy respect from higher motives: you must learn "to reverence yourself," that is, your intellectual existence; you must join my efforts, in endeavoring to adorn your mind, for, it is from the proper furnishing of that, you will become indeed a valuable person, you will, as I said, give birth to the most favorable impressions at first sight: but, how mortifying should this be all, if, upon a more extensive knowledge you should be discovered to possess no one mental charm, to be fit only at best, to be hung up as a pleasing picture among the paintings of some spacious hall. The flatterer, indeed, will still pursue you, but it will be from interested views, and he will smile at your undoing! Now, then, my best Love, is the time for you to lay in such a fund of useful knowledge, as shall continue, and augment every kind sentiment in regard to you, as shall set you above the snares of the artful betrayer.

Thus, that sweet form, shall serve but as a polished casket, which will contain a most beautiful gem, highly finished, and calculated for advantage, as well as ornament. Was she, I say, habituated thus to reflect, she would be taught to aspire; she would learn to estimate every accomplishment, according to its proper value; and, when the voice of adulation should assail her ear, as she had early been initiated into its true meaning, and from youth been accustomed to the language of praise; her attention would not be captivated, the Siren's song would not borrow the aid of novelty, her young mind would not be enervated or intoxicated, by a delicious surprise, she would possess her soul in serenity and by that means, rise superior to the deep-laid schemes which, too commonly, encompass the steps of beauty.

Neither should those to whom nature had been parsimonious, be tortured by me with degrading comparisons; every advantage I would expatiate upon, and there are few who possess not some personal charms; I would teach them to gloss over their imperfections, inasmuch as, I do think, an agreeable form, a very necessary introduction to society, and of course it behoves us to render our appearance as pleasing as possible: I would, I must repeat, by all means guard them against a low estimation of self, I would leave no charm undiscovered or unmarked, for the penetrating eye of the pretended admirer, to make unto himself a merit by holding up to her view; thus, I would destroy the weapons of flattery, or render them useless, by leaving not the least room for their operation.

A young lady, growing up with the idea, that she possesses few, or no personal attractions, and that her mental abilities are of an inferior kind, imbibing at the same time, a most melancholly idea of a female, descending down the vale of life in an unprotected state; taught also to regard her character ridiculously contemptible, will, too probably, throw herself away upon the first who approaches her with tenders of love, however indifferent may be her chance for happiness, least if she omits the present day of grace, she may never be so happy as to meet a second offer, and must then inevitably be stigmatized with that dreaded title, an Old Maid, must rank with a class whom she has been accustomed to regard as burthens upon society, and objects whom she might with impunity turn into ridicule! Certainly love, friendship and esteem, ought to take place of marriage, but, the woman thus circumstanced, will seldom regard these previous requisites to felicity, if she can but insure the honors, which she, in idea, associates with a matrimonial connection—

to prevent which great evil, I would early impress under proper regulations, a reverence of self; I would endeavor to rear to worth, and a consciousness thereof: I would be solicitous to inspire the glow of virtue, with that elevation of soul, that dignity, which is ever attendant upon self-approbation, arising from the genuine source of innate rectitude. I must be excused for thus insisting upon my hypothesis, as I am, from observation, persuaded, that many have suffered materially all their life long, from a depression of soul, early inculcated, in compliance to a false maxim, which hath supposed pride would thereby be eradicated. I know there is a contrary extreme, and I would, in almost all cases, prefer the happy medium. However, if these fugitive hints may induce some abler pen to improve thereon, the exemplification will give pleasure to the heart of CONSTANTIA.

Lines from On the Equality of the Sexes (1790)

That minds are not alike, full well I know,
This truth each day's experience will show;
To heights surprising some great spirits soar,
With inborn strength mysterious depths explore;
Their eager gaze surveys the path of light,
Confest it stood to Newton's piercing sight.
Deep science, like a bashful maid retires,
And but the *ardent* breast her worth inspires;
By perseverance the coy fair is won.
And Genius, led by Study, wears the crown.
But some there are who wish not to improve
Who never can the path of knowledge love,
Whose souls almost with the dull body one,
With anxious care each mental pleasure shun;
Weak is the level'd, enervated mind,
And but while here to vegetate design'd.
The torpid spirit mingling with its clod,
Can scarcely boast its origin from God;
Stupidly dull—they move progressing on—
They eat, and drink, and all their work is done.
While others, emulous of sweet applause,
Industrious seek for each event a cause,

Tracing the hidden springs whence knowledge flows,
Which nature all in beauteous order shows.
Yet cannot I their sentiments imbibe,
Who this distinction to the sex ascribe,
As if a woman's form must needs enrol,
A weak, a servile, an inferiour soul;
And that the guise of man must still proclaim,
Greatness of mind, and him, to be the same:
Yet as the hours revolve fair proofs arise,
Which the bright wreath of growing fame supplies;
And in past times some men have *sunk* so *low*,
That female records nothing *less* can show.
But imbecility is still confin'd,
And by the lordly sex to us consign'd;
They rob us of the power t'improve,
And then declare we only trifles love;
Yet haste the era, when the world shall know,
That such distinctions only dwell below;
The soul unfetter'd, to no sex confin'd,
Was for the abodes of cloudless day design'd.
Mean time we emulate their manly fires,
Though erudition all their thoughts inspires,
Yet nature with *equality* imparts
And *noble passions*, swell e'en *female hearts*.

Phillis Wheatley
(*ca. 1753–1784*)

orn in West Africa and brought to America as a slave around 1761, Phillis Wheatley was named by her owners, the Wheatley family in Boston. They quickly recognized her intelligence and gave her an excellent education. At the age of thirteen, she published her first poems. But when she could not find a publisher for a book in America, she went to England with Nathaniel Wheatley, her master's son, and found patrons who helped publish *Poems on Various Subjects* in London in 1773. Soon afterwards she was freed from slavery and married a freeman, but her husband left her, and her three children died in infancy. Wheatley herself died in poverty.

On Being Brought from Africa to America (1773)

'Twas mercy brought me from my pagan land,
Taught my benighted soul to understand
That there's a God, that there's a Savior too:
Once I redemption neither sought nor knew.
Some view our sable race with scornful eye,
"Their color is a diabolic dye."
Remember, Christians, Negroes, black as Cain,
May be refined, and join th' angelic train.

Susanna Haswell Rowson
(1762–1824)

he author of ten novels, seven plays, and numerous text-books and sketches, Susanna Haswell was born in Portsmouth, England, and spent most of her childhood in Massachusetts with her father, a Royal Navy lieutenant. During the Revolutionary War the family was placed under house arrest, and thirteen-year-old Susanna became their caretaker. In 1777, they sailed back to England in a prisoner exchange, and Rowson worked as a governess and writer. She published her first novel *Victoria* in 1786, and married William Rowson, a hardware merchant whose business failings prompted the couple onto the stage. They returned to America in 1793 to join a Philadelphia theater company. Her play *Slaves in Algiers* (1794), in which she also starred, was a hit, and the same year her fourth novel *Charlotte Temple*, which had originally been published in London in 1791, was pirated for American readers and became the first great bestseller in the colonies. Chapters VI and XVIII demonstrate Rowson's ability to tell an exciting story—the seduction of a young English girl by a glamorous British officer who takes her to New York and abandons her there with her child—and also to moralize about feminine virtue and obedience.

CHAPTER VI: An Intriguing Teacher, *from Charlotte Temple* (1791)

Madame Du Pont was a woman every way calculated to take the care of young ladies, had that care entirely devolved on herself; but it was impossible to attend the education of a numerous school without proper assistants; and those assistants were not always the kind of people whose conversation and morals were exactly such as parents of delicacy and refinement would wish a daughter to copy. Among the teachers at Madame Du Pont's school, was Mademoiselle La Rue, who added to a pleasing person and insinuating address, a liberal education and the manners of a gentlewoman. She was recommended to the school by a lady whose humanity overstepped the bounds of discretion: for though she knew Miss La Rue had eloped from a convent with a young officer, and, on coming to England, had lived with several different men in open defiance of all moral and religious duties, yet, finding her reduced to the most abject want, and believing the penitence which she professed to be sincere, she took her into her own family, and from thence recommended her to Madame Du Pont, as thinking the situation more suitable for a woman of her abilities. But Mademoiselle possessed too much of the spirit of intrigue to remain long without adventures. At church, where she constantly appeared, her person attracted the attention of a young man who was upon a visit at a gentleman's seat in the neighbourhood: she had met him several times clandestinely; and being invited to come out that evening, and eat some fruit and pastry in a summer-house belonging to the gentleman he was visiting, and requested to bring some of the ladies with her, Charlotte being her favourite, was fixed on to accompany her.

The mind of youth eagerly catches at promised pleasure: pure and innocent by nature, it thinks not of the dangers lurking beneath those pleasures, till too late to avoid them: when Mademoiselle asked Charlotte to go with her, she mentioned the gentleman as a relation, and spoke in such high terms of the elegance of his gardens, the sprightliness of his conversation, and the liberality with which he ever entertained his guests, that Charlotte thought only of the pleasure she should enjoy in the visit,—not on the imprudence of going without her governess's knowledge, or of the danger to which she exposed herself in visiting the house of a gay young man of fashion.

Madame Du Pont was gone out for the evening, and the rest of the ladies retired to rest, when Charlotte and the teacher stole out at the back gate, and in crossing the field, were accosted by Montraville, as mentioned in the first chapter.

Charlotte was disappointed in the pleasure she had promised herself from this visit. The levity of the gentlemen and the freedom of their conversation disgusted her. She was astonished at the liberties Mademoiselle permitted them to take; grew thoughtful and uneasy, and heartily wished herself at home again in her own chamber.

Perhaps one cause of that wish might be, an earnest desire to see the contents of the letter which had been put into her hand by Montraville.

Any reader who has the least knowledge of the world, will easily imagine the letter was made up of encomiums on her beauty, and vows of everlasting love and constancy; nor will he be surprised that a heart open to every gentle, generous sentiment, should feel itself warmed by gratitude for a man who professed to feel so much for her; nor is it improbable but her mind might revert to the agreeable person and martial appearance of Montraville.

In affairs of love, a young heart is never in more danger than when attempted by a handsome young soldier. A man of an indifferent appearance, will, when arrayed in a military habit, shew to advantage; but when beauty of person, elegance of manner, and an easy method of paying compliments, are united to the scarlet coat, smart cockade, and military sash, ah! well-a-day for the poor girl who gazes on him: she is in imminent danger; but if she listens to him with pleasure, 'tis all over with her, and from that moment she has neither eyes nor ears for any other object.

Now, my dear sober matron, (if a sober matron should deign to turn over these pages, before she trusts them to the eye of a darling daughter,) let me intreat you not to put on a grave face, and throw down the book in a passion and declare 'tis enough to turn the heads of half the girls in England; I do solemnly protest, my dear madam, I mean no more by what I have here advanced, than to ridicule those romantic girls, who foolishly imagine a red coat and silver epaulet constitute the fine gentleman; and should that fine gentleman make half a dozen fine speeches to them, they will imagine themselves so much in love as to fancy it a meritorious action to jump out of a two pair of stairs window, abandon their friends, and trust entirely to the honour of a man, who perhaps hardly knows the meaning of the word, and if he does, will be too much the modern man of refinement, to practice it in their favour.

Gracious heaven! when I think on the miseries that must rend the heart of a doting parent, when he sees the darling of his age at first seduced from his protection, and afterwards abandoned, by the very wretch whose promises of love decoyed her from the paternal roof— when he sees her poor and wretched, her bosom torn between remorse for her crime and love for her vile betrayer—when fancy paints to me the good old man stooping to raise the weeping penitent, while every tear from her eye is numbered by drops from his bleeding heart, my bosom glows with honest indignation, and I wish for power to extirpate those monsters of seduction from the earth.

Oh my dear girls—for to such only am I writing—listen not to the voice of love, unless sanctioned by paternal approbation: be assured, it is now past the days of romance: no woman can be run away with contrary to her own inclination: then kneel down each morning, and request kind heaven to keep you free from temptation, or, should it please to suffer you to be tried, pray for fortitude to resist the impulse of inclination when it runs counter to the precepts of religion and virtue.

CHAPTER XVIII: Reflections, *from Charlotte Temple* (1791)

"And am I indeed fallen so low," said Charlotte, "as to be only pitied? Will the voice of approbation no more meet my ear? and shall I never again possess a friend, whose face will wear a smile of joy whenever I approach? Alas! how thoughtless, how dreadfully imprudent have I been! I know not which is most painful to endure, the sneer of contempt, or the glance of compassion, which is depicted in the various countenances of my own sex: they are both equally humiliating. Ah! my dear parents, could you now see the child of your affections, the daughter whom you so dearly loved, a poor solitary being, without society, here wearing out her heavy hours in deep regret and anguish of heart, no kind friend of her own sex to whom she can unbosom her griefs, no beloved mother, no woman of character will appear in my company, and low as your Charlotte is fallen, she cannot associate with infamy."

These were the painful reflections which occupied the mind of Charlotte. Montraville had placed her in a small house a few miles from New-York: he gave her one female attendant, and supplied her with what money she wanted; but business and pleasure so entirely occupied his time, that he had little to devote to the woman, whom he had brought from all her connections, and robbed of innocence. Sometimes, indeed, he would steal out at the close of evening, and pass a few hours with her; and then so much was she attached to him, that all her sorrows were forgotten while blest with his society: she would enjoy a walk by moonlight, or sit by him in a little arbour at the bottom of the garden, and play on the harp, accompanying it with her plaintive, harmonious voice. But often, very often, did he promise to renew his visits, and, forgetful of his promise, leave her to mourn her disappointment. What painful hours of expectation would she pass! She would sit at a window which looked toward a field he used to cross, counting the minutes, and straining her eyes to catch the first glimpse of his person, till blinded with tears of disappointment, she would lean her head on her hands, and give free vent to her sorrows: then catching at some new hope, she would again renew her watchful position, till the shades of evening enveloped every object in a dusky cloud: she would then renew her complaints, and, with a heart bursting with disappointed love and wounded sensibility, retire to a bed which remorse had strewed with thorns, and court in vain that comforter of weary nature (who seldom visits the unhappy) to come and steep her senses in oblivion.

Who can form an adequate idea of the sorrow that preyed upon the mind of Charlotte? The wife, whose breast glows with affection to her husband, and who in return meets only indifference, can but faintly conceive her anguish. Dreadfully painful is the situation of such a woman, but she has many comforts of which our poor Charlotte was deprived. The duteous, faithful wife, though treated with indifference, has one solid pleasure within her own bosom, she can reflect that she has not deserved neglect—that she has ever fulfilled the duties of her station with the strictest exactness; she may hope, by constant assiduity and unremitted attention, to recall her wanderer, and be doubly happy in his returning affection; she knows he cannot leave her to unite himself to another: he cannot cast her out to poverty and contempt; she looks around her, and sees the smile of friendly welcome, or the tear of affectionate consolation, on the face of every person whom she favours with her esteem; and from all these circumstances she gathers comfort: but the poor girl by thoughtless passion led astray, who, in parting with her honour, has forfeited the esteem of the very man to whom she has sacrificed every thing dear and valuable in life, feels his indifference in the fruit of her own folly, and laments her want of power to recall his lost affection; she knows there is no tie but honour, and that, in a man who has been guilty of seduction, is but very feeble: he may leave her in a moment to shame and want; he may marry and forsake her for ever; and should he, she has no redress, no friendly, soothing companion to pour into her wounded mind the balm of consolation, no benevolent hand to lead her back to the path of rectitude; she has disgraced her friends, forfeited the good opinion of the world, and undone herself; she feels herself a poor solitary being in the midst of surrounding multitudes; shame bows her to the earth, remorse tears her distracted mind, and guilt, poverty, and disease close the dreadful scene: she sinks unnoticed to oblivion. The finger of contempt may point out to some passing daughter of youthful mirth, the humble bed where lies this frail sister of mortality; and will she, in the unbounded gaiety of her heart, exult in her own unblemished fame, and triumph over the silent ashes of the dead? Oh no! has she a heart of sensibility, she will stop, and thus address the unhappy victim of folly—

"Thou had'st thy faults, but sure thy sufferings have expiated them: thy errors brought thee to an early grave; but thou wert a fellow-creature—thou hast been unhappy—then be those errors forgotten."

Then, as she stoops to pluck the noxious weed from off the sod, a tear will fall, and consecrate the spot to Charity.

For ever honoured be the sacred drop of humanity; the angel of mercy shall record its source, and the soul from whence it sprang shall be immortal.

My dear Madam, contract not your brow into a frown of disapprobation. I mean not to extenuate the faults of those unhappy women who fall victims to guilt and folly; but surely, when we reflect how many errors we are ourselves subject to, how many secret faults lie hid in the recesses of our hearts, which we should blush to have brought into open day (and yet those faults require the lenity and pity of a benevolent judge, or awful would be our prospect of futurity) I say, my dear Madam, when we consider this, we surely may pity the faults of others.

Believe me, many an unfortunate female, who has once strayed into the thorny paths of vice, would gladly return to virtue, was any generous friend to endeavour to raise and re-assure her; but alas! it cannot be, you say; the world would deride and scoff. Then let me tell you, Madam, 'tis a very unfeeling world, and does not deserve half the blessings which a bountiful Providence showers upon it.

Oh, thou benevolent giver of all good! how shall we erring mortals dare to look up to thy mercy in the great day of retribution, if we now uncharitably refuse to overlook the errors, or alleviate the miseries, of our fellow-creatures.

Catharine Maria Sedgwick
(1789–1867)

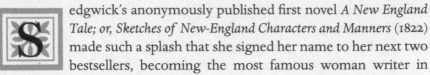 edgwick's anonymously published first novel *A New England Tale; or, Sketches of New-England Characters and Manners* (1822) made such a splash that she signed her name to her next two bestsellers, becoming the most famous woman writer in America. Though she continued to mold a distinctly American literature in her popular novels and short fiction for more than two decades, her short story *"Cacoethes Scribendi"* satirizes the wave of American women writers newly crowding the literary market. The title is a phrase from Juvenal's satires meaning "writer's itch," or "an irresistible urge to write."

Cacoethes Scribendi (1830)

> *Glory and gain the industrious tribe provoke.*
> —POPE

The little secluded and quiet village of H. lies at no great distance from our "literary emporium." It was never remarked or remarkable for any thing, save one mournful pre-eminence, to those who sojourned within its borders—it was duller, even, than common villages. The young men of the better class all emigrated. The most daring spirits adventured on the sea. Some went to Boston; some to the south; and some to the west; and left a community of women who lived like nuns, with the advantage of more liberty and fresh air, but without the consolation and excitement of a religious vow. Literally, there was not a single young gentleman in the village—nothing in manly shape to which these desperate circumstances could give the form and quality, and use of a beau. Some dashing city blades, who once strayed accidentally to this sequestered spot, averred that the girls stared at them as if, like Miranda, they would have exclaimed—

> *What is't? a spirit?*
> *Lord, how it looks about! Believe me, sir,*
> *It carries a brave form:—But 'tis a spirit.*

A peculiar fatality hung over this devoted place. If death seized on either head of a family, he was sure to take the husband; every woman in H. was a widow or maiden: and it is a sad fact, that when the holiest office of the church was celebrated, they were compelled to borrow deacons from an adjacent village. But, incredible as it may seem, there was no great diminution of happiness in consequence of the absence of the nobler sex. Mothers were occupied with their children and housewifery, and the young ladies read their books with as much interest as if they had lovers to discuss them with, and worked their frills and capes as diligently, and wore them as complacently, as if they were to be seen by manly eyes. Never were there pleasanter gatherings or parties (for that was the word even in their nomenclature) than those of the young girls of H. There was no mincing—no affectation—no hope of passing for what they were not—no envy of the pretty and fortunate—no insolent triumph over the plain, and demure, and neglected—but all was good-will and good-humour. They were a pretty circle of girls—a garland of bright fresh flowers. Never were there more sparkling glances—never sweeter smiles—nor more of them. Their present was all health and cheerfulness; and their future, not the gloomy perspective of dreary singleness, for somewhere in the passage of life they were sure to be mated. Most of the young men who had abandoned their native soil, as soon as they found themselves *getting along*, loyally returned to lay their fortunes at the feet of the companions of their childhood.

The girls made occasional visits to Boston, and occasional journeys to various parts of the country, for they were all enterprising and independent; and had the characteristic New England avidity for seizing a "privilege"; and in these various ways, to borrow a phrase of their good grandames, "a door was opened for them," and in due time they fulfilled the destiny of women.

We spoke strictly, and à la lettre, when we said that in the village of H. there was not a single *beau*. But on the outskirts of the town, at a pleasant farm, embracing hill and valley, upland and meadow land—in a neat house, looking to the south, with true economy of sunshine and comfort, and overlooking the prettiest winding stream that ever sent up its sparkling beauty to the eye; and flanked on the north by a rich maple grove, beautiful in spring and summer, and glorious in autumn, and the kindest defence in winter;—on this farm, and in this house dwelt a youth, to fame unknown; but known and loved by every inhabitant of H., old and young, grave and gay, lively and severe. Ralph Hepburn was one of nature's favourites. He had a figure that would have adorned courts and cities; and a face that adorned human nature, for it was full of good humour, kind-heartedness, spirit and intelligence; and, driving the plough, or wielding the scythe, his cheek flushed with manly and profitable exercise, he looked as if he had been moulded in a poet's fancy—as farmers look in Georgics and Pastorals. His gifts were by no means all external. He wrote verses in every album in the village, and very pretty album verses they were, and numerous too—for the number of albums was equivalent to the whole female population. He was admirable at pencil sketches; and once, with a little paint, the refuse of a house-painting, he achieved an admirable portrait of his grandmother and her cat. There was, to be sure, a striking likeness between the two figures; but he was limited to the same colours for both; and besides, it was not out of nature, for the old lady and her cat had purred together in the chimney corner, till their physiognomies bore an obvious resemblance to each other. Ralph had a talent for music too. His voice was the sweetest of all the Sunday choir; and one would have fancied, from the bright eyes that were turned on him, from the long line and double lines of treble and counter singers, that Ralph Hepburn was a notebook; or that the girls listened with their eyes as well as their ears. Ralph did not restrict himself to psalmody. He had an ear so exquisitely susceptible to the "touches of sweet harmony," that he discovered, by the stroke of his axe, the musical capacities of certain species of wood, and he made himself a violin of chestnut, and drew strains from it, that if they could not create a soul under the ribs of death, could make the prettiest feet and the lightest heart dance; an achievement far more to Ralph's taste than the aforesaid miracle. In short, it seemed as if nature, in her love of compensation, had showered on Ralph all the gifts that are usually diffused through a community of beaux. Yet Ralph was no prodigy; none of his talents were in excess, but all in moderate degree. No genius was ever so good humoured, so useful, so practical; and though, in his small and modest way, a Crichton, he was not, like most universal geniuses, good for nothing for any particular office in life. His farm was not a pattern farm—a prize farm, for an agricultural society; but in wonderful order, considering his miscellaneous pursuits. He was the delight of his grandfather, for his sagacity in hunting bees—the old man's favourite—in truth his only pursuit. He was so skilled in woodcraft, that the report of his gun was as certain a signal of death, as the tolling of a church bell. The fish always caught at his bait. He manufactured half his farming utensils; improved upon old inventions, and struck out some new ones; tamed partridges—

the most untameable of all the feathered tribe; domesticated squirrels; rivalled Scheherazade herself in telling stories, strange and long—the latter quality being essential at a country fireside; and, in short, Ralph made a perpetual holiday of a life of labour.

Every girl in the village-street knew when Ralph's waggon or sleigh traversed it; indeed, there was scarcely a house to which the horses did not, as if by instinct, turn up, while their master greeted its fair tenants. This state of affairs had continued for two winters and two summers, since Ralph came to his majority, and by the death of his father, to the sole proprietorship of the "Hepburn farm,"—the name his patrimonial acres had obtained from the singular circumstance, (in our *moving* country,) of their having remained in the same family for four generations. Never was the matrimonial destiny of a young lord, or heir just come to his estate, more thoroughly canvassed than young Hepburn's, by mothers, aunts, daughters, and nieces. But Ralph, perhaps from sheer good nature, seemed reluctant to give to one the heart, that diffused rays of sunshine through the whole village.

With all decent people, he eschewed the doctrines of a certain erratic female lecturer, on the odious monopoly of marriage; yet Ralph, like a tender-hearted judge, hesitated to place on a single brow the crown matrimonial, which so many deserved, and which, though Ralph was far enough from a coxcomb, he could not but see so many coveted.

Whether our hero perceived that his mind was becoming elated or distracted with this general favour, or that he observed a dawning of rivalry among the fair competitors, or whatever was the cause, the fact was, that he by degrees circumscribed his visits, and finally concentrated them in the family of his aunt Courland.

Mrs. Courland was a widow, and Ralph was the kindest of nephews to her, and the kindest of cousins to her children. To their mother, he seemed their guardian angel. That the five lawless, darling little urchins did not drown themselves when they were swimming, nor shoot themselves when they were shooting, was, in her eyes, Ralph's merit; and then, "he was so attentive to Alice, her only daughter—a brother could not be kinder." But who would not be kind to Alice?—She was a sweet girl of seventeen, not beautiful—not handsome, perhaps—but pretty enough—with soft hazel eyes; a profusion of light brown hair, always in the neatest trim; and a mouth, that could not but be lovely and loveable, for all kind and tender affections were playing about it. Though Alice was the only daughter of a doting mother, the only sister of five loving boys, the only niece of three single, fond aunts; and last and greatest, the only cousin of our only beau, Ralph Hepburn—no girl of seventeen was ever more disinterested, unassuming, unostentatious, and unspoiled. Ralph and Alice had always lived on terms of cousinly affection; an affection of a neutral tint, that they never thought of being shaded into the deep dye of a more tender passion. Ralph rendered her all cousinly offices. If he had twenty damsels to escort, not an uncommon case, he never forgot Alice. When he returned from any little excursion, he always brought some graceful offering to Alice.

He had lately paid a visit to Boston. It was at the season of the periodical inundation of annuals. He brought two of the prettiest to Alice. Ah! little did she think, they were to prove Pandora's box to her. Poor simple girl! she sat down to read them, as if an annual were meant to be read; and she was honestly interested and charmed. Her mother observed her delight. "What have you there, Alice?" she asked. "Oh, the prettiest story, mamma!—two such tried, faithful lovers, and married at last! It ends beautifully: I hate love stories that don't end in marriage!"

"And so do I, Alice," exclaimed Ralph, who entered at the moment; and, for the first time, Alice felt her cheeks tingle at his approach. He had brought a basket, containing a choice plant he had obtained for her; and she laid down the annual, and went with him to the garden, to see it set by his own hand.

Mrs. Courland seized upon the annual with avidity. She had imbibed a literary taste at Boston; where the best and happiest years of her life were passed. She had some literary ambition too. She read the North American Review from beginning to end; and she fancied no conversation could be sensible or improving, that was not about books. But she had been effectually prevented, by the necessities of a narrow income, and by the unceasing wants of five teasing boys, from indulging her literary inclinations; for Mrs. Courland, like all New England women, had been taught to consider domestic duties as the first temporal duties of her sex. She had recently seen some of the native productions with which the press is daily teeming; and which certainly have a tendency to dispel our early illusions about the craft of authorship. She had even felt some obscure intimations, within her secret soul, that she might herself become an author. The annual was destined to fix her fate. She opened it—the publisher had written the names of the authors of the anonymous pieces against their productions. Among them she found some of the familiar friends of her childhood and youth.

If, by a sudden gift of second sight, she had seen them enthroned as kings and queens, she would not have been more astonished. She turned to their pieces, and read them, as perchance no one else did, from beginning to end—faithfully. Not a sentence—a sentence! not a word was skipped. She paused to consider commas, colons, and dashes. All the art and magic of authorship were made level to her comprehension, and when she closed the book, she *felt a call* to become an author, and before she retired to bed she obeyed the call, as if it had been, in truth, a divinity stirring within her. In the morning she presented an article to *her* public, consisting of her own family and a few select friends. All applauded, and every voice, save one, was unanimous for publication— that one was Alice. She was a modest, prudent girl; she feared failure, and feared notoriety still more. Her mother laughed at her childish scruples. The piece was sent off, and in due time graced the pages of an annual. Mrs. Courland's fate was now decided. She had, to use her own phrase, started in the career of letters, and she was no Atalanta to be seduced from her straight onward way. She was a social, sympathetic, good-hearted creature too, and she could not bear to go forth in the golden field to reap alone.

She was, besides, a prudent woman, as most of her countrywomen are, and the little pecuniary equivalent for this delightful exercise of talent was not overlooked. Mrs. Courland, as we have somewhere said, had three single sisters—worthy women they were—but nobody ever dreamed of their taking to authorship. She, however, held them all in sisterly estimation. Their talents were magnified as the talents of persons who live in a circumscribed sphere are apt to be, particularly if seen through the dilating medium of affection.

Miss Anne, the eldest, was fond of flowers, a successful cultivator, and a diligent student of the science of botany. All this taste and knowledge, Mrs. Courland thought, might be turned to excellent account; and she persuaded Miss Anne to write a little book entitled "Familiar Dialogues on Botany." The second sister, Miss Ruth, had a turn for education, ("bachelor's wives and maid's children are always well taught,") and Miss Ruth undertook a popular treatise on that subject. Miss Sally, the youngest, was the saint of the family, and she doubted about the propriety of a literary occupation, till her scruples were overcome by the fortunate suggestion that her coup d'essai should be a Saturday night book, entitled "Solemn Hours,"—and solemn hours they were to their unhappy readers. Mrs. Courland next besieged her old mother. "You know, mamma," she said, "you have such a precious fund of anecdotes of the revolution and the French war, and you talk just like the 'Annals of the Parish,' and I am certain you can write a book fully as good."

"My child, you are distracted! I write a dreadfully poor hand, and I never learned to spell—no girls did in my time."

"Spell! that is not of the least consequence—the printers correct the spelling."

But the honest old lady would not be tempted on the crusade, and her daughter consoled herself with the reflection, that if she would not write, she was an admirable subject to be written about, and her diligent fingers worked off three distinct stories in which the old lady figured.

Mrs. Courland's ambition, of course, embraced within its widening circle her favourite nephew, Ralph. She had always thought him a genius, and genius in her estimation was the philosopher's stone. In his youth she had laboured to persuade his father to send him to Cambridge, but the old man uniformly replied that Ralph "was a smart lad on the farm, and steady, and by that he knew he was no genius." As Ralph's character was developed, and talent after talent broke forth, his aunt renewed her lamentations over his ignoble destiny. That Ralph was useful, good, and happy—the most difficult and rare results achieved in life—was nothing, so long as he was but a farmer in H. Once she did half persuade him to turn painter, but his good sense and filial duty triumphed over her eloquence, and suppressed the hankerings after distinction that are innate in every human breast, from the little ragged chimneysweep that hopes to be a *boss*, to the political aspirant, whose bright goal is the presidential chair.

Now Mrs. Courland fancied Ralph might climb the steep of fame without quitting his farm; occasional authorship was compatible with his vocation. But, alas! she could not persuade Ralph to pluck the laurels that she saw ready grown to his hand. She was not offended, for she was the best-natured woman in the world, but she heartily pitied him, and seldom mentioned his name without repeating that stanza of Gray's, inspired for the consolation of hopeless obscurity:

"Full many a gem of purest ray serene," &c.

Poor Alice's sorrows we have reserved to the last, for they were the heaviest. "Alice," her mother said, "was gifted; she was well educated, well informed; she was every thing necessary to be an author." But Alice resisted; and, though the gentlest and most complying of all good daughters, she would have resisted to the death—she would as soon have stood in a pillory as have appeared in print. Her mother, Mrs. Courland, was not an obstinate woman, and gave up in despair. But still our poor heroine was destined to be the victim of this *cacoethes scribendi*; for Mrs. Courland divided the world into two classes, or rather parts—authors and subjects for authors; the one active, and the other passive. At first blush one would have thought the village of H. rather a barren field for such a reaper as Mrs. Courland, but her zeal and indefatigableness worked wonders. She converted the stern scholastic divine of H. into as much of a La Roche as she could describe; a tall wrinkled bony old woman, who reminded her of Meg Merrilies sat for a witch; the schoolmaster for an Ichabod Crane; a poor half-witted boy was made to utter as much pathos, and sentiment, and wit, as she could put into his lips; and a crazy vagrant was a God-send to her. Then every "wide spreading elm," "blasted pine," or "gnarled oak," flourished on her pages. The village church and school-house stood there according to their actual dimensions. One old *pilgrim* house was as prolific as haunted tower or ruined abbey. It was surveyed outside, ransacked inside, and again made habitable for the reimbodied spirits of its founders.

The most kind-hearted of women, Mrs. Courland's interests came to be so at variance with the prosperity of the little community of H., that a sudden calamity, a death, a funeral, were fortunate events to her. To do her justice she felt them in a twofold capacity. She wept as a woman, and exulted as an author. The days of the calamities of authors have passed by. We have all wept over Otway, and shivered at the thought of Tasso. But times are changed. The lean sheaf is devouring the full one. A new class of sufferers has arisen, and there is nothing more touching in all the memoirs Mr. D'Israeli has collected, than the trials of poor Alice, tragi-comic though they were. Mrs. Courland's new passion ran most naturally in the worn channel of maternal affection. Her boys were too purely boys for her art—but Alice, her sweet Alice, was pre-eminently lovely in the new light in which she now placed every object. Not an incident in her life but was inscribed on her mother's memory, and thence transferred to her pages, by way of precept, or example, or pathetic or ludicrous circumstance. She regretted now, for the first time, that Alice had no lover whom she might introduce among her dramatis personæ. Once her thoughts did glance on Ralph, but she had not quite merged the woman in the author; she knew instinctively that Alice would be particularly offended at being thus paired with Ralph. But Alice's *public life* was not limited to her mother's productions. She was the darling niece of her three aunts. She had studied botany with the eldest, and Miss Anne had recorded in her private diary all her favourite's clever remarks during their progress in the science. This diary was now a mine of gold to her, and faithfully worked up for a circulating medium. But, most trying of all to poor Alice, was the attitude in which she appeared in her aunt Sally's "solemn hours." Every aspiration of piety to which her young lips had given utterance was there *printed*. She felt as if she were condemned to say her prayers in the market place. Every act of kindness, every deed of charity, she had ever performed, were produced to the public. Alice would have been consoled if she had known how small that public was; but, as it was, she felt like a modest country girl when she first enters an apartment hung on every side with mirrors, when, shrinking from observation, she sees in every direction her image multiplied and often distorted; for, notwithstanding Alice's dutiful respect for her good aunts, and her consciousness of their affectionate intentions, she could not but perceive that they were unskilled painters. She grew afraid to speak or to act, and from being the most artless, frank, and, at home, social little creature in the world, she became as silent and as still as a statue. And, in the circle of her young associates, her natural gaiety was constantly checked by their winks and smiles, and broader allusions to her multiplied portraits; for they had instantly recognized them through the thin veil of feigned names of persons and places. They called her a blue stocking too; for they had the vulgar notion that every body must be tinged that lived under the same roof with an author. Our poor victim was afraid to speak of a book—worse than that, she was afraid to touch one, and the last Waverley novel actually lay in the house a month before she opened it. She avoided wearing even a blue ribbon, as fearfully as a forsaken damsel shuns the colour of green.

It was during the height of this literary fever in the Courland family, that Ralph Hepburn, as has been mentioned, concentrated all his visiting there. He was of a compassionate disposition, and he knew Alice was, unless relieved by him, in solitary possession of their once social parlour, whilst her mother and aunts were driving their quills in their several apartments. Oh! what a changed place was that parlour! Not the tower of Babel, after the builders had forsaken it, exhibited a sadder reverse; not a Lancasterian school, when the boys have left it, a more striking contrast. Mrs. Courland and her sisters were all "talking women," and too generous to encroach on one another's rights and happiness. They had acquired the power to hear and speak simultaneously. Their parlour was the general gathering place, a sort of village exchange, where all the innocent gossips, old and young, met together. "There are tongues in trees," and surely there seemed to be tongues in the very walls of that

vocal parlour. Every thing there had a social aspect. There was some-
thing agreeable and conversable in the litter of netting and knitting
work, of sewing implements, and all the signs and shows of happy
female occupation.

Now, all was as orderly as a town drawing-room in company hours.
Not a sound was heard there save Ralph's and Alice's voices, mingling in
soft and suppressed murmurs, as if afraid of breaking the chain of their
aunt's ideas, or perchance, of too rudely jarring a tenderer chain. One
evening, after tea, Mrs. Courland remained with her daughter, instead of
retiring, as usual, to her writing desk. "Alice, my dear," said the good
mother, "I have noticed for a few days past that you look out of spirits.
You will listen to nothing I say on that subject; but if you would try it, my
dear, if you would only try it, you would find there is nothing so tran-
quillizing as the occupation of writing."

"I shall never try it, mamma."

"You are afraid of being called a blue stocking.—Ah! Ralph, how are
you?"—Ralph entered at this moment.—"Ralph, tell me honestly, do you
not think it a weakness in Alice to be afraid of blue stockings?"

"It would be a pity, aunt, to put blue stockings on such pretty feet as
Alice's."

Alice blushed and smiled, and her mother said—"Nonsense, Ralph;
you should bear in mind the celebrated saying of the Edinburgh wit—'no
matter how blue the stockings are, if the petticoats are long enough to
hide them.'"

"Hide Alice's feet! Oh aunt, worse and worse!"

"Better hide her feet, Ralph, than her talents—that is a sin for which
both she and you will have to answer. Oh! you and Alice need not
exchange such significant glances! You are doing yourselves and the pub-
lic injustice, and you have no idea how easy writing is."

"Easy writing, but hard reading, aunt."

"That's false modesty, Ralph. If I had but your opportunities to collect
materials"—Mrs. Courland did not know that in literature, as in some
species of manufacture, the most exquisite productions are wrought
from the smallest quantity of raw material—"There's your journey to
New York, Ralph," she continued, "you might have made three capital
articles out of that. The revolutionary officer would have worked up for
the 'Legendary;' the mysterious lady for the 'Token;' and the man in
black for the 'Remember Me;'—all founded on fact, all romantic and
pathetic."

"But mamma," said Alice, expressing in words what Ralph's arch smile expressed almost as plainly, "you know the officer drank too much; and the mysterious lady turned out to be a runaway milliner; and the man in black—oh! what a theme for a pathetic story!—the man in black was a widower, on his way to Newhaven, where he was to select his third wife from three *recommended* candidates."

"Pshaw! Alice: do you suppose it is necessary to tell things precisely as they are?"

"Alice is wrong, aunt, and you are right; and if she will open her writing desk for me, I will sit down this moment, and write a story—a true story—true from beginning to end; and if it moves you, my dear aunt, if it meets with your approbation, my destiny is decided."

Mrs. Courland was delighted; she had slain the giant, and she saw fame and fortune smiling on her favourite. She arranged the desk for him herself; she prepared a folio sheet of paper, folded the ominous margins, and was so absorbed in her bright visions, that she did not hear a little by-talk between Ralph and Alice, nor see the tell-tale flush on their cheeks, nor notice the perturbation with which Alice walked first to one window and then to another, and, finally, settled herself to that best of all seda-tives—hemming a handkerchief. Ralph chewed off the end of his quill, mended his pen twice, though his aunt assured him "printers did not mind the penmanship," and had achieved a single line when Mrs. Cour-land's vigilant eye was averted by the entrance of her servant girl, who put a packet into her hands. She looked at the direction, cut the string, broke the seals, and took out a periodical fresh from the publisher. She opened at the first article—a strangely-mingled current of maternal pride and literary triumph rushed through her heart and brightened her face. She whispered to the servant a summons to all her sisters to the par-lour, and an intimation, sufficiently intelligible to them, of her joyful rea-son for interrupting them.

Our readers will sympathize with her, and with Alice too, when we disclose to them the secret of her joy. The article in question was a clever composition written by our devoted Alice when she was at school. One of her fond aunts had preserved it; and aunts and mother had combined in the pious fraud of giving it to the public, unknown to Alice. They were perfectly aware of her determination never to be an author. But they fan-cied it was the mere timidity of an unfledged bird; and that when, by their innocent artifice, she found that her pinions could soar in a literary atmosphere, she would realize the sweet fluttering sensations they had experienced at their first flight. The good souls all hurried to the parlour, eager to witness the coup de théatre. Miss Sally's pen stood emblematically erect in her turban; Miss Ruth, in her haste, had overset her ink-stand, and the drops were trickling down her white dressing, or, as she now called it, writing gown; and Miss Anne had a wild flower in her hand, as she hoped, of an undescribed species, which in her joyful agitation, she most unluckily picked to pieces. All bit their lips to keep impatient congratulation from bursting forth. Ralph was so intent on his writing, and Alice on her hemming, that neither noticed the irruption; and Mrs. Courland was obliged twice to speak to her daughter before she could draw her attention.

"Alice, look here—Alice, my dear."

"What is it, mamma? something new of yours?"

"No; guess again, Alice."

"Of one of my aunts, of course?"

"Neither, dear, neither. Come and look for yourself, and see if you can then tell whose it is."

Alice dutifully laid aside her work, approached and took the book. The moment her eye glanced on the fatal page, all her apathy vanished—deep crimson overspread her cheeks, brow, and neck. She burst into tears of irrepressible vexation, and threw the book into the blazing fire.

The gentle Alice! Never had she been guilty of such an ebullition of temper. Her poor dismayed aunts retreated; her mother looked at her in mute astonishment; and Ralph, struck with her emotion, started from the desk, and would have asked an explanation, but Alice exclaimed—"Don't say any thing about it, mamma—I cannot bear it now."

Mrs. Courland knew instinctively that Ralph would sympathize entirely with Alice, and quite willing to avoid an éclaircissement, she said—"Some other time, Ralph, I'll tell you the whole. Show me now what you have written. How have you begun?"

Ralph handed her the paper with a novice's trembling hand.

"Oh! how very little! and so scratched and interlined! but never mind—'ce n'est que le premier pas qui coute.'"

While making these general observations, the good mother was getting out and fixing her spectacles, and Alice and Ralph had retreated behind her. Alice rested her head on his shoulder, and Ralph's lips were not far from her ear. Whether he was soothing her ruffled spirit, or what he was doing, is not recorded. Mrs. Courland read and re-read the sentence. She dropped a tear on it. She forgot her literary aspirations for Ralph and Alice—forgot she was herself an author—forgot every thing but the mother; and rising, embraced them both as her dear children, and expressed, in her raised and moistened eye, the consent to their union, which Ralph had dutifully and prettily asked in that short and true story of his love for his sweet cousin Alice.

In due time the village of H. was animated with the celebration of Alice's nuptials: and when her mother and aunts saw her the happy mistress of the Hepburn farm, and the happiest of wives, they relinquished, without a sigh, the hope of ever seeing her an AUTHOR.

Lydia Huntley Sigourney
(1791–1865)

he only daughter of a Connecticut handyman, Sigourney first entered the literary world through the patronage of her father's widowed employer. She also established a school for girls, and educational material for her students became her first book, *Moral Pieces in Prose and Verse* (1815). Her 1819 marriage to a prominent Hartford widower Charles Sigourney, who disapproved of her public authorship, forced her to publish her work anonymously for some time, but his declining finances and an exposé of her identity finally allowed her to write in her own name. While much of Sigourney's poetry focused on sentimental themes and Christian values, she was also one of the first American writers to sympathize with the plight of Native Americans and protest against Indian removal policies. Sigourney also had a sharp sense of humor, as her article on the endless and narcissistic solicitations of her fans demonstrates.

Indian Names (1849)

How can the red men be forgotten, while so many of our states and ter-
ritories, bays, lakes, and rivers, are indelibly stamped by names of
their giving?

Ye say they all have pass'd away,
    That noble race and brave;
That their light canoes have vanish'd
    From off the crested wave;
That, mid the forests where they roam'd,
    There rings no hunter's shout;
But their name is on your waters—
    Ye may not wash it out.

'Tis where Ontario's billow
    Like Ocean's surge is curl'd;

Where strong Niagara's thunders wake
   The echo of the world;
Where red Missouri bringeth
   Rich tribute from the west;
And Rappahannock sweetly sleeps
   On green Virginia's breast.

Ye say their conelike cabins,
   That cluster'd o'er the vale,
Have fled away like wither'd leaves
   Before the autumn's gale;
But their memory liveth on your hills,
   Their baptism on your shore,
Your everlasting rivers speak
   Their dialect of yore.

Old Massachusetts wears it
   Within her lordly crown,
And broad Ohio bears it
   Amid his young renown;
Connecticut hath wreath'd it
   Where her quiet foliage waves,
And bold Kentucky breathed it hoarse
   Through all her ancient caves.

Wachuset hides its lingering voice
   Within his rocky heart,
And Alleghany graves its tone
   Throughout his lofty chart.
Monadnock, on his forehead hoar,
   Doth seal the sacred trust:
Your mountains build their monument,
   Though ye destroy their dust.

Ye call these red-browed brethren
   The insects of an hour,
Crushed like the noteless worm amid
   The regions of their power;
Ye drive them from their fathers' lands,
   Ye break of faith the seal,

But can ye from the court of Heaven
    Exclude their last appeal?

Ye see their unresisting tribes,
    With toilsome step and slow,
On through the trackless desert pass,
    A caravan of woe;
Think ye the Eternal's ear is deaf?
    His sleepless vision dim?
Think ye the *soul's blood* may not cry
    From that far land to him?

Requests for Writing, *from Letters of Life* (1866)

With the establishment of a poetic name came a host of novel requisitions. Fame gathered from abroad cut out work at home. The number and nature of consequent applications were alike remarkable. Churches requested hymns, to be sung at consecrations, ordinations, and installations; charitable societies, for anniversaries; academies and schools, for exhibitions. Odes were desired for the festivities of New Year and the Fourth of July, for silver and golden weddings, for the voyager wherewith to express his leave-taking, and the lover to propitiate his mistress. Epistles from strangers often solicited elegies and epitaphs; and though the voice of bereavement was to me a sacred thing, yet I felt the inefficacy of balm thus offered to a heart that bled. Sometimes I consoled myself that the multitude of these solicitations bespoke an increasing taste for poetry among the people. But to gratify all was an impossibility. They would not only have covered the surface of one life, but of as many as ancient fable attributed to the feline race. I undertook at one time to keep a statement of the solicitations that showered upon me. A good-sized manuscript book was thus soon filled. It was commenced during what dear Mrs. Hemans used to call the "album persecution." It was then the fashion for school-girls, other youthful personages, and indeed people of every age, to possess themselves of a neatly-bound blank book, which was sent indiscriminately to any one whom they chose, with the request, or exaction, of a page or more in their own handwriting.

    Of those who were so unfortunate as to be known as rhymers, it was expressly stipulated that it must be original. Sometimes there would be a mass of these cormorant tax-gatherers in the house at the same time. To refuse compliance was accounted an offence, or an insult. I commuted the matter with my imperative engagements as well as I could, by setting aside a peculiar portion of time for these enforced subsidies. Happily this custom is now obsolete, having been merged in the slighter impost of autographs.

I feel an inclination to give you a few extracts from the manuscript catalogue before alluded to, which was not long continued. Perhaps they may amuse you, my sweetly patient friend. Some of them, you will observe, are not strictly poetical requisitions, but sprang from a position among poets.

> Requested to write dedication poems for three nicely-bound albums, brought by strangers.
>
> To ascertain and send an account of the comparative reputation, and terms of tuition and state of health of the female seminaries in this city, for a gentleman in a distant State who was thinking of sending a daughter to some boarding-school.
>
> To write an ode for the wedding of people in Maine, of whom I had never heard; the only fact mentioned by the expectant bridegroom, author of the letter, being that his chosen one was the youngest of ten brothers and sisters.
>
> To read critically, in one day, a manuscript of two hundred and sixty closely-written pages, and write a commendatory notice of it for some popular periodical.
>
> To obtain an accomplished female teacher for the children of a member of Congress, at the far South.
>
> A poem requested on the dog-star, Sirius.
>
> Desired to assist a servant-man not very well able to read, in getting his Sunday-school lessons, and to "write out all the answers for him, clear through the book, to save his time."
>
> A person feels inclined to offer a premium for some original piece of music, and would consider it "a favor if I would write six stanzas, each of eight lines, for it;" adding, that "the subject is to be Temperance," and he "does not know of any one that it possesses so much influence with as myself."
>
> A lady, whose husband expects to be absent on a journey for a month or two, wishes I would write a poem to testify her joy at his return.
>
> An almost illegible letter, requesting an elegy on a young man who was one of the nine children of a judge of probate, and "quite the Benjamin

of the family," the member of a musical society, and who, had he lived, "would likely have been married in about one year." It is added, that his funeral was attended by a large number of people; and "if I let them have a production on his death," I am desired to dedicate and have it published for the benefit of a society whose name I cannot decipher.

To prepare the memoir of a colored preacher, of whose character and existence I was ignorant. The document stated that the plan was to raise two thousand dollars by the publication of his biography and sermons, to present to his wife and nine children; who, it would seem, were all free, in health, and able to support themselves.

A hymn to be sung at the anniversary of a charitable society, for which I had recently furnished one; the argument adduced being that "a new one every year was interesting and advisable."

Epitaphs for a man and two children, with warning that only two hundred and fifty letters must be allowed in the whole, as the monument was not large enough to contain more.

A minister in Virginia encloses an urn, drawn with a pen, and colored by his son, a boy of fourteen, to be dedicated to the memory of Mrs. Judson. An acrostic is requested on the name of this son, whom he considers a genius, yet desires not to have it made "so personal" that it may not with propriety be published in one of their newspapers.

An ode, to be set to music, which must be finished early to-morrow morning, that copies may be struck off in season for the choir.

To write a publishing house in one of our large cities a laudatory notice of a volume I have never seen, by whose profits the author hopes to be able to travel in Europe.

A list of the female poets who have written in all languages, a statement of their births and deaths, with information of the best editions of their works, and where they may be obtained, for a gentleman resident in a distant State, who thinks of undertaking a compilation of feminine literature.

A piece to copy in the album of a lady of whom I had never heard, requested by a gentleman "to be sent as soon as Saturday afternoon, because then he is more at leisure to attend to it."

To punctuate a manuscript volume of three hundred pages, the author having always had a dislike to the business of punctuation, finding that it brings on a "pain in the back of the neck."

A poem, intended as a school premium for a young lady "not yet remarkable for neatness, but who might be encouraged to persevere if its beauties were set forth before her in attractive verse."

A letter from utter strangers, at a distance, stating that a person who had been in their employ had come to settle in this city, and they wished some pious individual to have charge over him, and warn him against evil company. That they should not thus have selected me, had they known of any other religious person in Hartford. They express apprehensions that he is going to set up the "rum-selling business," and propose, in a postscript, that when I obtain an interview, I should "wait and see whether he will own Christ unsolicited."

An album from a clerk in a store, given him by another clerk in another store, to be written in for a young lady, of whose name he was not quite certain, and the "most he knew about her was, that she was a very rich girl."

A new periodical desires a "touching tale, a bit of poetry, and an address to its readers," to be sent in the course of the week, and the printing will be stayed for the contributions.

The owner of a canary-bird, which had accidentally been starved to death, wishes some elegiac verses.

A stranger, whose son died at the age of nine months, "weighing just thirteen pounds, would be glad of some poetry to be framed, glazed, and hung over the chimney-piece, to keep the other children from forgetting him."

Solicitation from the far West, that I would "write out lengthy" a sketch of the loves of two personages, of whom no suggestive circumstances were related, one of whom was a journeyman tailor, and the name of the other, "Sister Babcock," as far as the chirography could be translated.

A poem proposed on the feather of a blue-bird picked up by the roadside.

A father requests elegiac lines on a young child, supplying, as the only suggestion for the tuneful Muse, the fact that he was unfortunately "drowned in a barrel of swine's food."

To draft a constitution for a society in a distant State, whose object is to diminish the reluctance of young people to the writing of compositions. . . .

Applications of a somewhat similar nature still occasionally occur, though I have ceased to take the trouble of recording them.

Caroline Kirkland
(1801–1864)

irkland was the oldest of eleven children, but she managed to get a good education at a Quaker school in New York run by an aunt. She met her husband while she was teaching school and he was a professor in foreign languages at Hamilton College. In 1837, the intrepid young couple boldly decided to start a model village in Pinckney, Michigan, in what was then the wild west. Under the pen name "Mary Clavers," Kirkland published a collection of "wicked glimpses of western life" titled *A New Home—Who'll Follow?* Such episodes as her candid portrayal of the ne'er-do-well Newlands and their fallen daughter Amelia outraged the local citizens, and in 1843 the Kirklands were forced to return to New York, where she ended her career as an editor and journalist.

CHAPTER XXVIII, *from A New Home—Who'll Follow?* (1839)

> *By sports like these are all their cares beguiled,*
> *The sports of children satisfy the child;*
> *Each nobler aim, repress'd by long control,*
> *Now sinks at last, or feebly mans the soul;*
> *While low delights succeeding fast behind,*
> *In happier meanness occupy the mind.*
> —Goldsmith, *The Traveller*

There is in our vicinity one class of settlers whose condition has always been inexplicable to me. They seem to work hard, to dress wretchedly, and to live in the most uncomfortable style in all respects, apparently denying themselves and their families every thing beyond the absolute necessaries of life. They complain most bitterly of poverty. They perform the severe labour which is shunned by their neighbours; they purchase the coarsest food, and are not too proud to ask for an old coat or a pair of cast boots, though it is always with the peculiar air of dignity and "don't care," which is characteristic of the country.

Yet instead of increasing their means by these penurious habits, they grow poorer every day. Their dwellings are more and more out of repair. There are more and more shingles in the windows, old hats and red petticoats cannot be spared; and an increasing dearth of cows, pigs, and chickens. The daughters go to service, and the sons "chore round" for every body and any body; and even the mamma, the centre of dignity, is fain to go out washing by the day.

A family of this description had fallen much under our notice. The father and his stout sons had performed a good deal of hard work in our service, and the females of the family had been employed on many occasions when "help" was scarce. Many requests for cast articles, or those of trifling value had been proffered during the course of our acquaintance; and in several attacks of illness, such comforts as our house afforded had been frequently sought, though no visit was ever requested.

They had been living through the summer in a shanty, built against a sloping bank, with a fire-place dug in the hill-side, and a hole pierced through the turf by way of chimney. In this den of some twelve feet square, the whole family had burrowed since April; but in October, a log-house of the ordinary size was roofed in, and though it had neither door nor window, nor chimney, nor hearth, they removed, and felt much elated with the change. Something like a door was soon after swinging on its leathern hinges, and the old man said they were now quite comfortable, though he should like to get a window!

The first intelligence we received from them after this, was that Mr. Newland, the father, was dangerously ill with inflammation of the lungs. This was not surprising, for a quilt is but a poor substitute for a window during a Michigan November. A window was supplied, and such alleviations as might be collected, were contributed by several of the neighbours. The old man lingered on, much to my surprise, and after two or three weeks we heard that he was better, and would be able to "kick round" pretty soon.

It was not long after, that we were enjoying the fine sleighing, which is usually so short-lived in this lakey region. The roads were not yet much beaten, and we had small choice in our drives, not desiring the troublesome honour of leading the way. It so happened that we found ourselves in the neighbourhood of Mr. Newland's clearing; and though the sun was low, we thought we might stop a moment to ask how the old man did.

We drove to the door, and so noiseless was our approach, guiltless of bells, that no one seemed aware of our coming. We tapped, and heard the usual reply, "Walk!" which I used to think must mean "Walk off."

I opened the door very softly, fearing to disturb the sick man; but I found this caution quite mal-apropos. Mrs. Newland was evidently in high holiday trim. The quilts had been removed from their stations round the bed, and the old man, shrunken and miserable-looking enough, sat on a chair in the corner. The whole apartment bore the marks of expected hilarity. The logs over-head were completely shrouded by broad hemlock boughs fastened against them; and evergreens of various kinds were disposed in all directions, while three tall slender candles, with the usual potato supporters, were placed on the cupboard shelf.

On the table, a cloth seemed to cover a variety of refreshments; and in front of this cloth stood a tin pail, nearly full of a liquid whose odour was but too discernible; and on the whiskey, for such it seemed, swam a small tin cup. But I forget the more striking part of the picture, the sons and daughters of the house. The former flaming in green stocks and scarlet watchguards, while the cut of their long dangling coats showed that whoever they might once have fitted, they were now exceedingly out of place; the latter decked in tawdry, dirty finery, and wearing any look but that of the modest country maiden, who, "in choosing her garments, counts no bravery in the world like decency."

The eldest girl, Amelia, who had lived with me at one time, had been lately at a hotel in a large village at some distance, and had returned but a short time before, not improved either in manners or reputation. Her tall commanding person was arrayed in far better taste than her sisters', and by contrast with the place and circumstances, she wore really a splendid air. Her dress was of rich silk, made in the extreme mode, and set off by elegant jewelry. Her black locks were drest with scarlet berries; most elaborate pendants of wrought gold hung almost to her shoulders; and above her glittering basilisk eyes, was a gold chain with a handsome clasp of cut coral. The large hands were covered with elegant gloves, and an embroidered handkerchief was carefully arranged in her lap.

I have attempted to give some idea of the appearance of things in this wretched log-hut, but I cannot pretend to paint the confusion into which our ill-timed visit threw the family, who had always appeared before us in such different characters. The mother asked us to sit down, however, and Mr. Newland muttered something, from which I gathered, that "the girls thought they must have a kind of a house-warmin' like."

We made our visit very short, of course; but before we could make our escape, an old fellow came in with a violin, and an ox-sled approached the door, loaded with young people of both sexes, who were all "spilt" into the deep snow, by a "mistake on purpose" of the driver. In the scramble which ensued, we took leave; wondering no longer at the destitution of the Newlands, or of the other families of the same class, whose young people we had recognized in the mêlée.

The Newland family did not visit us as usual after this. There was a certain consciousness in their appearance when we met, and the old man more than once alluded to our accidental discovery with evident uneasiness. He was a person not devoid of shrewdness, and he was aware that the utter discrepancy between his complaints, and the appearances we had witnessed, had given us but slight opinion of his veracity; and for some time we were almost strangers to each other.

How was I surprised some two months after at being called out of bed by a most urgent message from Mrs. Newland, that Amelia, her eldest daughter, was dying! The messenger could give no account of her condition, but that she was now in convulsions, and her mother despairing of her life.

I lost not a moment, but the way was long, and ere I entered the house, the shrieks of the mother and her children, told me I had come too late. Struck with horror I almost hesitated whether to proceed, but the door was opened, and I went in. Two or three neighbours with terrified countenances stood near the bed, and on it lay the remains of the poor girl, swollen and discoloured, and already so changed in appearance that I should not have recognized it elsewhere.

I asked for particulars, but the person whom I addressed, shook her head and declined answering; and there was altogether an air of horror and mystery which I was entirely unable to understand. Mrs. Newland, in her lamentations, alluded to the suddenness of the blow, and when I saw her a little calmed, I begged to know how long Amelia had been ill, expressing my surprise that I had heard nothing of it. She turned upon me as if I had stung her.

"What, you've heard their lies too, have ye!" she exclaimed fiercely, and she cursed in no measured terms those who meddled with what did not concern them. I felt much shocked: and disclaiming all intention of wounding her feelings, I offered the needful aid, and when all was finished, returned home uninformed as to the manner of Amelia Newland's death.

Yet I could not avoid noticing that all was not right.

Oft have I seen a timely-parted ghost
Of ashy semblance, meagre, pale and bloodless—

but the whole appearance of this sad wreck was quite different from that of any corpse I had ever viewed before. Nothing was done, but much said or hinted on all sides. Rumour was busy as usual; and I have been assured by those who ought to have warrant for their assertions, that this was but one fatal instance out of the *many cases*, wherein life was perilled in the desperate effort to elude the "slow unmoving finger" of public scorn.

That the class of settlers to which the Newlands belong, a class but too numerous in Michigan, is a vicious and degraded one, I cannot doubt: but whether the charge to which I have but alluded, is in any degree just, I am unable to determine. I can only repeat, "I say the tale as 't was said to me," and I may add that more than one instance of a similar kind, though with results less evidently fatal, has since come under my knowledge.

The Newlands have since left this part of the country, driving off with their own, as many of their neighbours' cattle and hogs as they could persuade to accompany them; and not forgetting one of the train of fierce dogs which have not only shown ample sagacity in getting their own living, but, "gin a' tales be true," assisted in supporting the family by their habits of nightly prowling.

I passed by their deserted dwelling. They had carried off the door and window, and some boys were busy pulling the shingles from the roof to make quail-traps. I trust we have few such neighbours left. Texas and the Canada war have done much for us in this way; and the wide west is rapidly drafting off those whom we shall regret as little as the Newlands.

Lydia Maria Child
(1802–1880)

ydia Maria Child spent her adolescence, after her mother's death, living with an older sister in Norridgewock, Maine. There she came to know many members of the Abenaki and Penobscot tribes who lived in the forest and learned their sad history. Child's sympathetic portrayal of Native Americans in her first novel, *Hobomok: A Tale of Early Times* (1824), drew on this experience and expressed her fierce belief in racial equality. Her story "The Church in the Wilderness" fictionalized the massacre of a village of Abenaki Indians and their Jesuit priest by English settlers, and dramatized the tragedy of mixed loyalties and identities. Child was an ambitious and versatile writer, equally capable of producing fiction, political essays including *An Appeal in Favor of that Class of Americans Called Africans* (1833), and even a domestic advice book called *The American Frugal Housewife* (1829). Recalling her ecstatic feelings in composing her early books, she described "the brightness and boundlessness" of her hopes and her "impetuous abundance" as an imaginative writer. But her marriage to a litigious and penniless radical journalist forced her to write out of financial pressure rather than literary ambition. By the end of her life, Child told her publisher, she found her Pegasus crippled "from having had a heavy cart of stones to drag for many years."

The Church in the Wilderness (1828)

There stood the Indian hamlet, there the lake
Spread its blue sheet, that flashed with many an oar,
Where the brown otter plunged him from the brake,
And the deer drank—as the light gale blew o'er,
The twinkling maze-field rustled on the shore;
And while that spot, so wild, and lone, and fair,
A look of glad and innocent beauty wore,
And peace was on the earth and in the air,
The warrior lit the pile and bound his captive there.
Not unavenged the foeman from the wood

Beheld the deed, and when the midnight shade
Was stillest, gorged his battle-axe with blood;
All died—the wailing babe—the shrieking maid—
And in the flood of fire, that scathed the glade,
The roofs went down; but deep the silence grew,
When on the dewy woods the day-beam played;
No more the cabin smokes rose wreathed and blue,
And ever by their lake, lay moored the light canoe.

—[WILLIAM CULLEN] BRYANT

There is a solitary spot, in a remote part of Maine, known by the name of Indian Old Point. The landscape has no peculiar beauty, save the little sparkling river, which winds gracefully and silently among the verdant hills, as if deeply contented with its sandy bed; and fields of Indian corn, tossing their silken tresses to the winds, as if conscious of rural beauty. Yet there is a charm thrown around this neglected and almost unknown place, by its association with some interesting passages in our earliest history. The soil is fertilized by the blood of a murdered tribe. Even now the spade strikes against wampum belts, which once covered hearts as bold and true, as ever beat beneath a crusader's shield, and gaudy beads are found, which once ornamented bosoms throbbing with as deep and fervent tenderness, as woman ever displayed in the mild courtesies of civilized life.

Here, one hundred years ago, stood the village of the Norridgewocks, one of the many tribes of the scattered Abnakis. These Indians have been less celebrated than many of their brethren; for they had not the fierce valor of the Pequods, the sinewy strength of the Delawares, or the bell-toned language of the Iroquois. They were, however, an influential nation; of consequence on account of their numbers, as well as their subtilty. The Jesuits, too, had long been among them, led by their zeal to fasten the strong girdle of an imposing faith around the habitable globe; and they had gained over the untutored minds of these savages, their usual mysterious and extraordinary power. The long continued state of effervescence, produced by the Reformation, tended to settle this country with rigid, restless, and ambitious spirits. Our broad lands were considered an ample tract of debatable ground, where the nations of the earth might struggle for disputed possession; and terrible indeed was the contest for religious supremacy between France and England, during the early part of the eighteenth century. Of the energy and perseverance displayed in this cause, there are few more striking examples than Sebastian

Rallè, the apostle of the Norridgewocks. His rude, cross-crowned church, standing in the heart of the American wilderness, proved the ambition and extent of that tremendous hierarchy, "whose roots were in another world, and whose far stretching shadow awed our own." Surrounded by the wigwams of the Abnakis, it seemed like an apostle of Antioch descended among savages, pointing out to them the heaven he had left. Our forefathers indeed thought it wore a different, and most unholy aspect; but to romantic minds, the Catholic church, even in its most degraded state, must ever be an object of interest. The majestic Latin, so lofty in its sound, and yet so soulless now to all save the learned, seems like the fragments of a mighty ruin, which Rome, in her decaying pride, scattered over the nations of the earth; and the innumerable ceremonies, more voiceless than the language in which they are preserved, forcibly remind one of the pomp and power rivalled only by attendant corruption. In this point of view only could the humble church of the Norridgewocks kindle the imagination; for it had little outward proportion, or inward splendor. It stood in a sheltered spot, between two small, verdant hills, with one graceful feathery elm at its side, bending forward, at every signal from the breeze, and half shading the cross, as if both bowed down in worship.

Various opinions were formed of the priest, who there administered the rites of a mysterious religion. All agreed that he was a learned man; some said he was benevolent and kind; while others pronounced him the most subtle and vindictive of hypocrites. The English settlers, who resided about three miles from the village of the Abnakis, regarded him with extreme aversion; but to the Indians he was the representative of the Good Spirit. It is true the maxims of the Jesuits had given something of sternness and cunning to a character naturally mild and frank; but he verily thought he was doing God's service, and he did it with a concentration of power and purpose well worthy of the respect it inspired. For thirty years he lived in the wilderness, sharing the dangers and privations incident to savage life. The languages of all the neighbouring tribes were familiar to him; and his utterance could not have been distinguished from that of a native, had it not been for a peculiarly softened cadence, and rapid enunciation. A restless light in his small, hazel eye, and the close compression of his lips, betokened one, who had, with a strong hand, thrown up dykes against the overflowing torrent of his own mad passions. The effort had likewise turned back many a gentle current of affection, which might have soothed and refreshed his heart; but let man do his worst, there are moments when nature will rebound from all the restraints imposed on her by pride, prejudice, or superstition.

There were two objects in the secluded residence of the self-denying Jesuit, on whom he poured forth in fullness the love he could not wholly stifle within him. When he came to america, he found among the savages the orphan son of the Baron de Castine, by a beautiful young Abnakis. The child was remarkably pretty and engaging; and the lonely priest, finding his heart daily warming toward him, induced the squaw who nursed him, to take up her abode in his own wigwam. The Indians called him Otoolpha, "The Son of the Stranger," and seemed to regard the adopted one with quite as much interest as their own offspring. Not a year after Otoolpha and his nurse were domesticated in the dwelling of the Jesuit, some of the tribe, on their return from Canada, found a nearly famished female infant in the wood. Had not Sebastian Rallè been of the party, its sufferings would, probably, have met a violent end; but at his suggestion, comfortable nourishment, and such care as they could give it were afforded. A nose slightly approaching to aquiline, and a complexion less darkly colored than usual, betrayed an origin half European; but as her parentage and tribe were unknown, they gave her the emphatic name of Saupoolah, "The Scattered Leaf," and engrafted her on the tree of Abnakis. From the first dawn of reason she gave indications of an impetuous, fearless, and romantic spirit. The squaw who nursed her, together with the little Otoolpha, tried in vain to curb her roving propensities. At four and five years old, she would frequently be absent several days, accompanied by her foster brother. The duties of the missionary often called him far from home, and it was absolutely impossible for him always to watch over them, either in kindness, or authority. Their long excursions during his absence, at first occasioned many anxious and wretched thoughts; but when he found his wayward protégés invariably returned, and when he saw they could cross streams, leap ditches, and thread their way through the labyrinths of the wilderness, with the boldness and sagacity of young hunters, he ceased to disturb himself on their account.

During the whole of their adventurous childhood but one accident ever happened to them. They had been at the English settlement to beg some beads in exchange for their little baskets, and on their return, they took a fancy to cross the Kennebec, when recent rains had swollen its deep and beautiful waters. Saupoolah's life nearly fell a sacrifice to the rapidity of the current; but her foster brother ran, with the speed of lightning, to call assistance from the village they had just left. A muscular, kind hearted woman, by the name of Allan, lived in a log-house, very near the river. In the midst of his terror, Otoolpha remembered this circumstance, and went there for succor. His frightened looks told his story,

even more plainly than his hurried exclamation;—"Ogh! Saupoolah die—
the Great Spirit drink her up!" Mrs. Allan saved the Indian child at the risk
of her own life, dried her clothes, gave them something warm and com-
fortable to eat, and conducted them into their homeward path in safety.
To this woman and her children Otoolpha and Saupoolah ever after
clung with singular intensity of affection. During their childish summers,
it was a daily occupation to fill baskets with berries for her little ones,
whom they always chose to feed with their own hands, watching every
morsel of the fruit as it disappeared between their rosy lips, with the
most animated expressions of delight; and when they arrived at maturer
years, they used the great influence they had with the tribe, to protect
Mrs. Allan from a thousand petty wrongs and insults, with which her
white brethren were not unfrequently visited.

Educated by the learned priest, as far as such fetterless souls could be
educated, and associating only with savages, these extraordinary young
people grew up with a strange mixture of European and aboriginal char-
acter. Both had the rapid, elastic tread of Indians; but the outlines of
their tall, erect figures possessed something of the pliant gracefulness of
France. When indignant, the expression of their eyes was like light from
a burning-glass; but in softer moments, they had a melting glance, which
belongs only to a civilized and voluptuous land. Saupoolah's hair, though
remarkably soft and fine, had the jet black hue of the savage; Otoolpha's
was brown, and when moistened by exercise, it sometimes curled
slightly around his high, prominent forehead. The same mixture of
nations was shown in their costume, as in their personal appearance.
Otoolpha usually wore a brown cloth tunic, with tight sleeves, and large
buttons, under which appeared a scarlet kilt to his knees, in heavy folds,
edged with the fur of the silver fox, and fastened at the waist by a broad
girdle, richly ornamented with Indian hieroglyphics. A coronet of scarlet
dyed fur, to which were fastened four silver bells, gave indication of his
noble descent; and from his neck were suspended a cross and rosary of
sandal wood, which Sebastian Rallè declared to have been sanctified by
the blessed touch of Innocent the Eleventh. Saupoolah's dress was nearly
similar. Her tunic was deep yellow; and her scarlet kilt touched the fur
edge of her high, closely fitted, and very gaudy moccasins. Her cap was
shaped not unlike a bishop's mitre; gaily ornamented with shells and
beadwork, and surmounted by the black feathers of three eagles her own
arrow had slain. In the chase, she was as eager and keen eyed as Otool-
pha. It was a noble sight to see them, equipped for the chase, bounding
along through the forest. The healthful and rapid blood, coursing

beneath their smooth, brown cheeks, gave a richness and vividness of beauty, which a fair, transparent complexion can never boast; and their motions had that graceful elasticity produced only by activity, unconsciousness, and freedom. Sebastian Rallè had been several years at Rome, in the service of the Pope, and had there acquired a refinement of taste uncommon at that early period. His adopted children sometimes accompanied him on his missionary expeditions to Canada and elsewhere, on which occasions the game they killed served for his support. When he saw them with their dark eyes fixed on a distant bird, arrows ready for flight, their majestic figures slightly bending backward, resting on one knee, with an advancing foot firmly fixed on the ground, displaying, by a natural bend of the limb, outlines most gracefully curved, he gazed upon them with uncontrolled delight; and he could not but acknowledge that the young savages, in their wild and careless beauty, rivalled the Apollos and woodnymphs to which classic imaginations had given birth. Such endowments are rare in Indian women; for the toils imposed upon them, usually weigh down the springs of the soul, till the body refuses to rebound at its feeble impulses; but when it does occur, it is the very perfection of ideal loveliness. Otoolpha would suffer no one to curb Saupoolah in her wildness and inspiration. To him and the Jesuit, she was docile and affectionate; to all others, haughty and impetuous. The Norridgewocks regarded them both with wonder and superstition, and frequently called them by a name, which signified the "Children of the Prophet." The distant tribes, who frequently met them in their hunting excursions, were lost in admiration of their swiftness and majesty, and called them, by one consent, the "Twin Eagles of Abnakis."

Contemptuously as some think of our red brethren, genius was no rare endowment among them; and seldom have souls been so rich in the wealth of nature, as the two powerful and peculiar beings, whom we have described. Many were the bold and beautiful thoughts which rushed upon their untutored imaginations, as they roamed over a picturesque country, sleeping in clefts where panthers hid themselves, and scaling precipices from which they scared the screaming eagles. Perhaps cultivated intellect never received brighter thoughts from the holy rays of the evening star, or a stormier sense of grandeur from the cataract, than did these children of the wilderness. Their far leaping ideas, clothed in brief, poetic language, were perhaps more pleasant to the secluded priest, than frequent intercourse with his own learned, but crafty order. To him they were indeed as "diamonds in the desert;" and long and painful were the penances he inflicted upon himself, for an all-absorbing love, which his erring conscience deemed a sin against that God, who bestowed such pure, delicious feelings on his mysterious creatures. The Jesuit was deeply read in human nature, and it needed but little sagacity to foresee that Saupoolah would soon be to her brother "something than sister dearer." When Otoolpha was but seventeen, and his companion not quite fifteen, their frank and childish affection had obviously assumed a different character. Restlessness when separated, and timidity and constraint when they met, betrayed their slavery to a new and despotic power. Sebastian Rallè observed it with joy. Early disappointment and voluntary vows had made the best and most luxurious emotions of our nature a sealed fountain within his own soul; but the old man had not forgotten youthful hopes and feelings, and for these beloved ones he coveted all earth had of happiness. They were married in presence of the whole tribe, with all the pomp and ceremony his limited means afforded. This event made no alteration in the household of the Jesuit. The old squaw, who had taken care of his adopted children from their infancy, performed all the services their half civilized way of life required, and the young hunters led the same wandering and fearless life as before. At the hour of sunset, it was the delight of the lonely priest to watch for their return, from a small opening, which served as a window to his study. It was a time he usually devoted to reflection and prayer; but the good man had virtues, which he called weaknesses and sins, and a spirit of devotion would not always remain with him at such seasons. The vine covered hills of France, his mother's kiss, and a bright, laughing girl, who had won his heart in early youth, would often rise before him with the distinctness of visions. The neglected rosary would fall from his hand, and love, as it first stole over a soul untainted by sensuality or selfishness, was the only heaven of which he dreamed. Such were the feelings with which he awaited the return of Otoolpha and Saupoolah, on the eleventh of December, 1719. Notwithstanding the lateness of the season, the day had been as mild as the first weeks of September. The drowsy sunshine dreaming on the hemlocks, pines, and cedars, had drawn forth an unusual fragrance; the children were at rest in the wigwams; most of the sanups had gone to Moose Head Lake, on a hunting expedition; and the few old men who remained, sat at the doors of their huts smoking their pipes in lazy silence.

Wautoconomese, an aged prophet among them, declared this unnatural warmth to be a prelude of terrible things. He had gained his power of judging by a close observation of electrical phenomena and all the various changes of the weather, and it was no difficult matter to make his tribe mistake experience for inspiration. The women were all in alarm at his predictions; nor is it strange that the learned Jesuit, living as he did in a superstitious age, and believing doctrines highly calculated to excite the imagination, should be more affected by their terrors than he was willing to acknowledge, even to himself. These feelings naturally embodied themselves in anxiety concerning the two eccentric beings, whose presence was as morning sunshine in his dreary dwelling. The hour at which they usually returned, had long since passed; and strong and vigilant as he knew them to be, fearful thoughts of panthers and wolves crowded on his heart. Waking, he knew the fiercest prowlers of the wilderness would have shunned them; but they might have slept where loup-cerviers were in ambush, and roused too late for safety.

While philosophy was struggling with these harassing ideas, and every moment growing weaker in the contest, he observed in the north a flash more brilliant than ever precedes the rising sun. For a moment it was stationary; then it moved, quivered, hurtled, and flashed, as if there had been "war in heaven," and the clouds, rolling themselves up "as a scroll," showed the gleaming of javelins, thrown thick and fast along the embattled line. All at once, a vivid stream of light from the south towered up, like Lucifer in his terrific greatness, and rushed onward with a mighty noise. The fiery forces, nearly meeting at the zenith, were separated only by a clear, deep spot of blue, surrounded by a few fleecy clouds. The effect was awful. It seemed as if the All-seeing Eye were looking down upon a sinful world, in mingled wrath and pity. The Catholic bowed his head, and his subdued spirit was mute in worship and fear. His solitude was soon interrupted by Wautoconomese, whose trembling agitation betrayed how little he had foreseen that his pompous prophecies would be thus sublimely fulfilled. Next the aged squaw, who, from fear of interrupting her master in his devotions, had long been crouching in her own corner of the wigwam, more dead than alive, came in, and reverentially crossing herself, implored permission to remain. To these were soon added an accession of almost all the women in the hamlet. Perhaps Sebastian Rallè was hardly aware how much the presence of these rude, uninformed beings relieved his spirit. His explanations to them, mixed with the consolations of religion, nerved his mind with new strength; and he began to look upon the awful appearance in the heavens with a calmness and rationality worthy of him. By degrees the light grew dim, then closed upon the speck of blue sky, which had appeared to keep watch over the souls of superstitious men, and the glorious scene seemed about to end. But suddenly a luminous bow shot from north to south with the rushing sound of a rocket, and divided the heavens with a broad belt of brightness. The phenomena of that night had been more extraordinary than any the Jesuit had ever witnessed; but until that moment he had known their name and nature; and, with that strange tendency to a belief in supernatural agency, which the greatest and wisest minds have, in a state of high excitement, his cheek now turned pale, and his heart dropped heavily within him, at what he deemed a sure presage of ruin to those he loved. Reason would have indeed told him that it did not comport with the economy of Providence to change the order of creation for so insignificant a thing as man; but who is not more under the influence of feeling than of reason?

Unable to endure the terrific creations of his own fancy, he left the house, followed only by one of the tribe, and entered the path by which the young hunters usually returned. He pursued this route, for nearly a mile, without seeing any traces of the objects of his anxiety. At last he heard a loud "Willoa." The source of the clear, ringing sound could not be mistaken; for Saupoolah alone could give the shrillest tones of the human voice such depth and smoothness of melody. The Jesuit, by his long residence with the savages, had acquired their quickness of eye and ear, and a few moments brought him within view of his adopted child. She was standing in a thickly shaded part of the wood, her hand resting on her brow, looking backward, apparently listening with eagerness to the coming footsteps. A slight shade of disappointment passed over her face when she saw Otoolpha was not with her father; but it soon gave place to an affectionate smile, at his enthusiastic demonstrations of joy. From her brief account it appeared they had early in the evening heard distressed noises apparently proceeding from a human voice; that they had separated in search of those from whom it came, and had thus lost each other. As she finished her story, another loud shout sent echoing through the forest, betrayed more anxiety than was common to her fearless nature. Yet even amid her doubt and perplexity, her romantic soul was open to the influence of the sublime scene above her. As they wound along through the forest, ever and anon shouting with their united voices, in hopes the echo would arouse Otoolpha, she occasionally fixed her eye on the bright arch, which still preserved its wavy radiance, though a little softened by light flashes of clouds, through which the stars were distinctly visible. "The arrows have been flying fast among the tribes of heaven to night," said she. "The stars have chased their enemies over the hills. They are returning victorious; and the moon has spread her mantle in their war path."

When such thoughts as these came over her, Saupoolah's eyes had a brightness totally different from the keenness and outward brilliancy common to fine looking Indians; it was a light that came from within, gleaming up from fires deep, deep down in the soul. It was probably this peculiarity, which had so universally gained for her the title of "Daughter of a Prophet;" and its effect on the savage, who had attended the Jesuit, was instantly observable, for he devoutly crossed himself, and walked at a great distance from the object of his veneration. Sebastian Rallè, accustomed as he was to the wild freaks, and almost infantile tenderness of his adopted children, had often smiled at their power over the tribe; yet something of pride, almost of deference, mingled with his own love of them. Saupoolah's remark, and the look of inspiration, with which she fixed her eye on the heavens, awakened in his mind the remembrance of many a season, when he had listened to their wild eloquence with wonder and delight. This train of thought betrayed itself in an eagerly affectionate glance at Saupoolah, and a loud shout to Otoolpha, that made the woods ring again. The young wife suddenly assumed the Indian attitude of intense listening; and joy flushed her whole face, like a sunbeam, as she exclaimed, "It is answered!" Another shout! there could be no mistake. It could not be the reverberation of an echo, for it was repeated louder and louder, at irregular intervals. A rapid and devious walk, guided by sounds which evidently grew nearer, brought Otoolpha in sight. Quick as a young fawn, overflowing with life and frolic, Saupoolah bounded forward, and sprang upon his neck. But the eye of the Jesuit, always rapid and restless in its movements, quickly glanced from his new found treasure to the objects around. A European lady, possessed of much matronly beauty, lay lifeless at his feet; and a fragile looking boy, apparently eight or nine years old, was bending over her, and weeping bitterly. This child, alone in the wilderness with his dead mother, had uttered those cries of distress and terror, which had startled Otoolpha and his companion. The sight of a white man seemed to the desolate boy a pledge of safety. He nestled close to the side of the priest, and looking up in his face imploringly, burst into tears. The heart of the Jesuit was touched. There was something in the boy's voice and the lady's features, that troubled the waters of a long sealed fountain. The Indians exchanged whispers with that air of solemnity, which the presence of the dead always inspires. They read a mixed feeling of agony and doubt in the countenance of Sebastian Rallè, but they did not ask, and they never knew its origin. After a moment's silence, during which he seemed struggling with powerful emotion, he placed his hand gently on the boy's head, and spoke soothing words in French, which the child understood with perfect facility. No sigh, no outward sign of despair escaped him; but there was a marble stillness, which, like the ominous quiet of a volcano, betrayed that raging materials were at work within.

He ordered the corpse to be borne to his wigwam with all possible gentleness; and when the unevenness of the path occasioned the least violence of motion, he would cringe, as if an adder had stung him. It was in vain that Wautoconomese and his frightened companion sought protection from him, on his return. Remarkable electrical appearances, in every variety of form, continued during the whole night; but the miserable man regarded them not. The lifeless mother was placed in his study, and he knelt down beside it with the boy, and spoke not a word. The old squaw brought in her tallest bayberry wax candles, and tried to prolong her stay in the room by a thousand little officious arts; but a gentle signal to withdraw was all she could gain from her heart stricken master. Day dawned, and found him unchanged in countenance or position. The boy, weary with grief and fatigue, had fallen asleep, and lay on the floor in a slumber as deep and peaceful as if unalloyed happiness had been his portion. The sight of his tranquil innocence, as the daylight shone upon his childish features, brought tears to the eyes of the rigid priest. It was a charm that broke the spell of agony which had bound down his spirit. The terribly cold and glassy look departed from him; but never, after that night, was Sebastian Rallè as he had been. Affliction did not soften and subdue him. It deepened the gloom with which he had long looked upon the world, and seemed to justify him in giving up his whole soul to the stern dictates of Jesuitical maxims. Even Otoolpha and Saupoolah met with occasional harshness; and William Ponsonby, the English boy, alone received uniform mildness and affection at his hands. He was a fair and delicate blossom; such a being as the heart would naturally cling to for its very fragility and dependence; but to none on earth, save Sebastian Rallè, was it known that there were other and deeper reasons for his peculiar tenderness.

The lady, whom he had loved in early youth, had been induced by her parents to marry a wealthy Englishman, in preference to the unportioned Frenchman, whom alone she had truly loved. Her husband lost much of his fortune, and joined his countrymen against the French, during the troubled period between 1690 and 1762. He was taken by the Indians, and his wife saw him suffer a horrid and lingering death. By the humanity of one of the savages, she made her escape, with her youngest son, the only one remaining of eight fine boys. She well knew the residence of that devoted lover, whom her weakness of purpose had driven to a life of solitude and self-denial; and to him she resolved to appeal for protection. Worn out with wandering and privation, she died suddenly in the wilderness, when her arduous journey was well nigh completed; and the conscientious priest, even in the anguish of a breaking heart, felt that it was well for him she had died; for to have seen the widowed one depending upon him for protection, when the solemn vows of his order had separated them forever, would have been worse than death to endure. The affection he had borne the mother rested on the child; and in him he found, what he had in vain wished for since his residence in the New World, a docile and intelligent scholar.

The boy was indeed a sort of "young Edwin;" a sad, imaginative child, fond of his books, and still more fond of rambling far and wide with the wayward Saupoolah. The log-house of good Mrs. Allan was the only place where William spoke in the language of his father; for English was a hateful sound to the ear of the Jesuit. The troubles between the neighbouring villages of English and Abnakis increased daily; and not a few of the latter were induced to revolt against their spiritual ruler. Distrust, jealousy, and weakness characterized all their councils. Their deep, but fluctuating feelings alternately showed themselves in insults to the priest, and acts of violence on their neighbours. Representatives were sent from the English villages on the Kennebec to the government at Boston, who protested against Sebastian Rallè, for constantly using his influence to excite Indian revenge to its utmost rancor; and letters filled with charges of this nature may still be seen in the records of the Historical Society. It is probable that they were, in some measure, well founded, for it was the dangerous creed of the Jesuits, that all human power, good or bad, should be made subservient to one grand end. Yet the Norridgewocks had so much reason to complain of the fraud and falsehood of the English, that it is difficult to decide to whom the greatest share of blame rightfully belongs. Be that as it may, affairs went from bad to worse. Mutual dislike became every day more inveterate; and Mrs. Allan was the only one who had not in some way or other suffered from the powerful arm of the implacable Otoolpha. His French origin, the great influence he had over his tribe, and his entire submission to the will of the Jesuit, procured for him a double portion of hatred. Dislike was returned with all the fierceness and impetuosity of his savage nature; and English mothers often frightened their children into obedience by the use of his terrible name. In the autumn of 1724, these discontents were obviously approaching a fearful crisis. A Council Fire was kindled at the village of the Abnakis; and fierce indeed were the imprecations uttered, and terrible the resolutions taken against the English.

Wautoconomese in his fury said, that the Evil Spirit had governed them ever since William Ponsonby came among them; and he demanded that the boy should at once be sacrificed to an offended Deity. The lip of the venerable priest quivered and turned pale for an instant; but it passed quickly, and so carefully had even the muscles of his face been trained in obedience to the Society of Jesus, that rigid indifference could alone be read there, as he carelessly asked, "Wherefore should the child die?" The fierce old prophet watched his emotions as the snake fixes her infernal eye on the bird she is charming unto death. "Because the Great Spirit, who dwells among the windy hills, and covers himself with the snow mantle, has whispered it in the ear of the wise man," said he proudly. "Wherefore else did he breathe softly on the wood, for four sleeps, and take his garments from the sun, that it might give warmth to the pale papoose, on his way through the wilderness? I tell you, he sent him to Wautoconomese, that he might sacrifice him instead of the young fawn and the beaver; for he loves not the white face and the double tongue of the Yengees."

"And the love I bear them is such as the panther gives the stricken deer," replied the Jesuit. "Ye are all one! ye are all one!" answered the raging prophet. "The Yengees say their king has counted more scalps than any other chief; and you say he is but a boy to the great king, who lives where the vines run with oil. Ye both have faces pale as a sick woman. One hisses like a snake, and the other chatters like a mad cat bird; but both hunt the poor Indian like a buffalo to his trap. Wautoconomese was once a very big prophet. The Great Spirit spoke to him loud, and his tribe opened their eyes wide, that they might look on him. What is Wautoconomese now? He speaks the words of the Great Spirit; and ye laugh when ye tell the young men of his tribe that his ears are old, and he cannot hear."

His stormy eloquence awakened the slumbering pride of his warlike nation; and against the whole race of white men they inwardly breathed a vow of extermination.

The boy was bound for sacrifice, and evil eyes were cast upon the Jesuit. The ingratitude of those for whom he had toiled thirty long years, and the threatened loss of the dearest object which God had left to cheer his lonely pilgrimage, seemed to freeze the faculties of the old man; and that day would have ended his trials with his life, had not Otoolpha stepped into the centre of the Council Circle, and, with a low bow to

Wautoconomese, demanded to be heard. He spoke reverently of the prophet; but, by all the sufferings and kindness of their French Father, he conjured them not to be ungrateful to him in his old age. He begged for the boy's life, and promised to lead his tribe to war against every white man, woman, and child, from Corratwick Falls to the Big Sea, if they would thus reward his victory.

He was a favorite with his tribe, and they listened to him. After much consultation, they determined on midnight marches at the end of three weeks, by which means they intended to surprise and put to death all the English soldiers on the Kennebec. If successful in this attempt, William Ponsonby was safe; if not, the innocent child must fall a victim to their savage hatred.

Saupoolah slept little the night after she listened to the Council of her tribe. She thought of Mrs. Allan's kind looks, when she saved her from drowning; and she remembered the happy hours when she used to feed the children from her little berry basket. Could she not save her from the general ruin? She asked Otoolpha if no stratagem could be devised. He told her it would lead to detection, and the life of William and the priest would be forfeited. In her uneasy slumbers she dreamed of the murder of her benefactress; and she started up, declaring she would save Mrs. Allan's life at the peril of her own. Otoolpha resolutely and somewhat harshly forbade her to do it. It was the first time he had ever spoken to her in a tone of authority; and her proud spirit rose against him. "I have loved him," thought she, "but not with tameness of a household drudge; if such is the service he wants, let him leave Saupoolah, and find a mate among the slaves of Abnakis." Her manner the next day was cold, suspicious, and constrained towards her husband. She said no more to him of her plans, but sought advice from the priest. The heart broken old man was roused into sudden energy, and solemnly and vehemently forbade her project. Saupoolah's soul struggled in cords to which she had been entirely unaccustomed. She was silent, but determined. That night she left Otoolpha in a sound sleep, and effected her dangerous purpose secretly. She told Mrs. Allan all the plans of the Norridgewocks, beseeching her to make no other use of the knowledge, than to save herself and family. The terrified matron promised she would not. But could, or ought, such a promise to be kept?

Time passed on, and threw no light on the dangerous deed Saupoolah had dared to perform. Fears of its consequences haunted her own soul, like a restless demon; and again and again did she extort from Mrs. Allan a vow never to betray her. More than half of her fault sprang from a kind and generous nature; but she could not forgive herself for the vexation that had mingled with better feelings. Her pride and her buoyancy were both gone; and upon Otoolpha, Sebastian Rallè, and William Ponsonby, she lavished the most anxious fondness.

The old priest cared little whether life or death were his portion; for he was old, and disappointment had ever been the shadow of his hopes. But for the dead mother's sake, his heart yearned for the life of the boy. Saupoolah, ever enthusiastic and self-sacrificing, promised to convey him away secretly, and place him under the protection of a Canadian priest. The time appointed was four days before the intended massacre of the English, when a Council Fire of one of the neighbouring tribes would induce most of the Norridgewocks to be absent. The night preceding his departure was a weary one to Sebastian Rallè. He spent it at William's couch in wakefulness and prayer. Affections, naturally intense, were all centered on this one object; and he had nerved himself to think that he must part with him, and then lay him down and die.

The gray tints of morning rose upon him, showing the whole of his miserable little apartment in cheerless obscurity. The old priest, stern, philosophic, and rigid elsewhere, was in the seclusion of his own apartment, as wayward and affectionate as a child. He stooped down, and parting William's soft hair, imprinted a kiss on his forehead. The boy, half unconscious what he did, fondly nestled his cheek into the hand that rested on him. Sebastian Rallè looked upward with an expression that seemed to say, "O Father, would that this cup might pass from me." Just then the church bell, with feeble but sweet tones, announced the hour of early mass. William was on his feet in an instant, and as quickly knelt to his venerable friend to receive his customary benediction. In a few minutes, every living soul in the hamlet was within the walls of the church. Wigwams were all quiet, and canoes were wimpling about in Sandy river. The savages had all bowed down and crossed themselves before the unseen God. The broken voice of the Jesuit was heard loudly beseeching; "*Ora, ora pro nobis,*" when armed men rushed in amid their peaceful worship. The dashing of swords, the groans of the dying, and the yells of the frantic, mingled in one horrid chaos of clamor. Not one escaped; not one. Some called out, "Save William Ponsonby and the priest!" Others aimed at the breast of the Jesuit, as if he had been the only victim desired. The English boy threw himself forward and received a stab, aimed at the heart of his old friend; and the priest, with one convulsive bound, and one loud shriek of agony, withdrew the sword and plunged it deeply in his own breast.

Saupoolah's noble heart broke with intensity of suffering. She fell life-less by the side of the murdered William, and a dozen swords at once were pointed at her. Otoolpha cast one hurried glance upon her; and man has no power to speak the mingled rage, despair, and anguish, which that wild glance expressed. With the concentrated strength of fifty savages, he forced his way unhurt to the river side, and sprung into Saupoolah's favorite canoe. The boat filled with water; and he found that even here the treacherous revenge of his enemies would reach his life. With desperate strength he gained the shore, and ran toward the forest. His coronet and belt made him a conspicuous victim; multitudes were in pursuit; and he died covered with wounds.

Before the setting of the sun, the pretty hamlet was reduced to ashes; and the Indians slept their last sleep beneath their own possessions.

For many years two white crosses marked the place where the Jesuit and his English boy were buried; but they have long since been removed. The white man's corn is nourished by the bones of the Abnakis; and the name of their tribe is well nigh forgotten.

Margaret Fuller
(1810–1850)

ducated at home by her father, a Massachusetts legislator, Fuller displayed a precocious brilliance from her earliest years. She began to publish essays and scholarly writing in 1834 and formed close relationships with Ralph Waldo Emerson and other leading Concord intellectuals, teaching for a time in Bronson Alcott's school. In 1839, Fuller launched a five-year series of formal conversations that showed the capabilities of women, leading to her women's rights manifesto *Woman in the Nineteenth Century* (1845). After two years as the editor of Emerson's Transcendentalist journal, *The Dial*, she joined the staff of Horace Greeley's *New York Tribune*, soon becoming a foreign correspondent in Europe. While reporting from Italy during the 1848 uprisings, Fuller had an affair with a twenty-six-year-old Italian Catholic radical, and had a child with him. She had always thought she would "write, like a man, of the world of intellect and action," not "like a woman, of love and hope and disappointment"; but the experience of passion and maternity changed her. Once the revolutions quieted in 1850, Fuller made the brave decision to return to America with her lover and son, face the sneers and social ostracism of her contemporaries, and take up her literary career; but all three drowned when their ship sank in a hurricane off Fire Island, less than a day before they were expected to arrive. She was only forty years old.

Her "Autobiographical Sketch," written when she was about thirty, was first published in *Memoirs of Margaret Fuller Ossoli* (1852), edited by Emerson along with William Henry Channing and James Freeman Clarke.

From Autobiographical Sketch (1852)

I. Youth

Parents

My father was a lawyer and a politician. He was a man largely endowed with that sagacious energy, which the state of New England society, for the last half century, has been so well fitted to develop. His father was a clergyman, settled as a pastor in Princeton, Massachusetts, within the bounds of whose parish-farm was Wachuset. His means were small, and the great object of his ambition was to send his sons to college. As a boy, my father was taught to think only of preparing himself for Harvard University, and when there of preparing himself for the profession of Law. As a Lawyer, again, the ends constantly presented were to work for distinction in the community, and for the means of supporting a family. To be an honored citizen, and to have a home on earth, were made the great aims of existence. To open the deeper fountains of the soul, to regard life here as the prophetic entrance to immortality, to develop his spirit to perfection,—motives like these had never been suggested to him, either by fellow-beings or by outward circumstances. The result was a character, in its social aspect, of quite the common sort. A good son and brother, a kind neighbor, an active man of business—in all these outward relations he was but one of a class, which surrounding conditions have made the majority among us. In the more delicate and individual relations, he never approached but two mortals, my mother and myself.

His love for my mother was the green spot on which he stood apart from the common-places of a mere bread-winning, bread-bestowing existence. She was one of those fair and flower-like natures, which sometimes spring up even beside the most dusty highways of life—a creature not to be shaped into a merely useful instrument, but bound by one law with the blue sky, the dew, and the frolic birds. Of all persons whom I have known, she had in her most of the angelic,—of that spontaneous love for every living thing, for man, and beast, and tree, which restores the golden age.

Death in the House

My earliest recollection is of a death,—the death of a sister, two years younger than myself. Probably there is a sense of childish endearments, such as belong to this tie, mingled with that of loss, of wonder, and mystery; but these last are prominent in memory. I remember coming home and meeting our nursery-maid, her face streaming with tears. That strange sight of tears made an indelible impression. I realize how little I was of stature, in that I looked up to this weeping face;—and it has often seemed since, that—full-grown for the life of this earth, I have looked up just so, at times of threatening, of doubt, and distress, and that just so has some being of the next higher order of existences looked down, aware of a law unknown to me, and tenderly commiserating the pain I must endure in emerging from my ignorance.

She took me by the hand and led me into a still and dark chamber,— then drew aside the curtain and showed me my sister. I see yet that beauty of death! The highest achievements of sculpture are only the reminder of its severe sweetness. Then I remember the house all still and dark,—the people in their black clothes and dreary faces,—the scent of the newly-made coffin,—my being set up in a chair and detained by a gentle hand to hear the clergyman,—the carriages slowly going, the procession slowly doling out their steps to the grave. But I have no remembrance of what I have since been told I did,—insisting, with loud cries, that they should not put the body in the ground. I suppose that my emotion was spent at the time, and so there was nothing to fix that moment in my memory.

I did not then, nor do I now, find any beauty in these ceremonies. What had they to do with the sweet playful child? Her life and death were alike beautiful, but all this sad parade was not. Thus my first experience of life was one of death. She who would have been the companion of my life was severed from me, and I was left alone. This has made a vast difference in my lot. Her character, if that fair face promised right, would have been soft, graceful and lively; it would have tempered mine to a gentler and more gradual course.

Overwork

My father,—all whose feelings were now concentrated on me,— instructed me himself. The effect of this was so far good that, not passing through the hands of many ignorant and weak persons as so many do at preparatory schools, I was put at once under discipline of considerable severity, and, at the same time, had a more than ordinarily high standard presented to me. My father was a man of business, even in literature; he had been a high scholar at college, and was warmly attached to all he had learned there, both from the pleasure he had derived in the exercise of his faculties and the associated memories of success and good repute. He was, beside, well read in French literature, and in English, a Queen Anne's man. He hoped to make me the heir of all he knew, and of as much more as the income of his profession enabled him to give me means of acquiring. At the very beginning, he made one great mistake, more common, it is to be hoped, in the last generation, than the warnings of physiologists will permit it to be with the next. He thought to gain time, by bringing forward the intellect as early as possible. Thus I had tasks given me, as many and various as the hours would allow, and on subjects beyond my age; with the additional disadvantage of reciting to him in the evening, after he returned from his office. As he was subject to many interruptions, I was often kept up till very late; and as he was a severe teacher, both from his habits of mind and his ambition for me, my feelings were kept on the stretch till the recitations were over. Thus frequently, I was sent to bed several hours too late, with nerves unnaturally stimulated. The consequence was a premature development of the brain, that made me a "youthful prodigy" by day, and by night a victim of spectral illusions, nightmare, and somnambulism, which at the time prevented the harmonious development of my bodily powers and checked my growth, while, later, they induced continual headache, weakness and nervous affections, of all kinds. As these again reacted on the brain, giving undue force to every thought and every feeling, there was finally produced a state of being both too active and too intense, which wasted my constitution, and will bring me,—even although I have learned to understand and regulate my now morbid temperament,—to a premature grave.

No one understood this subject of health then. No one knew why this child, already kept up so late, was still unwilling to retire. My aunts cried out upon the "spoiled child, the most unreasonable child that ever was,— if brother could but open his eyes to see it,—who was never willing to go to bed." They did not know that, so soon as the light was taken away, she seemed to see colossal faces advancing slowly towards her, the eyes dilating, and each feature swelling loathsomely as they came, till at last, when they were about to close upon her, she started up with a shriek which drove them away, but only to return when she lay down again. They did not know that, when at last she went to sleep, it was to dream of horses trampling over her, and to awake once more in fright; or, as she had just read in her Virgil, of being among trees that dripped with blood, where she walked and walked and could not get out, while the blood became a pool and splashed over her feet, and rose higher and higher, till soon she dreamed it would reach her lips. No wonder the child arose and walked in her sleep, moaning all over the house, till once, when they heard her, and came and waked her, and she told what she had dreamed, her father sharply bid her "leave off thinking of such nonsense, or she would be crazy,"—never knowing that he was himself the cause of all these horrors of the night. Often she dreamed of following to the grave the body of her mother, as she had done that of her sister, and woke to find the pillow drenched in tears. These dreams softened her heart too much, and cast a deep shadow over her young days; for then, and later, the life of dreams,—probably because there was in it less to distract the mind from its own earnestness,—has often seemed to her more real, and been remembered with more interest, than that of waking hours.

Poor child! Far remote in time, in thought, from that period, I look back on these glooms and terrors, wherein I was enveloped, and perceived that I had no natural childhood.

Books

Thus passed my first years. My mother was in delicate health, and much absorbed in the care of her younger children. In the house was neither dog nor bird, nor any graceful animated form of existence. I saw no persons who took my fancy, and real life offered no attraction. Thus my already over-excited mind found no relief from without, and was driven for refuge from itself to the world of books. I was taught Latin and English grammar at the same time, and began to read Latin at six years old, after which, for some years, I read it daily. In this branch of study, first by my father, and afterwards by a tutor, I was trained to quite a high degree of precision. I was expected to understand the mechanism of the language thoroughly, and in translating to give the thoughts in as few well-arranged words as possible, and without breaks or hesitation,—for with these my father had absolutely no patience.

Indeed, he demanded accuracy and clearness in everything: you must not speak, unless you can make your meaning perfectly intelligible to the person addressed; must not express a thought, unless you can give a reason for it, if required; must not make a statement, unless sure of all particulars—such were his rules. "But," "if," "unless," "I am mistaken," and "it may be so," were words and phrases excluded from the province where he held sway. Trained to great dexterity in artificial methods, accurate, ready, with entire command of his resources, he had no belief in minds that listen, wait, and receive. He had no conception of the subtle and indirect motions of imagination and feeling. His influence on me was great, and opposed to the natural unfolding of my character, which was fervent, of strong grasp, and disposed to infatuation, and self-forgetfulness. He made the common prose world so present to me, that my natural bias was controlled. I did not go mad, as many would do, at being continually roused from my dreams. I had too much strength to be crushed,—and since I must put on the fetters, could not submit to let them impede my motions. My own world sank deep within, away from the surface of my life; in what I did and said I learned to have reference to other minds. But my true life was only the dearer that it was secluded and veiled over by a thick curtain of available intellect, and that coarse, but wearable stuff woven by the ages,—Common Sense.

In accordance with this discipline in heroic common sense, was the influence of those great Romans, whose thoughts and lives were my daily food during those plastic years. The genius of Rome displayed itself in Character, and scarcely needed an occasional wave of the torch of thought to show its lineaments, so marble strong they gleamed in every light. Who, that has lived with those men, but admires the plain force of fact, of thought passed into action? They take up things with their naked hands. There is just the man, and the block he casts before you,—no divinity, no demon, no unfulfilled aim, but just the man and Rome, and what he did for Rome. Everything turns your attention to what a man can become, not by yielding himself freely to impressions, not by letting nature play freely through him, but by a single thought, an earnest purpose, an indomitable will, by hardihood, self-command, and force of expression. Architecture was the art in which Rome excelled, and this corresponds with the feeling these men of Rome excite. They did not grow,—they built themselves up, or were built up by the fate of Rome, as a temple for Jupiter Stator. The ruined Roman sits among the ruins; he flies to no green garden; he does not look to heaven; if his intent is defeated, if he is less than he meant to be, he lives no more. The names which end in "*us*," seem to speak with lyric cadence. That measured cadence,—that tramp and march,—which are not stilted, because they indicate real force, yet which seem so when compared with any other language,—make Latin a study in itself of mighty influence. The language alone, without the literature, would give one the *thought* of Rome. Man present in nature, commanding nature too sternly to be inspired by it, standing like the rock amid the sea, or moving like the fire over the land, either impassive, or irresistible; knowing not the soft mediums or fine flights of life, but by the force which he expresses, piercing to the centre.

We are never better understood than when we speak of a "Roman virtue," a "Roman outline." There is somewhat indefinite, somewhat yet unfulfilled in the thought of Greece, of Spain, of modern Italy; but ROME! it stands by itself, a clear Word. The power of will, the dignity of a fixed purpose is what it utters. Every Roman was an emperor. It is well that the infallible church should have been founded on this rock, that the presumptuous Peter should hold the keys, as the conquering Jove did before his thunderbolts, to be seen of all the world. The Apollo tends flocks with Admetus; Christ teaches by the lonely lake, or plucks wheat as he wanders through the fields some Sabbath morning. They never come to this stronghold; they could not have breathed freely where all became stone as soon as spoken, where divine youth found no horizon for its all-promising glance, but every thought put on, before it dared issue to the day in action, its *toga virilis*.

Suckled by this wolf, man gains a different complexion from that which is fed by the Greek honey. He takes a noble bronze in camps and battle-fields; the wrinkles of council will beseem his brow, and the eye cuts its way like the sword. The Eagle should never have been used as a symbol by any other nation: it belonged to Rome.

The history of Rome abides in mind, of course, more than the literature. It was degeneracy for a Roman to use the pen; his life was in the day. The "vaunting" of Rome, like that of the North American Indians, is her proper literature. A man rises; he tells who he is, and what he has done; he speaks of his country and her brave men; he knows that a conquering god is there, whose agent is his own right hand; and he should end like the Indian, "I have no more to say."

It never shocks us that the Roman is self-conscious. One wants no universal truths from him, no philosophy, no creation, but only his life, his Roman life felt in every pulse, realized in every gesture. The universal heaven takes in the Roman only to make us feel his individuality the more. The Will, the Resolve of Man!—it has been expressed,—fully expressed!

I steadily loved this ideal in my childhood, and this is the cause, probably, why I have always felt that man must know how to stand firm on the ground, before he can fly. In vain for me are men more, if they are less, than Romans. Dante was far greater than any Roman, yet I feel he was right to take the Mantuan as his guide through hell, and to heaven.

Horace was a great deal to me then, and is so still. Though his words do not abide in memory, his presence does: serene, courtly, of darting hazel eye, a self-sufficient grace, and an appreciation of the world of stern realities, sometimes pathetic, never tragic. He is the natural man of the world; he is what he ought to be, and his darts never fail of their aim. There is a perfume and raciness, too, which makes life a banquet, where the wit sparkles no less that the viands were bought with blood.

Ovid gave me not Rome, nor himself, but a view into the enchanted gardens of Greek mythology. This path I followed, have been following ever since; and now, life half over, it seems to me, as in my childhood, that every thought of which man is susceptible, is intimated there. In those young years, indeed, I did not see what I now see, but loved to creep from amid the Roman pikes to lie beneath this great vine, and see the smiling and serene shapes go by, woven from the finest fibres of all the elements. I knew not why, at that time,—but I loved to get away from the hum of the forum, and the mailed clang of Roman speech, to these shifting shows of nature, these Gods and Nymphs born of the sunbeam, the wave, the shadows on the hill.

As with Rome I antedated the world of deeds, so I lived in those Greek forms the true faith of a refined and intense childhood. So great was the force of reality with which these forms impressed me, that I prayed earnestly for a sign,—that it would lighten in some particular region of the heavens, or that I might find a bunch of grapes in the path, when I went forth in the morning. But no sign was given, and I was left a waif stranded upon the shores of modern life!

Of the Greek language, I knew only enough to feel that the sounds told the same story as the mythology;—that the law of life in that land was beauty, as in Rome it was a stern composure. I wish I had learned as much of Greece as of Rome,—so freely does the mind play in her sunny waters, where there is no chill, and the restraint is from within out; for these Greeks, in an atmosphere of ample grace, could not be impetuous, or stern, but loved moderation as equable life always must, for it is the law of beauty.

With these books I passed my days. The great amount of study exacted of me soon ceased to be a burden, and reading became a habit and a passion. The force of feeling, which, under other circumstances, might have ripened thought, was turned to learn the thoughts of others. This was not a tame state, for the energies brought out by rapid acquisition gave glow enough. I thought with rapture of the all-accomplished man, him of the many talents, wide resources, clear sight, and omnipotent will. A Caesar seemed great enough. I did not then know that such men impoverish the treasury to build the palace. I kept their statues as belonging to the hall of my ancestors, and loved to conquer obstacles, and fed my youth and strength for their sake.

Still, though this bias was so great that in earliest years I learned, in these ways, how the world takes hold of a powerful nature, I had yet other experiences. None of these were deeper than what I found in the happiest haunt of my childish years,—our little garden. Our house, though comfortable, was very ugly, and in a neighborhood which I detested,—every dwelling and its appurtenances having a *mesquin* and huddled look. I liked nothing about us except the tall graceful elms before the house, and the dear little garden behind. Our back door opened on a high flight of steps, by which I went down to a green plot, much injured in my ambitious eyes by the presence of the pump and the tool-house. This opened into a little garden, full of choice flowers and fruit-trees, which was my mother's delight, and was carefully kept. Here I felt at home. A gate opened thence into the fields,—a wooden gate made of boards, in a high, unpainted board wall, and embowered in the clematis creeper. This gate I used to open to see the sunset heaven; beyond this black frame I did not step, for I liked to look at the deep gold behind it. How exquisitely happy I was in its beauty, and how I loved the silvery wreaths of my protecting vine! I never would pluck one of its flowers at that time, I was so jealous of its beauty, but often since I carry off wreaths of it from the wild-wood, and it stands in nature to my mind as the emblem of domestic love.

Of late I have thankfully felt what I owe to that garden, where the best hours of my lonely childhood were spent. Within the house everything was socially utilitarian; my books told of a proud world, but in another temper were the teachings of the little garden. There my thoughts could lie callow in the nest, and only be fed and kept warm, not called to fly or sing before the time. I loved to gaze on the roses, the violets, the lilies, the pinks; my mother's hand had planted them, and they bloomed for me. I culled the most beautiful. I looked at them on every side. I kissed them, I pressed them to my bosom with passionate emotions, such as I have never dared express to any human being. An ambition swelled my heart to be as beautiful, as perfect as they. I have not kept my vow. Yet, forgive, ye wild asters, which gleam so sadly amid the fading grass; forgive me, ye golden autumn flowers, which so strive to reflect the glories of the parting distant sun; and ye silvery flowers, whose moonlight eyes I knew so well, forgive! Living and blooming in your unchecked law, ye know nothing of the blights, the distortions, which beset the human being; and which at such hours it would seem that no glories of free agency could ever repay!

There was, in the house, no apartment appropriated to the purpose of a library, but there was in my father's room a large closet filled with books, and to these I had free access when the task-work of the day was done. Its window overlooked wide fields, gentle slopes, a rich and smiling country, whose aspect pleased without much occupying the eye, while a range of blue hills, rising at about twelve miles distance, allured to reverie. "Distant mountains," says Tieck, "excite the fancy, for beyond them we place the scene of our Paradise." Thus, in the poems of fairy adventure, we climb the rocky barrier, pass fearless its dragon caves, and dark pine forests, and find the scene of enchantment in the vale behind. My hopes were never so definite, but my eye was constantly allured to that distant blue range, and I would sit, lost in fancies, till tears fell on my cheek. I loved this sadness; but only in later years, when the realities of life had taught me moderation, did the passionate emotions excited by seeing them again teach how glorious were the hopes that swelled my heart while gazing on them in those early days.

Melancholy attends on the best joys of a merely ideal life, else I should call most happy the hours in the garden, the hours in the book closet. Here were the best French writers of the last century; for my father had been more than half a Jacobin, in the time when the French Republic cast its glare of promise over the world. Here, too, were the Queen Anne authors, his models, and the English novelists; but among them I found none that charmed me. Smollett, Fielding, and the like, deal too broadly with the coarse actualities of life. The best of their men and women—so merely natural, with the nature found every day—do not meet our hopes. Sometimes the simple picture, warm with life and the light of the common sun, cannot fail to charm,—as in the wedded love of Fielding's Amelia,—but it is at a later day, when the mind is trained to comparison, that we learn to prize excellence like this as it deserves. Early youth is prince-like: it will bend only to "the king, my father." Various kinds of excellence please, and leave their impression, but the most commanding, alone, is duly acknowledged at that all-exacting age.

Three great authors it was my fortune to meet at this important period,—all, though of unequal, yet congenial powers,—all of rich and wide, rather than aspiring genius,—all free to the extent of the horizon their eye took in,—all fresh with impulse, racy with experience; never to be lost sight of, or superseded, but always to be apprehended more and more.

Ever memorable is the day on which I first took a volume of SHAKE-SPEARE in my hand to read. It was on a Sunday.

—This day was punctiliously set apart in our house. We had family prayers, for which there was no time on other days. Our dinners were different, and our clothes. We went to church. My father put some limitations on my reading, but—bless him for the gentleness which has left me a pleasant feeling for the day!—he did not prescribe what was, but only what was *not*, to be done. And the liberty this left was a large one. "You must not read a novel, or a play;" but all other books, the worst, or the best, were open to me. The distinction was merely technical. The day was pleasing to me, as relieving me from the routine of tasks and recitations; it gave me freer play than usual, and there were fewer things occurred in its course, which reminded me of the divisions of time; still the church-going, where I heard nothing that had any connection with my inward life, and these rules, gave me associations with the day of empty formalities, and arbitrary restrictions; but though the forbidden book or walk always seemed more charming then, I was seldom tempted to disobey.—

This Sunday—I was only eight years old—I took from the book-shelf a volume lettered SHAKESPEARE. It was not the first time I had looked at it, but before I had been deterred from attempting to read, by the broken appearance along the page, and preferred smooth narrative. But this time I held in my hand "Romeo and Juliet" long enough to get my eye fastened to the page. It was a cold winter afternoon. I took the book to the parlor fire, and had there been seated an hour or two, when my father looked up and asked what I was reading so intently. "Shakespeare," replied the child, merely raising her eye from the page. "Shakespeare,—that won't do; that's no book for Sunday; go put it away and take another." I went as I was bid, but took no other. Returning to my seat, the unfinished story, the personages to whom I was but just introduced, thronged and burnt my brain. I could not bear it long; such a lure it was impossible to resist. I went and brought the book again. There were several guests present, and I had got half through the play before I again attracted attention. "What is that child about that she don't hear a word that's said to her?" quoth my aunt. "What are you reading?" said my father. "Shakespeare" was again the reply, in a clear, though somewhat impatient, tone. "How?" said my father angrily,—then restraining himself before his guests,—"Give me the book and go directly to bed."

Into my little room no care of his anger followed me. Alone, in the dark, I thought only of the scene placed by the poet before my eye, where the free flow of life, sudden and graceful dialogue, and forms, whether grotesque or fair, seen in the broad lustre of his imagination, gave just what I wanted, and brought home the life I seemed born to live. My fancies swarmed like bees, as I contrived the rest of the story;—what all would do, what say, where go. My confinement tortured me. I could not go forth from this prison to ask after these friends; I could not make my pillow of the dreams about them which yet I could not forbear to frame. Thus was I absorbed when my father entered. He felt it right, before going to rest, to reason with me about my disobedience, shown in a way, as he considered, so insolent. I listened, but could not feel interested in what he said, nor turn my mind from what engaged it. He went away really grieved at my impenitence, and quite at a loss to understand conduct in me so unusual.

—Often since I have seen the same misunderstanding between parent and child,—the parent thrusting the morale, the discipline, of life upon the child, when just engrossed by some game of real importance and great leadings to it. That is only a wooden horse to the father,—the child was careering to distant scenes of conquest and crusade, through a country of elsewhere unimagined beauty. None but poets remember their youth; but the father who does not retain poetical apprehension of the world, free and splendid as it stretches out before the child, who cannot read his natural history, and follow out its intimations with reverence, must be a tyrant in his home, and the purest intentions will not prevent his doing much to cramp him. Each new child is a new Thought, and has bearings and discernings, which the Thoughts older in date know not yet, but must learn.—

My attention thus fixed on Shakespeare, I returned to him at every hour I could command. Here was a counterpoise to my Romans, still more forcible than the little garden. My author could read the Roman nature too,—read it in the sternness of Coriolanus, and in the varied wealth of Caesar. But he viewed these men of will as only one kind of men; he kept them in their place, and I found that he, who could understand the Roman, yet expressed in Hamlet a deeper thought.

In Cervantes, I found far less productive talent,—indeed, a far less powerful genius,—but the same wide wisdom, a discernment piercing the shows and symbols of existence, yet rejoicing in them all, both for their own life, and as signs of the unseen reality. Not that Cervantes philosophized,—his genius was too deeply philosophical for that; he took things as they came before him, and saw their actual relations and bearings. Thus the work he produced was of deep meaning, though he might never have expressed that meaning to himself. It was left implied in the whole. A Coleridge comes and calls Don Quixote the pure Reason, and Sancho the Understanding. Cervantes made no such distinctions in his own mind; but he had seen and suffered enough to bring out all his faculties, and to make him comprehend the higher as well as the lower part of our nature. Sancho is too amusing and sagacious to be contemptible; the Don too noble and clear-sighted towards absolute truth, to be ridiculous. And we are pleased to see manifested in this way, how the lower must follow and serve the higher, despite its jeering mistrust and the stubborn realities which break up the plans of this pure-minded champion.

The effect produced on the mind is nowise that described by Byron:—

"Cervantes smiled Spain's chivalry away," &c.

On the contrary, who is not conscious of a sincere reverence for the Don, prancing forth on his gaunt steed? Who would not rather be he than any of the persons who laugh at him?—Yet the one we would wish to be is thyself, Cervantes, unconquerable spirit! gaining flavor and color like wine from every change, while being carried round the world; in whose eye the serene sagacious laughter could not be dimmed by poverty, slavery, or unsuccessful authorship. Thou art to us still more the Man, though less the Genius, than Shakespeare; thou dost not evade our sight, but, holding the lamp to thine own magic shows, dost enjoy them with us.

My third friend was Molière, one very much lower, both in range and depth, than the others, but, as far as he goes, of the same character. Nothing secluded or partial is there about his genius,—a man of the world, and a man by himself, as he is. It was, indeed, only the poor social world of Paris that he saw, but he viewed it from the firm foundations of his manhood, and every lightest laugh rings from a clear perception, and teaches life anew.

These men were all alike in this,—they loved the *natural history* of man. Not what he should be, but what he is, was the favorite subject of their thought. Whenever a noble leading opened to the eye new paths of light, they rejoiced; but it was never fancy, but always fact, that inspired them. They loved a thorough penetration of the murkiest dens, and most tangled paths of nature; they did not spin from the desires of their own special natures, but reconstructed the world from materials which they collected on every side. Thus their influence upon me was not to prompt me to follow out thought in myself so much as to detect it everywhere, for each of these men is not only a nature, but a happy interpreter of many natures. They taught me to distrust all invention which is not based on a wide experience. Perhaps, too, they taught me to overvalue an outward experience at the expense of inward growth; but all this I did not appreciate till later.

It will be seen that my youth was not unfriended, since those great minds came to me in kindness. A moment of action in one's self, however, is worth an age of apprehension through others; not that our deeds are better, but that they produce a renewal of our being. I have had more productive moments and of deeper joy but never hours of more tranquil pleasure than those in which these demi-gods visited me,—and with a smile so familiar, that I imagined the world to be full of such. They did me good, for by them a standard was early given of sight and thought, from which I could never go back, and beneath which I cannot suffer patiently my own life or that of any friend to fall. They did me harm, too, for the child fed with meat instead of milk becomes too soon mature. Expectations and desires were thus early raised, after which I must long toil before they can be realized. How poor the scene around, how tame one's own existence, how meagre and faint every power, with these beings in my mind. Often I must cast them quite aside in order to grow in my small way, and not sink into despair. Certainly I do not wish that instead of these masters I had read baby books, written down to children, and with such ignorant dulness that they blunt the senses and corrupt the tastes of the still plastic human being. But I do wish that I had read no books at all till later,—that I had lived with toys, and played in the open air. Children should not cull the fruits of reflection and observation early, but expand in the sun, and let thoughts come to them. They should not through books antedate their actual experiences, but should take them gradually, as sympathy and interpretation are needed. With me, much of life was devoured in the bud.

First Friend

For a few months, this bookish and solitary life was invaded by interest in a living, breathing figure. At church, I used to look around with a feeling of coldness and disdain, which, though I now well understand its causes, seems to my wiser mind as odious as it was unnatural. The puny child sought everywhere for the Roman or Shakespeare figures, and she was met by the shrewd, honest eye, the homely decency, or the smartness of a New England village on Sunday. There was beauty, but I could not see it then; it was not of the kind I longed for. In the next pew sat a family who were my especial aversion. There were five daughters, the eldest not above four-and-twenty,—yet they had the old fairy, knowing look, hard, dry, dwarfed, strangers to the All-Fair,—were working-day residents in this beautiful planet. They looked as if their thoughts had never strayed beyond the jobs of the day, and they were glad of it. Their mother was one of those shrunken, faded patterns of woman who have never done anything to keep smooth the cheek and dignify the brow. The father had a Scotch look of shrewd narrowness, and entire self-complacency. I could not endure this family, whose existence contradicted all my visions; yet I could not forbear looking at them.

As my eye one day was ranging about with its accustomed coldness, and the proudly foolish sense of being in a shroud of thoughts that were not their thoughts, it was arrested by a face most fair, and well-known as it seemed at first glance,—for surely I had met her before and waited for her long. But soon I saw that she was a new apparition foreign to that scene, if not to me. Her dress,—the arrangement of her hair, which had the graceful pliancy of races highly cultivated for long,—the intelligent and full picture of her eye, whose reserve was in its self-possession, not in timidity,—all combined to make up a whole impression, which, though too young to understand, I was well prepared to feel.

How wearisome now appears that thorough-bred *millefleur* beauty, the distilled result of ages of European culture! Give me rather the wild heath on the lonely hill-side, than such a rose-tree from the daintily clipped garden. But, then, I had but tasted the cup, and knew not how little it could satisfy; more, more, was all my cry; continued through years, till I had been at the very fountain. Indeed, it was ruby-red, a perfumed draught, and I need not abuse the wine because I prefer water, but merely say I have had enough of it. Then, the first sight, the first knowledge of such a person was intoxication.

She was an English lady, who, by a singular chance, was cast upon this region for a few months. Elegant and captivating, her every look and gesture was tuned to a different pitch from anything I had ever known. She was in various ways "accomplished," as it is called, though to what degree I cannot now judge. She painted in oils;—I had never before seen any one use the brush, and days would not have been too long for me to watch the pictures growing beneath her hand. She played the harp; and its tones are still to me the heralds of the promised land I saw before me then. She rose, she looked, she spoke; and the gentle swaying motion she made all through life has gladdened memory, as the stream does the woods and meadows.

As she was often at the house of one of our neighbors, and afterwards at our own, my thoughts were fixed on her with all the force of my nature. It was my first real interest in my kind, and it engrossed me wholly. I had seen her,—I should see her,—and my mind lay steeped in the visions that flowed from this source. My task-work I went through with, as I have done on similar occasions all my life, aided by pride that could not bear to fail, or be questioned. Could I cease from doing the work of the day, and hear the reason sneeringly given,—"Her head is so completely taken up with ——— that she can do nothing?" Impossible.

Should the first love be blighted, they say, the mind loses its sense of eternity. All forms of existence seem fragile, the prison of time real, for a god is dead. Equally true is this of friendship. I thank Heaven that this first feeling was permitted its free flow. The years that lay between the woman and the girl only brought her beauty into perspective, and enabled me to see her as I did the mountains from my window, and made her presence to me a gate of Paradise. That which she was, that which she brought, that which she might have brought, were mine, and over a whole region of new life I ruled proprietor of the soil in my own right.

Her mind was sufficiently unoccupied to delight in my warm devotion. She could not know what it was to me, but the light cast by the flame through so delicate a vase cheered and charmed her. All who saw admired her in their way; but she would lightly turn her head from their hard or oppressive looks, and fix a glance of full-eyed sweetness on the child, who, from a distance, watched all her looks and motions. She did not say much to me—not much to any one; she spoke in her whole being rather than by chosen words. Indeed, her proper speech was dance or song, and what was less expressive did not greatly interest her. But she saw much, having in its perfection the woman's delicate sense for sympathies and attractions. We walked in the fields, alone. Though others were present, her eyes were gliding over all the field and plain for the objects of beauty to which she was of kin. She was not cold to her seeming companions; a sweet courtesy satisfied them, but it hung about her like her mantle that she wore without thinking of it; her thoughts were free, for these civilized beings can really live two lives at the same moment. With them she seemed to be, but her hand was given to the child at her side; others did not observe me, but to her I was the only human presence. Like a guardian spirit she led me through the fields and groves, and every tree, every bird greeted me, and said, what I felt, "She is the first angel of your life."

One time I had been passing the afternoon with her. She had been playing to me on the harp, and I sat listening in happiness almost unbearable. Some guests were announced. She went into another room to receive them, and I took up her book. It was Guy Mannering, then lately published, and the first of Scott's novels I had ever seen. I opened where her mark lay, and read merely with the feeling of continuing our mutual existence by passing my eyes over the same page where hers had been. It was the description of the rocks on the sea-coast where the little Harry Bertram was lost. I had never seen such places, and my mind was vividly stirred to imagine them. The scene rose before me, very unlike reality, doubtless, but majestic and wild. I was the little Harry Bertram, and had lost her,—all I had to lose,—and sought her vainly in long dark caves that had no end, splashing through the water; while the crags beetled above, threatening to fall and crush the poor child. Absorbed in the painful vision, tears rolled down my cheeks. Just then she entered with light step, and full-beaming eye. When she saw me thus, a soft cloud stole over her face, and clothed every feature with a lovelier tenderness than I had seen there before. She did not question, but fixed on me inquiring looks of beautiful love. I laid my head against her shoulder and wept,—dimly feeling that I must lose her and all,—all who spoke to me of the same things,—that the cold wave must rush over me. She waited till my tears were spent, then rising, took from a little box a bunch of golden amaranths or everlasting flowers, and gave them to me. They were very fragrant. "They came," she said, "from Madeira." These flowers stayed with me seventeen years. "Madeira" seemed to me the fortunate isle, apart in the blue ocean from all of ill or dread. Whenever I saw a sail passing in the distance,—if it bore itself with fulness of beautiful certainty,—I felt that it was going to Madeira. Those thoughts are all gone now. No Madeira exists for me now,—no fortunate purple isle,—and all these hopes and fancies are lifted from the sea into the sky. Yet I thank the charms that fixed them here so long,—fixed them till perfumes like those of the golden flowers were drawn from the earth, teaching me to know my birth-place.

I can tell little else of this time,—indeed, I remember little, except the state of feeling in which I lived. For I *lived*, and when this is the case, there is little to tell in the form of thought. We meet—at least those who are true to their instincts meet—a succession of persons through our lives, all of whom have some peculiar errand to us. There is an outer circle, whose existence we perceive, but with whom we stand in no real relation. They tell us the news, they act on us in the offices of society, they show us kindness and aversion; but their influence does not penetrate; we are nothing to them, nor they to us, except as a part of the world's furniture. Another circle, within this, are dear and near to us. We know them and of what kind they are. They are to us not mere facts, but intelligible thoughts of the divine mind. We like to see how they are unfolded; we like to meet them and part from them: we like their action upon us and the pause that succeeds and enables us to appreciate its quality. Often we leave them on our path, and return no more, but we bear them in our memory, tales which have been told, and whose meaning has been felt.

But yet a nearer group there are, beings born under the same star, and bound with us in a common destiny. These are not mere acquaintances, mere friends, but, when we meet, are sharers of our very existence. There is no separation; the same thought is given at the same moment to both,—indeed, it is born of the meeting, and would not otherwise have been called into existence at all. These not only know themselves more, but *are* more for having met, and regions of their being, which would else have laid sealed in cold obstruction, burst into leaf and bloom and song.

The times of these meetings are fated, nor will either party be able ever to meet any other person in the same way. Both seem to rise at a glance into that part of the heavens where the word can be spoken, by which they are revealed to one another and to themselves. The step in being thus gained, can never be lost, nor can it be re-trod; for neither party will be again what the other wants. They are no longer fit to inter-change mutual influence, for they do not really need it, and if they think they do, it is because they weakly pine after a past pleasure.

To the inmost circle of relations but few are admitted, because some prejudice or lack of courage has prevented the many from listening to their instincts the first time they manifested themselves. If the voice is once disregarded it becomes fainter each time, till, at last, it is wholly silenced, and the man lives in this world, a stranger to its real life, deluded like the maniac who fancies he has attained his throne, while in reality he is on a bed of musty straw. Yet, if the voice finds a listener and servant the first time of speaking, it is encouraged to more and more clearness. Thus it was with me,—from no merit of mine, but because I had the good for-tune to be free enough to yield to my impressions. Common ties had not bound me; there were no traditionary notions in my mind; I believed in nothing merely because others believed in it; I had taken no feelings on trust. Thus my mind was open to their sway.

This woman came to me, a star from the east, a morning star, and I worshipped her. She too was elevated by that worship, and her fairest self called out. To the mind she brought assurance that there was a region congenial with its tendencies and tastes, a region of elegant cul-ture and intercourse, whose object, fulfilled or not, was to gratify the sense of beauty, not the mere utilities of life. In our relation she was lifted to the top of her being. She had known many celebrities, had roused to passionate desire many hearts, and became afterwards a wife; but I do not believe she ever more truly realized her best self than towards the lonely child whose heaven she was, whose eye she met, and whose pos-sibilities she predicted. "He raised me," said a woman inspired by love, "upon the pedestal of his own high thoughts, and wings came at once, but I did not fly away. I stood there with downcast eyes worthy of his love, for he had made me so."

Thus we do always for those who inspire us to expect from them the best. That which they are able to be, they become, because we demand it of them. "We expect the impossible—and find it."

My English friend went across the sea. She passed into her former life, and into ties that engrossed her days. But she has never ceased to think of me. Her thoughts turn forcibly back to the child who was to her all she saw of the really New World. On the promised coasts she had found only cities, careful men and women, the aims and habits of ordinary life in her own land, without that elegant culture which she, probably, over-estimated, because it was her home. But in the mind of the child she found the fresh prairie, the untrodden forests for which she had longed. I saw in her the storied castles, the fair stately parks and the wind laden with tones from the past, which I desired to know. We wrote to one another for many years;—her shallow and delicate epistles did not disenchant me, nor did she fail to see something of the old poetry in my rude characters and stammering speech. But we must never meet again.

When this friend was withdrawn I fell into a profound depression. I knew not how to exert myself, but lay bound hand and foot. Melancholy enfolded me in an atmosphere, as joy had done. This suffering, too, was out of the gradual and natural course. Those who are really children could not know such love, or feel such sorrow. "I am to blame," said my father, "in keeping her at home so long merely to please myself. She needs to be with other girls, needs play and variety. She does not seem to me really sick, but dull rather. She eats nothing, you say. I see she grows thin. She ought to change the scene."

I was indeed *dull*. The books, the garden, had lost all charm. I had the excuse of headache, constantly, for not attending to my lessons. The light of life was set, and every leaf was withered. At such an early age there are no back or side scenes where the mind, weary and sorrowful, may retreat. Older, we realize the width of the world more, and it is not easy to despair on any point. The effort at thought to which we are compelled relieves and affords a dreary retreat, like hiding in a brick-kiln till the shower be over. But then all joy seemed to have departed with my friend, and the emptiness of our house stood revealed. This I had not felt while I every day expected to see or had seen her, or annoyance and dulness were unnoticed or swallowed up in the one thought that clothed my days with beauty. But now she was gone, and I was roused from habits of reading or reverie to feel the fiery temper of the soul, and to learn that it must have vent, that it would not be pacified by shadows, neither meet without consuming what lay around it. I avoided the table as much as possible, took long walks and lay in bed, or on the floor of my room. I complained of my head, and it was not wrong to do so, for a sense of dulness and suffocation, if not pain, was there constantly.

But when it was proposed that I should go to school, that was a remedy I could not listen to with patience for a moment. The peculiarity of my education had separated me entirely from the girls around, except that when they were playing at active games, I would sometimes go out and join them. I liked violent bodily exercise, which always relieved my nerves. But I had no success in associating with them beyond the mere play. Not only I was not their schoolmate, but my book-life and lonely habits had given a cold aloofness to my whole expression, and veiled my manner with a hauteur which turned all hearts away. Yet, as this reserve was superficial, and rather ignorance than arrogance, it produced no deep dislike. Besides, the girls supposed me really superior to themselves, and did not hate me for feeling it, but neither did they like me, nor wish to have me with them. Indeed, I had gradually given up all such wishes myself; for they seemed to me rude, tiresome, and childish, as I did to them dull and strange. This experience had been earlier, before I was admitted to any real friendship; but now that I had been lifted into the life of mature years, and into just that atmosphere of European life to which I had before been tending, the thought of sending me to school filled me with disgust.

Yet what could I tell my father of such feelings? I resisted all I could, but in vain. He had no faith in medical aid generally, and justly saw that this was no occasion for its use. He thought I needed change of scene, and to be roused to activity by other children. "I have kept you at home," he said, "because I took such pleasure in teaching you myself, and besides I knew that you would learn faster with one who is desirous to aid you. But you will learn fast enough wherever you are, and you ought to be more with others of your own age. I shall soon hear that you are better, I trust."

Frances Sargent Locke Osgood
(1811–1850)

sgood is among the nineteenth-century women poets who evaded the opposing categories of conventional sentimentality and light-hearted satire. She published her first poem at the age of fourteen, married the portraitist Samuel Stillman Osgood and moved with him to London for four years. She often wrote in the self-effacingly mournful style of "Ah! Woman Still," a lament for the social constraints placed on the free expression of the woman poet. But it was also known that her marriage was unhappy, that she had an intense relationship with Edgar Allan Poe, and that she could write sophisticated verse like "He Bade Me Be Happy," about women's romantic resilience.

He Bade Me Be Happy (1849)

He bade me "Be happy," he whisper'd "Forget me;"
   He vow'd my affection was cherish'd in vain.
"Be happy!" "Forget me!" I would, if he'd let me—
   Why will he keep coming to say so again?

He came—it was not the first time, by a dozen—
   To take, as he said, "an eternal adieu;"
He went, and, for comfort, I turn'd to—my cousin,
   When back stalk'd the torment his vows to renew.

"You must love me no longer!" he said but this morning.
   "I love you no longer!" I meekly replied.
"Is this my reward?" he cried; "falsehood and scorning
   From her who was ever my idol, my pride!"

He bade me "Be happy," he murmur'd "Forget me!—
   Go into the gayest society, Jane!"
And I would obey him, right well, if he'd let me;
   But, the moment I do, he comes loving again!

Ah! Woman Still (1850)

Ah! woman still
  Must veil the shrine,
Where feeling feeds the fire divine,
  Nor sing at will,
  Untaught by art,
The music prison'd in her heart!

Still gay the note,
  And light the lay,
The woodbird warbles on the spray,
  Afar to float;
  But homeward flown,
Within his nest, how changed the tone!

Oh! none can know,
  Who have not heard
The music-soul that thrills the bird,
  The carol low
  As coo of dove
He warbles to his woodland-love!

The world would say
  'Twas vain and wild,
The impassion'd lay of Nature's child;
  And Feeling so
  Should veil the shrine
Where softly glow her fires divine!

Frances Miriam Berry Whitcher
(1811–1852)

hitcher was the first American female humorist. Her short fiction about oblivious, self-important villagers so angered her fellow New York townspeople that she and her preacher husband felt compelled to switch parishes. Her popular 1846 series of magazine pieces about a voluble, sentimental, poeticizing Yankee widow, Priscilla Bedott, was posthumously collected as the bestselling *Widow Bedott Papers.*

The Widow Essays Poetry, *from The Widow Bedott Papers* (1856)

Yes—he was one o' the best men that ever trod shoe-leather husband was, though Miss Jinkins says (she 'twas Poll Bingham) *she* says, I never found it out till after he died, but that's the consarndest lie that ever was told, though it's jest of a piece with every thing else she says about me. I guess if every body could see the poitry I writ to his memory, nobody wouldent think I dident set store by him. Want to hear it? Well, I'll see if I can say it; it ginerally affects me wonderfully, seems to harrer up my feelins; but I'll try. Dident know I ever writ poetry? how you talk! used to make lots on 't; haint so much late years. I remember once when Parson Potter had a bee, I sent him an amazin' great cheese, and I writ a piece o' poitry and pasted on top on't. It says:

> *Teach him for to proclaim*
> *Salvation to the folks,*
> *No occasion give for any blame*
> *Nor wicked people's jokes.*

And so it goes on, but I guess I won't stop to say the rest on 't now, seein' there's seven and forty verses. Parson Potter and his wife was wonderfully pleased with it, used to sing it to the tune o' Haddem. But I was gwine to tell the one I made in relation to husband, it begins as follers:

> *He never jawed in all his life,*
> *He never was onkind—*

And (tho' I say it that was his wife)
Such men you seldom find.

(That's as true as the Scripturs, I never knowed him to say a harsh word.)

I never changed my single lot—
I thought 't would be a sin—

(though widder Jinkins says it's because I never had a chance.) Now 't ain't for me to say whether I ever had a numerous number o' chances or not, but there's them livin' that *might* tell if they was a mind to; why, this poitry was writ on account of being joked about Major Coon, three year after husband died. I guess the ginerality o' folks knows what was the nature o' Major Coon's feelins toward me, tho' his wife and Miss Jinkins *does* say I tried to ketch him. The fact is, Miss Coon feels wonderfully cut up 'cause she knows the Major took her "Jack at a pinch"—seein' he couldent get such as he wanted, he took such as he could get—but I goes on to say—

I never changed my single lot—
I thought 't would be a sin—
For I thought so much o' Deacon Bedott
I never got married agin.

If ever a hasty word he spoke
His anger dident last,
But vanished like tobacker smoke
Afore the wint'ry blast.

And since it was my lot to be
The wife of such a man,
tell the men that's after me
To ketch me if they can.

If I was sick a single jot
He called the doctor in—

That's a fact—he used to be scairt to death if any thing ailed me, now only jest think—widder Jinkins told Sam Pendergrasses wife (she 't was Sally Smith) that she guessed the deacon dident set no great store by me, or he wouldent a went off to confrence meetin' when I was down with the fever. The truth is, they couldent git along without him no way. Parson Potter seldom went to confrence meetin', and when he wa'n't there, who was ther, pray tell, that knowed enough to take the lead if husband dident do it? Deacon Kenipe hadent no gift, and Deacon Crosby hadent no inclination, and so it all come on to Deacon Bedott—and he was always ready and willin' to do his duty, you know; as long as he was able to stand on his legs he continued to go to confrence meetin'; why, I've knowed that man to go when he couldent scarcely crawl on account o' the pain in the spine of his back. He had a wonderful gift, and he wa'n't a man to keep his talents hid up in a napkin—so you see 't was from a sense o' duty he went when I was sick, whatever Miss Jinkins may say to the contrary. But where was I? O—

> If I was sick a single jot
>   He called the doctor in—
> I sot so much store by Deacon Bedott
>   I never got married agin.

> A wonderful tender heart he had
>   That felt for all mankind—
> It made him feel amazin' bad
>   To see the world so blind.

> Whiskey and rum he tasted not—

That's as true as the Scripturs—but if you'll believe it, Betsy, Ann Kenipe told my Melissy that Miss Jinkins said one day to their house how't she'd seen Deacon Bedott high, time and agin! did you ever! Well, I'm glad nobody don't pretend to mind any thing *she* says. I've knowed Poll Bingham from a gal, and she never knowed how to speak the truth—besides she always had a pertikkeler spite against husband and me, and between us tew, I'll tell you why if you won't mention it, for I make it a pint never to say nothin' to injure nobody. Well, she was a ravin-distracted after my husband herself, but it's a long story, I'll tell you about it some other time, and then you'll know why widder Jinkins is etarnally runnin' me down. See—where had I got to? O, I remember now—

> Whiskey and rum he tasted not—
>   He thought it was a sin—
> I thought so much o' Deacon Bedott
>   I never got married agin.

> *But now he's dead! the thought is killin'*
> *My grief I can't control—*
> *He never left a single shillin*
> *His widder to console.*

But that wa'n't his fault—he was so out o' health for a number o' year afore he died, it ain't to be wondered at he dident lay up nothin'—however it dident give him no great oneasiness—he never cared much for airthly riches, though Miss Pendergrass says she heard Miss Jinkins say Deacon Bedott was as tight as the skin on his back—begrudged folks their vittals when they came to his house! did you ever! why he was the hull-souldest man I ever see in all my born days. If I'd such a husband as Bill Jinkins was I'd hold my tongue about my neighbors' husbands. He was a dretful mean man, used to git drunk every day of his life—and he had an awful high temper—used to swear like all possest when he got mad—and I've heard my husband say—(and he wa'n't a man that ever said any thing that wa'n't true)—I've heard *him* say Bill Jinkins would cheat his own father out of his eye teeth if he had a chance. Where was I? O! "His widder to console"—there ain't but one more verse, 't ain't a very lengthy poim. When Parson Potter read it, he says to me, says he—"What did you stop so soon for?"—but Miss Jinkins told the Crosbys *she* thought I'd better a stopt afore I'd begun—she's a purty critter to talk so, I must say. I'd like to see some poitry o' hern—I guess it would be astonishin' stuff; and mor 'n all that, she said there wa'n't a word o' truth in the hull on 't— said I never cared tuppence for the deacon. What an everlastin' lie!! Why—when he died, I took it so hard I went deranged, and took on so for a spell they was afraid they should have to send me to a Lunattic Arsenal. But that's a painful subject, I won't dwell on 't. I conclude as follows:

> *I'll never change my single lot—*
> *I think 't would be a sin*
> *The inconsolable widder o' Deacon Bedott,*
> *Don't intend to get married agin.*

Excuse my cryin'—my feelins always overcomes me so when I say that poitry—O-o-o-o-o-o!

Fanny Fern
(*Sara Payson Willis Parton*)
(*1811–1872*)

fter losing her beloved first husband to typhoid fever, and divorcing a rich widower she had married out of financial desperation, Sara Payson Willis began writing newspaper columns under the pseudonym "Fanny Fern" to support her two daughters. In her lively and often funny articles, Fern encouraged her women readers in their ambitions, as in a sarcastic 1853 column mocking the envious antifeminist criticism of Harriet Beecher Stowe's bestseller *Uncle Tom's Cabin*. She would later praise Stowe for having "had the courage to assert herself—to be what nature intended her to be—a genius—even at the risk of being called unfeminine, eccentric, and unwomanly." In 1855, Fern's weekly column for the *New York Ledger* earned her $100 per week, making her the highest paid journalist in the country, and her autobiographical novel *Ruth Hall* (1855) became a bestseller. Her third marriage to the editor James Parton was a happy one, and the income from her columns, essay collections, novels, and children's books made her a wealthy woman.

Mrs. Stowe's Uncle Tom (1853)

> Mrs. Stowe's Uncle Tom *is too graphic ever to have been written by a* woman.
>
> —Exchange

"Too graphic to be written by a woman?" D'ye hear that, Mrs. Stowe? or has English thunder stopped your American ears? Oh, I can tell you, Mrs. "Tom Cabin," that you've got to pay "for the bridge that has carried you over." Do you suppose that you can quietly take the wind out of everybody's sails, the way you have, without having harpoons, and lampoons, and all sorts of *miss*-iles thrown after you? No indeed; every distanced scribbler is perfectly frantic; they stoutly protest your book shows no genius, which fact is unfortunately corroborated by the difficulty your publishers find in disposing of it; they are transported with rage in proportion as *you* are *translated*. Everybody whose cat ever ran through your great grandfather's entry "knows all about you," and how long it took you to cut your first "wisdom tooth." Then all the bitter sectarian enemies your wide awake brothers have evoked, and who are afraid to measure lances with them, huddle into a corner to revenge by "making mouths" at their sister!

Certainly; what right had you to get an "invitation to Scotland" free gratis? or to have "Apsley House" placed at your disposal, as soon as your orthodox toes touched English ground? or to have "a silver salver" presented to you? or to have lords and ladies, and dukes and duchesses paying homage to you? or in short to raise such a little tornado to sweep through the four quarters of the globe? *You?* nothing but a woman—an *American* woman! and a *Beecher* at that! It is perfectly insufferable—one genius in a family is enough. There's your old patriarch father—God bless him!—there's material enough in him to make a dozen ordinary men, to say nothing of "Henry Ward" who's not so great an idiot as he might be! You see you had no "call," Mrs. Tom Cabin, to drop your babies and darning-needle to immortalize your name.

Well, I hope your feminine shoulders are broad enough and strong enough to bear all the abuse your presumption will call down upon you. All the men in your family, your husband included, belong to "the cloth," and consequently can't practice pistol shooting; there's where your enemies have you, you little simpleton! that's the only objection I have to Mr. Fern's "taking orders," for I've quite a penchant for ministers.

I trust you are convinced by this time that "Uncle Tom's Cabin" is a "flash in the pan." I'm sorry you have lost so much money by it, but it will go to show you, that women should have their ambition bounded by a gridiron and a darning needle. If you had not meddled with your husband's *divine* inkstand for such a *dark* purpose, nobody would have said you was "40 years old and looked like a Irish woman;" and between you and me and the vestry door, I don't believe they've done with you yet; for I see that every steamer tosses fresh laurels on your orthodox head, from foreign shores, and foreign powers. Poor *unfortunate* Mrs. Tom Cabin! Ain't you to be pitied.

Harriet Beecher Stowe
(1811–1896)

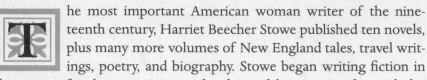he most important American woman writer of the nineteenth century, Harriet Beecher Stowe published ten novels, plus many more volumes of New England tales, travel writings, poetry, and biography. Stowe began writing fiction in the 1830s, after her marriage to the devoted but improvident scholar Calvin Stowe. As she explained to her friend Eliza Cabot Follen, she began to publish to support her family of seven children: "The nursery and the kitchen were my principle fields of labor. Then one of my friends pitying my toils copied and sent a number of little sketches from my pen to certain liberally paying 'Annuals' with my name. With the first money that I earned in this way I bought a feather bed! . . . And so I became an authoress." But beyond this modest and comic self-presentation, Stowe was an intellectual, an abolitionist, and a narrative innovator who corresponded with George Eliot about the art of fiction. *Uncle Tom's Cabin* (1852) was the first American novel to be internationally hailed as a great epic; George Sand, Tolstoy, and Turgenev read it with admiration.

While Stowe believed that slavery was the subject which offered the widest scope to a serious American novelist, she also wrote comic vernacular tales of New England life in the fictional village of Oldtown, and created Dickensian characters like Sam Lawson, the village do-nothing. As William Dean Howells, the editor of *The Atlantic Monthly*, noted, Sam's conversation came from "the naturalness of first-rate art."

The Village Do-Nothing, *from Oldtown Folks* (1869)

"Wal now, Horace, don't ye cry so. Why, I'm railly concerned for ye. Why, don't you s'pose your daddy' better off? Why, sartin *I* do. Don't cry, there's a good boy now. I'll give ye my jack-knife now."

This was addressed to me the day after my father's death while the preparations for the funeral hung like a pall over the house, and the terror of the last cold mystery, the tears of my mother, and a sort of bustling dreariness on the part of my aunts and grandmother, all conspired to bear down on my childish nerves with fearful power. It was a doctrine of those good old times, no less than of many in our present days, that a house invaded by death should be made as forlorn as hands could make it. It should be rendered as cold and stiff, as unnatural, as dead and corpse-like as possible, by closed shutters, looking-glasses pinned up in white sheets, and the locking up and hiding out of sight of any pleasant little familiar object which would be thought out of place in a sepulchre. This work had been driven through with unsparing vigor by Aunt Lois, who looked like one of the Fates as she remorselessly cleared away every little familiar object belonging to my father, and reduced every room to the shrouded stillness of a well-kept tomb.

Of course no one thought of looking after me. It was not the fashion of those days to think of children, if only they would take themselves off out of the way of the movements of the grown people; and so I had run out into the orchard back of the house, and, throwing myself down on my face under an apple tree in the tall clover, I gave myself up to despair, and was sobbing aloud in a nervous paroxysm of agony, when these words were addressed to me. The speaker was a tall, shambling, loose-jointed man, with a long, thin visage, prominent watery blue eyes, very fluttering and seedy habiliments, who occupied the responsible position of first do-nothing-in-ordinary in our village of Oldtown, and as such I must introduce him to my readers' notice.

Every New England village, if you only think of it, must have its do-nothing as regularly as it has its school-house or meeting house. Nature is always wide awake in the matter of compensation. Work, thrift, and industry are such an incessant steam power in Yankee life, that society would burn itself out with intense friction were there not interposed here and there the lubricating power of a decided do-nothing,—a man who won't be hurried, and won't work, and will take his ease in his own way, in spite of the whole protest of his neighborhood to the contrary. And there is on the face of the whole earth no do-nothing whose softness, idleness, general inaptitude to labor, and everlasting, universal shiftlessness can compare with that of this worthy, as found in a brisk Yankee village.

Sam Lawson filled this post with ample honor in Oldtown. He was a fellow dear to the souls of all "us boys" in the village, because, from the special nature of his position, he never had anything more pressing to do than croon and gossip with us. He was ready to spend hours in tinkering a boy's jack-knife, or mending his skate, or start at the smallest notice to watch at a woodchuck's hole, or give incessant service in tending a dog's sprained paw. He was always on hand to go fishing with us on Saturday afternoons; and I have known him to sit hour after hour on the bank, surrounded by a troop of boys, baiting our hooks and taking off our fish. He was a soft-hearted old body, and the wrigglings and contortions of our prey used to disturb his repose so that it was a regular part of his work to kill the fish by breaking their necks when he took them from the hook.

"Why, lordy massy, boys," he would say, "I can't bear to see no kind o' critter in torment. These 'ere pouts ain't to blame for bein' fish, and ye ought to put 'em out of their misery. Fish hes their rights as well as any on us."

Nobody but Sam would have thought of poking through the high grass and clover on our back lot to look me up, as I lay sobbing under the old apple-tree, the most insignificant little atom of misery that ever bewailed the inevitable.

Sam was of respectable family, and not destitute of education. He was an expert in at least five or six different kinds of handicraft, in all of which he had been pronounced by the knowing ones to be a capable workman, "if only he would stick to it." He had a blacksmith's shop, where, when the fit was on him, he would shoe a horse better than any man in the county. No one could supply a missing screw, or apply a timely brace, with more adroitness. He could mend cracked china so as to be almost as good as new; he could use carpenter's tools as well as a born carpenter, and would doctor a rheumatic door or a shaky window better than half the professional artisans in wood. No man could put a refractory clock to rights with more ingenuity than Sam,—that is, if you would give him his time to be about it.

I shall never forget the wrath and dismay which he roused in my Aunt Lois's mind by the leisurely way in which, after having taken our own venerable kitchen clock to pieces, and strewn the fragments all over the kitchen, he would roost over it in endless incubation, telling stories, entering into long-winded theological discussions, smoking pipes, and giving histories of all the other clocks in Oldtown, with occasional memoirs of those in Needmore, the North Parish, and Podunk, as placidly indifferent to all her volleys of sarcasm and contempt, her stinging expostulations and philippics, as the sailing old moon is to the frisky, animated barking of some puppy dog of earth.

"Why, ye see, Miss Lois," he would say, "clocks can't be druv; that's jest what they can't. Some things can be druv, and then agin some things can't, and clocks is that kind. They's jest got to be humored. Now this 'ere's a 'mazin' good clock, give me my time on it, and I'll have it so't will keep straight on to the Millennium."

"Millennium!" says Aunt Lois, with a snort of infinite contempt.

"Yes, the Millennium," says Sam, letting fall his work in a contemplative manner. "That 'ere's an interestin' topic now. Parson Lothrop, he don't think the Millennium will last a thousand years. What 's your 'pinion on that pint, Miss Lois?"

"My opinion is," said Aunt Lois, in her most nipping tones, "that if folks don't mind their own business, and do with their might what their hand finds to do, the Millennium won't come at all."

"Wal, you see, Miss Lois, it 's just here,—one day is with the Lord as a thousand years, and a thousand years as one day."

"I should think you thought a day was a thousand years, the way you work," said Aunt Lois.

"Wal," says Sam, sitting down with his back to his desperate litter of wheels, weights, and pendulums, and meditatively caressing his knee as he watched the sailing clouds in abstract meditation, "ye see, ef a thing 's ordained, why it 's got to be, ef you don't lift a finger. That 'ere 's so now, ain't it?"

"Sam Lawson, you are about the most aggravating creature I ever had to do with. Here you 've got our clock all to pieces and have been keeping up a perfect hurrah's nest in our kitchen for three days, and there you sit maundering and talking with your back to your work, fussin' about the Millennium, which is none of your business, or mine, as I know of! Do either put that clock together or let it alone!"

"Don't you be a grain uneasy, Miss Lois. Why, I 'll have your clock all right in the end, but I can't be druv. Wal, I guess I 'll take another spell on 't to-morrow or Friday."

Poor Aunt Lois, horror-stricken, but seeing herself actually in the hands of the imperturbable enemy, now essayed the tack of conciliation. "Now do, Lawson, just finish up this job, and I 'll pay you down, right on the spot; and you need the money."

"I 'd like to 'blige ye, Miss Lois; but ye see money ain't everything in this world. Ef I work tew long on one thing, my mind kind o' gives out, ye see; and besides, I 've got some 'sponsibilities to 'tend to. There 's Mrs. Captain Brown, she made me promise to come to-day and look at the nose o' that 'ere silver teapot o' hern; it 's kind o' sprung a leak. And then I 'greed to split a little oven-wood for the Widdah Pedee, that lives up on the Shelburn road. Must visit the widdahs in their affliction, Scriptur' says. And then there 's Hepsy: she 's allers a castin' it up at me that I don't do nothing for her and the chil'en; but then, lordy massy, Hepsy hain't no sort o' patience. Why jest this mornin' I was a tellin' her to count up her marcies, and, I 'clare for 't if I did n't think she 'd a throwed the tongs at me. That 'ere woman's temper railly makes me consarned. Wal good day, Miss Lois. I 'll be along again tomorrow or Friday or the first o' next week." And away he went with long, loose strides down the village street, while the leisurely wail of an old fuguing tune floated back after him,—

> *"Thy years are an*
> *Etarnal day,*
> *Thy years are an*
> *Etarnal day."*

"An eternal torment," said Aunt Lois, with a snap. "I am sure, if there 's a mortal creature on this earth that I pity, it 's Hepsy Lawson. Folks talk about her scolding,—that Sam Lawson is enough to make the saints in Heaven fall from grace. And you can't *do* anything with him: it 's like charging bayonet into a woolsack."

Now, the Hepsy thus spoken of was the luckless woman whom Sam's easy temper, and a certain youthful reputation for being a capable fellow, had led years before into the snares of matrimony with him, in consequence of which she was encumbered with the bringing up of six children on very short rations. She was a gnarly, compact, efficient little pepper-box of a woman, with snapping black eyes, pale cheeks, and a mouth always at half-cock, ready to go off with some sharp crack of reproof at the shoreless, bottomless, and tideless inefficiency of her husband. It seemed to be one of those facts of existence that she could not get used to, nor find anywhere in her brisk, fiery little body a grain of cool resignation for. Day after day she fought it with as bitter and intense a vigor, and with as much freshness of objurgation, as if it had come upon her for the first time,—just as a sharp, wiry little terrier will bark and bark from day to day, with never-ceasing pertinacity, into an empty squirrel-hole. She seemed to have no power within her to receive and assimilate the great truth that her husband was essentially, and was to be and always would be, only a do-nothing.

Poor Hepsy was herself quite as essentially a do-something,—an early-rising, bustling, driving, neat, efficient, capable little body,—who contrived, by going out to day's works,—washing, scrubbing, cleaning,—by making vests for the tailor, or closing and binding shoes for the shoemaker, by hoeing corn and potatoes in the garden at most unseasonable hours, actually to find bread to put into the mouths of the six young ravens aforesaid, and to clothe them decently. This might all do very well;

but when Sam—who believed with all his heart in the modern doctrines of woman's rights so far as to have no sort of objection to Hepsy's sawing wood or hoeing potatoes if she chose—would make the small degree of decency and prosperity the family had attained by these means a text on which to preach resignation, cheerfulness, and submission, then Hepsy's last cobweb of patience gave out, and she often became, for the moment, really dangerous, so that Sam would be obliged to plunge hastily out of doors to avoid a strictly personal encounter.

It was not to be denied that poor Hepsy really was a scold, in the strong old Saxon acceptation of the word. She had fought life single-handed, tooth and nail, with all the ferocity of outraged sensibilities, and had come out of the fight scratched and dishevelled, with few womanly graces. The good wives of the village, versed in the outs and ins of their neighbors' affairs, while they admitted that Sam was not all he should be, would sometimes roll up the whites of their eyes mysteriously, and say, "But then, poor man, what could you expect when he has n't a happy home? Hepsy's temper is, you know," etc., etc.

The fact is, that Sam's softly easy temper and habits of miscellaneous handiness caused him to have a warm corner in most of the households. No mothers ever are very hard on a man who always pleases the children; and every one knows the welcome of a universal gossip, who carries round a district a wallet of choice bits of neighborhood information.

Now Sam knew everything about everybody. He could tell Mrs. Major Broad just what Lady Lothrop gave for her best parlor carpet, that was brought over from England, and just on what occasions she used the big silver tankard, and on what they were content with the little one, and how many pairs of long silk stockings the minister had, and how many rows of stitching there were on the shoulders of his Sunday shirts. He knew just all that was in Deacon Badger's best room, and how many silver table-spoons and teaspoons graced the beaufet in the corner; and when each of his daughters was born, and just how Miss Susy came to marry as she did, and who wanted to marry her and could n't. He knew just the cost of Major Broad's scarlet cloak and shoe-buckles, and how Mrs. Major had a real *Ingy* shawl up in her "camphire" trunk, that cost nigh as much as Lady Lothrop's. Nobody had made love, or married, or had children born, or been buried, since Sam was able to perambulate the country, without his informing himself minutely of every available particular; and his unfathomable knowledge on these subjects was an unfailing source of popularity.

Besides this, Sam was endowed with no end of idle accomplishments.

His indolence was precisely of a turn that enjoyed the excitement of an occasional odd bit of work with which he had clearly no concern, and which had no sort of tendency toward his own support or that of his family. Something so far out of the line of practical utility as to be in a manner an artistic labor would awaken all the energies of his soul. His shop was a perfect infirmary for decayed articles of *virtu* from all the houses for miles around. Cracked china, lame tea-pots, broken shoe-buckles, rickety tongs, and decrepit fire-irons, all stood in melancholy proximity, awaiting Sam's happy hours of inspiration; and he was always happy to sit down and have a long, strictly confidential conversation concerning any of these with the owner, especially if Hepsy were gone out washing, or on any other work which kept her at a safe distance.

Sam could shave and cut hair as neatly as any barber, and was always in demand up and down the country to render these offices to the sick. He was ready to go for miles to watch with invalids, and a very acceptable watcher he made, beguiling the night hours with endless stories and legends. He was also an expert in psalmody, having in his youth been the pride of the village singing school. In those days he could perform reputably on the bass-viol in the choir of a Sunday with a dolefulness and solemnity of demeanor in the highest degree edifying,—though he was equally ready of a week-evening in scraping on a brisk little fiddle, if any of the thoughtless ones wanted a performer at a husking or a quilting frolic. Sam's obligingness was many-sided, and he was equally prepared at any moment to raise a funeral psalm or whistle the time of a double-shuffle.

But the more particular delight of Sam's heart was in funerals. He would walk miles on hearing the news of a dangerous illness, and sit roosting on the fence of the premises, delighted to gossip over the particulars, but ready to come down at any moment to do any of the odd turns which sickness in a family makes necessary; and when the last earthly scene was over, Sam was more than ready to render those final offices from which the more nervous and fastidious shrink, but in which he took almost a professional pride.

The business of an undertaker is a refinement of modern civilization. In simple old days neighbors fell into one another's hands for all the last wants of our poor mortality; and there were men and women of note who took a particular and solemn pride in these mournful offices. Sam had in fact been up all night in our house, and having set me up in the clover, and comforted me with a jack-knife, he proceeded to inform me of the particulars.

"Why, ye see! Horace, I ben up with 'em pretty much all night; and I laid yer father out myself, and I never see a better-lookin' corpse. It 's a 'mazin' pity your daddy hed such feelin's 'bout havin' people come to look at him, 'cause he does look beautiful, and it 's been a long time since we 've hed a funeral, anyway, and everybody was expectin' to come to his 'n, and they 'll all be dissipinted if the corpse ain't show 'd; but then, lordy massy, folks ought n't to think hard on't ef folks hes their own way 'bout their own funeral. That 'ere 's what I 've been a tellin' on 'em all, over to the tavern and round to the store. Why, you never see such a talk as there was about it. There was Aunt Sally Morse, and Betsey and Patsy Sawin, and Mis' Zeruiah Bacon, come over early to look at the corpse, and when they was n't let in, you never heerd sich a jawin'. Betsey and Patsy Sawin said that they allers suspected your father was an infidel, or some sich, and now they was clear; and Aunt Sally, she asked who made his shroud, and when she heerd there was n't to be none, he was laid out in his clothes, she said she never heerd such unchristian doin's,—that she always had heerd he had strange opinions, but she never thought it would come to that."

"My father is n't an infidel, and I wish I could kill 'em for talking so," said I, clenching my jack-knife in my small fist, and feeling myself shake with passion.

"Wal, wal, I kind o' spoke up to 'em about it. I was n't a-goin' to hear no sich jaw; and says I, 'I think ef there is any body that knows what 's what about funerals I 'm the man, fur I don't s'pose there 's a man in the county that 's laid out more folks, and set up with more corpses, and ben sent for fur and near, than I have, and my opinion is that mourners must always follow the last directions gi'n to 'em by the person. Ef a man has n't a right to have the say about his own body, what hes he a right to?' Wal, they said that it was putty well of me to talk so, when I had the privilege of sittin' up with him, and seein' all that was to be seen. 'Lordy massy,' says I, 'I don't see why ye need envi me; 't ain't my fault that folks thinks it 's agreeable to have me round. As to bein' buried in his clothes, why, lordy massy, 't ain't nothin' so extraordinary. In the old country great folks is very often laid out in their clothes. 'member, when I was a boy, old Mr. Sanger, the minister in Deerbrook, was laid out in his gown and bands, with a Bible in his hands, and he looked as nateral as a pictur. I was at Parson Rider's funeral, down to Wrentham. He was laid out in white flannel. But then there was old Captain Bigelow, down to the Pint there, he was laid out regular in his rigimentals, jest as he wore 'em in the war, epaulets and all.' Wal now, Horace, your daddy looks jest as peaceful as a psalm-tune. Now, you don't know,—jest as nateral as if he 'd only jest gone to sleep. So ye may set your heart at rest 'bout him."

It was one of those beautiful serene days of October, when the earth lies as bright and still as anything one can dream of in the New Jerusalem, and Sam's homely expressions of sympathy had quieted me somewhat. Sam, tired of his discourse, lay back in the clover, with his hands under his head, and went on with his moralizing.

"Lordy massy, Horace, to think on 't,—it 's so kind o' solemnizin'! It 's one's turn to-day, and another's to-morrow. We never know when our turn 'll come." And Sam raised a favorite stave,—

> "And must these active limbs of mine
> Lie moulderin' in the clay?"

"Active limbs! I guess so!" said a sharp voice, which came through the clover-heads like the crack of a rifle. "Well, I 've found you at last. Here you be, Sam Lawson, lyin' flat on your back at eleven o'clock in the morning, and not a potato dug, and not a stick of wood cut to get dinner with; and I won't cut no more if we never have dinner. It 's no use a humorin' you,—doin' your work for you. The more I do, the more I may do; so come home, won't you?"

"Lordy massy, Hepsy," said Sam, slowly erecting himself out of the grass, and staring at her with white eyes, "you don't ought to talk so. I ain't to blame. I hed to sit up with Mr. Holyoke all night, and help 'em lay him out at four o'clock this mornin'."

"You 're always everywhere but where you 've business to be," said Hepsy; "and helpin' and doin' for everybody but your own. For my part, I think charity ought to begin at home. You 're everywhere, up and down and round,—over to Shelbun, down to Podunk, up to North Parish; and here Abram and Kiah Stebbins have been waitin' all the morning with a horse they brought all the way from Boston to get you to shoe."

"Wal now, that 'ere shows they know what 's what. I told Kiah that ef they 'd bring that 'ere hoss to me I 'd 'tend to his huffs."

"And be off lying in the mowing, like a patridge, when they come after ye. That 's one way to do business," said Hepsy.

"Hepsy, I was just a miditatin'. Ef we don't miditate some times on all these 'ere things, it 'll be wus for us by and by."

"Meditate! I 'll help your meditations in a way you won't like, if you don't look out. So now you come home, and stop your meditatin', and go to doin' somethin'. I told 'em to come back this afternoon, and I 'd have you on the spot if 't was a possible thing," said the very practical Hepsy, laying firm hold of Sam's unresisting arm, and leading him away captive.

I stole into the darkened, silent room where my father had lain so long. Its desolate neatness struck a chill to my heart. Not even a bottle remained of the many familiar ones that used to cover the stand and the mantel-piece; but he, lying in his thread-bare Sunday coat, looked to me as I had often seen him in later days, when he had come from school exhausted, and fallen asleep in the bed. I crept to his side and nestled down on the floor as quietly as a dog lies down by the side of his master.

Elizabeth Stuart Phelps
(1815–1852)

lizabeth Stuart Phelps grew up in Andover, Massachusetts, where her father was a professor of theology at the seminary, and at sixteen began to publish articles in religious magazines under the pseudonym "H. Trusta," (an anagram of "Stuart"). In 1842, she married one of her father's students, Austin Phelps, and they spent their first six years together living in Boston, a stimulating period from which she drew on her urban experiences as a minister's wife for her second novel, *A Peep at Number Five* (1852). But her husband gave up his parish and joined the faculty at Andover Seminary, and Phelps struggled to combine her roles as faculty wife and mother with her imaginative writing. "The Angel Over the Right Shoulder" (1852) puts a cheerful face on the feelings of the woman torn between maternity and creativity, but Phelps died the same year at the age of thirty-seven. Toward the end of her life, she wrote, "I work in the dark. Everything lies in chaos before me. My life is a riddle to me." In the words of her daughter, Elizabeth Stuart Phelps Ward, who became a novelist as well, "Her last book and her last baby came together, and killed her."

The Angel over the Right Shoulder, or, The Beginning of a New Year (1852)

"There! a woman's work is never done," said Mrs. James. "I thought, for once, I was through; but just look at that lamp, now! it will not burn, and I must go and spend half an hour over it."

"Don't you wish you had never been married?" said Mr. James, with a good-natured laugh.

"Yes"—rose to her lips, but was checked by a glance at the group upon the floor, where her husband was stretched out, and two little urchins with sparkling eyes and glowing cheeks were climbing and tumbling over him, as if they found in this play the very essence of fun.

She did say, "I should like the good, without the evil, if I could have it."

"You have no evils to endure," replied her husband.

"That is just all you gentlemen know about it. What would you think, if you could not get an uninterrupted half hour to yourself, from morning till night? I believe you would give up trying to do anything."

"There is no need of that; all you want, is *system*. If you arranged your work systematically, you would find that you could command your time."

"Well," was the reply, "all I wish is, that you could just follow me around for one day, and see what I have to do. If you could reduce it all to system, I think you would show yourself a genius."

When the lamp was trimmed, the conversation was resumed. Mr. James had employed the "half hour," in meditating on this subject.

"Wife," said he, as she came in, "I have a plan to propose to you, and I wish you to promise me beforehand, that you will accede to it. It is to be an experiment, I acknowledge, but I wish it to have a fair trial. Now to please me, will you promise?"

Mrs. James hesitated. She felt almost sure that his plan would be quite impracticable, for what does a man know of a woman's work? Yet she promised.

"Now I wish you," said he, "to set apart two hours of every day for your own private use. Make a point of going to your room, and locking yourself in; and also make up your mind to let the work which is not done, go undone, if it must. Spend this time on just those things which will be most profitable to yourself. I shall bind you to your promise for one month—then, if it has proved a total failure, we will devise something else."

"When shall I begin?"

"To-morrow."

The morrow came. Mrs. James had chosen the two hours before dinner as being, on the whole, the most convenient and the least liable to interruption. They dined at one o'clock. She wished to finish her morning work, get dressed for the day, and enter her room at eleven.

Hearty as were her efforts to accomplish this, the hour of eleven found her with her work but half done; yet, true to her promise, she left all, retired to her room and locked the door.

With some interest and hope, she immediately marked out a course of reading and study, for these two precious hours: then arranging her table, her books, pen and paper, she commenced a schedule of her work with much enthusiasm. Scarcely had she dipped her pen in ink, when she heard the tramping of little feet along the hall, and then a pounding at her door.

"Mamma! mamma! I cannot find my mittens, and Hannah is going to slide without me."

"Go to Amy, my dear; mamma is busy."

"So Amy busy too; she say she can't leave baby."

The child began to cry, still standing close to the fastened door. Mrs. James knew the easiest, and indeed the only way of settling the trouble, was to go herself and hunt up the missing mittens. Then a parley must be held with Frank, to induce him to wait for his sister, and the child's tears must be dried, and little hearts must be all set right before the children went out to play; and so favorable an opportunity must not be suffered to slip, without impressing on young minds the importance of having a "place for everything, and everything in its place." This took time; and when Mrs. James returned to her study, her watch told her that *half* her portion had gone. Quietly resuming her work, she was endeavoring to mend her broken train of thought, when heavier steps were heard in the hall, and the fastened door was once more besieged. Now, Mr. James must be admitted.

"Mary," said he, "cannot you come and sew a string on for me? I do believe there is not a bosom in my drawer in order, and I am in a great hurry. I ought to have been down town an hour ago."

The schedule was thrown aside, the work-basket taken, and Mrs. James followed him. She soon sewed on the tape, but then a button needed fastening; and, at last, a rip in his glove was to be mended. As Mrs. James stitched away on the glove, a smile lurked in the corners of her mouth, which her husband observed.

"What are you laughing at?" asked he.

"To think how famously your plan works."

"I declare!" said he, "is this your study hour? I am sorry, but what can a man do? He cannot go down town without a shirt-bosom!"

"Certainly not," said his wife, quietly.

When her liege lord was fairly equipped and off, Mrs. James returned to her room. A half an hour yet remained to her, and of this she determined to make the most. But scarcely had she resumed her pen, when there was another disturbance in the entry. Amy had returned from walking out with the baby, and she entered the nursery with him, that she might get him to sleep. Now it happened that the only room in the house which Mrs. James could have to herself with a fire, was the one adjoining the nursery. She had become so accustomed to the ordinary noise of the children, that it did not disturb her; but the very extraordinary noise which master Charley sometimes felt called upon to make, when he was fairly on his back in the cradle, did disturb the unity of her thoughts. The words which she was reading rose and fell with the screams and lulls of the child, and she felt obliged to close her book, until the storm was over. When quiet was restored in the cradle, the children came in from sliding, crying with cold fingers; and just as she was going to them, the dinner-bell rang.

"How did your new plan work this morning?" inquired Mr. James.

"Famously," was the reply; "I read about seventy pages of German, and as many more in French."

"I am sure *I* did not hinder you long."

"No—yours was only one of a dozen interruptions."

"O, well! you must not get discouraged. Nothing succeeds well the first time. Persist in your arrangement, and by and by the family will learn that if they want anything of you, they must wait until after dinner."

"But what can a man do?" replied his wife; "he cannot go down town without a shirt-bosom."

"I was in a bad case," replied Mr. James, "it may not happen again. I am anxious to have you try the month out faithfully, and then we will see what has come of it."

The second day of trial was a stormy one. As the morning was dark, Bridget overslept, and consequently breakfast was too late by an hour. This lost hour Mrs. James could not recover. When the clock struck eleven, she seemed but to have commenced her morning's work, so much remained to be done. With mind disturbed and spirits depressed, she left her household matters "in the suds," as they were, and punctually retired to her study. She soon found, however, that she could not fix her attention upon any intellectual pursuit. Neglected duties haunted her, like ghosts around the guilty conscience. Perceiving that she was doing nothing with her books, and not wishing to lose the morning wholly, she commenced writing a letter. Bridget interrupted her before she had proceeded far on the first page.

"What, ma'am, shall we have for dinner? No marketing ha'n't come."

"Have some steaks, then."

"We ha'n't got none, ma'am."

"I will send out for some, directly."

Now there was no one to send but Amy, and Mrs. James knew it. With a sigh, she put down her letter and went into the nursery.

"Amy, Mr. James has forgotten our marketing. I should like to have you run over to the provision store, and order some beef-steaks; I will stay with the baby."

Amy was not much pleased to be sent out on this errand. She remarked, that she "must change her dress first."

"Be as quick as possible," said Mrs. James, "for I am particularly engaged at this hour."

Amy neither obeyed, nor disobeyed, but managed to take her own time, without any very deliberate intention to do so. Mrs. James, hoping to get along with a sentence or two, took her German book into the nursery. But this arrangement was not to master Charley's mind. A fig did he care for German, but "the kitties" he must have, whether or no— and kitties he would find in that particular book—so he turned its leaves over in great haste. Half of the time on the second day of trial had gone when Amy returned, and Mrs. James, with a sigh, left the nursery. Before one o'clock, she was twice called into the kitchen to superintend some important dinner arrangement, and thus it turned out that she did not finish one page of her letter.

On the third morning the sun shone, and Mrs. James rose early, made every provision which she deemed necessary for dinner, and for the comfort of her family; and then, elated by her success, in good spirits, and with good courage, she entered her study precisely at eleven o'clock, and locked her door. Her books were opened, and the challenge given to a hard German lesson. Scarcely had she made the first onset, when the door-bell was heard to ring, and soon Bridget, coming nearer and nearer,—then, tapping at the door.

"Somebodies wants to see you in the parlor, ma'am."

"Tell them I am engaged, Bridget."

"I told 'em you were to home, ma'am, and they sent up their names, but I ha'n't got 'em, jist."

There was no help for it—Mrs. James must go down to receive her callers. She had to smile when she felt little like it—to be sociable when her thoughts were busy with her task. Her friends made a long call—they had nothing else to do with their time, and when they went, others came. In very unsatisfactory chit-chat, her morning slipped away.

On the next day, Mr. James invited company to tea, and her morning was devoted to preparing for it; she did not enter her study. On the day following, a sick-head-ache confined her to her bed; and on Saturday, the care of the baby devolved upon her, as Amy had extra work to do. Thus passed the first week.

True to her promise, Mrs. James patiently persevered for a month, in her efforts to secure for herself this little fragment of her broken time, but with what success, the first week's history can tell. With its close, closed the month of December.

On the last day of the old year, she was so much occupied in her preparations for the morrow's festival, that the last hour of the day was approaching, before she made her good night's call in the nursery. She first went to the crib and looked at the baby. There he lay in his innocence and beauty, fast asleep. She softly stroked his golden hair—she kissed gently his rosy cheek—she pressed the little dimpled hand in hers; and then carefully drawing the coverlet over it, tucked it in,—and stealing yet another kiss, she left him to his peaceful dreams,—and sat down on her daughter's bed. She also slept sweetly, with her dolly hugged to her bosom. At this her mother smiled, but soon grave thoughts entered her mind, and these deepened into sad ones. She thought of her disappointment and the failure of her plans. To her, not only the past month but the whole past year, seemed to have been one of fruitless effort—all broken and disjointed— even her hours of religious duty had been encroached upon, and disturbed. She had accomplished nothing, that she could see, but to keep her house and family in order, and even this, to her saddened mind, seemed to have been but indifferently done. She was conscious of yearnings for a more earnest life than this. Unsatisfied longings for something which she had not attained, often clouded what, otherwise, would have been a bright day to her; and yet the causes of these feelings seemed to lie in a dim and misty region, which her eye could not penetrate.

What then did she need? To see some *results* from her life's work? To know that a golden cord bound her life-threads together into *unity* of purpose—notwithstanding they seemed, so often, single and broken?

She was quite sure that she felt no desire to shrink from duty, however humble, but she sighed for some comforting assurance of what *was duty.* Her employments, conflicting as they did with her tastes, seemed to her frivolous and useless. It seemed to her that there was some better way of living, which she, from deficiency in energy of character, or of principle, had failed to discover. As she leaned over her child, her tears fell fast upon its young brow.

Most earnestly did she wish, that she could shield that child from the disappointments and mistakes and self-reproach from which the mother was then suffering; that the little one might take up life where she could give it to her—all mended by her own experience. It would have been a comfort to have felt that, in fighting the battle, she had fought for both; yet she knew that so it could not be—that for ourselves must we all learn what are those things which "make for our peace."

The tears were in her eyes, as she gave the good-night to her sleeping daughter; then, with soft steps, she entered an adjoining room, and there fairly kissed out the old year on another chubby cheek, which nestled among the pillows. At length she sought her own rest.

Soon she found herself in a singular place. She was traversing a vast plain. No trees were visible, save those which skirted the distant horizon, and on their broad tops rested wreaths of golden clouds. Before her was a female, who was journeying towards that region of light. Little children were about her, now in her arms, now running by her side, and as they travelled, she occupied herself in caring for them. She taught them how to place their little feet; she gave them timely warnings of the pitfalls; she gently lifted them over the stumbling-blocks. When they were weary, she soothed them by singing of that brighter land, which she kept ever in view, and towards which she seemed hastening with her little flock. But what was most remarkable was, that, all unknown to her, she was constantly watched by two angels, who reposed on two golden clouds which floated above her. Before each was a golden book, and a pen of gold. One angel, with mild and loving eyes, peered constantly over her right shoulder; another, kept as strict watch over her left. Not a deed, not a word, not a look, escaped their notice. When a good deed, word, look, went from her, the angel over the right shoulder, with a glad smile, wrote it down in his book; when an evil, however trivial, the angel over the left shoulder recorded it in his book,—then, with sorrowful eyes, followed the pilgrim until he observed penitence for the wrong, upon which he dropped a tear on the record, and blotted it out, and both angels rejoiced.

To the looker-on, it seemed that the traveller did nothing which was worthy of such careful record.

Sometimes, she did but bathe the weary feet of her little children, but the angel over the *right shoulder*—wrote it down. Sometimes, she did but patiently wait to lure back a little truant who had turned his face away from the distant light, but the angel over the *right shoulder*—wrote it down. Sometimes, she did but soothe an angry feeling or raise a drooping eyelid, or kiss away a little grief; but the angel over the right shoulder—*wrote it down.*

Sometimes, her eye was fixed so intently on that golden horizon, and she became so eager to make progress thither, that the little ones, missing her care, did languish or stray. Then it was that the angel over the *left shoulder,* lifted his golden pen, and made the entry, and followed her with sorrowful eyes, until he could blot it out. Sometimes, she seemed to advance rapidly, but in her haste the little ones had fallen back, and it was the sorrowing angel who recorded her progress. Sometimes, so intent was she to gird up her loins, and have her lamp trimmed and burning, that the little children wandered away quite into forbidden paths, and it was the angel over the *left shoulder* who recorded her diligence.

Now the observer as she looked, felt that this was a faithful and true record, and was to be kept to that journey's end. The strong clasps of gold on those golden books, also impressed her with the conviction that, when they were closed, it would only be for a future opening.

Her sympathies were warmly enlisted for the gentle traveller, and with a beating heart she quickened her steps that she might overtake her. She wished to tell her of the angels keeping watch above her—to entreat her to be faithful and patient to the end—for her life's work was all written down—every item of it—and the *results* would be known when those golden books should be unclasped. She wished to beg of her to think no duty trivial which must be done, for over her right shoulder and over her left were recording angels, who would surely take note of all!

Eager to warn the traveller of what she had seen, she touched her. The traveller turned, and she recognized or seemed to recognize *herself*. Startled and alarmed, she awoke in tears. The gray light of morning struggled through the half-open shutter, the door ajar, and merry faces were peeping in.

"Wish you a happy new year, mamma!"—"Wish you a *Happy new Year!*—" "A happy noo ear!"

She returned the merry greeting most heartily. It seemed to her as if she had entered upon a new existence. She had found her way through the thicket in which she had been entangled, and a light was now about her path. The *Angel over the Right Shoulder* whom she had seen in her dream, would bind up in his golden book her life's work, if it were but well done. He required of her no great deeds, but faithfulness and patience to the end of the race which was set before her. Now she could see, plainly enough, that, though it was right and important for her to cultivate her own mind and heart, it was equally right and equally important, to meet and perform faithfully all those little household cares and duties on which the comfort and virtue of her family depended; for into these things the angels carefully looked—and these duties and cares acquired a dignity from the strokes of that golden pen—they could not be neglected without danger.

Sad thoughts and sadder misgivings—undefined yearnings and ungratified longings seemed to have taken their flight with the Old Year, and it was with fresh resolution and cheerful hope, and a happy heart, she welcomed the *Glad* New Year. The *Angel over the Right Shoulder* would go with her, and if she were found faithful, would strengthen and comfort her to its close.

Louise Amelia Knapp Smith Clappe
(1819–1906)

ne of the few women in California during the Gold Rush, Louise Knapp Smith was born in New Jersey and went West with her new husband, medical student Fayette Clapp, in 1849. In 1851 and 1852, while living in Rich Bar and Indian Bar, two mining camps in the Sierra Nevada mountains, she wrote a series of letters to her sister in Massachusetts, describing the tumult and violence of the period. Published in 1854 and 1855 in the San Francisco literary journal *Pioneer*, under the name "Dame Shirley," they were later collected as *The Shirley Letters* (1922). Once the Gold Rush had been exhausted, Clapp divorced her husband, added an "e" to her surname, and became a schoolteacher in San Francisco, where she taught for more than twenty years before returning to New England in 1878. Her description of a violent brawl between Spanish and American men in the town, and near-lynching that followed it, shows that women's writing during the 1850s could be graphic and dramatic, as well as sentimental.

Letter *19, from The Shirley Letters from the California Mines,*
1851–1852 (1922)

From our Log Cabin, Indian Bar, August 4, 1852

We have lived through so much of excitement for the last three weeks, dear M—, that I almost shrink from relating the gloomy events that have marked their flight. But if I leave out the darker shades of our mountain life, the picture will be very incomplete. In the short space of twenty-four days we have had murders, fearful accidents, bloody deaths, a mob, whippings, a hanging, an attempt at suicide, and a fatal duel. But to begin at the beginning, as, according to rule, one ought to do.

I think that, even among these beautiful hills, I never saw a more perfect "bridal of the earth and sky" than that of Sunday, the eleventh of July. On that morning I went with a party of friends to the head of the "Ditch," a walk of about three miles in length. I do not believe that Nature herself ever made anything so lovely as this artificial brooklet. It glides like a living thing through the very heart of the forest, sometimes creeping softly on, as though with muffled feet, through a wilderness of aquatic plants, sometimes dancing gaily over a white-pebbled bottom; now making a "sunshine in a shady place," across the mossy roots of the majestic old trees—and anon leaping with a grand anthem, adown the great, solemn rocks, which lie along its beautiful pathway. A sunny opening at the head of the ditch is a garden of perfumed shrubbery and many-tinted flowers—all garlanded with the prettiest vines imaginable, and peopled with an infinite variety of magnificent butterflies. These last were of every possible color—pink, blue, and yellow, shining black splashed with orange, purple flashed with gold, white, and even green. We returned about three in the evening, loaded with fragrant bundles, which, arranged in jars, tumblers, pitchers, bottles, and pails, (we are not particular as to the quality of our vases in the mountains, and love our flowers as well in their humble chalices as if their beautiful heads lay against a background of marble or porcelain) made the dark old cabin "a bower of beauty for us."

Shortly after our arrival, a perfectly deafening volley of shouts and yells elicited from my companion the careless remark that the customary Sabbath-day's fight was apparently more serious than usual. Almost as he spoke there succeeded a deathlike silence, broken in a minute after by a deep groan at the corner of the cabin, followed by the words, "Why, Tom, poor fellow, are you really wounded?" Before we could reach the door, it was burst violently open, by a person who inquired hurriedly for the Doctor—who, luckily, happened at that very moment to be approaching. The man who called him then gave us the following excited account of what had happened. He said that in a *melé* between the Americans and the foreigners, Domingo—a tall, majestic-looking Spaniard, a perfect type of the novelistic bandit of Old Spain—had stabbed Tom Somers, a young Irishman, but a naturalized citizen of the United States—and that, at the very moment, said Domingo, with a *Mejicana* hanging upon his arm, and brandishing threateningly the long, bloody knife with which he had inflicted the wound upon his victim, was parading up and down the street unmolested. It seems that when Tom Somers fell, the Americans, being unarmed, were seized with a sudden panic and fled. There was a rumor (unfounded, as it afterwards proved) to the effect that the Spaniards had on this day conspired to kill all the Americans on the river. In a few moments, however, the latter rallied and made a rush at the murderer, who immediately plunged into the river and swam across to Missouri Bar; eight or ten shots were fired at him while in the water, not one of which hit him. He ran like an antelope across the flat, swam thence to Smith's Bar, and escaped by the road leading out of the mountains from the Junction. Several men went in pursuit of him, but he was not taken, and without doubt, is now safe in Mexico.

In the meanwhile the consternation was terrific. The Spaniards, who, with the exception of six or eight knew no more of the affair than I did, thought that the Americans had arisen against them; and our own countrymen equally ignorant, fancied the same of the foreigners. About twenty of the latter, who were either sleeping or reading in their cabins at the time of the *émeute*, aroused by the cry of "Down with the Spaniards!" barricaded themselves in a drinking-saloon, determined to defend themselves as long as possible against the massacre, which was fully expected would follow this appalling shout. In the bake-shop, which stands next door to our cabin, young Tom Somers lay straightened for the grave (he lived but fifteen minutes after he was wounded), while over his dead body a Spanish woman was weeping and moaning in the most piteous and heart-rending manner. The Rich Barians, who had heard a most exaggerated account of the rising of the Spaniards against the Americans, armed with rifles, pistols, clubs, dirks, etc., were rushing down the hill by hundreds. Each one added fuel to his rage by crowding into the little bakery to gaze upon the blood-bathed bosom of the victim, yet warm with the life, which but an hour before it had so triumphantly worn. Then arose the most fearful shouts of "Down with the Spaniards!" "Drive every foreigner off the river!" "Don't let one of the murderous devils remain!" "Oh, if you have a drop of American blood in your veins, it must cry out for vengeance upon the cowardly assassins of poor Tom!" All this, mingled with the most horrible oaths and execrations, yelled up, as if in mockery, into that smiling heaven, which in its fair Sabbath calm, bent unmoved over the hell which was raging below.

After a time, the more sensible and sober part of the community succeeded in quieting, in a partial degree, the enraged and excited multitude. During the whole affair I had remained perfectly calm, in truth, much more so than I am now, when recalling it. The entire catastrophe had been so unexpected, and so sudden in its consummation, that I fancy I was stupefied into the most exemplary good behavior. F—— and several of his friends, taking advantage of the lull in the storm, came into the cabin and entreated me to join the two women who were living on the hill. At this time it seemed to be the general opinion that there would be a serious fight, and they said I might be wounded accidentally, if I remained on the Bar. As I had no fear of anything of the kind, I pleaded hard to be allowed to stop, but when told that my presence would increase the anxiety of our friends, of course, like a dutiful wife, I went on to the hill.

We three women, left entirely alone, seated ourselves upon a log overlooking the strange scene below. The Bar was a sea of heads, bristling with guns, rifles, and clubs. We could see nothing, but fancied from the apparent quiet of the crowd, that the miners were taking measures to investigate the sad event of the day. All at once, we were startled by the firing of a gun, and the next moment, the crowd dispersing, we saw a man led into the log cabin, while another was carried, apparently lifeless, into a Spanish drinking-saloon, from one end of which were burst off instantly several boards, evidently to give air to the wounded person. Of course we were utterly unable to imagine what had happened; and to all our perplexity and anxiety, one of the ladies insisted upon believing that it was her own husband who had been shot, and as she is a very nervous woman, you can fancy our distress. It was in vain to tell her—which we did over and over again—that that worthy individual wore a *blue* shirt, and the wounded person a *red* one. She doggedly insisted that her dear M—— had been shot, and, having informed us confidentially and rather inconsistently that "she should never see him again, never, never," plumped herself down upon the log in an attitude of calm and ladylike despair, which would have been infinitely amusing, had not the occasion been so truly a fearful one. Luckily for our nerves, a benevolent individual, taking pity upon our loneliness, came and told us what had happened.

It seems that an Englishman, the owner of a house of the vilest description, a person who is said to have been the primary cause of all the troubles of the day, attempted to force his way through the line of armed men which had been formed at each side of the street. The guard very properly refused to let him pass. In his drunken fury he tried to wrest a gun from one of them, which being accidentally discharged in the struggle, inflicted a severe wound upon a Mr. Oxley, and shattered in the most dreadful manner the thigh of Señor Pizarro, a man of high birth and breeding, a *porteño* of Buenos Aires. This frightful accident recalled the people to their senses, and they began to act a little less like madmen than they had previously done. They elected a Vigilance Committee, and authorized persons to go to the Junction and arrest the suspected Spaniards.

The first act of the Committee was to try a *Mejicana* who had been foremost in the fray. She has always worn male attire, and upon this occasion, armed with a pair of pistols, she fought like a very fury. Luckily, inexperienced in the use of fire-arms, she wounded no one. She was sentenced to leave the Bar by daylight, a perfectly just decision, for there is no doubt that she is a regular little demon. Some went so far as to say she ought to be hung, for she was the *indirect* cause of the fight. You see, always it is the old, cowardly excuse of Adam in Paradise: "The *woman* tempted me, and I did eat." As if the poor, frail head, once so pure and beautiful, had not sin enough of its own, dragging it forever downward, without being made to answer for the wrong-doing of a whole community of men.

The next day the Committee tried five or six Spaniards, who were proven to have been the ringleaders in the Sabbath-day riot. Two of them were sentenced to be whipped, the remainder to leave the Bar that evening; the property of all to be confiscated to the use of the wounded persons. O Mary! imagine my anguish when I heard the first blow fall upon those wretched men. I had never thought that I should be compelled to hear such fearful sounds, and, although I immediately buried my head in a shawl, nothing can efface from memory the disgust and horror of that moment. I had heard of such things, but heretofore had not realized that in the nineteenth century, men could be beaten like dogs, much less that other men not only could sentence such barbarism, but could actually stand by and see their own manhood degraded in such disgraceful manner. One of these unhappy persons was a very gentlemanly young Spaniard, who implored for death in the most moving terms. He appealed to his judges in the most eloquent manner—as gentlemen, as men of honor; representing to them that to be deprived of life, was nothing in comparison with the never-to-be-effaced stain of the vilest convict's punishment—to which they had sentenced him. Finding all his entreaties disregarded, he swore a most solemn oath, that he would murder every American that he should chance to meet alone, and as he is a man of the most dauntless courage, and rendered desperate by a burning sense of disgrace, which will cease only with his life, he will doubtless keep his word.

Although in my very humble opinion and in that of others more competent to judge of such matters than myself, these sentences were unnecessarily severe, yet so great was the rage and excitement of the crowd that the Vigilance Committee could do no less. The mass of the mob demanded fiercely the death of the prisoners, and it was evident that many of the Committee took side with the people. I shall never forget how horror-struck I was (bombastic as it *now* sounds) at hearing no less a personage than the Whig candidate for representative say "that the condemned had better fly for their lives, for the Avenger of Blood was on their tracks!" I am happy to say that said very worthy but sanguinary individual, "The Avenger of Blood!"—represented in this case by some half-dozen gambling rowdies—either changed his mind or lost scent of his prey; for the intended victims slept about two miles up the hill, quite peacefully until morning.

The following facts, elicited upon the trial, throw light upon this unhappy affair: seven miners from Old Spain, enraged at the cruel treatment which their countrymen had received on the "Fourth," and at the illiberal cry of "Down with the Spaniard," had united for the purpose of taking revenge on seven Americans whom they believed to be the originators of their insults. All well armed, they came from the Junction, where they were residing at the time, intending to challenge each one his man, and in fair fight compel their insolent aggressors to answer for the arrogance which they had exhibited more than once towards the Spanish race. Their first move on arriving at Indian Bar was to go and dine at the Humboldt, where they drank a most enormous quantity of champagne and claret. Afterwards they proceeded to the house of the Englishman whose brutal carelessness caused the accident which wounded Pizarro and Oxley, when one of them commenced a playful conversation with one of his countrywomen. This enraged the Englishman, who instantly struck the Spaniard a violent blow, and ejected him from the shanty. Thereupon ensued a spirited fight, which, through the exertion of a gentleman from Chile, a favorite with both nations, ended without bloodshed. This person knew nothing of the intended duel, or he might have prevented, by his wise counsels, what followed. Not suspecting for a moment anything of the kind, he went to Rich Bar. Soon after he left, Tom Somers, who is said always to have been a dangerous person when in liquor, without any apparent provocation struck Domingo (one of the original seven) a violent blow, which nearly felled him to the earth. The latter, a man of "dark antecedents" and the most reckless character, mad with wine, rage, and revenge, without an instant's pause drew his knife and inflicted a fatal wound upon his insulter. Thereupon followed the chapter of accidents which I have related.

On Tuesday following the fatal Sabbath, a man brought the news of the murder of a Mr. Bacon, a person well known on the river, who kept a ranch about twelve miles from Rich Bar. He was killed for his money, by his servant, a negro, who not three months ago was our own cook. He was the last one anybody would have suspected capable of such an act.

A party of men, appointed by the Vigilance Committee, left the Bar immediately in search of him. The miserable wretch was apprehended in Sacramento and part of the gold found upon his person. On the following Sunday he was brought in chains to Rich Bar. After a trial by the miners, he was sentenced to be hung at four o'clock in the evening. All efforts to make him confess proved futile. He said very truly, that whether innocent or guilty, they would hang him; and so he "died and made no sign" with a calm indifference, as the novelists say, "worthy of a better cause." The dreadful crime and death of "Josh," who, having been an excellent cook and very neat and respectful, was a favorite servant with us, added to the unhappiness which you can easily imagine that I was suffering under all these horrors.

On Saturday evening about eight o'clock, as we sat quietly conversing with the two ladies from the hill—whom, by the way, we found very agreeable additions to our society, hitherto composed entirely of gentlemen—we were startled by the loud shouting and rushing close by the door of the cabin, which stood open, of three or four hundred men. Of course we feminines, with nerves somewhat shattered from the events of the past week, were greatly alarmed.

We were soon informed that Henry Cook, *vice* "Josh," had, in a fit of delirium tremens, cut his throat from ear to ear. The poor wretch was alone when he committed the desperate deed, and in his madness, throwing the bloody razor upon the ground, ran part of the way up the hill. Here he was found almost senseless, and brought back to the Humboldt, where he was very nearly the cause of hanging poor "Paganini Ned"— who returned a few weeks since from the valley—for his first act on recovering himself, was to accuse that culinary individual of having attempted to murder him. The mob were for hanging our poor "Vattel" without judge or jury, and it was only through the most strenuous exertions of his friends, that the life of this illustrious person was saved. Poor Ned! it was forty-eight hours before his cork-screws returned to their original graceful curl; he threatens to leave us to our barbarism and no longer to waste his culinary talents upon an ungrateful and inappreciative people. He has sworn "war to the knife" against Henry, who was formerly his most intimate friend, as nothing can persuade him that the accusation did not proceed from the purest malice on the part of the suicide.

Their majesties the mob, with that beautiful consistency which usually distinguishes those august individuals, insisted upon shooting poor Henry—for said they, and the reasoning is remarkably conclusive and clear, "a man so hardened as to raise his hand against his *own* life, will never hesitate to murder another!" They almost mobbed F—— for bind-ing up the wounds of the unfortunate wretch and for saying that it was possible he might live. At last, however, they compromised the matter by determining that if Henry should recover, he should leave the Bar imme-diately. Neither contingency will probably take place, as it will be almost a miracle if he survives.

On the day following the attempted suicide, which was Sunday, noth-ing more exciting happened than a fight and the half-drowning of a drunken individual in the river, just in front of the Humboldt.

On Sunday last, the thigh of Señor Pizarro was amputated; but, alas, without success. He had been sick for many months with chronic dysen-tery, which after the operation returned with great violence, and he died at two o'clock on Monday morning with the same calm and lofty resig-nation which had distinguished him during his illness. When first wounded, believing his case hopeless, he had decidedly refused to submit to amputation, but as time wore on he was persuaded to take this one chance for his life for the sake of his daughter, a young girl of fifteen, at present at school in a convent in Chile, whom his death leaves without any near relative. I saw him several times during his illness, and it was melancholy indeed, to hear him talk of his motherless girl who, I have been told, is extremely beautiful, talented, and accomplished.

The state of society here has never been so bad as since the appoint-ment of a Committee of Vigilance. The rowdies have formed themselves into a company called the "Moguls," and they parade the streets all night, howling, shouting, breaking into houses, taking wearied miners out of their beds and throwing them into the river, and in short, "murdering sleep," in the most remorseless manner. Nearly every night they build bonfires fearfully near some rag shanty, thus endangering the lives (or I should rather say the property—for as it is impossible to sleep, lives are emphatically safe), of the whole community. They retire about five o'clock in the morning; previously to this blessed event posting notices to that effect, and that they will throw any one who may disturb them into the river. I am nearly worn out for want of rest, for truly they "make night hideous" with their fearful uproar. Mr. O——, who still lies dan-gerously ill from the wound received on what we call the "fatal Sunday," complains bitterly of the disturbances; and when poor Pizarro was dying, and one of his friends gently requested that they would be quiet for half an hour and permit the soul of the sufferer to pass in peace, they only laughed and yelled and hooted louder than ever, in the presence of the departing spirit, for the tenement in which he lay, being composed of green boughs only, could of course shut out no sounds. Without doubt if the Moguls had been sober, they would never have been guilty of such horrible barbarity as to compel the thoughts of a dying man to mingle with curses and blasphemies; but, alas! they were intoxicated, and may God forgive them, unhappy ones, for they knew not what they did. The poor, exhausted miners, for even well people cannot sleep in such a pandemonium, grumble and complain, but they—although far outnumbering the rioters—are too timid to resist. All say, "It is shameful; something ought to be done; something *must* be done," etc., and in the meantime the rioters triumph. You will wonder that the Committee of Vigilance does not interfere; it is said that some of that very Committee are the ringleaders among the "Moguls."

I believe I have related to you everything but the duel—and I will make the recital of this as short as possible, for I am sick of these sad subjects, and doubt not but you are the same. It took place on Tuesday morning, at eight o'clock, on Missouri Bar, when and where that same Englishman who has figured so largely in my letter, shot his best friend. The duelists were surrounded by a large crowd, I have been told, foremost among which stood the Committee of Vigilance! The man who received his dear friend's fatal shot was one of the most quiet and peaceable citizens on the Bar. He lived about ten minutes after he was wounded. He was from Ipswich, England, and only twenty-five years old when his own high passions snatched him from life. In justice to his opponent, it must be said that he would willingly have retired after the first shots had been exchanged, but poor Billy Leggett, as he was familiarly called, insisted upon having the distance between them shortened, and continuing the duel until one of them had fallen.

There, my dear M——, have I not fulfilled my promise of giving you a dish of horrors? And only think of such a shrinking, timid, frail thing as I *used* to be "long time ago" not only living right in the midst of them, but almost compelled to hear if not see the whole. I think that I may without vanity affirm, that I have "seen the elephant." "Did you see his tail?" asks innocent Ada J——, in her mother's letter. Yes, sweet Ada, the "entire Animal" has been exhibited to my view. "But you must remember that this is California," as the new comers are so fond of informing us! who consider ourselves "one of the oldest inhabitants" of the golden State.

And now, dear M——, *adiós*. Be thankful that you are living in the beautiful quiet of beautiful A——, and give up "hankering arter" (as you know what dear creature says—) California, for, believe me, this coarse, barbarous life would suit you even less than it does your sister.

Julia Ward Howe
(1819–1910)

owe is mainly remembered as the author of "The Battle Hymn of the Republic," and many poets would be proud to leave one such important poem to the national record. But she was also an ambitious, outspoken, fiery poet whose gifts were stifled in her stormy 1843 marriage to the celebrated doctor Samuel Gridley Howe. He wanted a decorous wife who would subjugate her own interests to his, and was shocked and enraged when he realized that she had published an anonymous volume of poems called *Passion-Flowers*, in 1853. He threatened to divorce her and take custody of their children from her if she ever wrote anything so personal again, and she gave in. Although she lived to be ninety years old, and became internationally known as an activist for women's rights, abolition, and world peace, Howe's contributions to the development of American poetry in the crucial decade of the 1850s were forgotten.

The Heart's Astronomy, *from Passion-Flowers* (1853)

This evening while the twilight fell,
My younger children watched for me;
Like cherubs in the window framed,
I saw the smiling group of three.

While round and round the house I trudged,
Intent to walk a weary mile,
Oft as I passed within their range,
The little things would beck and smile.

They watched me as Astronomers
Whose business lies in heaven afar,
Await, beside the slanting glass,
The reappearance of a star.

Not so, not so, my pretty ones,
Seek stars in yonder cloudless sky;

But mark no steadfast path for me,
A comet dire and strange am I.

Now to the inmost spheres of light
Lifted, my wondering soul dilates,
Now dropped to endless depth of night,
My hope God's slow recall awaits.

Among the shining I have shone,
Among the blessing, have been blest,
Then wearying years have held me bound
Where darkness deadness gives, not rest.

Between extremes distraught and rent,
I question not the way I go;
Who made me, gave it me, I deem,
Thus to aspire, to languish so.

But comets too have holy laws,
Their fiery sinews to restrain,
And from their outmost wanderings
Are drawn to heaven's dear heart again.

And ye, beloved ones, when ye know,
What wild, erratic natures are,
Pray that the laws of heavenly force,
Would hold and guide the Mother star.

The Battle Hymn of the Republic (1862)

Mine eyes have seen the glory of the coming of the Lord:
He is trampling out the vintage where the grapes of wrath are stored;
He hath loosed the fateful lightning of His terrible swift sword:
      His truth is marching on.

I have seen Him in the watch-fires of a hundred circling camps,
They have builded Him an altar in the evening dews and damps;
I can read His righteous sentence by the dim and flaring lamps:
      His day is marching on.

I have read a fiery gospel writ in burnished rows of steel:
"As ye deal with my contemners, so with you my grace shall deal;
Let the Hero, born of woman, crush the serpent with his heel,
    Since God is marching on."

He has sounded forth the trumpet that shall never call retreat;
He is sifting out the hearts of men before His judgment-seat:
Oh, be swift, my soul, to answer Him! be jubilant, my feet!
    Our God is marching on.

In the beauty of the lilies Christ was born across the sea,
With a glory in his bosom that transfigures you and me:
As he died to make men holy, let us die to make men free,
    While God is marching on.

Alice Cary
(1820–1871)

hough she was born to literate Universalist parents, Alice Cary received little formal education throughout her Ohio childhood. "We hungered and thirsted for knowledge," she wrote, "but there were not a dozen books on our family shelf, nor a library within our reach." Nonetheless, she began publishing poetry in local newspapers and magazines in her late teens, and by 1847 her work was reaching a national audience in the abolitionist *New Era*. After she and her younger sister Phoebe published a book of poems together in 1849, they moved to New York where they established a literary salon. In addition to five volumes of poetry, Alice Cary published three volumes of short stories about the fictional village of Clovernook, and three novels on feminist and social themes. Her defiant poem about marriage, "The Bridal Veil," expressed her view of women's spiritual and intellectual independence.

The Bridal Veil (1866)

We're married, they say, and you think you have won me,—
Well, take this white veil from my head, and look on me;
Here's matter to vex you, and matter to grieve you,
Here's doubt to distrust you, and faith to believe you,—
I am all as you see, common earth, common dew;
Be wary, and mould me to roses, not rue!

Ah! shake out the filmy thing, fold after fold,
And see if you have me to keep and to hold,—
Look close on my heart—see the worst of its sinning,—
It is not yours to-day for the yesterday's winning—
The past is not mine—I am too proud to borrow—
You must go to new heights if I love you to-morrow.

We're married! I'm plighted to hold up your praises,
As the turf at your feet does its handful of daisies;

That way lies my honor,—my pathway of pride,
But, mark you, if greener grass grow either side,
I shall know it, and keeping in body with you,
Shall walk in my spirit with feet on the dew!

We're married! Oh, pray that our love do not fail!
I have wings flattened down and hid under my veil:
They are subtle as light—you never undo them,
And swift in their flight—you can never pursue them,
And spite of all clasping, and spite of all bands,
I can slip like a shadow, a dream, from your hands.

Nay, call me not cruel, and fear not to take me,
I am yours for my life-time, to be what you make me,—
To wear my white veil for a sign, or a cover,
As you shall be proven my lord, or my lover;
A cover for peace that is dead, or a token
Of bliss that can never be written or spoken.

Elizabeth Drew Stoddard
(1823–1902)

The daughter of a prominent shipbuilder who often faced financial difficulties, Massachusetts-born Elizabeth Drew was both a social insider and an outsider. After her 1852 marriage to the poet and editor Richard Henry Stoddard, the couple moved to New York City, where he presided over the genteel male circle of "Drawing-Room Poets." Stoddard longed to be recognized as an important American writer who could be compared "with Shakespeare, Milton, Dante, and Co." Like many women writers of the period, she compared herself with only the greatest literary geniuses, and thus felt perennially unhappy and inadequate. Competition with her husband and his friends, and her sense that she was excluded as a woman poet, and trapped in old forms and myths, brought this phase of her writing to an end in 1860. "The Poet's Secret" and "Before the Mirror" express Stoddard's frustration and melancholy about her poetic role. She went on to write several short stories and three edgy, unconventional novels, but the critical praise she sought always eluded her.

The Poet's Secret (1860)

The poet's secret I must know,
    If that will calm my restless mind.
I hail the seasons as they go,
    I woo the sunshine, brave the wind.

I scan the lily and the rose,
    I nod to every nodding tree,
I follow every stream that flows,
    And wait beside the steadfast sea.

I question melancholy eyes,
    I touch the lips of women fair:
Their lips and eyes may make me wise,
    But what I seek for is not there.

In vain I watch the day and night,
    In vain the world through space may roll;
I never see the mystic light,
    Which fills the poet's happy soul.

To hear through life a rhythmic flow
    And into song its meaning turn—
The poet's secret I must know:—
    By pain and patience shall I learn?

Before the Mirror (1860)

Now like the Lady of Shalott,
    I dwell within an empty room,
And through the day, and through the night,
    I sit before an ancient loom.

And like the Lady of Shalott
    I look into a mirror wide,
Where shadows come, and shadows go,
    And ply my shuttle as they glide.

Not as she wove the yellow wool,
    Ulysses' wife, Penelope;
By day a queen among her maids,
    But in the night a woman, she,

Who, creeping from her lonely couch,
    Unraveled all the slender woof:
Or with a torch she climbed the towers,
    To fire the fagots on the roof!

But weaving with a steady hand,
    The shadows, whether false or true,
I put aside a doubt which asks,
    "Among these phantoms what are you?"

For not with altar, tomb, or urn,
    Or long-haired Greek with hollow shield,

Or dark-prowed ship with banks of oars,
   Or banquet in the tented field;

Or Norman knight in armor clad,
   Waiting a foe where four roads meet;
Or hawk and hound in bosky dell,
   Where dame and page in secret greet;

Or rose and lily, bud and flower,
   My web is broidered. Nothing bright
Is woven here: the shadows grow
   Still darker in the mirror's light!

And as my web grows darker too,
   Accursed seems this empty room;
For still I must forever weave
   These phantoms by this hateful loom.

Phoebe Cary
(1824–1871)

When her older sister Alice moved to New York, Phoebe Cary followed. In her mischievous *Poems and Parodies* (1854), she wrote feminist versions of classic poetry from Shakespeare to Longfellow, lampooning the portrayals of women in William Wordsworth's "She Dwelt Among the Untrodden Ways" and Oliver Goldsmith's novel *The Vicar of Wakefield*. In addition to her popular parodies, Cary also wrote religious hymns. Never married, she died only six months after the death of her sister.

Jacob (1886)

He dwelt among "apartments let,"
About five stories high;
A man I thought that none would get,
And very few would try.

A boulder, by a larger stone
Half hidden in the mud,
Fair as a man when only one
Is in the neighborhood.

He lived unknown, and few could tell
When Jacob was not free;
But he has got a wife,—and O!
The difference to me!

When Lovely Woman (1886)

When lovely woman wants a favor,
And finds, too late, that man won't bend,

What earthly circumstance can save her
From disappointment in the end?

The only way to bring him over,
The last experiment to try,
Whether a husband or a lover,
If he have feeling, is, to cry!

Lucy Larcom
(1824–1893)

hen her father, a sea captain in Beverly, Massachusetts, died, Larcom had to move to the bustling and progressive cotton mill town of Lowell. Her mother became a boardinghouse keeper for the young women who worked in the mills, and Larcom too became a spinner and mill-hand. In 1844, the Quaker poet John Greenleaf Whittier moved to Lowell to edit the local newspaper, and became her literary mentor when she published poems and stories in the mill magazine, the *Lowell Offering*. In 1849, Larcom's childhood sweetheart went to California for the Gold Rush, and she spent the middle years of her life as a schoolteacher in Illinois, Missouri, and Massachusetts, trying to decide whether to join him as his wife. In the end she could not bring herself to marry; "A Loyal Woman's No," a patriotic poem which appeared in *The Atlantic Monthly* in 1863, also seems to justify her refusal of a conventional domestic life. "Weaving," one of her many poems based on her experiences in the mills, appeared in her book *Poems* in 1869. Like Stoddard writing about "the Lady of Shalott," Larcom used the weaver as a metaphor for the woman cut off from the great events of her time.

A Loyal Woman's No (1863)

No! is my answer from this cold, bleak ridge,
    Down to your valley: you may rest you there:
The gulf is wide, and none can build a bridge
    That your gross weight would safely hither bear.

Pity me, if you will. I look at you
    With something that is kinder far than scorn,
And think, "Ah, well! I might have grovelled, too;
    I might have walked there, fettered and forsworn."

I am of nature weak as others are;
    I might have chosen comfortable ways;

Once from these heights I shrank, beheld afar,
　　In the soft lap of quiet, easy days.

I might,—(I will not hide it),—once I might
　　Have lost, in the warm whirlpools of your voice,
The sense of Evil, the stern cry of Right;
　　But Truth has steered me free, and I rejoice:

Not with the triumph that looks back to jeer
　　At the poor herd that call their misery bliss;
But as a mortal speaks when God is near,
　　I drop you down my answer; it is this:

I am not yours, because you prize in me
　　What is the lowest in my own esteem:
Only my flowery levels can you see,
　　Nor of my heaven-smit summits do you dream.

I am not yours, because you love yourself:
　　Your heart has scarcely room for me beside.
I could not be shut in with name and pelf;
　　I spurn the shelter of your narrow pride!

Not yours,—because you are not man enough
　　To grasp your country's measure of a man.
If such as you, when Freedom's ways are rough,
　　Cannot walk in them, learn that women can!

Not yours,—because, in this the nation's need,
　　You stoop to bend her losses to your gain,
And do not feel the meanness of your deed:
　　I touch no palm defiled with such a stain!

Whether man's thought can find too lofty steeps
　　For woman's scaling, care not I to know;
But when he falters by her side, or creeps,
　　She must not clog her soul with him to go.

Who weds me, must at least with equal pace
　　Sometimes move with me at my being's height:

To follow him to his superior place,
    His rarer atmosphere, were keen delight.

You lure me to the valley: men should call
    Up to the mountains, where the air is clear.
Win me and help me climbing, if at all!
    Beyond these peaks great harmonies I hear:—

The morning chant of Liberty and Law!
    The dawn pours in, to wash out Slavery's blot;
Fairer than aught the bright sun ever saw,
    Rises a nation without stain or spot!

The men and women mated for that time
    Tread not the soothing mosses of the plain;
Their hands are joined in sacrifice sublime;
    Their feet firm set in upward paths of pain.

Sleep your thick sleep, and go your drowsy way!
    You cannot hear the voices in the air!
Ignoble souls will shrivel in that day;
    The brightness of its coming can you bear?

For me, I do not walk these hills alone:
    Heroes who poured their blood out for the truth,
Women whose hearts bled, martyrs all unknown,
    Here catch the sunrise of immortal youth

On their pale cheeks and consecrated brows:—
    It charms me not, your call to rest below.
I press their hands, my lips pronounce their vows
    Take my life's silence for your answer: No!

Weaving (1869)

All day she stands before her loom;
    The flying shuttles come and go;
By grassy fields, and trees in bloom,
    She sees the winding river flow:

And fancy's shuttle flieth wide,
And faster than the waters glide.

Is she entangled in her dreams,
    Like that fair weaver of Shalott.
Who left her mystic mirror's-gleams,
    To gaze on light Sir Lancelot?
Her heart, a mirror sadly true,
Brings gloomier visions into view.

"I weave, and weave, the livelong day:
    The woof is strong, the warp is good:
I weave, to be my mother's stay;
    I weave, to win my daily food:
But ever as I weave," saith she,
"The world of women haunteth me.

"The river glides along, one thread
    In nature's mesh, so beautiful!
The stars are woven in; the red
    Of sunrise; and the rain-cloud dull.
Each seems a separate wonder wrought;
Each blends with some more wondrous thought.

"So, at the loom of life, we weave
    Our separate shreds, that varying fall,
Some stained, some fair; and, passing, leave
    To God the gathering up of all,
In that full pattern wherein man
Works blindly out the eternal plan.

"In his vast work, for good, or ill,
    The undone and the done he blends:
With whatsoever woof we fill,
    To our weak hands His might He lends,
And gives the threads beneath His eye
The texture of eternity.

"Wind on, by willow and by pine,
    Thou blue, untroubled Merrimack!
Afar, by sunnier streams than thine,

My sisters toil, with foreheads black;
And water with their blood this root,
Whereof we gather bounteous fruit.

"There be sad women, sick and poor;
    And those who walk in garments soiled:
Their shame, their sorrow, I endure;
    By their defect my hope is foiled:
The blot they bear is on my name;
Who sins, and I am not to blame?

"And how much of your wrong is mine,
    Dark women slaving at the South?
Of your stolen grapes I quaff the wine;
    The bread you starve for fills my mouth:
The beam unwinds, but every thread
With blood of strangled souls is red.

"If this be so, we win and wear
    A Nessus-robe of poisoned cloth;
Or weave them shrouds they may not wear,—
    Fathers and brothers falling both
On ghastly, death-sown fields, that lie
Beneath the tearless Southern sky.

"Alas! the weft has lost its white.
    It grows a hideous tapestry,
That pictures war's abhorrent sight:
    Unroll not, web of destiny!
Be the dark volume left unread,—
The tale untold,—the curse unsaid!"

So up and down before her loom
    She paces on, and to and fro,
Till sunset fills the dusty room,
    And makes the water redly glow,
As if the Merrimack's calm flood
Were changed into a stream of blood.

Too soon fulfilled, and all too true
    The words she murmured as she wrought:
But, weary weaver, not to you
    Alone was war's stern message brought:
"Woman!" it knelled from heart to heart,
"Thy sister's keeper know thou art!"

Frances E. W. Harper
(1825–1911)

ne of the first published African-American writers, Frances E. W. Harper lost her parents in Baltimore, Maryland, by the age of three and was raised by her abolitionist uncle, who educated her at his Academy for Negro Youth. She started publishing in antislavery journals in 1839, came out with her first book of poems, *Forest Leaves*, in 1845, and taught school for a few years before becoming a professional abolitionist lecturer in 1854. Harper incorporated her prose and poetry into her speeches and her politics into her creative writing. "The Triumph of Freedom—A Dream," first appeared in the *Anglo-African Magazine* in 1860, and was a parable about the arrest and execution of the white antislavery terrorist John Brown. Harper had visited him in prison and stayed with his wife for two weeks before he was hanged in December 1859. "Aunt Chloe," "Aunt Chloe's Politics," and "Learning to Read," from *Sketches of Southern Life* (1872), are vignettes of a black woman's life during slavery and reconstruction. In 1892, Harper published *Iola Leroy*, a novel about a beautiful Southern heiress whose racial identity is revealed when her father dies, and she is sold into slavery. Looking back at the Civil War from a black perspective, the novel helped form the literary convention of the tragic mulatto.

Aunt Chloe (1872)

I remember, well remember,
   That dark and dreadful day,
When they whispered to me, "Chloe,
   Your children's sold away!"

It seemed as if a bullet
   Had shot me through and through,
And I felt as if my heart-strings
   Was breaking right in two.

And I says to cousin Milly,
   "There must be some mistake;

Where's Mistus?" "In the great house crying—
   Crying like her heart would break.

"And the lawyer's there with Mistus;
   Says he's come to 'ministrate,
'Cause when master died he just left
   Heap of debt on the estate.

"And I thought 'twould do you good
   To bid your boys goodbye—
To kiss them both and shake their hands,
   And have a hearty cry.

"O! Chloe, I knows how you feel,
   'Cause I'se been through it all;
I thought my poor old heart would break
   When master sold my Saul."

Just then I heard the footsteps
   Of my children at the door,
And I rose right up to meet them.
   But I fell upon the floor.

And I heard poor Jakey saying,
   "Oh, mammy, don't you cry!"
And I felt my children kiss me
   And bid me, both, goodbye.

Then I had a mighty sorrow,
   Though I nursed it all alone;
But I wasted to a shadow,
   And turned to skin and bone.

But one day dear uncle Jacob
   (In heaven he's now a saint)
Said, "Your poor heart is in the fire,
   But child you must not faint."

Then I said to uncle Jacob,
   If I was good like you,

When the heavy trouble dashed me
  I'd know just what to do.

Then he said to me, "Poor Chloe,
  The way is open wide:"
And he told me of the Saviour,
  And the fountain in His side.

Then he said "Just take your burden
  To the blessed Master's feet;
I takes all my troubles, Chloe,
  Right unto the mercy-seat."

His words waked up my courage,
  And I began to pray,
And I felt my heavy burden
  Rolling like a stone away.

And a something seemed to tell me,
  You will see your boys again—
And that hope was like a poultice
  Spread upon a dreadful pain.

And it often seemed to whisper,
  Chloe, trust and never fear;
You'll get justice in the kingdom,
  If you do not get it here.

Aunt Chloe's Politics (1872)

Of course, I don't know very much
  About these politics,
But I think that some who run 'em,
  Do mighty ugly tricks.

I've seen 'em honey-fugle round,
  And talk so awful sweet,
That you'd think them full of kindness
  As an egg is full of meat.

Now I don't believe in looking
   Honest people in the face,
And saying when you're doing wrong,
   That "I haven't sold my race."

When we want to school our children,
   If the money isn't there,
Whether black or white have took it,
   The loss we all must share.

And this buying up each other
   Is something worse than mean,
Though I thinks a heap of voting,
   I go for voting clean.

Learning to Read (1872)

Very soon the Yankee teachers
   Came down and set up school;
But oh! how the Rebs did hate it,—
   It was agin' their rule.

Our masters always tried to hide
   Book learning from our eyes;
Knowledge did'nt agree with slavery—
   'Twould make us all too wise.

But some of us would try to steal
   A little from the book,
And put the words together,
   And learn by hook or crook.

I remember Uncle Caldwell,
   Who took pot-liquor fat
And greased the pages of his book,
   And hid it in his hat.

And had his master ever seen
   The leaves upon his head,

He'd have thought them greasy papers,
    But nothing to be read.

And there was Mr. Turner's Ben,
    Who heard the children spell,
And picked the words right up by heart,
    And learned to read 'em well.

Well, the Northern folks kept sending
    The Yankee teachers down
And they stood right up and helped us,
    Though Rebs did sneer and frown.

And, I longed to read my Bible,
    For precious words it said;
But when I begun to learn it,
    Folks just shook their heads,

And said there is no use trying,
    Oh! Chloe, you're too late;
But as I was rising sixty,
    I had no time to wait.

So I got a pair of glasses,
    And straight to work I went,
And never stopped till I could read
    The hymns and Testament.

Then I got a little cabin—
    A place to call my own—
And I felt as independent
    As the queen upon her throne.

The Triumph of Freedom—A Dream (1860)

It was a beautiful day in spring. The green sward stretched beneath my feet like a velvet carpet, fair flowers sprung up in my path, and peaceful streams swept laughingly by to gain their ocean home. Above me the heavens were eloquent with the praise of God, around me the earth was poetic with His ideas. It was one of those days when Nature, in the excess of her happiness, leans on the bosom of the balmy sunshine, listening to the gentle voices of the wooing winds. I had fallen into a state of dreamy, delicious languor, when I was roused to sudden consciousness by a startling shriek. I looked up, and, bending over me, I saw a spirit gazing upon me with a look of unmistakable sadness. "Come with me?" said she, laying her hand upon me and drawing me along with an irresistible impulse. Silently I followed, awed by her strange manner. "I wish," said she, after a few moments silence, "to show you the goddess of this place." Surely, thought I, that must be a welcome sight, for the loveliness of the place suggested to my mind a presiding genius of glorious beauty. "It is now her hour of worship, and I want to show you some of her rites and ceremonies, and also the priests of her shrine." Just then we came in sight of the goddess. She was seated on a glittering throne, all sparkling with precious gems and rubies; and, indeed, so bright was her throne, it threw a dazzling radiance over her sallow countenance. She wore a robe of flowing white, but it was not pure white, and I noticed that upon its hem and amid its seams and folds were great spots of blood. It was the hour of worship, and her priests were standing by, with their sacred books in their hands; it was one of their rites to search them for texts and passages to spread over the stains on her garment. When this was done, they bowed down their heads and worshipped, saying:— "Thou art the handmaid of Christianity; thy mission is heaven-appointed and divine." And all the people said "Amen." But during this worship I saw a young man arise, his face pale with emotion and horror, and he said, "It is false." That one word, so sublime in its brevity, sent a thrill of indignant fear through the hearts of the crowd. It lashed them into a tumultuous fury. Some of them dashed madly after the intruder, and hissed in his ears—"Fanatic, madman, traitor, and infidel." But the efforts they made to silence him only gained him a better hearing. They forced him into prison, but they had no chains strong enough to bind his freeborn spirit. A number of adherents gathered around the young man, and asked to know his meaning. "Come with me," said he, "and I will show you?" and while they still chanted the praises of the goddess, he drew them to the spot, where they might view the base and inside of the throne, and the foundation of her altar. I looked, (for I had joined them, led on by my guide,) and I saw a number of little hearts all filed together and quivering. "What," said I, "are these?" My guide answered, "They are the hearts of a hundred thousand new-born babes." I turned deathly sick, a fearful faintness swept over me, and I was about to fall, but she caught me in her arms, and said, "Look here," and beneath the throne were piles of hearts laid layer upon layer. I noticed that they seemed to be rocking to and fro, as if smitten with a great agony. "What are these?" said I, gazing horror-stricken upon them. "They are the hearts of desolate slave mothers, robbed of their little ones." I looked a little higher, and saw a row of poor, bruised and seared hearts. "What are these?" "These are the hearts out of which the manhood has been crushed; and these," said she, pointing to another pile of young, fresh hearts, from which the blood was constantly streaming, "are the hearts of young girls, sold from the warm clasp of their mothers' arms to the brutal clutches of a libertine or a profligate—from the temples of Christ to the altars of shame. And these," said she, looking sadly at a row of withered hearts, from which the blood still dropped, "are the hearts in which the manhood has never been developed." I turned away, heart-sickened, the blood almost freezing in my veins, and I saw the young man standing on an eminence, pointing to the throne and altar, his lips trembling with the burden of a heaven-sent message. He reminded me of the ancient seers, robed in the robes of prophecy, pronouncing the judgments of God against the oppressors of olden times. Some listened earnestly, and were roused by his words to deeds of noble daring. Others, within whose shrunken veins all noble blood was pale and thin, mocked him and breathed out their hatred against him; they set a price upon his head and tracked his steps with bitter malice, but he had awakened the spirit of Agitation, that would not slumber at their bidding.

The blood-stained goddess felt it shaking her throne, its earnest eye searching into the very depths of her guilty soul, and she said to her worshippers: "Hide me beneath your constitutions and laws—shield me beneath your parchments and opinions." And it was done; but the restless eye of Agitation pierced through all of them, as through the most transparent glass. "Hide me," she cried to the priests, "beneath the shadow of your pulpits; throw around me the robes of your religion; spread over me your altar clothes, and dye my lips with sacramental blood?" And yet, into the recesses of her guilty soul came the eye of this Agitation, and she trembled before its searching glance.

Then I saw an aged man standing before her altars; his gray hair floated in the air, a solemn radiance lit up his eye, and a lofty purpose sat enthroned upon his brow. He fixed his eye upon the goddess, and she cowered beneath his unfaltering gaze. He laid his aged hands upon her blood-cemented throne, and it shook and trembled to its base; her cheeks blanched with dread, her hands fell nerveless by her side. It seemed to me as if his very gaze would have almost annihilated her; but just then I saw, bristling with bayonets, a blood-stained ruffian, named the General Government, and he caught the hands of the aged man and fettered them, and he was then led to prison. I know not whether the angels of the living God walked to and fro in his prison—that, amid the silent watches of the night, he heard the rustling of their garments—I only know that the old man was a host within himself. The goddess gathered courage when she knew that she could rely on the arm of her ruffian accomplice; the old man offered her freedom, but she answered him with a scaffold—the gallows bent beneath his aged form. Her minions drained the blood from his veins, and they thought they had conquered him, but it was a delusion. From the prison came forth a cry of victory; from the gallows a shout of triumph over that power whose ethics are robbery of the weak and oppression of the feeble; the trophies of whose chivalry are a plundered cradle and a scourged and bleeding woman. I saw the green sward stained with his blood, but every drop of it was like the terrible teeth sown by Cadmus; they woke up armed men to smite the terror-stricken power that had invaded his life. It seemed as if his blood had been instilled into the veins of freemen and given them fresh vigor to battle against the hoary forms of gigantic Error and colossal Theory, who stood as sentinels around the throne of the goddess. His blood was a new baptism of Liberty. I noticed that they fought against her till she tottered and fell, amid the shouts of men who had burst their chains, and the rejoicings of women newly freed, and Freedom, like a glorified angel, smiled over the glorious jubilee and stood triumphant on the very spot where the terrible goddess had reigned for centuries. I saw Truth and Justice crown her radiant brow, from joyful lips floated anthems of praise and songs of deliverance—just such songs as one might expect to hear if a thousand rainbows would melt into speech, or the music of the spheres would translate itself into words. Peace, like light dew, descended where Slavery had spread ruin and desolation, and the guilty goddess, cowering beneath the clear, open gaze of Freedom, and ashamed of her meanness and guilt, skulked from the habitations of men, and ceased to curse the land with her presence; but the first stepping-stones of Freedom to power, were the lifeless bodies of the old man and his brave companions.

Rose Terry Cooke
(1827–1892)

ducated at the Hartford Female Seminary, Rose Terry Cooke had expected to support herself as a teacher, but a legacy from her great-uncle when she was twenty-one allowed her to become a full-time writer. Her poems and regional sketches inspired "every other young woman who turned the pages throughout the country," wrote her friend Harriet Spofford. But in her late forties, Cooke married a younger widower with two children, who could not keep a job, and whose father ruinously invested her money. By the end of her life, Cooke was reduced to begging her publisher for hack work.

Nonetheless, Cooke's writing is often powerful and moving. In "Blue-beard's Closet" she used a classic fairy tale to suggest the fears haunting a dependent wife, while the despairing "Arachne" makes the spider spinning her web out of her own body a metaphor for the woman poet. Hermione ("Miny") Todd, her heroine in the short story "Odd Miss Todd," is an isolated, self-educated, and eccentric old maid whose one romantic experience leaves her determined to embrace her oddity and singleness. Cooke's fiction both explored the options of marginal figures in New England village society and made a strong case for female independence.

Blue-beard's Closet (1861)

Fasten the chamber!
Hide the red key;
Cover the portal,
That eyes may not see.
Get thee to market,
To wedding and prayer;
Labor or revel,
The chamber is there!

In comes a stranger—
"Thy pictures how fine,

Titian or Guido,
Whose is the sign?"
Looks he behind them?
Ah! have a care!
"Here is a finer."
The chamber is there!

Fair spreads the banquet,
Rich the array;
See the bright torches
Mimicking day;
When harp and viol
Thrill the soft air,
Comes a light whisper:
The chamber is there!

Marble and painting,
Jasper and gold,
Purple from Tyrus,
Fold upon fold,
Blossoms and jewels,
Thy palace prepare:
Pale grows the monarch;
The chamber is there!

Once it was open
As shore to the sea;
White were the turrets,
Goodly to see;
All through the casements
Flowed the sweet air;
Now it is darkness;
The chamber is there!

Silence and horror
Brood on the walls;
Through every crevice
A little voice calls:
Quicken, mad footsteps,
On pavement and stair;

Look not behind thee,
The chamber is there!

Out of the gateway,
Through the wide world,
Into the tempest
Beaten and hurled,
Vain is thy wandering,
Sure thy despair,
Flying or staying,
The chamber is there!

Arachne (1881)

I watch her in the corner there,
As, restless, bold, and unafraid,
She slips and floats along the air
Till all her subtile house is made.

Her home, her bed, her daily food,
All from that hidden store she draws;
She fashions it and knows it good,
By instinct's strong and sacred laws.

No tenuous threads to weave her nest,
She seeks and gathers there or here;
But spins it from her faithful breast,
Renewing still, till leaves are sere.

Then, worn with toil, and tired of life,
In vain her shining traps are set.
Her frost hath hushed the insect strife
And gilded flies her charm forget.

But swinging in the snares she spun,
She sways to every wintry wind:
Her joy, her toil, her errand done,
Her corse the sport of storms unkind.

Poor sister of the spinster clan!
I too from out my store within
My daily life and living plan,
My home, my rest, my pleasure spin.

I know thy heart when heartless hands
Sweep all that hard-earned web away;
Destroy its pearled and glittering bands,
And leave thee homeless by the way.

I know thy peace when all is done.
Each anchored thread, each tiny knot,
Soft shining in the autumn sun;
A sheltered, silent, tranquil lot.

I know what thou hast never known,
—Sad presage to a soul allowed;—
That not for life I spin, alone,
But day by day I spin my shroud.

Odd Miss Todd (1882)

Her father was odd before her. Barzillai Todd was one of those men who crop out from the general level of other people like a bowlder from the soft green surface of a meadow.

He had a good farm, but he lived on it as Selkirk lived on his island. It was but half tilled; he never cut the huckleberry bushes or ploughed them up, for he ate little besides the hard yet juicy fruit while they lasted.

Then no persuasion would induce him to sell the woodland which rose all about his lonely brown house. The trees were his congeners; he knew them individually. It was his delight to lie at length under their aerial canopy, and see the golden flecks of sunshine dance athwart their perfect grace and verdure, or to watch for bits of blue sky, sapphire blue, "like the body of heaven in its clearness," revealed by the parting of a wind-swept bough. The light susurrus of stealing breezes made the purest music to his ear, and he loved to watch the thousand quaint insects that inhabited moss and bark, to trace the busy life of anthills, to track beetles on their laborious journeys, or to see how deftly the wren wove her mystic nest, and the partridge made of her pale eggs an open secret.

He was no farmer, as all Dorset knew. Hay just enough for his two lonely Ayrshire cows was all he cut, and root crops were unknown to his fields; he raised acres of strawberries, and, being a vegetarian, used them all their season, selling the vast surplus for money to buy books; corn he grew in abundance, for meal was a necessity, and waving crops of rye; a long range of beehives gave him honey, and he had a wild theory that honey was the cure-all, and that a man who had honey at hand and ate fruit in its season would live to an indefinite period.

Flowers did not come into his scheme of life, but flowers clustered about his brown house nevertheless, for he married late in life a pretty girl, below him in social position, but so devoted, intelligent, and lovely that in his silent fashion he worshiped her while she lived, and was constant to her memory when she died, leaving him only one solace, a girl of three, and one monument in profuse roses and honeysuckles at his door. Among the other oddities of the man was his absorbing passion for books. He bought every volume he could lay his hands on in days when books cost money.

Especially did he adore Shakespeare, and above almost all his characters he admired the lovely lady of the "Winter's Tale," and therefore, in spite of his wife's gentle remonstrance, their poor child figured in the family annals as Hermione Todd, a "concatenation accordingly" which use and time resented, and few people in Dorset ever knew that "Miny" Todd had any other name than this dissyllable.

After his wife's death Barzillai Todd lived a stranger life than ever. He hired an old deaf cousin to do his housework, instructing her himself in all the mysteries of rye mush, "whole-flour" bread, suppawn, samp, and other doubtful corn-bread dainties, which were only rendered eatable by lavish supplies of cream and fresh milk. For clothes little Miny depended on Hepsy's tasteless selection and clumsy fingers, and being a plain, dark, shy child, perhaps looked as well in the dull cotton fabrics and Shaker sun-scoops that were her uniform attire as in more dainty and warmer-hued garments. Education she had none, in the ordinary sense of the word: she learned how to read in a desultory way, and made out a cramped handwriting for herself by the time she was twelve years old. But it was another of her father's theories that women ought not to be educated. Nature, however, as nature often does, defied his opinion. Though Miny never went to school or to church, and taught herself to read and write, she found her way to the miscellaneous library that lay heaped on chairs, bureaus, tables, even the floor, everywhere in the old house, except in the kitchen and one sunny corner room reserved by Hepsy for her sewing and rare company. There were, no doubt, good materials for a liberal education, in these books, but, taken at haphazard, they were devoured on principles of natural selection, and the dry treatises thrown aside as they came uppermost; but the histories, travels, and, most eagerly of all, the biographies, were read over and over till Miny knew them by heart. There were no novels or poems, except Shakespeare, in the whole collection; these Barzillai Todd held in the highest contempt, and it was to the absence of all imaginative fiction, except as it is found more or less in biography, that the girl owed her strong common sense and her sturdy persistence in viewing things and people through its medium.

From her rambles at her father's heels—and she followed him everywhere with the mute fidelity of a dog—she learned to know and love all wild things, and inheriting from her dead mother a real passion for flowers, she soon made a garden for herself on the sunny slope before her windows that would have delighted a botanist; for every flower that sprung of itself in wood or field she transplanted thither, and with the reciprocal affection flowers show to those who love them, they all lived and blossomed.

In this way, like one of her own orchids, Miny Todd grew up to her womanhood. Lovers never came near her, and she had no friends. Dorset people did not offer civilities to her father, because he did not want or need them. Neither he nor Miny had ever been ill in their lives, and when his wife died of sudden congestion of the lungs, he had resented help and sympathy from every one, and shut himself in his lair as a beast of the forest might have done when sharply wounded.

A man in New England who gives no honor to church or school is ostracized at once, and Barzillai Todd's position toward these bulwarks of the state set him quite outside the pale of Dorset society. He did not care for this; he was a lazy, selfish dreamer, without natural energy or acquired industry; a few thousand dollars which his father left him—for he came of a highly respectable and once wealthy New England family— he had had the prudence to invest safely, and this income was enough, with the aid of his strawberry patch, to supply his needs. His luxuries nature purveyed for him, and life lapsed from him as the day died out of heaven, easily and unlamented. He came in tired one day, lay down on the rough chintz-covered sofa, from which he pushed a pile of books, and fell asleep, never to waken.

Miny was thirty years old when this happened, and her father eighty. It was time old Barzy Todd died, Dorset people thought, and a few kindly souls went out to the farm to help at his funeral, for Miny had not a relative in the world.

Miny had inherited her mother's warm feeling, and her biographical studies had awakened in her mind a strong wish to know other people. Her father had but one love in his strange gray life, and when that died, with his wife, his capacity for loving died too; but Miny had a broader nature, and when she found that the income which had supported her father was all her own, she rented the farm to an energetic young man, bought a little house in Dorset, and moving all her wild flowers to the small green yard in front of her new home, and the white roses and fragrant honeysuckle her mother had planted to either side of the door, she transplanted Hepsy also, with the best of the old furniture, and began at this late hour to make friends and to know the world,—as it wagged in Dorset, at least.

Of course the minister called on her at once, and great was the Reverend Mr. Fry's astonishment to find a real and practical heathen in the very midst of his flock; he hurried home to his study, and brought her immediately a Bible, which she received with gratitude, and set herself to read with the avidity that always possessed her at sight of a fresh book.

It would be incredible to an average sinner, hardened, as one may use the phrase, by continuous preaching and teaching, to hear, could it be described, what an effect this book had upon Miss Todd. The Word, indeed, fell into a good and honest heart, and was received with the simplicity and faith of a child. Mr. Fry, who continued his pastoral calls, was put to his wits' end to understand the mental and moral position of this queer woman.

She was converted, he could not doubt, but the process was so peculiar, so heterodox, that he could not perceive it to be a genuine conversion. She did not suffer from deep sense of sin, for she had not sinned as yet, for want of temptation. Her experience of life was so strange that her experience of religion was equally unexampled; but perceiving the one fact that Miny Todd earnestly desired to live according to the precepts of the Bible, and was ready to follow Christ as her leader and king, the deacons of Dorset church, never very rigid in their theology, this being an inland village far removed from the great centres of orthodoxy, consented to let Miss Todd slip easily through her examination, and join the church according to her desire. It was a long time, and the process would be tedious of detail, before Miss Miny understood the people about her or the life they led. She herself was busy always, trying to live up to her profession of religion; but the rest had something else to do, and put off their spiritual experience till Sunday. There were children, haying, harvesting, and all that sort of thing for her neighbors to live through; and all the more that she visited the sick, fed the hungry, and clothed the naked, they held themselves excused from such duty. Their gossip grated on her charity of soul, their little meannesses seemed to her unworthy of beings who had an eternity at stake, and her heart raged at the cruelties of domestic life which she could not but see among those about her.

If she had been less candid and simple-minded than she was, she would have turned bitter and scornful; but she was always ready to learn, to wait, and to love, so that if knowledge saddened, it also strengthened her, and what she deplored she directly tried to improve. Add to this disposition great plainness of speech,—such plainness as a real child may use and only provoke a smile, while custom and convention forbid it to grown people,—and it may be imagined that at thirty-five Miss Todd, ready for all good works, was yet no favorite in Dorset; and but for the fact that the Dorset and Albany Railroad had bought a hitherto unproductive part of the farm for track and station, and paid a good price for it, and another corner had been sold to a speculator, who fancied he had discovered a mine therein (though he only found a pocket of hematite ore which barely repaid his outlay),—all this making Miny a lady of "means," as Dorset people say,—she would have been as unpopular as heart could desire. But money appeals to the hearts of all mankind,—

> *"Age cannot wither it, nor custom stale."*

When Dorset knew that Miss Todd owned thirty thousand dollars besides her fifty-acre farm, it tacitly agreed that she could do and say what she pleased. Probably she would have done so if poverty had been her lot in life, yet she would not have done it with impunity; but her hand sweetened her speech, for it was always full of timely gifts.

Still, even her benevolence did not always offset her honesty. The Reverend Septimus Clark, a fine young clergyman from New York, who was traveling through Vermont, and, stopping at Dorset one Sunday, preached for Mr. Fry, will never till his dying day forget his encounter with Miss Miny. He had preached what Mrs. Deacon Norton pronounced "a most be-a-utiful discourse," as full of flowers as a greenhouse, liberally sprinkled with poetry, gently "picked out" with sentiment, and here and there a little natural religion put in, like cloves into a baked ham, more for ornament than use. It was a sermon a pagan or a Brahmin would have admired just as much as Mrs. Deacon Norton, but it stirred the depths of Miss Miny's soul. Her great honest gray eyes darkened, flashed, and at last dimmed with tears as she fixed them on the elegant youth supposed to be preaching the gospel; and when he ceased to discourse, and, pronouncing a graceful benediction, came down from the pulpit, he was surprised to see a short, dark, resolute-looking woman, with a pair of reproachful eyes fixed on him, draw nearer and nearer, and at last plant herself in the middle aisle just in his way.

He stopped, courteously, to let her move aside; but she never stirred, only looked straight at him, and said, "Do you believe the Bible?"

Mr. Clark was still more surprised, but answered civilly, "Certainly I do."

"You believe," she went on, "that all these folks you have been preaching to will be lost eternally if they don't believe on the Lord Jesus Christ?"

The Reverend Septimus stared blankly, yet her "glittering eye" compelled response. "Why, yes, madam: I am orthodox."

"And knowin' that, knowin' they will never see you again, 't is n't likely, and you have n't had but one chance to talk to 'em and tell what responsible bein's they are, you 've been and talked all this stuff about roses and clouds and brooks and things to dyin' souls! You poor deluded man, what is the Lord goin' to say to you in that Day?"

The Reverend Mr. Clark choked; he fairly became faint for a moment, for under his elegance and florality he had a conscience, and a somewhat dormant but living Christian faith; but he was not man enough to say, "Thank you;" he only pushed by Miss Miny, and asked Mr. Fry, who was waiting for him at the door, who the woman was who had stopped him.

"Oh, that is odd Miss Todd," said Mr. Fry, in such a matter-of-course way that Mr. Clark did not feel it necessary to mention her rebuke. But Miss Miny "builded better than she knew;" the youth never uttered such idle words again; he recognized the situation and accepted it, which is the key of all true life, and became one of the most fervid and spiritual preachers of his sect, though he never saw Miss Todd again.

Deacon Norton, too, winced under her lash, all the more that he was not sure his views of the matter were right. He felt called upon to deal with Miss Todd because she did not attend on weekly prayer-meetings, and paid her a visit for this purpose.

Miss Miny waited calmly till he had delivered his message, and her turn came.

"Look here, deacon," she said with quiet energy, "to begin with, I don't see any special obligation required in Scripter to have prayer-meetings. It says there folks must enter into their closets, and be secret about their praying."

"But what does Scripter say about two or three gatherin' together?"

"Well, that's another matter; that says if they 'll agree about something special to ask. I should b'lieve in that if there was a fever in Dorset, or a drought, or a big flood, or a time of wickedness being peculiar mighty; but you won't never make me believe that 'two or three' means twenty, or that agreeing about a thing to ask for means the broadcast sort of fashion you pray. Why, I did go once, and I was altogether taken down. The first man got up, and instead of praying, he told the Lord the longest string about Dorset people you ever heard,—how bad they were; and then he rambled off about the creation, and the state of the heathen. Deacon, I know that man. I know he 's as cross as a tiger to his wife, his boys hide when they see him coming, and he 's mean enough to take double toll out of a widow's meal bag. If he stopped reviling his neighbors, and lamentin' over the isles of the South, and tried to example after Jesus Christ, and be a 'livin' epistle,' as Paul says, I think he 'd do better. No; I sha'n't come to any more prayer-meetings. I believe in less prayin' and more practicing;" and with a flush on her dark cheek, and a light in her deep eyes that told how earnest her feeling was on the subject, Miss Miny took up the stocking she was knitting for an idiot boy in the poor-house, and clicked her needles faster than ever.

Deacon Norton uttered a horrified groan, and shook his hoary head ominously as he crossed the threshold; but he was a reflective man, and Miss Miny's ideas stirred a certain reformative conviction in his mind. He did not thereafter refrain from prayer-meetings, for it had been born and educated into him that they were a necessity of Christian life, but his prayers put on a new style. He was earnest in asking for spiritual gifts rather than in conveying information to his audience; and many an astonished soul discovered for the first time through those fervent petitions that religion is a matter of week-day life rather than Sunday solemnity.

Scandal, too, found little mercy at Miss Miny's door. There was a woman in Dorset who

> *"Made her enjoyment*
> *And only employment"*

in retailing some real or unreal story to somebody's disadvantage. Mrs. Peek was a little woman, with an indefinite sort of mouth, a pale face, and dead black eyes, with a furtive glitter that betrayed a lurking imp hidden in their dark pools. She was a mim, softspoken woman, but guileful and gliding as a snake. Miss Miny never visited her, though they met often at sewing circles, and it was at one of these social occasions that the venomous little creature began to retail some of her malice to Mrs. Norton, who was sitting sewing at one end of a sheet, with Miss Miny at the other. It was only a version of the old story,—a girl to whom a man had offered marriage, and then changed his mind without giving any reason.

"Well," said Mrs. Norton, "I think he 'd ought to have told her right out like a man, not to sneak off backhanded that way."

"M-m," responded Mrs. Peek, with an indescribable soft murmur. "Do you know, Mis' Norton, for certain, that he ever did ask Albiny to marry him?"

Mrs. Norton looked at her over her spectacles, with the peculiar glare of that sort of inspection. "I 'm as certain of it as though he told me, though I can't say he did tell me," she answered sharply.

"Well, m-m, she's a poor homeless cretur, and I wish her well. I wish her well. But maybe you 'll find out things ain't jest as you think they is; but I don't want to say nothin',—no I don't want to speak about it."

"I b'lieve she 's a good girl, Mis' Peek," said the deacon's wife angrily. "I b'lieve every word she says. I don' know as anybody asked him to make up to her, nor as anybody cares if he doos or doos n't, but I blame a man for keepin' company with any gal, an' then turnin' square round an' backin' down, without no reason nor rhyme to be given."

"Well, m-m, well, if so be, 't is so; but I 'm free to say I ain't by no means sure 't he ever did say snip to her, so to speak. I wish her well. I hope she 'll marry somebody that 'll make a good home for her, but— well, I don't want to say nothin'."

"What in the world do you keep doing it for, then?" curtly inquired Miss Miny.

An evil flash shot out of the dead black eyes, like flame out of thick smoke; but Mrs. Peek did not or could not answer, and Miss Todd went on:—

"If you wish Albiny Morse well, why do you keep insinuatin' against her? I guess you mistake; you don't like her, and you tell that it 's probable—well, that it 's likely she's told a lie about that fellow. I don't believe it, and I don't think, Mis' Peek, you remember what Scripter says

about doin' to others as you 'd have them do to you. 'T would n't be alto-
gether agreeable, I guess, to have folks say that you 'd asked Mr. Peek to
have ye before he 'd ever thought on 't, now would it?"

Mrs. Peek was hit on a sore spot by this pellet; she looked at Miss Miny
as if a dagger and a thrust would have interpreted her better than speech.

"I have n't nothin' to say to sech remarks," she murmured unctuously.
"No, I don't wish to say no more."

"Don't say it, then; nobody asked you to," stoutly replied Miss Todd.
"Least said is soonest mended, 'specially about your neighbors."

"Well, you sot her down consider'ble," said Mrs. Norton, as the small
serpent glided away, hissing gently.

"I don't like such talk," was Miss Todd's rejoinder. "I take a lot of inter-
est in other folks's affairs. I can't help it. I have n't got kith nor kin of my
own, and I do get to feel as though all Dorset was a sort of a family to
me; and I believe the Lord made folks to be int'rested in other folks, or
the world could n't gee, anyhow; but as for scandal and unfriendly talk, I
don't like it. If it 's got to be, why speak it out. I never could bear mice
because they always run round under things and rustle. It 's mean to
sneak, and hide, and burrow like that. I 've got as much respect again for
a man that swears right out as I have for one that keeps hintin'."

"For goodness' sake!" exclaimed the horrified listener.

Mrs. Norton had her own private grievances, and they were growing
fast. She had but one daughter, a pretty girl of sixteen, whose waving red
hair, white skin, blue eyes, and scarlet lips were mightily attractive to the
youths of Dorset; for though Dell Norton had a quick temper, she had a
merry wit, and was full of fun and brightness. Her father loved her with
all his shut-up heart, and her mother spoiled and scolded her by turns,
but if anybody else found fault with Dell she was as ready to fly at them
as an old hen whose chickens are profaned by mortal approach.

Now the girl had a girlish fashion of speech which Miss Todd did not
like, it seemed to her so near an approach to positive lying; and she at last
expressed her opinion, as usual, with entire frankness. She had gone into
Deacon Norton's of an errand one day, and Dell came hurrying in to ask
her mother if she might go to ride with Sam Elderkin, a youth of good
report, but a poor farmer, which is next door to being a pauper in New
England.

Regardless of poverty, however, Sam had "cast a wistful eye," as the
hymn-book says, into Deacon Norton's fold, and Mrs. Norton suspected
it. Dell liked him as she liked a dozen others, and her mother was wise
enough to say nothing till she should see real occasion.

Dell was all animation to-day.

"Oh, ma! Sam Elderkin 's got a new horse; his uncle down to Hartford sent it up to him. My! ain't it a splendid one! Its back 's three weeks broad, and it jest goes like a livin' storm. I don't believe lightnin' would more 'n keep up with it. I 'd jest like to ride behind it forever. Can't I go over to Wallingford with him?"

Mrs. Norton could say neither yes nor no, for Miss Miny asked so quickly and quietly, "You don't mean what you say, do ye, Adelye?"

"Why don't I?" snapped the girl.

"Why, forever 's a long time, and I don't believe even a Hartford horse could go like lightnin'. Seems as if your words was n't needed to be so big, are they?"

Dell sunk down in a chair and stared at this audacious female, but her mother blazed up.

"Look here, Miss Todd. I guess I 'm entire capable of bossin' Dell. She suits me, if she don't you. Go put on you bunnet, child, and go 'long. What in the world air you always meddlin' with other folks's business for, Miss Miny? Does it give you real satisfaction?"

"No," said Miss Miny quietly, with no trace of vexation on her homely face. "I don't know as I ought to have said what I did, but I do dislike to hear girls get into such a big way of talk; it seems so disrespectful to facts; and then it uses up words so fast,—makes idle words, seems to me. But I allow, Mrs. Norton, I had better not have spoke. I suppose I do seem to take more than my lawful int'rest in folks that ain't my folks; but you see I grew up in the wilderness, and I have n't got any people of my own, and I have to like them that don't belong to me, and I get to feeling as if they was my own."

"Well!" exclaimed Mrs. Norton, aghast at the honesty and humility of odd Miss Todd; but Dell rushed out of the bedroom where she had been prinking, threw her arms round Miss Miny, and gave her a hearty hug, exclaiming,—

"You dear old thing! you shall say just what you 're a mind to, for you 're just as clever as you can be, so there!"

Miss Miny laughed, though her eyes were very dim. Dell's generous young heart had been touched, and thereafter she found her way to the spinster's little house often, and through her confidences in the twilight, or beside the wood fire, Miss Miny discovered before many months that Sam Elderkin was resolved to marry Dell, and she was as determined to marry him; but both the deacon and Mrs. Norton were opposed with equal determination to the match.

"As obstinate as a Norton," was a Dorset proverb; but Miss Miny, unafraid of proverbs, determined to throw herself into the breach, and make things as right and straight as she could. For once she showed a little of the serpent's wisdom. Instinctively she understood, what the adherents of "women's rights" ignore, the fact that a woman can influence a man, or a man a woman, from the very reason of their difference in sex; so instead of going to Mrs. Norton, she cornered the deacon one day in the store, and asked him to step over to her house, and there laid the situation before him.

"'T ain't no use talkin'," he replied. "Sam Elderkin ain't worth a copper to-day over 'n' above his farm, and I ain't goin' to see Dell give over to want nor pestered with a shiftless husband."

"Well, now, Deacon Norton, who do you expect Dell will marry?"

The man looked puzzled, but went on: "Why, I expect she 'll come acrost some well-to-do feller some time that 'll make her comfortable."

"There ain't anybody in Dorset you want her to take up with?"

"I don't know as there *is*, and I don't know *as* there is. On the whole, I guess there ain't."

"Do you mean to send her away?"

"No, marm. I don't hold to gals goin' visitin' round; it sure turns their heads."

"Well, then, deacon, as sure as you set there, Sam is bound to marry Dell, and she is in the same mind, whether you let 'em or no. Now ain't it a lot better to give countenance to it than to have all Dorset talking about you and yours, saying hard things about your bein' a professor, yet so fond of money and so hard on your girl? Have you got any right to fetch reproach on the Church, jest to have your will done in this thing? Sam Elderkin is a good young man as ever was, only he's poor. Was n't Mis' Norton and you poor when you commenced in life; and are you willing to make Dell real unhappy, and give occasion to the enemy to revile, because you want her to do different from what you did?"

"You 're the peskiest woman I ever see!" roared the deacon, flinging out of the house and banging the door behind him. But he did not shut the truths he had heard inside that door; they rang in his ears wherever he went, followed him, like the frogs of Egypt's plague, even into his bed-chamber, tingled in his brain at every prayer-meeting, and, to use his own phrase, when he came to confession afterward, "Them things you said jest stuck to me like a bunch of burdocks to a dog's tail. I could n't neither drop 'em, nor claw 'em off."

But the result was that in due season Dell Norton was married properly at her father's house, and the farm Sam Elderkin owned dowered with four grade Alderneys from the Norton herd and a pair of great red oxen. Dell developed into a model wife and mother, and made such butter as Dorset never saw before; and when little hands grasped the old man's rough fingers, and little feet toddled beside him down to the garden gate, Deacon Norton, in his secret heart, felt a thrill of fervent gratitude to odd Miss Todd.

There lived in Dorset a poor widow with one son. Jonas Pringle was always a good boy,—in fact, rather a goody boy, one of the sort that usually boast of being the sons of poor but pious parents. He was lean and pale as a small boy, and seemed merely to draw out like a telescope rather than grow with advancing years. His hair was palely brown, his eyes palely blue, and his thin face and uncertain mouth could not be called lovely even by the extremest maternal partiality. His mother was a wailing female who would have wept for something she had not in the very lap of luxury, and life afforded her abundant grievances. If the sky shone cloudless, she shook her head and called the day "a real weather-breeder;" if it rained, she prognosticated blasted grain, rotted potatoes, floods, land slips, or any other evil she could think of.

Jonas had the hunger for books and education that his unhealthy sort of organization is so apt to foster. The truest kindness would have been to turn him out on a farm and make him work for his living, where sun and air, keen winds, and fresh earth would have brought life and color into his unwholesome visage, and hearty labor strengthened his flaccid muscles and knit his loose joints. He needed fibre and force, outward growth, and nourishing food. But his weak mother coddled him from babyhood,—kept him close by the stove, and taught him to knit and sew, when he should have been snowballing other boys or skating on Dorset Pond. She fed him on such cake and pie as her poverty of money and skill both allowed,—messes of poor flour, lard, soda, molasses, and allspice; she gave him strong green tea for the consequent headaches these viands surely caused, and tucked him up in bed with hot bricks and doses of herb tea, when boys of his own age, like Sam Elderkin, slept in the garret, with snowdrifts on their homespun blankets.

Miss Miny had only been established in Dorset a few years, and Jonas was a tall sallow youth of eighteen, when one fine day Mrs. Pringle took to her bed, to rise no more. Contradictory as women are, she endured her last illness with cheerful fortitude, and parted from Jonas with a smile, commending him in full faith to the widow's God. Jonas did not appear to suffer as much as would have pleased sympathizing friends.

The truth was, his bringing up had necessarily made him selfish, and while he really mourned for his mother, it was more because she had left him to take care of himself than for any deep filial love or sense of lost companionship.

It was the greatest comfort he could have, to be taken home by Miss Todd, installed in her comfortable spare room, and made much of, and Dorset people were not greatly surprised when they learned it was Miss Miny's intention to educate Jonas for the ministry, and give him a home. It required some self-denial on Miss Miny's part to do this; her old servant had died just before Mrs. Pringle, and as yet she had not replaced her. She resolved now to do her own work, and she also bought a knitting machine, and ground out dozens of pairs of worsted stockings, which she sold. Her money had been well invested, but her charities were exhaustive, and she would not discontinue one of them, but did her utmost in the way of work and economy for Jonas's sake, and felt herself repaid when in five years' time he came back a full-fledged minister of the gospel, and preached in the old church of his native village.

He did not at once attempt to settle anywhere. Dorset was pleasant to his soul. He was comfortably housed and fed, and it gave him keen pleasure to walk abroad among those who had looked down on his youthful poverty, and look down on them from his double pinnacle of education and office. Jonas was selfish, crafty, and plausible; his pale blue eyes were true to their usual index of character, an index that points to self-love and want of genuine honesty; and when he suggested that his health was injured by study, and he thought it would be best for him to spend the summer in Dorset and recruit, Miss Miny joyfully fell in with the arrangement.

It is a fixed law of our moral nature that we love those whom we befriend, and odd Miss Todd was not odd enough to evade this constitutional edict. She had spent time, money, and pains on Jonas as freely as if he had been her son, and she loved him with as pure and fervent affection as ever mother felt for her only boy, for in her nature lay that intense maternal feeling which is not given always to the physical mother,—that capacity of devotion, self-sacrifice, and powerful affection that makes a woman most womanly, most happy, yet capable of anguish unspeakable and mourning that will not be comforted. It did not matter to Miss Miny that Jonas was still lank, sallow, pale-haired, and the very conformation and likeness of a solemn prig; that he always spoke with the awful and lugubrious intonation of "the sacred desk." She did not see in him any distasteful trait or any uncomfortable habit; she enjoyed his intellectual conversation, his reading aloud, his rather obtrusive and outspoken piety. So Jonas basked in the comfort of Miss Miny's neat bright house all the long summer through, now and then exhorting at prayer-meetings or helping at a funeral just to keep his hand in.

He was not naturally an energetic man; his tastes were studious and dainty, his constitution frail, and all these combined to make him indolent. As Mrs. Deacon Norton pungently remarked, "He won't never eat smart man's bread: he likes to set on a fence and see folks mow."

As he whiled away the summer, it came into his head how pleasant life would be if one need not work for a living,—not a singular idea, and one that most of us who do work for a living frequently entertain, but with the thought arose a way of escape from this dreaded vista. Why should not he marry Miss Miny? He might perhaps have speculated on becoming her heir, but she had already confided to him that her property had been left to provide a free library and reading-room for the town of Dorset, and her will was in the judge of probate's hands.

It was an objection that she was twenty years older than he, but in New England country towns a woman is frequently some years older than her husband, and Miss Miny had no relatives to object, nor had he.

Once married, it would be easy to persuade her to destroy that will, and he had the acuteness for his own interest common to selfish men, and understood that odd Miss Todd could do an odd thing without provoking the comment of society. He had full faith in his own powers of fascination, as well as in her capacity for deep feeling, and after much consideration resolved to make cautious approaches. He became more devoted in manner; exerted himself to spare her fatigue and trouble; sighed occasionally, and fixed his eyes on her in a pathetic way; interspersed his readings with poetry; put on her shawl with almost an embrace; and never went out for a stroll without bringing her wild flowers that she loved, or berries from the hills and uplands.

Poor Miss Todd! in that lone bosom the girl's heart lay sleeping; no touch of prince's lips had ever disturbed its long sleep, but it was living still, and now with strange and almost painful throbs it began to dream, to stir. She resisted the unwonted trouble as a blind man might resist unknown approach and alien caresses, not knowing how to define the new and vague delight. She prayed fervently that she might not be given to idolatry, for she knew well that Jonas grew dearer to her daily, though she had not yet recognized the divine unrest that was sweeter than any foregone peace; her heart ached with feeling as we sometimes ache physically with laughter, for it was a pleasant pain. Does the aloe leave its long verdurous quiet and burst into stately bloom with such careless ease as the new-sprung violet blossoms? Does not some dull pang strike through the bulb that has lain all winter barren and hidden, when it sends upward its odorous spike of heaven-blue bells?

I do not know whether to weep or smile over this poor tale of genuine if delayed passion; it certainly is pitiful, yet it cannot help being ludicrous to betray what curious fancies possessed odd Miss Todd at this crisis of her life. No "sudden interposition of several guardian angels," such as saved dear old Hepzibah's turban from desecration, interfered in her behalf; she began to wear pink ribbons, which she had never yet indulged in; and further to set off her dark and dingy skin, bought herself a bright deep green gown; strove with the patient anguish only a woman knows to build her scant and crinkled hair up in some semblance of prevailing fashions; and illuminated her decent gray and black Sunday bonnet with a red rose outside and a blue bow inside. Dorset stared with all its eyes, but only laughed at odd Miss Todd. She lived behind her character as behind a shield; not a human being suspected that these outbursts of color, these shining eyes, this alert step, were not oddities at all, but genuine submissions to nature's commonest law, the law of love.

It occurred to Jonas as the long summer days went on that it would be very pleasant to drive about Dorset, and would give him more opportunity to hold private converse with Miss Miny; for her house was already like the cave of Adullam: "every one in distress, and everyone discontented," came there for help and counsel, and their *tête-à-têtes* were few and brief; so he borrowed some kind body's old horse and rattling wagon now and again, and drove Miss Todd through winding lanes, fragrant woods, up and down hills from whence the outlook was exquisite; or they wound along the edge of Dorset Pond, catching the too sweet breath of the white clethra on its shores, the finer odor of late wild roses, or the delicate perfume of grape blossoms,—all recalling Miss Miny's childhood to her mind and her heart, and putting the wistful girlish look into eyes that so long had gazed sadly on sin and sorrow. But all this took up her time. Housework languished, and she bethought herself of getting some help in her kitchen, when one hot August day Parson Fry stalked in to request aid from her ever-ready benevolence.

He had just received a letter from Mary Spencer, a former resident of Dorset, and distantly related to his wife, written on her death-bed. She had married a Southerner many years ago, a man of wealth, who had been attracted by her great beauty. She was but a poor girl, the tavern-keeper's daughter, and Mr. Spencer had taken her to Carolina, where for a year or two she lived an ideal life, happy as love and luxury can make a girl who has not known either before. Then the war came; her husband lost all his property, was killed in battle, and she returned to Champlin, a small town in Massachusetts, where her father had moved from Dorset, bringing with her a baby girl. There she had lived as before, helping in the tavern work till her child was eighteen years old. Her mother had died long ago, and she herself been wasting for years with slow consumption, when suddenly her father fell dead of apoplexy, and the shock hastened her own end. She had not a relative in the world or a friend to whose care she could leave Eleanor, except Parson Fry, and when he received her letter she was already dead, and Nora crying her heart out over her mother. Parson Fry was at his wits' end; he had not a spare inch of room in the parsonage. Indeed, if any brother minister happened in, as they are apt to do, Deacon Norton had to lodge him, for the "minister's blessing" was in full force in the parson's abode, ten small children and a baby giving him what Mrs. Norton rather sarcastically called "John Rogers's measure." She had been brought up on the old New England Primer, and the dim crowd that surrounded that martyr at the stake—ten children and one to carry—was present to her memory.

It was of course impossible to take Nora into his own house, so he came to consult with Miss Todd about her disposal, and found that good woman ready and glad to help him; indeed, she regarded it as a direct providence that the girl had been sent to her in time of need. Providence does not always work after our limited prescience, however, but it did prove to be the divinest of providences to Miss Miny that Nora arrived just then, though it wore a dark frown for a long time, and hid its "smiling face."

Eleanor Spencer had lived so long in the tavern at Champlin, and been made so useful in consequence of her mother's failing health, that Miss Miny's housework was mere play to her young strength and older experience. After the old patriarchal fashion of New England, she was made one of the family, and Jonas opened his eyes to their fullest extent when Nora appeared first at the breakfast-table, having arrived the night before, and already cooked the pink slice of savory ham, set about with milk-white eggs, the puffy biscuit, the spongy flapjacks, and clear coffee that his soul loved. She inherited her mother's beauty, with the coloring of her father's family: a brilliant complexion, great, soft dark eyes, bright hair that waved all over her shapely head and was gathered in coil on coil behind, and a slight and graceful figure, all of which her lilac print dress and spotless apron set off as green leaves do a rose. She was "a vision of delight" indeed, and Miss Miny, honest soul! looked at her with pleasure and admiration.

But as the summer days went on, and Nora became more wonted to her work, she learned to be more deft and nimble, and had many an hour to spend in the keeping-room, busy with her own sewing or Miss Miny's. She, too, listened to the readings and absorbed them into her quick and willing mind; her eyes darkened or shone at the lofty or passionate poetry, and her beautiful dimples danced, her red lips quivered with laughter, at whatever wit or humor lay among Jonas's selections. She was a whole audience in herself, and her attention and appreciation flattered the reader deeply, but her beauty did more potent execution.

For Jonas was young; and here, face to face with him day after day, was a girl beautiful as flesh and blood can be, and as intelligent as beautiful. It was altogether too much. His heart triumphed over his policy; in the madness of a real passion he was ready to go all lengths of labor and renunciation if Nora were his; and she began with that sort of hero worship inborn in most girls to look up adoringly at such wonders of education and intellect as his. She had seen hitherto only the commonest class of men, such as frequent a country tavern, and had no measure in her mind by which to test this man's real capacity; so she stood as ready to receive and respond to his first expression of feeling as a budded rose stands ready waiting for the expanding sun.

It was some time before Miss Miny's unsuspicious nature perceived the open secret that was acting in her quiet house. She was perceptive enough, but it seemed to her inexperience that Jonas was as much bound to prefer her to all other women as if he had sworn an oath of fealty. She was as odd in her ignorance of humanity as in everything else; a kiss would have been to this singular honesty of hers as sacred as a marriage vow; incredible as it may seem, she did not imagine it possible for a man to show every lover-like attention to a woman, and then "whistle down the wind" to a prettier face. This sort of thing, common as blades of grass, wore to her simplicity an aspect both tragic and brutal; dishonesty was an equal crime in her eyes with murder, for she took her ethical standard from the Bible, not from society, and found there no distinction in evil, no grades of sin,—save that awful exception, the sin unpardonable.

Yet before October poured its living dyes along the Dorset hills, odd Miss Todd began to see what no other woman could have so long misunderstood. She felt in her kind and faithful bosom the tortures that have no parallel in this world,—the remorseless tortures of jealousy. She had been all her life at peace with herself. Even Parson Fry had disturbed his soul over her religious experience because she never could truthfully say that she was the chief of sinners. But now she hated herself as earnestly as Calvin could have desired; for there developed within her such suspicion, such unkindness, something so near akin to hatred, that her prayers were mere utterances of agony, and her Bible a dead letter.

Sleep forsook her, and her daily food grew bitter. It was scarcely a relief to her when Jonas left Dorset to find, if possible, a parish where he was wanted; for she knew, with the fearful insight of jealousy, why Nora took her daily walk to the post-office, and why the letters she herself received from her boy were so dry and brief. She was too good to be positively unkind to Nora, and the girl was too deep in her bright dream to be troubled by Miss Todd's unusual silence and constrained manner. Her heart would have been shocked to pity—she had a kind heart—to know what a life her companion and friend was enduring.

Before Jonas had been prospecting—if that phrase is allowable—a month, he was engaged to fill the pulpit of a country church in Connecticut for a year, and with the characteristic imprudence of a man in love, he thought this was enough to warrant his marriage. He argued that one engagement would at least lead to another, and most probably to a settlement; for he had a certain floral eloquence and a "glittering generality" in his sermons that tickled people's ears, and did not disturb their consciences,—two qualifications which always make a clergyman popular. He had not an idea that he had treated Miss Todd in a way she could or should resent. He fell back on the patent fact that he had never asked her to marry him; and it is a general masculine code that up to this Rubicon you may fight or flee, as you like.

So he went back to Dorset in great glee; but his first entrance into the atmosphere of Miss Todd's house warned him of possible explosives. He sobered down his joy, was pleasant and deferential to Miss Miny, and devised private opportunities of speech with Nora; in fact, his final appeal to her, and her acceptance, took place in what he afterward recalled as "that sacred spot in front of the corner grocery."

It was agreed between the lovers that Miss Todd should not at present be taken into their confidence. They had an unacknowledged consciousness of her probable displeasure, so she was left to fight with her grief in that solitude that makes battle so hard, victory so long of coming. She was a reasonable woman ordinarily, but what jealous man or woman is reasonable? It was the most natural thing in the world that a young fellow like Jonas, ready to marry a plain, positive, odd, and old woman, from motives of policy, should be turned from his intent by the daily presence and contrast of abundant beauty and the divine charm of youth, but Miss Todd resented it in her soul as a real crime. There was nothing for it but to run from this conflict, and she could not run; she had nowhere to go. Fortunately for her, this inward storm disturbed the equilibrium of her strong constitution; she took to her bed, and in the comfortless tossings of a long low fever prayed day and night to die. No one dies, however, when they wish to; she had to submit to Nora's patient and careful nursing; for though the girl was too young to show much strength of character as yet, she was kind, and pitied Miss Miny from the heights of her own vernal joy, as a poor loveless old maid. Fortunately she did not put her feeling into words, but only put off her marriage, and took faithful care of Miss Todd through the long, dreary winter; and when the poor woman crept back to life again, it was to have Jonas's plans and happiness poured into her ears. She had a relapse, of course. People said she had been imprudent; and so she had, but long before her fever,—imprudent with the headlong carelessness of women who let themselves fall into an open pit, from which none can deliver them.

The relapse served one good purpose: it gave the best of reasons why this marriage should not take place at her house. She hired a nurse from another village, and sent Nora to the parsonage for her wedding; and when the happy pair came to say good-by, she was too ill to see them. It was a long time before Miss Miny recovered; but by June she declared herself well, and resumed her lonely life. Yet there was a great change in her, odd as she still was: a deeper, tenderer charity toward women, whom hitherto she had held in a sort of contempt; now she seemed to have a key to many of their shortcomings, and to sympathize with their pains and follies more than women often do with each other. Even to those whom society holds unpardonable—and in as small a place as Dorset there are such—she extended the very mercy of Christ, and with human love and pity helped Him to redeem them. Toward men she became pitiless and almost fierce. The injustice of their social position for the first time became visible to her eyes, and she resented it with the force of her nature. Whatever good she did was now turned into another channel: she cared no longer for the boys in the factory, but devoted herself to the teaching of the girls in Dorset, sending to Boston for a female teacher, and setting up a private school at her own expense, except the small fees charged for tuition, which went no further than to hire and heat the schoolrooms. Jonas and his wife rarely returned to the town, for Miss Todd never invited them, and Mr. Fry could not. Their first child was named Hermione Todd, but never profited thereby, and though

Jonas hoped to the end he received nothing. She had made a new will, and all her money went to found a female college of the smallest size, eligible for only ten members, and in its rigid rule resembling a nunnery.

For at length she did die, and during her last illness Mr. Fry, in pursuance of his office, had many serious conversations with her. One day he said, "And you feel in charity with all men, Sister Todd?"

"I don't know that," she replied sharply. "I suppose it is n't a duty to forgive folks unless they ask for forgiveness, is't?"

Parson Fry looked puzzled. "Well," he said meditatively, "I do suppose we ought to keep continooally in a forgiving frame."

"That is n't the point. You can't tell me about Scripter. The Lord never forgives folks without they repent. To offer such folks forgiveness would come the nearest of anything I can think of to throwin' pearls before swine; they 'd turn and rend you, surely."

"But you should be ready to forgive sech as do repent and seek pardon," solemnly replied the parson, a little disturbed by her contumacy.

"Well, I hope I am; but there 's small chance I shall be asked."

She never was. Though Jonas struggled with poverty, and Nora lost her beauty and grace in the hard life of a poor minister's wife, and her husband repented that he had not married Miss Todd, it was simply because he hungered for money with the primal instincts of a lazy and selfish man, from whom the brief insanity of passion had long fled, and who pined for the fleshpots of Egypt. That he had wronged her, or hurt her almost to the death, never occurred to him.

Miss Miny shocked the conventions of Dorset even to her last hour, for she extracted a promise solemn as an oath from her nurse with regard to her funeral.

"I want you should put on me a clean night-gownd and cap, Semanthy. I am going to sleep till the Lord comes, and I think it is a waste of good clothes to bury them. I wish to look conformable. Moreover, I want a plain pine coffin, and no plate about it. Money is n't plenty enough, as long as there's a poor woman livin', to make a vain show of it. I don't expect gown nor coffin to rise no more 'n this miserable old body, and I won't be answerable for foolish waste of what the Lord gave me."

After this she laid her cheek on her hand, sighed, and died, quietly as a brown leaf falls from the last tree that holds those tawny ghosts into the edge of winter.

Dorset people all came to her funeral, which was held in the meeting-house, and the universal grief discovered her secret benefactions as the early rains discover seeds long ago sown.

She had done a thousand kindnesses, small but helpful, that were all remembered now, and the lonely woman was mourned and missed as few women are except in their own households.

Mrs. Norton made the one characteristic comment of the day as she looked at the poor shrunken face of the dead: "Well, I never did! of all *things!* Laid out in a night-gownd and put into a pine coffin! She has n't never got over bein' odd Miss Todd."

Emily Dickinson
(1830–1886)

Though she is now widely known and lauded, in her lifetime Emily Dickinson was so private and reclusive that she published (anonymously) only seven of her almost two thousand poems. Born to a prominent family in Amherst, Massachusetts, Dickinson enjoyed a relatively typical adolescence but soon withdrew into her father's home, wearing only white and avoiding almost all direct contact with others, although she continued to write letters. Dickinson's poems, written on various scraps of paper, some of which were then copied and compiled into small, hand-bound volumes, are startlingly original explorations of love, loss, joy, and pain. Early editors of Dickinson's work tried to normalize her distinct style by assigning titles to her poems, fixing her punctuation (most notably removing her frequent dashes), and rearranging syntax. In 1955, T. H. Johnson published Dickinson's poems in their original forms for the first time, and in 1981, Ralph W. Franklin used physical evidence from Dickinson's hand-bound papers to restore her works to their original order, and numbered them.

138

To fight aloud, is very brave -
But *gallanter*, I know
Who charge within the bosom
The Cavalry of Wo -

Who win, and nations do not see -
Who fall - and none observe -
Whose dying eyes, no Country
Regards with patriot love -

We trust, in plumed procession
For such, the Angels go -
Rank after Rank, with even feet -
And Uniforms of snow.

269

Wild nights - Wild nights!
Were I with thee
Wild nights should be
Our luxury!

Futile - the winds -
To a Heart in port -
Done with the Compass -
Done with the Chart!

Rowing in Eden -
Ah, the Sea!
Might I but moor - tonight -
In thee!

339

I like a look of Agony,
Because I know it's true -
Men do not sham Convulsion,
Nor simulate, a Throe -

The Eyes glaze once - and that is Death -
Impossible to feign
The Beads upon the Forehead
By homely Anguish strung.

Helen Hunt Jackson
(1830–1885)

girlhood friend from Amherst, and a lifelong correspondent of Emily Dickinson, Helen Hunt Jackson took a very different path. A marriage to an army officer ended tragically with the death of her husband and then her nine-year-old son. With the encouragement of Thomas Higginson, she began to publish poems, short stories under the pseudonym "Saxe Holm," and an anonymous novel, *Mercy Philbrick's Choice* (1876), which some of her friends thought was based on Dickinson. In 1872, Jackson went west for her health, married a wealthy man she met in Colorado, and developed a passionate commitment to Indian rights. Her book *A Century of Dishonor* (1881) protested against government mistreatment of Indian tribes. Hoping to do "for the Indian a thousandth part of what *Uncle Tom's Cabin* did for the Negro," she published *Ramona* (1884), a love story about Native Americans and Latinos in California, which became a bestseller and is still a landmark in Californian literary history. But despite her own success, Jackson's skeptical view of the sacrifices women made for marriage never changed. In her feminist allegory "The Prince's Little Sweetheart," originally published in *Century* magazine, she questioned the fairy-tale image of marital bliss.

The Prince's Little Sweetheart (1885)

She was very young. No man had ever made love to her before. She belonged to the people, the common people. Her parents were poor, and could not buy any wedding trousseau for her. But that did not make any difference. A carriage was sent from the Court for her, and she was carried away "just as she was," in her stuff gown—the gown the Prince first saw her in. He liked her best in that, he said; and, moreover, what odds did it make about clothes? Were there not rooms upon rooms in the palace, full of the most superb clothes for Princes' Sweethearts?

It was into one of these rooms that she was taken first. On all sides of it were high glass cases reaching up to the ceiling, and filled with gowns, and mantles, and laces, and jewels: everything a woman could wear was there, and all of the very finest. What satins, what velvets, what feathers and flowers! Even down to shoes and stockings, every shade and color of stockings, of the daintiest silk. The Little Sweetheart gazed, breathless, at them all. But she did not have time to wonder, for in a moment more she was met by attendants, some young, some old, all dressed gayly. She did not dream at first that they were servants, till they began, all together, asking her what she would like to put on. Would she have a lace gown, or a satin? Would she like feathers, or flowers? And one ran this way, and one that; and among them all, the Little Sweetheart was so flustered she did not know if she were really alive and on the earth, or had been transported to some fairy land; and before she fairly realized what was being done, they had her clad in the most beautiful gown that was ever seen. White satin with gold butterflies on it, and a white lace mantle embroidered in gold butterflies; all white and gold she was, from top to toe, all but one foot; and there was something very odd about that. She heard one of the women whispering to the other, behind her back: "It is too bad there isn't any mate to this slipper! Well, she will have to wear this pink one. It is too big; but if we pin it up at the heel she can keep it on. The Prince really must get some more slippers."

And then they put on her left foot a pink satin slipper, which was so much too big it had to be pinned up in plaits at each side, and the pearl buckle on the top hid her foot quite out of sight. But the Little Sweetheart did not care. In fact, she had no time to think, for the Queen came sailing in and spoke to her, and crowds of ladies in dresses so bright and beautiful that they dazzled her eyes; and the Prince was there kissing her, and in a minute they were married, and went floating off in a dance, which was so swift it did not feel so much like dancing as it did like being carried through the air by a gentle wind.

Through room after room,—there seemed no end to the rooms, and each one more beautiful than the last,—from garden to garden, some full of trees, some with beautiful lakes in them, some full of solid beds of flowers, they went, sometimes dancing, sometimes walking, sometimes, it seemed to the Little Sweetheart, floating. Every hour there was some new beautiful thing to see, some new beautiful thing to do. And the Prince never left her for more than a few minutes; and when he came back he brought her gifts and kissed her. Gifts upon gifts he kept bringing, till the Little Sweetheart's hands were so full she had to lay the things down on tables or window-sills, wherever she could find place for them, which was not easy, for all the rooms were so full of beautiful things that it was difficult to move about without knocking something down.

The hours flew by like minutes. The sun came up high in the heavens, but nobody seemed tired; nobody stopped; dance, dance, whirl, whirl, song and laughter, and ceaseless motion. That was all that was to be seen or heard in this wonderful Court to which the Little Sweetheart had been brought.

Noon came, but nothing stopped. Nobody left off dancing, and the musicians played faster than ever.

And so it was all the long afternoon and through the twilight; and as soon as it was really dark, all the rooms, and the gardens, and the lakes blazed out with millions of lamps, till it was lighter far than day, and the ladies' dresses, as they danced back and forth, shone and sparkled like butterflies' wings.

At last the lamps began, one by one, to go out, and by degrees a soft sort of light, like moonlight, settled down on the whole place, and the fine-dressed servants that had robed the Little Sweetheart in her white satin gown took it off, and put her to bed in a gold bedstead, with golden silk sheets.

"Oh," thought the Little Sweetheart, "I shall never go to sleep in the world; and I'm sure I don't want to! I shall just keep my eyes open all night and see what happens next."

All the beautiful clothes she had taken off were laid on a sofa near the bed—the white satin dress at top, and the big pink satin slipper, with its huge pearl buckle, on the floor, in plain sight. "Where is the other?" thought the Little Sweetheart. "I do believe I lost it off. That's the way they come to have so many odd ones. But, how queer! I lost off the tight one! But the big one was pinned to my foot," she said, speaking out loud before she thought. "That was what kept it on."

"You are talking in your sleep, my love," said the Prince, who was close by her side, kissing her.

"Indeed, I am not asleep at all! I haven't shut my eyes," said the Little Sweetheart.

And the next thing she knew it was broad daylight, the sun streaming into her room, and the air resounding in all directions with music and laughter, and flying steps of dancers, just as it had been yesterday.

The Little Sweetheart sat up in bed and looked around her. She thought it very strange that she was all alone, the Prince gone, no one there to attend to her; in a few moments more she noticed that all her clothes were gone too.

"Oh," she thought, "I suppose one never wears the same clothes twice in this Court, and they will bring me others. I hope there will be two slippers alike to-day."

Presently she began to grow impatient; but, being a timid little crea-ture, and having never before seen the inside of a Court or been a Prince's Sweetheart, she did not venture to stir or to make any sound, only sat still in her bed, waiting to see what would happen. At last she could not bear the sounds of the dancing, and laughing, and playing, and singing any longer. So she jumped up, and, rolling one of the golden silk sheets around her, looked out of the window. There they all were, the crowds of gay people, just as they had been the day before when she was among them, whirling, dancing, laughing, singing. The tears came into the Little Sweetheart's eyes as she gazed. What could it mean that she was deserted in this way, not even her clothes left for her? She was as much a prisoner in her room as if the door had been locked.

As hour after hour passed, a new misery began to oppress her. She was hungry, seriously, distressingly hungry. She had been too happy to eat, the day before! Though she had sipped and tasted many delicious bever-ages and viands, which the Prince had pressed upon her, she had not taken any substantial food, and now she began to feel faint for the want of it. As noon drew near, the time at which she was accustomed in her father's house to eat dinner, the pangs of her hunger grew unbearable.

"I can't bear it another minute," she said to herself. "I must and I will have something to eat. I will slip down by some back way to the kitchen. There must be a kitchen, I suppose."

So saying, she opened one of the doors and timidly peered into the next room. It chanced to be the room with the great glass cases full of fine gowns and laces, where she had been dressed by the obsequious attendants on the previous day. No one was in the room. Glancing fear-fully in all directions, she rolled the golden silk sheet tightly around her, and flew, rather than ran, across the floor, and took hold of the handle of one of the glass doors. Alas, it was locked. She tried another, another; all were locked. In despair she turned to fly back to her bedroom, when sud-denly she spied on the floor, in a corner close by the case where hung her beautiful white satin dress, a little heap of what looked like brown rags. She darted toward it, snatched it from the floor, and in a second more was safe back in her room; it was her own old stuff gown.

"What luck!" said the Little Sweetheart; "nobody will ever know me in this. I'll put it on and creep down the back stairs, and beg a mouthful of food from some of the servants, and they'll never know who I am; and then I'll go back to bed, and stay there till the Prince comes to fetch me. Of course, he will come before long; and if he comes and finds me gone, I hope he will be frightened half to death, and think I have been carried off by robbers!"

Poor foolish Little Sweetheart! It did not take her many seconds to slip into the ragged old stuff gown; then she crept out, keeping close to the walls, so that she could hide behind the furniture if any one saw her.

She listened cautiously at each door before she opened it, and turned away from some where she heard sounds of merry talking and laughing. In the third room that she entered she saw a sight that arrested her instantly and made her cry out in astonishment: a girl who looked so much like her that she might have been her own sister, and, what was stranger, wore a brown stuff gown exactly like her own, was busily at work in this room with a big broom killing spiders. As the Little Sweetheart appeared in the doorway, this girl looked up, and said: "Oh, ho! there you are, are you? I thought you'd be out before long." And then she laughed unpleasantly.

"Who are you?" said the Little Sweetheart, beginning to tremble all over.

"Oh, I'm a Prince's Sweetheart!" said the girl, laughing still more unpleasantly; and, leaning on her broom, she stared at the Little Sweetheart from top to toe.

"But—" began the Little Sweetheart.

"Oh, we're all Princes' Sweethearts!" interrupted several voices, coming all at once from different corners of the big room; and before the Little Sweetheart could get out another word, she found herself surrounded by half a dozen or more girls and women, all carrying brooms, and all laughing unpleasantly as they looked at her.

"What!" she gasped, as she gazed at their stuff gowns and their brooms. "You were all of you Princes' Sweethearts? Is it only for one day, then?"

"Only for one day," they all replied.

"And always after that do you have to kill spiders?" she cried.

"Yes; that or nothing," they said. "You see it is a great deal of work to keep all the rooms in this Court clean."

"Isn't it very dull work to kill spiders?" said the Little Sweetheart.

"Yes, very," they said, all speaking at once. "But it's better than sitting still, doing nothing."

"Don't the Princes ever speak to you?" sobbed the Little Sweetheart.

"Yes, sometimes," they answered.

Just then the Little Sweetheart's own Prince came hurrying by, all in armor from head to foot, splendid shining armor that clinked as he walked.

"Oh, there he is!" cried the Little Sweetheart, springing forward; then suddenly she recollected her stuff gown, and shrunk back into the group. But the Prince had seen her.

"Oh, how d'do!" he said kindly. "I was wondering what had become of you. Good-bye! I'm off for the grand review to-day. Don't tire yourself out over the spiders. Good-bye!" and he was gone.

"I hate him!" cried the Little Sweetheart, her eyes flashing, and her cheeks scarlet.

"Oh no, you don't!" exclaimed all the spider-sweepers. "That's the worst of it. You may think you do; but you don't. You love him all the time after you've once begun."

"I'll go home!" said the Little Sweetheart.

"You can't," said the others. "It is not permitted."

"Is it always just like this, in this Court?" she asked.

"Yes, always the same. One day just like another; all whirl and dance from morning till night, and new people coming and going all the time, and spiders most of all. You can't think how fast brooms wear out in this Court!"

"I'll die!" said the Little Sweetheart.

"Oh no, you won't!" they said. "There are some of us, in some of the rooms here, that are wrinkled and gray-haired. The most of the Sweethearts live to be old."

"Do they?" said the Little Sweetheart, and burst into tears.

"Heavens!" cried I, "what a dream!" as I opened my eyes. There stood the Little Sweetheart in my room, vanishing away, so vivid had been the dream. "A most extraordinary dream!" said I. "I will write it out. Some of the Princes may read it!"

Rebecca Harding Davis
(1831–1910)

From her youth in a rapidly expanding West Virginia factory town, Rebecca Harding Davis became one of the first American realist writers, consistently engaged with the rights of women, racial minorities, and the working class. Her exploration of the harshness of urban factory life in her first publication, "Life in the Iron Mills," which appeared in *The Atlantic Monthly* in 1861, created a sensation and strongly influenced other women writers including Elizabeth Phelps Ward. Because she needed to support her husband and three children (including future journalist Richard Harding Davis), Davis had to write frequently for popular magazines, leaving less time for her serious fiction. "Marcia" (1876) reflects her sense of the secret tragedies of female authorship.

Marcia (1876)

One winter morning a few years ago the mail brought me a roll of MS. (with one stamp too many, as if to bribe the post to care for so precious a thing) and a letter. Every publisher, editor, or even the obscurest of writers receives such packages so often as to know them at a glance. Half a dozen poems and a story—a blur of sunsets, duchesses, violets, bad French, and worse English; not a solid grain of common-sense, not a hint of reality or even of possibility, in the whole of it. The letter—truth in every word: formal, hard, practical, and the meaning of it a woman's cry for bread for her hungry children. Each woman who writes such a letter fancies she is the first, that its pathos will move hard-hearted editors, and that the extent of her need will supply the lack of wit, wisdom, or even grammar in her verses or story. Such appeals pour in literally by the thousand every year to every publishing office. The sickly daughter of a poor family; the wife of a drunken husband; a widow; children that must be fed and clothed. What was the critic's honest opinion of her work? how much would it bring in dollars and cents? etc., etc.

I did not open the letter that day. When we reach middle age we have learned, through rough experiences, how many tragedies there are in our street or under our own roof which will be none the better for our handling, and are apt, selfishly, to try to escape the hearing of them.

This letter, however, when I opened it next morning, proved to be not of a tragical sort. The writer was "not dependent on her pen for support"; she "had vowed herself to literature"; she "was resolved to assist in the Progress of humanity." Scarcely had I laid down the letter when I was told that she waited below to see me. The card she sent up was a bit of the fly-leaf of a book, cut oblong with scissors, and the name—Miss Barr—written in imitation of engraving. Her back was toward me when I came down, and I had time to read the same sham stylishness written all over her thin little person. The sleazy black silk was looped in the prevailing fashion, a sweeping white plume drooped from the cheap hat, and on her hands were washed cotton gloves.

Instead of the wizened features of the "dead beat" which I expected, she turned to me a child's face: an ugly face, I believe other women called it, but one of the most innocent and honest in the world. Her brown eyes met yours eagerly, full of a joyous good-fellowship for every thing and every body alive. She poured out her story, too, in a light-hearted way, and in the lowest, friendliest of voices. To see the girl was to be her ally. "People will do any thing for me—but publish my manuscripts," she said.

She came from Mississippi; had been the only white child on a poor plantation on the banks of the Yazoo. "I have only had such teaching as my mother could give: she had but two years with a governess. We had no books nor newspapers, except an occasional copy of a magazine sent to us by friends in the North." Her mother was the one central figure in the world to her then. In our after-intercourse she talked of her continually. "She is a little woman—less than I; but she has one of the finest minds in the world," she would cry. "The sight of any thing beautiful or the sound of music sways her as the wind does a reed. But she never was twenty miles from the plantation; she has read nothing, knows nothing. My father thinks women are like mares—only useful to bring forth children. My mother's children all died in babyhood but me. There she has lived all her life, with the swamp on one side and the forest of live-oak on the other: nothing to do, nothing to think of. Oh, it was frightful! With a mind like hers, any woman would go mad, with that eternal forest and swamp, and the graves of her dead babies just in sight! She rubbed snuff a good deal to quiet herself, but of late years she has taken opium."

"And you?"

"I left her. I hoped to do something for us both. My mind is not of as high order as hers, but it is very different from that of most women. I shall succeed some day," in the most matter-of-fact tones. "As soon as I knew that I was a poet I determined to come to Philadelphia and go straight to real publishers and real editors. In my country nobody had ever seen a man who had written a book. Ever since I came here I find how hard it is to find out any thing about the business of authorship. Medicine, or law, or blacksmithing—every body knows the workings of those trades, but people with pens in their hands keep the secret of their craft like Freemasons," laughing.

"You came alone?"

"Quite alone. I hired a little room over a baker's shop in Pine Street. They are a very decent couple, the baker and his wife. I board myself, and send out my manuscripts. They always come back to me."

"Where do you send them?"

"Oh, everywhere. I can show you printed forms of rejection from every magazine and literary newspaper in the country," opening and shutting again a black sachel on her lap. "I have written three novels, and sent them to the ——s' and ——s'. They sent them back as unavailable. But they never read them. I trick them this a-way: I put a loose blue thread between the third and fourth pages of the manuscript, and it is always there when it comes back." Her voice broke a little, but she winked her brown eyes and laughed bravely.

"How long have you been here?"

"Three years."

"Impossible! You are but a child."

"I am twenty. I had an article published once in a Sunday paper," producing a slip about two inches long.

Three years, and only that little grain of success! She had supported herself meanwhile, as I learned afterward, by sewing men's socks for a firm in Germantown.

"You are ready to give up now?"

"No; not if it were ten years instead of three."

Yet I can swear there was not a drop of New England blood in her little body. One was certain, against all reason, that she would succeed. When even such puny creatures as this take the world by the throat in that fashion, they are sure to conquer it.

Her books and poems must, I think, have seemed unique to any editor. The spelling was atrocious; the errors of grammar in every line beyond remedy. The lowest pupil in our public schools would have detected her ignorance on the first page. There was, too, in all she said or wrote an occasional gross indecency, such as a child might show: her life on the plantation explained it. Like Juliet, she spoke the language of her nurse. But even Shakespeare's nurse and Juliet would not be allowed nowadays to chatter at will in the pages of a family magazine.

But in all her ignorance, mistakes, and weaknesses there was no trace of imitation. She plagiarized nobody. There was none of the usual talk of countesses, heather, larks, or emotions of which she knew nothing. She painted over and over again her own home on the Yazoo: the hot still sunshine, the silence of noon, the swamp, the slimy living things in the stagnant ponds, the semi-tropical forest, the house and negro quarters, with all their dirt and dreary monotony. It was a picture which remained in the mind strong and vivid as a desert by Gérôme or a moor by Boughton.

There could be but one kind of advice to give her—to put away pen and ink, and for three years at least devote herself to hard study. She would, of course, have none of such counsel. The popular belief in the wings of genius, which can carry it over hard work and all such obstacles as ignorance of grammar or even the spelling-book, found in her a marked example. Work was for commonplace talent, not for those whose veins were full of the divine ichor.

Meanwhile she went on sewing socks, and sending off her great yellow envelopes, with stamps to bring them back.

"Stamps and paper count up so fast!" she said, with a laugh, into which had grown a pitiful quaver. She would take not a penny of aid. "I shall not starve. When the time has come for me to know that I have failed, I can go back to my own country and live like the other women there."

Meanwhile her case very nearly reached starvation. I remember few things more pathetic than the damp, forlorn little figure in a shabby waterproof, black sachel in hand, which used to come to my door through the snows and drenching rains that winter. Her shoes were broken, and her hands shriveled blue with cold. But a plated gilt chain or a scarlet ribbon used to flaunt somewhere over the meagre, scant poverty. Sometimes she brought news with her. She had work given her—to collect a column of jokes for a Sunday paper, by which she made three dollars a week. But she lost it from trying to insert her own matter, which could not well be reckoned as funny sayings. One day she came flushed with excitement. Somebody had taken her through the Academy of Design and a private gallery of engravings then on exhibition. She had a keen, just eye for form and color, and the feeling of a true artist for both.

"That is what I could have done," she said, after keeping silence a long while. "But what chance had I? I never even saw a picture at home, except those which were cut out of illustrated papers. There seemed to be no way for me but to write."

It was suggested to her that she might find the other way even now. Painting, designing, wood-engraving, were expressions for a woman's mind, even though, like her own, it was "one of the finest in the world."

She did not smile. "It is too late," she said. "I will go on as I have begun. But it is a pity my mother and I had not known of such things."

After that her light-hearted courage seemed to give way. She persevered, but it was with dogged, indomitable resolution, and little hope.

One day in the spring I was summoned to see a visitor on business. I found a tall, lank young man stalking up and down the room, the most noticeable point about him the shock of red hair and whisker falling over his neck and greasy coat collar. The face was that of an ignorant, small-minded man. But it was candid and not sensual.

He came straight toward me. "Is Marcia Barr here?"

"No; she has been gone for an hour."

He damned his luck in a white heat of rage, which must, I thought, have required some time to kindle. Indeed, I found he had been pacing up and down the street half the morning, having seen her come in. She had gone out by a side door.

"I caught a glimpse of her half a mile off. I have come to Philadelphia three times this year to find her. Good God! how rank poor she is! Where does she live?"

I could not tell him, as Marcia had long ago left the baker's, and changed her quarters every month.

"And I reckon I'll have to wait until she comes hyah again. Tell her it's Zack Biron, the overseer's son, on—on business."

He was not long in unveiling his business, which any woman would soon have guessed. He had come to bring Marcia home and marry her. He had always "wanted her," and the old colonel, her father, had promised he should marry her provided he could bring her back from her mad flight. The colonel was dead, and he was now "runnin' the plantation for ole madam. She's no better than a walkin' corpse, with that damned drug she chews. She can't keep still now: walks, walks incessant about the place, with her eyes set an' the skin clingin' to her bones. I couldn't 'a borne it, I ashuah you, but for the sake of findin' Marcia."

Two months passed, in which he haunted the house. But Marcia did not come. She had begun to frequent newspaper offices, and occasionally was given a trifling bit of work by the managers of the reporting corps—a description of the dresses at a Männerchor ball to write, or a puff of some coming play, etc. She came at last to tell me of what she had done.

"It is miserable work. I would rather sew the heels of stockings; but the stocking looms have stopped, and I must live a little longer, at any rate. I think I have something to say, if people only would hear it."

I told her of Biron and his chase for her.

"I saw him outside the window the last time I was here. That was the reason I went out by the side street. I knew he was looking for me. You will not tell him I have been here?"

"But, Marcia, the man seems honest and kindly—"

"If he found me," in the same quiet tone, "he would marry me and take me back to the plantation."

"And you are not ready to give up?"

"No, I will not give up. I shall get into the right groove at last," with the infectious little laugh which nobody could resist.

The waterproof cloak was worn down quite into the cotton by this time, and the straw hat had been darned around the ragged edge. But there was a cheap red rose in it. Her cheekbones showed high, and her eyes shone out of black hollows.

"No, I have no cough, and I don't need medicine," she said, irritably, when questioned. "I have had plenty of offers of help. But I'd rather steal than take alms." She rose hastily and buttoned her cloak.

"This man Biron waits only a word to come to you. He is faithful as a dog."

She nodded carelessly. Biron, or a return to her old home, held no part in her world, it was plain to see.

I was out of the city for several months. A few weeks after my return I saw in the evening paper one day, in the usual list of crimes and casualties, an item headed *"Pitiable Case.*—A young woman named Burr was arrested yesterday on charge of theft, and taken to the Central Station. About eleven o'clock the other women in the cell where she was confined perceiving that she lay on a bench breathing in a stertorous manner, summoned Lieutenant Pardy, who found life to be almost extinct. A physician was called, who discovered that the woman had swallowed some poisonous drug. With her first breath of returning consciousness she protested her innocence of the charge. She appears to have been in an extreme state of want. But little hope is entertained of her recovery. Miss Burr is favorably known, we believe, as a writer of some ability for the daily press."

In spite of the difference of name, it must be Marcia.

When we reached the Central Station we were told that her discharge was already procured. She had friends who knew what wires to work. In the outer room were half a dozen young men, reporters, a foreman of a printing-room, and one or two women, dramatic or musical critics. There is as eager an *esprit de corps* among that class of journalists as among actors. They were all talking loudly, and zealous in defense of "little Marty," as they called her, whom they declared to be "a dunce so far as head went, but pure and guileless as a child."

"I knew she was devilishly hard up," said one, "but never suspected she was starving. She would not borrow a dollar, she had that pride in her."

Marcia was still in the cell, lying on an iron stretcher. The Mississippian, Biron, was with her, kneeling on the floor in his shirt sleeves, chafing her hand. He had taken off his coat to wrap about her.

"I've a good Quaker nurse and a room ready for her at the Continental the minute she can be moved," he whispered. "Look a-here!" turning down the poor bit of lace and red ribbon at her throat, his big hairy hand shaking. "Them bones is a'most through the skin! The doctor says it's hunger—hunger! And I was eatin' three solid meals a day—like a beast!"

Hunger had almost done its work. There was but a feeble flicker of life left in the emaciated little body; not enough to know or speak to us when at last she opened her dull eyes.

"None o' them folks need consarn themselves any furder about her," said Biron, savagely. "She'll come home to her own now, thank God, and be done with rubbishy book-makers. Mrs. Biron will live like a lady."

Two or three weeks later, the most splendid of hired phaetons stopped at my door, and Mr. and Mrs. Biron sent up their cards. Mr. Biron was glowing with happiness. It asserted itself offensively somehow in the very jingling of his watch chain and tie of his cravat.

"We return immediately to the plantation," he said, grandiloquently. "I reckon largely on the effect of her native air in restorin' Mrs. Biron to health."

Marcia was magnificent in silk and plumes, the costliest that her owner's money could buy. Her little face was pale, however, and she looked nobody in the eye.

"We leave for the South to-morrow," she said, calmly, "and I shall not return to Philadelphia. I have no wish to return."

"Shall I send you books or papers, Marcia?"

"No, I thank you; nothing."

When they rose to go, her husband said, "Mrs. Biron has some— rubbish she wishes to leave with you. Hyah!" calling out of the window. "You nigger, bring that thah bag!"

It was the old black sachel. Marcia took it in her white-gloved hands, half opened it, shut it quickly, came up closer.

"These are my manuscripts," she said. "Will you burn them for me? All: do not leave a line, a word. I could not do it."

I took the sachel, and they departed. Mr. Biron was vehement in his protestations of friendship and invitations to visit the plantation. But Marcia did not say a word, even of farewell.

Louisa May Alcott
(1832–1888)

ouisa May Alcott is world-famous as the author of books for girls, especially *Little Women* (1868) and its sequels, *Little Men* (1871) and *Jo's Boys* (1886). But she was also a writer for adults, who published novels, short stories, and satiric memoirs under her own name, as well as pulp fiction under the pseudonym "A. M. Barnard." "My Contraband," first published as "The Brothers" in *The Atlantic Monthly* in November 1863, and retitled for *Hospital Sketches and Camp and Fireside Stories* (1869), drew on Alcott's experiences as an army nurse at the Union Hotel Hospital in Georgetown in the Civil War. She intended the story to be a realistic portrayal of a wounded Confederate officer and his "contraband" half-brother, a slave who had escaped to join the Union forces. In a letter from Concord, Massachusetts, to her abolitionist friend Thomas Wentworth Higginson, Alcott apologized for her efforts to represent African-American dialect: "I knew that my contraband did not talk as he should, for even in Washington I had no time to study the genuine dialect, & when the story was written here I had no one to tell me how it should be."

"Transcendental Wild Oats," published in *The Independent* in 1873, was a fictionalized memoir of the Alcott family's disastrous efforts to establish a utopian community at Fruitlands in Harvard, Massachusetts, in 1843, when Louisa was ten years old. For six months, a small group led by Bronson Alcott ("Abel Lamb") and the fierce British reformer Charles Lane ("Timon Lion") tried to raise their own vegetables and lead model lives of self-denial. But their ignorance of farming, along with the eccentricities of the original members and the increasing tyranny of Lane, brought the group as a whole to the edge of starvation and Bronson Alcott to a suicidal breakdown, from which he was rescued by the support of his wife Abby ("Sister Hope"). Although young Louisa realized how dangerous and reckless an experiment it had been, she turned her bitter memories into a hilarious satire of all such well-intended but naïve enterprises.

My Contraband (1863)

Doctor Franck came in as I sat sewing up the rents in an old shirt, that Tom might go tidily to his grave. New shirts were needed for the living, and there was no wife or mother to "dress him handsome when he went to meet the Lord," as one woman said, describing the fine funeral she had pinched herself to give her son.

"Miss Dane, I'm in a quandary," began the Doctor, with that expression of countenance which says as plainly as words, "I want to ask a favor, but I wish you'd save me the trouble."

"Can I help you out of it?"

"Faith! I don't like to propose it, but you certainly can, if you please."

"Then give it a name, I beg."

"You see a Reb has just been brought in crazy with typhoid; a bad case every way; a drunken, rascally little captain somebody took the trouble to capture, but whom nobody wants to take the trouble to cure. The wards are full, the ladies worked to death, and willing to be for our own boys, but rather slow to risk their lives for a Reb. Now you've had the fever, you like queer patients, your mate will see to your ward for a while, and I will find you a good attendant. The fellow won't last long, I fancy; but he can't die without some sort of care, you know. I've put him in the fourth story of the west wing, away from the rest. It is airy, quiet, and comfortable there. I'm on that ward, and will do my best for you in every way. Now, then, will you go?"

"Of course I will, out of perversity, if not common charity; for some of these people think that because I'm an abolitionist I am also a heathen, and I should rather like to show them that, though I cannot quite love my enemies, I am willing to take care of them."

"Very good; I thought you'd go; and speaking of abolition reminds me that you can have a contraband for servant, if you like. It is that fine mulatto fellow who was found burying his Rebel master after the fight, and, being badly cut over the head, our boys brought him along. Will you have him?"

"By all means,—for I'll stand to my guns on that point, as on the other; these black boys are far more faithful and handy than some of the white scamps given me to serve, instead of being served by. But is this man well enough?"

"Yes, for that sort of work, and I think you'll like him. He must have been a handsome fellow before he got his face slashed; not much darker than myself; his master's son, I dare say, and the white blood makes him rather high and haughty about some things. He was in a bad way when he came in, but vowed he'd die in the street rather than turn in with the black fellows below; so I put him up in the west wing, to be out of the way, and he's seen to the captain all the morning. When can you go up?"

"As soon as Tom is laid out, Skinner moved, Haywood washed, Marble dressed, Charley rubbed, Downs taken up, Upham laid down, and the whole forty fed."

We both laughed, though the Doctor was on his way to the dead-house and I held a shroud on my lap. But in a hospital one learns that cheerfulness is one's salvation; for, in an atmosphere of suffering and death, heaviness of heart would soon paralyze usefulness of hand, if the blessed gift of smiles had been denied us.

In an hour I took possession of my new charge, finding a dissipated-looking boy of nineteen or twenty raving in the solitary little room, with no one near him but the contraband in the room adjoining. Feeling decidedly more interest in the black man than in the white, yet remembering the Doctor's hint of his being "high and haughty," I glanced furtively at him as I scattered chloride of lime about the room to purify the air, and settled matters to suit myself. I had seen many contrabands, but never one so attractive as this. All colored men are called "boys," even if their heads are white; this boy was five-and-twenty at least, strong-limbed and manly, and had the look of one who never had been cowed by abuse or worn with oppressive labor. He sat on his bed doing nothing; no book, no pipe, no pen or paper anywhere appeared, yet anything less indolent or listless than his attitude and expression I never saw. Erect he sat, with a hand on either knee, and eyes fixed on the bare wall opposite, so rapt in some absorbing thought as to be unconscious of my presence, though the door stood wide open and my movements were by no means noiseless. His face was half averted, but I instantly approved the Doctor's taste, for the profile which I saw possessed all the attributes of comeliness belonging to his mixed race. He was more quadroon than mulatto, with Saxon features, Spanish complexion, darkened by exposure, color in lips and cheek, waving hair, and an eye full of the passionate melancholy which in such men always seems to utter a mute protest against the broken law that doomed them at their birth. What could he be thinking of? The sick boy cursed and raved, I rustled to and fro, steps passed the door, bells rang, and the steady rumble of army-wagons came up from the street, still he never stirred. I had seen colored people in what they call "the black sulks," when, for days, they neither smiled nor spoke, and scarcely ate. But this was something more than that; for the man was not dully brooding over some small grievance; he seemed to see an all-absorbing fact or fancy recorded on the wall, which was a blank to me. I wondered if it were some deep wrong or sorrow, kept alive by memory and impotent regret; if he mourned for the dead master to whom he had been faithful to the end; or if the liberty now his were robbed of half its sweetness by the knowledge that someone near and dear to him still languished in the hell from which he had escaped. My heart warmed to him at that idea; I wanted to know and comfort him; and, following the impulse of the moment, I went in and touched him on the shoulder.

In an instant the man vanished and the slave appeared. Freedom was too new a boon to have wrought its blessed changes yet, and as he started up, with his hand at his temple, and an obsequious "Yes, Missis," any romance that had gathered round him fled away, leaving the saddest of all sad facts in living guise before me. Not only did the manhood seem to die out of him, but the comeliness that first attracted me; for, as he turned, I saw the ghastly wound that had laid open cheek and forehead. Being partly healed, it was no longer bandaged, but held together with strips of that transparent plaster which I never see without a shiver, and swift recollections of the scenes with which it is associated in my mind. Part of his black hair had been shorn away, and one eye was nearly closed; pain so distorted, and the cruel sabre-cut so marred that portion of his face, that, when I saw it, I felt as if a fine medal had been suddenly reversed, showing me a far more striking type of human suffering and wrong than Michelangelo's bronze prisoner. By one of those inexplicable processes that often teach us how little we understand ourselves, my purpose was suddenly changed; and, though I went in to offer comfort as a friend, I merely gave an order as a mistress.

"Will you open these windows? This man needs more air."

He obeyed at once, and, as he slowly urged up the unruly sash, the handsome profile was again turned toward me, and again I was possessed by my first impression so strongly that I involuntarily said,—

"Thank you."

Perhaps it was fancy, but I thought that in the look of mingled surprise and something like reproach which he gave me, there was also a trace of grateful pleasure. But he said, in that tone of spiritless humility these poor souls learn so soon,—

"I isn't a white man, Missis, I'se a contraband."

"Yes, I know it; but a contraband is a free man, and I heartily congratulate you."

He liked that; his face shone, he squared his shoulders, lifted his head, and looked me full in the eye with a brisk,—

"Thank ye, Missis; anything more to do fer yer?"

"Doctor Franck thought you would help me with this man, as there are many patients and few nurses or attendants. Have you had the fever?"

"No, Missis."

"They should have thought of that when they put him here; wounds and fevers should not be together. I'll try to get you moved."

He laughed a sudden laugh: if he had been a white man, I should have called it scornful; as he was a few shades darker than myself, I suppose it must be considered an insolent, or at least an unmannerly one.

"It don't matter, Missis. I'd rather be up here with the fever than down with those niggers; and there isn't no other place fer me."

Poor fellow! that was true. No ward in all the hospital would take him in to lie side by side with the most miserable white wreck there. Like the bat in Æsop's fable, he belonged to neither race; and the pride of one, the helplessness of the other, kept him hovering alone in the twilight a great sin has brought to overshadow the whole land.

"You shall stay, then; for I would far rather have you than my lazy Jack. But are you well and strong enough?"

"I guess I'll do, Missis."

He spoke with a passive sort of acquiescence,—as if it did not much matter, if he were not able, and no one would particularly rejoice, if he were.

"Yes, I think you will. By what name shall I call you?"

"Bob, Missis."

Every woman has her pet whim; one of mine was to teach the men self-respect by treating them respectfully. Tom, Dick and Harry would pass, when lads rejoiced in those familiar abbreviations; but to address men often old enough to be my father in that style did not suit my old-fashioned ideas of propriety. This "Bob" would never do; I should have found it as easy to call the chaplain "Gus" as my tragical-looking contra-band by a title so strongly associated with the tail of a kite.

"What is your other name?" I asked. "I like to call my attendants by their last names rather than by their first."

"I've got no other, Missis; we have our masters' names, or do without. Mine's dead, and I won't have anything of his 'bout me."

"Well, I'll call you Robert, then, and you may fill this pitcher for me, if you will be so kind."

He went; but, through all the tame obedience years of servitude had taught him, I could see that the proud spirit his father gave him was not yet subdued, for the look and gesture with which he repudiated his master's name were a more effective declaration of independence than any Fourth-of-July orator could have prepared.

We spent a curious week together. Robert seldom left his room, except upon my errands; and I was a prisoner all day, often all night, by the bedside of the Rebel. The fever burned itself rapidly away, for there seemed little vitality to feed it in the feeble frame of this old young man, whose life had been none of the most righteous, judging from the revelations made by his unconscious lips; since more than once Robert authoritatively silenced him, when my gentler hushings were of no avail, and blasphemous wanderings or ribald camp-songs made my cheeks burn and Robert's face assume an aspect of disgust. The captain was the gentleman in the world's eye, but the contraband was the gentleman in mine;—I was a fanatic, and that accounts for such depravity of taste, I hope. I never asked Robert of himself, feeling that somewhere there was a spot still too sore to bear the lightest touch; but, from his language, manner, and intelligence, I inferred that his color had procured for him the few advantages within the reach of a quick-witted, kindly-treated slave. Silent, grave, and thoughtful, but most serviceable, was my contraband; glad of the books I brought him, faithful in the performance of the duties I assigned to him, grateful for the friendliness I could not but feel and show toward him. Often I longed to ask what purpose was so visibly altering his aspect with such daily deepening gloom. But I never dared, and no one else had either time or desire to pry into the past of this specimen of one branch of the chivalrous "F.F.Vs."

On the seventh night, Dr. Franck suggested that it would be well for some one, besides the general watchman of the ward, to be with the captain, as it might be his last. Although the greater part of the two preceding nights had been spent there, of course I offered to remain,—for there is a strange fascination in these scenes, which renders one careless of fatigue and unconscious of fear until the crisis is passed.

"Give him water as long as he can drink, and if he drops into a natural sleep, it may save him. I'll look in at midnight, when some change will probably take place. Nothing but sleep or a miracle will keep him now. Good-night."

Away went the Doctor; and, devouring a whole mouthful of grapes, I lowered the lamp, wet the captain's head, and sat down on a hard stool to begin my watch. The captain lay with his hot, haggard face turned toward me, filling the air with his poisonous breath, and feebly muttering, with lips and tongue so parched that the sanest speech would have been difficult to understand. Robert was stretched on his bed in the inner room, the door of which stood ajar, that a fresh draught from his open window might carry the fever-fumes away through mine. I could just see a long, dark figure, with the lighter outline of a face, and, having little else to do just then I fell to thinking of this curious contraband, who evidently prized his freedom highly, yet seemed in no haste to enjoy it. Doctor Franck had offered to send him on to safer quarters, but he had said, "No, thank yer, sir, not yet," and then had gone away to fall into one of those black moods of his, which began to disturb me, because I had no power to lighten them. As I sat listening to the clocks from the steeples all about us, I amused myself with planning Robert's future, as I often did my own, and had dealt out to him a generous hand of trumps wherewith to play this game of life which hitherto had gone so cruelly against him, when a harsh, choked voice called,—

"Lucy!"

It was the captain, and some new terror seemed to have gifted him with momentary strength.

"Yes, here's Lucy," I answered, hoping that by the following fancy I might quiet him,—for his face was damp with the clammy moisture, and his frame shaken with the nervous tremor that so often precedes death. His dull eye fixed upon me, dilating with a bewildered look of incredulity and wrath, till he broke out fiercely,—

"That's a lie! she's dead,—and so's Bob, damn him!"

Finding speech a failure, I began to sing the quiet tune that had often soothed delirium like this; but hardly had the line,—

"See gentle patience smile on pain,"

passed my lips, when he clutched me by the wrist, whispering like one in mortal fear,—

"Hush! she used to sing that way to Bob, but she never would to me. I swore I'd whip the devil out of her, and I did; but you know before she cut her throat she said she'd haunt me, and there she is!"

He pointed behind me with an aspect of such pale dismay, that I involuntarily glanced over my shoulder and started as if I had seen a veritable ghost; for, peering from the gloom of that inner room, I saw a shadowy face, with dark hair all about it, and a glimpse of scarlet at the throat. An instant showed me that it was only Robert leaning from his bed's-foot, wrapped in a gray army-blanket, with his red shirt just visible above it, and his long hair disordered by sleep. But what a strange expression was on his face! The unmarred side was toward me, fixed and motionless as when I first observed it,—less absorbed now, but more intent. His eye glittered, his lips were apart like one who listened with every sense, and his whole aspect reminded me of a hound to which some wind had brought the scent of unsuspected prey.

"Do you know him, Robert? Does he mean you?"

"Laws, no, Missis; they all own half-a-dozen Bobs: but hearin' my name woke me; that's all."

He spoke quite naturally, and lay down again, while I returned to my charge, thinking that this paroxysm was probably his last. But by another hour I perceived a hopeful change; for the tremor had subsided, the cold dew was gone, his breathing was more regular, and Sleep, the healer, had descended to save or take him gently away. Doctor Franck looked in at midnight, bade me keep all cool and quiet, and not fail to administer a certain draught as soon as the captain woke. Very much relieved, I laid my head on my arms, uncomfortably folded on the little table, and fancied I was about to perform one of the feats which practice renders possible,—"sleeping with one eye open," as we say: a half-and-half doze, for all senses sleep but that of hearing; the faintest murmur, sigh, or motion will break it, and give one back one's wits much brightened by the brief permission to "stand at ease." On this night, the experiment was a failure, for previous vigils, confinement, and much care had rendered naps a dangerous indulgence. Having roused half-a-dozen times in an hour to find all quiet, I dropped my heavy head on my arms, and, drowsily resolving to look up again in fifteen minutes, fell fast asleep.

The striking of a deep-voiced clock woke me with a start. "That is one," thought I; but, to my dismay, two more strokes followed, and in remorseful haste I sprang up to see what harm my long oblivion had done. A strong hand put me back into my seat, and held me there. It was Robert. The instant my eye met his my heart began to beat, and all along my nerves tingled that electric flash which foretells a danger that we cannot see. He was very pale, his mouth grim, and both eyes full of sombre fire; for even the wounded one was open now, all the more sinister for the deep scar above and below. But his touch was steady, his voice quiet, as he said,—

"Sit still, Missis; I won't hurt yer, nor scare yer, ef I can help it, but yer waked too soon."

"Let me go, Robert,—the captain is stirring,—I must give him something."

"No, Missis, yer can't stir an inch. Look here!"

Holding me with one hand, with the other he took up the glass in which I had left the draught, and showed me it was empty.

"Has he taken it?" I asked, more and more bewildered.

"I flung it out o' winder, Missis; he'll have to do without."

"But why, Robert? why did you do it?"

"Kase I hate him!"

Impossible to doubt the truth of that; his whole face showed it, as he spoke through his set teeth, and launched a fiery glance at the unconscious captain. I could only hold my breath and stare blankly at him, wondering what mad act was coming next. I suppose I shook and turned white, as women have a foolish habit of doing when sudden danger daunts them; for Robert released my arm, sat down upon the bedside just in front of me, and said, with the ominous quietude that made me cold to see and hear,—

"Don't yer be frightened, Missis; don't try to run away, fer the door's locked and the key in my pocket; don't yer cry out, fer yer'd have to scream a long while, with my hand on yer mouth, 'efore yer was heard. Be still, an' I'll tell yer what I'm gwine to do."

"Lord help us! he has taken the fever in some sudden, violent way, and is out of his head. I must humor him till someone comes"; in pursuance of which swift determination, I tried to say, quite composedly,—

"I will be still and hear you; but open the window. Why did you shut it?"

"I'm sorry I can't do it, Missis; but yer'd jump out, or call, if I did, an' I'm not ready yet. I shut it to make yer sleep, an' heat would do it quicker'n anything else I could do."

The captain moved, and feebly muttered, "Water!" Instinctively I rose to give it to him, but the heavy hand came down upon my shoulder, and in the same decided tone Robert said,—

"'The water went with the physic; let him call."

"Do let me go to him! he'll die without care!"

"I mean he shall;—don't yer meddle, if yer please, Missis."

In spite of his quiet tone and respectful manner, I saw murder in his eyes, and turned faint with fear; yet the fear excited me, and, hardly knowing what I did, I seized the hands that had seized me, crying,—

"No, no, you shall not kill him! it is base to hurt a helpless man. Why do you hate him? He is not your master."

"He's my brother."

I felt that answer from head to foot, and seemed to fathom what was coming, with a prescience vague, but unmistakable. One appeal was left to me, and I made it.

"Robert, tell me what it means? Do not commit a crime and make me accessory to it. There is a better way of righting wrong than by violence;—let me help you find it."

My voice trembled as I spoke, and I heard the frightened flutter of my heart; so did he, and if any little act of mine had ever won affection or respect from him, the memory of it served me then. He looked down, and seemed to put some question to himself; whatever it was, the answer was in my favor, for when his eyes rose again, they were gloomy, but not desperate.

"I *will* tell yer, Missis; but mind, this makes no difference; the boy is mine. I'll give the Lord a chance to take him fust; if He don't, I shall."

"Oh, no! remember, he is your brother."

An unwise speech; I felt it as it passed my lips, for a black frown gathered on Robert's face, and his strong hands closed with an ugly sort of grip. But he did not touch the poor soul gasping there behind him, and seemed content to let the slow suffocation of that stifling room end his frail life.

"I'm not like to forgit dat, Missis, when I've been thinkin' of it all this week. I knew him when they fetched him in, an' would 'a' done it long 'fore this, but I wanted to ask where Lucy was; he knows,—he told - to-night,—an' now he's done for."

"Who is Lucy?" I asked hurriedly, intent on keeping his mind busy with any thought but murder.

With one of the swift transitions of a mixed temperament like this, at my question Robert's deep eyes filled, the clenched hands were spread before his face, and all I heard were the broken words,—

"My wife,—he took her—"

In that instant every thought of fear was swallowed up in burning indignation for the wrong, and a perfect passion of pity for the desperate man so tempted to avenge an injury for which there seemed no redress but this. He was no longer slave or contraband, no drop of black blood marred him in my sight, but an infinite compassion yearned to save, to help, to comfort him. Words seemed so powerless I offered none, only put my hand on his poor head, wounded, homeless, bowed down with grief for which I had no cure, and softly smoothed the long neglected hair, pitifully wondering the while where was the wife who must have loved this tender-hearted man so well.

The captain moaned again, and faintly whispered, "Air!" but I never stirred. God forgive me! just then I hated him as only a woman thinking of a sister woman's wrong could hate. Robert looked up; his eyes were dry again, his mouth grim. I saw that, said, "Tell me more," and he did; for sympathy is a gift the poorest may give, the proudest stoop to receive.

"Yer see, Missis, his father,—I might say ours, if I warn't ashamed of both of 'em,—his father died two years ago, an' left us all to Marster Ned,—that's him here, eighteen then. He always hated me, I looked so like old Marster: he don't,—only the light skin an' hair. Old Marster was kind to all of us, me 'specially, an' bought Lucy off the next plantation down there in South Car'lina, when he found I liked her. I married her, all I could; it warn't much, but we was true to one another till Marster Ned come home a year after an' made hell fer both of us. He sent my old mother to be used up in his rice-swamp in Georgy; he found me with my pretty Lucy, an' though young Miss cried, an I prayed to him on my knees, an' Lucy run away, he wouldn't have no mercy; he brought her back, an'—took her."

"Oh! what did you do?" I cried, hot with helpless pain and passion.

How the man's outraged heart sent the blood flaming up into his face and deepened the tones of his impetuous voice, as he stretched his arm across the bed, saying, with a terribly expressive gesture,—

"I half murdered him, an' to-night I'll finish."

"Yes, yes,—but go on now; what came next?"

He gave me a look that showed no white man could have felt a deeper degradation in remembering and confessing these last acts of brotherly oppression.

"They whipped me till I couldn't stand, an' then they sold me further South. Yer thought I was a white man once;—look here!"

With a sudden wrench he tore the shirt from neck to waist, and on his strong brown shoulders showed me furrows deeply ploughed, wounds which, though healed, were ghastlier to me than any in that house. I could not speak to him, and, with the pathetic dignity a great grief lends the humblest sufferer, he ended his brief tragedy by simply saying,—

"That's all, Missis. I'se never seen her since, an' now I never shall in this world,—maybe not in t'other."

"But, Robert, why think her dead? The captain was wandering when he said those sad things; perhaps he will retract them when he is sane. Don't despair; don't give up yet."

"No, Missis, I 'spect he's right; she was too proud to bear that long. It's like her to kill herself. I told her to, if there was no other way; an' she always minded me, Lucy did. My poor girl! Oh, it warn't right! No, by God, it warn't!"

As the memory of this bitter wrong, this double bereavement, burned in his sore heart, the devil that lurks in every strong man's blood leaped up; he put his hand upon his brother's throat, and, watching the white face before him, muttered low between his teeth,—

"I'm lettin' him go too easy; there's no pain in this; we a'n't even yet. I wish he knew me. Marster Ned! it's Bob; where's Lucy?"

From the captain's lips there came a long faint sigh, and nothing but a flutter of the eyelids showed that he still lived. A strange stillness filled the room as the elder brother held the younger's life suspended in his hand, while wavering between a dim hope and a deadly hate. In the whirl of thoughts that went on in my brain, only one was clear enough to act upon. I must prevent murder, if I could,—but how? What could I do up there alone, locked in with a dying man and a lunatic?—for any mind yielded utterly to any unrighteous impulse is mad while the impulse rules it. Strength I had not, nor much courage, neither time nor wit for stratagem, and chance only could bring me help before it was too late. But one weapon I possessed,—a tongue,—often a woman's best defense; and sympathy, stronger than fear, gave me power to use it. What I said Heaven only knows, but surely Heaven helped me; words burned on my lips, tears streamed from my eyes, and some good angel prompted me to use the one name that had power to arrest my hearer's hand and touch his heart. For at that moment I heartily believed that Lucy lived, and this earnest faith roused in him a like belief.

He listened with the lowering look of one in whom brute instinct was sovereign for the time,—a look that makes the noblest countenance base. He was but a man,—a poor, untaught, outcast, outraged man. Life had few joys for him; the world offered him no honors, no success, no home, no love. What future would this crime mar? and why should he deny himself that sweet, yet bitter morsel called revenge? How many white men, with all New England's freedom, culture, Christianity, would not have felt as he felt then? Should I have reproached him for a human anguish, a human longing for redress, all now left him from the ruin of his few poor hopes? Who had taught him that self-control, self-sacrifice, are attributes that make men masters of the earth and lift them nearer Heaven? Should I have urged the beauty of forgiveness, the duty of devout submission? He had no religion, for he was no saintly "Uncle Tom," and Slavery's black shadow seemed to darken all the world to him and shut out God. Should I have warned him of penalties, of judgments, and the potency of law? What did he know of justice, or the mercy that should temper that stern virtue, when every law, human and divine, had been broken on his hearthstone? Should I have tried to touch him by appeals to filial duty, to brotherly love? How had his appeals been answered? What memories had father and brother stored up in his heart to plead for either now? No,—all these influences, these associations, would have proved worse than useless, had I been calm enough to try them. I was not; but instinct, subtler than reason, showed me the one safe clue by which to lead this troubled soul from the labyrinth in which it groped and nearly fell. When I paused, breathless, Robert turned to me, asking, as if human assurances could strengthen his faith in Divine Omnipotence,—

"Do you believe, if I let Marster Ned live, the Lord will give me back my Lucy?"

"As surely as there is a Lord, you will find her here or in the beautiful hereafter, where there is no black or white, no master and no slave."

He took his hand from his brother's throat, lifted his eyes from my face to the wintry sky beyond, as if searching for that blessed country, happier even than the happy North. Alas, it was the darkest hour before the dawn!—there was no star above, no light below but the pale glimmer of the lamp that showed the brother who had made him desolate. Like a blind man who believes there is a sun, yet cannot see it, he shook his head, let his arms drop nervelessly upon his knees, and sat there dumbly asking that question which many a soul whose faith is firmer fixed than his had asked in hours less dark than this,—"Where is God?" I saw the tide had turned, and strenuously tried to keep this rudderless life-boat from slipping back into the whirlpool wherein it had been so nearly lost.

"I have listened to you, Robert; now hear me, and heed what I say, because my heart is full of pity for you, full of hope for your future, and a desire to help you now. I want you to go away from here, from the temptation of this place, and the sad thoughts that haunt it. You have conquered yourself once, and I honor you for it, because, the harder the battle, the more glorious the victory; but it is safer to put a greater distance between you and this man. I will write you letters, give you money, and send you to good old Massachusetts to begin your new life a freeman,—yes, and a happy man; for when the captain is himself again, I will learn where Lucy is, and move heaven and earth to find and give her back to you. Will you do this, Robert?"

Slowly, very slowly, the answer came; for the purpose of a week, perhaps a year, was hard to relinquish in an hour.

"Yes, Missis, I will."

"Good! Now you are the man I thought you, and I'll work for you with all my heart. You need sleep, my poor fellow; go, and try to forget.

The captain is still alive, and as yet you are spared that sin. No, don't look there; I'll care for him. Come, Robert, for Lucy's sake."

Thank Heaven for the immortality of love! for when all other means of salvation failed, a spark of this vital fire softened the man's iron will until a woman's hand could bend it. He let me take from him the key, let me draw him gently away and lead him to the solitude which now was the most healing balm I could bestow. Once in his little room, he fell down on his bed and lay there, as if spent with the sharpest conflict of his life. I slipped the bolt across his door, and unlocked my own, flung up the window, steadied myself with a breath of air, then rushed to Doctor Franck. He came; and till dawn we worked together, saving one brother's life, and taking earnest thought how best to secure the other's liberty. When the sun came up as blithely as if it shone only upon happy homes, the Doctor went to Robert. For an hour I heard the murmur of their voices; once I caught the sound of heavy sobs, and for a time reverent hush, as if in the silence that good man were ministering to soul as well as sense. When he departed he took Robert with him, pausing to tell me he should get him off as soon as possible, but not before we met again.

Nothing more was seen of them all day; another surgeon came to see the captain, and another attendant came to fill the empty place. I tried to rest, but could not, with the thought of poor Lucy tugging at my heart, and was soon back at my post again, anxiously hoping that my contraband had not been too hastily spirited away. Just as night fell there came a tap, and, opening, I saw Robert literally "clothed, and in his right mind." The Doctor had replaced the ragged suit with tidy garments, and no trace of that tempestuous night remained but deeper lines upon the forehead and the docile look of a repentant child. He did not cross the threshold, did not offer me his hand,—only took off his cap, saying, with a traitorous falter in his voice,—

"God bless yer, Missis! I'm gwine."

I put out both my hands, and held his fast.

"Good-by, Robert! Keep up good heart, and when I come home to Massachusetts we'll meet in a happier place than this. Are you quite ready, quite comfortable for your journey?"

"Yes, Missis, yes; the Doctor's fixed everything! I'se gwine with a friend of his; my papers are all right, an' I'm as happy as I can be till I find"—

He stopped there; then went on, with a glance into the room,—

"I'm glad I didn't do it, an' I thank yer, Missis, fer hinderin' me,—thank yer hearty; but I'm afraid I hate him jest the same."

Of course he did; and so did I; for these faulty hearts of ours cannot turn perfect in a night, but need frost and fire, wind and rain, to ripen and make them ready for the great harvest-home. Wishing to divert his mind, I put my poor mite into his hand, and, remembering the magic of a certain little book, I gave him mine, on whose dark cover whitely shone the Virgin Mother and the Child, the grand history of whose life the book contained. The money went into Robert's pocket with a grateful murmur, the book into his bosom, with a long look and a tremulous—

"I never saw *my* baby, Missis."

I broke down then; and though my eyes were too dim to see, I felt the touch of lips upon my hands, heard the sound of departing feet, and knew my contraband was gone.

When one feels an intense dislike, the less one says about the subject of it the better; therefore I shall merely record that the captain lived,—in time was exchanged; and that, whoever the other party was, I am convinced the Government got the best of the bargain. But long before this occurred, I had fulfilled my promise to Robert; for as soon as my patient recovered strength of memory enough to make his answer trustworthy, I asked, without any circumlocution,—

"Captain Fairfax, where is Lucy?"

And too feeble to be angry, surprised or insincere, he straightway answered,—

"Dead, Miss Dane."

"And she killed herself, when you sold Bob?"

"How the devil did you know that?" he muttered, with an expression half-remorseful, half-amazed; but I was satisfied, and said no more.

Of course, this went to Robert, waiting far away there in a lonely home,—waiting, working, hoping for his Lucy. It almost broke my heart to do it; but delay was weak, deceit was wicked; so I sent the heavy tidings, and very soon the answer came,—only three lines; but I felt that the sustaining power of the man's life was gone.

"I tort I'd never see her any more; I'm glad to know she's out of trouble. I thank yer, Missis; an' if they let us, I'll fight fer yer till I'm killed, which I hope will be 'fore long."

Six months later he had his wish, and kept his word.

Every one knows the story of the attack on Fort Wagner; but we should not tire yet of recalling how our Fifty-Fourth, spent with three sleepless nights, a day's fast, and a march under the July sun, stormed the fort as night fell, facing death in many shapes, following their brave leaders through a fiery rain of shot and shell, fighting valiantly for "God and Governor Andrew,"—how the regiment that went into action seven hundred strong, came out having had nearly half its number captured, killed, or wounded, leaving their young commander to be buried, like a chief of earlier times, with his body-guard around him, faithful to the death. Surely, the insult turns to honor, and the wide grave needs no monument but the heroism that consecrates it in our sight; surely, the hearts that held him nearest, see through their tears a noble victory in the seeming sad defeat; and surely, God's benediction was bestowed, when this loyal soul answered, as Death called the roll, "Lord, here am I, with the brothers Thou has given me!"

The future must show how well that fight was fought; for though Fort Wagner still defies us, public prejudice is down; and through the cannon-smoke of that black night the manhood of the colored race shines before many eyes that would not see, rings in many ears that would not hear, wins many hearts that would not hitherto believe.

When the news came that we were needed, there was none so glad as I to leave teaching contrabands, the new work I had taken up, and go to nurse "our boys," as my dusky flock so proudly called the wounded of the Fifty-Fourth. Feeling more satisfaction, as I assumed my big apron and turned up my cuffs, than if dressing for the President's levee, I fell to work in Hospital No. ID in Beaufort. The scene was most familiar, and yet strange; for only dark faces looked up at me from the pallets so thickly laid along the floor, and I missed the sharp accent of my Yankee boys in the slower, softer voices calling cheerily to one another, or answering my questions with a stout, "We'll never give it up, Missis, till the last Reb's dead," or, "If our people's free, we can afford to die."

Passing from bed to bed, intent on making one pair of hands do the work of three, at least, I gradually washed, fed, and bandaged my way down the long line of sable heroes, and coming to the very last, found that he was my contraband. So old, so worn, so deathly weak and wan, I never should have known him but for the deep scar on his cheek. That side lay uppermost, and caught my eye at once; but even then I doubted, such an awful change had come upon him, when, turning to the ticket just above his head, I saw the name, "Robert Dane." That both assured and touched me, for, remembering that he had no name, I knew that he had taken mine. I longed for him to speak to me, to tell how he had fared since I lost sight of him, and let me perform some little service for him in return for many he had done for me; but he seemed asleep; and as I stood re-living that strange night again, a bright lad, who lay next him softly waving an old fan across both beds, looked up and said,—

"I guess you know him, Missis?"

"You are right. Do you?"

"As much as any one was able to, Missis."

"Why do you say 'was,' as if the man were dead and gone?"

"I s'pose because I know he'll have to go. He's got a bad jab in the breast an' is bleedin' inside, the Doctor says. He don't suffer any, only gets weaker 'n' weaker every minute. I've been fannin' him this long while, an' he's talked a little; but he don't know me now, so he's most gone, I guess."

There was so much sorrow and affection in the boy's face, that I remembered something, and asked, with redoubled interest,—

"Are you the one that brought him off? I was told about a boy who nearly lost his life in saving that of his mate."

I dare say the young fellow blushed, as any modest lad might have done; I could not see it, but I heard the chuckle of satisfaction that escaped him, as he glanced from his shattered arm and bandaged side to the pale figure opposite.

"Lord, Missis, that's nothin'; we boys always stan' by one another, an' I warn't goin' to leave him to be tormented any more by them cussed Rebs. He's been a slave once, though he don't look half so much like it as me, an' I was born in Boston."

He did not; for the speaker was as black as the ace of spaces,—being a sturdy specimen, the knave of clubs would perhaps be a fitter representative,—but the dark freeman looked at the white slave with the pitiful, yet puzzled expression I have so often seen on the faces of our wisest men, when this tangled question of Slavery presents itself, asking to be cut or patiently undone.

"Tell me what you know of this man; for, even if he were awake, he is too weak to talk."

"I never saw him till I joined the regiment, an' no one 'peared to have got much out of him. He was a shut-up sort of feller, an' didn't seem to care for anything but gettin' at the Rebs. Some say he was the fust man of us that enlisted; I know he fretted till we were off, an' when we pitched into old Wagner, he fought like the devil."

"Were you with him when he was wounded? How was it?"

"Yes, Missis. There was somethin' queer about it; for he 'peared to know the chap that killed him, an' the chap knew him. I don't dare to ask, but I rather guess one owned the other some time; for, when they clinched, the chap sung out, 'Bob!' an' Dane, 'Marster Ned!'—then they went at it."

I sat down suddenly, for the old anger and compassion struggled in my heart, and I both longed and feared to hear what was to follow.

"You see, when the Colonel—Lord keep an' send him back to us!—it a'n't certain yet, you know, Missis, though it's two days ago we lost him,—well, when the Colonel shouted, 'Rush on, boys, rush on!' Dane tore away as if he was goin' to take the fort alone; I was next him, an' kept close as we went through the ditch an' up the wall. Hi! warn't that a rusher!" and the boy flung up his well arm with a whoop, as if the mere memory of that stirring moment came over him in a gust of irrepressible excitement.

"Were you afraid?" I said, asking the question women often put, and receiving the answer they seldom fail to get.

"No, Missis!"—emphasis on the "Missis,"—"I never thought of anything but the damn' Rebs, that scalp, slash, an' cut our ears off, when they git us. I was bound to let daylight into one of 'em at least, an' I did. Hope he liked it!"

"It is evident that you did, and I don't blame you in the least. Now go on about Robert, for I should be at work."

"He was one of the fust up; I was just behind, an' though the whole thing happened in a minute, I remember how it was, for all I was yellin' an' knockin' round like mad. Just where we were, some sort of an officer was wavin' his sword an' cheerin' on his men; Dane saw him by a big flash that come by; he flung away his gun, give a leap, an' went at that feller as if he was Jeff, Beauregard, an' Lee, all in one. I scrabbled after as quick as I could, but was only up in time to see him git the sword straight through him an' drop into the ditch. you needn't ask what I did next, Missis, for I don't quite know myself; all I'm clear about is, that I managed somehow to pitch that Reb into the fort as dead as Moses, git hold of Dane, an' bring him off. Poor old feller! we said we went in to live or die; he said he went in to die, an' he's done it."

I had been intently watching the excited speaker; but as he regretfully added those last words I turned again, and Robert's eyes met mine,—those melancholy eyes, so full of an intelligence that proved he had heard, remembered, and reflected with that preternatural power which often outlives all other faculties. He knew me, yet gave no greeting; was glad to see a woman's face, yet had no smile wherewith to welcome it; felt that he was dying, yet uttered no farewell. He was too far across the river to return or linger now; departing thought, strength, breath, were spent in one grateful look, one murmur of submission to the last pang he could ever feel. His lips moved, and, bending to them, a whisper chilled my cheek, as it shaped the broken words,—

"I'd 'a' done it,—but it's better so,—I'm satisfied."

Ah! well he might be,—for, as he turned his face from the shadow of the life that was, the sunshine of the life to be touched it with a beautiful content, and in the drawing of a breath my contraband found wife and home, eternal liberty and God. ·

Transcendental Wild Oats (1873)

On the first day of June, 184–, a large wagon, drawn by a small horse and containing a motley load, went lumbering over certain New England hills, with the pleasing accompaniments of wind, rain, and hail. A serene man with a serene child upon his knee was driving, or rather being driven, for the small horse had it all his own way. A brown boy with a William Penn style of countenance sat beside him, firmly embracing a bust of Socrates. Behind them was an energetic-looking woman, with a benevolent brow, satirical mouth, and eyes brimful of hope and courage. A baby reposed upon her lap, a mirror leaned against her knee, and a basket of provisions danced about at her feet, as she struggled with a large, unruly umbrella. Two blue-eyed little girls, with hands full of childish treasures, sat under one old shawl, chatting happily together.

In front of this lively party stalked a tall, sharp-featured man, in a long blue cloak; and a fourth small girl trudged along beside him through the mud as if she rather enjoyed it.

The wind whistled over the bleak hills; the rain fell in a despondent drizzle, and twilight began to fall. But the calm man gazed as tranquilly into the fog as if he beheld a radiant bow of promise spanning the gray sky. The cheery woman tried to cover every one but herself with the big umbrella. The brown boy pillowed his head on the bald pate of Socrates and slumbered peacefully. The little girls sang lullabies to their dolls in soft, maternal murmurs. The sharp-nosed pedestrian marched steadily on, with the blue cloak streaming out behind him like a banner; and the lively infant splashed through the puddles with a duck-like satisfaction pleasant to behold.

Thus these modern pilgrims journeyed hopefully out of the old world, to found a new one in the wilderness.

The editors of *The Transcendental Tripod* had received from Messrs. Lion & Lamb (two of the aforesaid pilgrims) a communication from which the following statement is an extract:

"We have made arrangements with the proprietor of an estate of about a hundred acres which liberates this tract from human ownership. Here we shall prosecute our effort to initiate a Family in harmony with the primitive instincts of man.

"Ordinary secular farming is not our object. Fruit, grain, pulse, herbs, flax, and other vegetable products, receiving assiduous attention, will afford ample manual occupation, and chaste supplies for the bodily needs. It is intended to adorn the pastures with orchards, and to supersede the labor of cattle by the spade and the pruning-knife.

"Consecrated to human freedom, the land awaits the sober culture of devoted men. Beginning with small pecuniary means, this enterprise must be rooted in a reliance on the succors of an ever-bounteous Providence, whose vital affinities being secured by this union with uncorrupted field and unworldly persons, the cares and injuries of a life of gain are avoided.

"The inner stature of each member of the Family is at no time neglected. Our plan contemplates all such disciplines, cultures, and habits as evidently conduce to the purifying of the inmates.

"Pledged to the spirit alone, the founders anticipate no hasty or numerous addition to their numbers. The kingdom of peace is entered only through the gates of self-denial; and felicity is the test and the reward of loyalty to the unswerving law of Love."

This prospective Eden at present consisted of an old red farm-house, a dilapidated barn, many acres of meadow-land, and a grove. Ten ancient apple-trees were all the "chaste supply" which the place offered as yet; but, in the firm belief that plenteous orchards were soon to be evoked from their inner consciousness, these sanguine founders had christened their domain Fruitlands.

Here Timon Lion intended to found a colony of Latter Day Saints, who, under his patriarchal sway, should regenerate the world and glorify his name for ever. Here Abel Lamb, with the devoutest faith in the high ideal which was to him a living truth, desired to plant a Paradise, where Beauty, Virtue, Justice, and Love might live happily together, without the possibility of a serpent entering in. And here his wife, unconverted but faithful to the end, hoped, after many wanderings over the face of the earth, to find rest for herself and a home for her children.

"There is our new abode," announced the enthusiast, smiling with a satisfaction quite undamped by the drops dripping from his hatbrim, as they turned at length into a cart-path that wound along a steep hillside into a barren looking valley.

"A little difficult of access," observed his practical wife, as she endeavored to keep her various household goods from going overboard with every lurch of the laden ark.

"Like all good things. But those who earnestly desire and patiently seek will soon find us," placidly responded the philosopher from the mud, through which he was now endeavoring to pilot the much-enduring horse.

"Truth lies at the bottom of a well, Sister Hope," said Brother Timon, pausing to detach his small comrade from a gate, whereon she was perched for a clearer gaze into futurity.

"That's the reason we so seldom get at it, I suppose," replied Mrs. Hope, making a vain clutch at the mirror, which a sudden jolt sent flying out of her hands.

"We want no false reflections here," said Timon, with a grim smile, as he crunched the fragments under foot in his onward march.

Sister Hope held her peace, and looked wistfully through the mist at her promised home. The old red house with a hospitable glimmer at its windows cheered her eyes; and considering the weather, was a fitter refuge than the sylvan bowers some of the more ardent souls might have preferred.

The newcomers were welcomed by one of the elect precious—a regenerate farmer, whose idea of reform consisted chiefly in wearing white cotton raiment and untanned leather. This costume, with a snowy beard, gave him a venerable, and at the same time a somewhat bridal appearance.

The goods and chattels of the Society not having arrived, the weary family reposed before the fire on blocks of wood, while Brother Moses White regaled them with roasted potatoes, brown bread and water, in two plates, a tin pan, and one mug—his table service being limited. But, having cast the forms and vanities of a depraved world behind them the elders welcomed hardship with the enthusiasm of new pioneers, and the children heartily enjoyed this foretaste of what they believed was to be a sort of perpetual Picnic.

During the progress of this frugal meal, two more brothers appeared. One a dark, melancholy man, clad in homespun, whose peculiar mission was to turn his name hind part before and use as few words as possible. The other was a bland, bearded Englishman, who expected to be saved by eating uncooked food and going without clothes. He had not yet adopted the primitive costume, however; but contented himself with meditatively chewing dry beans out of a basket.

"Every meal should be a sacrament, and the vessels used should be beautiful and symbolical," observed Brother Lamb, mildly, righting the tin pan slipping about on his knees. "I priced a silver service when in town, but it was too costly; so I got some graceful cups and vases of Britannia ware."

"Hardest things in the world to keep bright. Will whiting be allowed in the community?" inquired Sister Hope, with a housewife's interest in labor-saving institutions.

"Such trivial questions will be discussed at a more fitting time," answered Brother Lamb, sharply, as he burnt his fingers with a very hot potato. "Neither sugar, molasses, milk, butter, cheese, nor flesh are to be used among us, for nothing is to be admitted which has caused wrong or death to man or beast."

"Our garments are to be linen till we learn to raise our own cotton or some substitute for woollen fabrics," added Brother Abel, blissfully basking in an imaginary future as warm and brilliant as the generous fire before him.

"Haou abaout shoes?" asked Brother Moses, surveying his own with interest.

"We must yield that point till we can manufacture an innocent substitute for leather. Bark, wood, or some durable fabric will be invented in time. Meanwhile, those who desire to carry out our idea to the fullest extent can go barefooted," said Lion, who liked extreme measures.

"I never will, nor let my girls," murmured rebellious Sister Hope, under her breath.

"Haou do you cattle'ate to treat the ten-acre lot? Ef things ain't 'tended to right smart, we shan't hev no crops," observed the practical patriarch in cotton.

"We shall spade it," replied Abel, in such perfect good faith that Moses said no more, though he indulged in a shake of the head as he glanced at hands that had held nothing heavier than a pen for years. He was a paternal old soul and regarded the younger men as promising boys on a new sort of lark.

"What shall we do for lamps, if we cannot use any animal substance? I do hope light of some sort is to be thrown upon the enterprise," said Mrs. Lamb, with anxiety, for in those days kerosene and camphene were not, and gas unknown in the wilderness.

"We shall go without till we have discovered some vegetable oil or wax to serve us," replied Brother Timon, in a decided tone, which caused Sister Hope to resolve that her private lamp should be always trimmed, if not burning.

"Each member is to perform the work for which experience, strength, and taste best fit him," continued Dictator Lion. "Thus drudgery and disorder will be avoided and harmony prevail. We shall rise at dawn, begin the day by bathing, followed by music, and then a chaste repast of fruit and bread. Each one finds congenial occupation till the meridian meal; when some deep-searching conversation gives rest to the body and development to the mind. Healthful labor again engages us till the last meal, when we assemble in social communion, prolonged till sunset, when we retire to sweet repose, ready for the next day's activity."

"What part of the work do you incline to yourself?" asked Sister Hope, with a humorous glimmer in her keen eyes.

"I shall wait till it is made clear to me. Being in preference to doing is the great aim, and this comes to us rather by a resigned willingness than a willful activity, which is a check to all divine growth," responded Brother Timon.

"I thought so." And Mrs. Lamb sighed audibly, for during the year he had spent in her family Brother Timon had so faithfully carried out his idea of "being, not doing," that she had found his "divine growth" both an expensive and unsatisfactory process.

Here her husband struck into the conversation; his face shining with the light and joy of the splendid dreams and high ideals hovering before him.

"In these steps of reform, we do not rely so much on scientific reasoning or physiological skill as on the spirit's dictates. The greater part of man's duty consists in leaving alone much that he now does. Shall I stimulate with tea, coffee, or wine? No. Shall I consume flesh? Not if I value health. Shall I subjugate cattle? Shall I claim property in any created thing? Shall I trade? Shall I adopt a form of religion? Shall I interest myself in politics? To how many of these questions—could we ask them deeply enough and could they be heard as having relation to our eternal welfare—would the response be 'Abstain'?"

A mild snore seemed to echo the last word of Abel's rhapsody, for Brother Moses had succumbed to mundane slumber and sat nodding like a massive ghost. Forest Absalom, the silent man, and John Pease, the English member, now departed to the barn; and Mrs. Lamb led her flock to a temporary fold, leaving the founders of the "Consociate Family" to build castles in the air till the fire went out and the symposium ended in smoke.

The furniture arrived next day, and was soon bestowed; for the principal property of the community consisted in books. To this rare library was devoted the best room in the house, and the few busts and pictures that still survived many flittings were added to beautify the sanctuary, for here the family was to meet for amusement, instruction, and worship.

Any housewife can imagine the emotions of Sister Hope, when she took possession of a large, dilapidated kitchen, containing an old stove and the peculiar stores out of which food was to be evolved for her little family of eleven. Cakes of maple sugar, dried peas and beans, barley and hominy, meal of all sorts, potatoes, and dried fruit. No milk, butter, cheese, tea, or meat appeared. Even salt was considered a useless luxury and spice entirely forbidden by these lovers of Spartan simplicity. A ten years' experience of vegetarian vagaries had been good training for this new freak, and her sense of the ludicrous supported her through many trying scenes.

Unleavened bread, porridge, and water for breakfast; bread, vegetables, and water for dinner; bread, fruit, and water for supper was the bill of fare ordained by the elders. No teapot profaned that sacred stove, no gory steak cried aloud for vengeance from her chaste gridiron; and only a brave woman's taste, time, and temper were sacrificed on that domestic altar.

The vexed question of light was settled by buying a quantity of bayberry wax for candles; and, on discovering that no one knew how to make them, pine knots were introduced, to be used when absolutely necessary. Being summer, the evenings were not long, and the weary fraternity found it no great hardship to retire with the birds. The inner light was sufficient for most of them. But Mrs. Lamb rebelled. Evening was the only time she had to herself, and while the tired feet rested, the skilful hands mended torn frocks and little stockings, or the anxious heart forgot its burden in a book.

So "mother's lamp" burned steadily, while the philosophers built a new heaven and earth by moonlight; and through all the metaphysical mists and philanthropic pyrotechnics of that period Sister Hope played her own little game of "throwing light," and none but the moths were the worse for it.

Such farming probably was never seen before since Adam delved. The band of brothers began by spading garden and field; but a few days of it lessened their ardor amazingly. Blistered hands and aching backs suggested the expediency of permitting the use of cattle till the workers were better fitted for noble toil by a summer of the new life.

Brother Moses brought a yoke of oxen from his farm—at least, the philosophers thought so till it was discovered that one of the animals was a cow; and Moses confessed that he "must be let down easy, for he couldn't live on garden sarse entirely."

Great was Dictator Lion's indignation at this lapse from virtue. But time pressed, the work must be done; so the meek cow was permitted to wear the yoke and the recreant brother continued to enjoy forbidden draughts in the barn, which dark proceeding caused the children to regard him as one set apart for destruction.

The sowing was equally peculiar, for, owing to some mistake, the three brethren, who devoted themselves to this graceful task, found when about half through the job that each had been sowing a different sort of grain in the same field; a mistake which caused much perplexity, as it could not be remedied; but, after a long consultation and a good deal of laughter, it was decided to say nothing and see what would come of it.

The garden was planted with a generous supply of useful roots and herbs; but, as manure was not allowed to profane the virgin soil, few of these vegetable treasures ever came up. Purslane reigned supreme, and the disappointed planters ate it philosophically, deciding that Nature knew what was best for them, and would generously supply their needs, if they could only learn to digest her "sallets" and wild roots.

The orchard was laid out, a little grafting done, new trees and vines set, regardless of the unfit season and entire ignorance of the husband-men, who honestly believed that in the autumn they would reap a boun-teous harvest.

Slowly things got into order, and rapidly rumors of the new experi-ment went abroad, causing many strange spirits to flock thither, for in those days communities were the fashion and transcendentalism raged wildly. Some came to look on and laugh, some to be supported in poetic idleness, a few to believe sincerely and work heartily. Each member was allowed to mount his favorite hobby and ride it to his heart's content. Very queer were some of the riders, and very rampant some of the hob-bies.

One youth, believing that language was of little consequence if the spirit was only right startled newcomers by blandly greeting them with "good-morning, damn you," and other remarks of an equally mixed order. A second irrepressible being held that all the emotions of the soul should be freely expressed, and illustrated his theory by antics that would have sent him to a lunatic asylum, if, as an unregenerate wag said, he had not already been in one. When his spirit soared, he climbed trees and shouted; when doubt assailed him, he lay upon the floor and groaned lamentably. At joyful periods, he raced, leaped, and sang; when sad, he wept aloud; and when a great thought burst upon him in the watches of the night, he crowed like a jocund cockerel, to the great delight of the children and the great annoyance of the elders. One musical brother fiddled whenever so moved, sang sentimentally to the four little girls, and put a music-box on the wall when he hoed corn.

Brother Pease ground away at his uncooked food, or browsed over the farm on sorrel, mint, green fruit, and new vegetables. Occasionally he took his walks abroad, airily attired in an unbleached cotton *poncho*, which was the nearest approach to the primeval costume he was allowed to indulge in. At midsummer he retired to the wilderness, to try his plan where the woodchucks were without prejudices and huckleberry bushes were hospitably full. A sunstroke unfortunately spoilt his plan, and he returned to semi-civilization a sadder and wiser man.

Forest Absalom preserved his Pythagorean silence, cultivated his fine dark locks, and worked like a beaver, setting an excellent example of brotherly love, justice, and fidelity by his upright life. He it was who helped overworked Sister Hope with her heavy washes, kneaded the endless succession of batches of bread, watched over the children, and did the many tasks left undone by the brethren, who were so busy discussing and defining great duties that they forgot to perform the small ones.

Moses White placidly plodded about, "chorin' raound," as he called it, looking like an old-time patriarch, with his silver hair and flowing beard, and saving the community from many a mishap by his thrift and Yankee shrewdness.

Brother Lion domineered over the whole concern; for, having put the most money into the speculation, he was resolved to make it pay—as if anything founded on an ideal basis could be expected to do so by any but enthusiasts.

Abel Lamb simply revelled in the Newness, firmly believing that his dream was to be beautifully realized and in time not only little Fruitlands, but the whole earth, be turned into a Happy Valley. He worked with every muscle of his body, for *he* was in deadly earnest. He taught with his whole head and heart; planned and sacrificed, preached and prophesied, with a soul full of the purest aspirations, most unselfish purposes, and desires for a life devoted to God and man, too high and tender to bear the rough usage of this world.

It was a little remarkable that only one woman ever joined this community. Mrs. Lamb merely followed wheresoever her husband led—"as ballast for his balloon," as she said, in her bright way.

Miss Jane Gage was a stout lady of mature years, sentimental, amiable, and lazy. She wrote verses copiously, and had vague yearnings and graspings after the unknown, which led her to believe herself fitted for a higher sphere than any she had yet adorned.

Having been a teacher, she was set to instructing the children in the common branches. Each adult member took a turn at the infants; and, as each taught in his own way, the result was a chronic state of chaos in the minds of these much-afflicted innocents.

Sleep, food, and poetic musings were the desires of dear Jane's life, and she shirked all duties as clogs upon her spirit's wings. Any thought of lending a hand with the domestic drudgery never occurred to her; and when to the question, "Are there any beasts of burden on the place?" Mrs. Lamb answered, with a face that told its own tale, "Only one woman!" the buxom Jane took no shame to herself, but laughed at the joke, and let the stout-hearted sister tug on alone.

Unfortunately, the poor lady hankered after the flesh-pots, and endeavored to stay herself with private sips of milk, crackers, and cheese, and on one dire occasion she partook of fish at a neighbor's table.

One of the children reported this sad lapse from virtue, and poor Jane was Publicly reprimanded by Timon.

"I only took a little bit of the tail," sobbed the penitent poetess.

"Yes, but the whole fish had to be tortured and slain that you might tempt your carnal appetite with that one taste of the tail. Know ye not, consumers of flesh meat, that ye are nourishing the wolf and tiger in your bosoms?"

At this awful question and the peal of laughter which arose from some of the younger brethren, tickled by the ludicrous contrast between the stout sinner, the stern judge, and the naughty satisfaction of the young detective, poor Jane fled from the room to pack her trunk, and return to a world where fishes' tails were not forbidden fruit.

Transcendental wild oats were sown broadcast that year, and the fame thereof has not yet ceased in the land; for, futile as this crop seemed to outsiders, it bore an invisible harvest, worth much to those who planted in earnest. As none of the members of this particular community have ever recounted their experiences before, a few of them may not be amiss, since the interest in these attempts has never died out and Fruitlands was the most ideal of all these castles in Spain.

A new dress was invented since cotton, silk, and wool were forbidden as the product of slave labor, worm-slaughter, and sheep-robbery. Tunics and trowsers of brown linen were the only wear. The women's skirts were longer, and their straw hat-brims wider than the men's, and this was the only difference. Some persecution lent a charm to the costume, and the long-haired, linen-clad reformers quite enjoyed the mild martyrdom they endured when they left home.

Money was abjured, as the root of all evil. The produce of the land was to supply most of their wants, or be exchanged for the few things they could not grow. This idea had its inconveniences; but self-denial was the fashion, and it was surprising how many things one can do without. When they desired to travel, they walked, if possible, begged the loan of a vehicle, or boldly entered car or coach, and, stating their principles to the officials, took the consequences. Usually their dress, their earnest frankness, and gentle resolution won them a passage; but now and then they met with hard usage, and had the satisfaction of suffering for their principles.

On one of these penniless pilgrimages they took passage on a boat, and, when fare was demanded, artlessly offered to talk, instead of pay. As the boat was well under way and they actually had not a cent, there was no help for it. So Brothers Lion and Lamb held forth to the assembled passengers in their most eloquent style. There must have been something effective in this conversation, for the listeners were moved to take up a contribution for these inspired lunatics, who preached peace on earth and goodwill to man so earnestly, with empty pockets. A goodly sum was collected; but when the captain presented it the reformers proved that they were consistent even in their madness, for not a penny would they accept, saying, with a look at the group about them, whose indifference or contempt had changed to interest and respect, "You see how well we get on without money"; and so went serenely on their way, with their linen blouses flapping airily in the cold October wind.

They preached vegetarianism everywhere and resisted all temptations of the flesh, contentedly eating apples and bread at well-spread tables, and much afflicting hospitable hostesses by denouncing their food and taking away their appetites, discussing the "horrors of shambles," the "incorporation of the brute in man," and "on elegant abstinence the sign of a pure soul." But, when the perplexed or offended ladies asked what they should eat, they got in reply a bill of fare consisting of "bowls of sunrise for breakfast," "solar seeds of the sphere," "dishes from Plutarch's chaste table," and other viands equally hard to find in any modern market.

Reform conventions of all sorts were haunted by these brethren, who said many wise things and did many foolish ones. Unfortunately, these wanderings interfered with their harvest at home; but the rule was to do what the spirit moved, so they left their crops to Providence and went a-reaping in wider and, let us hope, more fruitful fields than their own.

Luckily, the earthly providence who watched over Abel Lamb was at hand to glean the scanty crop yielded by the "uncorrupted land," which, "consecrated to human freedom," had received "the sober culture of devout men."

About the time the grain was ready to house, some call of the Over-soul wafted all the men away. An easterly storm was coming up and the yellow stacks were sure to be ruined. Then Sister Hope gathered her forces. Three little girls, one boy (Timon's son), and herself, harnessed to clothes-baskets and Russia-linen sheets, were the only teams she could command; but with these poor appliances the indomitable woman got in the grain and saved food for her young, with the instinct and energy of a mother-bird with a brood of hungry nestlings to feed.

This attempt at regeneration had its tragic as well as comic side, though the world only saw the former.

With the first frosts, the butterflies, who had sunned themselves in the new light through the summer, took flight, leaving the few bees to see what honey they had stored for winter use. Precious little appeared beyond the satisfaction of a few months of holy living.

At first it seemed as if a chance to try holy dying also was to be offered them. Timon, much disgusted with the failure of the scheme, decided to retire to the Shakers, who seemed to be the only successful community going.

"What is to become of us?" asked Mrs. Hope, for Abel was heart-broken at the bursting of his lovely bubble.

"You can stay here, if you like, till a tenant is found. No more wood must be cut, however, and no more corn ground. All I have must be sold to pay the debts of the concern, as the responsibility is mine," was the cheering reply.

"Who is to pay us for what we have lost? I gave all I had—furniture, time, strength, six months of my children's lives—and all are wasted. Abel gave himself body and soul, and is almost wrecked by hard work and disappointment. Are we to have no return for this, but leave to starve and freeze in an old house, with winter at hand, no money, and hardly a friend left, for this wild scheme has alienated nearly all we had. You talk much about justice. Let us have a little, since there is nothing else left."

But the woman's appeal met with no reply but the old one: "It was an experiment. We all risked something, and must bear our losses as we can."

With this cold comfort, Timon departed with his son, and was absorbed into the Shaker brotherhood, where he soon found that the order of things was reversed, and it was all work and no play.

Then the tragedy began for the forsaken little family. Desolation and despair fell upon Abel. As his wife said, his new beliefs had alienated many friends. Some thought him mad, some unprincipled. Even the most kindly thought him a visionary, whom it was useless to help till he took more practical views of life. All stood aloof, saying: "Let him work out his own ideas, and see what they are worth."

He had tried, but it was a failure. The world was not ready for Utopia yet, and those who attempted to found it only got laughed at for their pains. In other days, men could sell all and give to the poor, lead lives devoted to holiness and high thought, and, after the persecution was over, find themselves honored as saints or martyrs. But in modern times these things are out of fashion. To live for one's principles, at all costs, is a dangerous speculation; and the failure of an ideal, no matter how humane and noble, is harder for the world to forgive and forget than bank robbery or the grand swindles of corrupt politicians.

Deep waters now for Abel, and for a time there seemed no passage through. Strength and spirits were exhausted by hard work and too much thought. Courage failed when, looking about for help, he saw no sympathizing face, no hand outstretched to help him, no voice to say cheerily:

"We all make mistakes, and it takes many experiences to shape a life. Try again, and let us help you."

Every door was closed, every eye averted, every heart cold, and no way open whereby he might earn bread for his children. His principles would not permit him to do many things that others did; and in the few fields where conscience would allow him to work, who would employ a man who had flown in the face of society, as he had done?

Then this dreamer, whose dream was the life of his life, resolved to carry out his idea to the bitter end. There seemed no place for him here—no work, no friend. To go begging conditions was as ignoble as to go begging money. Better perish of want than sell one's soul for the sustenance of his body. Silently he lay down upon his bed, turned his face to the wall, and waited with pathetic patience for death to cut the knot which he could not untie. Days and nights went by, and neither food nor water passed his lips. Soul and body were dumbly struggling together, and no word of complaint betrayed what either suffered.

His wife, when tears and prayers were unavailing, sat down to wait the end with a mysterious awe and submission; for in this entire resignation of all things there was an eloquent significance to her who knew him as no other human being did.

"Leave all to God," was his belief; and in this crisis the loving soul clung to this faith, sure that the All-wise Father would not desert this child who tried to live so near to Him. Gathering her children about her, she waited the issue of the tragedy that was being enacted in that solitary room, while the first snow fell outside, untrodden by the footprints of a single friend.

But the strong angels who sustain and teach perplexed and troubled souls came and went, leaving no trace without, but working miracles within. For, when all other sentiments had faded into dimness, all other hopes died utterly; when the bitterness of death was nearly over, when body was past any pang of hunger or thirst, and soul stood ready to depart, the love that outlives all else refused to die. Head had bowed to defeat, hand had grown weary with too heavy tasks, but heart could not grow cold to those who lived in its tender depths, even when death touched it.

"My faithful wife, my little girls—they have not forsaken me, they are mine by ties that none can break. What right have I to leave them alone? What right to escape from the burden and the sorrow I have helped to bring? This duty remains to me, and I must do it manfully. For their sakes, the world will forgive me in time; for their sakes, God will sustain me now."

Too feeble to rise, Abel groped for the food that always lay within his reach, and in the darkness and solitude of that memorable night ate and drank what was to him the bread and wine of a new communion, a new dedication of heart and life to the duties that were left him when the dreams fled.

In the early dawn, when that sad wife crept fearfully to see what change had come to the patient face on the pillow, she found it smiling at her, saw a wasted hand outstretched to her, and heard a feeble voice cry bravely, "Hope!"

What passed in that little room is not to be recorded except in the hearts of those who suffered and endured much for love's sake. Enough for us to know that soon the wan shadow of a man came forth, leaning on the arm that never failed him, to be welcomed and cherished by the children, who never forgot the experiences of that time.

"Hope" was the watchword now; and, while the last logs blazed on the hearth, the last bread and apples covered the table, the new com- mander, with recovered courage, said to her husband:

"Leave all to God—and me. He has done his part; now I will do mine."

"But we have no money, dear."

"Yes, we have. I sold all we could spare, and have enough to take us away from this snowbank."

"Where can we go?"

"I have engaged four rooms at our good neighbor, Lovejoy's. There we can live cheaply till spring. Then for new plans and a home of our own, please God."

"But, Hope, your little store won't last long, and we have no friends."

"I can sew and you can chop wood. Lovejoy offers you the same pay as he gives his other men; my old friend, Mrs. Truman, will send me all the work I want; and my blessed brother stands by us to the end. Cheer up, dear heart, for while there is work and love in the world we shall not suffer."

"And while I have my good angel Hope, I shall not despair, even if I wait another thirty years before I step beyond the circle of the sacred little world in which I still have a place to fill."

So one bleak December day, with their few possessions piled on an ox-sled, the rosy children perched atop, and the parents trudging arm in arm behind, the exiles left their Eden and faced the world again.

"Ah, me! my happy dream. How much I leave behind that never can be mine again," said Abel, looking back at the lost Paradise, lying white and chill in its shroud of snow.

"Yes, dear; but how much we bring away," answered brave-hearted Hope, glancing from husband to children.

"Poor Fruitlands! The name was as great a failure as the rest!" continued Abel, with a sigh, as a frostbitten apple fell from a leafless bough at his feet.

But the sigh changed to a smile as his wife added, in a half-tender, half-satirical tone:

"Don't you think Apple Slump would be a better name for it, dear?"

Harriet Prescott Spofford
(1835–1921)

o support her invalid parents and four younger siblings, Maine-born Harriet Prescott began writing pulp fiction for Boston newspapers. In 1859, when she was only twenty-three, *The Atlantic Monthly* published her mystery story set in Paris, "In a Cellar." Thomas Higginson, who had met and mentored Prescott when she was a gifted schoolgirl in Newburyport, Massachusetts, had to assure the editors "that a demure little Yankee girl had written it." On the strength of the story, Prescott was accepted in Boston literary circles and even invited to *The Atlantic*'s 1859 dinner honoring Harriet Beecher Stowe. In the 1860s she published two novels and a collection of short stories, as well as poems and children's books. Her marriage to the lawyer and poet Richard Spofford in 1865 was happy and prosperous; he supported her literary career and their home became the center of a circle of Boston writers.

"Circumstance," also published in *The Atlantic Monthly*, is the most influential and critically admired story that Spofford wrote. A gothic tale of a Puritan woman trapped in the Maine woods by a panther (probably a mountain lion) and forced to sing all night to distract the beast, it is sometimes read as an allegory of female creativity. But "Circumstance" is also about divine providence and salvation, and ends with a reference to Adam and Eve in Milton's *Paradise Lost*: "The world was all before them, where to choose." Emily Dickinson found the story both haunting and impressive, but Nathaniel Hawthorne's wife, Sophia, was offended by its sensuality.

Circumstance (1860)

She had remained, during all that day, with a sick neighbor,—those eastern wilds of Maine in that epoch frequently making neighbors and miles synonymous,—and so busy had she been with care and sympathy that she did not at first observe the approaching night. But finally the level rays, reddening the snow, threw their gleam upon the wall, and, hastily donning cloak and hood, she bade her friends farewell and sallied forth on her return. Home lay some three miles distant, across a copse, a meadow, and a piece of woods,—the woods being a fringe on the skirts of the great forests that stretch far away into the North. That home was one of a dozen log-houses lying a few furlongs apart from each other, with their half-cleared demesnes separating them at the rear from a wilderness untrodden save by stealthy native or deadly panther tribes.

She was in a nowise exalted frame of spirit,—on the contrary, rather depressed by the pain she had witnessed and the fatigue she had endured; but in certain temperaments such a condition throws open the mental pores, so to speak, and renders one receptive of every influence. Through the little copse she walked slowly, with her cloak folded about her, lingering to imbibe the sense of shelter, the sunset filtered in purple through the mist of woven spray and twig, the companionship of growth not sufficiently dense to band against her, the sweet home-feeling of a young and tender wintry wood. It was therefore just on the edge of the evening that she emerged from the place and began to cross the meadow-land. At one hand lay the forest to which her path wound; at the other the evening star hung over a tide of failing orange that slowly slipped down the earth's broad side to sadden other hemispheres with sweet regret. Walking rapidly now, and with her eyes wide-open, she distinctly saw in the air before her what was not there a moment ago, a winding-sheet,— cold, white, and ghastly, waved by the likeness of four wan hands,—that rose with a long inflation, and fell in rigid folds, while a voice, shaping itself from the hollowness above, spectral and melancholy, sighed,— "The Lord have mercy on the people! The Lord have mercy on the people!" Three times the sheet with its corpse-covering outline waved beneath the pale hands, and the voice, awful in its solemn and mysterious depth, sighed, "The Lord have mercy on the people!" Then all was gone, the place was clear again, the gray sky was obstructed by no deathly blot; she looked about her, shook her shoulders decidedly, and, pulling on her hood, went forward once more.

She might have been a little frightened by such an apparition, if she had led a life of less reality than frontier settlers are apt to lead; but dealing with hard fact does not engender a flimsy habit of mind, and this woman was too sincere and earnest in her character, and too happy in her situation, to be thrown by antagonism, merely, upon superstitious fancies and chimeras of the second-sight. She did not even believe herself subject to an hallucination, but smiled simply, a little vexed that her thought could have framed such a glamour from the day's occurrences, and not sorry to lift the bough of the warder of the woods and enter and disappear in their sombre path. If she had been imaginative, she would have hesitated at her first step into a region whose dangers were not visionary; but I suppose that the thought of a little child at home would conquer that propensity in the most habituated. So, biting a bit of spicy birch, she went along. Now and then she came to a gap where the trees had been partially felled, and here she found that the lingering twilight was explained by that peculiar and perhaps electric film which sometimes sheathes the sky in diffused light for many hours before a brilliant aurora. Suddenly, a swift shadow, like the fabulous flying-dragon, writhed through the air before her, and she felt herself instantly seized and borne aloft. It was that wild beast—the most savage and serpentine and subtle and fearless of our latitudes—known by hunters as the Indian Devil, and he held her in his clutches on the broad floor of a swinging fir-bough. His long sharp claws were caught in her clothing, he worried them sagaciously a little, then, finding that ineffectual to free them, he commenced licking her bare arm with his rasping tongue and pouring over her the wide streams of his hot, foetid breath. So quick had this flashing action been that the woman had had no time for alarm; moreover, she was not of the screaming kind: but now, as she felt him endeavoring to disentangle his claws, and the horrid sense of her fate smote her, and she saw instinctively the fierce plunge of those weapons, the long strips of living flesh torn from her bones, the agony, the quivering disgust, itself a worse agony,—while by her side, and holding her in his great lithe embrace, the monster crouched, his white tusks whetting and gnashing, his eyes glaring through all the darkness like balls of red fire,— a shriek, that rang in every forest hollow, that startled every winter-housed thing, that stirred and woke the least needle of the tasselled pines, tore through her lips. A moment afterward, the beast left the arm, once white, now crimson, and looked up alertly.

She did not think at this instant to call upon God. She called upon her husband. It seemed to her that she had but one friend in the world; that was he; and again the cry, loud, clear, prolonged, echoed through the woods. It was not the shriek that disturbed the creature at his relish; he was not born in the woods to be scared of an owl, you know; what then? It must have been the echo, most musical, most resonant, repeated and yet repeated, dying with long sighs of sweet sound, vibrated from rock to river and back again from depth to depth of cave and cliff. Her thought flew after it; she knew, that, even if her husband heard it, he yet could not reach her in time; she saw that while the beast listened he would not gnaw,—and this she *felt* directly, when the rough, sharp, and multiplied stings of his tongue retouched her arm. Again her lips opened by instinct, but the sound that issued thence came by reason. She had heard that music charmed wild beasts,—just this point between life and death intensified every faculty,—and when she opened her lips the third time, it was not for shrieking, but for singing.

A little thread of melody stole out, a rill of tremulous motion; it was the cradle-song with which she rocked her baby;—how could she sing that? And then she remembered the baby sleeping rosily on the long set-tee before the fire,—the father cleaning his gun, with one foot on the green wooden rundle,—the merry light from the chimney dancing out and through the room, on the rafters of the ceiling with their tassels of onions and herbs, on the log walls painted with lichens and festooned with apples, on the king's-arm slung across the shelf with the old pirate's-cutlass, on the snow-pile of the bed, and on the great brass clock,—dancing, too, and lingering on the baby, with his fringed-gentian eyes, his chubby fists clenched on the pillow, and his fine breezy hair fanning with the motion of his father's foot. All this struck her in one, and made a sob of her breath, and she ceased.

Immediately the long red tongue thrust forth again. Before it touched, a song sprang to her lips, a wild sea-song, such as some sailor might be singing far out on trackless blue water that night, the shrouds whistling with frost and the sheets glued in ice,—a song with the wind in its burden and the spray in its chorus. The monster raised his head and flared the fiery eyeballs upon her, then fretted the imprisoned claws a moment and was quiet; only the breath like the vapor from some hell-pit still swathed her. Her voice, at first faint and fearful, gradually lost its quaver, grew under her control and subject to her modulation; it rose on long swells, it fell in subtle cadences, now and then its tones pealed out like bells from distant belfries on fresh sonorous mornings. She sung the song through, and, wondering lest his name of Indian Devil were not his true name, and if he would not detect her, she repeated it. Once or twice now, indeed, the beast stirred uneasily, turned, and made the bough sway at his movement. As she ended, he snapped his jaws together, and tore away the fettered member, curling it under him with a snarl,—when she burst into the gayest reel that ever answered a fiddle-bow. How many a time she had heard her husband play it on the homely fiddle made by himself from birch and cherrywood! how many a time she had seen it danced on the floor of their one room, to the patter of wooden clogs and the rustle of homespun petticoat! how many a time she had danced it herself!—and did she not remember once, as they joined clasps for eight-hands-round, how it had lent its gay, bright measure to her life? And here she was singing it alone, in the forest, at midnight, to a wild beast! As she sent her voice trilling up and down its quick oscillations between joy and pain, the creature who grasped her uncurled his paw and scratched the bark from the bough; she must vary the spell; and her voice spun leaping along the projecting points of tune of a hornpipe. Still singing, she felt herself twisted about with a low growl and a lifting of the red lip from the glittering teeth; she broke the hornpipe's thread, and commenced unravelling a lighter, livelier thing, an Irish jig. Up and down and round about her voice flew, the beast threw back his head so that the diabolical face fronted hers, and the torrent of his breath prepared her for his feast as the anaconda slimes his prey. Franticly she darted from tune to tune; his restless movements followed her. She tired herself with dancing and vivid national airs, growing feverish and singing spasmodically as she felt her horrid tomb yawning wider. Touching in this manner all the slogan and keen clan cries, the beast moved again, but only to lay the disengaged paw across her with heavy satisfaction. She did not dare to pause; through the clear cold air, the frosty starlight, she sang. If there were yet any tremor in the tone, it was not fear,—she had learned the secret of sound at last; nor could it be chill,—far too high a fever throbbed her pulses; it was nothing but the thought of the log-house and of what might be passing within it. She fancied the baby stirring in his sleep and moving his pretty lips,—her husband rising and opening the door, looking out after her, and wondering at her absence. She fancied the light pouring through the chink and then shut in again with all the safety and comfort and joy, her husband taking down the fiddle and playing lightly with his head inclined, playing while she sang, while she sang for her life to an Indian Devil. Then she knew he was fumbling for and finding some shining fragment and scoring it down the yellowing hair, and unconsciously her voice forsook the wild war-tunes and drifted into the half-gay, half-melancholy "Rosin the Bow."

Suddenly she woke pierced with a pang, and the daggered tooth penetrating her flesh;—dreaming of safety, she had ceased singing and lost it. The beast had regained the use of all his limbs, and now, standing and raising his back, bristling and foaming, with sounds that would have been like hisses but for their deep and fearful sonority, he withdrew step by step toward the trunk of the tree, still with his flaming balls upon her. She was all at once free, on one end of the bough, twenty feet from the ground. She did not measure the distance, but rose to drop herself down, careless of any death, so that it were not this. Instantly, as if he scanned her thoughts, the creature bounded forward with a yell and caught her again in his dreadful hold. It might be that he was not greatly famished; for, as she suddenly flung up her voice again, he settled himself composedly on the bough, still clasping her with invincible pressure to his rough, ravenous breast, and listening in a fascination to the sad, strange U-la-lu that now moaned forth in loud, hollow tones above him. He half closed his eyes, and sleepily reopened and shut them again.

What rending pains were close at hand! Death! and what a death! worse than any other that is to be named! Water, be it cold or warm, that which buoys up blue icefields, or which bathes tropical coasts with currents of balmy bliss, is yet a gentle conqueror, kisses as it kills, and draws you down gently through darkening fathoms to its heart. Death at the sword is the festival of trumpet and bugle and banner, with glory ringing out around you and distant hearts thrilling through yours. No gnawing disease can bring such hideous end as this; for that is a fiend bred of your own flesh, and this—is it a fiend, this living lump of appetites? What dread comes with the thought of perishing in flames! but fire, let it leap and hiss never so hotly, is something too remote, too alien, to inspire us with such loathly horror as a wild beast; if it have a life, that life is too utterly beyond our comprehension. Fire is not half ourselves; as it devours, arouses neither hatred nor disgust; is not to be known by the strength of our lower natures let loose; does not drip our blood into our faces from foaming chaps, nor mouth nor slaver above us with vitality. Let us be ended by fire, and we are ashes, for the winds to bear, the leaves to cover; let us be ended by wild beasts, and the base, cursed thing howls with us forever through the forest. All this she felt as she charmed him, and what force it lent to her song God knows. If her voice should fail! If the damp and cold should give her any fatal hoarseness! If all the silent powers of the forest did not conspire to help her! The dark, hollow night rose indifferently over her; the wide, cold air breathed rudely past her, lifted her wet hair and blew it down again; the great boughs swung with a ponderous strength, now and then clashed their iron lengths together and shook off a sparkle of icy spears or some long-lain weight of snow from their heavy shadows. The green depths were utterly cold and silent and stern. These beautiful haunts that all the summer were hers and rejoiced to share with her their bounty, these heavens that had yielded their largess, these stems that had thrust their blossoms into her hands, all these friends of three moons ago forgot her now and knew her no longer.

Feeling her desolation, wild, melancholy, forsaken songs rose thereon from that frightful aerie,—weeping, wailing tunes, that sob among the people from age to age, and overflow with otherwise unexpressed sadness,—all rude, mournful ballads,—old tearful strains, that Shakespeare heard the vagrants sing, and that rise and fall like the wind and tide,—sailor-songs, to be heard only in lone mid-watches beneath the moon and stars,—ghastly rhyming romances, such as that famous one of the Lady Margaret, when

> She slipped on her gown of green
> A piece below the knee,—
> And 't was all a long cold winter's night
> A dead corse followed she.

Still the beast lay with closed eyes, yet never relaxing his grasp. Once a half-whine of enjoyment escaped him,—he fawned his fearful head upon her; once he scored her cheek with his tongue—savage caresses that hurt like wounds. How weary she was! and yet how terribly awake! How fuller and fuller of dismay grew the knowledge that she was only prolonging her anguish and playing with death! How appalling the thought that with her voice ceased her existence! Yet she could not sing forever; her throat was dry and hard; her very breath was a pain; her mouth was hotter than any desert-worn pilgrim's;—if she could but drop upon her burning tongue one atom of the ice that glittered about her!—but both of her arms were pinioned in the giant's vice. She remembered the winding-sheet, and for the first time in her life shivered with spiritual fear. Was it hers? She asked herself, as she sang, what sins she had committed, what life she had led, to find her punishment so soon and in these pangs,—and then she sought eagerly for some reason why her husband was not up and abroad to find her. He failed her,—her one sole hope in life; and without being aware of it, her voice forsook the songs of suffering and sorrow for old Covenanting hymns,—hymns with which her mother had lulled her, which the class-leader pitched in the chimney-corners,—grand and sweet Methodist hymns, brimming with melody and with all fantastic involutions of tune to suit that ecstatic worship,—hymns full of the beauty of holiness, steadfast, relying, sanctified by the salvation they had lent to those in worse extremity than hers,—for they had found themselves in the grasp of hell, while she was but in the jaws of death. Out of this strange music, peculiar to one character of faith, and than which there is none more beautiful in its degree nor owning a more potent sway of sound, her voice soared into the glorified chants of churches. What to her was death by cold or famine or wild beasts? "Though He slay me, yet will I trust in him," she sang. High and clear through the frore fair night, the level moonbeams splintering in the wood, the scarce glints of stars in the shadowy roof of branches, these sacred anthems rose,—rose as a hope from despair, as some snowy spray of flower-bells from blackest mould. Was she not in God's hands? Did not the world swing at his will? If this were in his great plan of providence, was it not best, and should she not accept it?

"He is the Lord our God; his judgments are in all the earth."

Oh, sublime faith of our fathers, where utter self-sacrifice alone was true love, the fragrance of whose unrequired subjection was pleasanter than that of golden censers swung in purple-vapored chancels!

Never ceasing in the rhythm of her thoughts, articulated in music as they thronged, the memory of her first communion flashed over her. Again she was in that distant place on that sweet spring morning. Again the congregation rustled out, and the few remained, and she trembled to find herself among them. How well she remembered the devout, quiet faces, too accustomed to the sacred feast to glow with their inner joy! how well the snowy linen at the altar, the silver vessels slowly and silently shifting! and as the cup approached and passed, how the sense of delicious perfume stole in and heightened the transport of her prayer, and she had seemed, looking up through the windows where the sky soared blue in constant freshness, to feel all heaven's balms dripping from the portals, and to scent the lilies of eternal peace! Perhaps another would not have felt so much ecstasy as satisfaction on that occasion; but it is a true, if a later disciple, who has said, "The Lord bestoweth his blessings there, where he findeth the vessels empty."

"And does it need the walls of a church to renew my communion?" she asked. "Does not every moment stand a temple four-square to God? And in that morning, with its buoyant sunlight, was I any dearer to the Heart of the World than now?—'My beloved is mine, and I am his'," she sang over and over again, with all varied inflection and profuse tune. How gently all the winter-wrapt things bent toward her then! into what relation with her had they grown! how this common dependence was the spell of their intimacy! how at one with Nature had she become! how all the night and the silence and the forest seemed to hold its breath, and to send its soul up to God in her singing! It was no longer despondency, that singing. It was neither prayer nor petition. She had left imploring, "How long wilt thou forget me, O Lord? Lighten mine eyes, lest I sleep the sleep of death! For in death there is no remembrance of thee,"—with countless other such fragments of supplication. She cried rather, "Yea, though I walk through the valley of the shadow of death, I will fear no evil: for thou art with me; thy rod and thy staff, they comfort me,"—and lingered, and repeated, and sang again, "I shall be satisfied, when I awake, with thy likeness."

Then she thought of the Great Deliverance, when he drew her up out of many waters, and the flashing old psalm pealed forth triumphantly:

> *The lord descended from above,*
> *   and bow'd the heavens hie:*
> *And underneath his feet he cast*
> *   the darknesse of the skie.*
> *On cherubs and on cherubins*
> *   full royally he road:*
> *And on the wings of all the winds*
> *   came flying all abroad.*

She forgot how recently, and with what a strange pity for her own shapeless form that was to be, she had quaintly sung,—

> *Oh, lovely appearance of death!*
> *   What sight upon earth is so fair?*
> *Not all the gay pageants that breathe*
> *   Can with a dead body compare!*

She remembered instead,—"In thy presence is fulness of joy; at thy right hand there are pleasures forevermore. God will redeem my soul from the power of the grave: for he shall receive me. He will swallow up death in victory." Not once now did she say, "Lord, how long wilt thou look on? rescue my soul from their destructions, my darling from the lions,"—for she knew that the young lions roar after their prey and seek their meat from God. "O Lord, thou preservest man and beast!" she said.

She had no comfort or consolation in this season, such as sustained the Christian martyrs in the amphitheatre. She was not dying for her faith; there were no palms in heaven for her to wave; but how many a time had she declared,—"I had rather be a doorkeeper in the house of my God, than to dwell in the tents of wickedness!" And as the broad rays here and there broke through the dense covert of shade and lay in rivers of lustre on crystal sheathing and frozen fretting of trunk and limb and on the great spaces of refraction, they builded up visibly that house, the shining city on the hill, and singing, "Beautiful for situation, the joy of the whole earth, is Mount Zion, on the sides of the North, the city of the Great King," her vision climbed to that higher picture where the angel shows the dazzling thing, the holy Jerusalem descending out of heaven from God, with its splendid battlements and gates of pearls, and its foundations, the eleventh a jacinth, the twelfth an amethyst,—with its great white throne, and the rainbow round about it, in sight like unto an emerald: "And there shall be no night there,—for the Lord God giveth them light," she sang.

What whisper of dawn now rustled through the wilderness? How the night was passing? And still the beast crouched upon the bough, changing only the posture of his head, that again he might command her with those charmed eyes;—half their fire was gone; she could almost have released herself from his custody; yet, had she stirred, no one knows what malevolent instinct might have dominated anew. But of that she did not dream; long ago stripped of any expectation, she was experiencing in her divine rapture how mystically true it is that "he that dwelleth in the secret place of the Most High shall abide under the shadow of the Almighty."

Slow clarion cries now wound from the distance as the cocks caught the intelligence of day and re-echoed it faintly from farm to farm,— sleepy sentinels of night, sounding the foe's invasion, and translating that dim intuition to ringing notes of warning. Still she chanted on. A remote crash of brushwood told of some other beast on his depredations, or some night-belated traveller groping his way through the narrow path. Still she chanted on. The far, faint echoes of the chanticleers died into distance,—the crashing of the branches grew nearer. No wild beast that, but a man's step,—a man's form in the moonlight, stalwart and strong,— on one arm slept a little child, in the other hand he held his gun. Still she chanted on.

Perhaps, when her husband last looked forth, he was half ashamed to find what a fear he felt for her. He knew she would never leave the child so long but for some direst need,—and yet he may have laughed at himself, as he lifted and wrapped it with awkward care, and, loading his gun and strapping on his horn, opened the door again and closed it behind him, going out and plunging into the darkness and dangers of the forest. He was more singularly alarmed than he would have been willing to acknowledge; as he had sat with his bow hovering over the strings, he had half believed to hear her voice mingling gayly with the instrument, till he paused and listened if she were not about to lift the latch and enter. As he drew nearer the heart of the forest, that intimation of melody seemed to grow more actual, to take body and breath, to come and go on long swells and ebbs of the night-breeze, to increase with tune and words, till a strange shrill singing grew ever clearer, and, as he stepped into an open space of moonbeams, far up in the branches, rocked by the wind, and singing, "How beautiful upon the mountains are the feet of him that bringeth good tidings, that publisheth peace," he saw his wife,—his wife,—but, great God in heaven! how? Some mad exclamation escaped him, but without diverting her. The child knew the singing voice, though never heard before in that unearthly key, and turned toward it through the veiling dreams. With a celerity almost instantaneous, it lay, in the twinkling of an eye, on the ground at the father's feet, while his gun was raised to his shoulder and levelled at the monster covering his wife with shaggy form and flaming gaze,—his wife so ghastly white, so rigid, so stained with blood, her eyes so fixedly bent above, and her lips, that had indurated into the chiselled pallor of marble, parted only with that flood of solemn song.

I do not know if it were the mother-instinct that for a moment lowered her eyes,—those eyes, so lately riveted on heaven, now suddenly seeing all life-long bliss possible. A thrill of joy pierced and shivered through her like a weapon, her voice trembled in its course, her glance lost its steady strength, fever-flushes chased each other over her face, yet she never once ceased chanting. She was quite aware, that, if her husband shot now, the ball must pierce her body before reaching any vital part of the beast,—and yet better that death, by his hand, than the other. But this her husband also knew, and he remained motionless, just covering the creature with the sight. He dared not fire, lest some wound not mortal should break the spell exercised by her voice, and the beast, enraged with pain, should rend her in atoms; moreover, the light was too uncertain for his aim. So he waited. Now and then he examined his gun to see if the damp were injuring its charge, now and then he wiped the great drops from his forehead. Again the cocks crowed with the passing hour,—the last time they were heard on that night. Cheerful home sound then, how full of safety and all comfort and rest it seemed! what sweet morning incidents of sparkling fire and sunshine, of gay household bustle, shining dresser, and cooing baby, of steaming cattle in the yard, and brimming milk-pails at the door! what pleasant voices! what laughter! what security! and here—

Now, as she sang on in the slow, endless, infinite moments, the fervent vision of God's peace was gone. Just as the grave had lost its sting, she was snatched back again into the arms of earthly hope. In vain she tried to sing, "There remaineth a rest for the people of God,"—her eyes trembled on her husband's, and she could only think of him, and of the child, and of happiness that yet might be, but with what a dreadful gulf of doubt between! She shuddered now in the suspense; all calm forsook her; she was tortured with dissolving heats or frozen with icy blasts; her face contracted, growing small and pinched; her voice was hoarse and sharp,—every tone cut like a knife,—the notes became heavy to lift,— withheld by some hostile pressure,—impossible. One gasp, a convulsive effort, and there was silence,—she had lost her voice.

The beast made a sluggish movement,—stretched and fawned like one awakening,—then, as if he would have yet more of the enchantment, stirred her slightly with his muzzle. As he did so, a sidelong hint of the man standing below with the raised gun smote him; he sprung round furiously, and, seizing his prey, was about to leap into some unknown airy den of the topmost branches now waving to the slow dawn. The late moon had rounded through the sky so that her gleam at last fell full upon the bough with fairy frosting; the wintry morning light did not yet penetrate the gloom. The woman, suspended in mid-air an instant, cast only one agonized glance beneath,—but across and through it, ere the lids could fall, shot a withering sheet of flame,—a rifle-crack, half-heard, was lost in the terrible yell of desperation that bounded after it and filled her ears with savage echoes, and in the wide arc of some eternal descent she was falling;—but the beast fell under her.

I think that the moment following must have been too sacred for us, and perhaps the three have no special interest again till they issue from the shadows of the wilderness upon the white hills that skirt their home. The father carries the child hushed again into slumber, the mother follows with no such feeble step as might be anticipated. It is not time for reaction,—the tension not yet relaxed, the nerves still vibrant, she seems to herself like some one newly made; the night was a dream; the present stamped upon her in deep satisfaction, neither weighed nor compared with the past; if she has the careful tricks of former habit, it is as an automaton; and as they slowly climb the steep under the clear gray vault and the paling morning star, and as she stops to gather a spray of the red-rose berries or a feathery tuft of dead grasses for the chimney-piece of the log-house, or a handful of brown cones for the child's play,—of these quiet, happy folk you would scarcely dream how lately they had stolen from under the banner and encampment of the great King Death. The husband proceeds a step or two in advance; the wife lingers over a singular foot-print in the snow, stoops and examines it, then looks up with a hurried word. Her husband stands alone on the hill, his arms folded across the babe, his gun fallen,—stands defined as a silhouette against the pallid sky. What is there in their home, lying below and yellowing in the light, to fix him with such a stare? She springs to his side. There is no home there. The log-house, the barns, the neighboring farms, the fences, are all blotted out and mingled in one smoking ruin. Desolation and death were indeed there, and beneficence and life in the forest. Tomahawk and scalping-knife, descending during that night, had left behind them only this work of their accomplished hatred and one subtle footprint in the snow.

For the rest,—the world was all before them, where to choose.

Sarah Piatt
(1836–1919)

escendant of an old pioneer family, Kentuckian poet Sarah Piatt composed poems upholding traditional Victorian values in her books but included more subtly ironic and playful poetry in her work for magazines. By the time she married fellow journalist and poet John James Piatt in 1861, she was already a popular magazine poet. Moving with her new husband to Washington, D.C., at the start of the Civil War, Piatt wrote poems exploring the tension between romantic notions of the South and the brutality of slavery. In collaboration with her husband, she published the first of many books of poetry, *The Nests at Washington and Other Poems*, in 1864. "The Palace-Burner" is Piatt's response to women's involvement in the Paris Commune in the spring of 1871, while "A New Thanksgiving" is her fierce antiwar take on the complacent holiday poem.

The Palace-Burner (1872)
(A Picture in a Newspaper.)

She has been burning palaces. "To see
    The sparks look pretty in the wind?" Well, yes—
And something more. But women brave as she
    Leave much for cowards such as I to guess.

But this is old, so old that everything
    Is ashes here—the woman and the rest.
Two years are oh! so long. Now you may bring
    Some newer pictures. You like this one best?

You wish that you had lived in Paris then?
    You would have loved to burn a palace, too?
But they had guns in France, and Christian men
    Shot wicked little Communists, like you.

You would have burned the palace? Just because
    You did not live in it yourself! Oh! why?

Have I not taught you to respect the laws?
   You would have burned the palace. Would not *I*?

Would I? Go to your play. Would I, indeed?
   I? Does the boy not know my soul to be
Languid and worldly, with a dainty need
   For light and music? Yet he questions me.

Can he have seen my soul more near than I?
   Ah! in the dusk and distance sweet she seems,
With lips to kiss away a baby's cry,
   Hands fit for flowers, and eyes for tears and dreams.

Can he have seen my soul? And could she wear
   Such utter life upon a dying face,
Such unappealing, beautiful despair,
   Such garments—soon to be a shroud—with grace?

Has she a charm so calm that it could breathe
   In damp, low places, till some frightened hour;
Then start, like a fair, subtle snake, and wreathe
   A stinging poison with a shadowy power?

Would *I* burn palaces? The child has seen
   In this fierce creature of the Commune here,
So bright with bitterness and so serene,
   A being finer than my soul, I fear.

A New Thanksgiving (1910)

For war, plague, pestilence, flood, famine, fire,
   For Christ discrowned, for false gods set on high;
For fools, whose hands must have their hearts' desire,
We thank Thee—in the darkness—and so die.

For shipwreck: Oh, the sob of strangling seas!—
   No matter. For the snake that charms the dove;

And (is it not the bitterest of all these?)
   We thank Thee—in our blind faith—even for Love.

For breaking hearts; for all that breaks the heart;
   For Death, the one thing after all the rest,
We thank Thee, O our Father! Thou who art,
   And wast, and shalt be—knowing these are best.

Constance Fenimore Woolson
(1840–1894)

ne of the finest short-story writers of the post–Civil War period, Woolson began publishing her writing in 1869 to support her newly widowed mother. Her acutely observed short stories were quickly accepted by prestigious magazines such as *Harper's*, *Century*, and *The Atlantic Monthly*. When Woolson moved from her native Ohio to Florida in 1873 and then in 1879 to Europe (where she met and became friends with Henry James), her fiction followed, reflecting her experiences in the Reconstructionist South and among American expatriates abroad. In an 1882 letter to James, Woolson had declared that she would "never dare put down what men are thinking," but two of her most original stories are written from a male point of view. "Miss Grief" describes the humbling encounter of a fashionable male writer with a female literary genius. "Rodman the Keeper" is an ironic and provocative story about a Union officer who has become the keeper of the national Civil War cemetery in the south. A lifetime sufferer from severe hereditary depression, Woolson died in 1894 in Venice, in fall from a window that was probably a suicide.

Miss Grief (1880)

"A conceited fool" is a not uncommon expression. Now, I know that I am not a fool, but I also know that I am conceited. But, candidly, can it be helped if one happens to be young, well and strong, passably good-looking, with some money that one has inherited and more that one has earned—in all, enough to make life comfortable—and if upon this foundation rests also the pleasant superstructure of a literary success? The success is deserved, I think: certainly it was not lightly gained. Yet even with this I fully appreciate its rarity. Thus, I find myself very well entertained in life: I have all I wish in the way of society, and a deep, though of course carefully concealed, satisfaction in my own little fame; which fame I foster by a gentle system of non-interference. I know that I am spoken of as "that quiet young fellow who writes those delightful little studies of society, you know"; and I live up to that definition.

A year ago I was in Rome, and enjoying life particularly. I had a large number of my acquaintances there, both American and English, and no day passed without its invitation. Of course I understood it: it is seldom that you find a literary man who is good tempered, well dressed, sufficiently provided with money, and amiably obedient to all the rules and requirements of "society." "When found, make a note of it"; and the note was generally an invitation.

One evening, upon returning to my lodgings, my man Simpson informed me that a person had called in the afternoon, and upon learning that I was absent had left not a card, but her name—"Miss Grief." The title lingered—Miss Grief! "Grief has not so far visited me here," I said to myself, dismissing Simpson and seeking my little balcony for a final smoke, "and she shall not now. I shall take care to be 'not at home' to her if she continues to call." And then I fell to thinking of Isabel Abercrombie, in whose society I had spent that and many evenings: they were golden thoughts.

The next day there was an excursion; it was late when I reached my rooms, and again Simpson informed me that Miss Grief had called.

"Is she coming continuously?" I said, half to myself.

"Yes, sir: she mentioned that she should call again."

"How does she look?"

"Well, sir, a lady, but not so prosperous as she was, I should say," answered Simpson, discreetly.

"Young?"

"No, sir."

"Alone?"

"A maid with her, sir."

But once outside in my little high-up balcony with my cigar, I again forgot Miss Grief and whatever she might represent. Who would not forget in that moonlight, with Isabel Abercrombie's face to remember?

The stranger came a third time, and I was absent; then she let two days pass, and began again. It grew to be a regular dialogue between Simpson and myself when I came in at night: "Grief today?"

"Yes, sir."

"What time?"

"Four, sir."

"Happy the man," I thought, "who can keep her confined to a particular hour!"

But I should not have treated my visitor so cavalierly if I had not felt sure that she was eccentric and unconventional—qualities extremely tiresome in a woman no longer young or attractive. If she were not eccentric, she would not have persisted in coming to my door day after day in this silent way, without stating her errand, leaving a note, or presenting her credentials in any shape. I made up my mind that she had something to sell—a bit of carving or some intaglio supposed to be antique. It was known that I had a fancy for oddities. I said to myself, "She has read or heard of my 'Old Gold' story, or else 'The Buried God,' and she thinks me an idealizing ignoramus upon whom she can impose. Her sepulchral name is at least not Italian; probably she is a sharp countrywoman of mine, turning, by means of the present æsthetic craze, an honest penny when she can."

She had called seven times during a period of two weeks without seeing me, when one day I happened to be at home in the afternoon, owing to a pouring rain and a fit of doubt concerning Miss Abercrombie. For I had constructed a careful theory of that young lady's characteristics in my own mind, and she had lived up to it delightfully until the previous evening, when with one word she had blown it to atoms and taken flight, leaving me standing, as it were, on a desolate shore, with nothing but a handful of mistaken inductions wherewith to console myself. I do not know a more exasperating frame of mind, at least for a constructor of theories. I could not write, and so I took up a French novel (I model myself a little on Balzac). I had been turning over its pages but a few moments when Simpson knocked, and, entering softly, said, with just a shadow of a smile on his well-trained face, "Miss Grief." I briefly consigned Miss Grief to all the Furies, and then, as he still lingered—perhaps not knowing where they resided—I asked where the visitor was.

"Outside, sir—in the hall. I told her I would see if you were at home."

"She must be unpleasantly wet if she had no carriage."

"No carriage, sir: they always come on foot. I think she *is* a little damp, sir."

"Well, let her in; but I don't want the maid. I may as well see her now, I suppose, and end the affair."

"Yes, sir."

I did not put down my book. My visitor should have a hearing, but not much more: she had sacrificed her womanly claims by her persistent attacks upon my door. Presently Simpson ushered her in. "Miss Grief," he said, and then went out, closing the curtain behind him.

A woman—yes, a lady—but shabby, unattractive, and more than middle-aged.

I rose, bowed slightly, and then dropped into my chair again, still keeping the book in my hand. "Miss Grief?" I said interrogatively as I indicated a seat with my eyebrows.

"Not Grief," she answered—"Crief: my name is Crief."

She sat down, and I saw that she held a small flat box.

"Not carving, then," I thought—"probably old lace, something that belonged to Tullia or Lucrezia Borgia." But, as she did not speak, I found myself obliged to begin: "You have been here, I think, once or twice before?"

"Seven times; this is the eighth."

A silence.

"I am often out; indeed, I may say that I am never in," I remarked carelessly.

"Yes; you have many friends."

"—Who will perhaps buy old lace," I mentally added. But this time I too remained silent; why should I trouble myself to draw her out? She had sought me; let her advance her idea, whatever it was, now that entrance was gained.

But Miss Grief (I preferred to call her so) did not look as though she could advance anything; her black gown, damp with rain, seemed to retreat fearfully to her thin self, while her thin self retreated as far as possible from me, from the chair, from everything. Her eyes were cast down; an old-fashioned lace veil with a heavy border shaded her face. She looked at the floor, and I looked at her.

I grew a little impatient, but I made up my mind that I would continue silent and see how long a time she would consider necessary to give due effect to her little pantomime. Comedy? Or was it tragedy? I suppose full five minutes passed thus in our double silence; and that is a long time when two persons are sitting opposite each other alone in a small still room.

At last my visitor, without raising her eyes, said slowly, "You are very happy, are you not, with youth, health, friends, riches, fame?"

It was a singular beginning. Her voice was clear, low, and very sweet as she thus enumerated my advantages one by one in a list. I was attracted by it, but repelled by her words, which seemed to me flattery both dull and bold.

"Thanks," I said, "for your kindness, but I fear it is undeserved. I seldom discuss myself even when with my friends."

"I am your friend," replied Miss Grief. Then, after a moment, she added slowly, "I have read every word you have written."

I curled the edges of my book indifferently; I am not a fop, I hope, but—others have said the same.

"What is more, I know much of it by heart," continued my visitor. "Wait: I will show you;" and then, without pause, she began to repeat something of mine word for word, just as I had written it. On she went, and I—listened. I intended interrupting her after a moment, but I did not, because she was reciting so well, and also because I felt a desire gaining upon me to see what she would make of a certain conversation which I knew was coming—a conversation between two of my characters which was, to say the least, sphinx-like, and somewhat incandescent as well. What won me a little, too, was the fact that the scene she was reciting (it was hardly more than that, though called a story) was secretly my favorite among all the sketches from my pen which a gracious public has received with favor. I never said so, but it was; and I had always felt a wondering annoyance that the aforesaid public, while kindly praising beyond their worth other attempts of mine, had never noticed the higher purpose of this little shaft, aimed not at the balconies and lighted windows of society, but straight up toward the distant stars. So she went on, and presently reached the conversation: my two people began to talk. She had raised her eyes now, and was looking at me soberly as she gave the words of the woman, quiet, gentle, cold, and the replies of the man, bitter, hot, and scathing. Her very voice changed, and took, though always sweetly, the different tones required, while no point of meaning, however small, no breath of delicate emphasis which I had meant, but which the dull types could not give, escaped an appreciative and full, almost overfull, recognition which startled me. For she had understood me—understood me almost better than I had understood myself. It seemed to me that while I had labored to interpret, partially, a psychological riddle, she, coming after, had comprehended its bearings better than I had, though confining herself strictly to my own words and emphasis. The scene ended (and it ended rather suddenly), she dropped her eyes, and moved her hand nervously to and fro over the box she held; her gloves were old and shabby, her hands small.

I was secretly much surprised by what I had heard, but my ill humor was deep-seated that day, and I still felt sure, besides, that the box contained something which I was expected to buy.

"You recite remarkably well," I said carelessly, "and I am much flattered also by your appreciation of my attempt. But it is not, I presume, to that alone that I owe the pleasure of this visit?"

"Yes," she answered, still looking down, "it is, for if you had not written that scene I should not have sought you. Your other sketches are interiors—exquisitely painted and delicately finished, but of small scope.

This is a sketch in a few bold, masterly lines—work of entirely different spirit and purpose."

I was nettled by her insight. "You have bestowed so much of your kind attention upon me that I feel your debtor," I said, conventionally. "It may be that there is something I can do for you—connected, possibly, with that little box?"

It was impertinent, but it was true; for she answered, "Yes."

I smiled, but her eyes were cast down and she did not see the smile.

"What I have to show you is a manuscript," she said after a pause which I did not break; "it is a drama. I thought that perhaps you would read it."

"An authoress! This is worse than old lace," I said to myself in dismay.—Then, aloud, "My opinion would be worth nothing, Miss Crief."

"Not in a business way, I know. But it might be—an assistance personally." Her voice had sunk to a whisper; outside, the rain was pouring steadily down. She was a very depressing object to me as she sat there with her box.

"I hardly think I have the time at present—" I began.

She had raised her eyes and was looking at me; then, when I paused, she rose and came suddenly toward my chair. "Yes, you will read it," she said with her hand on my arm—"you will read it. Look at this room; look at yourself; look at all you have. Then look at me, and have pity."

I had risen, for she held my arm, and her damp skirt was brushing my knees.

Her large dark eyes looked intently into mine as she went on; "I have no shame in asking. Why should I have? It is my last endeavor; but a calm and well-considered one. If you refuse I shall go away, knowing that Fate has willed it so. And I shall be content."

"She is mad," I thought. But she did not look so, and she had spoken quietly, even gently. "Sit down," I said, moving away from her. I felt as if I had been magnetized; but it was only the nearness of her eyes to mine, and their intensity. I drew forward a chair, but she remained standing.

"I cannot," she said in the same sweet, gentle tone, "unless you promise."

"Very well, I promise; only sit down."

As I took her arm to lead her to the chair, I perceived that she was trembling, but her face continued unmoved.

"You do not, of course, wish me to look at your manuscript now?" I said, temporizing; "it would be much better to leave it. Give me your address, and I will return it to you with my written opinion; though, I repeat, the latter will be of no use to you. It is the opinion of an editor or publisher that you want."

"It shall be as you please. And I will go in a moment," said Miss Grief, pressing her palms together, as if trying to control the tremor that had seized her slight frame.

She looked so pallid that I thought of offering her a glass of wine; then I remembered that if I did it might be a bait to bring her there again, and this I was desirous to prevent. She rose while the thought was passing through my mind. Her pasteboard box lay on the chair she had first occupied; she took it, wrote an address on the cover, laid it down, and then, bowing with a little air of formality, drew her black shawl round her shoulders and turned toward the door.

I followed, after touching the bell. "You will hear from me by letter," I said.

Simpson opened the door, and I caught a glimpse of the maid, who was waiting in the anteroom. She was an old woman, shorter than her mistress, equally thin, and dressed like her in rusty black. As the door opened she turned toward it a pair of small, dim blue eyes with a look of furtive suspense. Simpson dropped the curtain, shutting me into the inner room; he had no intention of allowing me to accompany my visitor further. But I had the curiosity to go to a bay window in an angle from whence I could command the street door, and presently I saw them issue forth in the rain and walk away side by side, the mistress, being the taller, holding the umbrella: probably there was not much difference in rank between persons so poor and forlorn as these.

It grew dark. I was invited out for the evening, and I knew that if I should go I should meet Miss Abercrombie. I said to myself that I would not go. I got out my paper for writing, I made my preparations for a quiet evening at home with myself; but it was of no use. It all ended slavishly in my going. At the last allowable moment I presented myself, and—as a punishment for my vacillation, I suppose—I never passed a more disagreeable evening. I drove homeward in a murky temper; it was foggy without, and very foggy within. What Isabel really was, now that she had broken through my elaborately built theories, I was not able to decide. There was, to tell the truth, a certain young Englishman—But that is apart from this story.

I reached home, went up to my rooms, and had a supper. It was to console myself; I am obliged to console myself scientifically once in a while. I was walking up and down afterward, smoking and feeling somewhat better, when my eye fell upon the pasteboard box. I took it up; on the cover was written an address which showed that my visitor must have walked a long distance in order to see me: "A. Crief."—"A Grief," I thought; "and so she is. I positively believe she has brought all this trouble upon me: she has the evil eye." I took out the manuscript and looked at it. It was in the form of a little volume, and clearly written; on the cover was the word "Armor" in German text, and, underneath, a pen-and-ink sketch of a helmet, breastplate, and shield.

"Grief certainly needs armor," I said to myself, sitting down by the table and turning over the pages. "I may as well look over the thing now; I could not be in a worse mood." And then I began to read.

Early the next morning Simpson took a note from me to the given address, returning with the following reply: "No; I prefer to come to you; at four; A. CRIEF." These words, with their three semicolons, were written in pencil upon a piece of coarse printing paper, but the handwriting was as clear and delicate as that of the manuscript in ink.

"What sort of a place was it, Simpson?"

"Very poor, sir, but I did not go all the way up. The elder person came down, sir, took the note, and requested me to wait where I was."

"You had no chance, then, to make inquiries?" I said, knowing full well that he had emptied the entire neighborhood of any information it might possess concerning these two lodgers.

"Well, sir, you know how these foreigners will talk, whether one wants to hear or not. But it seems that these two persons have been there but a few weeks; they live alone, and are uncommonly silent and reserved. The people round there call them something that signifies 'the Madames American, thin and dumb.'"

At four the "Madames American" arrived; it was raining again, and they came on foot under their old umbrella. The maid waited in the ante-room, and Miss Grief was ushered into my bachelor's parlor. I had thought that I should meet her with great deference; but she looked so forlorn that my deference changed to pity. It was the woman that impressed me then, more than the writer—the fragile, nerveless body more than the inspired mind. For it was inspired; I had sat up half the night over her drama, and had felt thrilled through and through more than once by its earnestness, passion, and power.

No one could have been more surprised than I was to find myself thus enthusiastic. I thought I had outgrown that sort of thing. And one would have supposed, too (I myself should have supposed so the day before), that the faults of the drama, which were many and prominent, would have chilled any liking I might have felt, I being a writer myself, and therefore critical; for writers are as apt to make much of the "how," rather than the "what," as painters, who, it is well known, prefer an exquisitely rendered representation of a commonplace theme to an imperfectly executed picture of even the most striking subject. But in this case, on the contrary, the scattered rays of splendor in Miss Grief's drama had made me forget the dark spots, which were numerous and disfiguring; or, rather, the splendor had made me anxious to have the spots removed. And this also was a philanthropic state very unusual with me. Regarding unsuccessful writers, my motto had been "Væ victis!"

My visitor took a seat and folded her hands; I could see, in spite of her quiet manner, that she was in breathless suspense. It seemed so pitiful that she should be trembling there before me—a woman so much older than I was, a woman who possessed the divine spark of genius, which I was by no means sure (in spite of my success) had been granted to me— that I felt as if I ought to go down on my knees before her, and entreat her to take her proper place of supremacy at once. But there! one does not go down on one's knees, combustively, as it were, before a woman over fifty, plain in feature, thin, dejected, and ill dressed. I contented myself with taking her hands (in their miserable old gloves) in mine, while I said cordially, "Miss Crief, your drama seems to me full of original power. It has roused my enthusiasm: I sat up half the night reading it."

The hands I held shook, but something (perhaps a shame for having evaded the knees business) made me tighten my hold and bestow upon her also a reassuring smile. She looked at me for a moment, and then, suddenly and noiselessly, tears rose and rolled down her cheeks. I dropped her hands and retreated. I had not thought her tearful: on the contrary, her voice and face had seemed rigidly controlled. But now here she was bending herself over the side of the chair with her head resting on her arms, not sobbing aloud, but her whole frame shaken by the strength of her emotion. I rushed for a glass of wine; I pressed her to take it. I did not quite know what to do, but, putting myself in her place, I decided to praise the drama; and praise it I did. I do not know when I have used so many adjectives. She raised her head and began to wipe her eyes.

"Do take the wine," I said, interrupting myself in my cataract of language.

"I dare not," she answered; then added humbly, "that is, unless you have a biscuit here or a bit of bread."

I found some biscuit; she ate two, and then slowly drank the wine, while I resumed my verbal Niagara. Under its influence—and that of the wine too, perhaps—she began to show new life. It was not that she looked radiant—she could not—but simply that she looked warm. I now perceived what had been the principal discomfort of her appearance heretofore: it was that she had looked all the time as if suffering from cold.

At last I could think of nothing more to say, and stopped. I really admired the drama, but I thought I had exerted myself sufficiently as an anti-hysteric, and that adjectives enough, for the present at least, had been administered. She had put down her empty wineglass, and was resting her hands on the broad cushioned arms of her chair with, for a thin person, a sort of expanded content.

"You must pardon my tears," she said, smiling; "it was the revulsion of feeling. My life was at a low ebb: if your sentence had been against me, it would have been my end."

"Your end?"

"Yes, the end of my life; I should have destroyed myself."

"Then you would have been a weak as well as wicked woman," I said in a tone of disgust. I do hate sensationalism.

"Oh no, you know nothing about it. I should have destroyed only this poor worn tenement of clay. But I can well understand how *you* would look upon it. Regarding the desirableness of life, the prince and the beggar may have different opinions. We will say no more of it, but talk of the drama instead." As she spoke the word "drama" a triumphant brightness came into her eyes.

I took the manuscript from a drawer and sat down beside her. "I suppose you know that there are faults," I said, expecting ready acquiescence.

"I was not aware that there were any," was her gentle reply.

Here was a beginning! After all my interest in her—and, I may say under the circumstances, my kindness—she received me in this way! However, my belief in her genius was too sincere to be altered by her whimsies; so I persevered. "Let us go over it together," I said. "Shall I read it to you, or will you read it to me?"

"I will not read it, but recite it."

"That will never do; you will recite it so well that we shall see only the good points, and what we have to concern ourselves with now is the bad ones."

"I will recite it," she repeated.

"Now, Miss Crief," I said bluntly, "for what purpose did you come to me? Certainly not merely to recite: I am no stage manager. In plain English, was it not your idea that I might help you in obtaining a publisher?"

"Yes, yes," she answered, looking at me apprehensively, all her old manner returning.

I followed up my advantage, opened the little paper volume and began. I first took the drama line by line, and spoke of the faults of expression and structure; then I turned back and touched upon two or three glaring impossibilities in the plot. "Your absorbed interest in the motive of the whole no doubt made you forget these blemishes," I said apologetically.

But, to my surprise, I found that she did not see the blemishes—that she appreciated nothing I had said, comprehended nothing. Such unaccountable obtuseness puzzled me. I began again, going over the whole with even greater minuteness and care. I worked hard: the perspiration stood in beads upon my forehead as I struggled with her—what shall I call it—obstinacy? But it was not exactly obstinacy. She simply could not see the faults of her own work, any more than a blind man can see the smoke that dims a patch of blue sky. When I had finished my task the second time, she still remained as gently impassive as before. I leaned back in my chair exhausted, and looked at her.

Even then she did not seem to comprehend (whether she agreed with it or not) what I must be thinking. "It is such a heaven to me that you like it!" she murmured dreamily, breaking the silence. Then, with more animation, "And *now* you will let me recite it?"

I was too weary to oppose her; she threw aside her shawl and bonnet, and, standing in the center of the room, began.

And she carried me along with her: all the strong passages were doubly strong when spoken, and the faults, which seemed nothing to her, were made by her earnestness to seem nothing to me, at least for that moment. When it was ended, she stood looking at me with a triumphant smile.

"Yes," I said, "I like it, and you see that I do. But I like it because my taste is peculiar. To me originality and force are everything—perhaps because I have them not to any marked degree myself—but the world at large will not overlook as I do your absolutely barbarous shortcomings on account of them. Will you trust me to go over the drama and correct it at my pleasure?" This was a vast deal for me to offer; I was surprised at myself.

"No," she answered softly, still smiling. "There shall not be so much as a comma altered." Then she sat down and fell into a reverie as though she were alone.

"Have you written anything else?" I said after a while, when I had become tired of the silence.

"Yes."

"Can I see it? Or is it *them*?"

"It is *them*. Yes, you can see all."

"I will call upon you for the purpose."

"No, you must not," she said, coming back to the present nervously. "I prefer to come to you."

At this moment Simpson entered to light the room, and busied himself rather longer than was necessary over the task. When he finally went out I saw that my visitor's manner had sunk into its former depression: the presence of the servant seemed to have chilled her.

"When did you say I might come?" I repeated, ignoring her refusal.

"I did not say it. It would be impossible."

"Well, then, when will you come here?" There was, I fear, a trace of fatigue in my tone.

"At your good pleasure, sir," she answered humbly.

My chivalry was touched by this: after all, she was a woman. "Come tomorrow," I said. "By the way, come and dine with me then; why not?" I was curious to see what she would reply.

"Why not, indeed? Yes, I will come. I am forty-three: I might have been your mother."

This was not quite true, as I am over thirty: but I look young, while she—Well, I had thought her over fifty. "I can hardly call you 'mother,' but we might compromise upon 'aunt,'" I said, laughing. "Aunt what?"

"My name is Aaronna," she gravely answered. "My father was much disappointed that I was not a boy, and gave me as nearly as possible the name he had prepared—Aaron."

"Then come and dine with me tomorrow, and bring with you the other manuscripts, Aaronna," I said, amused at the quaint sound of the name. On the whole, I did not like "aunt."

"I will come," she answered.

It was twilight and still raining, but she refused all offers of escort or carriage, departing with her maid, as she had come, under the brown umbrella. The next day we had the dinner. Simpson was astonished—and more than astonished, grieved—when I told him that he was to dine with the maid; but he could not complain in words, since my own guest, the mistress, was hardly more attractive. When our preparations were complete, I could not help laughing: the two prim little tables, one in the parlor and one in the anteroom, and Simpson disapprovingly going back and forth between them, were irresistible.

I greeted my guest hilariously when she arrived, and, fortunately, her manner was not quite so depressed as usual: I could never have accorded myself with a tearful mood. I had thought that perhaps she would make, for the occasion, some change in her attire; I have never known a woman who had not some scrap of finery, however small, in reserve for that unexpected occasion of which she is ever dreaming. But no: Miss Grief wore the same black gown, unadorned and unaltered. I was glad that there was no rain that day, so that the skirt did not at least look so damp and rheumatic.

She ate quietly, almost furtively, yet with a good appetite, and she did not refuse the wine. Then, when the meal was over and Simpson had removed the dishes, I asked for the new manuscripts. She gave me an old green copybook filled with short poems, and a prose sketch by itself; I lit a cigar and sat down at my desk to look them over.

"Perhaps you will try a cigarette?" I suggested, more for amusement than anything else, for there was not a shade of Bohemianism about her; her whole appearance was puritanical.

"I have not yet succeeded in learning to smoke."

"You have tried?" I said, turning round.

"Yes: Serena and I tried, but we did not succeed."

"Serena is your maid?"

"She lives with me."

I was seized with inward laughter, and began hastily to look over her manuscripts with my back toward her, so that she might not see it. A vision had risen before me of those two forlorn women, alone in their room with locked doors, patiently trying to acquire the smoker's art.

But my attention was soon absorbed by the papers before me. Such a fantastic collection of words, lines, and epithets I had never before seen, or even in dreams imagined. In truth, they were like the work of dreams: they were *Kubla Khan*, only more so. Here and there was radiance like the flash of a diamond, but each poem, almost each verse and line, was marred by some fault or lack which seemed wilful perversity, like the work of an evil sprite. It was like a case of jeweller's wares set before you, with each ring unfinished, each bracelet too large or too small for its purpose, each breastpin without its fastening, each necklace purposely broken. I turned the pages, marvelling. When about half an hour had passed, and I was leaning back for a moment to light another cigar, I glanced toward my visitor. She was behind me, in an easy chair before my small fire, and she was—fast asleep! In the relaxation of her unconsciousness I was struck anew by the poverty her appearance expressed; her feet were visible, and I saw the miserable worn old shoes which hitherto she had kept concealed.

After looking at her for a moment, I returned to my task and took up the prose story; in prose she must be more reasonable. She was less fantastic perhaps, but hardly more reasonable. The story was that of a profligate and commonplace man forced by two of his friends, in order not to break the heart of a dying girl who loves him, to live up to a high imaginary ideal of himself which her pure but mistaken mind has formed. He has a handsome face and sweet voice, and repeats what they tell him. Her long, slow decline and happy death, and his own inward ennui and profound weariness of the rôle he has to play, made the vivid points of the story. So far, well enough, but here was the trouble: through the whole narrative moved another character, a physician of tender heart and exquisite mercy, who practiced murder as a fine art, and was regarded (by the author) as a second Messiah! This was monstrous. I read it through twice, and threw it down; then, fatigued, I turned round and leaned back, waiting for her to wake. I could see her profile against the dark hue of the easy chair.

Presently she seemed to feel my gaze, for she stirred, then opened her eyes. "I have been asleep," she said, rising hurriedly.

"No harm in that, Aaronna."

But she was deeply embarrassed and troubled, much more so than the occasion required; so much so, indeed, that I turned the conversation back upon the manuscripts as a diversion. "I cannot stand that doctor of yours," I said, indicating the prose story; "no one would. You must cut him out."

Her self-possession returned as if by magic. "Certainly not," she answered haughtily.

"Oh, if you do not care—I had labored under the impression that you were anxious these things should find a purchaser."

"I am, I am," she said, her manner changing to deep humility with wonderful rapidity. With such alternations of feeling as this sweeping over her like great waves, no wonder she was old before her time.

"Then you must take out that doctor."

"I am willing, but do not know how," she answered, pressing her hands together helplessly. "In my mind he belongs to the story so closely that he cannot be separated from it."

Here Simpson entered, bringing a note for me: it was a line from Miss Abercrombie inviting me for that evening—an unexpected gathering, and therefore likely to be all the more agreeable. My heart bounded in spite of me; I forgot Miss Grief and her manuscripts for the moment as completely as though they had never existed. But, bodily, being still in the same room with her, her speech brought me back to the present.

"You have had good news?" she said.

"Oh no, nothing especial—merely an invitation."

"But good news also," she repeated. "And now, as for me, I must go."

Not supposing that she would stay much later in any case, I had that morning ordered a carriage to come for her at about that hour. I told her this. She made no reply beyond putting on her bonnet and shawl.

"You will hear from me soon," I said; "I shall do all I can for you."

She had reached the door, but before opening it she stopped, turned and extended her hand. "You are good," she said: "I give you thanks. Do not think me ungrateful or envious. It is only that you are young, and I am so—so old." Then she opened the door and passed through the ante-room without pause, her maid accompanying her and Simpson with gladness lighting the way. They were gone. I dressed hastily and went out—to continue my studies in psychology.

Time passed; I was busy, amused and perhaps a little excited (sometimes psychology is exciting). But, though much occupied with my own affairs, I did not altogether neglect my self-imposed task regarding Miss Grief. I began by sending her prose story to a friend, the editor of a monthly magazine, with a letter making a strong plea for its admittance. It should have a chance first on its own merits. Then I forwarded the drama to a publisher, also an acquaintance, a man with a taste for phantasms and a soul above mere common popularity, as his own coffers knew to their cost. This done, I waited with conscience clear.

Four weeks passed. During this waiting period I heard nothing from Miss Grief. At last one morning came a letter from my editor. "The story has force, but I cannot stand that doctor," he wrote. "Let her cut him out, and I might print it." Just what I myself had said. The package lay there on my table, travel worn and grimed; a returned manuscript is, I think, the most melancholy object on earth. I decided to wait, before writing to Aaronna, until the second letter was received. A week later it came. "Armor" was declined. The publisher had been "impressed" by the power displayed in certain passages, but the "impossibilities of the plot" rendered it "unavailable for publication"—in fact, would "bury it in ridicule" if brought before the public, a public "lamentably" fond of amusement, "seeking it, undaunted, even in the cannon's mouth." I doubt if he knew himself what he meant. But one thing, at any rate, was clear: "Armor" was declined.

Now, I am, as I have remarked before, a little obstinate. I was determined that Miss Grief's work should be received. I would alter and improve it myself, without letting her know: the end justified the means. Surely the sieve of my own good taste, whose mesh had been pronounced so fine and delicate, would serve for two. I began; and utterly failed.

I set to work first upon "Armor." I amended, altered, left out, put in, pieced, condensed, lengthened; I did my best, and all to no avail. I could not succeed in completing anything that satisfied me, or that approached, in truth, Miss Grief's own work just as it stood. I suppose I went over that manuscript twenty times: I covered sheets of paper with my copies. But the obstinate drama refused to be corrected; as it was it must stand or fall.

Wearied and annoyed, I threw it aside and took up the prose story: that would be easier. But, to my surprise, I found that that apparently gentle "doctor" would not out: he was so closely interwoven with every part of the tale that to take him out was like taking out one especial figure in a carpet: that is, impossible, unless you unravel the whole. At last I did unravel the whole, and then the story was no longer good, or Aaronna's: it was weak, and mine. All this took time, for of course I had much to do in connection with my own life and tasks. But, though slowly and at my leisure, I really did try my best as regarded Miss Grief, and without success. I was forced at last to make up my mind that either my own powers were not equal to the task, or else that her perversities were as essential a part of her work as her inspirations, and not to be separated from it. Once during this period I showed two of the short poems to Isabel, withholding of course the writer's name. "They were written by a woman," I explained.

"Her mind must have been disordered, poor thing!" Isabel said in her gentle way when she returned them—"at least, judging by these. They are hopelessly mixed and vague."

Now, they were not vague so much as vast. But I knew that I could not make Isabel comprehend it, and (so complex a creature is man) I do not know that I wanted her to comprehend it. These were the only ones in the whole collection that I would have shown her, and I was rather glad that she did not like even these. Not that poor Aaronna's poems were evil: they were simply unrestrained, large, vast, like the skies or the wind.

Isabel was bounded on all sides, like a violet in a garden bed. And I liked her so.

One afternoon, about the time when I was beginning to see that I could not "improve" Miss Grief, I came upon the maid. I was driving, and she had stopped on the crossing to let the carriage pass. I recognized her at a glance (by her general forlornness), and called to the driver to stop: "How is Miss Grief?" I said. "I have been intending to write to her for some time."

"And your note, when it comes," answered the old woman on the crosswalk fiercely, "she shall not see."

"What?"

"I say she shall not see it. Your patronizing face shows that you have no good news, and you shall not rack and stab her any more on *this* earth, please God, while I have authority."

"Who has racked or stabbed her, Serena?"

"Serena, indeed! Rubbish! I'm no Serena: I'm her aunt. And as to who has racked and stabbed her, I say you, *you*—YOU literary men!" She had put her old head inside my carriage, and flung out these words at me in a shrill, menacing tone. "But she shall die in peace in spite of you," she continued. "Vampires! you take her ideas and fatten on them, and leave her to starve. You know you do—*you* who have had her poor manuscripts these months and months!"

"Is she ill?" I asked in real concern, gathering that much at least from the incoherent tirade.

"She is dying," answered the desolate old creature, her voice softening and her dim eyes filling with tears.

"Oh, I trust not. Perhaps something can be done. Can I help you in any way?"

"In all ways if you would," she said, breaking down and beginning to sob weakly, with her head resting on the sill of the carriage window. "Oh, what have we not been through together, we two! Piece by piece I have sold all."

I am goodhearted enough, but I do not like to have old women weeping across my carriage door. I suggested, therefore, that she should come inside and let me take her home. Her shabby old skirt was soon beside me, and, following her directions, the driver turned toward one of the most wretched quarters of the city, the abode of poverty, crowded and unclean. Here, in a large bare chamber up many flights of stairs, I found Miss Grief.

As I entered I was startled: I thought she was dead. There seemed no life present until she opened her eyes, and even then they rested upon us vaguely, as though she did not know who we were. But as I approached a light came into them: she recognized me, and this sudden revivification, this return of the soul to the almost deserted body, was the most wonderful thing I ever saw. "You have good news of the drama?" she whispered as I bent over her: "tell me. I *know* you have good news."

What was I to answer? Pray, what would you have answered, puritan?

"Yes, I have good news, Aaronna," I said. "The drama will appear." (And who knows? Perhaps it will in some other world.)

She smiled, and her now brilliant eyes did not leave my face.

"He knows I'm your aunt: I told him," said the old woman, coming to the bedside.

"Did you?" whispered Miss Grief, still gazing at me with a smile. "Then please, dear Aunt Martha, give me something to eat."

Aunt Martha hurried across the room, and I followed her. "It's the first time she's asked for food in weeks," she said in a husky tone.

She opened a cupboard door vaguely, but I could see nothing within. "What have you for her?" I asked with some impatience, though in a low voice.

"Please God, nothing!" answered the poor old woman, hiding her reply and her tears behind the broad cupboard door. "I was going out to get a little something when I met you."

"Good Heavens! is it money you need? Here, take this and send; or go yourself in the carriage waiting below."

She hurried out breathless, and I went back to the bedside, much disturbed by what I had seen and heard. But Miss Grief's eyes were full of life, and as I sat down beside her she whispered earnestly, "Tell me."

And I did tell her—a romance invented for the occasion. I venture to say that none of my published sketches could compare with it. As for the lie involved, it will stand among my few good deeds; I know, at the judgment bar.

And she was satisfied. "I have never known what it was," she whispered, "to be fully happy until now." She closed her eyes, and when the lids fell I again thought that she had passed away. But no, there was still pulsation in her small, thin wrist. As she perceived my touch she smiled. "Yes, I am happy," she said again, though without audible sound.

The old aunt returned; food was prepared, and she took some. I myself went out after wine that should be rich and pure. She rallied a little, but I did not leave her: her eyes dwelt upon me and compelled me to stay, or rather my conscience compelled me. It was a damp night, and

I had a little fire made. The wine, fruit, flowers, and candles I had ordered made the bare place for the time being bright and fragrant. Aunt Martha dozed in her chair from sheer fatigue—she had watched many nights—but Miss Grief was awake, and I sat beside her.

"I make you my executor," she murmured, "as to the drama. But my other manuscripts place, when I am gone, under my head, and let them be buried with me. They are not many—those you have and these. See!"

I followed her gesture, and saw under her pillows the edges of two more copybooks like the one I had. "Do not look at them—my poor dead children!" she said tenderly. "Let them depart with me—unread, as I have been."

Later she whispered, "Did you wonder why I came to you? It was the contrast. You were young—strong—rich—praised—loved—successful: all that I was not. I wanted to look at you—and imagine how it would feel. You had success—but I had the greater power. Tell me, did I not have it?"

"Yes, Aaronna."

"It is all in the past now. But I am satisfied."

After another pause she said with a faint smile, "Do you remember when I fell asleep in your parlor? It was the good and rich food. It was so long since I had had food like that!"

I took her hand and held it, conscience stricken, but now she hardly seemed to perceive my touch. "And the smoking?" she whispered. "Do you remember how you laughed? I saw it. But I had heard that smoking soothed—that one was no longer tired and hungry—with a cigar."

In little whispers of this sort, separated by long rests and pauses, the night passed. Once she asked if her aunt was asleep, and when I answered in the affirmative she said, "Help her to return home—to America: the drama will pay for it. I ought never to have brought her away."

I promised, and she resumed her bright-eyed silence.

I think she did not speak again. Toward morning the change came, and soon after sunrise, with her old aunt kneeling by her side, she passed away.

All was arranged as she had wished. Her manuscripts, covered with violets, formed her pillow. No one followed her to the grave save her aunt and myself; I thought she would prefer it so. Her name was not "Crief," after all, but "Moncrief;" I saw it written out by Aunt Martha for the coffin plate, as follows: "Aaronna Moncrief, aged forty-three years, two months, and eight days."

I never knew more of her history than is written here. If there was more that I might have learned, it remained unlearned, for I did not ask.

And the drama? I keep it here in this locked case. I could have had it published at my own expense; but I think that now she knows its faults herself, perhaps, and would not like it.

I keep it; and, once in a while, I read it over—not as a *memento mori* exactly, but rather as a memento of my own good fortune, for which I should continually give thanks. The want of one grain made all her work void, and that one grain was given to me. She, with the greater power, failed—I, with the less, succeeded. But no praise is due to me for that. When I die "Armor" is to be destroyed unread: not even Isabel is to see it. For women will misunderstand each other; and, dear and precious to me as my sweet wife is, I could not bear that she or anyone should cast so much as a thought of scorn upon the memory of the writer, upon my poor dead, "unavailable," unaccepted "Miss Grief."

Rodman the Keeper (1880)

The long years come and go,
    And the Past,
The sorrowful, splendid Past,
With its glory and its woe,
    Seems never to have been.
    ——Seems never to have been?
    O somber days and grand,
    How ye crowd back once more,
Seeing our heroes' graves are green
By the Potomac and the Cumberland,
And in the valley of the Shenandoah!

When we remember how they died,—
In dark ravine and on the mountain-side,
In leaguered fort and fire-encircled town,
And where the iron ships went down,—
How their dear lives were spent
In the weary hospital-tent,
In the cockpit's crowded hive,

———it seems
Ignoble to be alive!

—THOMAS BAILEY ALDRICH

"Keeper of what? Keeper of the dead. Well, it is easier to keep the dead than the living; and as for the gloom of the thing, the living among whom I have been lately were not a hilarious set."

John Rodman sat in the doorway and looked out over his domain. The little cottage behind him was empty of life save himself alone. In one room the slender appointments provided by government for the keeper, who being still alive must sleep and eat, made the bareness doubly bare; in the other the desk and the great ledgers, the ink and pens, the register, the loud-ticking clock on the wall, and the flag folded on a shelf, were all for the kept, whose names, in hastily written, blotted rolls of manuscript, were waiting to be transcribed in the new red-bound ledgers in the keeper's best handwriting day by day, while the clock was to tell him the hour when the flag must rise over the mounds where reposed the bodies of fourteen thousand United States soldiers—who had languished where once stood the prison pens, on the opposite slopes, now fair and peaceful in the sunset; who had fallen by the way in long marches to and fro under the burning sun; who had fought and died on the many battlefields that reddened the beautiful state, stretching from the peaks of the marble mountains in the smoky west down to the sea islands of the ocean border. The last rim of the sun's red ball had sunk below the horizon line, and the western sky glowed with deep rose-color, which faded away above into pink, into the salmon tint, into shades of that far-away heavenly emerald which the brush of the earthly artist can never reproduce, but which is found sometimes in the iridescent heart of the opal. The small town, a mile distant, stood turning its back on the cemetery; but the keeper could see the pleasant, rambling old mansions, each with its rose garden and neglected outlying fields, the empty Negro quarters falling into ruin, and everything just as it stood when on that April morning the first gun was fired on Sumter; apparently not a nail added, not a brushful of paint applied, not a fallen brick replaced, or latch or lock repaired. The keeper had noted these things as he strolled through the town, but not with surprise; for he had seen the South in its first estate, when, fresh, strong, and fired with enthusiasm, he, too, had marched away from his village home with the colors flying above and the girls waving their handkerchiefs behind, as the regiment, a thousand strong, filed down the dusty road. That regiment, a weak, scarred two hundred, came back a year later with lagging step and colors tattered and scorched, and the girls could not wave their handkerchiefs, wet and sodden with tears. But the keeper, his wound healed, had gone again; and he had seen with his New England eyes the magnificence and the carelessness of the South, her splendor and negligence, her wealth and thriftlessness, as through Virginia and the fair Carolinas, across Georgia and into sunny Florida, he had marched month by month, first a lieutenant, then captain, and finally major and colonel, as death mowed down those above him, and he and his good conduct were left. Everywhere magnificence went hand in hand with neglect, and he had said so as chance now and then threw a conversation in his path.

"We have no such shiftless ways," he would remark, after he had furtively supplied a prisoner with hardtack and coffee.

"And no such grand ones either," Johnny Reb would reply, if he was a man of spirit; and generally he was.

The Yankee, forced to acknowledge the truth of this statement, qualified it by observing that he would rather have more thrift with a little less grandeur; whereupon the other answered that _he_ would not; and there the conversation rested. So now ex-Colonel Rodman, keeper of the national cemetery, viewed the little town in its second estate with philosophic eyes. "It is part of a great problem now working itself out; I am not here to tend the living, but the dead," he said.

Whereupon, as he walked among the long mounds, a voice seemed to rise from the still ranks below: "While ye have time, do good to men," it said. "Behold, we are beyond your care." But the keeper did not heed.

This still evening in early February he looked out over the level waste. The little town stood in the lowlands; there were no hills from whence cometh help—calm heights that lift the soul above earth and its cares; no river to lead the aspirations of the children outward toward the great sea. Everything was monotonous, and the only spirit that rose above the waste was a bitterness for the gained and sorrow for the lost cause. The keeper was the only man whose presence personated the former in their sight, and upon him therefore, as representative, the bitterness fell, not in words, but in averted looks, in sudden silences when he approached, in withdrawals and avoidance, until he lived and moved in a vacuum; wherever he went there was presently no one save himself; the very shopkeeper who sold him sugar seemed turned into a man of wood, and took his money reluctantly, although the shilling gained stood perhaps for that day's dinner. So Rodman withdrew himself, and came and went among them no more; the broad acres of his domain gave him as much exercise as his shattered ankle could bear; he ordered his few supplies by the quantity, and began the life of a solitary, his island marked out by the massive granite wall with which the United States Government has carefully surrounded those sad Southern cemeteries of hers; sad, not so much from the number of the mounds representing youth and strength cut off in their bloom, for that is but the fortune of war, as for the complete isolation which marks them. "Strangers in a strange land" is the thought of all who, coming and going to and from Florida, turn aside here and there to stand for a moment among the closely ranged graves which seem already a part of the past, that near past which in our hurrying American life is even now so far away. The government work was completed before the keeper came; the lines of the trenches were defined by low granite copings, and the comparatively few single mounds were headed by trim little white boards bearing generally the word "Unknown," but here and there a name and an age, in most cases a boy from some far-away Northern State; "twenty-one," "twenty-two," said the inscriptions; the dates were those dark years among the sixties, measured now more than by anything else in the number of maidens widowed in heart, and women widowed indeed, who sit still and remember, while the world rushes by. At sunrise the keeper ran up the stars and stripes; and so precise were his ideas of the accessories belonging to the place, that from his own small store of money he had taken enough, by stinting himself, to buy a second flag for stormy weather, so that, rain or not, the colors should float over the dead. This was not patriotism so-called, or rather miscalled, it was not sentimental fancy, it was not zeal or triumph; it was simply a sense of the fitness of things, a conscientiousness which had in it nothing of religion, unless indeed a man's endeavor to live up to his own ideal of his duty be a religion. The same feeling led the keeper to spend hours in copying the rolls. "John Andrew Warren, Company G, Eighth New Hampshire Infantry," he repeated, as he slowly wrote the name, giving "John Andrew" clear, bold capitals and a lettering impossible to mistake; "died August 15, 1863, aged twenty-two years. He came from the prison pen yonder, and lies somewhere in those trenches, I suppose. Now then, John Andrew, don't fancy I am sorrowing for you; no doubt you are better off than I am at this very moment. But none the less, John Andrew, shall pen, ink, and hand do their duty to you. For that I am here."

Infinite pains and labor went into these records of the dead; one hair's-breadth error, and the whole page was replaced by a new one. The same spirit kept the grass carefully away from the low coping of the trenches, kept the graveled paths smooth and the mounds green, and the

bare little cottage neat as a man-of-war. When the keeper cooked his din-
ner, the door toward the east, where the dead lay, was scrupulously
closed, nor was it opened until everything was in perfect order again. At
sunset the flag was lowered, and then it was the keeper's habit to walk
slowly up and down the path until the shadows veiled the mounds on
each side, and there was nothing save the peaceful green of earth. "So
time will efface our little lives and sorrows," he mused, "and we shall be
as nothing in the indistinguishable past." Yet nonetheless did he fulfill the
duties of every day and hour with exactness. "At least they shall not say
that I was lacking," he murmured to himself as he thought vaguely of
the future beyond these graves. Who "they" were, it would have
troubled him to formulate, since he was one of the many sons whom
New England in this generation sends forth with a belief composed
entirely of negatives. As the season advanced, he worked all day in the
sunshine. "My garden looks well," he said. "I like this cemetery because
it is the original resting place of the dead who lie beneath. They were not
brought here from distant places, gathered up by contract, numbered,
and described like so much merchandise; their first repose has not been
broken, their peace has been undisturbed. Hasty burials the prison
authorities gave them; the thin bodies were tumbled into the trenches by
men almost as thin, for the whole state went hungry in those dark days.
There were not many prayers, no tears, as the dead carts went the
rounds. But the prayers had been said, and the tears had fallen, while the
poor fellows were still alive in the pens yonder; and when at last death
came, it was like a release. They suffered long; and I for one believe that
therefore shall their rest be long—long and sweet."

After a time began the rain, the soft, persistent, gray rain of the South-
ern lowlands, and he stayed within and copied another thousand names
into the ledger. He would not allow himself the companionship of a dog
lest the creature should bark at night and disturb the quiet. There was no
one to hear save himself, and it would have been a friendly sound as he
lay awake on his narrow iron bed, but it seemed to him against the spirit
of the place. He would not smoke, although he had the soldier's fond-
ness for a pipe. Many a dreary evening, beneath a hastily built shelter of
boughs, when the rain poured down and everything was comfortless, he
had found solace in the curling smoke; but now it seemed to him that it
would be incongruous, and at times he almost felt as if it would be selfish
too. "*They* cannot smoke, you know, down there under the wet grass," he
thought, as standing at the window he looked toward the ranks of the
mounds stretching across the eastern end from side to side—"my

parade-ground," he called it. And then he would smile at his own fancies, draw the curtain, shut out the rain and the night, light his lamp, and go to work on the ledgers again. Some of the names lingered in his memory; he felt as if he had known the men who bore them, as if they had been boys together, and were friends even now although separated for a time. "James Marvin, Company B, Fifth Maine. The Fifth Maine was in the seven days' battle. I say, do you remember that retreat down the Quaker church road, and the way Phil Kearney held the rearguard firm?" And over the whole seven days he wandered with his mute friend, who remembered everything and everybody in the most satisfactory way. One of the little headboards in the parade ground attracted him peculiarly because the name inscribed was his own: "———Rodman, Company A, One Hundred and Sixth New York."

"I remember that regiment; it came from the extreme northern part of the state. Blank Rodman must have melted down here, coming as he did from the half-arctic region along the St. Lawrence. I wonder what he thought of the first hot day, say in South Carolina, along those simmering rice fields?" He grew into the habit of pausing for a moment by the side of this grave every morning and evening. "Blank Rodman. It might easily have been John. And then, where should I be?"

But Blank Rodman remained silent, and the keeper, after pulling up a weed or two and trimming the grass over his relative, went off to his duties again. "I am convinced that Blank is a relative," he said to himself, "distant, perhaps, but still a kinsman."

One April day the heat was almost insupportable; but the sun's rays were not those brazen beams that sometimes in Northern cities burn the air and scorch the pavements to a white heat; rather were they soft and still; the moist earth exhaled her richness, not a leaf stirred, and the whole level country seemed sitting in a hot vapor bath. In the early dawn the keeper had performed his outdoor tasks, but all day he remained almost without stirring in his chair between two windows, striving to exist. At high noon out came a little black bringing his supplies from the town, whistling and shuffling along, gay as a lark. The keeper watched him coming slowly down the white road, loitering by the way in the hot blaze, stopping to turn a somersault or two, to dangle over a bridge rail, to execute various impromptu capers all by himself. He reached the gate at last, entered, and, having come all the way up the path in a hornpipe step, he set down his basket at the door to indulge in one long and final double-shuffle before knocking. "Stop that!" said the keeper through the closed blinds. The little darkey darted back; but as nothing further came

out of the window—a boot, for instance, or some other stray missile—
he took courage, showed his ivories, and drew near again. "Do you sup-
pose I am going to have you stirring up the heat in that way?" demanded
the keeper.

The little black grinned, but made no reply, unless smoothing the hot
white sand with his black toes could be construed as such; he now
removed his rimless hat and made a bow.

"Is it, or is it not warm?" asked the keeper, as a naturalist might inquire
of a salamander, not referring to his own so much as to the salamander's
ideas on the subject.

"Dunno, mars'," replied the little black.

"How do *you* feel?"

"'Spects I feel all right, mars'."

The keeper gave up the investigation, and presented to the salamander
a nickel cent. "I suppose there is no such thing as a cool spring in all this
melting country," he said.

But the salamander indicated with his thumb a clump of trees on the
green plain north of the cemetery. "Ole Mars' Ward's place—cole spring
dah." He then departed, breaking into a run after he had passed the gate,
his ample mouth watering at the thought of a certain chunk of taffy at
the mercantile establishment kept by Aunt Dinah in a corner of her one-
roomed cabin. At sunset the keeper went thirstily out with a tin pail on
his arm, in search of the cold spring. "If it could only be like the spring
down under the rocks where I used to drink when I was a boy!" he
thought. He had never walked in that direction before. Indeed, now that
he had abandoned the town, he seldom went beyond the walls of the
cemetery. An old road led across to the clump of trees, through fields run
to waste, and following it he came to the place, a deserted house with
tumble-down fences and overgrown garden, the outbuildings indicating
that once upon a time there were many servants and a prosperous mas-
ter. The house was of wood, large on the ground, with encircling piaz-
zas; across the front door rough bars had been nailed, and the closed
blinds were protected in the same manner; from long want of paint the
clapboards were gray and mossy, and the floor of the piazza had fallen in
here and there from decay. The keeper decided that his cemetery was a
much more cheerful place than this, and then he looked around for the
spring. Behind the house the ground sloped down; it must be there. He
went around and came suddenly upon a man lying on an old rug outside
of a back door. "Excuse me. I thought nobody lived here," he said.

"Nobody does," replied the man; "I am not much of a body, am I?"

His left arm was gone, and his face was thin and worn with long ill-ness; he closed his eyes after speaking, as though the few words had exhausted him.

"I came for water from a cold spring you have here, somewhere," pur-sued the keeper, contemplating the wreck before him with the interest of one who has himself been severely wounded and knows the long, weary pain. The man waved his hand toward the slope without unclosing his eyes, and Rodman went off with his pail and found a little shady hollow, once curbed and paved with white pebbles, but now neglected, like all the place. The water was cold, however, deliciously cold. He filled his pail and thought that perhaps after all he would exert himself to make coffee, now that the sun was down; it would taste better made of this cold water. When he came up the slope the man's eyes were open.

"Have some water?" asked Rodman.

"Yes; there's a gourd inside."

The keeper entered, and found himself in a large, bare room; in one corner was some straw covered with an old counterpane, in another a table and chair; a kettle hung in the deep fireplace, and a few dishes stood on a shelf; by the door on a nail hung a gourd; he filled it and gave it to the host of this desolate abode. The man drank with eagerness.

"Pomp has gone to town," he said, "and I could not get down to the spring today, I have had so much pain."

"And when will Pomp return?"

"He should be here now; he is very late tonight."

"Can I get you anything?"

"No, thank you; he will soon be here."

The keeper looked out over the waste; there was no one in sight. He was not a man of any especial kindliness—he had himself been too hardly treated in life for that—but he could not find it in his heart to leave this helpless creature all alone with night so near. So he sat down on the doorstep. "I will rest awhile," he said, not asking but announcing it. The man had turned away and closed his eyes again, and they both remained silent, busy with their own thoughts; for each had recognized the ex-soldier, Northern and Southern, in portions of the old uniforms, and in the accent. The war and its memories were still very near to the maimed, poverty-stricken Confederate; and the other knew that they were, and did not obtrude himself.

Twilight fell, and no one came.

"Let me get you something," said Rodman; for the face looked ghastly as the fever abated. The other refused. Darkness came; still, no one.

"Look here," said Rodman, rising, "I have been wounded myself, was in hospital for months; I know how you feel. You must have food—a cup of tea, now, and a slice of toast, brown and thin."

"I have not tasted tea or wheaten bread for weeks," answered the man; his voice died off into a wail, as though feebleness and pain had drawn the cry from him in spite of himself. Rodman lighted a match; there was no candle, only a piece of pitch pine stuck in an iron socket on the wall; he set fire to this primitive torch and looked around.

"There is nothing there," said the man outside, making an effort to speak carelessly; "my servant went to town for supplies. Do not trouble yourself to wait; he will come presently, and—and I want nothing."

But Rodman saw through proud poverty's lie; he knew that irregular quavering of the voice, and that trembling of the hand; the poor fellow had but one to tremble. He continued his search; but the bare room gave back nothing, not a crumb.

"Well, if you are not hungry," he said, briskly, "I am, hungry as a bear; and I'll tell you what I am going to do. I live not far from here, and I live all alone too; I haven't a servant as you have. Let me take supper here with you, just for a change; and, if your servant comes, so much the better, he can wait upon us. I'll run over and bring back the things."

He was gone without waiting for reply; the shattered ankle made good time over the waste, and soon returned, limping a little, but bravely hasting, while on a tray came the keeper's best supplies, Irish potatoes, corned beef, wheaten bread, butter, and coffee; for he would not eat the hot biscuits, the corncake, the bacon and hominy of the country, and constantly made little New England meals for himself in his prejudiced little kitchen. The pine torch flared in the doorway; a breeze had come down from the far mountains and cooled the air. Rodman kindled a fire on the cavernous hearth, filled the kettle, found a saucepan, and commenced operations, while the other lay outside and watched every movement in the lighted room.

"All ready; let me help you in. Here we are now; fried potatoes, cold beef, mustard, toast, butter, and tea. Eat, man; and the next time I am laid up you shall come over and cook for me."

Hunger conquered, and the other ate, ate as he had not eaten for months. As he was finishing a second cup of tea, a slow step came around the house; it was the missing Pomp, an old Negro, bent and shriveled, who carried a bag of meal and some bacon in his basket. "That is what they live on," thought the keeper.

He took leave without more words. "I suppose now I can be allowed to go home in peace," he grumbled to conscience. The Negro followed him across what was once the lawn. "Fin' Mars' Ward mighty low," he said apologetically, as he swung open the gate which still hung between its posts, although the fence was down, "but I hurred and hurred as fas' as I could; it's mighty fur to de town. Proud to see you, sah; hope you'll come again. Fine fambly, de Wards, sah, befo' de war."

"How long has he been in this state?" asked the keeper.

"Ever sence one ob de las' battles, sah; but he's worse sence we come yer, 'bout a mont' back."

"Who owns the house? Is there no one to see to him? Has he no friends?"

"House b'long to Mars' Ward's uncle; fine place once, befo' de war; he's dead now, and dah's nobuddy but Miss Bettina, an' she's gone off somewhuz. Propah place, sah, fur Mars' Ward—own uncle's house," said the old slave, loyally striving to maintain the family dignity even then.

"Are there no better rooms—no furniture?"

"Sartin; but—but Miss Bettina, she took de keys; she didn't know we was comin'—"

"You had better send for Miss Bettina, I think," said the keeper, starting homeward with his tray, washing his hands, as it were, of any future responsibility in the affair.

The next day he worked in his garden, for clouds veiled the sun and exercise was possible; but, nevertheless, he could not forget the white face on the old rug. "Pshaw!" he said to himself, "haven't I seen tumble-down old houses and battered human beings before this?"

At evening came a violent thunderstorm, and the splendor of the heavens was terrible. "We have chained you, mighty spirit," thought the keeper as he watched the lightning, "and some time we shall learn the laws of the winds and foretell the storms; then, prayers will no more be offered in churches to alter the weather than they would be offered now to alter an eclipse. Yet back of the lightning and the wind lies the power of the great Creator, just the same.".

But still into his musings crept, with shadowy persistence, the white face on the rug.

"Nonsense!" he exclaimed; "if white faces are going around as ghosts, how about the fourteen thousand white faces that went under the sod down yonder? If they could arise and walk, the whole state would be filled and no more carpetbaggers needed." So, having balanced the one with the fourteen thousand, he went to bed.

Daylight brought rain—still, soft, gray rain; the next morning showed the same, and the third likewise, the nights keeping up their part with low-down clouds and steady pattering on the roof. "If there was a river here, we should have a flood," thought the keeper, drumming idly on his window-pane. Memory brought back the steep New England hillsides shedding their rain into the brooks, which grew in a night to torrents and filled the rivers so that they overflowed their banks; then, suddenly, an old house in a sunken corner of a waste rose before his eyes, and he seemed to see the rain dropping from a moldy ceiling on the straw where a white face lay.

"Really, I have nothing else to do today, you know," he remarked in an apologetic way to himself, as he and his umbrella went along the old road; and he repeated the remark as he entered the room where the man lay, just as he had fancied, on the damp straw.

"The weather *is* unpleasant," said the man. "Pomp, bring a chair."

Pomp brought one, the only one, and the visitor sat down. A fire smoldered on the hearth and puffed out acrid smoke now and then, as if the rain had clogged the soot in the long-neglected chimney; from the streaked ceiling oozing drops fell with a dull splash into little pools on the decayed floor; the door would not close; the broken panes were stopped with rags, as if the old servant had tried to keep out the damp; in the ashes a corncake was baking.

"I am afraid you have not been so well during these long rainy days," said the keeper, scanning the face on the straw.

"My old enemy, rheumatism," answered the man; "the first sunshine will drive it away."

They talked awhile, or rather the keeper talked, for the other seemed hardly able to speak, as the waves of pain swept over him; then the visitor went outside and called Pomp out. "*Is* there any one to help him, or not?" he asked impatiently.

"Fine fambly, befo' de war," began Pomp.

"Never mind all that; is there any one to help him now—yes or no?"

"No," said the old black with a burst of despairing truthfulness. "Miss Bettina, she's as poor as Mars' Ward, an' dere's no one else. He's had noth'n but hard corncake for three days, an' he can't swaller it no more."

The next morning saw Ward De Rosset lying on the white pallet in the keeper's cottage, and old Pomp, marveling at the cleanliness all around him, installed as nurse. A strange asylum for a Confederate soldier, was it not? But he knew nothing of the change, which he would have fought with his last breath if consciousness had remained; returning fever, however, had absorbed his senses, and then it was that the keeper and the slave had borne him slowly across the waste, resting many times, but accomplishing the journey at last.

That evening John Rodman, strolling to and fro in the dusky twilight, paused alongside of the other Rodman. "I do not want him here, and that is the plain truth," he said, pursuing the current of his thoughts. "He fills the house; he and Pomp together disturb all my ways. He'll be ready to fling a brick at me too, when his senses come back; small thanks shall I have for lying on the floor, giving up all my comforts, and, what is more, riding over the spirit of the place with a vengeance!" He threw himself down on the grass beside the mound and lay looking up toward the stars, which were coming out, one by one, in the deep blue of the Southern night. "With a vengeance, did I say? That is it exactly—the vengeance of kindness. The poor fellow has suffered horribly in body and in estate, and now ironical Fortune throws him in my way, as if saying, 'Let us see how far your selfishness will yield.' This is not a question of magnanimity; there is no magnanimity about it, for the war is over, and you Northerners have gained every point for which you fought. This is merely a question between man and man; it would be the same if the sufferer was a poor Federal, one of the carpetbaggers, whom you despise so, for instance, or a pagan Chinaman. And Fortune is right; don't you think so, Blank Rodman? I put it to you, now, to one who has suffered the extreme rigor of the other side—those prison pens yonder."

Whereupon Blank Rodman answered that he had fought for a great cause, and that he knew it, although a plain man and not given to speech-making; he was not one of those who had sat safely at home all through the war, and now belittled it and made light of its issues. (Here a murmur came up from the long line of the trenches, as though all the dead had cried out.) But now the points for which he had fought being gained, and strife ended, it was the plain duty of every man to encourage peace. For his part he bore no malice; he was glad the poor Confederate was up in the cottage, and he did not think any the less of the keeper for bringing him there. He would like to add that he thought more of him; but he was sorry to say that he was well aware what an effort it was, and how almost grudgingly the charity began.

If Blank Rodman did not say this, at least the keeper imagined that he did. "That is what he would have said," he thought. "I am glad you do not object," he added, pretending to himself that he had not noticed the rest of the remark.

"We do not object to the brave soldier who honestly fought for his cause, even though he fought on the other side," answered Blank Rodman for the whole fourteen thousand. "But never let a coward, a double-face, or a flippant-tongued idler walk over our heads. It would make us rise in our graves!"

And the keeper seemed to see a shadowy pageant sweep by—gaunt soldiers with white faces, arming anew against the subtle product of peace: men who said, "It was nothing! Behold, we saw it with our eyes!"—stay-at-home eyes.

The third day the fever abated, and Ward De Rosset noticed his surroundings. Old Pomp acknowledged that he had been moved, but veiled the locality: "To a frien's house, Mars' Ward."

"But I have no friends now, Pomp," said the weak voice.

Pomp was very much amused at the absurdity of this. "No frien's! Mars' Ward, no frien's!" He was obliged to go out of the room to hide his laughter. The sick man lay feebly thinking that the bed was cool and fresh, and the closed green blinds pleasant; his thin fingers stroked the linen sheet, and his eyes wandered from object to object. The only thing that broke the rule of bare utility in the simple room was a square of white drawing paper on the wall, upon which was inscribed in ornamental text the following verse:

> *Toujours femme varie,*
> *Bien fou qui s'y fie;*
> *Une femme souvent*
> *N'est qu'une plume au vent.*

With the persistency of illness the eyes and mind of Ward De Rosset went over and over this distich; he knew something of French, but was unequal to the effort of translating; the rhymes alone caught his vagrant fancy. "Toujours femme varie," he said to himself over and over again; and when the keeper entered, he said it to him.

"Certainly," answered the keeper; "bien fou qui s'y fie. How do you find yourself this morning?"

"I have not found myself at all, so far. Is this your house?"

"Yes."

"Pomp told me I was in a friend's house," observed the sick man, vaguely.

"Well, it isn't an enemy's. Had any breakfast? No? Better not talk, then."

He went to the detached shed which served for a kitchen, upset all Pomp's clumsy arrangements, and ordered him outside; then he set to work and prepared a delicate breakfast with his best skill. The sick man eagerly eyed the tray as he entered. "Better have your hands and face sponged off, I think," said Rodman; and then he propped him up skillfully, and left him to his repast. The grass needed mowing on the parade ground; he shouldered his scythe and started down the path, viciously kicking the gravel aside as he walked. "Wasn't solitude your principal idea, John Rodman, when you applied for this place?" he demanded of himself. "How much of it are you likely to have with sick men, and sick men's servants, and so forth?"

The "and so forth," thrown in as a rhetorical climax, turned into reality and arrived bodily upon the scene—a climax indeed. One afternoon, returning late to the cottage, he found a girl sitting by the pallet—a girl young and dimpled and dewy; one of the creamy roses of the South that, even in the bud, are richer in color and luxuriance than any Northern flower. He saw her through the door, and paused; distressed old Pomp met him and beckoned him cautiously outside. "Miss Bettina," he whispered gutturally; "she's come back from somewhuz, an' she's awful mad 'cause Mars' Ward's here. I tole her all 'bout 'em—de leaks an' de rheumatiz an' de hard corncake, but she done gone scole me; and Mars' Ward, he know now whar he is, an' he mad too."

"Is the girl a fool?" said Rodman. He was just beginning to rally a little. He stalked into the room and confronted her. "I have the honor of addressing—"

"Miss Ward."

"And I am John Rodman, keeper of the national cemetery."

This she ignored entirely; it was as though he had said, "I am John Jones, the coachman." Coachmen were useful in their way; but their names were unimportant.

The keeper sat down and looked at his new visitor. The little creature fairly radiated scorn; her pretty head was thrown back, her eyes, dark brown fringed with long dark lashes, hardly deigned a glance; she spoke to him as though he was something to be paid and dismissed like any other mechanic.

"We are indebted to you for some days' board, I believe, keeper—medicines, I presume, and general attendance. My cousin will be removed today to our own residence; I wish to pay now what he owes."

The keeper saw that her dress was old and faded; the small black shawl had evidently been washed and many times mended; the old-fashioned knitted purse she held in her hand was lank with long famine.

"Very well," he said; "if you choose to treat a kindness in that way, I consider five dollars a day none too much for the annoyance, expense, and trouble I have suffered. Let me see: five days—or is it six? Yes. Thirty dollars, Miss Ward."

He looked at her steadily; she flushed. "The money will be sent to you," she began haughtily; then, hesitatingly, "I must ask a little time—"

"O Betty, Betty, you know you can not pay it. Why try to disguise— But that does not excuse *you* for bringing me here," said the sick man, turning toward his host with an attempt to speak fiercely, which ended in a faltering quaver.

All this time the old slave stood anxiously outside of the door; in the pauses they could hear his feet shuffling as he waited for the decision of his superiors. The keeper rose and threw open the blinds of the window that looked out on the distant parade ground. "Bringing you here," he repeated—"*here*; that is my offense, is it? There they lie, fourteen thousand brave men and true. Could they come back to earth they would be the first to pity and aid you, now that you are down. So would it be with you if the case were reversed; for a soldier is generous to a soldier. It was not your own heart that spoke then; it was the small venom of a woman, that here, as everywhere through the South, is playing its rancorous part."

The sick man gazed out through the window, seeing for the first time the far-spreading ranks of the dead. He was very weak, and the keeper's words had touched him; his eyes were suffused with tears. But Miss Ward rose with a flashing glance. She turned her back full upon the keeper and ignored his very existence. "I will take you home immediately, Ward— this very evening," she said.

"A nice, comfortable place for a sick man," commented the keeper, scornfully. "I am going out now, De Rosset, to prepare your supper; you had better have one good meal before you go."

He disappeared, but as he went he heard the sick man say, deprecatingly: "It isn't very comfortable over at the old house now, indeed it isn't, Betty; I suffered"—and the girl's passionate outburst in reply. Then he closed his door and set to work.

When he returned, half an hour later, Ward was lying back exhausted on the pillows, and his cousin sat leaning her head upon her hand; she had been weeping, and she looked very desolate, he noticed, sitting there in what was to her an enemy's country. Hunger is a strong master, however, especially when allied to weakness; and the sick man ate with eagerness.

"I must go back," said the girl, rising. "A wagon will be sent out for you, Ward; Pomp will help you."

But Ward had gained a little strength as well as obstinacy with the nourishing food. "Not tonight," he said.

"Yes, tonight."

"But I can not go tonight; you are unreasonable, Bettina. Tomorrow will do as well, if go I must."

"If go you must! You do not want to go, then—to go to our own home—and with me" —Her voice broke; she turned toward the door.

The keeper stepped forward. "This is all nonsense, Miss Ward," he said, "and you know it. Your cousin is in no state to be moved. Wait a week or two, and he can go in safety. But do not dare to offer me your money again; my kindness was to the soldier, not to the man, and as such he can accept it. Come out and see him as often as you please. I shall not intrude upon you. Pomp, take the lady home."

And the lady went.

Then began a remarkable existence for the four: a Confederate soldier lying ill in the keeper's cottage of a national cemetery; a rampant little rebel coming out daily to a place which was to her anathema-maranatha; a cynical, misanthropic keeper sleeping on the floor and enduring every variety of discomfort for a man he never saw before—a man belonging to an idle, arrogant class he detested; and an old black freedman allowing himself to be taught the alphabet in order to gain permission to wait on his master—master no longer in law—with all the devotion of his loving old heart. For the keeper had announced to Pomp that he must learn his alphabet or go; after all these years of theory, he, as a New-Englander, could not stand by and see precious knowledge shut from the black man. So he opened it, and mighty dull work he found it.

Ward De Rosset did not rally as rapidly as they expected. The white-haired doctor from the town rode out on horseback, pacing slowly up the graveled roadway with a scowl on his brow, casting, as he dismounted, a furtive glance down toward the parade ground. His horse and his coat were alike old and worn, and his broad shoulders were bent with long service in the miserably provided Confederate hospitals, where he had striven to do his duty through every day and every night of those shadowed years. Cursing the incompetency in high places, cursing the mismanagement of the entire medical department of the Confederate army, cursing the recklessness and indifference which left the men suffering for want of proper hospitals and hospital stores, he yet went on resolutely doing his best with the poor means in his control until the last. Then he came home, he and his old horse, and went the rounds again, he prescribing for whooping cough or measles, and Dobbin waiting outside;

the only difference was that fees were small and good meals scarce for both, not only for the man but for the beast. The doctor sat down and chatted awhile kindly with De Rosset, whose father and uncle had been dear friends of his in the bright, prosperous days; then he left a few harmless medicines and rose to go, his gaze resting a moment on Miss Ward, then on Pomp, as if he were hesitating. But he said nothing until on the walk outside he met the keeper, and recognized a person to whom he could tell the truth. "There is nothing to be done; he may recover, he may not; it is a question of strength merely. He needs no medicines, only nourishing food, rest, and careful tendance."

"He shall have them," answered the keeper briefly. And then the old gentleman mounted his horse and rode away, his first and last visit to a national cemetery.

"National!" he said to himself—"national!"

All talk of moving De Rosset ceased, but Miss Ward moved into the old house. There was not much to move: herself, her one trunk, and Marí, a black attendant, whose name probably began life as Maria, since the accent still dwelt on the curtailed last syllable. The keeper went there once, and once only, and then it was an errand for the sick man, whose fancies came sometimes at inconvenient hours—when Pomp had gone to town, for instance. On this occasion the keeper entered the mockery of a gate and knocked at the front door, from which the bars had been removed; the piazza still showed its decaying planks, but quick-growing summer vines had been planted, and were now encircling the old pillars and veiling all defects with their greenery. It was a woman's pathetic effort to cover up what can not be covered—poverty. The blinds on one side were open, and white curtains waved to and fro in the breeze; into this room he was ushered by Marí. Matting lay on the floor, streaked here and there ominously by the dampness from the near ground. The furniture was of dark mahogany, handsome in its day: chairs, a heavy pier table with low-down glass, into which no one by any possibility could look unless he had eyes in his ankles, a sofa with a stiff round pillow of hair cloth under each curved end, and a mirror with a compartment framed off at the top, containing a picture of shepherds and shepherdesses, and lambs with blue ribbons around their necks, all enjoying themselves in the most natural and lifelike manner. Flowers stood on the high mantelpiece, but their fragrance could not overcome the faint odor of the damp straw-matting. On a table were books—a life of General Lee, and three or four shabby little volumes printed at the South during the war, waifs of prose and poetry of that highly wrought, richly colored style which seems indigenous to Southern soil.

"Some way, the whole thing reminds me of a funeral," thought the keeper.

Miss Ward entered, and the room bloomed at once; at least that is what a lover would have said. Rodman, however, merely noticed that she bloomed, and not the room, and he said to himself that she would not bloom long if she continued to live in such a moldy place. Their conversation in these days was excessively polite, shortened to the extreme minimum possible, and conducted without the aid of the eyes, at least on one side. Rodman had discovered that Miss Ward never looked at him, and so he did not look at her—that is, not often; he was human, however, and she was delightfully pretty. On this occasion they exchanged exactly five sentences, and then he departed, but not before his quick eyes had discovered that the rest of the house was in even worse condition than this parlor, which, by the way, Miss Ward considered quite a grand apartment; she had been down near the coast, trying to teach school, and there the desolation was far greater than here, both armies having passed back and forward over the ground, foragers out, and the torch at work more than once.

"Will there ever come a change for the better?" thought the keeper, as he walked homeward. "What an enormous stone has got to be rolled up hill! But at least, John Rodman, *you* need not go to work at it; *you* are not called upon to lend your shoulder."

Nonetheless, however, did he call out Pomp that very afternoon and sternly teach him "E" and "F," using the smooth white sand for a blackboard, and a stick for chalk. Pomp's primer was a government placard hanging on the wall of the office. It read as follows:

IN THIS CEMETERY REPOSE THE REMAINS OF
FOURTEEN THOUSAND THREE HUNDRED AND TWENTY-ONE
UNITED STATES SOLDIERS.

> *Tell me not in mournful numbers*
> *Life is but an empty dream;*
> *For the soul is dead that slumbers,*
> *And things are not what they seem.*
>
> *Life is real! Life is earnest!*
> *And the grave is not its goal;*

Dust thou art, to dust returnest,
    Was not written of the soul!

"The only known instance of the government's condescending to
poetry," the keeper had thought, when he first read this placard. It was
placed there for the instruction and edification of visitors; but, no visitors
coming, he took the liberty of using it as a primer for Pomp. The large
letters served the purpose admirably, and Pomp learned the entire quo-
tation; what he thought of it has not transpired. Miss Ward came over
daily to see her cousin. At first she brought him soups and various con-
coctions from her own kitchen—the leaky cavern, once the dining room,
where the soldier had taken refuge after his last dismissal from hospital;
but the keeper's soups were richer, and free from the taint of smoke; his
martial laws of neatness even disorderly old Pomp dared not disobey, and
the sick man soon learned the difference. He thanked the girl, who came
bringing the dishes over carefully in her own dimpled hands, and then,
when she was gone, he sent them untasted away. By chance Miss Ward
learned this, and wept bitter tears over it; she continued to come, but her
poor little soups and jellies she brought no more.

One morning in May the keeper was working near the flag staff, when
his eyes fell upon a procession coming down the road which led from the
town and turning toward the cemetery. No one ever came that way:
what could it mean? It drew near, entered the gate, and showed itself to
be Negroes walking two and two—old uncles and aunties, young men
and girls, and even little children, all dressed in their best; a very poor
best, sometimes gravely ludicrous imitations of "ole mars'" or "ole
miss'," sometimes mere rags bravely patched together and adorned with
a strip of black calico or rosette of black ribbon; not one was without a
badge of mourning. All carried flowers, common blossoms from the
little gardens behind the cabins that stretched around the town on the
outskirts—the new forlorn cabins with their chimneys of piled stones
and ragged patches of corn; each little darkey had his bouquet and
marched solemnly along, rolling his eyes around, but without even the
beginning of a smile, while the elders moved forward with gravity, the
bubbling, irrepressible gayety of the Negro subdued by the newborn dig-
nity of the freedman.

"Memorial Day," thought the keeper; "I had forgotten it."

"Will you do us de hono', sah, to take de head ob de processio', sah?"
said the leader, with a ceremonious bow. Now, the keeper had not much
sympathy with the strewing of flowers, North or South; he had seen the

beautiful ceremony more than once turned into a political demonstration. Here, however, in this small, isolated, interior town, there was nothing of that kind; the whole population of white faces laid their roses and wept true tears on the graves of their lost ones in the village churchyard when the Southern Memorial Day came round, and just as naturally the whole population of black faces went out to the national cemetery with their flowers on the day when, throughout the North, spring blossoms were laid on the graves of the soldiers, from the little Maine village to the stretching ranks of Arlington, from Greenwood to the far Western burial places of San Francisco. The keeper joined the procession and led the way to the parade ground. As they approached the trenches, the leader began singing and all joined. "Swing low, sweet chariot," sang the freedmen, and their hymn rose and fell with strange, sweet harmony—one of those wild, unwritten melodies which the North heard with surprise and marveling when, after the war, bands of singers came to their cities and sang the songs of slavery, in order to gain for their children the coveted education. "Swing low, sweet chariot," sang the freedmen, and two by two they passed along, strewing the graves with flowers till all the green was dotted with color. It was a pathetic sight to see some of the old men and women, ignorant field hands, bent, dull eyed, and past the possibility of education even in its simplest forms, carefully placing their poor flowers to the best advantage. They knew dimly that the men who lay beneath those mounds had done something wonderful for them and for their children; and so they came bringing their blossoms, with little intelligence but with much love.

The ceremony over, they retired. As he turned, the keeper caught a glimpse of Miss Ward's face at the window.

"Hope we 's not makin' too free, sah," said the leader, as the procession, with many a bow and scrape, took leave, "but we 's kep' de day now two years, sah, befo' you came, sah, an we's teachin' de chil'en to keep it, sah."

The keeper returned to the cottage. "Not a white face," he said.

"Certainly not," replied Miss Ward, crisply.

"I know some graves at the North, Miss Ward, graves of Southern soldiers, and I know some Northern women who do not scorn to lay a few flowers on the lonely mounds as they pass by with their blossoms on our Memorial Day."

"You are fortunate. They must be angels. We have no angels here."

"I am inclined to believe you are right," said the keeper.

That night old Pomp, who had remained invisible in the kitchen during the ceremony; stole away in the twilight and came back with a few flowers. Rodman saw him going down toward the parade ground, and watched. The old man had but a few blossoms; he arranged them hastily on the mounds with many a furtive glance toward the house, and then stole back, satisfied; he had performed his part.

Ward De Rosset lay on his pallet, apparently unchanged; he seemed neither stronger nor weaker. He had grown childishly dependent upon his host, and wearied for him, as the Scotch say; but Rodman withstood his fancies, and gave him only the evenings, when Miss Bettina was not there. One afternoon, however, it rained so violently that he was forced to seek shelter; he set himself to work on the ledgers; he was on the ninth thousand now. But the sick man heard his step in the outer room, and called in his weak voice, "Rodman, Rodman." After a time he went in, and it ended in his staying; for the patient was nervous and irritable, and he pitied the nurse, who seemed able to please him in nothing. De Rosset turned with a sigh of relief toward the strong hands that lifted him readily, toward the composed manner, toward the man's voice that seemed to bring a breeze from outside into the close room; animated, cheered, he talked volubly. The keeper listened, answered once in a while, and quietly took the rest of the afternoon into his own hands. Miss Ward yielded to the silent change, leaned back, and closed her eyes. She looked exhausted and for the first time pallid; the loosened dark hair curled in little rings about her temples, and her lips were parted as though she was too tired to close them; for hers were not the thin, straight lips that shut tight naturally, like the straight line of a closed box. The sick man talked on. "Come, Rodman," he said, after a while, "I have read that lying verse of yours over at least ten thousand and fifty-nine times; please tell me its history; I want to have something definite to think of when I read it for the ten thousand and sixtieth."

> *Toujours femme varie,*
> *Bien fou qui s'y fie;*
> *Une femme souvent*
> *N'est qu'une plume au vent.*

read the keeper slowly, with his execrable English accent. "Well, I don't know that I have any objection to telling the story. I am not sure but that it will do me good to hear it all over myself in plain language again."

"Then it concerns yourself," said De Rosset; "so much the better. I hope it will be, as the children say, the truth, and long."

"It will be the truth, but not long. When the war broke out I was twenty-eight years old, living with my mother on our farm in New England. My father and two brothers had died and left me the homestead; otherwise I should have broken away and sought fortune farther westward, where the lands are better and life is more free. But mother loved the house, the fields, and every crooked tree. She was alone, and so I staid with her. In the center of the village green stood the square, white meeting-house, and near by the small cottage where the pastor lived; the minister's daughter, Mary, was my promised wife. Mary was a slender little creature with a profusion of pale flaxen hair, large, serious blue eyes, and small, delicate features; she was timid almost to a fault; her voice was low and gentle. She was not eighteen, and we were to wait a year. The war came, and I volunteered, of course, and marched away; we wrote to each other often; my letters were full of the camp and skirmishes; hers told of the village, how the widow Brown had fallen ill, and how it was feared that Squire Stafford's boys were lapsing into evil ways. Then came the day when my regiment marched to the field of its slaughter, and soon after our shattered remnant went home. Mary cried over me, and came out every day to the farmhouse with her bunches of violets; she read aloud to me from her good little books, and I used to lie and watch her profile bending over the page, with the light falling on her flaxen hair low down against the small, white throat. Then my wound healed, and I went again, this time for three years; and Mary's father blessed me, and said that when peace came he would call me son, but not before, for these were no times for marrying or giving in marriage. He was a good man, a red-hot abolitionist, and a roaring lion as regards temperance; but nature had made him so small in body that no one was much frightened when he roared. I said that I went for three years; but eight years have passed and I have never been back to the village. First, mother died. Then Mary turned false. I sold the farm by letter and lost the money three months afterward in an unfortunate investment; my health failed. Like many another Northern soldier, I remembered the healing climate of the South; its soft airs came back to me when the snow lay deep on the fields and the sharp wind whistled around the poor tavern where the moneyless, half-crippled volunteer sat coughing by the fire. I applied for this place and obtained it. That is all."

"But it is not all," said the sick man, raising himself on his elbow; "you have not told half yet, nor anything at all about the French verse."

"Oh—that? There was a little Frenchman staying at the hotel; he had formerly been a dancing master, and was full of dry, withered conceits, although he looked like a thin and bilious old ape dressed as a man. He taught me, or tried to teach me, various wise sayings, among them this one, which pleased my fancy so much that I gave him twenty-five cents to write it out in large text for me."

"Toujours femme varie," repeated De Rosset; "but you don't really think so, do you, Rodman?"

"I do. But they cannot help it; it is their nature. I beg your pardon, Miss Ward. I was speaking as though you were not here."

Miss Ward's eyelids barely acknowledged his existence; that was all. But some time after she remarked to her cousin that it was only in New England that one found that pale flaxen hair.

June was waning, when suddenly the summons came. Ward De Rosset died. He was unconscious toward the last, and death, in the guise of sleep, bore away his soul. They carried him home to the old house, and from there the funeral started, a few family carriages, dingy and battered, following the hearse, for death revived the old neighborhood feeling; that honor at least they could pay—the sonless mothers and the widows who lived shut up in the old houses with everything falling into ruin around them, brooding over the past. The keeper watched the small procession as it passed his gate on its way to the churchyard in the village. "There he goes, poor fellow, his sufferings over at last," he said; and then he set the cottage in order and began the old solitary life again.

He saw Miss Ward but once.

It was a breathless evening in August, when the moonlight flooded the level country. He had started out to stroll across the waste; but the mood changed, and climbing over the eastern wall he had walked back to the flag staff, and now lay at its foot gazing up into the infinite sky. A step sounded on the gravel walk; he turned his face that way, and recognized Miss Ward. With confident step she passed the dark cottage, and brushed his arm with her robe as he lay unseen in the shadow. She went down toward the parade ground, and his eyes followed her. Softly outlined in the moonlight, she moved to and fro among the mounds, pausing often, and once he thought she knelt. Then slowly she returned, and he raised himself and waited; she saw him, started, then paused.

"I thought you were away," she said; "Pomp told me so."

"You set him to watch me?"

"Yes. I wished to come here once, and I did not wish to meet you."

"Why did you wish to come?"

"Because Ward was here—and because—because—never mind. It is enough that I wished to walk once among those mounds."

"And pray there?"

"Well—and if I did!" said the girl defiantly.

Rodman stood facing her, with his arms folded; his eyes rested on her face; he said nothing.

"I am going away tomorrow," began Miss Ward again, assuming with an effort her old, pulseless manner. "I have sold the place, and I shall never return, I think; I am going far away."

"Where?"

"To Tennessee."

"That is not so very far," said the keeper, smiling.

"There I shall begin a new existence," pursued the voice, ignoring the comment.

"You have scarcely begun the old; you are hardly more than a child, now. What are you going to do in Tennessee?"

"Teach."

"Have you relatives there?"

"No."

"A miserable life—a hard, lonely, loveless life," said Rodman. "God help the woman who must be that dreary thing, a teacher from necessity!"

Miss Ward turned swiftly, but the keeper kept by her side. He saw the tears glittering on her eyelashes, and his voice softened. "Do not leave me in anger," he said; "I should not have spoken so, although indeed it was the truth. Walk back with me to the cottage, and take your last look at the room where poor Ward died, and then I will go with you to your home."

"No; Pomp is waiting at the gate," said the girl, almost inarticulately.

"Very well; to the gate, then."

They went toward the cottage in silence; the keeper threw open the door. "Go in," he said. "I will wait outside."

The girl entered and went into the inner room, throwing herself down upon her knees at the bedside. "O Ward, Ward!" she sobbed; "I am all alone in the world now, Ward, all alone!" She buried her face in her hands and gave way to a passion of tears; and the keeper could not help but hear as he waited outside. Then the desolate little creature rose and came forth, putting on, as she did so, her poor armor of pride. The keeper had not moved from the doorstep. Now he turned his face. "Before you go,—go away for ever from this place—will you write your name in my register," he said, "the visitors' register? The government had it prepared for the throngs who would visit these graves; but with the exception of the blacks, who cannot write, no one has come, and the register is empty. Will you write your name? Yet do not write it unless you can think gently of the men who lie there under the grass. I believe you do think gently of them, else why have you come of your own accord to stand by the side of their graves?" As he said this, he looked fixedly at her.

Miss Ward did not answer; but neither did she write.

"Very well," said the keeper; "come away. You will not, I see."

"I cannot! Shall I, Bettina Ward, set my name down in black and white as a visitor to this cemetery, where lie fourteen thousand of the soldiers who killed my father, my three brothers, my cousins; who brought desolation upon all our house, and ruin upon all our neighborhood, all our State, and all our country?—for the South *is* our country, and not your icy North. Shall I forget these things? Never! Sooner let my right hand wither by my side! I was but a child; yet I remember the tears of my mother, and the grief of all around us. There was not a house where there was not one dead."

"It is true," answered the keeper; "at the South, all went."

They walked down to the gate together in silence. "Good-by," said John, holding out his hand; "you will give me yours or not as you choose, but I will not have it as a favor."

She gave it.

"I hope that life will grow brighter to you as the years pass. May God bless you."

He dropped her hand; she turned, and passed through the gateway; then he sprang after her. "Nothing can change you," he said; "I know it, I have known it all along; you are part of your country, part of the time, part of the bitter hour through which she is passing. Nothing can change you; if it could, you would not be what you are, and I should not—But you cannot change. Good-by, Bettina, poor little child; good-by. Follow your path out into the world. Yet do not think, dear, that I have not seen—have not understood."

He bent and kissed her hand; then he was gone, and she went on alone.

A week later the keeper strolled over toward the old house. It was twilight, but the new owner was still at work. He was one of those sandy-haired, energetic Maine men, who, probably on the principle of extremes, were often found through the South, making new homes for themselves in the pleasant land.

"Pulling down the old house, are you?" said the keeper, leaning idly on the gate, which was already flanked by a new fence.

"Yes," replied the Maine man, pausing; "it was only an old shell, just ready to tumble on our heads. You're the keeper over yonder, an't you?" (He already knew everybody within a circle of five miles.)

"Yes. I think I should like those vines if you have no use for them," said Rodman, pointing to the uprooted greenery that once screened the old piazza.

"Wuth about twenty-five cents, I guess," said the Maine man, handing them over.

Elizabeth Stuart Phelps Ward
(1844–1911)

fter her mother's death, eight-year-old Mary Gray Phelps changed her name to Elizabeth Stuart Phelps in honor of her. Her mother, she believed, had been "torn by the civil war of the dual nature which can be given to women only"—the conflict between creativity and maternity. Phelps Ward had no children, but unlike her mother she used her married name, Ward; though her marriage was late and short-lived. Phelps Ward published fifty-seven books of socially conscious, feminist fiction, poetry, children's literature, and essays. Her feminist vision of a domestic heaven became *The Gates Ajar* (1868), a bestselling novel for grieving Civil War widows and orphans. Inspired by a fatal 1859 mill fire in Lawrence, Massachusetts, on a date as iconic for the time as September 11, Phelps Ward published "The Tenth of January" in *The Atlantic Monthly* in 1868. Rebecca Harding Davis's "Life in the Iron Mills" was among her literary models. Her finest novel, *The Story of Avis* (1877), was about the struggles of a great woman painter to be both an artist and a mother.

The Tenth of January (1868)

The city of Lawrence is unique in its way.

For simooms that scorch you and tempests that freeze; for sand-heaps and sand-hillocks and sand-roads; for men digging sand, for women shaking off sand, for minute boys crawling in sand; for sand in the church-slips and the gingerbread-windows, for sand in your eyes, your nose, your mouth, down your neck, up your sleeves, under your *chignon*, down your throat; for unexpected corners where tornadoes lie in wait; for "bleak, uncomforted" sidewalks, where they chase you, dog you, confront you, strangle you, twist you, blind you, turn your umbrella wrong side out; for "dimmykhrats" and bad ice-cream; for unutterable circus-bills and religious tea-parties; for uncleared ruins, and mills that spring up in a night; for jaded faces and busy feet; for an air of youth and incompleteness at which you laugh, and a consciousness of growth and greatness which you respect,—it—

I believe, when I commenced that sentence, I intended to say that it would be difficult to find Lawrence's equal.

Of the twenty-five thousand souls who inhabit that city, ten thousand are operatives in the factories. Of these ten thousand two thirds are girls.

These pages are written as one sets a bit of marble to mark a mound. I linger over them as we linger beside the grave of one who sleeps well; half sadly, half gladly,—more gladly than sadly,—but hushed.

The time to see Lawrence is when the mills open or close. So languidly the dull-colored, inexpectant crowd wind in! So briskly they come bounding out! Factory faces have a look of their own,—not only their common dinginess, and a general air of being in a hurry to find the wash-bowl, but an appearance of restlessness,—often of envious restlessness, not habitual in most departments of "healthy labor." Watch them closely you can read their histories at a venture. A widow this, in the dusty black, with she can scarcely remember how many mouths to feed at home. Worse than widowed that one: she has put her baby out to board,—and humane people know what that means,—to keep the little thing beyond its besotted father's reach. There is a group who have "just come over." A child's face here, old before its time. That girl—she climbs five flights of stairs twice a day—will climb no more stairs for herself or another by the time clover-leaves are green. "The best thing about one's grave is that it will be level," she was heard once to say. Somebody muses a little here,—she is to be married this winter. There is a face just behind her whose fixed eyes repel and attract you; there may be more love than guilt in them, more despair than either.

Had you stood in some unobserved corner of Essex Street, at four o'clock one Saturday afternoon towards the last of November, 1859, watching the impatient stream pour out of the Pemberton Mill, eager with a saddening eagerness for its few holiday hours, you would have observed one girl who did not bound.

She was slightly built, and undersized; her neck and shoulders were closely muffled, though the day was mild; she wore a faded scarlet hood which heightened the pallor of what must at best have been a pallid face. It was a sickly face, shaded off with purple shadows, but with a certain wiry nervous strength about the muscles of the mouth and chin: it would have been a womanly, pleasant mouth, had it not been crossed by a white scar, which attracted more of one's attention than either the womanliness or pleasantness. Her eyes had light long lashes, and shone through them steadily.

You would have noticed as well, had you been used to analyzing crowds, another face,—the two were side by side,—dimpled with pink and white flushes, and framed with bright black hair. One would laugh at this girl and love her, scold her and pity her, caress her and pray for her, then forget her perhaps.

The girls from behind called after her: "Del! Del Ivory! look over there!"

Pretty Del turned her head. She had just flung a smile at a young clerk who was petting his mustache in a shop-window, and the smile lingered.

One of the factory boys was walking alone across the Common in his factory clothes. "Why, there's Dick! Sene, do you see?"

Sene's scarred mouth moved slightly, but she made no reply. She had seen him five minutes ago.

One never knows exactly whether to laugh or cry over them, catching their chatter as they file past the show-windows of the long, showy street.

"Look a' that pink silk with the figures on it!"

"I 've seen them as is betther nor that in the ould counthree.—Patsy Malorrn, let alon' hangin' onto the shawl of me!"

"That's Mary Foster getting out of that carriage with the two white horses,—she that lives in the brown house with the cupilo."

"Look at her dress trailin' after her. I'd like my dresses trailin' after me."

"Well, may they be good,—these rich folks!"

"That's so. I'd be good if I was rich; wouldn't you, Moll?"

"You'd keep growing wilder than ever, if you went to hell, Meg Match: yes you would, because my teacher said so."

"So, then, he wouldn't marry her, after all; and she—"

"Going to the circus to-night, Bess?"

"I can't help crying, Jenny. You don't *know* how my head aches! It aches, and it aches, and it seems as if it would never stop aching. I wish—I wish I was dead, Jenny!"

They separated at last, going each her own way,—pretty Del Ivory to her boarding-place by the canal, her companion walking home alone.

This girl, Asenath Martyn, when left to herself, fell into a contented dream not common to girls who have reached her age,—especially girls who have seen the phases of life which she had seen. Yet few of the faces in the streets that led her home were more gravely lined. She puzzled one at the first glance, and at the second. An artist, meeting her musing on a canal-bridge one day, went home and painted a Mayflower budding in February.

It was a damp unwholesome place, the street in which she lived, cut short by a broken fence, a sudden steep, and the water; filled with children,—they ran from the gutters after her, as she passed,—and filled to the brim; it tipped now and then, like an over-full soup-plate, and spilled out two or three through the break in the fence.

Down in the corner, sharp upon the water, the east-winds broke about a little yellow house, where no children played; an old man's face watched at a window, and a nasturtium-vine crawled in the garden. The broken panes of glass about the place were well mended, and a clever little gate, extemporized from a wild grape-vine, swung at the entrance. It was not an old man's work.

Asenath went in with expectant eyes; they took in the room at a glance, and fell.

"Dick has n't come, father?"

"Come and gone child; didn't want any supper, he said. You're an hour before time, Senath."

"Yes. Did n't want any supper, you say? I don't see why not."

"No more do I, but it's none of our concern as I knows on; very like the pickles hurt him for dinner; Dick never had an o'er-strong stomach, as you might say. But you don't tell me how it m' happen you're let out at four o'clock, Senath," half complaining.

"O, something broke in the machinery, father; you know you would n't understand if I told you what."

He looked up from his bench,—he cobbled shoes there in the corner on his strongest days, and after her as she turned quickly away and up stairs to change her dress. She was never exactly cross with her father; but her words rang impatiently sometimes.

She came down presently, transformed, as only factory-girls are trans-formed, by the simple little toilet she had been making; her thin, soft hair knotted smoothly, the tips of her fingers rosy from the water, her pale neck well toned by her gray stuff dress and cape;—Asenath always wore a cape: there was one of crimson flannel, with a hood, that she had meant to wear to-night; she had thought about it coming home from the mill; she was apt to wear it on Saturdays and Sundays; Dick had more time at home. Going up stairs to-night, she had thrown it away into a drawer, and shut the drawer with a snap; then opened it softly, and cried a little; but she had not taken it out.

As she moved silently about the room, setting the supper-table for two, crossing and recrossing the broad belt of sunlight that fell upon the floor, it was easy to read the sad story of the little hooded capes.

They might have been graceful shoulders. The hand which had scarred her face had rounded and bent them,—her own mother's hand.

Of a bottle always on the shelf; of brutal scowls where smiles should be; of days when she wandered dinnerless and supperless in the streets through loathing of her home; of nights when she sat out in the snow-drifts through terror of her home; of a broken jug one day, a blow, a fall, then numbness, and the silence of the grave,—she had her distant memories of waking on a sunny afternoon, in bed, with a little cracked glass upon the opposite wall; of creeping out and up to it in her night-dress; of the ghastly twisted thing that looked back at her. Through the open window she heard the children laughing and leaping in the sweet summer air. She crawled into bed and shut her eyes. She remembered stealing out at last, after many days, to the grocery round the corner for a pound of coffee. "Humpback! humpback!" cried the children,—the very children who could leap and laugh.

One day she and little Del Ivory made mud-houses after school.

"I'm going to have a house of my own, when I'm grown up," said pretty Del; "I shall have a red carpet and some curtains; my husband will buy me a piano."

"So will mine, I guess," said Sene, simply.

"*Yours!*" Del shook back her curls; "who do you suppose would ever marry *you?*"

One night there was a knocking at the door, and a hideous, sodden thing borne in upon a plank.

The crowded street, tired of tipping out little children, had tipped her mother staggering through the broken fence. At the funeral she heard some one say, "How glad Sene must be!"

Since that, life had meant three things,—her father, the mills, and Richard Cross.

"You're a bit put out that the young fellow did n't stay to supper,—eh, Senath?" the old man said, laying down his boot.

"Put out! Why should I be? His time is his own. It's likely to be the Union that took him out, such a fine day for the Union! I'm sure I never expected him to go to walk with me *every* Saturday afternoon. I'm not a fool to tie him up to the notions of a crippled girl. Supper is ready, father."

But her voice rasped bitterly. Life's pleasures were so new and late and important to her, poor thing! It went hard to miss the least of them. Very happy people will not understand exactly how hard.

Old Martyn took off his leather apron with a troubled face, and, as he passed his daughter, gently laid his tremulous, stained hand upon her head. He felt her least uneasiness, it would seem, as a chameleon feels a cloud upon the sun.

She turned her face softly and kissed him. But she did not smile.

She had planned a little for this holiday supper; saving three mellow-cheeked Louise Bonnes—expensive pears just then—to add to their bread and molasses. She brought them out from the closet, and watched her father eat them.

"Going out again Senath?" he asked, seeing that she went for her hat and shawl, "and not a mouthful have you eaten! Find your old father dull company hey? Well, well!"

She said something about needing the air; the mill was hot; she should soon be back; she spoke tenderly and she spoke truly, but she went out into the windy sunset with her little trouble, and forgot him. The old man, left alone, sat for a while with his head sunk upon his breast. She was all he had in the world,—this one little crippled girl that the world had dealt hardly with. She loved him; but he was not, probably would never be, to her exactly what she was to him. Usually he forgot this. Sometimes he quite understood it, as to-night.

Asenath, with the purpose only of avoiding Dick, and of finding a still spot where she might think her thoughts undisturbed, wandered away over the eastern bridge, and down to the river's brink. It was a moody place; such a one as only apathetic or healthy natures (I wonder if that is tautology!) can healthfully yield to the bank sloped steeply; a fringe of stunted aspens and willows sprang from the frozen sand: it was a sickening, airless place in summer,—it was damp and desolate now. There was a sluggish wash of water under foot, and a stretch of dreary flats behind. Belated locomotives shrieked to each other across the river, and the wind bore down the current the roar and rage of the dam. Shadows were beginning to skulk under the huge brown bridge. The silent mills stared up and down and over the streams with a blank, unvarying stare. An oriflamme of scarlet burned in the west, flickered dully in the dirty, curdling water, flared against the windows of the Pemberton, which quivered and dripped, Asenath thought, as if with blood.

She sat down on a gray stone, wrapped in her gray shawl, curtained about by the aspens from the eye of passers on the bridge. She had a fancy for this place when things went ill with her. She had always borne her troubles alone, but she must be alone to bear them.

She knew very well that she was tired and nervous that afternoon, and that, if she could reason quietly about this little neglect of Dick's, it would cease to annoy her. Indeed, why should she be annoyed? Had he not done everything for her, been everything to her, for two long, sweet years? She dropped her head with a shy smile. She was never tired of living over these two years. She took positive pleasure in recalling the wretchedness in which they found her, for the sake of their dear relief. Many a time, sitting with her happy face hidden in his arms, she had laughed softly, to remember the day on which he came to her. It was at twilight, and she was tired. Her reels had troubled her all the afternoon; the overseer was cross; the day was hot and long. Somebody on the way home had said in passing her: "Look at that girl! I'd kill myself if I looked like that": it was in a whisper, but she heard it. All life looked hot and long; the reels would always be out of order; the overseer would never be kind. Her temples would always throb, and her back would ache. People would always say, "Look at that girl!"

"Can you direct me to—" She looked up; she had been sitting on the door-step with her face in her hands. Dick stood there with his cap off. He forgot that he was to inquire the way to Newbury Street, when he saw the tears on her shrunken cheeks. Dick could never bear to see a woman suffer.

"I would n't cry," he said simply, sitting down beside her. Telling a girl not to cry is an infallible recipe for keeping her at it. What could the child do, but sob as if her heart would break? Of course he had the whole story in ten minutes, she his in another ten. It was common and short enough:—a "Down-East" boy, fresh from his father's farm, hunting for work and board,—a bit homesick here in the strange, unhomelike city, it might be, and glad of some one to say so to.

What more natural than that, when her father came out and was pleased with the lad, there should be no more talk of Newbury Street; that the little yellow house should become his home; that he should swing the fantastic gate, and plant the nasturtiums; that his life should grow to be one within hers and the old man's, his future and theirs unite unconsciously?

She remembered—it was not exactly pleasant, somehow, to remember it to-night—just the look of his face when they came into the house that summer evening, and he for the first time saw what she was, her cape having fallen off, in the full lamplight. His kindly blue eyes widened within shocked surprise, and fell; when he raised them, a pity like a mother's had crept into them; it broadened and brightened as time slid by, but it never left them.

So you see, after that, life unfolded in a burst of little surprises for Asenath. If she came home very tired, some one said, "I am sorry." If she wore a pink ribbon, she heard a whisper, "It suits you." If she sang a little song, she knew that somebody listened.

"I did not know the world was like this!" cried the girl.

After a time there came a night that he chanced to be out late,—they had planned an arithmetic lesson together, which he had forgotten,—and she sat grieving by the kitchen fire.

"You missed me so much then?" he said regretfully, standing within his hand upon her chair.

She was trying to shell some corn; she dropped the pan, and the yellow kernels rolled away on the floor.

"What should I have if I did n't have you?" she said, and caught her breath.

The young man paced to the window and back again. The firelight touched her shoulders, and the sad, white scar.

"You shall have me always, Asenath," he made answer. He took her face within his hands and kissed it; and so they shelled the corn together, and nothing more was said about it.

He had spoken this last spring of their marriage; but the girl, like all girls, was shyly silent, and he had not urged it.

Asenath started from her pleasant dreaming just as the oriflamme was furling into gray, suddenly conscious that she was not alone. Below her, quite on the brink of the water, a girl was sitting,—a girl with a bright plaid shawl, and a nodding red feather in her hat. Her head was bent, and her hair fell against a profile cut in pink-and-white.

"Del is too pretty to be here alone so late," thought Asenath, smiling tenderly. Good-natured Del was kind to her in a certain way, and she rather loved the girl. She rose to speak to her, but concluded, on a second glance through the aspens, that Miss Ivory was quite able to take care of herself.

Del was sitting on an old log that jutted into the stream, dabbling in the water within the tips of her feet. (Had she lived on The Avenue she could not have been more particular about her shoemaker.) Some one— it was too dark to see distinctly—stood beside her, his eyes upon her face. Asenath could hear nothing, but she needed to hear nothing to know how the young fellow's eyes drank in the coquettish picture. Besides, it was an old story. Del counted her rejected lovers by the score.

"It's no wonder," she thought in her honest way, standing still to watch them with a sense of puzzled pleasure much like that with which she watched the print-windows,—"it's no wonder they love her. I'd love her if I was a man: so pretty! so pretty! She's just good for nothing, Del is;—would let the kitchen fire go out, and would n't mend the baby's aprons; but I'd love her all the same; marry her, probably, and be sorry all my life."

Pretty Del! Poor Del! Asenath wondered whether she wished that she were like her; she could not quite make out; it would be pleasant to sit on a log and look like that; it would be more pleasant to be watched as Del was watched just now: it struck her suddenly that Dick had never looked like this at her.

The hum of their voices ceased while she stood there with her eyes upon them; Del turned her head away with a sudden movement, and the young man left her, apparently without bow or farewell, sprang up the bank at a bound, and crushed the undergrowth with quick, uneasy strides.

Asenath, with some vague idea that it would not be honorable to see his face,—poor fellow!—shrank back into the aspens and the shadow.

He towered tall in the twilight as he passed her, and a dull, umber gleam, the last of the sunset, struck him from the west.

Struck it out into her sight,—the haggard struggling face,—Richard Cross's face.

Of course you knew it from the beginning, but remember that the girl did not. She might have known it, perhaps, but she had not.

Asenath stood up, sat down again.

She had a distinct consciousness, for the moment, of seeing herself crouched down there under the aspens and the shadow, a humpbacked white creature, with distorted face and wide eyes. She remembered a picture she had somewhere seen of a little chattering goblin in a graveyard, and was struck with the resemblance. Distinctly, too, she heard herself saying, with a laugh, she thought, "I might have known it; I might have known."

Then the blood came through her heart with a hot rush, and she saw Del on the log, smoothing the red feather of her hat. She heard a man's step, too, that rang over the bridge, passed the toll-house, grew faint, grew fainter, died in the sand by the Everett Mill.

Richard's face! Richard's face, looking—God help her!—as it had never looked at her; struggling—God pity him!—as it had never struggled for her.

She shut her hands into each other, and sat still a little while. A faint hope came to her then perhaps, after all; her face lightened grayly, and she crept down the bank to Del.

"I won't be a fool," she said, "I'll make sure,—I'll make as sure as death."

"Well, where did *you* drop down from, Sene?" said Del, with a guilty start.

"From over the bridge, to be sure. Did you think I swam, or flew, or blew?"

"You came on me so sudden!" said Del, petulantly; "you nearly frightened the wits out of me. You did n't meet anybody on the bridge?" with a quick look.

"Let me see." Asenath considered gravely. "There was one small boy making faces, and two—no, three—dogs, I believe; that was all."

"Oh!"

Del looked relieved, but fell silent.

"You're sober, Del. Been sending off a lover, as usual?"

"I don't know anything about its being usual," answered Del, in an aggrieved, coquettish way, "but there's been somebody here that liked me well enough."

"You like him, maybe? It's time you liked somebody, Del."

Del curled the red feather about her fingers, and put her hat on over her eyes, then a little cry broke from her, half sob, half anger.

"I might, perhaps,—I don't know. He's good. I think he'd let me have a parlor and a door-bell. But he's going to marry somebody else, you see. I sha' n't tell you his name, so you need n't ask."

Asenath looked out straight upon the water. A dead leaf that had been caught in an eddy attracted her attention; it tossed about for a minute, then a tiny whirlpool sucked it down.

"I wasn't going to ask; it's nothing to me, of course. He does n't care for her then,—this other girl?"

"Not so much as he does for me. He did n't mean to tell me, but he said that I—that I looked so—pretty, it came right out. But there! I mustn't tell you any more."

Del began to be frightened; she looked up sideways at Asenath's quiet face. "I won't say another word," and so chattered on, growing a little cross; Asenath need not look so still, and sure of herself,—a mere humpbacked fright!

"He'll never break his engagement, not even for me; he's sorry for her, and all that. I think it's too bad. He's handsome. He makes me feel like saying my prayers, too, he's so good! Besides, I want to be married. I hate the mill. I hate to work. I'd rather be taken care of;—a sight rather. I feel bad enough about it to cry."

Two tears rolled over her cheeks, and fell on the soft plaid shawl. Del wiped them away carefully with her rounded fingers.

Asenath turned and looked at this Del Ivory long and steadily through the dusk. The pretty, shallow thing! The worthless, bewildering thing!

A fierce contempt for her pink-and-white, and tears and eyelashes and attitudes, came upon her; then a sudden sickening jealousy that turned her faint where she sat.

What did God mean,—Asenath believed in God, having so little else to believe in,—what did he mean, when he had blessed the girl all her happy life with such wealth of beauty, by filling her careless hands with this one best, last gift? Why, the child could not hold such golden love! She would throw it away by and by. What a waste it was!

Not that she had these words for her thought, but she had the thought distinctly through her dizzy pain.

"So there's nothing to do about it," said Del, pinning her shawl. "We can't have anything to say to each other,—unless anybody should die, or anything; and of course I'm not wicked enough to think of *that.—Sene!* Sene! what are you doing?"

Sene had risen slowly, stood upon the log, caught at an aspen-top, and swung out within it its whole length above the water. The slight tree writhed and quivered about the roots. Sene looked down and moved her marred lips without sound.

Del screamed and wrung her hands. It was an ugly sight!

"O don't, Sene, *don't!* You'll drown yourself! you will be drowned! you will be—O, what a start you gave me! What *were* you doing, Senath Martyn?"

Sene swung slowly back, and sat down.

"Amusing myself a little;—well, unless somebody died, you said? But I believe I won't talk any more to-night. My head aches. Go home, Del."

Del muttered a weak protest at leaving her there alone; but, with her bright face clouded and uncomfortable, went.

Asenath turned her head to listen for the last rustle of her dress, then folded her arms, and, with her eyes upon the sluggish current, sat still.

An hour and a half later, an Andover farmer, driving home across the bridge, observed on the river's edge—a shadow cut within a shadow— the outline of a woman's figure, sitting perfectly still with folded arms. He reined up and looked down; but it sat quite still.

"Hallo there!" he called; "you'll fall in if you don't look out!" for the wind was strong, and it blew against the figure; but it did not move nor make reply. The Andover farmer looked over his shoulder with the sudden recollection of a ghost-story which he had charged his grandchildren not to believe last week, cracked his whip, and rumbled on.

Asenath began to understand by and by that she was cold, so climbed the bank, made her way over the windy flats, the railroad, and the western bridge confusedly with an idea of going home. She turned aside by the toll-gate. The keeper came out to see what she was doing, but she kept out of his sight behind the great willow and his little blue house,—the blue house with the green blinds and red moulding. The dam thundered that night, the wind and the water being high. She made her way up above it, and looked in. She had never seen it so black and smooth there. As she listened to the roar, she remembered something that she had read—was it in the Bible or the Ledger?—about seven thunders uttering their Voices.

"He's sorry for her, and all that," they said.

A dead bough shot down the current while she stood there, went over and down, and out of sight, throwing up its little branches like helpless hands.

It fell in with a thought of Asenath's, perhaps; at any rate she did not like the looks of it, and went home.

Over the bridge, and the canal, and the lighted streets, the falls called after her: "He's sorry for her, and all that." The curtain was drawn aside when she came home, and she saw her father through the window, sitting alone, with his gray head bent.

It occurred to her that she had often left him alone,—poor old father! It occurred to her, also, that she understood now what it was to be alone. Had she forgotten him in these two comforted, companioned years?

She came in weakly, and looked about.

"Dick's in, and gone to bed," said the old man, answering her look. "You're tired, Senath."

"I am tired, father."

She sunk upon the floor,—the heat of the room made her a little faint,—and laid her head upon his knee; oddly enough, she noticed that the patch on it had given way,—wondered how many days it had been so,—whether he had felt ragged and neglected while she was busy about that blue neck-tie for Dick. She put her hand up and smoothed the corners of the rent.

"You shall be mended up to-morrow, poor father!"

He smiled, pleased like a child to be remembered. She looked up at him,—at his gray hair and shrivelled face, at his blackened hands and bent shoulders, and dusty, ill-kept coat. What would it be like, if the days brought her nothing but him?

"Something's the matter with my little gal? Tell father, can't ye?"

Her face flushed hot, as if she had done him wrong. She crept up into his arms, and put her hands behind his rough old neck.

"Would you kiss me, father? You don't think I'm too ugly to kiss, maybe,—you?"

She felt better after that. She had not gone to sleep now for many a night unkissed; it had seemed hard at first.

When she had gone half-way up stairs, Dick came to the door of his room on the first floor, and called her. He held the little kerosene lamp over his head; his face was grave and pale.

"I have n't said good night, Sene."

She made no reply.

"Asenath, good night."

She stayed her steps upon the stairs without turning her head. Her father had kissed her to-night. Was not that enough?

"Why, Sene, what's the matter with you?"

Dick mounted the stairs, and touched his lips to her forehead with a gently compassionate smile.

She fled from him with a cry like the cry of a suffocated creature, shut her door, and locked it with a ringing clang.

"She's walked too far, and got a little nervous," said Dick, screwing up his lamp; "poor thing!"

Then he went into his room to look at Del's photograph awhile before he burned it up; for he meant to burn it up.

Asenath, when she had locked her door, put her lamp before the looking-glass and tore off her gray cape; tore it off so savagely that the button snapped and rolled away,—two little crystal semicircles like tears upon the floor.

There was no collar about the neck of her dress, and this heightened the plainness and the pallor of her face. She shrank instinctively at the first sight of herself; and opened the drawer where the crimson cape was folded, but shut it resolutely.

"I'll see the worst of it," she said with pinched lips. She turned herself about and about before the glass, letting the cruel light gloat over her shoulders, letting the sickly shadows grow purple on her face. Then she put her elbows on the table and her chin into her hands, and so, for a motionless half-hour, studied the unrounded, uncolored, unlightened face that stared back at her; her eyes darkening at its eyes, her hair touching its hair, her breath dimming the outline of its repulsive mouth.

By and by she dropped her head into her hands. The poor, mistaken face! She felt as if she would like to blot it out of the world, as her tears used to blot out the wrong sums upon her slate. It had been so happy! But he was sorry for it, and all that. Why did a good God make such faces?

She slipped upon her knees, bewildered.

"He *can't* mean any harm nohow," she said, speaking fast, and knelt there and said it over till she felt sure of it.

Then she thought of Del once more,—of her colors and sinuous springs, and little cries and chatter.

After a time she found that she was growing faint, and so stole down into the kitchen for some food. She stayed a minute to warm her feet. The fire was red and the clock was ticking. It seemed to her home-like and comfortable, and she seemed to herself very homeless and lonely; so she sat down on the floor, with her head in a chair, and cried as hard as she ought to have done four hours ago.

She climbed into bed about one o'clock, having decided, in a dull way, to give Dick up tomorrow.

But when to-morrow came he was up with a bright face, and built the kitchen fire for her, and brought in all the water, and helped her fry the potatoes, and whistled a little about the house, and worried at her paleness, and so she said nothing about it.

"I'll wait till night," she planned, making ready for the mill.

"O, I can't!" she cried at night. So other mornings came, and other nights.

I am quite aware that, according to all romantic precedents, this conduct was preposterous in Asenath. Floracita, in the novel, never so far forgets the whole duty of a heroine as to struggle, waver, doubt, delay. It is proud and proper to free the young fellow; proudly and properly she frees him; "suffers in silence"—till she marries another man; and (having had a convenient opportunity to refuse the original lover) overwhelms the reflective reader with a sense of poetic justice and the eternal fitness of things.

But I am not writing a novel, and, as the biographer of this simple factory girl, am offered few advantages.

Asenath was no heroine, you see. Such heroic elements as were in her—none could tell exactly what they were, or whether there were any: she was one of those people in whom it is easy to be quite mistaken;—her life had not been one to develop. She might have a certain pride of her own, under given circumstances; but plants grown in a cellar will turn to the sun at any cost; how could she go back into her dark?

As for the other man to marry, he was out of the question. Then, none love with the tenacity of the unhappy; no life is so lavish of itself as the denied life: to him that hath not shall be given,—and Asenath loved this Richard Cross.

It might be altogether the grand and suitable thing to say to him, "I will not be your wife." It might be that she would thus regain a strong shade of lost self-respect. It might be that she would make him happy, and give pleasure to Del. It might be that the two young people would be her "friends," and love her in a way.

But all this meant that Dick must go out of her life. Practically, she must make up her mind to build the fires, and pump the water, and mend the windows alone. In dreary fact, he would not listen when she sung; would not say, "You are tired, Sene"; would never kiss away an undried tear. There would be nobody to notice the crimson cape, nobody to make blue neck-ties for; none for whom to save the Bonnes de Jersey, or to take sweet, tired steps, or make dear, dreamy plans. To be sure, there was her father; but fathers do not count for much in a time like this on which Sene had fallen.

That Del Ivy was—Del Ivory, added intricacies to the question. It was a very unpoetic but undoubted fact that Asenath could in no way so insure Dick's unhappiness as to pave the way to his marriage with the woman whom he loved. There would be a few merry months, then slow worry and disappointment; pretty Del accepted at last, not as the crown of his young life, but as its silent burden and misery. Poor Dick! good Dick! Who deserved more wealth of wifely sacrifice? Asenath, thinking this, crimsoned with pain and shame. A streak of good common sense in the girl told her—though she half scorned herself for the conviction— that even a crippled woman who should bear all things and hope all things for his sake might blot out the memory of this rounded Del; that, no matter what the motive with which he married her, he would end by loving his wife like other people.

She watched him sometimes in the evenings, as he turned his kind eyes after her over the library book which he was reading.

"I know I could make him happy! I *know* I could!" she muttered fiercely to herself.

November blew into December, December congealed into January, while she kept her silence. Dick, in his honorable heart, seeing that she suffered, wearied himself with plans to make her eyes shine; brought her two pails of water instead of one, never forgot the fire, helped her home from the mill. She saw him meet Del Ivory once upon Essex Street with a grave and silent bow; he never spoke with her now. He meant to pay the debt he owed her down to the uttermost farthing; that grew plain. Did she try to speak her wretched secret, he suffocated her with kindness, struck her dumb with tender words.

She used to analyze her life in those days, considering what it would be without him. To be up by half past five o'clock in the chill of all the winter mornings, to build the fire and cook the breakfast and sweep the floor, to hurry away, faint and weak, over the raw, slippery streets, to climb at half past six the endless stairs and stand at the endless loom, and hear the endless wheels go buzzing round, to sicken in the oily smells, and deafen at the remorseless noise, and weary of the rough girl swearing at the other end of the pass; to eat her cold dinner from a little cold tin pail out on the stairs in the three-quarters-of-an-hour recess; to come exhausted home at half past six at night, and get the supper, and brush up about the shoemaker's bench, and be too weak to eat; to sit with aching shoulders and make the button-holes of her best dress, or darn her father's stockings, till nine o'clock; to hear no bounding step or cheery whistle about the house; to creep into bed and lie there trying not to think, and wishing that so she might creep into her grave,—this not for one winter, but for all the winters,—how should *you* like it, you young girls, with whom time runs like a story?

The very fact that her employers dealt honorably by her; that she was fairly paid, and promptly, for her wearing toil; that the limit of endurance was consulted in the temperature of the room, and her need of rest in an occasional holiday,—perhaps, after all, in the mood she was in, did not make this factory life more easy. She would have found it rather a relief to have somebody to complain of,—wherein she was like the rest of us, I fancy.

But at last there came a day—it chanced to be the ninth of January— when Asenath went away alone at noon, and sat where Merrimack sung his songs to her. She hid her face upon her knees, and listened and thought her own thoughts, till they and the slow torment of the winter seemed greater than she could bear. So, passing her hands confusedly over her forehead, she said at last aloud, "That's what God means, Asenath Martyn!" and went back to work with a purpose in her eyes.

She "asked out" a little earlier than usual, and went slowly home. Dick was there before her; he had been taking a half-holiday. He had made the tea and toasted the bread for a little surprise. He came up and said, "Why, Sene, your hands are cold!" and warmed them for her in his own.

After tea she asked him, would he walk out with her for a little while?

and he in wonder went. The streets were brightly lighted, and the moon was up. The ice cracked crisp under their feet.

Sleighs, with two riders in each, shot merrily by. People were laughing in groups before the shop-windows. In the glare of a jeweller's counter somebody was buying a wedding-ring, and a girl with red cheeks was looking hard the other way.

"Let's get away," said Asenath,—"get away from here!"

They chose by tacit consent that favorite road of hers over the eastern bridge. Their steps had a hollow, lonely ring on the frosted wood; she was glad when the softness of the snow in the road received them. She looked back once at the water, wrinkled into thin ice on the edge for a foot or two, then open and black and still.

"What are you doing?" asked Dick. She said that she was wondering how cold it was, and Dick laughed at her.

They strolled on in silence for perhaps a mile of the desolate road.

"Well, this is social!" said Dick at length; "how much farther do you want to go? I believe you'd walk to Reading if nobody stopped you!"

She was taking slow, regular steps like an automaton, and looking straight before her. "How much farther? Oh!" She stopped and looked about her.

A wide young forest spread away at their feet, to the right and to the left. There was ice on the tiny oaks and miniature pines; it glittered sharply under the moon; the light upon the snow was blue; cold roads wound away through it, deserted; little piles of dead leaves shivered; a fine keen spray ran along the tops of the drifts; inky shadows lurked and dodged about the undergrowth; in the broad spaces the snow glared; the lighted mills, a zone of fire, blazed from east to west; the skies were bare, and the wind was up, and Merrimack in the distance chanted solemnly.

"Dick," said Asenath, "this is a dreadful place! Take me home."

But when he would have turned, she held him back with a sudden cry, and stood still. "I meant to tell you—I meant to say—Dick! I was going to say—"

But she did not say it. She opened her lips to speak once and again, but no sound came from them.

"Sene! why, Sene, what ails you?"

He turned, and took her in his arms.

"Poor Sene!"

He kissed her, feeling sorry for her unknown trouble. He wondered why she sobbed. He kissed her again. She broke from him, and away with a great bound upon the snow.

"You make it so hard! You've no right to make it so hard! It ain't as if you loved me, Dick! I know I'm not like other girls! Go home and let me be!"

But Dick drew her arm through his, and led her gravely away. "I like you well enough, Asenath," he said, with that motherly pity in his eyes; "I've always liked you. So don't let us have any more of this."

So Asenath said nothing more.

The sleek black river beckoned to her across the snow as they went home. A thought came to her as she passed the bridge,—it is a curious study what wicked thoughts will come to good people!—she found herself considering the advisability of leaping the low brown parapet, and if it would not be like Dick to go over after her; if there would be a chance for them, even should he swim from the banks; how soon the icy current would paralyze him; how sweet it would be to chill to death there in his arms; how all this wavering and pain would be over; how Del would look when they dragged them out down below the machine-shop!

"Sene, are you cold?" asked puzzled Dick. She was warmly wrapped in her little squirrel furs; but he felt her quivering upon his arm, like one in an ague, all the way home.

About eleven o'clock that night her father waked from an exciting dream concerning the best method of blacking patent-leather; Sene stood beside his bed with her gray shawl thrown over her night-dress.

"Father, suppose some time there should be only you and me—"

"Well, well, Sene," said the old man sleepily,—"very well."

"I'd try to be a good girl! Could you love me enough to make up?"

He told her indistinctly that she always was a good girl; she never had a whipping from the day her mother died. She turned away impatiently; then cried out and fell upon her knees.

"Father, father! I'm in a great trouble. I have n't got any mother, any friend, anybody. Nobody helps me! Nobody knows. I've been thinking such things—O, such wicked things—up in my room! Then I got afraid of myself. You're good. You love me. I want you to put your hand on my head and say, 'God bless you, child, and show you how.'"

Bewildered, he put his hand upon her unbound hair, and said: "God bless you, child, and show you how!"

Asenath looked at the old withered hand a moment, as it lay beside her on the bed, kissed it, and went away.

There was a scarlet sunrise the next morning. A pale pink flush stole through a hole in the curtain, and fell across Asenath's sleeping face, and lay there like a crown. It woke her, and she threw on her dress, and sat down for a while on the window-sill, to watch the coming-on of the day.

The silent city steeped and bathed itself in rose-tints; the river ran red, and the snow crimsoned on the distant New Hampshire hills; Pemberton, mute and cold, frowned across the disk of the climbing sun, and dripped, as she had seen it drip before, with blood.

The day broke softly, the snow melted, the wind blew warm from the river. The factory-bell chimed cheerily, and a few sleepers, in safe, luxurious beds, were wakened by hearing the girls sing on their way to work.

Asenath came down with a quiet face. In her communing with the sunrise helpful things had been spoken to her. Somehow, she knew not how, the peace of the day was creeping into her heart. For some reason, she knew not why, the torment and unrest of the night were gone. There was a future to be settled, but she would not trouble herself about that just now. There was breakfast to get; and the sun shone, and a snow-bird was chirping outside of the door. She noticed how the tea-kettle hummed, and how well the new curtain, with the castle and waterfall on it, fitted the window. She thought that she would scour the closet at night, and surprise her father by finishing those last slippers. She kissed him when she had tied on the red hood, and said good-by to Dick, and told them just where to find the squash-pie for dinner.

When she had closed the twisted gate, and taken a step or two upon the snow, she came thoughtfully back. Her father was on his bench, mending one of Meg Match's shoes. She pushed it gently out of his hands, sat down upon his lap, and stroked the shaggy hair away from his forehead.

"Father!"

"Well, what now, Sene?—what now?"

"Sometimes I believe I've forgotten you a bit, you know. I think we're going to be happier after this. That's all."

She went out singing, and he heard the gate shut again with a click.

Sene was a little dizzy that morning,—the constant palpitation of the floors always made her dizzy after a wakeful night,—and so her colored cotton threads danced out of place, and troubled her.

Del Ivory, working beside her, said, "How the mill shakes! What's going on?"

"It's the new machinery they're h'isting in," observed the overseer, carelessly. "Great improvement, but heavy, very heavy; they calc'late on getting it all into place to-day; you'd better be tending to your frame, Miss Ivory."

As the day wore on, the quiet of Asenath's morning deepened. Round and round with the pulleys over her head she wound her thoughts of Dick. In and out with her black and dun-colored threads she spun her future. Pretty Del, just behind her, was twisting a pattern like a rainbow. She noticed this, and smiled.

"Never mind!" she thought, "I guess God knows."

Was He ready "to bless her, and show her how"? She wondered. If, indeed, it were best that she should never be Dick's wife, it seemed to her that He would help her about it. She had been a coward last night; her blood leaped in her veins with shame at the memory of it. Did He understand? Did He not know how she loved Dick, and how hard it was to lose him?

However that might be, she began to feel at rest about herself. A curious apathy about means and ways and decisions took possession of her. A bounding sense that a way of escape was provided from all her troubles, such as she had when her mother died, came upon her.

Years before, an unknown workman in South Boston, casting an iron pillar upon its core, had suffered it to "float" a little, a very little more, till the thin, unequal side cooled to the measure of an eighth of an inch. That man had provided Asenath's way of escape.

She went out at noon with her luncheon, and found a place upon the stairs, away from the rest, and sat there awhile, with her eyes upon the river, thinking. She could not help wondering a little, after all, why God needed to have made her so unlike the rest of his fair handiwork. Del came bounding by, and nodded at her carelessly. Two young Irish girls, sisters, the beauties of the mill,—magnificently colored creatures,—were singing a little love-song together, while they tied on their hats to go home.

"There *are* such pretty things in the world!" thought poor Sene.

Did anybody speak to her after the girls were gone? Into her heart these words fell suddenly, "*He* hath no form nor comeliness. *His* visage was so marred more than any man."

They clung to her fancy all the afternoon. She liked the sound of them. She wove them in with her black and dun-colored threads.

The wind began—at last to blow chilly up the staircases, and in at the cracks; the melted drifts out under the walls to harden; the sun dipped above the dam; the mill dimmed slowly; shadows crept down between the frames.

"It's time for lights," said Meg Match, and swore a little at her spools. Sene, in the pauses of her thinking, heard snatches of the girls' talk. "Going to ask out to-morrow, Meg?"

"Guess so, yes; me and Bob Smith we thought we'd go to Boston, and come up in the theatre train."

"Del Ivory, I want the pattern of your zouave."

"Did I go to church? No, you don't catch me! If I slave all the week, I'll do what I please on Sunday."

"Hush-sh! There's the boss looking over here!"

"Kathleen Donnavon, be still with your ghost-stories. There's one thing in the world I never will hear about, and that's dead people."

"Del," said Sene, "I think to-morrow—"

She stopped. Something strange had happened to her frame; it jarred, buzzed, snapped; the threads untwisted and flew out of place.

"Curious!" she said, and looked up.

Looked up to see her overseer turn wildly, clap his hands to his head, and fall; to hear a shriek from Del that froze her blood; to see the solid ceiling gape above her; to see the walls and windows stagger; to see iron pillars reel, and vast machinery throw up its helpless, giant arms, and a tangle of human faces blanch and writhe!

She sprang as the floor sunk. As pillar after pillar gave way, she bounded up an inclined plane, with the gulf yawning after her. It gained upon her, leaped at her, caught her; beyond were the stairs and an open door; she threw out her arms, and struggled on with hands and knees, tripped in the gearing, and saw, as she fell, a square, oaken beam above her yield and crash; it was of a fresh red color; she dimly wondered why,—as she felt her hands slip, her knees slide, support, time, place, and reason, go utterly out.

"At ten minutes before five, on Tuesday, the tenth of January, the Pemberton Mill, all hands being at the time on duty, fell to the ground."

So the record flashed over the telegraph wires, sprang into large type in the newspapers, passed from lip to lip, a nine days' wonder, gave place to the successful candidate, and the muttering South, and was forgotten.

Who shall say what it was to the seven hundred and fifty souls who were buried in the ruins?

What to the eighty-eight who died that death of exquisite agony? What to the wrecks of men and women who endure unto this day a life that is worse than death? What to that architect and engineer who, when the fatal pillars were first delivered to them for inspection, had found one broken under their eyes, yet accepted the contract, and built with them a mill whose thin walls and wide, unsupported stretches might have tottered over massive columns and on flawless ore?

One that we love may go upon the battle-ground, and we are ready for the worst: we have said our good-bys; our hearts wait and pray: it is his life, not his death, which is the surprise. But that he should go out to his safe, daily, commonplace occupations, unnoticed and uncaressed,— scolded a little, perhaps, because he leaves the door open, and tells us how cross we are this morning; and they bring him up the steps by and by, a mangled mass of death and horror,—that is hard.

Old Martyn, working at Meg Match's shoes,—she was never to wear those shoes, poor Meg!—heard, at ten minutes before five, what he thought to be the rumble of an earthquake under his very feet, and stood with bated breath, waiting for the crash. As nothing further appeared to happen, he took his stick and limped out into the street.

A vast crowd surged through it from end to end. Women with white lips were counting the mills,—Pacific, Atlantic, Washington,—Pemberton? Where was Pemberton?

Where Pemberton had winked its many eyes last night, and hummed with its iron lips this noon, a cloud of dust, black, silent, horrible, puffed a hundred feet into the air.

Asenath opened her eyes after a time. Beautiful green and purple lights had been dancing about her, but she had had no thoughts. It occurred to her now that she must have been struck upon the head. The church-clocks were striking eight. A bonfire which had been built at a distance, to light the citizens in the work of rescue, cast a little gleam in through the *débris* across her two hands, which lay clasped together at her side. One of her fingers, she saw, was gone; it was the finger which held Dick's little engagement ring. The red beam lay across her forehead, and drops dripped from it upon her eyes. Her feet, still tangled in the gearing which had tripped her, were buried beneath a pile of bricks.

A broad piece of flooring, that had fallen slantwise, roofed her in, and saved her from the mass of ironwork overhead, which would have crushed the breath out of Titans. Fragments of looms, shafts, and pillars were in heaps about. Some one whom she could not see was dying just behind her. A little girl who worked in her room—a mere child—was crying, between her groans, for her mother. Del Ivory sat in a little open space, cushioned about with reels of cotton; she had a shallow gash upon her cheek; she was wringing her hands. They were at work from the outside, sawing entrances through the labyrinth of planks. A dead woman lay close by, and Sene saw them draw her out. It was Meg Match. One of the pretty Irish girls was crushed quite out of sight; only one hand was free; she moved it feebly. They could hear her calling for Jimmy

Mahoney, Jimmy Mahoney! and would they be sure and give him back the handkerchief? Poor Jimmy Mahoney! By and by she called no more; and in a little while the hand was still. On the other side of the slanted flooring some one prayed aloud. She had a little baby at home. She was asking God to take care of it for her. "For Christ's sake," she said. Sene listened long for the Amen, but it was never spoken. Beyond, they dug a man out from under a dead body, unhurt. He crawled to his feet, and broke into furious blasphemies.

As consciousness came fully, agony grew. Sene shut her lips and folded her bleeding hands together and uttered no cry. Del did screaming enough for two, she thought. She pondered things calmly as the night deepened, and the words that the workers outside were saying came brokenly to her. Her hurt, she knew, was not unto death; but it must be cared for before very long; how far could she support this slow bleeding away? And what were the chances that they could hew their way to her without crushing her?

She thought of her father, of Dick; of the bright little kitchen and supper-table set for three; of the song that she had sung in the flush of the morning. Life—even her life—grew sweet, now that it was slipping from her.

Del cried presently that they were cutting them out. The glare of the bonfires struck through an opening; saws and axes flashed; voices grew distinct.

"They never can get at me," said Sene. "I must be able to crawl. If you could get some of those bricks off of my feet, Del!"

Del took off two or three in a frightened way; then, seeing the blood on them, sat down and cried.

A Scotch girl, with one arm shattered, crept up and removed the pile, then fainted.

The opening broadened, brightened; the sweet night-wind blew in; the safe night-sky shone through. Sene's heart leaped within her. Out in the wind and under the sky she should stand again, after all! Back in the little kitchen, where the sun shone, and she could sing a song, there would yet be a place for her. She worked her head from under the beam, and raised herself upon her elbow.

At that moment she heard a cry:

"Fire! *fire!* GOD ALMIGHTY HELP THEM,—THE RUINS ARE ON FIRE!"

A man working over the *débris* from the outside had taken the notion—it being rather dark just there—to carry a lantern with him.

"For God's sake," a voice cried from the crowd, "don't stay there with that light!"

But before the words had died upon the air, it was the dreadful fate of the man with the lantern to let it fall,—and it broke upon the ruined mass.

That was at nine o'clock. What there was to see from then till morning could never be told or forgotten.

A network twenty feet high, of rods and girders, of beams, pillars, stairways, gearing, roofing, ceiling, walling; wrecks of looms, shafts, twisters, pulleys, bobbins, mules, locked and interwoven; wrecks of human creatures wedged in; a face that you know turned up at you from some pit which twenty-four hours' hewing could not open; a voice that you know crying after you from God knows where; a mass of long, fair hair visible here, a foot there, three fingers of a hand over there; the snow bright-red under foot; charred limbs and headless trunks tossed about; strong men carrying covered things by you, at the sight of which other strong men have fainted; the little yellow jet that flared up, and died in smoke, and flared again, leaped out, licked the cotton-bales, tasted the oiled machinery, crunched the netted wood, danced on the heaped-up stone, threw its cruel arms high into the night, roared for joy at helpless firemen, and swallowed wreck, death, and life together out of your sight,—the lurid thing stands alone in the gallery of tragedy.

"Del," said Sene, presently, "I smell the smoke." And in a little while, "How red it is growing away over there at the left!"

To lie here and watch the hideous redness crawling after her, springing at her!—it had seemed greater than reason could bear, at first.

Now it did not trouble her. She grew a little faint, and her thoughts wandered. She put her head down upon her arm, and shut her eyes. Dreamily she heard them saying a dreadful thing outside, about one of the overseers; at the alarm of fire he had cut his throat, and before the flames touched him he was taken out.

Dreamily she heard Del cry that the shaft behind the heap of reels was growing hot. Dreamily she saw a tiny puff of smoke struggle through the cracks of a broken fly-frame.

They were working to save her, with rigid, stern faces. A plank snapped, a rod yielded; they drew out the Scotch girl; her hair was singed; then a man with blood upon his face and wrists held down his arms.

"There's time for one more! God save the rest of ye,—I can't!"

Del sprang; then stopped,—even Del,—stopped ashamed, and looked back at the cripple. Asenath at this sat up erect. The latent heroism in her awoke. All her thoughts grew clear and bright. The tangled skein of her perplexed and troubled winter unwound suddenly. This, then, was the way. It was better so. God had provided himself a lamb for the burnt-offering.

So she said, "Go, Del, and tell him I sent you with my dear love, and that it's all right." And Del at the first word went.

Sene sat and watched them draw her out; it was a slow process; the loose sleeve of her factory sack was scorched.

Somebody at work outside turned suddenly and caught her. It was Dick. The love which he had fought so long broke free of barrier in that hour. He kissed her pink arm where the burnt sleeve fell off. He uttered a cry at the blood upon her face. She turned faint with the sense of safety; and, with a face as white as her own, he bore her away in his arms to the hospital, over the crimson snow.

Asenath looked out through the glare and smoke with parched lips. For a scratch upon the girl's smooth cheek, he had quite forgotten her. They had left her, tombed alive here in this furnace, and gone their happy way. Yet it gave her a curious sense of relief and triumph. If this were all that she could be to him, the thing which she had done was right, quite right. God must have known. She turned away, and shut her eyes again.

When she opened them, neither Dick, nor Del, nor crimsoned snow, nor sky, were there; only the smoke writhing up a pillar of blood-red flame.

The child who had called for her mother began to sob out that she was afraid to die alone. "Come here, Molly," said Sene. "Can you crawl around?"

Molly crawled around.

"Put your head in my lap, and your arms about my waist, and I will put my hands in yours, so. There! I guess that's better."

But they had not given them up yet. In the still unburnt rubbish at the right, some one had wrenched an opening within a foot of Sene's face. They clawed at the solid iron pintles like savage things. A fireman fainted in the glow.

"Give it up!" cried the crowd from behind. "It can't be done! Fall back!"—then hushed, awestruck.

An old man was crawling along upon his hands and knees over the heated bricks. He was a very old man. His gray hair blew about in the wind.

"I want my little gal!" he said. "Can't anybody tell me where to find my little gal?" A rough-looking young fellow pointed in perfect silence through the smoke.

"I'll have her out yet. I'm an old man, but I can help. She's my little gal, ye see. Hand me that there dipper of water; it'll keep her from choking, may be. Now! Keep cheery, Sene! Your old father'll get ye out. Keep up good heart, child! That's it!"

"It's no use, father. Don't feel bad, father. I don't mind it very much."

He hacked at the timber; he tried to laugh; he bewildered himself with cheerful words.

"No more ye need n't, Senath, for it'll be over in a minute. Don't be downcast yet! We'll have ye safe at home before ye know it. Drink a little more water,—do now! They'll get at ye now, sure!"

But above the crackle and the roar a woman's voice rang out like a bell:—

"*We're going home, to die no more.*"

A child's notes quavered in the chorus. From sealed and unseen graves, white young lips swelled the glad refrain,—

"*We're going, going home.*"

The crawling smoke turned yellow, turned red. Voice after voice broke and hushed utterly. One only sang on like silver. It flung defiance down at death. It chimed into the lurid sky without a tremor. For one stood beside her in the furnace, and his form was like unto the form of the Son of God. Their eyes met. Why should not Asenath sing?

"Senath!" cried the old man out upon the burning bricks; he was scorched now, from his gray hair to his patched boots.

The answer came triumphantly,—

"*To die no more, no more, no more!*"

"Sene! little Sene!"

But some one pulled him back.

Emma Lazarus
(1849–1887)

he fourth daughter of a wealthy New York Jewish family, Emma Lazarus was encouraged in her writing by her father, who provided her with a superb education and helped her publish her first collection, *Poems and Translations: Written Between the Ages of Fourteen and Sixteen* (1866). Although she sometimes wrote, as in "Echoes," about women's lack of poetic confidence, Lazarus was among the most confident and courageous women writers of her age. She undertook the commitment to write about specifically Jewish themes, and about the persecution of Jews in Eastern Europe; and spoke for all American immigrants in her most famous poem "The New Colossus," inscribed on the pedestal of the Statue of Liberty.

Echoes (1880)

Late-born and woman-souled, I dare not hope,
The freshness of the elder lays, the might
Of manly, modern passion shall alight
Upon my Muse's lips, nor may I cope
(Who veiled and screened by womanhood must grope)
With the world's strong-armed warriors and recite
The dangers, wounds, and triumphs of the fight;
Twanging the full-stringed lyre through all its scope.
But if thou ever in some lake-floored cave
O'erbrowed by rocks, a wild voice wooed and heard,
Answering at once from heaven and earth and wave,
Lending elf-music to thy harshest word,
Misprize thou not these echoes that belong
To one in love with solitude and song.

The New Colossus (1883)

Not like the brazen giant of Greek fame,
With conquering limbs astride from land to land;
Here at our sea-washed, sunset gates shall stand
A mighty woman with a torch, whose flame
Is the imprisoned lightning, and her name
Mother of Exiles. From her beacon-hand
Glows world-wide welcome; her mild eyes command
The air-bridged harbor that twin cities frame.
"Keep, ancient lands, your storied pomp!" cries she
With silent lips. "Give me your tired, your poor,
Your huddled masses yearning to breathe free,
The wretched refuse of your teeming shore.
Send these, the homeless, tempest-tost to me,
I lift my lamp beside the golden door!"

Sarah Orne Jewett
(1849–1909)

ewett grew up in South Berwick, Maine, one of three daughters of a doctor who took her with him on his country rounds, as well as giving her access to his library, where she read Austen and Flaubert. She started to write fiction as a young woman, and decided early that her forte was short stories rather than the novel, a decision some critics have seen as confining her to minor literary status, what Henry James called her "beautiful little quantum of achievement." But Jewett's local color, regionalist, and psychological stories have stood up to contemporary judgments, while many nineteenth-century novels have lost their readership. In "The Circus at Denby," which is one of the earliest stories to use the freak as an emblem for oppressed women, two friends on summer holiday from Boston take an excursion to see a traveling circus. "A White Heron," one of Jewett's most anthologized stories, is a parable about a girl's refusal to enter the heterosexual and urban worlds, a fairy tale about a New England princess who refuses to be rescued from her isolation by the handsome prince.

After her father's death in 1882, Jewett formed an intimate friendship with Annie Fields, who was mourning the death of her husband. In May 1882 they traveled together to Europe, visiting Ireland, England, Norway, Belgium, Italy, France, and Switzerland; and upon their return in the fall, Jewett collected her clothes from the family home and moved into the Fields's house at 148 Charles Street in Boston. Their relationship was one of the most celebrated and accepted of the "Boston marriages," or female romantic partnerships, characteristic of the late nineteenth century.

The Circus at Denby (1877)

Kate and I looked forward to a certain Saturday with as much eagerness as if we had been little school-boys, for on that day we were to go to a circus at Denby, a town perhaps eight miles inland. There had not been a circus so near Deephaven for a long time, and nobody had dared to believe the first rumor of it, until two dashing young men had deigned to come themselves to put up the big posters on the end of 'Bijah Mauley's barn. All the boys in town came as soon as possible to see these amazing pictures, and some were wretched in their secret hearts at the thought that they might not see the show itself. Tommy Dockum was more interested than any one else, and mentioned the subject so frequently one day when he went blackberrying with us, that we grew enthusiastic, and told each other what fun it would be to go, for everybody would be there, and it would be the greatest loss to us if we were absent. I thought I had lost my childish fondness for circuses, but it came back redoubled; and Kate may contradict me if she chooses, but I am sure she never looked forward to the Easter Oratorio with half the pleasure she did to this "caravan," as most of the people called it.

We felt that it was a great pity that any of the boys and girls should be left lamenting at home, and finding that there were some of our acquaintances and Tommy's who saw no chance of going, we engaged Jo Sands and Leander Dockum to carry them to Denby in two fish-wagons, with boards laid across for the extra seats. We saw them join the straggling train of carriages which had begun to go through the village from all along shore, soon after daylight, and they started on their journey shouting and carousing, with their pockets crammed with early apples and other provisions. We thought it would have been fun enough to see the people go by, for we had had no idea until then how many inhabitants that country held.

We had asked Mrs. Kew to go with us; but she was half an hour later than she had promised, for, since there was no wind, she could not come ashore in the sail-boat, and Mr. Kew had had to row her in in the dory. We saw the boat at last nearly in shore, and drove down to meet it: even the horse seemed to realize what a great day it was, and showed a disposition to friskiness, evidently as surprising to himself as to us.

Mrs. Kew was funnier that day than we had ever known her, which is saying a great deal, and we should not have had half so good a time if she had not been with us; although she lived in the lighthouse, and had no chance to "see passing," which a woman prizes so highly in the country, she had a wonderful memory for faces, and could tell us the names of all Deephaveners and of most of the people we met outside its limits. She looked impressed and solemn as she hurried up from the water's edge, giving Mr. Kew some parting charges over her shoulder as he pushed off the boat to go back; but after we had convinced her that the delay had not troubled us, she seemed more cheerful. It was evident that she felt the importance of the occasion, and that she was pleased at our having chosen her for company. She threw back her veil entirely, sat very straight, and took immense pains to bow to every acquaintance whom she met. She wore her best Sunday clothes, and her manner was formal for the first few minutes; it was evident that she felt we were meeting under unusual circumstances, and that, although we had often met before on the friendliest terms, our having asked her to make this excursion in public required a different sort of behavior at her hands, and a due amount of ceremony and propriety. But this state of things did not last long, as she soon made a remark at which Kate and I laughed so heartily in lighthouse-acquaintance fashion, that she unbent, and gave her whole mind to enjoying herself.

When we came by the store where the post-office was kept we saw a small knot of people gathered round the door, and stopped to see what had happened. There was a forlorn horse standing near, with his harness tied up with fuzzy ends of rope, and the wagon was cobbled together with pieces of board; the whole craft looked as if it might be wrecked with the least jar. In the wagon were four or five stupid-looking boys and girls, one of whom was crying softly. Their father was sick, some one told us. "He was took faint, but he is coming to all right; they have give him something to take: their name is Craper, and they live way over beyond the Ridge, on Stone Hill. They were goin' over to Denby to the circus, and the man was calc'lating to get doctored, but I d' know 's he can get so fur; he's powerful slim-looking to me." Kate and I went to see if we could be of any use, and when we went into the store we saw the man leaning back in his chair, looking ghastly pale, and as if he were far gone in consumption. Kate spoke to him, and he said he was better: he had felt bad all the way along, but he hadn't given up. He was pitiful, poor fellow, with his evident attempt at dressing up. He had the bushiest, dustiest red hair and whiskers, which made the pallor of his face still more striking, and his illness had thinned and paled his rough, clumsy hands. I thought what a hard piece of work it must have been for him to start for the circus that morning, and how kind-hearted he must be to have made such an effort for his children's pleasure. As we went out they stared at us gloomily. The shadow of their disappointment touched and chilled our pleasure.

Somebody had turned the horse so that he was heading toward home, and by his actions he showed that he was the only one of the party who was glad. We were so sorry for the children; perhaps it had promised to be the happiest day of their lives, and now they must go back to their uninteresting home without having seen the great show.

"I am so sorry you are disappointed," said Kate, as we were wondering how the man who had followed us could ever climb into the wagon.

"Heh?" said he, blankly, as if he did not know what her words meant. "What fool has been a turning o' this horse?" he asked a man who was looking on.

"Why, which way be ye goin'?"

"To the circus," said Mr. Craper, with decision, "where d' ye s'pose? That's where I started for, anyways." And he climbed in and glanced round to count the children, struck the horse with the willow switch, and they started off briskly, while everybody laughed. Kate and I joined Mrs. Kew, who had enjoyed the scene.

"Well, there!" said she, "I wonder the folks in the old North burying-ground ain't a-rising up to go to Denby to that caravan!"

We reached Denby at noon; it was an uninteresting town which had grown up around some mills. There was a great commotion in the streets, and it was evident that we had lost much in not having seen the procession. There was a great deal of business going on in the shops, and there were two or three hand-organs at large, near one of which we stopped awhile to listen, just after we had met Leander and given the horse into his charge. Mrs. Kew finished her shopping as soon as possible, and we hurried toward the great tents, where all the flags were flying. I think I have not told you that we were to have the benefit of seeing a menagerie in addition to the circus, and you may be sure we went faithfully round to see everything that the cages held.

I cannot truthfully say that it was a good show; it was somewhat dreary, now that I think of it quietly and without excitement. The creatures looked tired, and as if they had been on the road for a great many years. The animals were all old, and there was a shabby great elephant whose look of general discouragement went to my heart, for it seemed as if he were miserably conscious of a misspent life. He stood dejected and motionless at one side of the tent, and it was hard to believe that there was a spark of vitality left in him. A great number of the people had never seen an elephant before, and we heard a thin little old man, who stood near us, say delightedly, "There's the old creatur', and no mistake, Ann 'Liza. I wanted to see him most of anything. My sakes alive, ain't he big!"

And Ann 'Liza, who was stout and sleepy-looking, droned out, "Ye-es, there's consider'ble of him; but he looks as if he ain't got no animation."

Kate and I turned away and laughed, while Mrs. Kew said confidentially, as the couple moved away, "*She* needn't be a reflectin' on the poor beast. That's Mis Seth Tanner, and there isn't a woman in Deephaven nor East Parish to be named the same day with her for laziness. I'm glad she didn't catch sight of me; she'd have talked about nothing for a fortnight."

There was a picture of a huge snake in Deephaven, and I was just wondering where he could be, or if there ever had been one, when we heard a boy ask the same question of the man whose thankless task it was to stir up the lions with a stick to make them roar. "The snake's dead," he answered good-naturedly. "Didn't you have to dig an awful long grave for him?" asked the boy; but the man said he reckoned they curled him up some, and smiled as he turned to his lions, who looked as if they needed a tonic. Everybody lingered longest before the monkeys, who seemed to be the only lively creatures in the whole collection; and finally we made our way into the other tent, and perched ourselves on a high seat, from whence we had a capital view of the audience and the ring, and could see the people come in. Mrs. Kew was on the lookout for acquaintances, and her spirits as well as our own seemed to rise higher and higher. She was on the alert, moving her head this way and that to catch sight of people, giving us running commentary in the mean time. It was very pleasant to see a person so happy as Mrs. Kew was that day, and I dare say in speaking of the occasion she would say the same thing of Kate and me,—for it was such a good time! We bought some peanuts, without which no circus seems complete, and we listened to the conversations which were being carried on around us while we were waiting for the performance to begin. There were two old farmers whom we had noticed occasionally in Deephaven; one was telling the other, with great confusion of pronouns, about a big pig which had lately been killed. "John did feel dreadful disappointed at having to kill now," we heard him say, "bein' as he had calc'lated to kill along near Thanksgivin' time; there was goin' to be a new moon then, and he expected to get seventy-five or a hundred pound more on to him. But he didn't seem to gain, and me and 'Bijah both told him he'd be better to kill now, while everything was favor'ble, and if he set out to wait something might happen to him, and then I've always held that you can't get no hog only just so fur, and for my part I don't like these great overgrown creatur's. I like well enough to see a hog that'll weigh six hundred, just for the beauty on 't, but for my eatin' give me one that'll just rise three. 'Bijah's accurate, and he says he is goin' to weigh risin' five hundred and fifty. I shall stop, as I go home, to John's wife's brother's and see if they've got the particulars yet; John was goin' to get the scales this morning. I guess likely consider'ble many'll gather there tomorrow after meeting. John didn't calc'late to cut up till Monday."

"I guess likely I'll stop in tomorrow," said the other man; "I like to see a han'some hog. Chester White, you said? Consider them best, don't ye?" But this question never was answered, for the greater part of the circus company in gorgeous trappings came parading in.

The circus was like all other circuses, except that it was shabbier than most, and the performers seemed to have less heart in it than usual. They did their best, and went through with their parts conscientiously, but they looked as if they never had had a good time in their lives. The audience was hilarious, and cheered and laughed at the tired clown until he looked as if he thought his speeches might possibly be funny, after all. We were so glad we had pleased the poor thing; and when he sang a song our satisfaction was still greater, and so he sang it all over again. Perhaps he had been associating with people who were used to circuses. The afternoon was hot, and the boys with Japanese fans and trays of lemonade did a remarkable business for so late in the season; the brass band on the other side of the tent shrieked its very best, and all the young men of the region had brought their girls, and some of these countless pairs of country lovers we watched a great deal, as they "kept company" with more or less depth of satisfaction in each other. We had a grand chance to see the fashions, and there were many old people and a great number of little children, and some families had evidently locked their house door behind them, since they had brought both the dog and the baby.

"Doesn't it seem as if you were a child again?" Kate asked me. "I am sure this is just the same as the first circus I ever saw. It grows more and more familiar, and it puzzles me to think they should not have altered in the least while I have changed so much, and have even had time to grow up. You don't know how it is making me remember other things of which I have not thought for years. I was seven years old when I went that first time. Uncle Jack invited me. I had a new parasol, and he laughed because I would hold it over my shoulder when the sun was in my face. He took me into the side-shows and bought me everything I asked for, on the way home, and we did not get home until twilight. The rest of the family had dined at four o'clock and gone out for a long drive, and it was such fun to have our dinner by ourselves. I sat at the head of the table in mamma's place, and when Bridget came down and insisted that I must go to bed, Uncle Jack came softly up stairs and sat by the window, smoking and telling me stories. He ran and hid in the closet when we heard mamma coming up, and when she found him out by the cigar-smoke, and made believe scold him, I thought she was in earnest, and begged him off. Yes; and I remember that Bridget sat in the next room, making her new dress so she could wear it to church next day. I thought it was a beautiful dress, and besought mamma to have one like it. It was bright green with yellow spots all over it," said Kate. "Ah, poor Uncle Jack! He was so good to me! We were always telling stories of what we would do when I was grown up. He died in Canton the next year, and I cried myself ill; but for a long time I thought he might not be dead, after all, and might come home any day. He used to seem so old to me, and he really was just out of college and not so old as I am now. That day at the circus he had a pink rosebud in his buttonhole, and—ah! when have I ever thought of this before!—a woman sat before us who had a stiff little cape on her bonnet like a shelf, and I carefully put peanuts round the edge of it, and when she moved her head they would fall. I thought it was the best fun in the world, and I wished Uncle Jack to ride the donkey; I was sure he could keep on, because his horse had capered about with him one day on Beacon Street, and I thought him a perfect rider, since nothing had happened to him then."

"I remember," said Mrs. Kew, presently, "that just before I was married 'he' took me over to Wareham Corners to a caravan. My sister Hannah and the young man who was keeping company with her went too. I haven't been to one since till today, and it does carry me back same's it does you, Miss Kate. It doesn't seem more than five years ago, and what would I have thought if I had known 'he' and I were going to keep a light-house and be contented there, what's more, and sometimes not get ashore for a fortnight; settled, gray-headed old folks! We were gay enough in those days. I know old Miss Sabrina Smith warned me that I'd better think twice before I took up with Tom Kew, for he was a light-minded young man. I speak o' that to him in the winter-time, when he sets reading the almanac half asleep and I'm knitting, and the wind's a'howling and the waves coming ashore on those rocks as if they wished they could put out the light and blow down the lighthouse. We were reflected on a good deal for going to that caravan; some of the old folks didn't think it was improvin'—Well, I should think that man was a trying to break his neck!"

Coming out of the great tent was disagreeable enough, and we seemed to have chosen the worst time, for the crowd pushed fiercely, though I suppose nobody was in the least hurry, and we were all severely jammed, while from somewhere underneath came the wails of a deserted dog. We had not meant to see the side-shows, and went carelessly past two or three tents; but when we came in sight of the picture of the Kentucky giantess, we noticed that Mrs. Kew looked at it wistfully, and we immediately asked if she cared anything about going to see the wonder, whereupon she confessed that she never heard of such a thing as a woman's weighing six hundred and fifty pounds, so we all three went in. There were only two or three persons inside the tent, beside a little boy who played the hand-organ.

The Kentucky giantess sat in two chairs on a platform, and there was a large cage of monkeys just beyond, toward which Kate and I went at once. "Why, she isn't more than two-thirds as big as the picture," said Mrs. Kew, in a regretful whisper; "but I guess she's big enough; doesn't she look discouraged, poor creatur'?" Kate and I felt ashamed of ourselves for being there. No matter if she had consented to be carried round for a show, it must have been horrible to be stared at and joked about day after day; and we gravely looked at the monkeys, and in a few minutes turned to see if Mrs. Kew were not ready to come away, when to our surprise we saw that she was talking to the giantess with great interest, and we went nearer.

"I thought your face looked natural the minute I set foot inside the door," said Mrs. Kew; "but you've—altered some since I saw you, and I couldn't place you till I heard you speak. Why, you used to be spare; I am amazed, Marilly! Where are your folks?"

"I don't wonder you are surprised," said the giantess. "I was a good ways from this when you knew me, wasn't I? But father he run through with every cent he had before he died, and 'he' took to drink and it killed him after a while, and then I begun to grow worse and worse, till I couldn't do nothing to earn a dollar, and everybody was a coming to see me, till at last I used to ask 'em ten cents apiece, and I scratched along somehow till this man came round and heard of me, and he offered me my keep and good pay to go along with him. He had another giantess before me, but she had begun to fall away consider'ble, so he paid her off and let her go. This other giantess was an awful expense to him, she was such an eater; now I don't have no great of an appetite,"—this was said plaintively,—"and he's raised my pay since I've been with him because we did so well. I took up with his offer because I was nothing but a drag and never will be. I'm as comfortable as I can be, but it's a pretty hard business. My oldest boy is able to do for himself, but he's married this last year, and his wife don't want me. I don't know's I blame her either. It would be something like if I had a daughter now; but there, I'm getting to like travelling first-rate; it gives anybody a good deal to think of."

"I was asking the folks about you when I was up home the early part of the summer," said Mrs. Kew, "but all they knew was that you were living out in New York State. Have you been living in Kentucky long? I saw it on the picture outside."

"No," said the giantess, "that was a picture the man bought cheap from another show that broke up last year. It says six hundred and fifty pounds, but I don't weigh more than four hundred. I haven't been weighed for some time past. Between you and me I don't weigh so much as that, but you mustn't mention it, for it would spoil my reputation, and might hender my getting another engagement." And then the poor giantess lost her professional look and tone as she said, "I believe I'd rather die than grow any bigger. I do lose heart sometimes, and wish I was a smart woman and could keep house. I'd be smarter than ever I was when I had the chance; I tell you that! Is Tom along with you?"

"No. I came with these young ladies, Miss Lancaster and Miss Denis, who are stopping over to Deephaven for the summer." Kate and I turned as we heard this introduction; we were standing close by, and I am proud to say that I never saw Kate treat any one more politely than she did that absurd, pitiful creature with the gilt crown and many bracelets. It was not that she said much, but there was such an exquisite courtesy in her manner, and an apparent unconsciousness of there being anything in the least surprising or uncommon about the giantess.

Just then a party of people came in, and Mrs. Kew said good by reluctantly. "It has done me sights of good to see you," said our new acquaintance; "I was feeling down-hearted just before you came in. I'm pleased to see somebody that remembers me as I used to be." And they shook hands in a way that meant a great deal, and when Kate and I said good afternoon the giantess looked at us gratefully, and said, "I'm very much obliged to you for coming in, young ladies."

"Walk in! walk in!" the man was shouting as we came away. "Walk in and see the wonder of the world, ladies and gentlemen,—the largest woman ever seen in America,—the great Kentucky giantess!"

"Wouldn't you have liked to stay longer?" Kate asked Mrs. Kew as we came down the street. But she answered that it would be no satisfaction; the people were coming in, and she would have no chance to talk. "I never knew her very well; she is younger than I, and she used to go to meeting where I did, but she lived five or six miles from our house. She's had a hard time of it, according to her account," said Mrs. Kew. "She used to be a dreadful flighty, high-tempered girl, but she's lost that now, I can see by her eyes. I was running over in my mind to see if there was anything I could do for her, but I don't know as there is. She said the man who hired her was kind. I guess your treating her so polite did her as much good as anything. She used to be real ambitious. I had it on my tongue's end to ask her if she couldn't get a few days' leave and come out to stop with me, but I thought just in time that she'd sink the dory in a minute. There! seeing her has took away all the fun," said Mrs. Kew ruefully; and we were all dismal for a while, but at last, after we were fairly started for home, we began to be merry again.

We passed the Craper family whom we had seen at the store in the morning; the children looked as stupid as ever, but the father, I am sorry to say, had been tempted to drink more whiskey than was good for him. He had a bright flush on his cheeks, and he was flourishing his whip, and hoarsely singing some meaningless tune. "Poor creature!" said I, "I should think this day's pleasuring would kill him." "Now, wouldn't you think so?" said Mrs. Kew, sympathizingly; "but the truth is, you couldn't kill one of those Crapers if you pounded him in a mortar."

We had a pleasant drive home, and we kept Mrs. Kew to supper, and afterward went down to the shore to see her set sail for home. Mr. Kew had come in some time before, and had been waiting for the moon to rise. Mrs. Kew told us that she should have enough to think of for a year, she had enjoyed the day so much; and we stood on the pebbles watching the boat out of the harbor, and wishing ourselves on board, it was such a beautiful evening.

We went to another show that summer, the memory of which will never fade. It is somewhat impertinent to call it a show, and "public entertainment" is equally inappropriate, though we certainly were entertained. It had been raining for two or three days; the Deephavenites spoke of it as "a spell of weather." Just after tea, one Thursday evening, Kate and I went down to the post-office. When we opened the great hall door, the salt air was delicious, but we found the town apparently wet through and discouraged; and though it had almost stopped raining just then, there was a Scotch mist, like a snow-storm with the chill taken off, and the Chantrey elms dripped hurriedly, and creaked occasionally in the east-wind.

"There will not be a cap'n on the wharves for a week after this," said I to Kate; "only think of the cases of rheumatism!"

We stopped for a few minutes at the Carews', who were as much surprised to see us as if we had been mermaids out of the sea, and begged us to give ourselves something warm to drink, and to change our boots the moment we got home. Then we went on to the post-office. Kate went in, but stopped, as she came out with our letters, to read a written notice securely fastened to the grocery door by four large carpet-tacks with wide leathers round their necks.

"Dear," said she, exultantly, "there's going to be a lecture tonight in the church,—a free lecture on the Elements of True Manhood. Wouldn't you like to go?" And we went.

We were fifteen minutes later than the time appointed, and were sorry to find that the audience was almost imperceptible. The dampness had affected the antiquated lamps so that those on the walls and on the front of the gallery were the dimmest lights I ever saw, and sent their feeble rays through a small space the edges of which were clearly defined. There were two rather more energetic lights on the table near the pulpit, where the lecturer sat, and as we were in the rear of the church, we could see the yellow fog between ourselves and him. There were fourteen persons in the audience, and we were all huddled together in a cowardly way in the pews nearest the door: three old men, four women, and four children, besides ourselves and the sexton, a deaf little old man with a wooden leg.

The children whispered noisily, and soon, to our surprise, the lecturer rose and began. He bowed, and treated us with beautiful deference, and read his dreary lecture with enthusiasm. I wish I could say, for his sake, that it was interesting; but I cannot tell a lie, and it was so long! He went on and on, until it seemed as if I had been there ever since I was a little girl. Kate and I did not dare to look at each other, and in my desperation at feeling her quiver with laughter, I moved to the other end of the pew, knocking over a big hymn-book on the way, which attracted so much attention that I have seldom felt more embarrassed in my life. Kate's great dog rose several times to shake himself and yawn loudly, and then lie down again despairingly.

You would have thought the man was addressing an enthusiastic Young Men's Christian Association. He exhorted with fervor upon our duties as citizens and as voters, and told us a great deal about George Washington and Benjamin Franklin, whom he urged us to choose as our examples. He waited for applause after each of his outbursts of eloquence, and presently went on again, in no wise disconcerted at the silence, and as if he were sure that he would fetch us next time. The rain began to fall again heavily, and the wind wailed around the meeting-house. If the lecture had been upon any other subject it would not have been so hard for Kate and me to keep sober faces; but it was directed entirely toward young men, and there was not a young man there.

The children in front of us mildly scuffled with each other at one time, until the one at the end of the pew dropped a marble, which struck the floor and rolled with a frightful noise down the edge of the aisle where there was no carpet. The congregation instinctively started up to look after it, but we recollected ourselves and leaned back again in our places, while the awed children, after keeping unnaturally quiet, fell asleep, and tumbled against each other helplessly. After a time the man sat down and wiped his forehead, looking well satisfied; and when we were wondering whether we might with propriety come away, he rose again, and said it was a free lecture, and he thanked us for our kind patronage on that inclement night; but in other places which he had visited there had been a contribution taken up for the cause. It would, perhaps, do no harm,—would the sexton—

But the sexton could not have heard the sound of a cannon at that distance, and slumbered on. Neither Kate nor I had any money, except a twenty-dollar bill in my purse, and some coppers in the pocket of her water-proof cloak which she assured me she was prepared to give; but we saw no signs of the sexton's waking, and as one of the women kindly went forward to wake the children, we all rose and came away.

After we had made as much fun and laughed as long as we pleased that night, we became suddenly conscious of the pitiful side of it all; and being anxious that every one should have the highest opinion of Deephaven, we sent Tom Dockum early in the morning with an anonymous note to the lecturer, whom he found without much trouble; but afterward we were disturbed at hearing that he was going to repeat his lecture that evening,—the wind having gone round to the northwest,—and I have no doubt there were a good many women able to be out, and that he harvested enough ten-cent pieces to pay his expenses without our help; though he had particularly told us it was for "the cause," the evening before, and that ought to have been a consolation.

A White Heron (1886)

I

The woods were already filled with shadows one June evening, just before eight o'clock, though a bright sunset still glimmered faintly among the trunks of the trees. A little girl was driving home her cow, a plodding, dilatory, provoking creature in her behavior, but a valued companion for all that. They were going away from whatever light there was, and striking deep into the woods, but their feet were familiar with the path, and it was no matter whether their eyes could see it or not.

There was hardly a night the summer through when the old cow could be found waiting at the pasture bars; on the contrary, it was her greatest pleasure to hide herself away among the huckleberry bushes, and though she wore a loud bell she had made the discovery that if one stood perfectly still it would not ring. So Sylvia had to hunt for her until she found her, and call Co'! Co'! with never an answering Moo, until her childish patience was quite spent. If the creature had not given good milk and plenty of it, the case would have seemed very different to her owners. Besides, Sylvia had all the time there was, and very little use to make of it. Sometimes in pleasant weather it was a consolation to look upon the cow's pranks as an intelligent attempt to play hide and seek, and as the child had no playmates she lent herself to this amusement with a good deal of zest. Though this chase had been so long that the wary animal herself had given an unusual signal of her whereabouts, Sylvia had only laughed when she came upon Mistress Moolly at the swamp-side, and urged her affectionately homeward with a twig of birch leaves. The old cow was not inclined to wander farther, she even turned in the right direction for once as they left the pasture, and stepped along the road at a good pace. She was quite ready to be milked now, and seldom stopped to browse. Sylvia wondered what her grandmother would say because they were so late. It was a great while since she had left home at half-past five o'clock, but everybody knew the difficulty of making this errand a short one. Mrs. Tilley had chased the horned torment too many summer evenings herself to blame any one else for lingering, and was only thankful as she waited that she had Sylvia, nowadays, to give such valuable assistance. The good woman suspected that Sylvia loitered occasionally on her own account; there never was such a child for straying about out-of-doors since the world was made! Everybody said that it was a good change for a little maid who had tried to grow for eight years in a crowded manufacturing town, but, as for Sylvia herself, it seemed as if she never had been alive at all before she came to live at the farm. She thought often with wistful compassion of a wretched dry geranium that belonged to a town neighbor.

"'Afraid of folks,'" old Mrs. Tilley said to herself, with a smile, after she had made the unlikely choice of Sylvia from her daughter's houseful of children, and was returning to the farm. "'Afraid of folks,' they said! I guess she won't be troubled no great with 'em up to the old place!" When they reached the door of the lonely house and stopped to unlock it, and the cat came to purr loudly, and rub against them, a deserted pussy, indeed, but fat with young robins, Sylvia whispered that this was a beautiful place to live in, and she never should wish to go home.

The companions followed the shady wood-road, the cow taking slow steps, and the child very fast ones. The cow stopped long at the brook to drink, as if the pasture were not half a swamp, and Sylvia stood still and waited, letting her bare feet cool themselves in the shoal water, while the great twilight moths struck softly against her. She waded on through the brook as the cow moved away, and listened to the thrushes with a heart that beat fast with pleasure. There was a stirring in the great boughs overhead. They were full of little birds and beasts that seemed to be wide-awake, and going about their world, or else saying good-night to each other in sleepy twitters. Sylvia herself felt sleepy as she walked along. However, it was not much farther to the house, and the air was soft and sweet. She was not often in the woods so late as this, and it made her feel as if she were a part of the gray shadows and the moving leaves. She was just thinking how long it seemed since she first came to the farm a year ago, and wondering if everything went on in the noisy town just the same as when she was there; the thought of the great red-faced boy who used to chase and frighten her made her hurry along the path to escape from the shadow of the trees.

Suddenly this little woods-girl is horror-stricken to hear a clear whistle not very far away. Not a bird's whistle, which would have a sort of friendliness, but a boy's whistle, determined, and somewhat aggressive. Sylvia left the cow to whatever sad fate might await her, and stepped discreetly aside into the bushes, but she was just too late. The enemy had discovered her, and called out in a very cheerful and persuasive tone, "Halloa, little girl, how far is it to the road?" and trembling Sylvia answered almost inaudibly, "A good ways."

She did not dare to look boldly at the tall young man, who carried a gun over his shoulder, but she came out of her bush and again followed the cow, while he walked alongside.

"I have been hunting for some birds," the stranger said kindly, "and I have lost my way, and need a friend very much. Don't be afraid," he added gallantly. "Speak up and tell me what your name is, and whether you think I can spend the night at your house, and go out gunning early in the morning."

Sylvia was more alarmed than before. Would not her grandmother consider her much to blame? But who could have foreseen such an accident as this? It did not appear to be her fault, and she hung her head as if the stem of it were broken, but managed to answer "Sylvy," with much effort when her companion again asked her name.

Mrs. Tilley was standing in the doorway when the trio came into view. The cow gave a loud moo by way of explanation.

"Yes, you'd better speak up for yourself, you old trial! Where'd she tucked herself away this time, Sylvy?" Sylvia kept an awed silence; she knew by instinct that her grandmother did not comprehend the gravity of the situation. She must be mistaking the stranger for one of the farmer-lads of the region.

The young man stood his gun beside the door, and dropped a heavy game-bag beside it; then he bade Mrs. Tilley good-evening, and repeated his wayfarer's story, and asked if he could have a night's lodging.

"Put me anywhere you like," he said. "I must be off early in the morning, before day; but I am very hungry, indeed. You can give me some milk at any rate, that's plain."

"Dear sakes, yes," responded the hostess, whose long slumbering hospitality seemed to be easily awakened. "You might fare better if you went out on the main road a mile or so, but you're welcome to what we've got. I'll milk right off, and you make yourself at home. You can sleep on husks or feathers," she proffered graciously. "I raised them all myself. There's good pasturing for geese just below here towards the ma'sh. Now step round and set a plate for the gentleman, Sylvy!" And Sylvia promptly stepped. She was glad to have something to do, and she was hungry herself.

It was a surprise to find so clean and comfortable a little dwelling in this New England wilderness. The young man had known the horrors of its most primitive housekeeping, and the dreary squalor of that level of society which does not rebel at the companionship of hens. This was the best thrift of an old-fashioned farmstead, though on such a small scale that it seemed like a hermitage. He listened eagerly to the old woman's quaint talk, he watched Sylvia's pale face and shining gray eyes with ever growing enthusiasm, and insisted that this was the best supper he had eaten for a month, and afterward the new-made friends sat down in the door-way together while the moon came up.

Soon it would be berry-time, and Sylvia was a great help at picking. The cow was a good milker, though a plaguy thing to keep track of, the hostess gossiped frankly, adding presently that she had buried four children, so that Sylvia's mother, and a son (who might be dead) in California were all the children she had left. "Dan, my boy, was a great hand to go gunning," she explained sadly. "I never wanted for pa'tridges or gray squer'ls while he was to home. He's been a great wanderer, I expect, and he's no hand to write letters. There, I don't blame him, I'd ha' seen the world myself if it had been so I could.

"Sylvy takes after him," the grandmother continued affectionately, after a minute's pause. "There ain't a foot o' ground she don't know her way over, and the wild creatures counts her one o' themselves. Squer'ls she'll tame to come an' feed right out o' her hands, and all sorts o' birds. Last winter she got the jay-birds to bangeing here, and I believe she'd 'a' scanted herself of her own meals to have plenty to throw out amongst 'em, if I hadn't kep' watch. Anything but crows, I tell her, I'm willin' to help support—though Dan he went an' tamed one o' them that did seem to have reason same as folks. It was round here a good spell after he went away. Dan an' his father they didn't hitch,—but he never held up his head ag'in after Dan had dared him an' gone off."

The guest did not notice this hint of family sorrows in his eager interest in something else.

"So Sylvy knows all about birds, does she?" he exclaimed, as he looked round at the little girl who sat, very demure but increasingly sleepy, in the moonlight. "I am making a collection of birds myself. I have been at it ever since I was a boy." (Mrs. Tilley smiled.) "There are two or three very rare ones I have been hunting for these five years. I mean to get them on my own ground if they can be found."

"Do you cage 'em up?" asked Mrs. Tilley doubtfully, in response to this enthusiastic announcement.

"Oh, no, they're stuffed and preserved, dozens and dozens of them," said the ornithologist, "and I have shot or snared every one myself. I caught a glimpse of a white heron a few miles from here on Saturday, and I have followed it in this direction. They have never been found in this district at all. The little white heron, it is," and he turned again to look at Sylvia with the hope of discovering that the rare bird was one of her acquaintances.

But Sylvia was watching a hop-toad in the narrow footpath.

"You would know the heron if you saw it," the stranger continued eagerly. "A queer tall white bird with soft feathers and long thin legs. And it would have a nest perhaps in the top of a high tree, made of sticks, something like a hawk's nest."

Sylvia's heart gave a wild beat; she knew that strange white bird, and had once stolen softly near where it stood in some bright green swamp grass, away over at the other side of the woods. There was an open place where the sunshine always seemed strangely yellow and hot, where tall, nodding rushes grew, and her grandmother had warned her that she might sink in the soft black mud underneath and never be heard of more. Not far beyond were the salt marshes just this side the sea itself, which Sylvia wondered and dreamed much about, but never had seen, whose great voice could sometimes be heard above the noise of the woods on stormy nights.

"I can't think of anything I should like so much as to find that heron's nest," the handsome stranger was saying. "I would give ten dollars to anybody who could show it to me," he added desperately, "and I mean to spend my whole vacation hunting for it if need be. Perhaps it was only migrating, or had been chased out of its own region by some bird of prey."

Mrs. Tilley gave amazed attention to all this, but Sylvia still watched the toad, not divining, as she might have done at some calmer time, that the creature wished to get to its hole under the door-step, and was much hindered by the unusual spectators at that hour of the evening. No amount of thought, that night, could decide how many wished-for treasures the ten dollars, so lightly spoken of, would buy.

The next day the young sportsman hovered about the woods, and Sylvia kept him company, having lost her first fear of the friendly lad, who proved to be most kind and sympathetic. He told her many things about the birds and what they knew and where they lived and what they did with themselves. And he gave her a jack-knife, which she thought as great a treasure as if she were a desert-islander. All day long he did not once make her troubled or afraid except when he brought down some unsuspecting singing creature from its bough. Sylvia would have liked him vastly better without his gun; she could not understand why he killed the very birds he seemed to like so much. But as the day waned, Sylvia still watched the young man with loving admiration. She had never seen anybody so charming and delightful; the woman's heart, asleep in the child, was vaguely thrilled by a dream of love. Some premonition of that great power stirred and swayed these young foresters who traversed the solemn woodlands with soft-footed silent care. They stopped to listen to a bird's song; they pressed forward again eagerly, parting the branches,—speaking to each other rarely and in whispers; the young man going first and Sylvia following, fascinated, a few steps behind, with her gray eyes dark with excitement.

She grieved because the longed-for white heron was elusive, but she did not lead the guest, she only followed, and there was no such thing as speaking first. The sound of her own unquestioned voice would have terrified her—it was hard enough to answer yes or no when there was need of that. At last evening began to fall, and they drove the cow home together, and Sylvia smiled with pleasure when they came to the place where she heard the whistle and was afraid only the night before.

II

Half a mile from home, at the farther edge of the woods, where the land was highest, a great pine-tree stood, the last of its generation. Whether it was left for a boundary mark, or for what reason, no one could say; the wood-choppers who had felled its mates were dead and gone long ago, and a whole forest of sturdy trees, pines and oaks and maples, had grown again. But the stately head of this old pine towered above them all and made a landmark for sea and shore miles and miles away. Sylvia knew it well. She had always believed that whoever climbed to the top of it could see the ocean; and the little girl had often laid her hand on the great rough trunk and looked up wistfully at those dark boughs that the wind always stirred, no matter how hot and still the air might be below. Now she thought of the tree with a new excitement, for why, if one climbed it at break of day, could not one see all the world, and easily discover from whence the white heron flew, and mark the place, and find the hidden nest?

What a spirit of adventure, what wild ambition! What fancied triumph and delight and glory for the later morning when she could make known the secret! It was almost too real and too great for the childish heart to bear.

All night the door of the little house stood open, and the whippoorwills came and sang on the very step. The young sportsman and his old hostess were sound asleep, but Sylvia's great design kept her broad awake and watching. She forgot to think of sleep. The short summer night seemed as long as the winter darkness, and at last when the whippoorwills ceased, and she was afraid the morning would after all come too soon, she stole out of the house and followed the pasture path through the woods, hastening toward the open ground beyond, listening with a sense of comfort and companionship to the drowsy twitter of a half-awakened bird, whose perch she had jarred in passing. Alas, if the great wave of human interest which flooded for the first time this dull little life should sweep away the satisfactions of an existence heart to heart with nature and the dumb life of the forest!

There was the huge tree asleep yet in the paling moonlight, and small and hopeful Sylvia began with utmost bravery to mount to the top of it, with tingling, eager blood coursing the channels of her whole frame, with her bare feet and fingers, that pinched and held like bird's claws to the monstrous ladder reaching up, up, almost to the sky itself. First she must mount the white oak tree that grew alongside, where she was almost lost among the dark branches and the green leaves heavy and wet with dew; a bird fluttered off its nest, and a red squirrel ran to and fro and scolded pettishly at the harmless housebreaker. Sylvia felt her way easily. She had often climbed there, and knew that higher still one of the oak's upper branches chafed against the pine trunk, just where its lower boughs were set close together. There, when she made the dangerous pass from one tree to the other, the great enterprise would really begin.

She crept out along the swaying oak limb at last, and took the daring step across into the old pine-tree. The way was harder than she thought; she must reach far and hold fast, the sharp dry twigs caught and held her and scratched her like angry talons, the pitch made her thin little fingers clumsy and stiff as she went round and round the tree's great stem, higher and higher upward. The sparrows and robins in the woods below were beginning to wake and twitter to the dawn, yet it seemed much lighter there aloft in the pine-tree, and the child knew that she must hurry if her project were to be of any use.

The tree seemed to lengthen itself out as she went up, and to reach farther and farther upward. It was like a great main-mast to the voyaging earth; it must truly have been amazed that morning through all its ponderous frame as it felt this determined spark of human spirit wending its way from higher branch to branch. Who knows how steadily the least twigs held themselves to advantage this light, weak creature on her way! The old pine must have loved his new dependent. More than all the hawks, and bats, and moths, and even the sweet voiced thrushes, was the brave, beating heart of the solitary gray-eyed child. And the tree stood still and held away the winds that June morning while the dawn grew bright in the east.

Sylvia's face was like a pale star, if one had seen it from the ground, when the last thorny bough was past, and she stood trembling and tired but wholly triumphant, high in the tree-top. Yes, there was the sea with the dawning sun making a golden dazzle over it, and toward that glorious east flew two hawks with slow-moving pinions. How low they looked in the air from that height when before one had only seen them far up, and dark against the blue sky. Their gray feathers were as soft as moths; they seemed only a little way from the tree, and Sylvia felt as if she too could go flying away among the clouds. Westward, the woodlands and farms reached miles and miles into the distance; here and there were church steeples, and white villages; truly it was a vast and awesome world.

The birds sang louder and louder. At last the sun came up bewilderingly bright. Sylvia could see the white sails of ships out at sea, and the clouds that were purple and rose-colored and yellow at first began to fade away. Where was the white heron's nest in the sea of green branches, and was this wonderful sight and pageant of the world the only reward for having climbed to such a giddy height? Now look down again, Sylvia, where the green marsh is set among the shining birches and dark hemlocks; there where you saw the white heron once you will see him again; look, look! a white spot of him like a single floating feather comes up from the dead hemlock and grows larger, and rises, and comes close at last, and goes by the landmark pine with steady sweep of wing and outstretched slender neck and crested head. And wait! wait! do not move a foot or a finger, little girl, do not send an arrow of light and consciousness from your two eager eyes, for the heron has perched on a pine bough not far beyond yours, and cries back to his mate on the nest and plumes his feathers for the new day!

The child gives a long sigh a minute later when a company of shouting cat-birds comes also to the tree, and vexed by their fluttering and lawlessness the solemn heron goes away. She knows his secret now, the wild, light, slender bird that floats and wavers, and goes back like an arrow presently to his home in the green world beneath. Then Sylvia, well satisfied, makes her perilous way down again, not daring to look far below the branch she stands on, ready to cry sometimes because her fingers ache and her lamed feet slip. Wondering over and over again what the stranger would say to her, and what he would think when she told him how to find his way straight to the heron's nest.

"Sylvy, Sylvy!" called the busy old grandmother again and again, but nobody answered, and the small husk bed was empty, and Sylvia had disappeared.

The guest waked from a dream, and remembering his day's pleasure hurried to dress himself that it might sooner begin. He was sure from the way the shy little girl looked once or twice yesterday that she had at least seen the white heron, and now she must really be made to tell. Here she comes now, paler than ever, and her worn old frock is torn and tattered, and smeared with pine pitch. The grandmother and the sportsman stand in the door together and question her, and the splendid moment has come to speak of the dead hemlock-tree by the green marsh.

But Sylvia does not speak after all, though the old grandmother fretfully rebukes her, and the young man's kind, appealing eyes are looking straight in her own. He can make them rich with money; he has promised it, and they are poor now. He is so well worth making happy, and he waits to hear the story she can tell.

No, she must keep silence! What is it that suddenly forbids her and makes her dumb? Has she been nine years growing, and now, when the great world for the first time puts out a hand to her, must she thrust it aside for a bird's sake? The murmur of the pine's green branches is in her ears, she remembers how the white heron came flying through the golden air and how they watched the sea and the morning together, and Sylvia cannot speak; she cannot tell the heron's secret and give its life away.

Dear loyalty, that suffered a sharp pang as the guest went away disappointed later in the day, that could have served and followed him and loved him as a dog loves! Many a night Sylvia heard the echo of his whistle haunting the pasture path as she came home with the loitering cow. She forgot even her sorrow at the sharp report of his gun and the sight of thrushes and sparrows dropping silent to the ground, their songs hushed and their pretty feathers stained and wet with blood. Were the birds better friends than their hunter might have been,—who can tell? Whatever treasures were lost to her, woodlands and summer-time, remember! Bring your gifts and graces and tell your secrets to this lonely country child!

Mary Noailles Murfree
(*Charles Egbert Craddock*)
(*1850–1922*)

ne of the few American women writers who used a male pseudonym, Murfree published her short stories about Tennessee mountain folk under the name "Charles Egbert Craddock." She successfully maintained her disguise as "Mr. Craddock" for seven years. Over her career, she published fourteen novels and forty-five short stories set in the Appalachian Mountains. One of her most popular Tennessee dialect tales, "The 'Harnt' That Walks Chilhowee" is both a love story and a feminist protest against the law.

The "Harnt" That Walks Chilhowee (1884)

June had crossed the borders of Tennessee. Even on the summit of Chilhowee Mountain the apples in Peter Giles's orchard were beginning to redden, and his Indian corn, planted on so steep a declivity that the stalks seemed to have much ado to keep their footing, was crested with tassels and plumed with silk. Among the dense forests, seen by no man's eye, the elder was flying its creamy banners in honor of June's coming, and, heard by no man's ear, the pink and white bells of the azalea rang out melodies of welcome.

"An' it air a toler'ble for'ard season. Yer wheat looks likely; an' yer gyarden truck air thrivin' powerful. Even that cold spell we-uns hed about the full o' the moon in May ain't done sot it back none, it 'pears like ter me. But, 'cording ter my way o' thinkin', ye hev got chickens enough hyar ter eat off every peabloom ez soon ez it opens." And Simon Burney glanced with a gardener's disapproval at the numerous fowls, lifting their red combs and tufted top-knots here and there among the thick clover under the apple-trees.

"Them's Clarsie's chickens,—my darter, ye know," drawled Peter Giles, a pale, listless, and lank mountaineer. "An' she hev been gin ter onderstand ez they hev got ter be kep' out 'n the gyarden; 'thout," he added indulgently,—"'thout I'm a-plowin', when I lets 'em foller in the furrow ter pick up worms. But law! Clarsie is so spry that she don't ax no better 'n ter be let ter run them chickens off 'n the peas."

Then the two men tilted their chairs against the posts of the little porch in front of Peter Giles's log cabin and puffed their pipes in silence. The panorama spread out before them showed misty and dreamy among the delicate spiral wreaths of smoke. But was that gossamer-like illusion, lying upon the far horizon, the magic of nicotian, or the vague presence of distant heights? As ridge after ridge came down from the sky in ever-graduating shades of intenser blue, Peter Giles might have told you that this parallel system of enchantment was only "the mountings:" that here was Foxy, and there was Big Injun, and still beyond was another, which he had "hearn tell ran spang up into Virginny." The sky that bent to clasp this kindred blue was of varying moods. Floods of sunshine submerged Chilhowee in liquid gold, and revealed that dainty outline limned upon the northern horizon; but over the Great Smoky mountains clouds had gathered, and a gigantic rainbow bridged the valley.

Peter Giles's listless eyes were fixed upon a bit of red clay road, which was visible through a gap in the foliage far below. Even a tiny object, that ant-like crawled upon it, could be seen from the summit of Chilhowee. "I reckon that's my brother's wagon an' team," he said, as he watched the moving atom pass under the gorgeous triumphal arch. "He 'lowed he war goin' ter the Cross-Roads ter-day."

Simon Burney did not speak for a moment. When he did, his words seemed widely irrelevant. "That's a likely gal o' yourn," he drawled, with an odd constraint in his voice,—"a likely gal, that Clarsie."

There was a quick flash of surprise in Peter Giles's dull eyes. He covertly surveyed his guest, with an astounded curiosity rampant in his slow brains. Simon Burney had changed color; an expression of embarrassment lurked in every line of his honest, florid, hard-featured face. An alert imagination might have detected a deprecatory self-consciousness in every gray hair that striped the black beard raggedly fringing his chin.

"Yes," Peter Giles at length replied, "Clarsie air a likely enough gal. But she air mightily sot ter hevin' her own way. An' ef 't ain't give ter her peaceable-like, she jes' takes it, whether or no."

This statement, made by one presumably fully informed on the subject, might have damped the ardor of many a suitor,—for the monstrous truth was dawning on Peter Giles's mind that suitor was the position to which this slow, elderly widower aspired. But Simon Burney, with that odd, all-pervading constraint still prominently apparent, mildly observed, "Waal, ez much ez I hev seen of her goin's-on, it 'pears ter me ez her way air a mighty good way. An' it ain't comical that she likes it."

Urgent justice compelled Peter Giles to make some amends to the absent Clarissa. "That's a fac'," he admitted. "An' Clarsie ain't no hand ter jaw. She don't hev no words. But then," he qualified, truth and consistency alike constraining him, "she air a toler'ble hard-headed gal. That air a true word. Ye mought ez well try ter hender the sun from shining ez ter make that thar Clarsie Giles do what she don't want ter do."

To be sure, Peter Giles had a right to his opinion as to the hardness of his own daughter's head. The expression of his views, however, provoked Simon Burney to wrath; there was something astir within him that in a worthier subject might have been called a chivalric thrill, and it forbade him to hold his peace. He retorted: "Of course ye kin say that, ef so minded; but ennybody ez hev got eyes kin see the change ez hev been made in this hyar place sence that thar gal hev been growed. I ain't a-purtendin' ter know that thar Clarsie ez well ez you-uns knows her hyar at home, but I hev seen enough, an' a deal more 'n enough, of her goin's-on, ter know that what she does ain't done fur *herself*. An' ef she will hev her way, it air fur the good of the whole tribe of ye. It 'pears ter me ez thar ain't many gals like that thar Clarsie. An' she air a merciful critter. She air mighty savin' of the feelin's of everything, from the cow an' the mare down ter the dogs, an' pigs, an' chickens; always a-feedin' of 'em jes' ter the time, an' never draggin', an' clawin', an' beatin' of 'em. Why, that thar Clarsie can't put her foot out 'n the door, that every dumb beastis on this hyar place ain't a-runnin' ter git nigh her. I hev seen them pigs mos' climb the fence when she shows her face at the door. 'Pears ter me ez that thar Clarsie could tame a b'ar, ef she looked at him a time or two, she's so savin' o' the critter's feelin's! An' thar's that old yaller dog o' yourn," pointing to an ancient cur that was blinking in the sun, "he's older 'n Clarsie, an' no 'count in the worl'. I hev hearn ye say forty times that ye would kill him, 'ceptin' that Clarsie purtected him, an' hed sot her heart on his a-livin' along. An' all the home-folks, an' everybody that kems hyar to sot an' talk awhile, never misses a chance ter kick that thar old dog, or poke him with a stick, or cuss him. But Clarsie!—I hev seen that gal take the bread an' meat off'n her plate, an' give it ter that old dog, ez 'pears ter me ter be the worst dispositionest dog I ever see, an' no thanks lef' in him. He hain't hed the grace ter wag his tail fur twenty year. That thar Clarsie air surely a merciful critter, an' a mighty spry, likely young gal, besides."

Peter Giles sat in stunned astonishment during this speech, which was delivered in a slow, drawling monotone, with frequent meditative pauses, but nevertheless emphatically. He made no reply, and as they were once more silent there rose suddenly the sound of melody upon the air. It came from beyond that tumultuous stream that raced with the wind down the mountain's side; a great log thrown from bank to bank served as bridge. The song grew momentarily more distinct; among the leaves there were fugitive glimpses of blue and white, and at last Clarsie appeared, walking lightly along the log, clad in her checked homespun dress, and with a pail upon her head.

She was a tall, lithe girl, with that delicately transparent complexion often seen among the women of these mountains. Her lustreless black hair lay along her forehead without a ripple or wave; there was something in the expression of her large eyes that suggested those of a deer,— something free, untamable, and yet gentle. "'T ain't no wonder ter me ez Clarsie is all tuk up with the wild things, an' critters ginerally," her mother was wont to say. "She sorter looks like 'em, I'm a-thinkin'."

As she came in sight there was a renewal of that odd constraint in Simon Burney's face and manner, and he rose abruptly. "Waal," he said, hastily, going to his horse, a raw-boned sorrel, hitched to the fence, "it's about time I war a-startin' home, I reckons."

He nodded to his host, who silently nodded in return, and the old horse jogged off with him down the road, as Clarsie entered the house and placed the pail upon a shelf.

"Who d' ye think hev been hyar a-speakin' of compli*mints* on ye, Clarsie?" exclaimed Mrs. Giles, who had overheard through the open door every word of the loud, drawling voice on the porch.

Clarsie's liquid eyes widened with surprise, and a faint tinge of rose sprang into her pale face, as she looked an expectant inquiry at her mother.

Mrs. Giles was a slovenly, indolent woman, anxious, at the age of forty-five, to assume the prerogatives of advanced years. She had placed all her domestic cares upon the shapely shoulders of her willing daughter, and had betaken herself to the chimney-corner and a pipe.

"Yes, thar hev been somebody hyar a-speakin' of compli*mints* on ye, Clarsie," she reiterated, with chuckling amusement. "He war a mighty peart, likely boy,—that he war!"

Clarsie's color deepened.

"Old Simon Burney!" exclaimed her mother, in great glee at the incongruity of the idea. "*Old Simon Burney!*—jes' a-sittin' out thar, a-wastin' the time, an' a-burnin' of daylight—jes' ez perlite an' smilin' ez a basket of chips—a-speakin' of compli*mints* on ye!"

There was a flash of laughter among the sylvan suggestions of Clarsie's eyes,—a flash as of sudden sunlight upon water. But despite her mirth she seemed to be unaccountably disappointed. The change in her manner was not noticed by her mother, who continued banteringly,—

"Simon Burney air a mighty pore old man. Ye oughter be sorry fur him, Clarsie. Ye mustn't think less of folks than ye does of the dumb beastis,—that ain't religion. Ye knows ye air sorry fur mos' everything; why not fur this comical old consarn? Ye oughter marry him ter take keer of him. He said ye war a merciful critter; now is yer chance ter show it! Why, air ye a-goin' ter weavin', Clarsie, jes' when I wants ter talk ter ye 'bout 'n old Simon Burney? But law! I knows ye kerry him with ye in yer heart."

The girl summarily closed the conversation by seating herself before a great hand-loom; presently the persistent thump, thump, of the batten and the noisy creak of the treadle filled the room, and through all the long, hot afternoon her deft, practiced hands lightly tossed the shuttle to and fro.

The breeze freshened, after the sun went down, and the hop and gourd vines were all astir as they clung about the little porch where Clarsie was sitting now, idle at last. The rain clouds had disappeared, and there bent over the dark, heavily wooded ridges a pale blue sky, with here and there the crystalline sparkle of a star. A halo was shimmering in the east, where the mists had gathered about the great white moon, hanging high above the mountains. Noiseless wings flitted through the dusk; now and then the bats swept by so close as to wave Clarsie's hair with the wind of their flight. What an airy, glittering, magical thing was that gigantic spider-web suspended between the silver moon and her shining eyes! Ever and anon there came from the woods a strange, weird, long-drawn sigh, unlike the stir of the wind in the trees, unlike the fret of the water on the rocks. Was it the voiceless sorrow of the sad earth? There were stars in the night besides those known to astronomers: the stellular fire-flies gemmed the black shadows with a fluctuating brilliancy; they circled in and out of the porch, and touched the leaves above Clarsie's head with quivering points of light. A steadier and an intenser gleam was advancing along the road, and the sound of languid footsteps came with it; the aroma of tobacco graced the atmosphere, and a tall figure walked up to the gate.

"Come in, come in," said Peter Giles, rising, and tendering the guest a chair. "Ye air Tom Pratt, ez well ez I kin make out by this light. Waal, Tom, we hain't furgot ye sence ye done been hyar."

As Tom had been there on the previous evening, this might be considered a joke, or an equivocal compliment. The young fellow was restless and awkward under it, but Mrs. Giles chuckled with great merriment.

"An' how air ye a-comin' on, Mrs. Giles?" he asked propitiatorily.

"Jes' toler'ble, Tom. Air they all well ter yer house?"

"Yes, they 're toler'ble well, too." He glanced at Clarsie, intending to address to her some polite greeting, but the expression of her shy, half-startled eyes, turned upon the far-away moon, warned him. "Thar never war a gal so skittish," he thought. "She'd run a mile, skeered ter death, ef I said a word ter her."

And he was prudently silent.

"Waal," said Peter Giles, "what's the news out yer way, Tom? Enny-thing a-goin' on?"

"Thar war a shower yander on the Backbone; it rained toler'ble hard fur a while, an' sot up the corn wonderful. Did ye git enny hyar?"

"Not a drap."

"'Pears ter me ez I kin see the clouds a-circlin' round Chilhowee, an' a-rainin' on everybody's corn-field 'ceptin' ourn," said Mrs. Giles. "Some folks is the favored of the Lord, an' t' others hev ter work fur everything an' git nuthin'. Waal, waal; we-uns will see our reward in the nex' worl'. Thar 's a better worl' than this, Tom."

"That's a fac'," said Tom, in orthodox assent.

"An' when we leaves hyar once, we leaves all trouble an' care behind us, Tom; fur we don't come back no more." Mrs. Giles was drifting into one of her pious moods.

"I dunno," said Tom. "Thar hev been them ez hev."

"Hev what?" demanded Peter Giles, startled.

"Hev come back ter this hyar yearth. Thar's a harnt that walks Chil-howee every night o' the worl'. I know them ez hev seen him."

Clarsie's great dilated eyes were fastened on the speaker's face. There was a dead silence for a moment, more eloquent with these looks of amazement than any words could have been.

"I reckons ye remember a puny, shriveled little man, named Reuben Crabb, ez used ter live yander, eight mile along the ridge ter that thar big sulphur spring," Tom resumed, appealing to Peter Giles. "He war born with only one arm."

"I 'members him," interpolated Mrs. Giles, vivaciously. "He war a mighty porely, sickly little critter, all the days of his life. 'T war a wonder he war ever raised ter be a man,—an' a pity, too. An' 't war powerful comical, the way of his takin' off; a stunted, one-armed little critter a-ondertakin' ter fight folks an' shoot pistols. He hed the use o' his one arm, sure."

"Waal," said Tom, "his house ain't thar now, 'kase Sam Grim's broth-ers burned it ter the ground fur his a-killin' of Sam. That warn't all that war done ter Reuben fur killin' of Sam. The sheriff run Reuben Crabb down this hyar road 'bout a mile from hyar,—mebbe less,—an' shot him dead in the road, jes' whar it forks. Waal, Reuben war in company with another evil-doer,—*he* war from the Cross-Roads, an' I furgits what he hed done, but he war a-tryin' ter hide in the mountings, too; an' the sher-iff lef' Reuben a-lyin' thar in the road, while he tries ter ketch up with t'other; but his horse got a stone in his hoof, an' he los' time, an' hed ter gin it up. An' when he got back ter the forks o' the road whar he had lef' Reuben a-lyin' dead, thar war nuthin' thar 'ceptin' a pool o' blood. Waal, he went right on ter Reuben's house, an' them Grim boys hed burnt it ter the ground; but he seen Reuben's brother Joel. An' Joel, he tole the sher-iff that late that evenin' he hed tuk Reuben's body out'n the road an' buried it, 'kase it hed been lyin' thar in the road ever sence early in the mornin', an' he couldn't leave it thar all night, an' he hed n't no shelter fur it, sence the Grim boys hed burnt down the house. So he war obleeged ter bury it. An' Joel showed the sheriff a new-made grave, an' Reuben's coat whar the sheriff's bullet hed gone in at the back an' kem out'n the breast. The sheriff 'lowed ez they'd fine Joel fifty dollars fur a-buryin' of Reuben afore the cor'ner kem; but they never done it, ez I knows on. The sheriff said that when the cor'ner kem the body would be tuk up fur a 'quest. But thar hed been a powerful big frishet, an' the river 'twixt the cor'ner's house an' Chilhowee couldn't be forded fur three weeks. The cor'ner never kem, an' so thar it all stayed. That war four year ago."

"Waal," said Peter Giles, dryly, "I ain't seen no harnt yit. I knowed all that afore."

Clarsie's wondering eyes upon the young man's moonlit face had elicited these facts, familiar to the elders, but strange, he knew, to her.

"I war jes' a-goin' on ter tell," said Tom, abashed. "Waal, ever sence his brother Joel died, this spring, Reuben's harnt walks Chilhowee. He war seen week afore las', 'bout daybreak, by Ephraim Blenkins, who hed been a-fishin', an' war a-goin' home. Eph happened ter stop in the laurel ter wind up his line, when all in a minit he seen the harnt go by, his face white, an' his eye-balls like fire, an' puny an' one-armed, jes' like he lived. Eph, he owed me a haffen day's work; I holped him ter plow las' month, an' so he kem ter-day an' hoed along cornsider'ble ter pay fur it. He say he believes the harnt never seen him, 'kase it went right by. He 'lowed ef the harnt hed so much ez cut one o' them blazin' eyes round at him he could n't but hev drapped dead. Waal, this mornin', 'bout sunrise, my brother Bob's little gal, three year old, strayed off from home while her mother war out milkin' the cow. An' we went a-huntin' of her, mightily worked up, 'kase thar hev been a b'ar prowlin' round our cornfield twict this summer. An' I went to the right, an' Bob went to the lef'. An' he say ez he war a-pushin' 'long through the laurel, he seen the bushes ahead of him a-rustlin'. An' he jes' stood still an' watched 'em. An' fur a while the bushes war still too; an' then they moved jes' a little, fust this way an' then that, till all of a suddint the leaves opened, like the mouth of hell mought hev done, an' thar he seen Reuben Crabb's face. He say he never seen sech a face! Its mouth war open, an' its eyes war a-startin' out 'n its head, an' its skin war white till it war blue; an' ef the devil hed hed it a-hangin' over the coals that minit it could n't hev looked no more skeered. But that war all that Bob seen, 'kase he jes' shet his eyes an' screeched an' screeched like he war destracted. An' when he stopped a second ter ketch his breath he hearn su'thin' a-answerin' him back, sorter weak-like, an' thar war little Peggy a-pullin' through the laurel. Ye know she's too little ter talk good, but the folks down ter our house believes she seen the harnt, too."

"My Lord!" exclaimed Peter Giles. "I 'low I could n't live a minit ef I war ter see that thar harnt that walks Chilhowee!"

"I know *I* could n't," said his wife.

"Nor me, nuther," murmured Clarsie.

"Waal," said Tom, resuming the thread of his narrative, "we hev all been a-talkin' down yander ter our house ter make out the reason why Reuben Crabb's harnt hev sot out ter walk *jes' sence his brother Joel died,—* 'kase it war never seen afore then. An' ez nigh ez we kin make it out, the reason is 'kase thar 's nobody lef' in this hyar worl' what believes he war n't ter blame in that thar killin' o' Sam Grim. Joel always swore ez Reuben never killed him no more 'n nuthin'; that Sam's own pistol went off in his own hand, an' shot him through the heart jes' ez he war a-drawin' of it ter shoot Reuben Crabb. An' I hev hearn other men ez war a-standin' by say the same thing, though them Grims tells another tale; but ez Reuben never owned no pistol in his life, nor kerried one, it don't 'pear ter me ez what them Grims say air reasonable. Joel always swore ez Sam Grim war a mighty mean man,—a great big feller like him a-rockin' of a deformed little critter, an' a-mockin' of him, an' a hittin' of him. An' the day of the fight Sam jes' knocked him down fur nuthin' at all; an' afore ye could wink Reuben jumped up suddint, an' flew at him like an eagle, an' struck him in the face. An' then Sam drawed his pistol, an' it went off in his own hand, an' shot him through the heart, an' killed him dead. Joel said that ef he could hev kep' that pore little critter Reuben still, an' let the sheriff arrest him peaceable-like, he war sure the jury would hev let him off; 'kase how war Reuben a-goin' ter shoot ennybody when Sam Grim never left a-holt of the only pistol between 'em, in life, or in death? They tells me they hed ter bury Sam Grim with that thar pistol in his hand; his grip war too tight fur death to unloose it. But Joel said that Reuben war sartain they'd hang him. He hed n't never seen no jestice from enny one man, an' he could n't look fur it from twelve men. So he jes' sot out ter run through the woods, like a painter or a wolf, ter be hunted by the sheriff, an' he war run down an' kilt in the road. Joel said *he* kep' up arter the sheriff ez well ez he could on foot,—fur the Crabbs never hed no horse,—ter try ter beg fur Reuben, ef he war cotched, an' tell how little an' how weakly he war. I never seen a young man's head turn white like Joel's done; he said he reckoned it war his troubles. But ter the las' he stuck ter his rifle faithful. He war a powerful hunter; he war out rain or shine, hot or cold, in sech weather ez other folks would think thar war n't no use in tryin' ter do nuthin' in. I'm mightily afeard o' seein' Reuben, now, that's a fac'," concluded Tom, frankly; "kase I hev hearn tell, an' I believes it, that ef a harnt speaks ter ye, it air sartain ye 're bound ter die right then."

"'Pears ter me," said Mrs. Giles, "ez many mountings ez thar air round hyar, he mought hev tuk ter walkin' some o' them, stiddier Chilhowee."

There was a sudden noise close at hand: a great inverted splint-basket, from which came a sound of flapping wings, began to move slightly back and forth. Mrs. Giles gasped out an ejaculation of terror, the two men sprang to their feet, and the coy Clarsie laughed aloud in an exuberance of delighted mirth, forgetful of her shyness. "I declar' ter goodness, you-uns air all skeered fur true! Did ye think it war the harnt that walks Chilhowee?"

"What's under that thar basket?" demanded Peter Giles, rather sheepishly, as he sat down again.

"Nuthin' but the duck-legged Dominicky," said Clarsie, "what air bein' broke up from settin'." The moonlight was full upon the dimpling merriment in her face, upon her shining eyes and parted red lips, and her gurgling laughter was pleasant to hear. Tom Pratt edged his chair a trifle nearer, as he, too, sat down.

"Ye ought'nt never ter break up a duck-legged hen, nor a Dominicky, nuther," he volunteered, "'kase they air sech a good kind o' hen ter kerry chickens; but a hen that is duck-legged an' Dominicky too oughter be let ter set, whether or no."

Had he been warned in a dream, he could have found no more secure road to Clarsie's favor and interest than a discussion of the poultry. "I 'm a-thinkin'," she said, "that it air too hot fur hens ter set now, an' 't will be till the las' of August."

"It don't 'pear ter me ez it air hot much in June up hyar on Chilhowee,— thar 's a differ, I know, down in the valley; but till July, on Chilhowee, it don't 'pear ter me ez it air too hot ter set a hen. An' a duck-legged Dominicky air mighty hard ter break up."

"That's a fac'," Clarsie admitted; "but I 'll hev ter do it, somehow, 'kase I ain't got no eggs fur her. All my hens air kerryin' of chickens."

"Waal!" exclaimed Tom, seizing his opportunity, "I'll bring ye some ter-morrer night, when I come agin. We-uns hev got eggs ter our house."

"Thanky," said Clarsie, shyly smiling.

This unique method of courtship would have progressed very pros- perously but for the interference of the elders, who are an element always more or less adverse to love-making. "Ye oughter turn out yer hen now, Clarsie," said Mrs. Giles, "ez Tom air a-goin' ter bring ye some eggs ter-morrer. I wonder ye don't think it 's mean ter keep her up longer 'n ye air obleeged ter. Ye oughter remember ye war called a merciful critter jes' ter-day."

Clarsie rose precipitately, raised the basket, and out flew the "duck- legged Dominicky," with a frantic flutter and hysterical cackling. But Mrs. Giles was not to be diverted from her purpose; her thoughts had recurred to the absurd episode of the afternoon, and with her relish of the incongruity of the joke she opened upon the subject at once.

"Waal, Tom," she said, "we'll be hevin' Clarsie married, afore long, I'm a-thinkin'." The young man sat bewildered. He, too, had entertained views concerning Clarsie's speedy marriage, but with a distinctly per- sonal application; and this frank mention of the matter by Mrs. Giles had a sinister suggestion that perhaps her ideas might be antagonistic. "An' who d 'ye think hev been hyar ter-day, a-speakin' of compli*mints* on Clar- sie?" He could not answer, but he turned his head with a look of inquiry, and Mrs. Giles continued, "He is a mighty peart, likely boy,—*he* is."

There was a growing anger in the dismay on Tom Pratt's face; he leaned forward to hear the name with a fiery eagerness, altogether incongruous with his usual lack-lustre manner.

"Old Simon Burney!" cried Mrs. Giles, with a burst of laughter. "*Old Simon Burney! Jes*' a-speakin' of compli*mints* on Clarsie!"

The young fellow drew back with a look of disgust. "Why, he's a old man; he ain't no fit husband fur Clarsie."

"Don't ye be too sure ter count on that. I war jes' a-layin' off ter tell Clarsie that a gal oughter keep mighty clar o' widowers, 'thout she wants ter marry one. Fur I believes," said Mrs. Giles, with a wild flight of imagination, "ez them men hev got some sort 'n trade with the Evil One, an' he gives 'em the power ter witch the gals, somehow, so 's ter git 'em ter marry; 'kase I don't think that any gal that 's got good sense air a-goin' ter be a man's second ch'ice, an' the mother of a whole pack of stepchil'ren, 'thout she air under some sort 'n spell. But them men carries the day with the gals, ginerally, an' I 'm a-thinkin' they 're banded with the devil. Ef I war a gal, an' a smart, peart boy like Simon Burney kem around a-speakin' of compli*mints*, an' sayin' I war a merciful critter, I 'd jes' give it up, an' marry him fur second ch'ice. Thar's one blessin'," she continued, contemplating the possibility in a cold-blooded fashion positively revolting to Tom Pratt: "he ain't got no tribe of chil'ren fur Clarsie ter look arter; nary chick nor child hev old Simon Burney got. He hed two, but they died."

The young man took leave presently, in great depression of spirit,— the idea that the widower was banded with the powers of evil was rather overwhelming to a man whose dependence was in merely mortal attractions; and after he had been gone a little while Clarsie ascended the ladder to a nook in the roof, which she called her room.

For the first time in her life her slumber was fitful and restless, long intervals of wakefulness alternating with snatches of fantastic dreams. At last she rose and sat by the rude window, looking out through the chestnut leaves at the great moon, which had begun to dip toward the dark uncertainty of the western ridges, and at the shimmering, translucent, pearly mists that filled the intermediate valleys. All the air was dew and incense; so subtle and penetrating an odor came from that fir-tree beyond the fence that it seemed as if some invigorating infusion were thrilling along her veins; there floated upward, too, the warm fragrance of the clover, and every breath of the gentle wind brought from over the stream a thousand blended, undistinguishable perfumes of the deep forests beyond. The moon's idealizing glamour had left no trace of the uncouthness of the place which the daylight revealed; the little log house, the great overhanging chestnut-oaks, the jagged precipice before the door, the vague outlines of the distant ranges, all suffused with a magic sheen, might have seemed a stupendous alto-rilievo in silver repoussé. Still, there came here and there the sweep of the bat's dusky wings; even they were a part of the night's witchery. A tiny owl perched for a moment or two amid the dew-tipped chestnut-leaves, and gazed with great round eyes at Clarsie as solemnly as she gazed at him.

"I'm thankful enough that ye hed the grace not ter screech while ye war hyar," she said, after the bird had taken his flight. "I ain't ready ter die yit, an' a screech-owel air the sure sign."

She felt now and then a great impatience with her wakeful mood. Once she took herself to task: "Jes' a-sittin' up hyar all night, the same ez ef I war a fox, or that thar harnt that walks Chilhowee!"

And then her mind reverted to Tom Pratt, to old Simon Burney, and to her mother's emphatic and oracular declaration that widowers are in league with Satan, and that the girls upon whom they cast the eye of supernatural fascination have no choice in the matter. "I wish I knowed ef that thar sayin' war true," she murmured, her face still turned to the western spurs, and the moon sinking so slowly toward them.

With a sudden resolution she rose to her feet. She knew a way of telling fortunes which was, according to tradition, infallible, and she determined to try it, and ease her mind as to her future. Now was the propitious moment. "I hev always hearn that it won't come true 'thout ye try it jes' before daybreak, an' a-kneelin' down at the forks of the road." She hesitated a moment and listened intently. "They'd never git done a-laffin' at me, ef they fund it out," she thought.

There was no sound in the house, and from the dark woods arose only those monotonous voices of the night,—so familiar to her ears that she accounted their murmurous iteration as silence too. She leaned far out of the low window, caught the wide-spreading branches of the tree beside it, and swung herself noiselessly to the ground. The road before her was dark with the shadowy foliage and dank with the dew; but now and then, at long intervals, there lay athwart it a bright bar of light, where the moonshine fell through a gap in the trees. Once, as she went rapidly along her way, she saw speeding across the white radiance, lying just before her feet, the ill-omened shadow of a rabbit. She paused, with a superstitious sinking of the heart, and she heard the animal's quick, leaping rush through the bushes near at hand; but she mustered her courage, and kept steadily on. "'T ain't no use a-goin' back ter git shet o' bad luck," she argued. "Ef old Simon Burney air my fortune, he'll come whether or no,—ef all they say air true."

The serpentine road curved to the mountain's brink before it forked, and there was again that familiar picture of precipice, and far-away ridges, and shining mist, and sinking moon, which was visibly turning from silver to gold. The changing lustre gilded the feathery ferns that grew in the marshy dip. Just at the angle of the divergent paths there rose into the air a great mass of indistinct white blossoms, which she knew were the exquisite mountain azaleas, and all the dark forest was starred with the blooms of the laurel.

She fixed her eyes upon the mystic sphere dropping down the sky, knelt among the azaleas at the forks of the road, and repeated the time-honored invocation:—

"Ef I 'm a-goin' ter marry a young man, whistle, Bird, whistle. Ef I 'm a-goin' ter marry an old man, low, Cow, low. Ef I ain't a-goin' ter marry nobody, knock, Death, knock."

There was a prolonged silence in the matutinal freshness and perfume of the woods. She raised her head, and listened attentively. No chirp of half-awakened bird, no tapping of woodpecker, or the mysterious death-watch; but from far along the dewy aisles of the forest, the ungrateful Spot, that Clarsie had fed more faithfully than herself, lifted up her voice, and set the echoes vibrating. Clarsie, however, had hardly time for a pang of disappointment. While she still knelt among the azaleas her large, deer-like eyes were suddenly dilated with terror. From around the curve of the road came the quick beat of hastening footsteps, the sobbing sound of panting breath, and between her and the sinking moon there passed an attenuated, one-armed figure, with a pallid, sharpened face, outlined for a moment on its brilliant disk, and dreadful starting eyes, and quivering open mouth. It disappeared in an instant among the shadows of the laurel, and Clarsie, with a horrible fear clutching at her heart, sprang to her feet.

Her flight was arrested by other sounds. Before her reeling senses could distinguish them, a party of horsemen plunged down the road. They reined in suddenly as their eyes fell upon her, and their leader, an eager, authoritative man, was asking her a question. Why could she not understand him? With her nerveless hands feebly catching at the shrubs for support, she listened vaguely to his impatient, meaningless words, and saw with helpless deprecation the rising anger in his face. But there was no time to be lost. With a curse upon the stupidity of the mountaineer, who could n't speak when she was spoken to, the party sped on in a sweeping gallop, and the rocks and the steeps were hilarious with the sound.

When the last faint echo was hushed, Clarsie tremblingly made her way out into the road; not reassured, however, for she had a frightful conviction that there was now and then a strange stir in the laurel, and that she was stealthily watched. Her eyes were fixed upon the dense growth with a morbid fascination, as she moved away; but she was once more rooted to the spot when the leaves parted and in the golden moonlight the ghost stood before her. She could not nerve herself to run past him, and he was directly in her way homeward. His face was white, and lined, and thin; that pitiful quiver was never still in the parted lips; he looked at her with faltering, beseeching eyes. Clarsie's merciful heart was stirred. "What ails ye, ter come back hyar, an' foller me?" she cried out, abruptly. And then a great horror fell upon her. Was not one to whom a ghost should speak doomed to death, sudden and immediate?

The ghost replied in a broken, shivering voice, like a wail of pain, "I war a-starvin',—I war a-starvin'," with despairing iteration.

It was all over, Clarsie thought. The ghost had spoken, and she was a doomed creature. She wondered that she did not fall dead in the road. But while those beseeching eyes were fastened in piteous appeal on hers, she could not leave him. "I never hearn that 'bout ye," she said, reflectively. "I knows ye hed awful troubles while ye war alive, but I never knowed ez ye war starved."

Surely that was a gleam of sharp surprise in the ghost's prominent eyes, succeeded by a sly intelligence.

"Day is nigh ter breakin'," Clarsie admonished him, as the lower rim of the moon touched the silver mists of the west. "What air ye a-wantin' of me?"

There was a short silence. Mind travels far in such intervals. Clarsie's thoughts had overtaken the scenes when she should have died that sudden terrible death: when there would be no one left to feed the chickens; when no one would care if the pigs cried with the pangs of hunger, unless, indeed, it were time for them to be fattened before killing. The mare,—how often would she be taken from the plow, and shut up for the night in her shanty without a drop of water, after her hard day's work! Who would churn, or spin, or weave? Clarsie could not understand how the machinery of the universe could go on without her. And Towse, poor Towse! He was a useless cumberer of the ground, and it was hardly to be supposed that after his protector was gone he would be spared a blow or a bullet, to hasten his lagging death. But Clarsie still stood in the road, and watched the face of the ghost, as he, with his eager, starting eyes, scanned her open, ingenuous countenance.

"Ye do ez ye air bid, or it 'll be the worse for ye," said the "harnt," in the same quivering, shrill tone. "Thar 's hunger in the nex' worl' ez well ez in this, an' ye bring me some vittles hyar this time ter-morrer, an' don't ye tell nobody ye hev seen me, nether, or it 'll be the worse for ye."

There was a threat in his eyes as he disappeared in the laurel, and left the girl standing in the last rays of moonlight.

A curious doubt was stirring in Clarsie's mind when she reached home, in the early dawn, and heard her father talking about the sheriff and his posse, who had stopped at the house in the night, and roused its inmates, to know if they had seen a man pass that way.

"Clarsie never hearn none o' the noise, I'll be bound, 'kase she always sleeps like a log," said Mrs. Giles, as her daughter came in with the pail, after milking the cow. "Tell her 'bout 'n it."

"They kem a-bustin' along hyar a while afore day-break, a-runnin' arter the man," drawled Mr. Giles, dramatically. "An' they knocked me up, ter know ef ennybody hed passed. An' one o' them men—I never seen none of 'em afore; they's all valley folks, I'm a-thinkin'—an' one of 'em bruk his saddle-girt' a good piece down the road, an' he kem back ter borrer mine; an' ez we war a-fixin' of it, he tole me what they war all arter. He said that word war tuk ter the sheriff down yander in the valley—'pears ter me them town-folks don't think nobody in the mount-ings hev got good sense—word war tuk ter the sheriff 'bout this one-armed harnt that walks Chilhowee; an' he sot it down that Reuben Crabb war n't dead at all, an' Joel jes' purtended ter hev buried him, an' it air Reuben hisself that walks Chilhowee. An' thar air two hunderd dol-lars blood-money reward fur ennybody ez kin ketch him. These hyar valley folks air powerful cur'ous critters,—two hunderd dollars blood-money reward fur that thar harnt that walks Chilhowee! I jes' sot myself ter laffin' when that thar cuss tole it so solemn. I jes' 'lowed ter him ez he could n't shoot a harnt nor hang a harnt, an' Reuben Crabb hed about got done with his persecutions in this worl'. An' he said that by the time they hed scoured this mounting, like they hed laid off ter do, they would find that that thar puny little harnt war nuthin' but a mortal man, an' could be kep' in a jail ez handy ez enny other flesh an' blood. He said the sheriff 'lowed ez the reason Reuben hed jes' taken ter walk Chilhowee sence Joel died is 'kase thar air nobody ter feed him, like Joel done, mebbe, in the nights; an' Reuben always war a pore, one-armed, weakly critter, what can't even kerry a gun, an' he air driv by hunger out'n the hole whar he stays, ter prowl round the cornfields an' hencoops ter steal suthin',—an' that's how he kem ter be seen frequent. The sheriff 'lowed that Reuben can't find enough roots an' yerbs ter keep him up; but law!— a harnt eatin'! It jes' sot me off ter laffin'. Reuben Crabb hev been too busy in torment fur the las' four year ter be a-studyin' 'bout eatin'; an' it air his harnt that walks Chilhowee."

The next morning, before the moon sank, Clarsie, with a tin pail in her hand, went to meet the ghost at the appointed place. She understood now why the terrible doom that falls upon those to whom a spirit may chance to speak had not descended upon her, and that fear was gone; but the secrecy of her errand weighed heavily. She had been scrupulously careful to put into the pail only such things as had fallen to her share at the table, and which she had saved from the meals of yesterday. "A gal that goes a-robbin' fur a hongry harnt," was her moral reflection, "oughter be throwed bodaciously off'n the bluff."

She found no one at the forks of the road. In the marshy dip were only the myriads of mountain azaleas, only the masses of feathery ferns, only the constellated glories of the laurel blooms. A sea of shining white mist was in the valley, with glinting golden rays striking athwart it from the great cresses of the sinking moon; here and there the long, dark, horizontal line of a distant mountain's summit rose above the vaporous shimmer, like a dreary, sombre island in the midst of enchanted waters. Her large, dreamy eyes, so wild and yet so gentle, gazed out through the laurel leaves upon the floating gilded flakes of light, as in the deep coverts of the mountain, where the fulvous-tinted deer were lying, other eyes, as wild and as gentle, dreamily watched the vanishing moon. Overhead, the filmy, lace-like clouds, fretting the blue heavens, were tinged with a faint rose. Through the trees she caught a glimpse of the red sky of dawn, and the glister of a great lucent, tremulous star. From the ground, misty blue exhalations were rising, alternating with the long lines of golden light yet drifting through the woods. It was all very still, very peaceful, almost holy. One could hardly believe that these consecrated solitudes had once reverberated with the echoes of man's death-dealing ingenuity, and that Reuben Crabb had fallen, shot through and through, amid that wealth of flowers at the forks of the road. She heard suddenly the far-away baying of a hound. Her great eyes dilated, and she lifted her head to listen. Only the solemn silence of the woods, the slow sinking of the noiseless moon, the voiceless splendor of that eloquent day-star.

Morning was close at hand, and she was beginning to wonder that the ghost did not appear, when the leaves fell into abrupt commotion, and he was standing in the road, beside her. He did not speak, but watched her with an eager, questioning intentness, as she placed the contents of the pail upon the moss at the roadside. "I'm a-comin' agin ter-morrer," she said, gently. He made no reply, quickly gathered the food from the ground, and disappeared in the deep shades of the woods.

She had not expected thanks, for she was accustomed only to the gratitude of dumb beasts; but she was vaguely conscious of something wanting, as she stood motionless for a moment, and watched the burnished rim of the moon slip down behind the western mountains. Then she slowly walked along her misty way in the dim light of the coming dawn. There was a footstep in the road behind her; she thought it was the ghost once more. She turned, and met Simon Burney, face to face. His rod was on his shoulder, and a string of fish was in his hand.

"Ye air a-doin' wrongful, Clarsie," he said, sternly. "It air agin the law fur folks ter feed an' shelter them ez is a-runnin' from jestice. An' ye 'll git yerself inter trouble. Other folks will find ye out, besides me, an' then the sheriff 'll be up hyar arter ye."

The tears rose to Clarsie's eyes. This prospect was infinitely more terrifying than the awful doom which follows the horror of a ghost's speech.

"I can't holp it," she said, however, doggedly swinging the pail back and forth. "I can't gin my consent ter starvin' of folks, even ef they air a-hidin' an' a-runnin' from jestice."

"They mought put ye in jail, too,—I dunno," suggested Simon Burney.

"I can't holp that, nether," said Clarsie, the sobs rising, and the tears falling fast. "Ef they comes an' gits me, and puts me in the pen'tiary away down yander, somewhars in the valley, like they done Jane Simpkins, fur a-cuttin' of her step-mother's throat with a butcherknife, while she war asleep,—though some said Jane war crazy,—I can't gin my consent ter starvin' of folks."

A recollection came over Simon Burney of the simile of "hendering the sun from shining."

"She hev done sot it down in her mind," he thought, as he walked on beside her and looked at her resolute face. Still he did not relinquish his effort.

"Doin' wrong, Clarsie, ter aid folks what air a-doin' wrong, an' mebbe *hev* done wrong, air powerful hurtful ter everybody, an' henders the law an' jestice."

"I can't holp it," said Clarsie.

"It 'pears tolerable comical ter me," said Simon Burney, with a sudden perception of a curious fact which has proved a marvel to wiser men, "that no matter how good a woman is, she ain't got no respect fur the laws of the country, an' don't sot no store by jestice." After a momentary silence he appealed to her on another basis. "Somebody will ketch him arter a while, ez sure en ye air born. The sheriff's a-sarchin' now, an' by the time that word gits around, all the mounting boys 'll turn out, 'kase thar air two hunderd dollars blood-money fur him. An' then he 'll think, when they ketches him,—an' everybody 'll say so, too,—ez ye war constant in feedin' him jes' ter 'tice him ter comin' ter one place, so ez ye could tell somebody whar ter go ter ketch him, an' make them gin ye haffen the blood-money, mebbe. That's what the mounting will say, mos' likely."

"I can't holp it," said Clarsie, once more.

He left her walking on toward the rising sun, and retraced his way to the forks of the road. The jubilant morning was filled with the song of birds; the sunlight flashed on the dew; all the delicate enameled bells of the pink and white azaleas were swinging tremulously in the wind; the aroma of ferns and mint rose on the delicious fresh air. Presently he checked his pace, creeping stealthily on the moss and grass beside the road rather than in the beaten path. He pulled aside the leaves of the laurel with no more stir than the wind might have made, and stole cautiously through its dense growth, till he came suddenly upon the puny little ghost, lying in the sun at the foot of a tree. The frightened creature sprang to his feet with a wild cry of terror, but before he could move a step he was caught and held fast in the strong grip of the stalwart mountaineer beside him. "I hey kem hyar ter tell ye a word, Reuben Crabb," said Simon Burney. "I hev kem hyar ter tell ye that the whole mounting air a-goin' ter turn out ter sarch fur ye; the sheriff air a-ridin' now, an' ef ye don't come along with me they 'll hev ye afore night, 'kase thar air two hunderd dollars reward fur ye."

What a piteous wail went up to the smiling blue sky, seen through the dappling leaves above them! What a horror, and despair, and prescient agony were in the hunted creature's face! The ghost struggled no longer; he slipped from his feet down upon the roots of the tree, and turned that woful face, with its starting eyes and drawn muscles and quivering parted lips, up toward the unseeing sky.

"God Almighty, man!" exclaimed Simon Burney, moved to pity. "Why n't ye quit this hyar way of livin' in the woods like ye war a wolf? Why n't ye come back an' stand yer trial? From all I 've hearn tell, it 'pears ter me ez the jury air obleeged ter let ye off, an' I 'll take keer of ye agin them Grims."

"I hain't got no place ter live in," cried out the ghost, with a keen despair.

Simon Burney hesitated. Reuben Crabb was possibly a murderer,—at the best could but be a burden. The burden, however, had fallen in his way, and he lifted it.

"I tell ye now, Reuben Crabb," he said, "I ain't a-goin' ter holp no man ter break the law an' hender jestice; but ef ye will go an' stand yer trial, I'll take keer of ye agin them Grims ez long ez I kin fire a ride. An' arter the jury hev done let ye off, ye air welcome ter live along o' me at my house till ye die. Ye air no-'count ter work, I know, but I ain't a-goin' ter grudge ye fur a livin' at my house."

And so it came to pass that the reward set upon the head of the harnt that walked Chilhowee was never claimed.

With his powerful ally, the forlorn little spectre went to stand his trial, and the jury acquitted him without leaving the box. Then he came back to the mountains to live with Simon Burney. The cruel gibes of his burly mockers that had beset his feeble life from his childhood up, the deprivation and loneliness and despair and fear that had filled those days when he walked Chilhowee, had not improved the harnt's temper. He was a helpless creature, not able to carry a gun or hold a plow, and the years that he spent smoking his cobpipe in Simon Burney's door were idle years and unhappy. But Mrs. Giles said she thought he was "a mighty lucky little critter: fust, he hed Joel ter take keer of him an' feed him, when he tuk ter the woods ter portend he war a harnt; an' they do say now that Clarsie Pratt, afore she war married, used ter kerry him vittles, too; an' then old Simon Burney tuk him up an' fed him ez plenty ez ef he war a good workin' hand, an' gin him clothes an' house-room, an' put up with his jawin' jes' like he never hearn a word of it. But law! some folks dunno when they air well off."

There was only a sluggish current of peasant blood in Simon Burney's veins, but a prince could not have dispensed hospitality with a more royal hand. Ungrudgingly he gave of his best; valiantly he defended his thankless guest at the risk of his life; with a moral gallantry he struggled with his sloth, and worked early and late, that there might be enough to divide. There was no possibility of a recompense for him, not even in the encomiums of discriminating friends, nor the satisfaction of tutored feelings and a practiced spiritual discernment; for he was an uncouth creature, and densely ignorant.

The grace of culture is, in its way, a fine thing, but the best that art can do—the polish of a gentleman—is hardly equal to the best that Nature can do in her higher moods.

Kate Chopin
(1850–1904)

fter her wealthy father died when she was four years old, Kate O'Flaherty grew up in St. Louis, where she received a strict Catholic convent education. In 1870 she married Oscar Chopin, a Creole cotton broker, and they moved to New Orleans where she had six children. Upon his death in 1882, she brought her children back to her family in St. Louis, and began writing to support her family, publishing her first poem in 1889 and her first novel, *At Fault*, in 1890. By this time she had begun reading widely in evolutionary science and French naturalist fiction, including the work of de Maupassant, Flaubert, and Zola. Chopin was the first American woman to write openly about female sexuality, and to challenge bourgeois social views of feminine decorum and maternal fulfillment. She set her fiction in the Creole and Cajun societies of New Orleans, and in works such as "The Story of an Hour," "At the 'Cadian Ball," and "The Storm," portrayed the desire for autonomy beneath the façade of the respectable Southern lady, and the sensuality of the Cajun woman. When her frank portrayal of a woman's sexual and artistic rebellion in her novel *The Awakening* (1899) scandalized readers, Chopin refused to apologize but her literary career came to an abrupt and premature end.

The Story of an Hour (1894)

Knowing that Mrs. Mallard was afflicted with a heart trouble, great care was taken to break to her as gently as possible the news of her husband's death.

It was her sister Josephine who told her, in broken sentences; veiled hints that revealed in half concealing. Her husband's friend Richards was there, too, near her. It was he who had been in the newspaper office when intelligence of the railroad disaster was received, with Brently Mallard's name leading the list of "killed." He had only taken the time to assure himself of its truth by a second telegram, and had hastened to forestall any less careful, less tender friend in bearing the sad message.

She did not hear the story as many women have heard the same, with a paralyzed inability to accept its significance. She wept at once, with sudden, wild abandonment, in her sister's arms. When the storm of grief had spent itself she went away to her room alone. She would have no one follow her.

There stood, facing the open window, a comfortable, roomy armchair. Into this she sank, pressed down by a physical exhaustion that haunted her body and seemed to reach into her soul.

She could see in the open square before her house the tops of trees that were all aquiver with the new spring life. The delicious breath of rain was in the air. In the street below a peddler was crying his wares. The notes of a distant song which some one was singing reached her faintly, and countless sparrows were twittering in the eaves.

There were patches of blue sky showing here and there through the clouds that had met and piled one above the other in the west facing her window.

She sat with her head thrown back upon the cushion of the chair, quite motionless, except when a sob came up into her throat and shook her, as a child who has cried itself to sleep continues to sob in its dreams.

She was young, with a fair, calm face, whose lines bespoke repression and even a certain strength. But now there was a dull stare in her eyes, whose gaze was fixed away off yonder on one of those patches of blue sky. It was not a glance of reflection, but rather indicated a suspension of intelligent thought.

There was something coming to her and she was waiting for it, fearfully. What was it? She did not know; it was too subtle and elusive to name. But she felt it, creeping out of the sky, reaching toward her through the sounds, the scents, the color that filled the air.

Now her bosom rose and fell tumultuously. She was beginning to recognize this thing that was approaching to possess her, and she was striving to beat it back with her will—as powerless as her two white slender hands would have been.

When she abandoned herself a little whispered word escaped her slightly parted lips. She said it over and over under her breath: "free, free, free!" The vacant stare and the look of terror that had followed it went from her eyes. They stayed keen and bright. Her pulses beat fast, and the coursing blood warmed and relaxed every inch of her body.

She did not stop to ask if it were or were not a monstrous joy that held her. A clear and exalted perception enabled her to dismiss the suggestion as trivial.

She knew that she would weep again when she saw the kind, tender hands folded in death; the face that had never looked save with love upon her, fixed and gray and dead. But she saw beyond that bitter moment a long procession of years to come that would belong to her absolutely. And she opened and spread her arms out to them in welcome.

There would be no one to live for during those coming years; she would live for herself. There would be no powerful will bending hers in that blind persistence with which men and women believe they have a right to impose a private will upon a fellow-creature. A kind intention or a cruel intention made the act seem no less a crime as she looked upon it in that brief moment of illumination.

And yet she had loved him—sometimes. Often she had not. What did it matter! What could love, the unsolved mystery, count for in face of this possession of self-assertion which she suddenly recognized as the strongest impulse of her being!

"Free! Body and soul free!" she kept whispering.

Josephine was kneeling before the closed door with her lips to the key-hole, imploring for admission. "Louise, open the door! I beg, open the door—you will make yourself ill. What are you doing, Louise? For heaven's sake open the door."

"Go away. I am not making myself ill." No; she was drinking in a very elixir of life through that open window.

Her fancy was running riot along those days ahead of her. Spring days, and summer days, and all sorts of days that would be her own. She breathed a quick prayer that life might be long. It was only yesterday she had thought with a shudder that life might be long.

She arose at length and opened the door to her sister's importunities. There was a feverish triumph in her eyes, and she carried herself unwittingly like a goddess of Victory. She clasped her sister's waist, and together they descended the stairs. Richards stood waiting for them at the bottom.

Some one was opening the front door with a latchkey. It was Brently Mallard who entered, a little travel-stained, composedly carrying his grip-sack and umbrella. He had been far from the scene of accident, and did not even know there had been one. He stood amazed at Josephine's piercing cry; at Richards' quick motion to screen him from the view of his wife.

But Richards was too late.

When the doctors came they said she had died of heart disease—of joy that kills.

At the 'Cadian Ball (1894)

Bobinôt, that big, brown, good-natured Bobinôt, had no intention of going to the ball, even though he knew Calixta would be there. For what came of those balls but heartache, and a sickening disinclination for work the whole week through, till Saturday night came again and his tortures began afresh? Why could he not love Ozéina, who would marry him tomorrow; or Fronie, or any one of a dozen others, rather than that little Spanish vixen? Calixta's slender foot had never touched Cuban soil; but her mother's had, and the Spanish was in her blood all the same. For that reason the prairie people forgave her much that they would not have overlooked in their own daughters or sisters.

Her eyes,—Bobinôt thought of her eyes, and weakened,—the bluest, the drowsiest, most tantalizing that ever looked into a man's; he thought of her flaxen hair that kinked worse than a mulatto's close to her head; that broad smiling mouth and tiptilted nose, that full-figure; that voice like a rich contralto song, with cadences in it that must have been taught by Satan, for there was no one else to teach her tricks on that 'Cadian prairie. Bobinôt thought of them all as he plowed his rows of cane.

There had even been a breath of scandal whispered about her a year ago, when she went to Assumption,—but why talk of it? No one did now. "C'est Espagnol, ça," most of them said with lenient shoulder-shrugs. "Bon chien tient de race," the old men mumbled over their pipes, stirred by recollections. Nothing was made of it, except that Fronie threw it up to Calixta when the two quarreled and fought on the church steps after mass one Sunday, about a lover. Calixta swore roundly in fine 'Cadian French and with true Spanish spirit, and slapped Fronie's face. Fronie had slapped her back; "Tiens, cocotte, va!" "Espèce de lionèse; prends ça, et ça!" till the curé himself was obliged to hasten and make peace between them. Bobinôt thought of it all, and would not go to the ball.

But in the afternoon, over at Friedheimer's store, where he was buying a trace-chain, he heard some one say that Alcée Laballière would be there. Then wild horses could not have kept him away. He knew how it would be—or rather he did not know how it would be—if the handsome young planter came over to the ball as he sometimes did. If Alcée happened to be in a serious mood, he might only go to the card-room and play a round or two; or he might stand out on the galleries talking crops and politics with the old people. But there was no telling. A drink or two could put the devil in his head,—that was what Bobinôt said to himself, as he wiped the sweat from his brow with his red bandanna; a gleam from Calixta's eyes, a flash of her ankle, a twirl of her skirts could do the same. Yes, Bobinôt would go to the ball.

That was the year Alcée Laballière put nine hundred acres in rice. It was putting a good deal of money into the ground but the returns promised to be glorious. Old Madame Laballière, sailing about the spacious galleries in her white *volante*, figured it all out in her head. Clarisse, her goddaughter, helped her a little, and together they built more air-castles than enough. Alcée worked like a mule that time; and if he did not kill himself, it was because his constitution was an iron one. It was an every-day affair for him to come in from the field well-nigh exhausted, and wet to the waist. He did not mind if there were visitors; he left them to his mother and Clarisse. There were often guests: young men and women who came up from the city, which was but a few hours away, to visit his beautiful kinswoman. She was worth going a good deal farther than that to see. Dainty as a lily; hardy as a sunflower; slim, tall, graceful, like one of the reeds that grew in the marsh. Cold and kind and cruel by turn, and everything that was aggravating to Alcée.

He would have liked to sweep the place of those visitors, often. Of the men, above all, with their ways and their manners; their swaying of fans like women, and dandling about hammocks. He could have pitched them over the levee into the river, if it hadn't meant murder. That was Alcée. But he must have been crazy the day he came in from the rice-field, and, toil-stained as he was, clasped Clarisse by the arms and panted a volley of hot, blistering love-words into her face. No man had ever spoken love to her like that.

"Monsieur!" she exclaimed, looking him full in the eyes, without a quiver. Alcée's hands dropped and his glance wavered before the chill of her calm, clear eyes.

"*Par exemple!*" she muttered disdainfully, as she turned from him, deftly adjusting the careful toilet that he had so brutally disarranged.

That happened a day or two before the cyclone came that cut into the rice like fine steel. It was an awful thing, coming so swiftly, without a moment's warning in which to light a holy candle or set a piece of blessed palm burning. Old madame wept openly and said her beads, just as her son Didier, the New Orleans one, would have done. If such a thing had happened to Alphonse, the Laballière planting cotton up in Natchitoches, he would have raved and stormed like a second cyclone, and made his surroundings unbearable for a day or two. But Alcée took the misfortune differently. He looked ill and gray after it, and said nothing. His speechlessness was frightful. Clarisse's heart melted with tenderness; but when she offered her soft, purring words of condolence, he accepted them with mute indifference. Then she and her nénaine wept afresh in each other's arms.

A night or two later, when Clarisse went to her window to kneel there in the moonlight and say her prayers before retiring, she saw that Bruce, Alcée's negro servant, had led his master's saddle-horse noiselessly along the edge of the sward that bordered the gravel-path, and stood holding him near by. Presently, she heard Alcée quit his room, which was beneath her own, and traverse the lower portico. As he emerged from the shadow and crossed the strip of moonlight, she perceived that he carried a pair of well-filled saddle-bags which he at once flung across the animal's back. He then lost no time in mounting, and after a brief exchange of words with Bruce, went cantering away, taking no precaution to avoid the noisy gravel as the negro had done.

Clarisse had never suspected that it might be Alcée's custom to sally forth from the plantation secretly, and at such an hour; for it was nearly midnight. And had it not been for the telltale saddle-bags, she would only have crept to bed, to wonder, to fret, and dream unpleasant dreams. But her impatience and anxiety would not be held in check. Hastily unbolting the shutters of her door that opened upon the gallery, she stepped outside and called softly to the old negro.

"Gre't Peter! Miss Clarisse. I was n' sho it was a ghos' o' w'at, stan'in' up dah, plumb in de night, dataway."

He mounted halfway up the long, broad flight of stairs. She was standing at the top.

"Bruce, w'ere has Monsieur Alcée gone?" she asked.

"W'y, he gone 'bout he business, I reckin," replied Bruce, striving to be non-committal at the outset.

"W'ere has Monsieur Alcée gone?" she reiterated, stamping her bare foot. "I won't stan' any nonsense or any lies; mine, Bruce."

"I don' ric'lic ez I eva tole you lie *yit*, Miss Clarisse. Mista Alcée, he all broke up, sho."

"W'ere—has—he gone? Ah Sainte Vierge! Faut de la patience! butor, va!"

"W'en I was in he room, a-breshin' off he clo'es to-day," the darkey began, settling himself against the stair-rail, "he look dat speechless an' down, I say, 'You 'pear to me like some pussun w'at gwine have a spell o' sickness, Mista Alcée.' He say, 'You reckin?' 'I dat he git up, go look hisse'f stiddy in de glass. Den he go to de chimbly an'jerk up de quinine bottle an' po' a gre't hoss-dose on to he han'. An' he swalla dat mess in a wink, an' wash hit down wid a big dram o' w'iskey w'at he keep in he room, aginst he come all soppin' wet outen de fiel'.

"He 'lows, 'No, I ain' gwine be sick, Bruce.' Den he square off. He say, 'I kin mak out to stan' up an' gi' an' take wid any man I knows, lessen hit's John L. Sulvun. But w'en God A'mighty an' a 'oman jines fo'ces agin me, dat 's one too many fur me.' I tell 'im, 'Jis so,' whils' I 'se makin' out to bresh a spot off w'at ain' dah, on he coat colla. I tell 'im, 'You wants li'le res', suh.' He say, 'No, I wants li'le fling; dat w'at I wants; an' I gwine git it. Pitch me a fis'ful o' clo'es in dem 'ar saddle-bags.' Dat w'at he say. Don't you bodda, missy. He jis' gone a-caperin' yonda to de Cajun ball. Uh—uh—de skeeters is fair' a-swarmin' like bees roun' yo' foots!"

The mosquitoes were indeed attacking Clarisse's white feet savagely. She had unconsciously been alternately rubbing one foot over the other during the darkey's recital.

"The 'Cadian ball," she repeated contemptuously. "Humph! *Par exemple!* Nice conduc' for a Laballière. An' he needs a saddle-bag, fill' with clothes, to go to the 'Cadian ball!"

"Oh, Miss Clarisse; you go on to bed, chile; git yo' soun' sleep. He 'low he come back in couple weeks o' so. I kiarn be repeatin' lot o' truck w'at young mans say, out heah face o' young gal."

Clarisse said no more, but turned and abruptly reëntered the house.

"You done talk too much wid yo' mouf a'ready, you ole fool nigga, you," muttered Bruce to himself as he walked away.

Alcée reached the ball very late, of course—too late for the chicken gumbo which had been served at midnight.

The big, low-ceiled room—they called it a hall—was packed with men and women dancing to the music of three fiddles. There were broad galleries all around it. There was a room at one side where sober-faced men were playing cards. Another, in which babies were sleeping, was called *le parc aux petits*. Any one who is white may go to a 'Cadian ball, but he must pay for his lemonade, his coffee and chicken gumbo. And he must behave himself like a 'Cadian. Grosbœuf was giving this ball. He had been giving them since he was a young man, and he was a middle-aged one, now. In that time he could recall but one disturbance, and that was caused by American railroaders, who were not in touch with their surroundings and had no business there. "Ces maudits gens du raiderode," Grosbœuf called them.

Alcée Laballière's presence at the ball caused a flutter even among the men, who could not but admire his "nerve" after such misfortune befalling him. To be sure, they knew the Laballières were rich—that there were resources East, and more again in the city. But they felt it took a *brave homme* to stand a blow like that philosophically. One old gentleman, who was in the habit of reading a Paris newspaper and knew things, chuckled gleefully to everybody that Alcée's conduct was altogether *chic, mais chic*. That he had more *panache* than Boulanger. Well, perhaps he had.

But what he did not show outwardly was that he was in a mood for ugly things to-night. Poor Bobinôt alone felt it vaguely. He discerned a gleam of it in Alcée's handsome eyes, as the young planter stood in the doorway, looking with rather feverish glance upon the assembly, while he laughed and talked with a 'Cadian farmer who was beside him.

Bobinôt himself was dull-looking and clumsy. Most of the men were. But the young women were very beautiful. The eyes that glanced into Alcée's as they passed him were big, dark, soft as those of the young heifers standing out in the cool prairie grass.

But the belle was Calixta. Her white dress was not nearly so handsome or well made as Fronie's (she and Fronie had quite forgotten the battle on the church steps, and were friends again), nor were her slippers so stylish as those of Ozéina; and she fanned herself with a handkerchief, since she had broken her red fan at the last ball, and her aunts and uncles were not willing to give her another. But all the men agreed she was at her best to-night. Such animation! and abandon! such flashes of wit!

"Hé, Bobinôt! *Mais* w'at 's the matta? W'at you standin' *planté là* like ole Ma'ame Tina's cow in the bog, you?"

That was good. That was an excellent thrust at Bobinôt, who had forgotten the figure of the dance with his mind bent on other things, and it started a clamor of laughter at his expense. He joined good-naturedly. It was better to receive even such notice as that from Calixta than none at all. But Madame Suzonne, sitting in a corner, whispered to her neighbor that if Ozéina were to conduct herself in a like manner, she should immediately be taken out to the mule-cart and driven home. The women did not always approve of Calixta.

Now and then there were short lulls in the dance, when couples flocked out upon the galleries for a brief respite and fresh air. The moon had gone down pale in the west, and in the east was yet no promise of day. After such an interval, when the dancers again assembled to resume the interrupted quadrille, Calixta was not among them.

She was sitting upon a bench out in the shadow, with Alcée beside her.

They were acting like fools. He had attempted to take a little gold ring from her finger; just for the fun of it, for there was nothing he could have done with the ring but replace it again. But she clinched her hand tight. He pretended that it was a very difficult matter to open it. Then he kept the hand in his. They seemed to forget about it. He played with her earring, a thin crescent of gold hanging from her small brown ear. He caught a wisp of the kinky hair that had escaped its fastening, and rubbed the ends of it against his shaven cheek.

"You know, last year in Assumption, Calixta?" They belonged to the younger generation, so preferred to speak English.

"Don't come say Assumption to me, M'sieur Alcée. I done yeard Assumption till I 'm plumb sick."

"Yes, I know. The idiots! Because you were in Assumption, and I happened to go to Assumption, they must have it that we went together. But it was nice—*hein*, Calixta?—in Assumption?"

They saw Bobinôt emerge from the hall and stand a moment outside the lighted doorway, peering uneasily and searchingly into the darkness. He did not see them, and went slowly back.

"There is Bobinôt looking for you. You are going to set poor Bobinôt crazy. You'll marry him someday; *hein*, Calixta?"

"I don't say no, me," she replied, striving to withdraw her hand, which he held more firmly for the attempt.

"But come, Calixta; you know you said you would go back to Assumption, just to spite them."

"No, I neva said that, me. You mus' dreamt that."

"Oh, I thought you did. You know I'm going down to the city."

"W'en?"

"To-night."

"Betta make has'e, then; it 's mos' day."

"Well, to-morrow 'll do."

"W'at you goin' do, yonda?"

"I don't know. Drown myself in the lake, maybe; unless you go down there to visit your uncle."

Calixta's senses were reeling; and they well-nigh left her when she felt Alcée's lips brush her ear like the touch of a rose.

"Mista Alcée! Is dat Mista Alcée?" the thick voice of a negro was asking; he stood on the ground, holding to the banister-rails near which the couple sat.

"W'at do you want now?" cried Alcée impatiently. "Can't I have a moment of peace?"

"I ben huntin' you high an' low, suh," answered the man. "Dey—dey some one in de road, onda de mulbare-tree, want see you a minute."

"I would n't go out to the road to see the Angel Gabriel. And if you come back here with any more talk, I 'll have to break your neck." The negro turned mumbling away.

Alcée and Calixta laughed softly about it. Her boisterousness was all gone. They talked low, and laughed softly, as lovers do.

"Alcée! Alcée Laballière!"

It was not the negro's voice this time; but one that went through Alcée's body like an electric shock, bringing him to his feet.

Clarisse was standing there in her riding-habit, where the negro had stood. For an instant confusion reigned in Alcée's thoughts, as with one who awakes suddenly from a dream. But he felt that something of serious import had brought his cousin to the ball in the dead of night.

"W'at does this mean, Clarisse?" he asked.

"It means something has happen' at home. You mus' come."

"Happened to maman?" he questioned, in alarm.

"No; nénaine is well, and asleep. It is something else. Not to frighten you. But you mus' come. Come with me, Alcée."

There was no need for the imploring note. He would have followed the voice anywhere.

She had now recognized the girl sitting back on the bench.

"Ah, c'est vous, Calixta? Comment ça va, mon enfant?"

"Tcha va b'en; et vous, mam'zélle?"

Alcée swung himself over the low rail and started to follow Clarisse, without a word, without a glance back at the girl. He had forgotten he was leaving her there. But Clarisse whispered something to him, and he turned back to say "Good-night, Calixta," and offer his hand to press through the railing. She pretended not to see it.

"How come that? You settin' yere by yo'self, Calixta?" It was Bobinôt who had found her there alone. The dancers had not yet come out. She looked ghastly in the faint, gray light struggling out of the east.

"Yes, that's me. Go yonda in the *parc aux petits* an' ask Aunt Olisse fu' my hat. She knows w'ere 't is. I want to go home, me."

"How you came?"

"I come afoot, with the Cateaus. But I 'm goin' now. I ent goin' wait fu' 'em. I'm plumb wo' out, me."

"Kin I go with you, Calixta?"

"I don' care."

They went together across the open prairie and along the edge of the fields, stumbling in the uncertain light. He told her to lift her dress that was getting wet and bedraggled; for she was pulling at the weeds and grasses with her hands.

"I don' care; it's got to go in the tub, anyway. You been sayin' all along you want to marry me, Bobinôt. Well, if you want, yet, I don' care, me."

The glow of a sudden and overwhelming happiness shone out in the brown, rugged face of the young Acadian. He could not speak, for very joy. It choked him.

"Oh well, if you don' want," snapped Calixta, flippantly, pretending to be piqued at his silence.

"*Bon Dieu!* You know that makes me crazy, w'at you sayin'. You mean that, Calixta? You ent goin' turn roun' agin?"

"I neva tole you that much yet, Bobinôt. I mean that. *Tiens,*" and she held her hand in the business-like manner of a man who clinches a bargain with a hand-clasp. Bobinôt grew bold with happiness and asked Calixta to kiss him. She turned her face, that was almost ugly after the night's dissipation, and looked steadily into his.

"I don' want to kiss you, Bobinôt," she said, turning away again, "not to-day. Some other time. *Bonté divine!* Ent you satisfy, *yet!*"

"Oh, I 'm satisfy, Calixta," he said.

Riding through a patch of wood, Clarisse's saddle became ungirted, and she and Alcée dismounted to readjust it.

For the twentieth time he asked her what had happened at home.

"But, Clarisse, w'at is it? Is it a misfortune?"

"Ah, *Dieu sait!* It's only something that happen' to me."

"To you!"

"I saw you go away las' night, Alcée, with those saddle-bags," she said, haltingly, striving to arrange something about the saddle, "an' I made Bruce tell me. He said you had gone to the ball, an' wouldn' be home for weeks an' weeks. I thought, Alcée—maybe you were going to—to Assumption. I got wild. An' then I knew if you didn't come back, *now*, to-night. I couldn't stan' it,—again."

She had her face hidden in her arm that she was resting against the saddle when she said that.

He began to wonder if this meant love. But she had to tell him so, before he believed it. And when she told him, he thought the face of the Universe was changed—just like Bobinôt. Was it last week the cyclone had well-nigh ruined him? The cyclone seemed a huge joke, now. It was he, then, who, an hour ago was kissing Calixta's ear and whispering non-sense into it. Calixta was like a myth, now. The one, only, great reality in the world was Clarisse standing before him, telling him that she loved him.

In the distance they heard the rapid discharge of pistol-shots; but it did not disturb them. They knew it was only the negro musicians who had gone into the yard to fire their pistols into the air, as the custom is, and to announce *"le bal est fini."*

The Storm (1898)

I

The leaves were so still that even Bibi thought it was going to rain. Bobinôt, who was accustomed to converse on terms of perfect equality with his little son, called the child's attention to certain sombre clouds that were rolling with sinister intention from the west, accompanied by a sullen, threatening roar. They were at Friedheimer's store and decided to remain there till the storm had passed. They sat within the door on two empty kegs. Bibi was four years old and looked very wise.

"Mama'll be 'fraid, yes," he suggested with blinking eyes.

"She'll shut the house. Maybe she got Sylvie helpin' her this evenin'," Bobinôt responded reassuringly.

"No; she ent got Sylvie. Sylvie was helpin' her yistiday," piped Bibi.

Bobinôt arose and going across to the counter purchased a can of shrimps, of which Calixta was very fond. Then he returned to his perch on the keg and sat stolidly holding the can of shrimps while the storm burst. It shook the wooden store and seemed to be ripping great furrows in the distant field. Bibi laid his little hand on his father's knee and was not afraid.

II

Calixta, at home, felt no uneasiness for their safety. She sat at a side win-dow sewing furiously on a sewing machine. She was greatly occupied and did not notice the approaching storm. But she felt very warm and often stopped to mop her face on which the perspiration gathered in beads. She unfastened her white sacque at the throat. It began to grow dark, and suddenly realizing the situation she got up hurriedly and went about closing windows and doors.

Out on the small front gallery she had hung Bobinôt's Sunday clothes to dry and she hastened out to gather them before the rain fell. As she stepped outside, Alcée Laballière rode in at the gate. She had not seen him very often since her marriage, and never alone. She stood there with Bobinôt's coat in her hands, and the big rain drops began to fall. Alcée rode his horse under the shelter of a side projection where the chickens had huddled and there were plows and a harrow piled up in the corner.

"May I come and wait on your gallery till the storm is over, Calixta?" he asked.

"Come 'long in, M'sieur Alcée."

His voice and her own startled her as if from a trance, and she seized Bobinôt's vest. Alcée, mounting to the porch, grabbed the trousers and snatched Bibi's braided jacket that was about to be carried away by a sudden gust of wind. He expressed an intention to remain outside, but it was soon apparent that he might as well have been out in the open: the water beat in upon the boards in driving sheets, and he went inside, closing the door after him. It was even necessary to put something beneath the door to keep the water out.

"My! what a rain! It's good two years sence it rain' like that," exclaimed Calixta as she rolled up a piece of bagging and Alcée helped her to thrust it beneath the crack.

She was a little fuller of figure than five years before when she married; but she had lost nothing of her vivacity. Her blue eyes still retained their melting quality; and her yellow hair, dishevelled by the wind and rain, kinked more stubbornly than ever about her ears and temples.

The rain beat upon the low, shingled roof with a force and clatter that threatened to break an entrance and deluge them there. They were in the dining room—the sitting room—the general utility room. Adjoining was her bed room, with Bibi's couch along side her own. The door stood open, and the room with its white, monumental bed, its closed shutters, looked dim and mysterious.

Alcée flung himself into a rocker and Calixta nervously began to gather up from the floor the lengths of a cotton sheet which she had been sewing.

"If this keeps up, *Dieu sait* if the levees goin' to stan' it!" she exclaimed.

"What have you got to do with the levees?"

"I got enough to do! An' there's Bobinôt with Bibi out in that storm— if he only didn' left Friedheimer's!"

"Let us hope, Calixta, that Bobinôt's got sense enough to come in out of a cyclone."

She went and stood at the window with a greatly disturbed look on her face. She wiped the frame that was clouded with moisture. It was stiflingly hot. Alcée got up and joined her at the window, looking over her shoulder. The rain was coming down in sheets obscuring the view of far-off cabins and enveloping the distant wood in a gray mist. The playing of the lightning was incessant. A bolt struck a tall chinaberry tree at the edge of the field. It filled all visible space with a blinding glare and the crash seemed to invade the very boards they stood upon.

Calixta put her hands to her eyes, and with a cry, staggered backward. Alcée's arm encircled her, and for an instant he drew her close and spasmodically to him.

"*Bonté!*" she cried, releasing herself from his encircling arm and retreating from the window, "the house'll go next! If I only knew w'ere Bibi was!" She would not compose herself; she would not be seated. Alcée clasped her shoulders and looked into her face. The contact of her warm, palpitating body when he had unthinkingly drawn her into his arms, had aroused all the old-time infatuation and desire for her flesh.

"Calixta," he said, "don't be frightened. Nothing can happen. The house is too low to be struck, with so many tall trees standing about. There! aren't you going to be quiet? say, aren't you?" He pushed her hair back from her face that was warm and steaming. Her lips were as red and moist as pomegranate seed. Her white neck and a glimpse of her full, firm bosom disturbed him powerfully. As she glanced up at him the fear in her liquid blue eyes had given place to a drowsy gleam that unconsciously betrayed a sensuous desire. He looked down into her eyes and there was nothing for him to do but to gather her lips in a kiss. It reminded him of Assumption.

"Do you remember—in Assumption, Calixta?" he asked in a low voice broken by passion. Oh! she remembered; for in Assumption he had kissed her and kissed and kissed her; until his senses would well nigh fail, and to save her he would resort to a desperate flight. If she was not an immaculate dove in those days, she was still inviolate; a passionate creature whose very defenselessness had made her defense, against which his honor forbade him to prevail. Now—well, now—her lips seemed in a manner free to be tasted, as well as her round, white throat and her whiter breasts.

They did not heed the crashing torrents, and the roar of the elements made her laugh as she lay in his arms. She was a revelation in that dim, mysterious chamber; as white as the couch she lay upon. Her firm, elastic flesh that was knowing for the first time its birthright, was like a creamy lily that the sun invites to contribute its breath and perfume to the undying life of the world.

The generous abundance of her passion, without guile or trickery, was like a white flame which penetrated and found response in depths of his own sensuous nature that had never yet been reached.

When he touched her breasts they gave themselves up in quivering ecstasy, inviting his lips. Her mouth was a fountain of delight. And when he possessed her, they seemed to swoon together at the very borderland of life's mystery.

He stayed cushioned upon her, breathless, dazed, enervated, with his heart beating like a hammer upon her. With one hand she clasped his head, her lips lightly touching his forehead. The other hand stroked with a soothing rhythm his muscular shoulders.

The growl of the thunder was distant and passing away. The rain beat softly upon the shingles, inviting them to drowsiness and sleep. But they dared not yield.

The rain was over; and the sun was turning the glistening green world into a palace of gems. Calixta, on the gallery, watched Alcée ride away. He turned and smiled at her with a beaming face; and she lifted her pretty chin in the air and laughed aloud.

III

Bobinôt and Bibi, trudging home, stopped without at the cistern to make themselves presentable.

"My! Bibi, w'at will yo' mama say! You ought to be ashame'. You oughta' put on those good pants. Look at 'em! An' that mud on yo' collar! How you got that mud on yo' collar, Bibi? I never saw such a boy!" Bibi was the picture of pathetic resignation. Bobinôt was the embodiment of serious solicitude as he strove to remove from his own person and his son's the signs of their tramp over heavy roads and through wet fields. He scraped the mud off Bibi's bare legs and feet with a stick and carefully removed all traces from his heavy brogans. Then, prepared for the worst—the meeting with an over-scrupulous housewife, they entered cautiously at the back door.

Calixta was preparing supper. She had set the table and was dripping coffee at the hearth. She sprang up as they came in.

"Oh, Bobinôt! You back! My! but I was uneasy. W'ere you been during the rain? An' Bibi? he ain't wet? he ain't hurt?" She had clasped Bibi and was kissing him effusively. Bobinôt's explanations and apologies which he had been composing all along the way, died on his lips as Calixta felt him to see if he were dry, and seemed to express nothing but satisfaction at their safe return.

"I brought you some shrimps, Calixta," offered Bobinôt, hauling the can from his ample side pocket and laying it on the table.

"Shrimps! Oh, Bobinôt! you too good fo' anything!" and she gave him a smacking kiss on the cheek that resounded, "J'vous réponds, we'll have a feas' to-night! umph-umph!"

Bobinôt and Bibi began to relax and enjoy themselves, and when the three seated themselves at table they laughed much and so loud that any- one might have heard them as far away as Laballière's.

IV

Alcée Laballière wrote to his wife, Clarisse, that night. It was a loving let- ter, full of tender solicitude. He told her not to hurry back, but if she and the babies liked it at Biloxi, to stay a month longer. He was getting on nicely; and though he missed them, he was willing to bear the separation a while longer—realizing that their health and pleasure were the first things to be considered.

V

As for Clarisse, she was charmed upon receiving her husband's letter. She and the babies were doing well. The society was agreeable; many of her old friends and acquaintances were at the bay. And the first free breath since her marriage seemed to restore the pleasant liberty of her maiden days. Devoted as she was to her husband, their intimate conjugal life was something which she was more than willing to forego for a while.

So the storm passed and every one was happy.

Mary E. Wilkins Freeman
(1852–1930)

ary E. Wilkins spent her childhood in Randolph, Massachusetts, and Brattleboro, Vermont, and attended Mount Holyoke Female Seminary for a year. After the deaths of her parents and sister, she went in 1883 to live with her childhood friend Mary Wales in a "Boston marriage" that lasted almost twenty years. But in 1902 Mary Wilkins married Charles M. Freeman, a doctor, and moved with him to New Jersey. Publishing as "Mary E. Wilkins" before her marriage, she is now known as "Freeman," although Dr. Freeman was an alcoholic who was eventually institutionalized, and the couple separated legally.

Freeman's long and prolific career extended from the 1870s to 1918, and she published seven novels as well as almost two hundred fifty short stories. "A New England Nun" lovingly explores the domestic world of an unmarried woman and asks whether her refusal to leave it is a choice for freedom or morbid isolation. "Old Woman Magoun" was Freeman's most sinister and gothic rendition of this ambiguous female withdrawal. In a little-known story, "Noblesse," Freeman wrote from the point of view of a circus fat lady in a freak story like Jewett's "The Circus at Denby."

A New England Nun (1891)

It was late in the afternoon, and the light was waning. There was a difference in the look of the tree shadows out in the yard. Somewhere in the distance cows were lowing and a little bell was tinkling; now and then a farm-wagon tilted by, and the dust flew; some blue-shirted laborers with shovels over their shoulders plodded past; little swarms of flies were dancing up and down before the peoples' faces in the soft air. There seemed to be a gentle stir arising over everything for the mere sake of subsidence—a very premonition of rest and hush and night.

This soft diurnal commotion was over Louisa Ellis also. She had been peacefully sewing at her sitting-room window all the afternoon. Now she quilted her needle carefully into her work, which she folded precisely, and laid in a basket with her thimble and thread and scissors. Louisa Ellis could not remember that ever in her life she had mislaid one of these little feminine appurtenances, which had become, from long use and constant association, a very part of her personality.

Louisa tied a green apron round her waist, and got out a flat straw hat with a green ribbon. Then she went into the garden with a little blue crockery bowl, to pick some currants for her tea. After the currants were picked she sat on the back door-step and stemmed them, collecting the stems carefully in her apron, and afterwards throwing them into the hen-coop. She looked sharply at the grass beside the step to see if any had fallen there.

Louisa was slow and still in her movements; it took her a long time to prepare her tea; but when ready it was set forth with as much grace as if she had been a veritable guest to her own self. The little square table stood exactly in the centre of the kitchen, and was covered with a starched linen cloth whose border pattern of flowers glistened. Louisa had a damask napkin on her tea-tray, where were arranged a cut-glass tumbler full of teaspoons, a silver cream-pitcher, a china sugar-bowl, and one pink china cup and saucer. Louisa used china every day—something which none of her neighbors did. They whispered about it among themselves. Their daily tables were laid with common crockery, their sets of best china stayed in the parlor closet, and Louisa Ellis was no richer nor better bred than they. Still she would use the china. She had for her supper a glass dish full of sugared currants, a plate of little cakes, and one of light white biscuits. Also a leaf or two of lettuce, which she cut up daintily. Louisa was very fond of lettuce, which she raised to perfection in her little garden. She ate quite heartily, though in a delicate, pecking way; it seemed almost surprising that any considerable bulk of the food should vanish.

After tea she filled a plate with nicely baked thin corn-cakes, and carried them out into the back-yard.

"Caesar!" she called. "Caesar! Caesar!"

There was a little rush, and the clank of a chain, and a large yellow-and-white dog appeared at the door of his tiny hut, which was half hidden among the tall grasses and flowers. Louisa patted him and gave him the corn-cakes. Then she returned to the house and washed the tea-things, polishing the china carefully. The twilight had deepened; the chorus of the frogs floated in at the open window wonderfully loud and shrill, and once in a while a long sharp drone from a tree-toad pierced it. Louisa took off her green gingham apron, disclosing a shorter one of pink-and-white print. She lighted her lamp, and sat down again with her sewing.

In about half an hour Joe Dagget came. She heard his heavy step on the walk, and rose and took off her pink-and-white apron. Under that was still another—white linen with a little cambric edging on the bottom; that was Louisa's company apron. She never wore it without her calico sewing apron over it unless she had a guest. She had barely folded the pink-and-white one with methodical haste and laid it in a table-drawer when the door opened and Joe Dagget entered.

He seemed to fill up the whole room. A little yellow canary that had been asleep in his green cage at the south window woke up and fluttered wildly, beating his little yellow wings against the wires. He always did so when Joe Dagget came into the room.

"Good-evening," said Louisa. She extended her hand with a kind of solemn cordiality.

"Good-evening, Louisa," returned the man, in a loud voice.

She placed a chair for him, and they sat facing each other, with the table between them. He sat bolt-upright, toeing out his heavy feet squarely, glancing with a good-humored uneasiness around the room. She sat gently erect, folding her slender hands in her white-linen lap.

"Been a pleasant day," remarked Dagget.

"Real pleasant," Louisa assented, softly. "Have you been haying?" she asked, after a little while.

"Yes, I've been haying all day, down in the ten-acre lot. Pretty hot work."

"It must be."

"Yes, it's pretty hot work in the sun."

"Is your mother well to-day?"

"Yes, mother's pretty well."

"I suppose Lily Dyer's with her now?"

Dagget colored. "Yes, she's with her," he answered, slowly.

He was not very young, but there was a boyish look about his large face. Louisa was not quite as old as he, her face was fairer and smoother, but she gave people the impression of being older.

"I suppose she's a good deal of help to your mother," she said, further.

"I guess she is; I don't know how mother'd get along without her," said Dagget, with a sort of embarrassed warmth.

"She looks like a real capable girl. She's pretty-looking too," remarked Louisa.

"Yes, she is pretty fair looking."

Presently Dagget began fingering the books on the table. There was a square red autograph album, and a Young Lady's Gift-Book which had belonged to Louisa's mother. He took them up one after the other and opened them; then laid them down again, the album on the Gift-Book.

Louisa kept eying them with mild uneasiness. Finally she rose and changed the position of the books, putting the album underneath. That was the way they had been arranged in the first place.

Dagget gave an awkward little laugh. "Now what difference did it make which book was on top?" said he.

Louisa looked at him with a deprecating smile. "I always keep them that way," murmured she.

"You do beat everything," said Dagget, trying to laugh again. His large face was flushed.

He remained about an hour longer, then rose to take leave. Going out, he stumbled over a rug, and trying to recover himself, hit Louisa's work-basket on the table, and knocked it on the floor.

He looked at Louisa, then at the rolling spools; he ducked himself awkwardly toward them, but she stopped him. "Never mind," said she; "I'll pick them up after you're gone."

She spoke with a mild stiffness. Either she was a little disturbed, or his nervousness affected her, and made her seem constrained in her effort to reassure him.

When Joe Dagget was outside he drew in the sweet evening air with a sigh, and felt much as an innocent and perfectly well-intentioned bear might after his exit from a china shop.

Louisa, on her part, felt much as the kind-hearted, long-suffering owner of the china shop might have done after the exit of the bear.

She tied on the pink, then the green apron, picked up all the scattered treasures and replaced them in her work-basket, and straightened the rug. Then she set the lamp on the floor, and began sharply examining the carpet. She even rubbed her fingers over it, and looked at them.

"He's tracked in a good deal of dust," she murmured. "I thought he must have."

Louisa got a dust-pan and brush, and swept Joe Dagget's track carefully.

If he could have known it, it would have increased his perplexity and uneasiness, although it would not have disturbed his loyalty in the least. He came twice a week to see Louisa Ellis, and every time, sitting there in her delicately sweet room, he felt as if surrounded by a hedge of lace. He was afraid to stir lest he should put a clumsy foot or hand through the fairy web, and he had always the consciousness that Louisa was watching fearfully lest he should.

Still the lace and Louisa commanded perforce his perfect respect and patience and loyalty. They were to be married in a month, after a singular courtship which had lasted for a matter of fifteen years. For fourteen out of the fifteen years the two had not once seen each other, and they had seldom exchanged letters. Joe had been all those years in Australia, where he had gone to make his fortune, and where he had stayed until he made it. He would have stayed fifty years if it had taken so long, and come home feeble and tottering, or never come home at all, to marry Louisa.

But the fortune had been made in the fourteen years, and he had come home now to marry the woman who had been patiently and unquestioningly waiting for him all that time.

Shortly after they were engaged he had announced to Louisa his determination to strike out into new fields, and secure a competency before they should be married. She had listened and assented with the sweet serenity which never failed her, not even when her lover set forth on that long and uncertain journey. Joe, buoyed up as he was by his sturdy determination, broke down a little at the last, but Louisa kissed him with a mild blush, and said good-by.

"It won't be for long," poor Joe had said, huskily; but it was for fourteen years.

In that length of time much had happened. Louisa's mother and brother had died, and she was all alone in the world. But greatest happening of all—a subtle happening which both were too simple to understand—Louisa's feet had turned into a path, smooth maybe under a calm, serene sky, but so straight and unswerving that it could only meet a check at her grave, and so narrow that there was no room for any one at her side.

Louisa's first emotion when Joe Dagget came home (he had not apprised her of his coming) was consternation, although she would not admit it to herself, and he never dreamed of it. Fifteen years ago she had been in love with him—at least she considered herself to be. Just at that time, gently acquiescing with and falling into the natural drift of girlhood, she had seen marriage ahead as a reasonable feature and a probable desirability of life. She had listened with calm docility to her mother's views upon the subject. Her mother was remarkable for her cool sense and sweet, even temperament. She talked wisely to her daughter when Joe Dagget presented himself, and Louisa accepted him with no hesitation. He was the first lover she had ever had.

She had been faithful to him all these years. She had never dreamed of the possibility of marrying any one else. Her life, especially for the last seven years, had been full of a pleasant peace, she had never felt discontented nor impatient over her lover's absence; still she had always looked forward to his return and their marriage as the inevitable conclusion of things. However, she had fallen into a way of placing it so far in the future that it was almost equal to placing it over the boundaries of another life.

When Joe came she had been expecting him, and expecting to be married for fourteen years, but she was as much surprised and taken aback as if she had never thought of it.

Joe's consternation came later. He eyed Louisa with an instant confirmation of his old admiration. She had changed but little. She still kept her pretty manner and soft grace, and was, he considered, every whit as attractive as ever. As for himself, his stent was done; he had turned his face away from fortune-seeking, and the old winds of romance whistled as loud and sweet as ever through his ears. All the song which he had been wont to hear in them was Louisa; he had for a long time a loyal belief that he heard it still, but finally it seemed to him that although the winds sang always that one song, it had another name. But for Louisa the wind had never more than murmured; now it had gone down, and everything was still. She listened for a little while with half-wistful attention; then she turned quietly away and went to work on her wedding clothes.

Joe had made some extensive and quite magnificent alterations in his house. It was the old homestead; the newly-married couple would live there, for Joe could not desert his mother, who refused to leave her old home. So Louisa must leave hers. Every morning, rising and going about among her neat maidenly possessions, she felt as one looking her last upon the faces of dear friends. It was true that in a measure she could take them with her, but, robbed of their old environments, they would appear in such new guises that they would almost cease to be themselves. Then there were some peculiar features of her happy solitary life which she would probably be obliged to relinquish altogether. Sterner tasks than these graceful but half-needless ones would probably devolve upon her. There would be a large house to care for; there would be company to entertain; there would be Joe's rigorous and feeble old mother to wait upon; and it would be contrary to all thrifty village traditions for her to keep more than one servant. Louisa had a little still, and she used to occupy herself pleasantly in summer weather with distilling the sweet and aromatic essences from roses and peppermint and spearmint. By-

and-by her still must be laid away. Her store of essences was already considerable, and there would be no time for her to distil for the mere pleasure of it. Then Joe's mother would think it foolishness; she had already hinted her opinion in the matter. Louisa dearly loved to sew a linen seam, not always for use, but for the simple, mild pleasure which she took in it. She would have been loath to confess how more than once she had ripped a seam for the mere delight of sewing it together again. Sitting at her window during long sweet afternoons, drawing her needle gently through the dainty fabric, she was peace itself. But there was small chance of such foolish comfort in the future. Joe's mother, domineering, shrewd old matron that she was even in her old age, and very likely even Joe himself, with his honest masculine rudeness, would laugh and frown down all these pretty but senseless old maiden ways.

Louisa had almost the enthusiasm of an artist over the mere order and cleanliness of her solitary home. She had throbs of genuine triumph at the sight of the window-panes which she had polished until they shone like jewels. She gloated gently over her orderly bureau-drawers, with their exquisitely folded contents redolent with lavender and sweet clover and very purity. Could she be sure of the endurance of even this? She had visions, so startling that she half repudiated them as indelicate, of coarse masculine belongings strewn about in endless litter; of dust and disorder arising necessarily from a coarse masculine presence in the midst of all this delicate harmony.

Among her forebodings of disturbance, not the least was with regard to Caesar. Caesar was a veritable hermit of a dog. For the greater part of his life he had dwelt in his secluded hut, shut out from the society of his kind and all innocent canine joys. Never had Caesar since his early youth watched at a woodchuck's hole; never had he known the delights of a stray bone at a neighbor's kitchen door. And it was all on account of a sin committed when hardly out of his puppyhood. No one knew the possible depth of remorse of which this mild-visaged, altogether innocent-looking old dog might be capable; but whether or not he had encountered remorse, he had encountered a full measure of righteous retribution. Old Caesar seldom lifted up his voice in a growl or a bark; he was fat and sleepy; there were yellow rings which looked like spectacles around his dim old eyes; but there was a neighbor who bore on his hand the imprint of several of Caesar's sharp white youthful teeth, and for that he had lived at the end of a chain, all alone in a little hut, for fourteen years. The neighbor, who was choleric and smarting with the pain of his wound, had demanded either Caesar's death or complete ostracism. So

Louisa's brother, to whom the dog had belonged, had built him his little kennel and tied him up. It was now fourteen years since, in a flood of youthful spirits, he had inflicted that memorable bite, and with the exception of short excursions, always at the end of the chain, under the strict guardianship of his master or Louisa, the old dog had remained a close prisoner. It is doubtful if, with his limited ambition, he took much pride in the fact, but it is certain that he was possessed of considerable cheap fame. He was regarded by all the children in the village and by many adults as a very monster of ferocity. St. George's dragon could hardly have surpassed in evil repute Louisa Ellis's old yellow dog. Mothers charged their children with solemn emphasis not to go too near to him, and the children listened and believed greedily, with a fascinated appetite for terror, and ran by Louisa's house stealthily, with many sidelong and backward glances at the terrible dog. If perchance he sounded a hoarse bark, there was a panic. Wayfarers chancing into Louisa's yard eyed him with respect, and inquired if the chain were stout. Caesar at large might have seemed a very ordinary dog, and excited no comment whatever; chained, his reputation overshadowed him, so that he lost his own proper outlines and looked darkly vague and enormous. Joe Dagget, however, with his good-humored sense and shrewdness, saw him as he was. He strode valiantly up to him and patted him on the head, in spite of Louisa's soft clamor of warning, and even attempted to set him loose. Louisa grew so alarmed that he desisted, but kept announcing his opinion in the matter quite forcibly at intervals. "There ain't a better-natured dog in town," he would say, "and it's downright cruel to keep him tied up there. Some day I'm going to take him out."

Louisa had very little hope that he would not, one of these days, when their interests and possessions should be more completely fused in one. She pictured to herself Caesar on the rampage through the quiet and unguarded village. She saw innocent children bleeding in his path. She was herself very fond of the old dog, because he had belonged to her dead brother, and he was always very gentle with her; still she had great faith in his ferocity. She always warned people not to go too near him. She fed him on ascetic fare of corn-mush and cakes, and never fired his dangerous temper with heating and sanguinary diet of flesh and bones. Louisa looked at the old dog munching his simple fare, and thought of her approaching marriage and trembled. Still no anticipation of disorder and confusion in lieu of sweet peace and harmony, no forebodings of Caesar on the rampage, no wild fluttering of her little yellow canary, were sufficient to turn her a hair's-breadth. Joe Dagget had been fond of her and working for her all these years. It was not for her, whatever came to pass, to prove untrue and break his heart. She put the exquisite little stitches into her wedding-garments, and the time went on until it was only a week before her wedding-day. It was a Tuesday evening, and the wedding was to be a week from Wednesday.

There was a full moon that night. About nine o'clock Louisa strolled down the road a little way. There were harvest-fields on either hand, bordered by low stone walls. Luxuriant clumps of bushes grew beside the wall, and trees—wild cherry and old apple-trees—at intervals. Presently Louisa sat down on the wall and looked about her with mildly sorrowful reflectiveness. Tall shrubs of blueberry and meadow-sweet, all woven together and tangled with blackberry vines and horsebriers, shut her in on either side. She had a little clear space between them. Opposite her, on the other side of the road, was a spreading tree; the moon shone between its boughs, and the leaves twinkled like silver. The road was bespread with a beautiful shifting dapple of silver and shadow; the air was full of a mysterious sweetness. "I wonder if it's wild grapes?" murmured Louisa. She sat there some time. She was just thinking of rising, when she heard footsteps and low voices, and remained quiet. It was a lonely place, and she felt a little timid. She thought she would keep still in the shadow and let the persons, whoever they might be, pass her.

But just before they reached her the voices ceased, and the footsteps. She understood that their owners had also found seats upon the stone wall. She was wondering if she could not steal away unobserved, when the voice broke the stillness. It was Joe Dagget's. She sat still and listened.

The voice was announced by a loud sigh, which was as familiar as itself. "Well," said Dagget, "you've made up your mind, then, I suppose?"

"Yes," returned another voice; "I'm going day after to-morrow."

"That's Lily Dyer," thought Louisa to herself. The voice embodied itself in her mind. She saw a girl tall and full-figured, with a firm, fair face, looking fairer and firmer in the moonlight, her strong yellow hair braided in a close knot. A girl full of a calm rustic strength and bloom, with a masterful way which might have beseemed a princess. Lily Dyer was a favorite with the village folk; she had just the qualities to arouse the admiration. She was good and handsome and smart. Louisa had often heard her praises sounded.

"Well," said Joe Dagget, "I ain't got a word to say."

"I don't know what you could say," returned Lily Dyer.

"Not a word to say," repeated Joe, drawing out the words heavily. "I ain't sorry," he began at last, "that that happened yesterday—that we kind of let on how we felt to each other. I guess it's just as well we knew. Of course I can't do anything any different. I'm going right on an' get married next week. I ain't going back on a woman that's waited for me fourteen years, an' break her heart."

"If you should jilt her to-morrow, I wouldn't have you," spoke up the girl, with sudden vehemence.

"Well, I ain't going to give you the chance," said he; "but I don't believe you would, either."

"You'd see I wouldn't. Honor's honor, an' right's right. An' I'd never think anything of any man that went against 'em for me or any other girl; you'd find that out, Joe Dagget."

"Well, you'll find out fast enough that I ain't going against 'em for you or any other girl," returned he. Their voices sounded almost as if they were angry with each other. Louisa was listening eagerly.

"I'm sorry you feel as if you must go away," said Joe, "but I don't know but it's best."

"Of course it's best. I hope you and I have got common-sense."

"Well, I suppose you're right." Suddenly Joe's voice got an undertone of tenderness. "Say, Lily," said he, "I'll get along well enough myself, but I can't bear to think—You don't suppose you're going to fret much over it?"

"I guess you'll find out I sha'n't fret much over a married man."

"Well, I hope you won't—I hope you won't, Lily. God knows I do. And—I hope—one of these days—you'll—come across somebody else—"

"I don't see any reason why I shouldn't." Suddenly her tone changed. She spoke in a sweet, clear voice, so loud that she could have been heard across the street. "No, Joe Dagget," said she, "I'll never marry any other man as long as I live. I've got good sense, an' I ain't going to break my heart nor make a fool of myself; but I'm never going to be married, you can be sure of that. I ain't that sort of a girl to feel this way twice."

Louisa heard an exclamation and a soft commotion behind the bushes; then Lily spoke again—the voice sounded as if she had risen. "This must be put a stop to," said she. "We've stayed here long enough. I'm going home."

Louisa sat there in a daze, listening to their retreating steps. After a while she got up and slunk softly home herself. The next day she did her housework methodically; that was as much a matter of course as breathing; but she did not sew on her wedding-clothes. She sat at her window and meditated. In the evening Joe came. Louisa Ellis had never known that she had any diplomacy in her, but when she came to look for it that night she found it, although meek of its kind, among her little feminine weapons. Even now she could hardly believe that she had heard aright, and that she would not do Joe a terrible injury should she break her troth-plight. She wanted to sound him without betraying too soon her own inclinations in the matter. She did it successfully, and they finally came to an understanding; but it was a difficult thing, for he was as afraid of betraying himself as she.

She never mentioned Lily Dyer. She simply said that while she had no cause of complaint against him, she had lived so long in one way that she shrank from making a change.

"Well, I never shrank, Louisa," said Dagget. "I'm going to be honest enough to say that I think maybe it's better this way; but if you'd wanted to keep on, I'd have stuck to you till my dying day. I hope you know that."

"Yes, I do," said she.

That night she and Joe parted more tenderly than they had done for a long time. Standing in the door, holding each other's hands, a last great wave of regretful memory swept over them.

"Well, this ain't the way we've thought it was all going to end, is it, Louisa?" said Joe.

She shook her head. There was a little quiver on her placid face.

"You let me know if there's ever anything I can do for you," said he. "I ain't ever going to forget you, Louisa." Then he kissed her, and went down the path.

Louisa, all alone by herself that night, wept a little, she hardly knew why; but the next morning, on waking, she felt like a queen who, after fearing lest her domain be wrested away from her, sees it firmly insured in her possession.

Now the tall weeds and grasses might cluster around Caesar's little hermit hut, the snow might fall on its roof year in and year out, but he never would go on a rampage through the unguarded village. Now the little canary might turn itself into a peaceful yellow ball night after night, and have no need to wake and flutter with wild terror against its bars. Louisa could sew linen seams, and distil roses, and dust and polish and fold away in lavender, as long as she listed. That afternoon she sat with her needle-work at the window, and felt fairly steeped in peace. Lily Dyer, tall and erect and blooming, went past; but she felt no qualm. If Louisa Ellis had sold her birthright she did not know it, the taste of the pottage was so delicious, and had been her sole satisfaction for so long. Serenity and placid narrowness had become to her as the birthright itself.

She gazed ahead through a long reach of future days strung together like pearls in a rosary, every one like the others, and all smooth and flawless and innocent, and her heart went up in thankfulness. Outside was the fervid summer afternoon; the air was filled with the sounds of the busy harvest of men and birds and bees; there were halloos, metallic clatterings, sweet calls, and long hummings. Louisa sat, prayerfully numbering her days, like an uncloistered nun.

Old Woman Magoun (1909)

The hamlet of Barry's Ford is situated in a sort of high valley among the mountains. Below it the hills lie in moveless curves like a petrified ocean; above it they rise in green-cresting waves which never break. It is *Barry's* Ford because at one time the Barry family was the most important in the place; and *Ford* because just at the beginning of the hamlet the little turbulent Barry River is fordable. There is, however, now a rude bridge across the river.

Old Woman Magoun was largely instrumental in bringing the bridge to pass. She haunted the miserable little grocery, wherein whiskey and hands of tobacco were the most salient features of the stock in trade, and she talked much. She would elbow herself into the midst of a knot of idlers and talk.

"That bridge ought to be built this very summer," said Old Woman Magoun. She spread her strong arms like wings, and sent the loafers, half laughing, half angry, flying in every direction. "If I were a *man*," said she, "I'd go out this very minute and lay the fust log. If I were a passel of lazy men layin' round, I'd start up for once in my life, I would." The men cowered visibly—all except Nelson Barry; he swore under his breath and strode over to the counter.

Old Woman Magoun looked after him majestically. "You can cuss all you want to, Nelson Barry," said she; "I ain't afraid of you. I don't expect you to lay ary log of the bridge, but I'm goin' to have it built this very summer." She did. The weakness of the masculine element in Barry's Ford was laid low before such strenuous feminine assertion.

Old Woman Magoun and some other women planned a treat—two sucking pigs, and pies, and sweet cake—for a reward after the bridge should be finished. They even viewed leniently the increased consumption of ardent spirits.

"It seems queer to me," Old Woman Magoun said to Sally Jinks, "that men can't do nothin' without havin' to drink and chew to keep their sperits up. Lord! I've worked all my life and never done nuther."

"Men is different," said Sally Jinks.

"Yes, they be," assented Old Woman Magoun, with open contempt.

The two women sat on a bench in front of Old Woman Magoun's house, and little Lily Barry, her granddaughter, sat holding her doll on a small mossy stone near by. From where they sat they could see the men at work on the new bridge. It was the last day of the work.

Lily clasped her doll—a poor old rag thing—close to her childish bosom, like a little mother, and her face, round which curled her long yellow hair, was fixed upon the men at work. Little Lily had never been allowed to run with the other children of Barry's Ford. Her grandmother had taught her everything she knew—which was not much, but tending at least to a certain measure of spiritual growth—for she, as it were, poured the goodness of her own soul into this little receptive vase of another. Lily was firmly grounded in her knowledge that it was wrong to lie or steal or disobey her grandmother. She had also learned that one should be very industrious. It was seldom that Lily sat idly holding her doll-baby, but this was a holiday because of the bridge. She looked only a child, although she was nearly fourteen; her mother had been married at sixteen. That is, Old Woman Magoun said that her daughter, Lily's mother, had married at sixteen; there had been rumors, but no one had dared openly gainsay the old woman. She said that her daughter had married Nelson Barry, and he had deserted her. She had lived in her mother's house, and Lily had been born there, and she had died when the baby was only a week old. Lily's father, Nelson Barry, was the fairly dangerous degenerate of a good old family. Nelson's father before him had been bad. He was now the last of the family, with the exception of a sister of feeble intellect, with whom he lived in the old Barry house. He was a middle-aged man, still handsome. The shiftless population of Barry's Ford looked up to him as to an evil deity. They wondered how Old Woman Magoun dared brave him as she did. But Old Woman Magoun had within her a mighty sense of reliance upon herself as being on the right track in the midst of a maze of evil, which gave her courage. Nelson Barry had manifested no interest whatever in his daughter. Lily seldom saw her father. She did not often go to the store which was his favorite haunt. Her grandmother took care that she should not do so.

However, that afternoon she departed from her usual custom and sent Lily to the store.

She came in from the kitchen, whither she had been to baste the roasting pig. "There's no use talkin'," said she, "I've got to have some more salt. I've jest used the very last I had to dredge over that pig. I've got to go to the store."

Sally Jinks looked at Lily. "Why don't you send her?" she asked.

Old Woman Magoun gazed irresolutely at the girl. She was herself very tired. It did not seem to her that she could drag herself up the dusty hill to the store. She glanced with covert resentment at Sally Jinks. She thought that she might offer to go. But Sally Jinks said again, "Why don't you let her go?" and looked with a languid eye at Lily holding her doll on the stone.

Lily was watching the men at work on the bridge, with her childish delight in a spectacle of any kind, when her grandmother addressed her.

"Guess I'll let you go down to the store an' git some salt, Lily," said she.

The girl turned uncomprehending eyes upon her grandmother at the sound of her voice. She had been filled with one of the innocent reveries of childhood. Lily had in her the making of an artist or a poet. Her prolonged childhood went to prove it, and also her retrospective eyes, as clear and blue as blue light itself, which seemed to see past all that she looked upon. She had not come of the old Barry family for nothing. The best of the strain was in her, along with the splendid stanchness in humble lines which she had acquired from her grandmother.

"Put on your hat," said Old Woman Magoun; "the sun is hot, and you might git a headache." She called the girl to her, and put back the shower of fair curls under the rubber band which confined the hat. She gave Lily some money, and watched her knot it into a corner of her little cotton handkerchief. "Be careful you don't lose it," said she, "and don't stop to talk to anybody, for I am in a hurry for that salt. Of course, if anybody speaks to you answer them polite, and then come right along."

Lily started, her pocket-handkerchief weighted with the small silver dangling from one hand, and her rag doll carried over her shoulder like a baby. The absurd travesty of a face peeped forth from Lily's yellow curls. Sally Jinks looked after her with a sniff.

"She ain't goin' to carry that rag doll to the store?" said she.

"She likes to," replied Old Woman Magoun, in a half-shamed yet defiantly extenuating voice.

"Some girls at her age is thinkin' about beaux instead of rag dolls," said Sally Jinks.

The grandmother bristled, "Lily ain't big nor old for her age," said she. "I ain't in any hurry to have her git married. She ain't none too strong."

"She's got a good color," said Sally Jinks. She was crocheting white cotton lace, making her thick fingers fly. She really knew how to do scarcely anything except to crochet that coarse lace; somehow her heavy brain or her fingers had mastered that.

"I know she's got a beautiful color," replied Old Woman Magoun, with an odd mixture of pride and anxiety, "but it comes an' goes."

"I've heard that was a bad sign," remarked Sally Jinks, loosening some thread from her spool.

"Yes, it is," said the grandmother. "She's nothin' but a baby, though she's quicker than most to learn."

Lily Barry went on her way to the store. She was clad in a scanty short frock of blue cotton; her hat was tipped back, forming an oval frame for her innocent face. She was very small, and walked like a child, with the clap-clap of little feet of babyhood. She might have been considered, from her looks, under ten.

Presently she heard footsteps behind her; she turned around a little timidly to see who was coming. When she saw a handsome, well-dressed man, she felt reassured. The man came alongside and glanced down carelessly at first, then his look deepened. He smiled, and Lily saw he was very handsome indeed, and that his smile was not only reassuring but wonderfully sweet and compelling.

"Well, little one," said the man, "where are you bound, you and your dolly?"

"I am going to the store to buy some salt for grandma," replied Lily, in her sweet treble. She looked up in the man's face, and he fairly started at the revelation of its innocent beauty. He regulated his pace by hers, and the two went on together. The man did not speak again at once. Lily kept glancing timidly up at him, and every time that she did so the man smiled and her confidence increased. Presently when the man's hand grasped her little childish one hanging by her side, she felt a complete trust in him. Then she smiled up at him. She felt glad that this nice man had come along, for just here the road was lonely.

After a while the man spoke. "What is your name, little one?" he asked, caressingly.

"Lily Barry."

The man started. "What is your father's name?"

"Nelson Barry," replied Lily.

The man whistled. "Is your mother dead?"

"Yes, sir."

"How old are you, my dear?"

"Fourteen," replied Lily.

The man looked at her with surprise. "As old as that?"

Lily suddenly shrank from the man. She could not have told why. She pulled her little hand from his, and he let it go with no remonstrance. She clasped both her arms around her rag doll, in order that her hand should not be free for him to grasp again.

She walked a little farther away from the man, and he looked amused.

"You still play with your doll?" he said, in a soft voice.

"Yes, sir," replied Lily. She quickened her pace and reached the store.

When Lily entered the store, Hiram Gates, the owner, was behind the counter. The only man besides in the store was Nelson Barry. He sat tipping his chair back against the wall; he was half asleep, and his handsome face was bristling with a beard of several days' growth and darkly flushed. He opened his eyes when Lily entered, the strange man following. He brought his chair down on all fours, and he looked at the man— not noticing Lily at all—with a look compounded of defiance and uneasiness.

"Hullo, Jim!" he said.

"Hullo, old man!" returned the stranger.

Lily went over to the counter and asked for the salt, in her pretty little voice. When she had paid for it and was crossing the store, Nelson Barry was on his feet.

"Well, how are you, Lily? It is Lily, isn't it?" he said.

"Yes, sir," replied Lily, faintly.

Her father bent down and, for the first time in her life, kissed her, and the whiskey odor of his breath came into her face.

Lily involuntarily started, and shrank away from him. Then she rubbed her mouth violently with her little cotton handkerchief, which she held gathered up with the rag doll.

"Damn it all! I believe she is afraid of me," said Nelson Barry, in a thick voice.

"Looks a little like it," said the other man, laughing.

"It's that damned old woman," said Nelson Barry. Then he smiled again at Lily. "I didn't know what a pretty little daughter I was blessed with," said he, and he softly stroked Lily's pink cheek under her hat.

Now Lily did not shrink from him. Hereditary instincts and nature itself were asserting themselves in the child's innocent, receptive breast.

Nelson Barry looked curiously at Lily. "How old are you, anyway, child?" he asked.

"I'll be fourteen in September," replied Lily.

"But you still play with your doll?" said Barry, laughing kindly down at her.

Lily hugged her doll more tightly, in spite of her father's kind voice. "Yes, sir," she replied.

Nelson glanced across at some glass jars filled with sticks of candy. "See here, little Lily, do you like candy?" said he.

"Yes, sir."

"Wait a minute."

Lily waited while her father went over to the counter. Soon he returned with a package of the candy.

"I don't see how you are going to carry so much," he said, smiling. "Suppose you throw away your doll?"

Lily gazed at her father and hugged the doll tightly, and there was all at once in the child's expression something mature. It became the reproach of a woman. Nelson's face sobered.

"Oh, it's all right, Lily," he said; "keep your doll. Here, I guess you can carry this candy under your arm."

Lily could not resist the candy. She obeyed Nelson's instructions for carrying it, and left the store laden. The two men also left, and walked in the opposite direction, talking busily.

When Lily reached home, her grandmother, who was watching for her, spied at once the package of candy.

"What's that?" she asked, sharply.

"My father gave it to me," answered Lily, in a faltering voice. Sally regarded her with something like alertness.

"Your father?"

"Yes, ma'am."

"Where did you see him?"

"In the store."

"He gave you this candy?"

"Yes, ma'am."

"What did he say?"

"He asked me how old I was, and—"

"And what?"

"I don't know," replied Lily; and it really seemed to her that she did not know, she was so frightened and bewildered by it all, and, more than anything else, by her grandmother's face as she questioned her.

Old Woman Magoun's face was that of one upon whom a long-anticipated blow had fallen. Sally Jinks gazed at her with a sort of stupid alarm.

Old Woman Magoun continued to gaze at her grandchild with that look of terrible solicitude, as if she saw the girl in the clutch of a tiger. "You can't remember what else he said?" she asked, fiercely, and the child began to whimper softly.

"No, ma'am," she sobbed. "I—don't know, and—"

"And what? Answer me."

"There was another man there. A real handsome man."

"Did he speak to you?" asked Old Woman Magoun.

"Yes, ma'am; he walked along with me a piece," confessed Lily, with a sob of terror and bewilderment.

"What did *he* say to you?" asked Old Woman Magoun, with a sort of despair.

Lily told, in her little, faltering, frightened voice, all of the conversation which she could recall. It sounded harmless enough, but the look of the realization of a long-expected blow never left her grandmother's face.

The sun was getting low, and the bridge was nearing completion. Soon the workmen would be crowding into the cabin for their promised supper. There became visible in the distance, far up the road, the heavily plodding figure of another woman who had agreed to come and help. Old Woman Magoun turned again to Lily.

"You go right up-stairs to your own chamber now," said she.

"Good land! ain't you goin' to let that poor child stay up and see the fun?" said Sally Jinks.

"You jest mind your own business," said Old Woman Magoun, forcibly, and Sally Jinks shrank. "You go right up there now, Lily," said the grandmother, in a softer tone, "and grandma will bring you up a nice plate of supper."

"When be you goin' to let that girl grow up?" asked Sally Jinks, when Lily had disappeared.

"She'll grow up in the Lord's good time," replied Old Woman Magoun, and there was in her voice something both sad and threatening. Sally Jinks again shrank a little.

Soon the workmen came flocking noisily into the house. Old Woman Magoun and her two helpers served the bountiful supper. Most of the men had drunk as much as, and more than, was good for them, and Old Woman Magoun had stipulated that there was to be no drinking of anything except coffee during supper.

"I'll git you as good a meal as I know how," she said, "but if I see ary one of you drinkin' a drop, I'll run you all out. If you want anything to drink, you can go up to the store afterward. That's the place for you to go to, if you've got to make hogs of yourselves. I ain't goin' to have no hogs in my house."

Old Woman Magoun was implicitly obeyed. She had a curious authority over most people when she chose to exercise it. When the supper was in full swing, she quietly stole up-stairs and carried some food to Lily. She found the girl, with the rag doll in her arms, crouching by the window in her little rocking-chair—a relic of her infancy, which she still used.

"What a noise they are makin', grandma!" she said, in a terrified whisper, as her grandmother placed the plate before her on a chair.

"They've 'most all of 'em been drinkin'. They air a passel of hogs," replied the old woman.

"Is the man that was with—with my father down there?" asked Lily, in a timid fashion. Then she fairly cowered before the look in her grandmother's eyes.

"No, he ain't; and what's more, he never will be down there if I can help it," said Old Woman Magoun, in a fierce whisper. "I know who he is. They can't cheat me. He's one of them Willises—that family the Barrys married into. They're worse than the Barrys, ef they *have* got money. Eat your supper, and put him out of your mind, child."

It was after Lily was asleep, when Old Woman Magoun was alone, clearing away her supper dishes, that Lily's father came. The door was closed, and he knocked, and the old woman knew at once who was there. The sound of that knock meant as much to her as the whir of a bomb to the defender of a fortress. She opened the door, and Nelson Barry stood there.

"Good-evening, Mrs. Magoun," he said.

Old Woman Magoun stood before him, filling up the doorway with her firm bulk.

"Good-evening, Mrs. Magoun," said Nelson Barry again.

"I ain't got no time to waste," replied the old woman, harshly. "I've got my supper dishes to clean up after them men."

She stood there and looked at him as she might have looked at a rebellious animal which she was trying to tame. The man laughed.

"It's no use," said he. "You know me of old. No human being can turn me from my way when I am once started in it. You may as well let me come in."

Old Woman Magoun entered the house, and Barry followed her.

Barry began without any preface. "Where is the child?" asked he.

"Up-stairs. She has gone to bed."

"She goes to bed early."

"Children ought to," returned the old woman, polishing a plate.

Barry laughed. "You are keeping her a child a long while," he remarked, in a soft voice which had a sting in it.

"She *is* a child," returned the old woman, defiantly.

"Her mother was only three years older when Lily was born."

The old woman made a sudden motion toward the man which seemed fairly menacing. Then she turned again to her dish-washing.

"I want her," said Barry.

"You can't have her," replied the old woman, in a still stern voice.

"I don't see how you can help yourself. You have always acknowledged that she was my child."

The old woman continued her task, but her strong back heaved. Barry regarded her with an entirely pitiless expression.

"I am going to have the girl, that is the long and short of it," he said, "and it is for her best good, too. You are a fool, or you would see it."

"Her best good?" muttered the old woman.

"Yes, her best good. What are you going to do with her, anyway? The girl is a beauty, and almost a woman grown, although you try to make out that she is a baby. You can't live forever."

"The Lord will take care of her," replied the old woman, and again she turned and faced him, and her expression was that of a prophetess.

"Very well, let Him," said Barry, easily. "All the same I'm going to have her, and I tell you it is for her best good. Jim Willis saw her this afternoon, and—"

Old Woman Magoun looked at him. "Jim Willis!" she fairly shrieked.

"Well, what of it?"

"One of them Willises!" repeated the old woman, and this time her voice was thick. It seemed almost as if she were stricken with paralysis. She did not enunciate clearly.

The man shrank a little. "Now what is the need of your making such a fuss?" he said. "I will take her, and Isabel will look out for her."

"Your half-witted sister?" said Old Woman Magoun.

"Yes, my half-witted sister. She knows more than you think."

"More wickedness."

"Perhaps. Well, a knowledge of evil is a useful thing. How are you going to avoid evil if you don't know what it is like? My sister and I will take care of my daughter."

The old woman continued to look at the man, but his eyes never fell.

Suddenly her gaze grew inconceivably keen. It was as if she saw through all externals.

"I know what it is!" she cried. "You have been playing cards and you lost, and this is the way you will pay him."

Then the man's face reddened, and he swore under his breath.

"Oh, my God!" said the old woman; and she really spoke with her eyes aloft as if addressing something outside of them both. Then she turned again to her dish-washing.

The man cast a dogged look at her back. "Well, there is no use talking. I have made up my mind," said he, "and you know me and what that means. I am going to have the girl."

"When?" said the old woman, without turning around.

"Well, I am willing to give you a week. Put her clothes in good order before she comes."

The old woman made no reply. She continued washing dishes. She even handled them so carefully that they did not rattle.

"You understand," said Barry. "Have her ready a week from to-day."

"Yes," said Old Woman Magoun, "I understand."

Nelson Barry, going up the mountain road, reflected that Old Woman Magoun had a strong character, that she understood much better than her sex in general the futility of withstanding the inevitable.

"Well," he said to Jim Willis when he reached home, "the old woman did not make such a fuss as I expected."

"Are you going to have the girl?"

"Yes; a week from to-day. Look here, Jim; you've got to stick to your promise."

"All right," said Willis. "Go you one better."

The two were playing at cards in the old parlor, once magnificent, now squalid, of the Barry house. Isabel, the half-witted sister, entered, bringing some glasses on a tray. She had learned with her feeble intellect some tricks, like a dog. One of them was the mixing of sundry drinks. She set the tray on a little stand near the two men, and watched them with her silly simper.

"Clear out now and go to bed," her brother said to her, and she obeyed.

Early the next morning Old Woman Magoun went up to Lily's little sleeping-chamber, and watched her a second as she lay asleep, with her yellow locks spread over the pillow. Then she spoke. "Lily," said she— "Lily, wake up. I am going to Greenham across the new bridge, and you can go with me."

Lily immediately sat up in bed and smiled at her grandmother. Her eyes were still misty, but the light of awakening was in them.

"Get right up," said the old woman. "You can wear your new dress if you want to."

Lily gurgled with pleasure like a baby. "And my new hat?" asked she.

"I don't care."

Old Woman Magoun and Lily started for Greenham before Barry's Ford, which kept late hours, was fairly awake. It was three miles to Greenham. The old woman said that, since the horse was a little lame, they would walk. It was a beautiful morning, with a diamond radiance of dew over everything. Her grandmother had curled Lily's hair more punctiliously than usual. The little face peeped like a rose out of two rows of golden spirals. Lily wore her new muslin dress with a pink sash, and her best hat of a fine white straw trimmed with a wreath of rosebuds; also the neatest black open-work stockings and pretty shoes. She even had white cotton gloves. When they set out, the old, heavily stepping woman, in her black gown and cape and bonnet, looked down at the little pink fluttering figure. Her face was full of the tenderest love and admiration, and yet there was something terrible about it. They crossed the new bridge—a primitive structure built of logs in a slovenly fashion. Old Woman Magoun pointed to a gap.

"Jest see that," said she. "That's the way men work."

"Men ain't very nice, be they?" said Lily, in her sweet little voice.

"No, they ain't, take them all together," replied her grandmother.

"That man that walked to the store with me was nicer than some, I guess," Lily said, in a wishful fashion. Her grandmother reached down and took the child's hand in its small cotton glove. "You hurt me, holding my hand so tight," Lily said presently, in a deprecatory little voice.

The old woman loosened her grasp. "Grandma didn't know how tight she was holding your hand," said she. "She wouldn't hurt you for nothin', except it was to save your life, or somethin' like that." She spoke with an undertone of tremendous meaning which the girl was too childish to grasp. They walked along the country road. Just before they reached Greenham they passed a stone wall overgrown with blackberry-vines, and, an unusual thing in that vicinity, a lusty spread of deadly nightshade full of berries.

"Those berries look good to eat, grandma," Lily said.

At that instant the old woman's face became something terrible to see. "You can't have any now," she said, and hurried Lily along.

"They look real nice," said Lily.

When they reached Greenham, Old Woman Magoun took her way straight to the most pretentious house there, the residence of the lawyer, whose name was Mason. Old Woman Magoun bade Lily wait in the yard for a few moments, and Lily ventured to seat herself on a bench beneath an oak-tree; then she watched with some wonder her grandmother enter the lawyer's office door at the right of the house. Presently the lawyer's wife came out and spoke to Lily under the tree. She had in her hand a little tray containing a plate of cake, a glass of milk, and an early apple. She spoke very kindly to Lily; she even kissed her, and offered her the tray of refreshments, which Lily accepted gratefully. She sat eating, with Mrs. Mason watching her, when Old Woman Magoun came out of the lawyer's office with a ghastly face.

"What are you eatin'?" she asked Lily, sharply. "Is that a sour apple?"

"I thought she might be hungry," said the lawyer's wife, with loving, melancholy eyes upon the girl.

Lily had almost finished the apple. "It's real sour, but I like it; it's real nice, grandma," she said.

"You ain't been drinkin' milk with a sour apple?"

"It was real nice milk, grandma."

"You ought never to have drunk milk and eat a sour apple," said her grandmother. "Your stomach was all out of order this mornin', an' sour apples and milk is always apt to hurt anybody."

"I don't know but they are," Mrs. Mason said, apologetically, as she stood on the green lawn with her lavender muslin sweeping around her. "I am real sorry, Mrs. Magoun. I ought to have thought. Let me get some soda for her."

"Soda never agrees with her," replied the old woman, in a harsh voice. "Come," she said to Lily, "it's time we were goin' home."

After Lily and her grandmother had disappeared down the road, Lawyer Mason came out of his office and joined his wife, who had seated herself on the bench beneath the tree. She was idle, and her face wore the expression of those who review joys forever past. She had lost a little girl, her only child, years ago, and her husband always knew when she was thinking about her. Lawyer Mason looked older than his wife; he had a dry, shrewd, slightly one-sided face.

"What do you think, Maria?" he said. "That old woman came to me with the most pressing entreaty to adopt that little girl."

"She is a beautiful little girl," said Mrs. Mason, in a slightly husky voice.

"Yes, she is a pretty child," assented the lawyer, looking pityingly at his wife; "but it is out of the question, my dear. Adopting a child is a serious measure, and in this case a child who comes from Barry's Ford."

"But the grandmother seems a very good woman," said Mrs. Mason.

"I rather think she is. I never heard a word against her. But the father! No, Maria, we cannot take a child with Barry blood in her veins. The stock has run out; it is vitiated physically and morally. It won't do, my dear."

"Her grandmother had her dressed up as pretty as a little girl could be," said Mrs. Mason, and this time the tears welled into her faithful, wistful eyes.

"Well, we can't help that," said the lawyer, as he went back to his office.

Old Woman Magoun and Lily returned, going slowly along the road to Barry's Ford. When they came to the stone wall where the blackberry-vines and the deadly nightshade grew, Lily said she was tired, and asked if she could not sit down for a few minutes. The strange look on her grandmother's face had deepened. Now and then Lily glanced at her and had a feeling as if she were looking at a stranger.

"Yes, you can set down if you want to," said Old Woman Magoun, deeply and harshly.

Lily started and looked at her, as if to make sure that it was her grandmother who spoke. Then she sat down on a stone which was comparatively free of the vines.

"Ain't you goin' to set down, grandma?" Lily asked, timidly.

"No; I don't want to get into that mess," replied her grandmother. "I ain't tired. I'll stand here."

Lily sat still; her delicate little face was flushed with heat. She extended her tiny feet in her best shoes and gazed at them. "My shoes are all over dust," said she.

"It will brush off," said her grandmother, still in that strange voice.

Lily looked around. An elm-tree in the field behind her cast a spray of branches over her head; a little cool puff of wind came on her face. She gazed at the low mountains on the horizon, in the midst of which she lived, and she sighed, for no reason that she knew. She began idly picking at the blackberry-vines; there were no berries on them; then she put her little fingers on the berries of the deadly nightshade. "These look like nice berries," she said.

Old Woman Magoun, standing stiff and straight in the road, said nothing.

"They look good to eat," said Lily.

Old Woman Magoun still said nothing, but she looked up into the ineffable blue of the sky, over which spread at intervals great white clouds shaped like wings.

Lily picked some of the deadly nightshade berries and ate them. "Why, they are real sweet," said she. "They are nice." She picked some more and ate them.

Presently her grandmother spoke. "Come," she said, "it is time we were going. I guess you have set long enough."

Lily was still eating the berries when she slipped down from the wall and followed her grandmother obediently up the road.

Before they reached home, Lily complained of being very thirsty. She stopped and made a little cup of a leaf and drank long at a mountain brook. "I am dreadful dry, but it hurts me to swallow," she said to her grandmother when she stopped drinking and joined the old woman waiting for her in the road. Her grandmother's face seemed strangely dim to her. She took hold of Lily's hand as they went on. "My stomach burns," said Lily, presently. "I want some more water."

"There is another brook a little farther on," said Old Woman Magoun, in a dull voice.

When they reached that brook, Lily stopped and drank again, but she whimpered a little over her difficulty in swallowing. "My stomach burns, too," she said, walking on, "and my throat is so dry, grandma." Old Woman Magoun held Lily's hand more tightly. "You hurt me holding my hand so tight, grandma," said Lily, looking up at her grandmother, whose face she seemed to see through a mist, and the old woman loosened her grasp.

When at last they reached home, Lily was very ill. Old Woman Magoun put her on her own bed in the little bedroom out of the kitchen. Lily lay there and moaned, and Sally Jinks came in.

"Why, what ails her?" she asked. "She looks feverish."

Lily unexpectedly answered for herself. "I ate some sour apples and drank some milk," she moaned.

"Sour apples and milk are dreadful apt to hurt anybody," said Sally Jinks. She told several people on her way home that Old Woman Magoun was dreadful careless to let Lily eat such things.

Meanwhile Lily grew worse. She suffered cruelly from the burning in her stomach, the vertigo, and the deadly nausea. "I am so sick, I am so sick, grandma," she kept moaning. She could no longer see her grandmother as she bent over her, but she could hear her talk.

Old Woman Magoun talked as Lily had never heard her talk before, as nobody had ever heard her talk before. She spoke from the depths of her soul; her voice was as tender as the coo of a dove, and it was grand and exalted. "You'll feel better very soon, little Lily," said she.

"I am so sick, grandma."

"You will feel better very soon, and then—"

"I am sick."

"You shall go to a beautiful place."

Lily moaned.

"You shall go to a beautiful place," the old woman went on.

"Where?" asked Lily, groping feebly with her cold little hands. Then she moaned again.

"A beautiful place, where the flowers grow tall."

"What color? Oh, grandma, I am so sick."

"A blue color," replied the old woman. Blue was Lily's favorite color. "A beautiful blue color, and as tall as your knees, and the flowers always stay there, and they never fade."

"Not if you pick them, grandma? Oh!"

"No, not if you pick them; they never fade, and they are so sweet you can smell them a mile off; and there are birds that sing, and all the roads have gold stones in them, and the stone walls are made of gold."

"Like the ring grandpa gave you? I am so sick, grandma."

"Yes, gold like that. And all the houses are built of silver and gold, and the people all have wings, so when they get tired walking they can fly, and—"

"I am so sick, grandma."

"And all the dolls are alive," said Old Woman Magoun. "Dolls like yours can run, and talk, and love you back again."

Lily had her poor old rag doll in bed with her, clasped close to her agonized little heart. She tried very hard with her eyes, whose pupils were so dilated that they looked black, to see her grandmother's face when she said that, but she could not. "It is dark," she moaned, feebly.

"There where you are going it is always light," said the grandmother, "and the commonest things shine like that breastpin Mrs. Lawyer Mason had on to-day."

Lily moaned pitifully, and said something incoherent. Delirium was commencing. Presently she sat straight up in bed and raved; but even then her grandmother's wonderful compelling voice had an influence over her.

"You will come to a gate with all the colors of the rainbow," said her grandmother; "and it will open, and you will go right in and walk up the gold street, and cross the field where the blue flowers come up to your knees, until you find your mother, and she will take you home where you are going to live. She has a little white room all ready for you, white curtains at the windows, and a little white looking-glass, and when you look in it you will see—"

"What will I see? I am so sick, grandma."

"You will see a face like yours, only it's an angel's; and there will be a little white bed, and you can lay down an' rest."

"Won't I be sick, grandma?" asked Lily. Then she moaned and babbled wildly, although she seemed to understand through it all what her grandmother said.

"No, you will never be sick anymore. Talkin' about sickness won't mean anything to you."

It continued. Lily talked on wildly, and her grandmother's great voice of soothing never ceased, until the child fell into a deep sleep, or what resembled sleep; but she lay stiffly in that sleep, and a candle flashed before her eyes made no impression on them.

Then it was that Nelson Barry came. Jim Willis waited outside the door. When Nelson entered he found Old Woman Magoun on her knees beside the bed, weeping with dry eyes and a might of agony which fairly shook Nelson Barry, the degenerate of a fine old race.

"Is she sick?" he asked, in a hushed voice.

Old Woman Magoun gave another terrible sob, which sounded like the gasp of one dying.

"Sally Jinks said that Lily was sick from eating milk and sour apples," said Barry, in a tremulous voice. "I remember that her mother was very sick once from eating them."

Lily lay still, and her grandmother on her knees shook with her terrible sobs.

Suddenly Nelson Barry started. "I guess I had better go to Greenham for a doctor if she's as bad as that," he said. He went close to the bed and looked at the sick child. He gave a great start. Then he felt of her hands and reached down under the bedclothes for her little feet. "Her hands and feet are like ice," he cried out. "Good God! why didn't you send for some one—for me—before? Why, she's dying; she's almost gone!"

Barry rushed out and spoke to Jim Willis, who turned pale and came in and stood by the bedside.

"She's almost gone," he said, in a hushed whisper.

"There's no use going for the doctor; she'd be dead before he got here," said Nelson, and he stood regarding the passing child with a strange, sad face—unutterably sad, because of his incapability of the truest sadness.

"Poor little thing, she's past suffering, anyhow," said the other man, and his own face also was sad with a puzzled, mystified sadness.

Lily died that night. There was quite a commotion in Barry's Ford until after the funeral, it was all so sudden, and then everything went on as usual. Old Woman Magoun continued to live as she had done before. She supported herself by the produce of her tiny farm; she was very industrious, but people said that she was a trifle touched, since every time she went over the log bridge with her eggs or her garden vegetables to sell in Greenham, she carried with her, as one might have carried an infant, Lily's old rag doll.

Noblesse (1914)

Margaret Lee encountered in her late middle age the rather singular strait of being entirely alone in the world. She was unmarried, and as far as relatives were concerned, she had none except those connected with her by ties not of blood, but by marriage.

Margaret had not married when her flesh had been comparative; later, when it had become superlative, she had no opportunities to marry. Life would have been hard enough for Margaret under any circumstances, but it was especially hard, living, as she did, with her father's stepdaughter and that daughter's husband.

Margaret's stepmother had been a child in spite of her two marriages, and a very silly, although pretty child. The daughter, Camille, was like her, although not so pretty, and the man whom Camille had married was what Margaret had been taught to regard as "common." His business pursuits were irregular and partook of mystery. He always smoked cigarettes and chewed gum. He wore loud shirts and a diamond scarfpin which had upon him the appearance of stolen goods. The gem had belonged to Margaret's own mother, but when Camille expressed a desire to present it to Jack Desmond, Margaret had yielded with no outward hesitation, but afterward she wept miserably over its loss when alone in her room. The spirit had gone out of Margaret, the little which she had possessed. She had always been a gentle, sensitive creature, and was almost helpless before the wishes of others.

After all, it had been a long time since Margaret had been able to force the ring even upon her little finger, but she had derived a small pleasure from the reflection that she owned it in its faded velvet box, hidden under laces in her top bureau drawer. She did not like to see it blazing forth from the tie of this very ordinary young man who had married Camille. Margaret had a gentle, high-bred contempt for Jack Desmond, but at the same time a vague fear of him. Jack had a measure of unscrupulous business shrewdness, which spared nothing and nobody, and that in spite of the fact that he had not succeeded.

Margaret owned the old Lee place, which had been magnificent, but of late years the expenditures had been reduced and it had deteriorated. The conservatories had been closed. There was only one horse in the stable. Jack had bought him. He was a worn-out trotter with legs carefully bandaged. Jack drove him at reckless speed, not considering those slender, braceleted legs. Jack had a racing-gig, and when in it, with striped coat, cap on one side, cigarette in mouth, lines held taut, skimming along the roads in clouds of dust, he thought himself the man and true sportsman which he was not. Some of the old Lee silver had paid for that waning trotter.

Camille adored Jack, and cared for no associations, no society, for which he was not suited. Before the trotter was bought she told Margaret that the kind of dinners which she was able to give in Fairhill were awfully slow. "If we could afford to have some men out from the city, some nice fellers that Jack knows, it would be worth while," said she, "but we have grown so hard up we can't do a thing to make it worth their while. Those men haven't got any use for a back-number old place like this. We can't take them round in autos, nor give them a chance at cards, for Jack couldn't pay if he lost, and Jack is awful honorable. We can't have the right kind of folks here for any fun. I don't propose to ask the rector and his wife, and old Mr. Harvey, or people like the Leaches."

"The Leaches are a very good old family," said Margaret, feebly.

"I don't care for good old families when they are so slow," retorted Camille. "The fellers we could have here, if we were rich enough, come from fine families, but they are up-to-date. It's no use hanging on to old silver dishes we never use and that I don't intend to spoil my hands shining. Poor Jack don't have much fun, anyway. If he wants that trotter—he says it's going dirt cheap—I think it's mean he can't have it, instead of your hanging on to a lot of out-of-style old silver; so there."

Two generations ago there had been French blood in Camille's family. She put on her clothes beautifully; she had a dark, rather fine-featured, alert little face, which gave a wrong impression, for she was essentially vulgar. Sometimes poor Margaret Lee wished that Camille had been def-initely vicious, if only she might be possessed of more of the characteris-tics of breeding. Camille so irritated Margaret in those somewhat abstruse traits called sensibilities that she felt as if she were living with a sort of spiritual nutmeg grater. Seldom did Camille speak that she did not jar Margaret, although unconsciously. Camille meant to be kind to the stout woman, whom she pitied as far as she was capable of pitying without understanding. She realized that it must be horrible to be no longer young, and so stout that one was fairly monstrous, but how hor-rible she could not with her mentality conceive. Jack also meant to be kind. He was not of the brutal—that is, intentionally brutal—type, but he had a shrewd eye to the betterment of himself, and no realization of the torture he inflicted upon those who opposed that betterment.

For a long time matters had been worse than usual financially in the Lee house. The sisters had been left in charge of the sadly dwindled estate, and had depended upon the judgment, or lack of judgment, of Jack. He approved of taking your chances and striking for larger income. The few good old grandfather securities had been sold, and wild ones from the very jungle of commerce had been substituted. Jack, like most of his type, while shrewd, was as credulous as a child. He lied himself, and expected all men to tell him the truth. Camille at his bidding mort-gaged the old place, and Margaret dared not oppose. Taxes were not paid; interest was not paid; credit was exhausted. Then the house was put up at public auction, and brought little more than sufficient to pay the creditors. Jack took the balance and staked it in a few games of chance, and of course lost. The weary trotter stumbled one day and had to be shot. Jack became desperate. He frightened Camille. He was suddenly morose. He bade Camille pack, and Margaret also, and they obeyed. Camille stowed away her crumpled finery in the bulging old trunks, and Margaret folded daintily her few remnants of past treasures. She had an old silk gown or two, which resisted with their rich honesty the inroads of time, and a few pieces of old lace, which Camille understood no bet-ter than she understood their owner.

Then Margaret and the Desmonds went to the city and lived in a hor-rible, tawdry little flat in a tawdry locality. Jack roared with bitter mirth when he saw poor Margaret forced to enter her tiny room sidewise; Camille laughed also, although she chided Jack gently. "Mean of you to make fun of poor Margaret, Jacky dear," she said.

For a few weeks Margaret's life in that flat was horrible; then it became still worse. Margaret nearly filled with her weary, ridiculous bulk her little room, and she remained there most of the time, although it was sunny and noisy, its one window giving on a courtyard strung with clothes-lines and teeming with boisterous life. Camille and Jack went trolley riding, and made shift to entertain a little, merry but questionable people, who gave them passes to vaudeville and entertained in their turn until the small hours. Unquestionably these people suggested to Jack Desmond the scheme which spelled tragedy to Margaret.

She always remembered one little dark man with keen eyes who had seen her disappearing through her door of a Sunday night when all these gay, bedraggled birds were at liberty and the fun ran high. "Great Scott!" the man had said, and Margaret had heard him demand of Jack that she be recalled. She obeyed, and the man was introduced, also the other members of the party. Margaret Lee stood in the midst of this throng and heard their repressed titters of mirth at her appearance. Everybody there was in good humor with the exception of Jack, who was still nursing his bad luck, and the little dark man, whom Jack owed. The eyes of Jack and the little dark man made Margaret cold with a terror of something, she knew not what. Before that terror the shame and mortification of her exhibition to that merry company was of no import.

She stood among them, silent, immense, clad in her dark purple silk gown spread over a great hoop skirt. A real lace collar lay softly over her enormous, billowing shoulders; real lace ruffles lay over her great, shapeless hands. Her face, the delicacy of whose features was veiled with flesh, flushed and paled. Not even flesh could subdue the sad brilliancy of her dark-blue eyes, fixed inward upon her own sad state, unregardful of the company. She made an indefinite murmur of response to the salutations given her, and then retreated. She heard the roar of laughter after she had squeezed through the door of her room. Then she heard eager conversation, of which she did not catch the real import, but which terrified her with chance expressions. She was quite sure that she was the subject of that eager discussion. She was quite sure that it boded her no good.

In a few days she knew the worst; and the worst was beyond her utmost imaginings. This was before the days of moving-picture shows; it was the day of humiliating spectacles of deformities, when inventions of amusements for the people had not progressed. It was the day of exhibitions of sad freaks of nature, calculated to provoke tears rather than laughter in the healthy-minded, and poor Margaret Lee was a chosen victim. Camille informed her in a few words of her fate. Camille was sorry for her, although not in the least understanding why she was sorry. She realized dimly that Margaret would be distressed, but she was unable from her narrow point of view to comprehend fully the whole tragedy.

"Jack has gone broke," stated Camille. "He owes Bill Stark a pile, and he can't pay a cent of it; and Jack's sense of honor about a poker debt is about the biggest thing in his character. Jack has got to pay. And Bill has a little circus, going to travel all summer, and he's offered big money for you. Jack can pay Bill what he owes him, and we'll have enough to live on, and have lots of fun going around. You hadn't ought to make a fuss about it."

Margaret, pale as death, stared at the girl, pertly slim, and common and pretty, who stared back laughingly, although still with the glimmer of uncomprehending pity in her black eyes.

"What does—he—want—me—for?" gasped Margaret.

"For a show, because you are so big," replied Camille. "You will make us all rich, Margaret. Ain't it nice?"

Then Camille screamed, the shrill raucous scream of the women of her type, for Margaret had fallen back in a dead faint, her immense bulk inert in her chair. Jack came running in alarm. Margaret had suddenly gained value in his shrewd eyes. He was as pale as she.

Finally Margaret raised her head, opened her miserable eyes, and regained her consciousness of herself and what lay before her. There was no course open but submission. She knew that from the first. All three faced destitution; she was the one financial asset, she and her poor flesh. She had to face it, and with what dignity she could muster.

Margaret had great piety. She kept constantly before her mental vision the fact in which she believed, that the world which she found so hard, and which put her to unspeakable torture, was not all.

A week elapsed before the wretched little show of which she was to be a member went on the road, and night after night she prayed. She besieged her God for strength. She never prayed for respite. Her realization of the situation and her lofty resolution prevented that. The awful, ridiculous combat was before her; there was no evasion; she prayed only for the strength which leads to victory.

However, when the time came, it was all worse than she had imagined. How could a woman gently born and bred conceive of the horrible ignominy of such a life? She was dragged hither and yon, to this and that little town. She traveled through sweltering heat on jolting trains; she slept in tents; she lived—she, Margaret Lee—on terms of equality with the common and the vulgar. Daily her absurd unwieldiness was exhibited to crowds screaming with laughter. Even her faith wavered. It seemed to her that there was nothing forevermore beyond those staring, jeering faces of silly mirth and delight at sight of her, seated in two chairs, clad in a pink spangled dress, her vast shoulders bare and sparkling with a tawdry necklace, her great, bare arms covered with brass bracelets, her hands incased in short, white kid gloves, over the fingers of which she wore a number of rings—stage properties.

Margaret became a horror to herself. At times it seemed to her that she was in the way of fairly losing her own identity. It mattered little that Camille and Jack were very kind to her, that they showed her the nice things which her terrible earnings had enabled them to have. She sat in her two chairs—the two chairs proved a most successful advertisement—with her two kid-cushiony hands clenched in her pink spangled lap, and she suffered agony of soul, which made her inner self stern and terrible, behind that great pink mask of face. And nobody realized until one sultry day when the show opened at a village in a pocket of green hills—indeed, its name was Greenhill—and Sydney Lord went to see it.

Margaret, who had schooled herself to look upon her audience as if they were not, suddenly comprehended among them another soul who understood her own. She met the eyes of the man, and a wonderful comfort, as of a cool breeze blowing over the face of clear water, came to her. She knew that the man understood. She knew that she had his fullest sympathy. She saw also a comrade in the toils of comic tragedy, for Sydney Lord was in the same case. He was a mountain of flesh. As a matter of fact, had he not been known in Greenhill and respected as a man of weight of character as well as of body, and of an old family, he would have rivaled Margaret. Beside him sat an elderly woman, sweet-faced, slightly bent as to her slender shoulders, as if with a chronic attitude of submission. She was Sydney's widowed sister, Ellen Waters. She lived with her brother and kept his house, and had no will other than his.

Sydney Lord and his sister remained when the rest of the audience had drifted out, after the privileged handshakes with the queen of the show. Every time a coarse, rustic hand reached familiarly after Margaret's Sydney shrank.

He motioned his sister to remain seated when he approached the stage. Jack Desmond, who had been exploiting Margaret, gazed at him with admiring curiosity. Sydney waved him away with a commanding gesture. "I wish to speak to her a moment. Pray leave the tent," he said, and Jack obeyed. People always obeyed Sydney Lord.

Sydney stood before Margaret, and he saw the clear crystal, which was herself, within all the flesh, clad in tawdry raiment, and she knew that he saw it.

"Good God!" said Sydney, "you are a lady!"

He continued to gaze at her, and his eyes, large and brown, became blurred; at the same time his mouth tightened.

"How came you to be in such a place as this?" demanded Sydney. He spoke almost as if he were angry with her.

Margaret explained briefly.

"It is an outrage," declared Sydney. He said it, however, rather absently. He was reflecting. "Where do you live?" he asked.

"Here."

"You mean—?"

"They make up a bed for me here, after the people have gone."

"And I suppose you had—before this—a comfortable house."

"The house which my grandfather Lee owned, the old Lee mansion-house, before we went to the city. It was a very fine old Colonial house," explained Margaret, in her finely modulated voice.

"And you had a good room?"

"The southeast chamber had always been mine. It was very large, and the furniture was old Spanish mahogany."

"And now—" said Sydney.

"Yes," said Margaret. She looked at him, and her serious blue eyes seemed to see past him. "It will not last," she said.

"What do you mean?"

"I try to learn a lesson. I am a child in the school of God. My lesson is one that always ends in peace."

"Good God!" said Sydney.

He motioned to his sister, and Ellen approached in a frightened fashion. Her brother could do no wrong, but this was the unusual, and alarmed her.

"This lady—" began Sydney.

"Miss Lee," said Margaret. "I was never married. I am Miss Margaret Lee."

"This," said Sydney, "is my sister Ellen, Mrs. Waters. Ellen, I wish you to meet Miss Lee."

Ellen took into her own Margaret's hand, and said feebly that it was a beautiful day and she hoped Miss Lee found Greenhill a pleasant place to—visit.

Sydney moved slowly out of the tent and found Jack Desmond. He was standing near with Camille, who looked her best in a pale-blue summer silk and a black hat trimmed with roses. Jack and Camille never really knew how the great man had managed, but presently Margaret had gone away with him and his sister.

Jack and Camille looked at each other.

"Oh, Jack, ought you to have let her go?" said Camille.

"What made you let her go?" asked Jack.

"I—don't know. I couldn't say anything. That man has a tremendous way with him. Goodness!"

"He is all right here in the place, anyhow," said Jack. "They look up to him. He is a big bug here. Comes of a family like Margaret's, though he hasn't got much money. Some chaps were braggin' that they had a bigger show than her right here, and I found out."

"Suppose," said Camille, "Margaret does not come back?"

"He could not keep her without bein' arrested," declared Jack, but he looked uneasy. He had, however, looked uneasy for some time. The fact was, Margaret had been very gradually losing weight. Moreover, she was not well. That very night, after the show was over, Bill Stark, the little dark man, had a talk with the Desmonds about it.

"Truth is, before long, if you don't look out, you'll have to pad her," said Bill; "and giants don't amount to a row of pins after that begins."

Camille looked worried and sulky. "She ain't very well, anyhow," said she. "I ain't going to kill Margaret."

"It's a good thing she's got a chance to have a night's rest in a house," said Bill Stark.

"The fat man has asked her to stay with him and his sister while the show is here," said Jack.

"The sister invited her," said Camille, with a little stiffness. She was common, but she had lived with Lees, and her mother had married a Lee. She knew what was due Margaret, and also due herself.

"The truth is," said Camille, "this is an awful sort of life for a woman like Margaret. She and her folks were never used to anything like it."

"Why didn't you make your beauty husband hustle and take care of her and you, then?" demanded Bill, who admired Camille, and disliked her because she had no eyes for him.

"My husband has been unfortunate. He has done the best he could," responded Camille. "Come, Jack; no use talking about it any longer. Guess Margaret will pick up. Come along. I'm tired out."

That night Margaret Lee slept in a sweet chamber with muslin curtains at the windows, in a massive old mahogany bed, much like hers which had been sacrificed at an auction sale. The bed linen was linen, and smelled of lavender. Margaret was too happy to sleep. She lay in the cool, fragrant sheets and was happy, and convinced of the presence of the God to whom she had prayed. All night Sydney Lord sat down stairs in his book-walled sanctum and studied over the situation. It was a crucial one. The great psychological moment of Sydney Lord's life for knight errantry had arrived. He studied the thing from every point of view. There was no romance about it. These were hard, sordid, tragic, ludicrous facts with which he had to deal. He knew to a nicety the agonies which Margaret suffered. He knew, because of his own capacity for sufferings of like stress. "And she is a woman and a lady," he said, aloud.

If Sydney had been rich enough, the matter would have been simple. He could have paid Jack and Camille enough to quiet them, and Margaret could have lived with him and his sister and their two old servants. But he was not rich; he was even poor. The price to be paid for Margaret's liberty was a bitter one, but it was that or nothing. Sydney faced it. He looked about the room. To him the walls lined with the dull gleams of old books were lovely. There was an oil portrait of his mother over the mantelshelf. The weather was warm now, and there was no need for a hearth fire, but how exquisitely homelike and dear that room could be when the snow drove outside and there was the leap of flame on the hearth! Sydney was a scholar and a gentleman. He had led a gentle and sequestered life. Here in his native village there were none to gibe and sneer. The contrast of the traveling show would be as great for him as it had been for Margaret, but he was the male of the species, and she the female. Chivalry, racial, harking back to the beginning of nobility in the human, to its earliest dawn, fired Sydney. The pale daylight invaded the study. Sydney, as truly as any knight of old, had girded himself, and with no hope, no thought of reward, for the battle in the eternal service of the strong for the weak, which makes the true worth of the strong.

There was only one way. Sydney Lord took it. His sister was spared the knowledge of the truth for a long while. When she knew, she did not lament; since Sydney had taken the course, it must be right. As for Margaret, not knowing the truth, she yielded. She was really on the verge of illness. Her spirit was of too fine a strain to enable her body to endure long. When she was told that she was to remain with Sydney's sister while Sydney went away on business, she made no objection. A wonderful sense of relief, as of wings of healing being spread under her despair, was upon her. Camille came to bid her good-by.

"I hope you have a nice visit in this lovely house," said Camille, and kissed her. Camille was astute, and to be trusted. She did not betray Sydney's confidence. Sydney used a disguise—a dark wig over his partially bald head and a little make-up—and he traveled about with the show and sat on three chairs, and shook hands with the gaping crowd, and was curiously happy. It was discomfort; it was ignominy; it was maddening to support by the exhibition of his physical deformity a perfectly worthless young couple like Jack and Camille Desmond, but it was all superbly ennobling for the man himself.

Always as he sat on his three chairs, immense, grotesque—the more grotesque for his splendid dignity of bearing—there was in his soul of a gallant gentleman the consciousness of that other, whom he was shielding from a similar ordeal. Compassion and generosity, so great that they comprehended love itself and excelled its highest type, irradiated the whole being of the fat man exposed to the gaze of his inferiors. Chivalry, which rendered him almost godlike, strengthened him for his task. Sydney thought always of Margaret as distinct from her physical self, a sort of crystalline, angelic soul, with no encumbrance of earth. He achieved a purely spiritual conception of her. And Margaret, living again her gentle lady life, was likewise ennobled by a gratitude which transformed her. Always a clear and beautiful soul, she gave out new lights of character like a jewel in the sun. And she also thought of Sydney as distinct from his physical self. The consciousness of the two human beings, one of the other, was a consciousness as of two wonderful lines of good and beauty, moving forever parallel, separate, and inseparable in an eternal harmony of spirit.

Grace King
(1852–1932)

hen Grace King was nine years old, New Orleans fell to Federal troops, and her mother fled the occupied city with her children to hide downriver at a plantation. After the war the family returned but had lost their home and property. Grace was educated in a French Creole school in New Orleans, and determined to be a writer; but after her father died in 1881, she feared that she would have to give up her plans. Yet she kept writing, and published her first novel in 1888. In "The Little Convent Girl," collected in *Balcony Stories* (1893), King wrote hauntingly about race and identity in the South after the Civil War. But after *Balcony Stories*, King did not publish any books of fiction for twenty-three years. Instead, she wrote biographies and histories. Until the end of her life she could not untangle the mixed threads of her identity as Southerner, woman, and writer.

The Little Convent Girl (1893)

She was coming down on the boat from Cincinnati, the little convent girl. Two sisters had brought her aboard. They gave her in charge of the captain, got her a state-room, saw that the new little trunk was put into it, hung the new little satchel up on the wall, showed her how to bolt the door at night, shook hands with her for good-by (good-bys have really no significance for sisters), and left her there. After a while the bells all rang, and the boat, in the awkward elephantine fashion of boats, got into midstream. The chambermaid found her sitting on the chair in the stateroom where the sisters had left her, and showed her how to sit on a chair in the saloon. And there she sat until the captain came and hunted her up for supper. She could not do anything of herself; she had to be initiated into everything by some one else.

She was known on the boat only as "the little convent girl." Her name, of course, was registered in the clerk's office, but on a steamboat no one thinks of consulting the clerk's ledger. It is always the little widow, the fat madam, the tall colonel, the parson, etc. The captain, who pronounced by the letter, always called her the little con*vent* girl. She was the beau-ideal of the little convent girl. She never raised her eyes except when spoken to. Of course she never spoke first, even to the chambermaid, and when she did speak it was in the wee, shy, furtive voice one might imagine a just-budding violet to have; and she walked with such soft, easy, carefully calculated steps that one naturally felt the penalties that must have secured them—penalties dictated by a black code of deportment.

She was dressed in deep mourning. Her black straw hat was trimmed with stiff new crape, and her stiff new bombazine dress had crape collar and cuffs. She wore her hair in two long plaits fastened around her head tight and fast. Her hair had a strong inclination to curl, but that had been taken out of it as austerely as the noise out of her footfalls. Her hair was as black as her dress; her eyes, when one saw them, seemed blacker than either, on account of the bluishness of the white surrounding the pupil. Her eyelashes were almost as thick as the black veil which the sisters had fastened around her hat with an extra pin the very last thing before leaving. She had a round little face, and a tiny pointed chin; her mouth was slightly protuberant from the teeth, over which she tried to keep her lips well shut, the effort giving them a pathetic little forced expression. Her complexion was sallow, a pale sallow, the complexion of a brunette bleached in darkened rooms. The only color about her was a blue taffeta ribbon from which a large silver medal of the Virgin hung over the place where a breastpin should have been. She was so little, so little, although she was eighteen, as the sisters told the captain; otherwise they would not have permitted her to travel all the way to New Orleans alone.

Unless the captain or the clerk remembered to fetch her out in front, she would sit all day in the cabin, in the same place, crocheting lace, her spool of thread and box of patterns in her lap, on the handkerchief spread to save her new dress. Never leaning back—oh, no! always straight and stiff, as if the conventual back board were there within call. She would eat only convent fare at first, notwithstanding the importunities of the waiters, and the jocularities of the captain, and particularly of the clerk. Every one knows the fund of humor possessed by a steamboat clerk, and what a field for display the table at meal-times affords. On Friday she fasted rigidly, and she never began to eat, or finished, without a little Latin movement of the lips and a sign of the cross. And always at six o'clock of the evening she remembered the angelus, although there was no church bell to remind her of it.

She was in mourning for her father, the sisters told the captain, and she was going to New Orleans to her mother. She had not seen her mother since she was an infant, on account of some disagreement between the parents, in consequence of which the father had brought her to Cincinnati, and placed her in the convent. There she had been for twelve years, only going to her father for vacations and holidays. So long as the father lived he would never let the child have any communication with her mother. Now that he was dead all that was changed, and the first thing that the girl herself wanted to do was to go to her mother.

The mother superior had arranged it all with the mother of the girl, who was to come personally to the boat in New Orleans, and receive her child from the captain, presenting a letter from the mother superior, a facsimile of which the sisters gave the captain.

It is a long voyage from Cincinnati to New Orleans, the rivers doing their best to make it interminable, embroidering themselves *ad libitum* all over the country. Every five miles, and sometimes oftener, the boat would stop to put off or take on freight, if not both. The little convent girl, sitting in the cabin, had her terrible frights at first from the hideous noises attendant on these landings—the whistles, the ringings of the bells, the running to and fro, the shouting. Every time she thought it was shipwreck, death, judgment, purgatory; and her sins! her sins! She would drop her crochet, and clutch her prayer-beads from her pocket, and relax the constraint over her lips, which would go to rattling off prayers with the velocity of a relaxed windlass. That was at first, before the captain took to fetching her out in front to see the boat make a landing. Then she got to liking it so much that she would stay all day just where the captain put her, going inside only for her meals. She forgot herself at times so much that she would draw her chair a little closer to the railing, and put up her veil, actually, to see better. No one ever usurped her place, quite in front, or intruded upon her either with word or look; for every one learned to know her shyness, and began to feel a personal interest in her, and all wanted the little convent girl to see everything that she possibly could.

And it was worth seeing—the balancing and *chasséing* and waltzing of the cumbersome old boat to make a landing. It seemed to be always attended with the difficulty and the improbability of a new enterprise; and the relief when it did sidle up anywhere within rope's-throw of the spot aimed at! And the roustabout throwing the rope from the perilous end of the dangling gang-plank! And the dangling roustabouts hanging like drops of water from it—dropping sometimes twenty feet to the land, and not infrequently into the river itself. And then what a rolling of barrels, and shouldering of sacks, and singing of Jim Crow songs, and pacing of Jim Crow steps; and black skins glistening through torn shirts, and white teeth gleaming through red lips, and laughing, and talking and—bewildering! entrancing! Surely the little convent girl in her convent walls never dreamed of so much unpunished noise and movement in the world!

The first time she heard the mate—it must have been like the first time woman ever heard man—curse and swear, she turned pale, and ran quickly, quickly into the saloon, and—came out again? No, indeed! not with all the soul she had to save, and all the other sins on her conscience. She shook her head resolutely, and was not seen in her chair on deck again until the captain not only reassured her, but guaranteed his reassurance. And after that, whenever the boat was about to make a landing, the mate would first glance up to the guards, and if the little convent girl was sitting there he would change his invective to sarcasm, and politely request the colored gentlemen not to hurry themselves—on no account whatever; to take their time about shoving out the plank; to send the rope ashore by post-office—write him when it got there; begging them not to strain their backs; calling them mister, colonel, major, general, prince, and your royal highness, which was vastly amusing. At night, however, or when the little convent girl was not there, language flowed in its natural curve, the mate swearing like a pagan to make up for lost time.

The captain forgot himself one day: it was when the boat ran aground in the most unexpected manner and place, and he went to work to express his opinion, as only steamboat captains can, of the pilot, mate, engineer, crew, boat, river, country, and the world in general, ringing the bell, first to back, then to head, shouting himself hoarser than his own whistle—when he chanced to see the little black figure hurrying through the chaos on the deck; and the captain stuck as fast aground in midstream as the boat had done.

In the evening the little convent girl would be taken on the upper deck, and going up the steep stairs there was such confusion, to keep the black skirts well over the stiff white petticoats; and, coming down, such blushing when suspicion would cross the unprepared face that a rim of white stocking might be visible; and the thin feet, laced so tightly in the glossy new leather boots, would cling to each successive step as if they could never, never make another venture; and then one boot would (there is but that word) hesitate out, and feel and feel around, and have such a pause of helpless agony as if indeed the next step must have been wilfully removed, or was nowhere to be found on the wide, wide earth.

It was a miracle that the pilot ever got her up into the pilot-house; but pilots have a lonely time, and do not hesitate even at miracles when there is a chance for company. He would place a box for her to climb to the tall bench behind the wheel, and he would arrange the cushions, and open a window here to let in air, and shut one there to cut off a draft, as if there could be no tenderer consideration in life for him than her comfort. And he would talk of the river to her, explain the chart, pointing out eddies, whirlpools, shoals, depths, new beds, old beds, cut-offs, caving banks, and making banks, as exquisitely and respectfully as if she had been the River Commission.

It was his opinion that there was as great a river as the Mississippi flowing directly under it—an underself of a river, as much a counterpart of the other as the second story of a house is of the first; in fact, he said they were navigating through the upper story. Whirlpools were holes in the floor of the upper river, so to speak; eddies were rifts and cracks. And deep under the earth, hurrying toward the subterranean stream, were other streams, small and great, but all deep, hurrying to and from that great mother-stream underneath, just as the small and great overground streams hurry to and from their mother Mississippi. It was almost more than the little convent girl could take in: at least such was the expression of her eyes; for they opened as all eyes have to open at pilot stories. And he knew as much of astronomy as he did of hydrology, could call the stars by name, and define the shapes of the constellations; and she, who had studied astronomy at the convent, was charmed to find that what she had learned was all true. It was in the pilot-house, one night, that she forgot herself for the first time in her life, and stayed up until after nine o'clock. Although she appeared almost intoxicated at the wild pleasure, she was immediately overwhelmed at the wickedness of it, and observed much more rigidity of conduct thereafter. The engineer, the boiler-men, the firemen, the stokers, they all knew when the little convent girl was up in the pilot-house: the speaking-tube became so mild and gentle.

With all the delays of river and boat, however, there is an end to the journey from Cincinnati to New Orleans. The latter city, which at one time to the impatient seemed at the terminus of the never, began, all of a sudden, one day to make its nearingness felt; and from that period every other interest paled before the interest in the immanence of arrival into port, and the whole boat was seized with a panic of preparation, the little convent girl with the others. Although so immaculate was she in person and effects that she might have been struck with a landing, as some good people might be struck with death, at any moment without fear of results, her trunk was packed and repacked, her satchel arranged and rearranged, and, the last day, her hair was brushed and plaited and smoothed over and over again until the very last glimmer of a curl disappeared. Her dress was whisked, as if for microscopic inspection; her face was washed; and her finger-nails were scrubbed with the hard convent nail-brush, until the disciplined little tips ached with a pristine soreness. And still there were hours to wait, and still the boat added up delays. But she arrived at last, after all, with not more than the usual and expected difference between the actual and the advertised time of arrival.

There was extra blowing and extra ringing, shouting, commanding, rushing up the gangway and rushing down the gangway. The clerks, sitting behind tables on the first deck, were plied, in the twinkling of an eye, with estimates, receipts, charges, countercharges, claims, reclaims, demands, questions, accusations, threats, all at topmost voices. None but steamboat clerks could have stood it. And there were throngs composed of individuals every one of whom wanted to see the captain first and at once: and those who could not get to him shouted over the heads of the others; and as usual he lost his temper and politeness, and began to do what he termed "hustle."

"Captain! Captain!" a voice called him to where a hand plucked his sleeve, and a letter was thrust toward him. "The cross, and the name of the convent." He recognized the envelope of the mother superior. He read the duplicate of the letter given by the sisters. He looked at the woman—the mother—casually, then again and again.

The little convent girl saw him coming, leading some one toward her. She rose. The captain took her hand first, before the other greeting, "Good-by, my dear," he said. He tried to add something else, but seemed undetermined what. "Be a good little girl—" It was evidently all he could think of. Nodding to the woman behind him, he turned on his heel, and left.

One of the deck-hands was sent to fetch her trunk. He walked out behind them, through the cabin, and the crowd on deck, down the stairs, and out over the gangway. The little convent girl and her mother went with hands tightly clasped. She did not turn her eyes to the right or left, or once (what all passengers do) look backward at the boat which, however slowly, had carried her surely over dangers that she wot not of. All looked at her as she passed. All wanted to say good-by to the little convent girl, to see the mother who had been deprived of her so long. Some expressed surprise in a whistle; some in other ways. All exclaimed audibly, or to themselves, "Colored!"

It takes about a month to make the round trip from New Orleans to

Cincinnati and back, counting five days' stoppage in New Orleans. It was a month to a day when the steamboat came puffing and blowing up to the wharf again, like a stout dowager after too long a walk; and the same scene of confusion was enacted, as it had been enacted twelve times a year, at almost the same wharf for twenty years; and the same calm, a death calmness by contrast, followed as usual the next morning.

The decks were quiet and clean; one cargo had just been delivered, part of another stood ready on the levee to be shipped. The captain was there waiting for his business to begin, the clerk was in his office getting his books ready, the voice of the mate could be heard below, mustering the old crew out and a new crew in; for if steamboat crews have a single principle,—and there are those who deny them any,—it is never to ship twice in succession on the same boat. It was too early yet for any but roustabouts, marketers, and church-goers; so early that even the river was still partly mist-covered; only in places could the swift, dark current be seen rolling swiftly along.

"Captain!" A hand plucked at his elbow, as if not confident that the mere calling would secure attention. The captain turned. The mother of the little convent girl stood there, and she held the little convent girl by the hand. "I have brought her to see you," the woman said. "You were so kind—and she is so quiet, so still, all the time, I thought it would do her a pleasure."

She spoke with an accent, and with embarrassment; otherwise one would have said that she was bold and assured enough.

"She don't go nowhere, she don't do nothing but make her crochet and her prayers, so I thought I would bring her for a little visit of 'How d' ye do' to you."

There was, perhaps, some inflection in the woman's voice that might have made known, or at least awakened, the suspicion of some latent hope or intention, had the captain's ear been fine enough to detect it. There might have been something in the little convent girl's face, had his eye been more sensitive—a trifle paler, maybe, the lips a little tighter drawn, the blue ribbon a shade faded. He may have noticed that, but— And the visit of "How d' ye do" came to an end.

They walked down the stairway, the woman in front, the little convent girl—her hand released to shake hands with the captain—following, across the bared deck, out to the gangway, over to the middle of it. No one was looking, no one saw more than a flutter of white petticoats, a show of white stockings, as the little convent girl went under the water.

The roustabout dived, as the roustabouts always do, after the drowning, even at the risk of their good-for-nothing lives. The mate himself jumped overboard; but she had gone down in a whirlpool. Perhaps, as the pilot had told her whirlpools always did, it may have carried her through to the underground river, to that vast, hidden, dark Mississippi that flows beneath the one we see; for her body was never found.

Charlotte Perkins Gilman
(1860–1935)

An internationally known feminist theorist, editor, and lecturer, Charlotte Perkins Stetson Gilman wrote utopian novels, poems, stories, an autobiography, and several works of social science, but she is best known today as the author of a short story based on her own postpartum depression and treatment. After the birth of her daughter, Katharine, in 1885, she had a complete breakdown and was treated by the famous neurologist Silas Weir Mitchell, who had invented the "rest cure" for neurotic intellectual women. In his Philadelphia sanitarium, Gilman was forbidden all physical and mental activity, including writing. It was a disastrous regimen for her and almost drove her mad. In 1888 she came to the decision that she must divorce her husband Charles Walter Stetson, move to California with her child, and start a new life as a writer, or she would never recover her mental health. Her subsequent decision to let the child be raised by Stetson and his second wife created a scandal, but Gilman's rejection of conventional domesticity enabled her to have a productive career, and even to marry a more egalitarian man in 1900. Gilman's claim that the story changed Weir Mitchell's medical practice, however, is unproven.

The Yellow Wall-Paper (1892)

It is very seldom that mere ordinary people like John and myself secure ancestral halls for the summer.

A colonial mansion, a hereditary estate, I would say a haunted house, and reach the height of romantic felicity—but that would be asking too much of fate!

Still I will proudly declare that there is something queer about it.

Else, why should it be let so cheaply? And why have stood so long untenanted?

John laughs at me, of course, but one expects that in marriage.

John is practical in the extreme. He has no patience with faith, an intense horror of superstition, and he scoffs openly at any talk of things not to be felt and seen and put down in figures.

John is a physician, and *perhaps*—(I would not say it to a living soul, of course, but this is dead paper and a great relief to my mind)—*perhaps* that is one reason I do not get well faster.

You see he does not believe I am sick!

And what can one do?

If a physician of high standing, and one's own husband, assures friends and relatives that there is really nothing the matter with one but temporary nervous depression—a slight hysterical tendency—what is one to do?

My brother is also a physician, and also of high standing, and he says the same thing.

So I take phosphates or phosphites—whichever it is, and tonics, and journeys, and air, and exercise, and am absolutely forbidden to "work" until I am well again.

Personally, I disagree with their ideas.

Personally, I believe that congenial work, with excitement and change, would do me good.

But what is one to do?

I did write for a while in spite of them; but it *does* exhaust me a good deal—having to be so sly about it, or else meet with heavy opposition.

I sometimes fancy that in my condition if I had less opposition and more society and stimulus—but John says the very worst thing I can do is to think about my condition, and I confess it always makes me feel bad.

So I will let it alone and talk about the house.

The most beautiful place! It is quite alone, standing well back from the road, quite three miles from the village. It makes me think of English places that you read about, for there are hedges and walls and gates that lock, and lots of separate little houses for the gardeners and people.

There is a *delicious* garden! I never saw such a garden—large and shady, full of box-bordered paths, and lined with long grape-covered arbors with seats under them.

There were greenhouses, too, but they are all broken now.

There was some legal trouble, I believe, something about the heirs and co-heirs; anyhow, the place has been empty for years.

That spoils my ghostliness, I am afraid, but I don't care—there is something strange about the house—I can feel it.

I even said so to John one moonlight evening, but he said what I felt was a *draught*, and shut the window.

I get unreasonably angry with John sometimes. I'm sure I never used to be so sensitive. I think it is due to this nervous condition.

But John says if I feel so, I shall neglect proper self-control; so I take pains to control myself—before him, at least, and that makes me very tired.

I don't like our room a bit. I wanted one downstairs that opened onto the piazza and had roses all over the window, and such pretty old-fashioned chintz hangings! but John would not hear of it.

He said there was only one window and not room for two beds, and no near room for him if he took another.

He is very careful and loving, and hardly lets me stir without special direction.

I have a schedule prescription for each hour in the day; he takes all care from me, and so I feel basely ungrateful not to value it more.

He said we came here solely on my account, that I was to have perfect rest and all the air I could get. "Your exercise depends on your strength, my dear," said he, "and your food somewhat on your appetite; but air you can absorb all the time." So we took the nursery at the top of the house.

It is a big, airy room, the whole floor nearly, with windows that look all ways, and air and sunshine galore. It was nursery first and then play-room and gymnasium, I should judge; for the windows are barred for little children, and there are rings and things in the walls.

The paint and paper look as if a boys' school had used it. It is stripped off—the paper—in great patches all around the head of my bed, about as far as I can reach, and in a great place on the other side of the room low down. I never saw a worse paper in my life.

One of those sprawling flamboyant patterns committing every artistic sin.

It is dull enough to confuse the eye in following, pronounced enough to constantly irritate and provoke study, and when you follow the lame uncertain curves for a little distance they suddenly commit suicide—plunge off at outrageous angles, destroy themselves in unheard of contradictions.

The color is repellent, almost revolting; a smouldering unclean yellow, strangely faded by the slow-turning sunlight.

It is a dull yet lurid orange in some places, a sickly sulphur tint in others.

No wonder the children hated it! I should hate it myself if I had to live in this room long.

There comes John, and I must put this away,—he hates to have me write a word.

We have been here two weeks, and I haven't felt like writing before, since that first day.

I am sitting by the window now, up in this atrocious nursery, and there is nothing to hinder my writing as much as I please, save lack of strength.

John is away all day, and even some nights when his cases are serious.

I am glad my case is not serious!

But these nervous troubles are dreadfully depressing.

John does not know how much I really suffer. He knows there is no reason to suffer, and that satisfies him.

Of course it is only nervousness. It does weigh on me so not to do my duty in any way!

I meant to be such a help to John, such a real rest and comfort, and here I am a comparative burden already!

Nobody would believe what an effort it is to do what little I am able,— to dress and entertain, and order things.

It is fortunate Mary is so good with the baby. Such a dear baby!

And yet I *cannot* be with him, it makes me so nervous.

I suppose John never was nervous in his life. He laughs at me so about this wall-paper!

At first he meant to repaper the room, but afterwards he said that I was letting it get the better of me, and that nothing was worse for a nervous patient than to give way to such fancies.

He said that after the wall-paper was changed it would be the heavy bedstead, and then the barred windows, and then that gate at the head of the stairs, and so on.

"You know the place is doing you good," he said, "and really, dear, I don't care to renovate the house just for a three months' rental."

"Then do let us go downstairs," I said, "there are such pretty rooms there."

Then he took me in his arms and called me a blessed little goose, and said he would go down cellar, if I wished, and have it whitewashed into the bargain.

But he is right enough about the beds and windows and things.

It is an airy and comfortable room as anyone need wish, and, of course, I would not be so silly as to make him uncomfortable just for a whim.

I'm really getting quite fond of the big room, all but that horrid paper.

Out of one window I can see the garden, those mysterious deep-shaded arbors, the riotous old-fashioned flowers, and bushes and gnarly trees.

Out of another I get a lovely view of the bay and a little private wharf belonging to the estate. There is a beautiful shaded lane that runs down there from the house. I always fancy I see people walking in these numerous paths and arbors, but John has cautioned me not to give way to fancy in the least. He says that with my imaginative power and habit of story-making, a nervous weakness like mine is sure to lead to all manner of excited fancies, and that I ought to use my will and good sense to check the tendency. So I try.

I think sometimes that if I were only well enough to write a little it would relieve the press of ideas and rest me.

But I find I get pretty tired when I try.

It is so discouraging not to have any advice and companionship about my work. When I get really well, John says we will ask Cousin Henry and Julia down for a long visit; but he says he would as soon put fireworks in my pillow-case as to let me have those stimulating people about now.

I wish I could get well faster.

But I must not think about that. This paper looks to me as if it knew what a vicious influence it had!

There is a recurrent spot where the pattern lolls like a broken neck and two bulbous eyes stare at you upside down.

I get positively angry with the impertinence of it and the everlasting-ness. Up and down and sideways they crawl, and those absurd, unblinking eyes are everywhere. There is one place where two breadths didn't match, and the eyes go all up and down the line, one a little higher than the other.

I never saw so much expression in an inanimate thing before, and we all know how much expression they have! I used to lie awake as a child and get more entertainment and terror out of blank walls and plain furniture than most children could find in a toy-store.

I remember what a kindly wink the knobs of our big, old bureau used to have, and there was one chair that always seemed like a strong friend.

I used to feel that if any of the other things looked too fierce I could always hop into that chair and be safe.

The furniture in this room is no worse than inharmonious, however, for we had to bring it all from downstairs. I suppose when this was used as a playroom they had to take the nursery things out, and no wonder! I never saw such ravages as the children have made here.

The wall-paper, as I said before, is torn off in spots, and it sticketh closer than a brother—they must have had perseverance as well as hatred.

Then the floor is scratched and gouged and splintered, the plaster itself is dug out here and there, and this great heavy bed, which is all we found in the room, looks as if it had been through the wars.

But I don't mind it a bit—only the paper.

There comes John's sister. Such a dear girl as she is, and so careful of me! I must not let her find me writing.

She is a perfect and enthusiastic housekeeper, and hopes for no better profession. I verily believe she thinks it is the writing which made me sick!

But I can write when she is out, and see her a long way off from these windows.

There is one that commands the road, a lovely shaded winding road, and one that just looks off over the country. A lovely country, too, full of great elms and velvet meadows.

This wallpaper has a kind of sub-pattern in a different shade, a particularly irritating one, for you can only see it in certain lights, and not clearly then.

But in the places where it isn't faded and where the sun is just so—I can see a strange, provoking, formless sort of figure, that seems to skulk about behind that silly and conspicuous front design.

There's sister on the stairs!

Well, the Fourth of July is over! The people are all gone and I am tired out. John thought it might do me good to see a little company, so we just had mother and Nellie and the children down for a week.

Of course I didn't do a thing. Jennie sees to everything now.

But it tired me all the same.

John says if I don't pick up faster he shall send me to Weir Mitchell in the fall.

But I don't want to go there at all. I had a friend who was in his hands once, and she says he is just like John and my brother, only more so!

Besides, it is such an undertaking to go so far.

I don't feel as if it was worthwhile to turn my hand over for anything, and I'm getting dreadfully fretful and querulous.

I cry at nothing, and cry most of the time.

Of course I don't when John is here, or anybody else, but when I am alone.

And I am alone a good deal just now. John is kept in town very often by serious cases, and Jennie is good and lets me alone when I want her to.

So I walk a little in the garden or down that lovely lane, sit on the porch under the roses, and lie down up here a good deal.

I'm getting really fond of the room in spite of the wallpaper. Perhaps *because* of the wallpaper.

It dwells in my mind so!

I lie here on this great immovable bed—it is nailed down, I believe—and follow that pattern about by the hour. It is as good as gymnastics, I assure you. I start, we'll say, at the bottom, down in the corner over there where it has not been touched, and I determine for the thousandth time that I *will* follow that pointless pattern to some sort of a conclusion.

I know a little of the principle of design, and I know this thing was not arranged on any laws of radiation, or alternation, or repetition, or symmetry, or anything else that I ever heard of.

It is repeated, of course, by the breadths, but not otherwise.

Looked at in one way each breadth stands alone, the bloated curves and flourishes—a kind of "debased Romanesque" with *delirium tremens*—go waddling up and down in isolated columns of fatuity.

But, on the other hand, they connect diagonally, and the sprawling outlines run off in great slanting waves of optic horror, like a lot of wallowing seaweeds in full chase.

The whole thing goes horizontally, too, at least it seems so, and I exhaust myself in trying to distinguish the order of its going in that direction.

They have used a horizontal breadth for a frieze, and that adds wonderfully to the confusion.

There is one end of the room where it is almost intact, and there, when the crosslights fade and the low sun shines directly upon it, I can almost fancy radiation after all,—the interminable grotesques seem to form around a common centre and rush off in headlong plunges of equal distraction.

It makes me tired to follow it. I will take a nap, I guess.

I don't know why I should write this.

I don't want to.

I don't feel able.

And I know John would think it absurd. But I *must* say what I feel and think in some way—it is such a relief!

But the effort is getting to be greater than the relief.

Half the time now I am awfully lazy, and lie down ever so much.

John says I mustn't lose my strength, and has me take cod liver oil and lots of tonics and things, to say nothing of ale and wine and rare meat.

Dear John! He loves me very dearly, and hates to have me sick. I tried to have a real earnest reasonable talk with him the other day, and tell him how I wish he would let me go and make a visit to Cousin Henry and Julia.

But he said I wasn't able to go, nor able to stand it after I got there; and I did not make out a very good case for myself, for I was crying before I had finished.

It is getting to be a great effort for me to think straight. Just this nervous weakness I suppose.

And dear John gathered me up in his arms, and just carried me upstairs and laid me on the bed, and sat by me and read to me till it tired my head.

He said I was his darling and his comfort and all he had, and that I must take care of myself for his sake, and keep well.

He says no one but myself can help me out of it, that I must use my will and self-control and not let any silly fancies run away with me.

There's one comfort, the baby is well and happy, and does not have to occupy this nursery with the horrid wall-paper.

If we had not used it, that blessed child would have! What a fortunate escape! Why, I wouldn't have a child of mine, an impressionable little thing, live in such a room for worlds.

I never thought of it before, but it is lucky that John kept me here after all, I can stand it so much easier than a baby, you see.

Of course I never mention it to them any more—I am too wise, but I keep watch of it all the same.

There are things in the wall-paper that nobody knows but me, or ever will.

Behind that outside pattern the dim shapes get clearer every day.

It is always the same shape, only very numerous.

And it is like a woman stooping down and creeping about behind that pattern. I don't like it a bit. I wonder—I begin to think—I wish John would take me away from here!

It is so hard to talk with John about my case, because he is so wise, and because he loves me so.

But I tried it last night.

It was moonlight. The moon shines in all around just as the sun does.

I hate to see it sometimes, it creeps so slowly, and always comes in by one window or another.

John was asleep and I hated to waken him, so I kept still and watched the moonlight on that undulating wallpaper till I felt creepy.

The faint figure behind seemed to shake the pattern, just as if she wanted to get out.

I got up softly and went to feel and see if the paper *did* move, and when I came back John was awake.

"What is it, little girl?" he said. "Don't go walking about like that— you'll get cold."

I thought it was a good time to talk, so I told him that I really was not gaining here, and that I wished he would take me away.

"Why, darling!" said he, "our lease will be up in three weeks, and I can't see how to leave before.

"The repairs are not done at home, and I cannot possibly leave town just now. Of course if you were in any danger, I could and would, but you really are better, dear, whether you can see it or not. I am a doctor, dear, and I know. You are gaining flesh and color, your appetite is better, I feel really much easier about you."

"I don't weigh a bit more," said I, "nor as much; and my appetite may be better in the evening when you are here but it is worse in the morning when you are away!"

"Bless her little heart!" said he with a big hug, "she shall be as sick as she pleases! But now let's improve the shining hours by going to sleep, and talk about it in the morning!"

"And you won't go away?" I asked gloomily.

"Why, how can I, dear? It is only three weeks more and then we will take a nice little trip of a few days while Jennie is getting the house ready. Really dear you are better!"

"Better in body perhaps—" I began, and stopped short, for he sat up straight and looked at me with such a stern, reproachful look that I could not say another word.

"My darling," said he, "I beg of you, for my sake and for our child's sake, as well as for your own, that you will never for one instant let that idea enter your mind! There is nothing so dangerous, so fascinating, to a temperament like yours. It is a false and foolish fancy. Can you trust me as a physician when I tell you so?"

So of course I said no more on that score, and we went to sleep before long. He thought I was asleep first, but I wasn't, and lay there for hours trying to decide whether that front pattern and the back pattern really did move together or separately.

On a pattern like this, by daylight, there is a lack of sequence, a defiance of law, that is a constant irritant to a normal mind.

The color is hideous enough, and unreliable enough, and infuriating enough, but the pattern is torturing.

You think you have mastered it, but just as you get well underway in following, it turns a back somersault and there you are. It slaps you in the face, knocks you down, and tramples upon you. It is like a bad dream.

The outside pattern is a florid arabesque, reminding one of a fungus. If you can imagine a toadstool in joints, an interminable string of toadstools, budding and sprouting in endless convolutions—why, that is something like it.

That is, sometimes!

There is one marked peculiarity about this paper, a thing nobody seems to notice but myself, and that is that it changes as the light changes.

When the sun shoots in through the east window—I always watch for that first long, straight ray—it changes so quickly that I never can quite believe it.

That is why I watch it always.

By moonlight—the moon shines in all night when there is a moon—I wouldn't know it was the same paper.

At night in any kind of light, in twilight, candlelight, lamplight, and worst of all by moonlight, it becomes bars! The outside pattern I mean, and the woman behind it is as plain as can be.

I didn't realize for a long time what the thing was that showed behind, that dim sub-pattern, but now I am quite sure it is a woman.

By daylight she is subdued, quiet. I fancy it is the pattern that keeps her so still. It is so puzzling. It keeps me quiet by the hour.

I lie down ever so much now. John says it is good for me, and to sleep all I can.

Indeed he started the habit by making me lie down for an hour after each meal.

It is a very bad habit I am convinced, for you see I don't sleep.

And that cultivates deceit, for I don't tell them I'm awake—O no!

The fact is I am getting a little afraid of John.

He seems very queer sometimes, and even Jennie has an inexplicable look.

It strikes me occasionally, just as a scientific hypothesis,—that perhaps it is the paper!

I have watched John when he did not know I was looking, and come into the room suddenly on the most innocent excuses, and I've caught him several times *looking at the paper*! And Jennie too. I caught Jennie with her hand on it once.

She didn't know I was in the room, and when I asked her in a quiet, a very quiet voice, with the most restrained manner possible, what she was doing with the paper—she turned around as if she had been caught stealing, and looked quite angry—asked me why I should frighten her so!

Then she said that the paper stained everything it touched, that she had found yellow smooches on all my clothes and John's, and she wished we would be more careful!

Did not that sound innocent? But I know she was studying that pattern, and I am determined that nobody shall find it out but myself!

Life is very much more exciting now than it used to be. You see I have something more to expect, to look forward to, to watch. I really do eat better, and am more quiet than I was.

John is so pleased to see me improve! He laughed a little the other day, and said I seemed to be flourishing in spite of my wall-paper.

I turned it off with a laugh. I had no intention of telling him it was *because* of the wall-paper—he would make fun of me. He might even want to take me away.

I don't want to leave now until I have found it out. There is a week more, and I think that will be enough.

I'm feeling ever so much better! I don't sleep much at night, for it is so interesting to watch developments; but I sleep a good deal in the daytime.

In the daytime it is tiresome and perplexing.

There are always new shoots on the fungus, and new shades of yellow all over it. I cannot keep count of them, though I have tried conscientiously.

It is the strangest yellow, that wall-paper! It makes me think of all the yellow things I ever saw—not beautiful ones like buttercups, but old foul, bad yellow things.

But there is something else about that paper—the smell! I noticed it the moment we came into the room, but with so much air and sun it was not bad. Now we have had a week of fog and rain, and whether the windows are open or not, the smell is here.

It creeps all over the house.

I find it hovering in the dining-room, skulking in the parlor, hiding in the hall, lying in wait for me on the stairs.

It gets into my hair.

Even when I go to ride, if I turn my head suddenly and surprise it—there is that smell!

Such a peculiar odor, too! I have spent hours in trying to analyze it, to find what it smelled like.

It is not bad—at first, and very gentle, but quite the subtlest, most enduring odor I ever met.

In this damp weather it is awful, I wake up in the night and find it hanging over me.

It used to disturb me at first. I thought seriously of burning the house—to reach the smell.

But now I am used to it. The only thing I can think of that it is like is the *color* of the paper! A yellow smell.

There is a very funny mark on this wall, low down, near the mop-board. A streak that runs round the room. It goes behind every piece of furniture, except the bed, a long, straight, even *smooch*, as if it had been rubbed over and over.

I wonder how it was done and who did it, and what they did it for. Round and round and round—round and round and round—it makes me dizzy!

I really have discovered something at last.

Through watching so much at night, when it changes so, I have finally found out.

The front pattern *does* move—and no wonder! The woman behind shakes it!

Sometimes I think there are a great many women behind, and sometimes only one, and she crawls around fast, and her crawling shakes it all over.

Then in the very bright spots she keeps still, and in the very shady spots she just takes hold of the bars and shakes them hard.

And she is all the time trying to climb through. But nobody could climb through that pattern—it strangles so; I think that is why it has so many heads.

They get through, and then the pattern strangles them off and turns them upside down, and makes their eyes white!

If those heads were covered or taken off it would not be half so bad.

I think that woman gets out in the daytime!

And I'll tell you why—privately—I've seen her!

I can see her out of every one of my windows!

It is the same woman, I know, for she is always creeping, and most women do not creep by daylight.

I see her in that long shaded lane, creeping up and down. I see her in those dark grape arbors, creeping all around the garden.

I see her on that long road under the trees, creeping along, and when a carriage comes she hides under the blackberry vines.

I don't blame her a bit. It must be very humiliating to be caught creeping by daylight!

I always lock the door when I creep by daylight. I can't do it at night, for I know John would suspect something at once.

And John is so queer now, that I don't want to irritate him. I wish he would take another room! Besides, I don't want anybody to get that woman out at night but myself.

I often wonder if I could see her out of all the windows at once.

But, turn as fast as I can, I can only see out of one at one time.

And though I always see her, she *may* be able to creep faster than I can turn!

I have watched her sometimes away off in the open country, creeping as fast as a cloud shadow in a high wind.

If only that top pattern could be gotten off from the under one! I mean to try it, little by little.

I have found out another funny thing, but I shan't tell it this time! It does not do to trust people too much.

There are only two more days to get this paper off, and I believe John is beginning to notice. I don't like the look in his eyes.

And I heard him ask Jennie a lot of professional questions, about me. She had a very good report to give.

She said I slept a good deal in the daytime.

John knows I don't sleep very well at night, for all I'm so quiet!

He asked me all sorts of questions too, and pretended to be very loving and kind.

As if I couldn't see through him!

Still, I don't wonder he acts so, sleeping under this paper for three months.

It only interests me, but I feel sure John and Jennie are secretly affected by it.

Hurrah! This is the last day, but it is enough. John to stay in town over night, and won't be out until this evening.

Jennie wanted to sleep with me—the sly thing! but I told her I should undoubtedly rest better for a night all alone.

That was clever, for really I wasn't alone a bit! As soon as it was moonlight and that poor thing began to crawl and shake the pattern, I got up and ran to help her.

I pulled and she shook, I shook and she pulled, and before morning we had peeled off yards of that paper.

A strip about as high as my head and half around the room.

And then when the sun came and that awful pattern began to laugh at me, I declared I would finish it to-day!

We go away to-morrow, and they are moving all my furniture down again to leave things as they were before.

Jennie looked at the wall in amazement, but I told her merrily that I did it out of pure spite at the vicious thing.

She laughed and said she wouldn't mind doing it herself, but I must not get tired.

How she betrayed herself that time!

But I am here, and no person touches this paper but me,—not *alive*!

She tried to get me out of the room—it was too patent! But I said it was so quiet and empty and clean now that I believed I would lie down again and sleep all I could, and not to wake me even for dinner—I would call when I woke.

So now she is gone, and the servants are gone, and the things are gone, and there is nothing left but that great bedstead nailed down, with the canvas mattress we found on it.

We shall sleep downstairs to-night, and take the boat home to-morrow.

I quite enjoy the room, now it is bare again.

How those children did tear about here!

This bedstead is fairly gnawed!

But I must get to work.

I have locked the door and thrown the key down into the front path.

I don't want to go out, and I don't want to have anybody come in, till John comes.

I want to astonish him.

I've got a rope up here that even Jennie did not find. If that woman does get out, and tries to get away, I can tie her!

But I forgot I could not reach far without anything to stand on!

This bed will *not* move!

I tried to lift and push it until I was lame, and then I got so angry I bit off a little piece at one corner—but it hurt my teeth.

Then I peeled off all the paper I could reach standing on the floor. It sticks horribly and the pattern just enjoys it! All those strangled heads and bulbous eyes and waddling fungus growths just shriek with derision!

I am getting angry enough to do something desperate. To jump out of the window would be admirable exercise, but the bars are too strong even to try.

Besides I wouldn't do it. Of course not. I know well enough that a step like that is improper and might be misconstrued.

I don't like to *look* out of the windows even—there are so many of those creeping women, and they creep so fast.

I wonder if they all come out of that wall-paper as I did?

But I am securely fastened now by my well-hidden rope—you don't get *me* out in the road there!

I suppose I shall have to get back behind the pattern when it comes night, and that is hard!

It is so pleasant to be out in this great room and creep around as I please!

I don't want to go outside. I won't, even if Jennie asks me to.

For outside you have to creep on the ground, and everything is green instead of yellow.

But here I can creep smoothly on the floor, and my shoulder just fits in that long smooch around the wall, so I cannot lose my way.

Why, there's John at the door!

It is no use, young man, you can't open it!

How he does call and pound!

Now he's crying for an axe.

It would be a shame to break down that beautiful door!

"John dear!" said I in the gentlest voice, "the key is down by the front steps, under a plantain leaf!"

That silenced him for a few moments.

Then he said—very quietly indeed, "Open the door, my darling!"

"I can't," said I. "The key is down by the front door under a plantain leaf!"

And then I said it again, several times, very gently and slowly, and said it so often that he had to go and see, and he got it of course, and came in. He stopped short by the door.

"What is the matter?" he cried. "For God's sake, what are you doing!"

I kept on creeping just the same, but I looked at him over my shoulder.

"I've got out at last," said I, "in spite of you and Jane. And I've pulled off most of the paper, so you can't put me back!"

Now why should that man have fainted? But he did, and right across my path by the wall, so that I had to creep over him every time!

Why I Wrote "The Yellow Wall-Paper" (1913)

Many and many a reader has asked that. When the story first came out, in the *New England Magazine* about 1891, a Boston physician made protest in *The Transcript*. Such a story ought not to be written, he said; it was enough to drive anyone mad to read it.

Another physician, in Kansas I think, wrote to say that it was the best description of incipient insanity he had ever seen, and—begging my pardon—had I been there?

Now the story of the story is this:

For many years I suffered from a severe and continuous nervous breakdown tending to melancholia—and beyond. During about the third year of this trouble I went, in devout faith and some faint stir of hope, to a noted specialist in nervous diseases, the best known in the country. This wise man put me to bed and applied the rest cure, to which a still-good physique responded so promptly that he concluded there was nothing much the matter with me, and sent me home with solemn advice to "live as domestic a life as far as possible," to "have but two hours' intellectual life a day," and "never to touch pen, brush or pencil again as long as I lived." This was in 1887.

I went home and obeyed those directions for some three months, and came so near the border line of utter mental ruin that I could see over.

Then, using the remnants of intelligence that remained, and helped by a wise friend, I cast the noted specialist's advice to the winds and went to work again—work, the normal life of every human being; work, in which is joy and growth and service, without which one is a pauper and a parasite; ultimately recovering some measure of power.

Being naturally moved to rejoicing by this narrow escape, I wrote "The Yellow Wall-Paper," with its embellishments and additions to carry out the ideal (I never had hallucinations or objections to my mural decorations) and sent a copy to the physician who so nearly drove me mad. He never acknowledged it.

The little book is valued by alienists and as a good specimen of one kind of literature. It has to my knowledge saved one woman from a similar fate—so terrifying her family that they let her out into normal activity and she recovered.

But the best result is this. Many years later I was told that the great specialist had admitted to friends of his that he had altered his treatment of neurasthenia since reading "The Yellow Wall-Paper."

It was not intended to drive people crazy, but to save people from being driven crazy, and it worked.

Edith Wharton
(1862–1937)

orn to an upper-class family in New York, Edith Newbold Jones had been expected to be beautiful, elegant, and well dressed, certainly not to think of herself as intelligent, creative, or sexual. She made a socially acceptable marriage in 1885, to Harvard graduate Edward Wharton, and they traveled to Europe and then lived elegantly in New York. But Edith's repressed ambition and intellectual frustration led her to a neurasthenic breakdown at the end of the 1890s; she was treated by a rest cure in Philadelphia at the clinic of Silas Weir Mitchell. The treatment worked better for Wharton than for Charlotte Perkins Gilman. By 1899, she had published her first book of short stories, *The Greater Inclination*, and started to think of herself as an artist. With her first novel, *The House of Mirth* (1905), Wharton made herself into a professional writer. Two years later, at the age of forty-six, she had an ecstatic sexual affair in Paris with the bisexual American journalist Morton Fullerton. The affair did not last, but in 1913 she divorced her husband; and for most of her literary career as a distinguished novelist, she lived in Paris. Wharton's "The Valley of Childish Things," published in 1896, was one of the many parables and fairy tales written by American women at the end of the century that acknowledged the bitter disappointments of their romantic ideals and their longing for a more significant life.

The Valley of Childish Things (1896)

I

Once upon a time a number of children lived together in the Valley of Childish Things, playing all manner of delightful games, and studying the same lesson-books. But one day a little girl, one of their number, decided that it was time to see something of the world about which the lesson-books had taught her; and as none of the other children cared to leave their games, she set out alone to climb the pass which led out of the valley.

It was a hard climb, but at length she reached a cold, bleak table-land beyond the mountains. Here she saw cities and men, and learned many useful arts, and in so doing grew to be a woman. But the table-land was bleak and cold, and when she had served her apprenticeship she decided to return to her old companions in the Valley of Childish Things, and work with them instead of with strangers.

It was a weary way back, and her feet were bruised by the stones, and her face was beaten by the weather; but half way down the pass she met a man, who kindly helped her over the roughest places. Like herself, he was lame and weather-beaten; but as soon as he spoke she recognised him as one of her old playmates. He too had been out in the world, and was going back to the valley; and on the way they talked together of the work they meant to do there. He had been a dull boy, and she had never taken much notice of him; but as she listened to his plans for building bridges and draining swamps and cutting roads through the jungle, she thought to herself, "Since he has grown into such a fine fellow, what splendid men and women my other playmates must have become!"

But what was her surprise to find, on reaching the valley, that her former companions, instead of growing into men and women, had all remained little children. Most of them were playing the same old games, and the few who affected to be working were engaged in such strenuous occupations as building mudpies and sailing paper boats in basins. As for the lad who had been the favourite companion of her studies, he was playing marbles with all the youngest boys in the valley.

At first the children seemed glad to have her back, but soon she saw that her presence interfered with their games; and when she tried to tell them of the great things that were being done on the table-land beyond the mountains, they picked up their toys and went farther down the valley to play.

Then she turned to her fellow-traveller, who was the only grown man in the valley; but he was on his knees before a dear little girl with blue eyes and a coral necklace, for whom he was making a garden out of cockle-shells and bits of glass, and broken flowers stuck in sand.

The little girl was clapping her hands and crowing (she was too young to speak articulately); and when she who had grown to be a woman laid her hand on the man's shoulder, and asked him if he did not want to set to work with her building bridges, draining swamps, and cutting roads through the jungle, he replied that at that particular moment he was too busy.

And as she turned away, he added in the kindest possible way, "Really, my dear, you ought to have taken better care of your complexion."

Sui Sin Far
(Edith Maude Eaton)
(1865–1914)

he daughter of a financially struggling English landscape painter and a Chinese mother adopted by English missionaries, Edith Maude Eaton was born in England. As a young woman, she moved to Montreal, Canada, and got a job as a journalist at the *Montreal Star* to help support her thirteen siblings. In 1888 she began publishing articles in Montreal magazines under her adopted Chinese name "Sui Sin Far" (the translation of the Chinese symbol for water lily). Moving frequently around the United States and Canada, Sui Sin Far wrote stories and articles about Chinese culture in North America, and in 1900 began publishing her sympathetic portrayals of Chinese and Chinese Americans in national magazines such as *Century* and *Ladies' Home Journal*. In "The Inferior Woman," Mrs. Spring Fragrance, the heroine of twelve of her stories about the Americanization of a Chinese wife living in Seattle, decides to become a writer and takes up questions of love, class, and culture that overturn American stereotypes.

The Inferior Woman (1912)

I

Mrs. Spring Fragrance walked through the leafy alleys of the park, admiring the flowers and listening to the birds singing. It was a beautiful afternoon with the warmth from the sun cooled by a refreshing breeze. As she walked along she meditated upon a book which she had some notion of writing. Many American women wrote books. Why should not a Chinese? She would write a book about Americans for her Chinese women friends. The American people were so interesting and mysterious. Something of pride and pleasure crept into Mrs. Spring Fragrance's heart as she pictured Fei and Sie and Mai Gwi Far listening to Lae-Choo reading her illuminating paragraphs.

As she turned down a by-path she saw Will Carman, her American neighbor's son, coming towards her, and by his side a young girl who seemed to belong to the sweet air and brightness of all the things around her. They were talking very earnestly and the eyes of the young man were on the girl's face.

"Ah!" murmured Mrs. Spring Fragrance, after one swift glance. "It is love."

She retreated behind a syringa bush, which completely screened her from view.

Up the winding path went the young couple.

"It is love," repeated Mrs. Spring Fragrance, "and it is the 'Inferior Woman.'"

She had heard about the Inferior Woman from the mother of Will Carman.

After tea that evening Mrs. Spring Fragrance stood musing at her front window. The sun hovered over the Olympic mountains like a great, golden red-bird with dark purple wings, its long tail of light trailing underneath in the waters of Puget Sound.

"How very beautiful!" exclaimed Mrs. Spring Fragrance; then she sighed.

"Why do you sigh?" asked Mr. Spring Fragrance.

"My heart is sad," answered the wife.

"Is the cat sick?" inquired Mr. Spring Fragrance.

Mrs. Spring Fragrance shook her head. "It is not our Wise One who troubles me today," she replied. "It is our neighbors. The sorrow of the Carman household is that the mother desires for her son the Superior Woman, and his heart enshrines but the Inferior. I have seen them together today, and I know."

"What do you know?"

"That the Inferior Woman is the mate for young Carman."

Mr. Spring Fragrance elevated his brows. Only the day before, his wife's arguments had all been in favor of the Superior Woman. He uttered some words expressive of surprise, to which Mrs. Spring Fragrance retorted:

"Yesterday, O Great Man, I was a caterpillar!"

Just then young Carman came strolling up the path. Mr. Spring Fragrance opened the door to him. "Come in, neighbor," said he. "I have received some new books from Shanghai."

"Good," replied young Carman, who was interested in Chinese literature. While he and Mr. Spring Fragrance discussed the "Odes of Chow" and the "Sorrows of Han," Mrs. Spring Fragrance, sitting in a low easy-chair of rose-colored silk, covertly studied her visitor's countenance.

Why was his expression so much more grave than gay? It had not been so a year ago—before he had known the Inferior Woman. Mrs. Spring Fragrance noted other changes, also, both in speech and manner. "He is no longer a boy," mused she. "He is a man, and it is the work of the Inferior Woman."

"And when, Mr. Carman," she inquired, "will you bring home a daughter to your mother?"

"And when, Mrs. Spring Fragrance, do you think I should?" returned the young man.

Mrs. Spring Fragrance spread wide her fan and gazed thoughtfully over its silver edge.

"The summer moons will soon be over," said she. "You should not wait until the grass is yellow."

> *"The woodmen's blows responsive ring,*
> *As on the trees they fall,*
> *And when the birds their sweet notes sing,*
> *They to each other call.*
> *From the dark valley comes a bird,*
> *And seeks a lofty tree,*
> *Ying goes its voice, and thus it cries:*
> *'Companion, come to me'*
> *The bird, although a creature small,*
> *Upon its mate depends,*
> *And shall we men, who rank o'er all,*
> *Not seek to have our friends?"*

quoted Mr. Spring Fragrance.

Mrs. Spring Fragrance tapped his shoulder approvingly with her fan.

"I perceive," said young Carman, "that you are both allied against my peace."

"It is for your mother," replied Mrs. Spring Fragrance soothingly. "She will be happy when she knows that your affections are fixed by marriage."

There was a slight gleam of amusement in the young man's eyes as he answered: "But if my mother has no wish for a daughter—at least, no wish for the daughter I would want to give her?"

"When I first came to America," returned Mrs. Spring Fragrance, "my husband desired me to wear the American dress. I protested and declared that never would I so appear. But one day he brought home a gown fit for a fairy, and ever since then I have worn and adored the American dress."

"Mrs. Spring Fragrance," declared young Carman, "your argument is incontrovertible."

II

A young man with a determined set to his shoulders stood outside the door of a little cottage perched upon a bluff overlooking the Sound. The chill sea air was sweet with the scent of roses, and he drew in a deep breath of inspiration before he knocked.

"Are you not surprised to see me?" he inquired of the young person who opened the door.

"Not at all," replied the young person demurely.

He gave her a quick almost fierce look. At their last parting he had declared that he would not come again unless she requested him, and that she assuredly had not done.

"I wish I could make you feel," said he.

She laughed—a pretty infectious laugh which exorcised all his gloom. He looked down upon her as they stood together under the cluster of electric lights in her cozy little sitting-room. Such a slender, girlish figure! Such a soft cheek, red mouth, and firm little chin! Often in his dreams of her he had taken her into his arms and coaxed her into a good humor. But, alas! dreams are not realities, and the calm friendliness of this young person made any demonstration of tenderness well-nigh impossible. But for the shy regard of her eyes, you might have thought that he was no more to her than a friendly acquaintance.

"I hear," said she, taking up some needlework, "that your Welland case comes on tomorrow."

"Yes," answered the young lawyer, "and I have all my witnesses ready."

"So, I hear, has Mr. Greaves," she retorted. "You are going to have a hard fight."

"What of that, when in the end I'll win."

He looked over at her with a bright gleam in his eyes.

"I wouldn't be too sure," she warned demurely. "You may lose on a technicality."

He drew his chair a little nearer to her side and turned over the pages of a book lying on her work-table. On the fly-leaf was inscribed in a man's writing: "To the dear little woman whose friendship is worth a fortune."

Another book beside it bore the inscription: "With the love of all the firm, including the boys," and a volume of poems above it was dedicated to the young person "with the high regards and staunch affection" of some other masculine person.

Will Carman pushed aside these evidences of his sweetheart's popularity with his own kind and leaned across the table.

"Alice," said he, "once upon a time you admitted that you loved me."

A blush suffused the young person's countenance.

"Did I?" she queried.

"You did, indeed."

"Well?"

"Well! If you love me and I love you—"

"Oh, please!" protested the girl, covering her ears with her hands.

"I *will* please," asserted the young man. "I have come here tonight, Alice, to ask you to marry me—and at once."

"Deary me!" exclaimed the young person; but she let her needlework fall into her lap as her lover, approaching nearer, laid his arm around her shoulders and, bending his face close to hers, pleaded his most important case.

If for a moment the small mouth quivered, the firm little chin lost its firmness, and the proud little head yielded to the pressure of a lover's arm, it was only for a moment so brief and fleeting that Will Carman had hardly become aware of it before it had been passed.

"No," said the young person sorrowfully but decidedly. She had arisen and was standing on the other side of the table facing him. "I cannot marry you while your mother regards me as beneath you."

"When she knows you she will acknowledge you are above me. But I am not asking you to come to my mother, I am asking you to come to me, dear. If you will put your hand in mine and trust to me through all the coming years, no man or woman born can come between us."

But the young person shook her head.

"No," she repeated. "I will not be your wife unless your mother welcomes me with pride and pleasure."

The night air was still sweet with the perfume of roses as Will Carman passed out of the little cottage door; but he drew in no deep breath of inspiration. His impetuous Irish heart was too heavy with disappointment. It might have been a little lighter, however, had he known that the eyes of the young person who gazed after him were misty with a love and yearning beyond expression.

III

"Will Carman has failed to snare his bird," said Mr. Spring Fragrance to Mrs. Spring Fragrance. Their neighbor's son had just passed their veranda without turning to bestow upon them his usual cheerful greeting.

"It is too bad," sighed Mrs. Spring Fragrance sympathetically. She clasped her hands together and exclaimed:

"Ah, these Americans! These mysterious, inscrutable, incomprehensible Americans! Had I the divine right of learning I would put them into an immortal book!"

"The divine right of learning," echoed Mr. Spring Fragrance, "Humph!"

Mrs. Spring Fragrance looked up into her husband's face in wonderment.

"Is not the authority of the scholar, the student, almost divine?" she queried.

"So 'tis said," responded he. "So it seems."

The evening before, Mr. Spring Fragrance, together with several Seattle and San Francisco merchants, had given a dinner to a number of young students who had just arrived from China. The morning papers had devoted several columns to laudation of the students, prophecies as to their future, and the great influence which they would exercise over the destiny of their nation; but no comment whatever was made on the givers of the feast, and Mr. Spring Fragrance was therefore feeling somewhat unappreciated. Were not he and his brother merchants worthy of a little attention? If the students had come to learn things in America, they, the merchants, had accomplished things. There were those amongst them who had been instrumental in bringing several of the students to America. One of the boys was Mr. Spring Fragrance's own young brother, for whose maintenance and education he had himself sent the wherewithal every year for many years. Mr. Spring Fragrance, though well read in the Chinese classics, was not himself a scholar. As a boy he had come to the shores of America, worked his way up, and by dint of painstaking study after working hours acquired the Western language and Western business ideas. He had made money, saved money, and sent money home. The years had flown, his business had grown. Through his efforts trade between his native town and the port city in which he lived had greatly increased. A school in Canton was being builded in part with funds furnished by him and a railway syndicate, for the purpose of constructing a line of railway from the big city of Canton to his own native town, was under process of formation, with the name of Spring Fragrance at its head.

No wonder then that Mr. Spring Fragrance muttered "Humph!" when Mrs. Spring Fragrance dilated upon the "divine right of learning," and that he should feel irritated and humiliated, when, after explaining to her his grievances, she should quote in the words of Confutze: "Be not concerned that men do not know you; be only concerned that you do not know them." And he had expected wifely sympathy.

He was about to leave the room in a somewhat chilled state of mind when she surprised him again by pattering across to him and following up a low curtsy with these words:

"I bow to you as the grass bends to the wind. Allow me to detain you for just one moment."

Mr. Spring Fragrance eyed her for a moment with suspicion.

"As I have told you, O Great Man," continued Mrs. Spring Fragrance, "I desire to write an immortal book, and now that I have learned from you that it is not necessary to acquire the 'divine right of learning' in order to accomplish things, I will begin the work without delay. My first subject will be 'The Inferior Woman of America.' Please advise me how I shall best inform myself concerning her."

Mr. Spring Fragrance, perceiving that his wife was now serious, and being easily mollified, sat himself down and rubbed his head. After thinking for a few moments he replied:

"It is the way in America, when a person is to be illustrated, for the illustrator to interview the person's friends. Perhaps, my dear, you had better confer with the Superior Woman."

"Surely," cried Mrs. Spring Fragrance, "no sage was ever so wise as my Great Man."

"But I lack the 'divine right of learning,'" dryly deplored Mr. Spring Fragrance.

"I am happy to hear it," answered Mrs. Spring Fragrance. "If you were a scholar you would have no time to read American poetry and American newspapers."

Mr. Spring Fragrance laughed heartily.

"You are no Chinese woman," he teased. "You are an American."

"Please bring me my parasol and my folding fan," said Mrs. Spring Fragrance. "I am going out for a walk."

And Mr. Spring Fragrance obeyed her.

IV

"This is from Mary Carman, who is in Portland," said the mother of the Superior Woman, looking up from the reading of a letter, as her daughter came in from the garden.

"Indeed," carelessly responded Miss Evebrook.

"Yes, it's chiefly about Will."

"Oh, is it? Well, read it then, dear. I'm interested in Will Carman, because of Alice Winthrop."

"I had hoped, Ethel, at one time that you would have been interested in him for his own sake. However, this is what she writes:

"I came here chiefly to rid myself of a melancholy mood which has taken possession of me lately, and also because I cannot bear to see my boy so changed towards me, owing to his infatuation for Alice Winthrop. It is incomprehensible to me how a son of mine can find any pleasure whatever in the society of such a girl. I have traced her history, and find that she is not only uneducated in the ordinary sense, but her environment, from childhood up, has been the sordid and demoralizing one of extreme poverty and ignorance. This girl, Alice, entered a law office at the age of fourteen, supposedly to do the work of an office boy. Now, after seven years in business, through the friendship and influence of men far above her socially, she holds the position of private secretary to the most influential man in Washington—a position which by rights belongs only to a well-educated young woman of good family. Many such applied. I myself sought to have Jane Walker appointed. Is it not disheartening to our woman's cause to be compelled to realize that girls such as this one can win men over to be friends and lovers, when there are so many splendid young women who have been carefully trained to be companions and comrades of educated men?"

"Pardon me, mother," interrupted Miss Evebrook, "but I have heard enough. Mrs. Carman is your friend and a well-meaning woman sometimes; but a woman suffragist, in the true sense, she certainly is not. Mark my words: If any young man had accomplished for himself what Alice Winthrop has accomplished, Mrs. Carman could not have said enough in his praise. It is women such as Alice Winthrop who, in spite of every drawback, have raised themselves to the level of those who have had every advantage, who are the pride and glory of America. There are thousands of them, all over this land: women who have been of service to others all their years and who graduated from the university of life with honor. Women such as I, who are called the Superior Women of America, are after all nothing but school-girls in comparison."

Mrs. Evebrook eyed her daughter mutinously. "I don't see why you should feel like that," said she. "Alice is a dear bright child, and it is prejudice engendered by Mary Carman's disappointment about you and Will which is the real cause of poor Mary's bitterness towards her; but to my mind, Alice does not compare with my daughter. She would be frightened to death if she had to make a speech."

"You foolish mother!" rallied Miss Evebrook. "To stand upon a platform at woman suffrage meetings and exploit myself is certainly a great recompense to you and father for all the sacrifices you have made in my behalf. But since it pleases you, I do it with pleasure even on the nights when my beau should 'come a courting.'"

"There is many a one who would like to come, Ethel. You're the handsomest girl in this Western town—and you know it."

"Stop that, mother. You know very well I have set my mind upon having ten years' freedom; ten years in which to love, live, suffer, see the world, and learn about men (not schoolboys) before I choose one."

"Alice Winthrop is the same age as you are, and looks like a child beside you."

"Physically, maybe; but her heart and mind are better developed. She has been out in the world all her life, I only a few months."

"Your lecture last week on 'The Opposite Sex' was splendid."

"Of course. I have studied one hundred books on the subject and attended fifty lectures. All that was necessary was to repeat in an original manner what was not by any means original."

Miss Evebrook went over to a desk and took a paper therefrom.

"This," said she, "is what Alice has written me in reply to my note suggesting that she attend next week the suffrage meeting, and give some of the experiences of her business career. The object I had in view when I requested the relation of her experiences was to use them as illustrations of the suppression and oppression of women by men. Strange to say, Alice and I have never conversed on this particular subject. If we had I would not have made this request of her, nor written her as I did. Listen:

"I should dearly love to please you, but I am afraid that my experiences, if related, would not help the cause. It may be, as you say, that men prevent women from rising to their level; but if there are such men, I have not met them. Ever since, when a little girl, I walked into a law office and asked

*for work, and the senior member kindly looked me over through his
spectacles and inquired if I thought I could learn to index books, and the
junior member glanced under my hat and said: "This is a pretty little girl
and we must be pretty to her," I have loved and respected the men amongst
whom I have worked and wherever I have worked. I may have been
exceptionally fortunate, but I know this: the men for whom I have worked
and amongst whom I have spent my life, whether they have been business
or professional men, students or great lawyers and politicians, all alike
have upheld me, inspired me, advised me, taught me, given me a broad
outlook upon life for a woman; interested me in themselves and in their
work. As to corrupting my mind and my morals, as you say so many men
do, when they have young and innocent girls to deal with: As a woman I
look back over my years spent amongst business and professional men,
and see myself, as I was at first, an impressionable, ignorant little girl,
born a Bohemian, easy to lead and easy to win, but borne aloft and
morally supported by the goodness of my brother men, the men amongst
whom I have worked. That is why, dear Ethel, you will have to forgive me,
because I cannot carry out your design, and help your work, as otherwise
I would like to do."*

"That, mother," declared Miss Evebrook, "answers all Mrs. Carman's
insinuations, and should make her ashamed of herself. Can any one
know the sentiments which little Alice entertains towards men, and won-
der at her winning out as she has?"

Mrs. Evebrook was about to make a reply, when her glance happening
to stray out of the window, she noticed a pink parasol.

"Mrs. Spring Fragrance!" she ejaculated, while her daughter went to
the door and invited in the owner of the pink parasol, who was seated in
a veranda rocker calmly writing in a note-book.

"I'm so sorry that we did not hear your ring, Mrs. Spring Fragrance,"
said she.

"There is no necessity for you to sorrow," replied the little Chinese
woman. "I did not expect you to hear a ring which rang not. I failed to
pull the bell."

"You forgot, I suppose," suggested Ethel Evebrook.

"Is it wise to tell secrets?" ingenuously inquired Mrs. Spring Fra-
grance.

"Yes, to your friends. Oh, Mrs. Spring Fragrance, you are *so* refresh-
ing."

"I have pleasure, then, in confiding to you. I have an ambition to accomplish an immortal book about the Americans, and the conversation I heard through the window was so interesting to me that I thought I would take some of it down for my book before I intruded myself. With your kind permission I will translate for your correction."

"I shall be delighted—honored," said Miss Evebrook, her cheeks glowing and her laugh rippling, "if you will promise me that you will also translate for our friend, Mrs. Carman."

"Ah, yes, poor Mrs. Carman! My heart is so sad for her," murmured the little Chinese woman.

V

When the mother of Will Carman returned from Portland, the first person upon whom she called was Mrs. Spring Fragrance. Having lived in China while her late husband was in the customs service there, Mrs. Carman's prejudices did not extend to the Chinese, and ever since the Spring Fragrances had become the occupants of the villa beside the Carmans, there had been social good feeling between the American and Chinese families. Indeed, Mrs. Carman was wont to declare that amongst all her acquaintances there was not one more congenial and interesting than little Mrs. Spring Fragrance. So after she had sipped a cup of delicious tea, tasted some piquant candied limes and told Mrs. Spring Fragrance all about her visit to the Oregon city and the Chinese people she had met there, she reverted to a personal trouble confided to Mrs. Spring Fragrance some months before and dwelt upon it for more than half an hour. Then she checked herself and gazed at Mrs. Spring Fragrance in surprise. Hitherto she had found the little Chinese woman sympathetic and consoling. Chinese ideals of filial duty chimed in with her own. But today Mrs. Spring Fragrance seemed strangely uninterested and unresponsive.

"Perhaps," gently suggested the American woman, who was nothing if not sensitive, "you have some trouble yourself. If so, my dear, tell me all about it."

"Oh no!" answered Mrs. Spring Fragrance brightly. "I have no troubles to tell; but all the while I am thinking about the book I am writing."

"A book!"

"Yes, a book about Americans, an immortal book."

"My dear Mrs. Spring Fragrance!" exclaimed her visitor in amazement.

"The American woman writes books about the Chinese. Why not a Chinese woman write books about the Americans?"

"I see what you mean. Why, yes, of course. What an original idea!"

"Yes, I think that is what it is. My book I shall take from the words of others."

"What do you mean, my dear?"

"I listen to what is said, I apprehend, I write it down. Let me illustrate by the 'Inferior Woman' subject. The Inferior Woman is most interesting to me because you have told me that your son is in much love with her. My husband advised me to learn about the Inferior Woman from the Superior Woman. I go to see the Superior Woman. I sit on the veranda of the Superior Woman's house. I listen to her converse with her mother about the Inferior Woman. With the speed of flames I write down all I hear. When I enter the house the Superior Woman advises me that what I write is correct. May I read to you?"

"I shall be pleased to hear what you have written; but do not think you were wise in your choice of subject," returned Mrs. Carman somewhat primly.

"I am sorry I am not wise. Perhaps I had better not read?" said Mrs. Spring Fragrance with humility.

"Yes, yes, do, please."

There was eagerness in Mrs. Carman's voice. What could Ethel Eve-brook have to say about that girl!

When Mrs. Spring Fragrance had finished reading, she looked up into the face of her American friend—a face in which there was nothing now but tenderness.

"Mrs. Mary Carman," said she, "you are so good as to admire my husband because he is what the Americans call 'a man who has made himself.' Why then do you not admire the Inferior Woman who is a woman who has made herself?"

"I think I do," said Mrs. Carman slowly.

VI

It was an evening that invited to reverie. The far stretches of the sea were gray with mist, and the city itself, lying around the sweep of the Bay, seemed dusky and distant. From her cottage window Alice Winthrop looked silently at the open world around her. It seemed a long time since she had heard Will Carman's whistle. She wondered if he were still angry with her. She was sorry that he had left her in anger, and yet not sorry. If she had not made him believe that she was proud and selfish, the parting would have been much harder; and perhaps had he known the truth and realized that it was for his sake, and not for her own, that she was sending him away from her, he might have refused to leave her at all. His was such an imperious nature. And then they would have married—right away. Alice caught her breath a little, and then she sighed. But they would not have been happy. No, that could not have been possible if his mother did not like her. When a gulf of prejudice lies between the wife and mother of a man, that man's life is not what it should be. And even supposing she and Will could have lost themselves in each other, and been able to imagine themselves perfectly satisfied with life together, would it have been right? The question of right and wrong was a very real one to Alice Winthrop. She put herself in the place of the mother of her lover—a lonely elderly woman, a widow with an only son, upon whom she had expended all her love and care ever since, in her early youth, she had been bereaved of his father. What anguish of heart would be hers if that son deserted her for one whom she, his mother, deemed unworthy! Prejudices are prejudices. They are like diseases.

The poor, pale, elderly woman, who cherished bitter and resentful feelings towards the girl whom her son loved, was more an object of pity than condemnation to the girl herself.

She lifted her eyes to the undulating line of hills beyond the water. From behind them came a silver light. "Yes," said she aloud to herself—and, though she knew it not, there was an infinite pathos in such philosophy from one so young—"if life cannot be bright and beautiful for me, at least it can be peaceful and contented."

The light behind the hills died away; darkness crept over the sea. Alice withdrew from the window and went and knelt before the open fire in her sitting-room. Her cottage companion, the young woman who rented the place with her, had not yet returned from town.

Alice did not turn on the light. She was seeing pictures in the fire, and in every picture was the same face and form—the face and form of a fine, handsome young man with love and hope in his eyes. No, not always love and hope. In the last picture of all there was an expression which she wished she could forget. And yet she would remember—ever—always—and with it, these words: "Is it nothing to you—nothing—to tell a man that you love him, and then to bid him go?"

Yes, but when she had told him she loved him she had not dreamed that her love for him and his for her would estrange him from one who, before ever she had come to this world, had pillowed his head on her breast.

Suddenly this girl, so practical, so humorous, so clever in every-day life, covered her face with her hands and sobbed like a child. Two roads of life had lain before her and she had chosen the hardest.

The warning bell of an automobile passing the cross-roads checked her tears. That reminded her that Nellie Blake would soon be home. She turned on the light and went to the bedroom and bathed her eyes. Nellie must have forgotten her key. There she was knocking.

The chill sea air was sweet with the scent of roses as Mary Carman stood upon the threshold of the little cottage, and beheld in the illumination from within the young girl whom she had called "the Inferior Woman."

"I have come, Miss Winthrop," said she, "to beg of you to return home with me. Will, reckless boy, met with a slight accident while out shooting, so could not come for you himself. He has told me that he loves you, and if you love him, I want to arrange for the prettiest wedding of the season. Come dear!"

"I am so glad," said Mrs. Spring Fragrance, "that Will Carman's bird is in his nest and his felicity is assured."

"What about the Superior Woman?" asked Mr. Spring Fragrance.

"Ah, the Superior Woman! Radiantly beautiful, and gifted with the divine right of learning! I love well the Inferior Woman; but, O Great Man, when we have a daughter, may Heaven ordain that she walk in the groove of the Superior Woman."

Mary Austin
(1868–1934)

 ary Austin's family moved from a small town in Illinois to a California homestead after her graduation from college. She was fascinated by the San Joaquin Valley and Inyo County, where she took long walks and came to know Native Americans, sheepherders, and miners. Her 1891 marriage was unhappy, with the birth of a severely handicapped daughter adding to its stresses. After 1899 Austin often lived apart from her husband, and they divorced in 1905. Over her lifetime she sought alternative families in writers' communities from Pasadena, Carmel, and Santa Fe to Greenwich Village. Austin's fiction and essays about the West emphasized its natural beauty, ethnic diversity, and mythic spaces. Sherwood Anderson told her that "what Twain and Harte have missed, you have found." In "The Walking Woman," set in the San Joaquin Valley, Austin created a paradigmatic female wanderer, a New Woman who finds her destiny in the loneliness of the desert. Her autobiographical story "Frustrate" (published in the *Century* in 1912) explores what might have happened to Austin had she not found fulfillment and independence as a writer.

The Walking Woman (1907)

The first time of my hearing of her was at Temblor. We had come all one day between blunt, whitish cliffs rising from mirage water, with a thick, pale wake of dust billowing from the wheels, all the dead wall of the foothills sliding and shimmering with heat, to learn that the Walking Woman had passed us somewhere in the dizzying dimness, going down to the Tulares on her own feet. We heard of her again in the Carrisal, and again at Adobe Station, where she had passed a week before the shearing, and at last I had a glimpse of her at the Eighteen-Mile House as I went hurriedly northward on the Mojave stage; and afterward sheepherders at whose camps she slept, and cowboys at rodeos, told me as much of her way of life as they could understand. Like enough they told her as much of mine. That was very little. She was the Walking Woman, and no one knew her name, but because she was a sort of whom men speak respectfully, they called her to her face Mrs. Walker, and she answered to it if she was so inclined. She came and went about our western world on no discoverable errand, and whether she had some place of refuge where she lay by in the interim, or whether between her seldom, unaccountable appearances in our quarter she went on steadily walking, was never learned. She came and went, oftenest in a kind of muse of travel which the untrammelled space begets, or at rare intervals flooding wondrously with talk, never of herself, but of things she had known and seen. She must have seen some rare happenings, too—by report. She was at Maverick the time of the Big Snow, and at Tres Piños when they brought home the body of Morena; and if anybody could have told whether De Borba killed Mariana for spite or defence, it would have been she, only she could not be found when most wanted. She was at Tunawai at the time of the cloud-burst, and if she had cared for it could have known most desirable things of the ways of trail-making, burrow-habiting small things.

All of which should have made her worth meeting, though it was not, in fact, for such things I was wishful to meet her; and as it turned out, it was not of these things we talked when at last we came together. For one thing, she was a woman, not old, who had gone about alone in a country where the number of women is as one in fifteen. She had eaten and slept at the herder's camps, and laid by for days at one-man stations whose masters had no other touch of human kind than the passing of chance prospectors, or the halting of the tri-weekly stage. She had been set on her way by teamsters who lifted her out of white, hot desertness and put her down at the crossing of unnamed ways, days distant from anywhere. And through all this she passed unarmed and unoffended. I had the best testimony to this, the witness of the men themselves. I think they talked of it because they were so much surprised at it. It was not, on the whole, what they expected of themselves.

Well I understand that nature which wastes its borders with too eager burning, beyond which rim of desolation it flares forever quick and white, and have had some inkling of the isolating calm of a desire too high to stoop to satisfaction. But you could not think of these things pertaining to the Walking Woman; and if there were ever any truth in the exemption from offense residing in a frame of behavior called ladylike, it should have been inoperative here. What this really means is that you get no affront so long as your behavior in the estimate of the particular audience invites none. In the estimate of the immediate audience—conduct which affords protection in Mayfair gets you no consideration in Maverick. And by no canon could it be considered ladylike to go about on your own feet, with a blanket and a black bag and almost no money in your purse, in and about the haunts of rude and solitary men.

There were other things that pointed the wish for a personal encounter with the Walking Woman. One of them was the contradiction of reports of her—as to whether she was comely, for example. Report said yes, and again, plain to the point of deformity. She had a twist to her face, some said; a hitch to one shoulder; they averred she limped as she walked. But by the distance she covered she should have been straight and young. As to sanity, equal incertitude. On the mere evidence of her way of life she was cracked; not quite broken, but unserviceable. Yet in her talk there was both wisdom and information, and the word she brought about trails and water-holes was as reliable as an Indian's.

By her own account she had begun by walking off an illness. There had been an invalid to be taken care of for years, leaving her at last broken in body, and with no recourse but her own feet to carry her out of that predicament. It seemed there had been, besides the death of her invalid, some other worrying affairs, upon which, and the nature of her illness, she was never quite clear, so that it might well have been an unsoundness of mind which drove her to the open, sobered and healed at last by the large soundness of nature. It must have been about that time that she lost her name. I am convinced that she never told it because she did not know it herself. She was the Walking Woman, and the country people called her Mrs. Walker. At the time I knew her, though she wore short hair and a man's boots, and had a fine down over all her face from exposure to the weather, she was perfectly sweet and sane.

I had met her occasionally at ranch-houses and road-stations, and had got as much acquaintance as the place allowed; but for the things I wished to know there wanted a time of leisure and isolation. And when the occasion came we talked altogether of other things.

It was at Warm Springs in the Little Antelope I came upon her in the heart of a clear forenoon. The spring lies off a mile from the main trail, and has the only trees about it known in that country. First you come upon a pool of waste full of weeds of a poisonous dark green, every reed ringed about the water-level with a muddy white incrustation. Then the three oaks appear staggering on the slope, and the spring sobs and blubbers below them in ashy-colored mud. All the hills of that country have the down plunge toward the desert and back abruptly toward the Sierra. The grass is thick and brittle and bleached straw-color toward the end of the season. As I rode up the swale of the spring I saw the Walking Woman sitting where the grass was deepest, with her black bag and blanket, which she carried on a stick, beside her. It was one of those days when the genius of talk flows as smoothly as the rivers of mirage through the blue hot desert morning.

You are not to suppose that in my report of a Borderer I give you the words only, but the full meaning of the speech. Very often the words are merely the punctuation of thought; rather, the crests of the long waves of inter-communicative silences. Yet the speech of the Walking Woman was fuller than most.

The best of our talk that day began in some dropped word of hers from which I inferred that she had had a child. I was surprised at that, and then wondered why I should have been surprised, for it is the most natural of all experiences to have children. I said something of that purport, and also that it was one of the perquisites of living I should be least willing to do without. And that led to the Walking Woman saying that there were three things which if you had known you could cut out all the rest, and they were good any way you got them, but best if, as in her case, they were related to and grew each one out of the others. It was while she talked that I decided that she really did have a twist to her face, a sort of natural warp or skew into which it fell when it was worn merely as a countenance, but which disappeared the moment it became the vehicle of thought or feeling.

The first of the experiences the Walking Woman had found most worth while had come to her in a sand-storm on the south slope of Tehachapi in a dateless spring. I judged it should have been about the time she began to find herself, after the period of worry and loss in which her wandering began. She had come, in a day pricked full of intimations of a storm, to the camp of Filon Geraud, whose companion shepherd had gone a three days' *pasear* to Mojave for supplies. Geraud was of great hardihood, red-blooded, of a full laughing eye, and an indubitable spark for women. It was the season of the year when there is a soft bloom on the days, but the nights are cowering cold and the lambs tender, not yet flockwise. At such times a sand-storm works incalculable disaster. The lift of the wind is so great that the whole surface of the ground appears to travel upon it slantwise, thinning out miles high in air. In the intolerable smother the lambs are lost from the ewes; neither dogs nor man make headway against it.

The morning flared through a horizon of yellow smudge, and by midforenoon the flock broke.

"There were but the two of us to deal with the trouble," said the Walking Woman. "Until that time I had not known how strong I was, nor how good it is to run when running is worth while. The flock travelled down the wind, the sand bit our faces; we called, and after a time heard the words broken and beaten small by the wind. But after a while we had not to call. All the time of our running in the yellow dusk of day and the black dark of night, I knew where Filon was. A flock-length away, I knew him. Feel? What should I feel? I knew. I ran with the flock and turned it this way and that as Filon would have.

"Such was the force of the wind that when we came together we held by one another and talked a little between pantings. We snatched and ate what we could as we ran. All that day and night until the next afternoon the camp kit was not out of the cayaques. But we held the flock. We herded them under a butte when the wind fell off a little, and the lambs sucked; when the storm rose they broke, but we kept upon their track and brought them together again. At night the wind quieted, and we slept by turns; at least Filon slept. I lay on the ground when my turn was and beat with the storm. I was no more tired than the earth was. The sand filled in the creases of the blanket, and where I turned, dripped back upon the ground. But we saved the sheep. Some ewes there were that would not give down their milk because of the worry of the storm, and the lambs died. But we kept the flock together. And I was not tired."

The Walking Woman stretched out her arms and clasped herself, rocking in them as if she would have hugged the recollection to her breast.

"For you see," said she, "I worked with a man, without excusing, without any burden on me of looking or seeming. Not fiddling or fumbling as women work, and hoping it will all turn out for the best. It was not for Filon to ask, Can you, or Will you. He said, Do, and I did. And my work was good. We held the flock. And that," said the Walking Woman, the twist coming in her face again, "is one of the things that make you able to do without the others."

"Yes," I said; and then, "What others?"

"Oh," she said, as if it pricked her, "the looking and the seeming."

And I had not thought until that time that one who had the courage to be the Walking Woman would have cared! We sat and looked at the pattern of the thick crushed grass on the slope, wavering in the fierce noon like the waterings in the coat of a tranquil beast; the ache of a world-old bitterness sobbed and whispered in the spring. At last—

"It is by the looking and the seeming," said I, "that the opportunity finds you out."

"Filon found out," said the Walking Woman. She smiled; and went on from that to tell me how, when the wind went down about four o'clock and left the afternoon clear and tender, the flock began to feed, and they had out the kit from the cayaques, and cooked a meal. When it was over, and Filon had his pipe between his teeth, he came over from his side of the fire, of his own notion, and stretched himself on the ground beside her. Of his own notion. There was that in the way she said it that made it seem as if nothing of that sort had happened before to the Walking Woman, and for a moment I thought she was about to tell me of the things I wished to know; but she went on to say what Filon had said to her of her work with the flock. Obvious, kindly things, such as any man in sheer decency would have said, so that there must have something more gone with the words to make them so treasured of the Walking Woman.

"We were very comfortable," said she, "and not so tired as we expected to be. Filon leaned upon his elbow. I had not noticed until then how broad he was in the shoulders, and how strong in the arms. And we had saved the flock together. We felt that. There was something that said together, in the slope of his shoulders toward me. It was around his mouth and on the cheek high up under the shine of his eyes. And under the shine the look—the look that said, 'We are of one sort and one mind'—his eyes that were the color of the flat water in the toulares—do you know the look?"

"I know it."

"The wind was stopped and all the earth smelled of dust, and Filon understood very well that what I had done with him I could not have done so well with another. And the look—the look in the eyes—"

"Ah-ah—!"

I have always said, I will say again, I do not know why at this point the Walking Woman touched me. If it were merely a response to my unconscious throb of sympathy, or the unpremeditated way of her heart to declare that this, after all, was the best of all indispensable experiences; or in some flash of forward vision, encompassing the unimpassioned years, the stir, the movement of tenderness were for *me*—but no; as often as I have thought of it, I have thought of a different reason, but no conclusive one, why the Walking Woman should have put out her hand and laid it on my arm.

"To work together, to love together," said the Walking Woman, withdrawing her hand again; "there you have two of the things; the other you know."

"The mouth at the breast," said I.

"The lips and the hands," said the Walking Woman. "The little, pushing hands and the small cry." There ensued a pause of fullest understanding, while the land before us swam in the noon, and a dove in the oaks behind the spring began to call. A little red fox came out of the hills and lapped delicately at the pool.

"I stayed with Filon until the fall," said she. "All that summer in the Sierras, until it was time to turn south on the trail. It was a good time, and longer than he could be expected to have loved one like me. And besides, I was no longer able to keep the trail. My baby was born in October."

Whatever more there was to say to this, the Walking Woman's hand said it, straying with remembering gesture to her breast. There are so many ways of loving and working, but only one way of the first-born. She added after an interval that she did not know if she would have given up her walking to keep at home and tend him, or whether the thought of her son's small feet running beside her in the trails would have driven her to the open again. The baby had not stayed long enough for that. "And whenever the wind blows in the night," said the Walking Woman, "I wake and wonder if he is well covered."

She took up her black bag and her blanket; there was the ranch-house at Dos Palos to be made before night, and she went as outliers do, without a hope expressed of another meeting and no word of good-bye. She was the Walking Woman. That was it. She had walked off all sense of society-made values, and, knowing the best when the best came to her, was able to take it. Work—as I believed; love—as the Walking Woman had proved it; a child—as you subscribe to it. But look you: it was the naked thing the Walking Woman grasped, not dressed and tricked out, for instance, by prejudices in favor of certain occupations; and love, man love, taken as it came, not picked over and rejected if it carried no obligation of permanency; and a child; *any* way you get it, a child is good to have, say nature and the Walking Woman; to have it and not to wait upon a proper concurrence of so many decorations that the event may not come at all.

At least one of us is wrong. To work and to love and to bear children. *That* sounds easy enough. But the way we live establishes so many things of much more importance.

Far down the dim, hot valley I could see the Walking Woman with her blanket and black bag over her shoulder. She had a queer, sidelong gait, as if in fact she had a twist all through her.

Recollecting suddenly that people called her lame, I ran down to the open place below the spring where she had passed. There in the bare, hot sand the track of her two feet bore evenly and white.

Frustrate (1912)

I know that I am a disappointed woman and that nobody cares at all about it, not even Henry; and if anybody thought of it, it would only be to think it ridiculous. It is ridiculous, too, with my waist, and not knowing how to do my hair or anything. I look at Henry sometimes of evenings, when he has his feet on the fender, and wonder if he has the least idea how disappointed I am. I even have days of wondering if Henry isn't disappointed, too. He might be disappointed in himself, which would be even more dreadful; but I don't suppose we shall ever find out about each other. It is part of my disappointment that Henry has never seemed to want to find out.

There are people who think it is somehow discreditable to be disappointed; and whatever comes, you must pretend to like it, and just keep on pretending. I don't know why. It must be that some things are right in life and some others are not, and unless somebody has the courage to speak up about it, I don't know how we are ever to find it out. I don't see, if nobody else is hurt by it, why we shouldn't have what we like out of life; and if there's a way of getting or not getting it, people have a right to know. Sometimes I think if I'd known a little more, just a very little . . . !

It all began, I suppose, in the kind of people I was brought up among. They'd none of them had the kind of things I wanted, so of course they couldn't tell me anything about the way to get them. There was my mother. She had to work hard, and had never been anywhere but to a Methodist conference and once to the capital when father was a delegate or something, and her black silk had been turned twice; but she didn't seem the least disappointed. I think it must have been the way things were between her and my father. Father died when I was sixteen, so I couldn't tell much about it, but I know mother never so much as thought of marrying again. She was like a person who has had a full meal, but I— I am just kind of hungry . . . *always*. My mother never talked to me about her relations to my father. Mothers didn't; it wasn't thought suitable. I think sometimes, if she had, it might have made a difference about my marrying Henry.

The trouble was in the beginning, that though I knew the world was all full of exciting, interesting things, I thought they came to you just by living. I had no idea there was a particular way you had to go to work to get them. I think my people weren't the kind to make very nice discriminations about experiences or anything. They wouldn't have thought one way of being in love, for instance, was much better or different from another. They had everything sort of ticketed off and done with: such as that all church-members were happier than unbelievers, and all men naturally more competent and intelligent than their women. They must have known, some of them, that things didn't always work out that way; but they never let on about it—anyway, not to us young people. And if married couples weren't happy together, it wasn't considered decent to speak of it.

I suppose that was what got me to thinking about all the deep and high and shining things that I had a kind of instinct went with being married, belonged to it naturally, and, when you had found a suitable man, came along in their proper place without much thinking. And that was about all I knew when Henry proposed to me at the Odd Fellows' Festival. We were both on the decoration committee, and drove out to the old Lawson place that afternoon for roses. I remember the feel of them against my cheek, hot and sweet, and the smell of the syringa, and a great gold-and-black butterfly that fled and flitted down the green country road, mottled black and gold with shadows. Things like that gave me a strange kind of excitement, and yet a kind of lonesomeness, too, so I didn't mind Henry holding my hand between us in the buggy. I thought he must be feeling something of the same sort, and it didn't seem friendly to take my hand away. But I did take it away a moment later when he proposed. It turned me kind of cold. Of course I meant to accept him after a while. I liked him, and he was what my folks called suitable; but I seemed to want a little time to think about it.

Henry didn't want me to think. He kept hinting, and that evening under the grape-arbor at the minister's, where we had gone to get the sewing society's ice-cream freezer, he kissed me. I'd heard about engaged kisses, but this wasn't anything but just a kiss—like when you have been playing drop the handkerchief. I'd always had a feeling that when you had an engaged kiss something beautiful happened. There were times afterward when it almost seemed about to, and I would want to be kissed again to see if the next time . . . Henry said he was glad I had turned out to have an affectionate disposition.

My family thought I was doing well to marry Henry. He had no bad habits, and his people were well-to-do; and then I wasn't particularly pretty or rich or anything. I had never been very popular with young men; I was too eager. Not for them, you understand; but just living and doing things seemed to me such a good game. I suppose it is difficult for some folks to understand how you can be excited by the way a shadow falls, or a bird singing on a wet bough; and somehow young men seemed to get the idea that the excitement had something to do with them. It made them feel as if something was expected of them; and you know how it is with young men: they sort of pull back from the thing that is expected of them just because it is expected. I always thought it rather small, but I suppose they can't help it. There was a woman I met at Fair-shore who explained how that was; but I didn't know it then, and I was rather sensitive about it. Anyway, it came about that I hadn't many beaux, and my mother was a good deal relieved when I settled down to Henry. And we hadn't any more than got the furniture as he wanted it when I discovered that there hadn't anything happened at all! Instead of living with my mother, I was just living with Henry; I've never done anything else.

There are things nobody ever tells young girls about marriage. Sometimes I think it is because, if they knew how to estimate their experience in the beginning, there is such a lot they wouldn't go on with; and when I was married, nobody ever thought of anything but that you had to go on with it. There were times when it seemed as if all it needed was just going on: there was a dizzying point just about to be reached from which Henry and I should really set out for somewhere.

It took me fifteen years to realize that we hadn't set out for anything, and would never get anywhere in particular.

I know I tried. Times I would explain to Henry what I wanted until he seemed to want it as much as I did; and then we would begin whatever we had to do,—at least I would begin,—and then I would find out that Henry had forgotten what we were doing it for—like the time we saved to set out the south lot in apricots, and Henry bought water-shares with the money. He said it would be cheaper to own the water for the apricots; but then we hadn't anything left to pay for the planting, and the man who had sold Henry the shares turned out not to own them. After a while I gave up saving.

The trouble was, Henry said, I was too kind of simple. It always seemed to me, if you wanted things, you picked out the one nearest to you, and made a mark so you could keep tab on whether you were getting it or not; and then you picked out the next nearest, and went for that, and after a while you had all of them. But Henry said when it came to business it was a good deal more complicated, and you had to look on all sides of a thing. Henry was strong on looking on all sides; anybody that had any kind of reasonableness could always get over him, like that man with the water-shares. That was when I was trying to make myself believe that if we could get a little money together, we might be in things. I had been reading the magazines, and I knew that there were big, live things with feelers out all over creation, and if I could just get the least little tip of one . . . But I knew it wasn't money. When I wasn't too sick and overworked and worn out trying to keep track of Henry's reasons, I knew that the thing I was aching for was close beside me . . . when I heard the wind walk on the roof at night, . . . or heard music playing . . . and I would be irritated with Henry because he couldn't help me lay hold of it. It is ridiculous, I know, but there were times when it seemed to me if Henry had been fatter, it would have helped some. I don't mean to say that I had wanted to marry a fat man, but Henry hadn't filled out any, not like it seems men ought to: he just got dry and thinner. It used to make me kind of exasperated. Henry was always patient with me; he thought it was because I hadn't any children. He would have liked children. So would I when I thought I was to have one, but I was doing my own housework, and I was never strong. I cried about it a good deal at the time; but I don't suppose I really wanted it very much or I would have adopted one. I will tell you—there are women that want children just for the sake of having them, but the most of them want them because there is a man—And the man they want gets to hear of it, and whenever a woman is in any way unhappy, they think all she needs is a baby. But there's something else ought to happen first, and I never gave up thinking it was going to happen; all the time I kept looking out, like Sister Anne in the fairy-tale, and it seemed to me a great many times I saw dust moving. I never understood why we couldn't do things right here at home—big things. There were those people I'd read about in Germany—just plain carpenters and butchers and their wives—giving passion-plays. They didn't know anything about plays; they just felt grateful, and they did something like they felt. I spoke to the minister's wife about it once—not about a passion-play, of course, that wouldn't have done; but about our just taking hold of something as if we thought we were as good as those Germans,—but she didn't seem to think we could. She kind of pursed up her mouth and said, "Well, we must remember that they had the advantage of having lived abroad." It was always like that. You had to have lived somewhere or been taught or had things different; you couldn't just start right off from where you were. It was all of a piece with Henry's notion of business; there was always some kind of queer mixed-up-ness about it that I couldn't understand. But still I didn't give up thinking that somehow I was going to pull the right string at last, and then things would begin to happen. Not knowing what it was I wanted to happen, I couldn't be expected to realize that it couldn't happen now on account of my being married to Henry. It was at Fairshore that I found out.

It was when we had been married eighteen years that Aunt Lucy died and left me all her property. It wasn't very much, but it was more than Henry would ever have, and I just made up my mind that I was going to have the good of it. Henry didn't make any objection, and the first thing I did was to go down to Fairshore for the summer. I chose Fairshore because I had heard about all the authors and painters being there. You see, when you never have any real life except what you get from reading, you have a kind of feeling that writers are the only real *own* folks you've got. You even get to thinking sometimes that maybe, if you had known how to go about it, you could have written yourself, though perhaps you'd feel that way about bridge-building or soldiering, if it was the only real kind of work you saw much of. Not that I ever thought I could write; but I had so many ideas that were exactly like what I'd read that I thought if I could only just get somebody to write them for me—But you can't; they've all got things of their own. Still, you would think the way they get inside the people they write about that they would be able to see what is going on inside of you, and be a little kind.

You see, it had come over me that away deep inside of me there was a really beautiful kind of life, singing, and burning blue and red and gold as it sang, and there were days when I couldn't bear to think of it wasting there and nobody to know.

Not that Henry didn't take an interest in me,—his kind of interest,—if I was sick or hurt, or seeing that I had a comfortable chair. But if I should say to Henry to lean upon my heart and listen to the singing there, he would have sent for the doctor. Nobody talks like that here in Castroville: only in books I thought I had heard the people calling to one another quietly and apart over all the world, like birds waking in a wood. I've wondered since I came back from Fairshore if people put things in books because they would like to have them that way.

It is difficult to tell what happened to me at Fairshore. It didn't really happen—just the truth of things coming over me in a slow, acrid dribble. Sometimes in the night I can feel the recollection of it all awash at the bottom of my heart, cold and stale. But nothing happened. Nobody took any notice of me but one woman. She was about my age, plain-looking and rather sad. I'd be proud to mention her name; but I've talked about her a great deal, and, with all my being so disappointed, it isn't so bad but it might be worse if everybody got to find out about it. She was really a much greater writer than the rest of them; but, I am ashamed to say it, just at first, perhaps because she was so little different from me on the outside, and perhaps just because she was a woman, I didn't seem to care much about her. I don't know why I shouldn't say it, but I did want to have something to do with interesting men. People seem to think that when a woman is married she has got all that's coming to her; but we're not very different from men, and *they* have to have things. There are days sometimes when it seems to me that never to have known any kind of men but Henry and the minister and old man Truett, who does our milking, would be more than I could bear. I thought if I could get to know a man who was big enough so I couldn't walk all around him, so to speak,—somebody that I could reach and reach and not find the end of,—I shouldn't feel so—so frustrated. There was a man there who wrote things that made you feel like that,—as if you could take hands with him and go out and rescue shipwrecked men and head rebellions. And when I tried to talk to him, I found him looking at me the way young men used to before I married Henry—as if he thought I wanted something, and it was rather clever of him not to give it to me. It was after that that I took to sitting with the writer woman. I'd noticed that though the men seemed to respect her, and you saw them in corners sometimes reading manuscripts to her, they never took her to walk, or to see the moon rise, or the boats come in. They spent all that on the pretty women, young and kind of empty-headed. I'd heard them talk when they thought I wasn't listening. And the writer woman sat about with the other women, and didn't seem to mind it.

I hoped when people saw me with her, they'd think it was because she was so famous, and not guess how terrible it was to find yourself all at once a middle-aged woman sitting on a bench, and all the world going by as if it was just what they expected. It came over me that here were all the things I had dreamed about,—the great sea roaring landward, music, quick and gay; looks, little incidents,—and I wasn't in it; I wasn't in it at all.

I suppose the writer woman must have seen how it was with me, but I thought at first she was talking of herself.

"It's all very wonderful out there, isn't it?" she said, looking toward the blue water and the beach shining like a shell, with the other writers and painters walking up and down and making it into world stuff. "Very wonderful—when you have the price to pay for it!"

"It *is* expensive." I was thinking of the hotel, but I saw in a minute she meant something else.

"The price you pay," she said, "it isn't being fit to be in the Great World or being able to appreciate it when you're in; it is what you contribute to keep other people in, I suppose."

I must have said something about not being able to see what the kind of women who were in contributed—just girls and flirty kind of married women.

"It's a kind of game, keeping other people in," said the writer woman. "They don't know much else, but they know the game. We are, most of us," she said, "like those matches that will not light unless they are struck upon the box: there is a particular sort of person that sets us off. It's a business, being that sort of person."

"If anybody could only learn it—" I tried to seem only polite.

"It is the whole art," she said, "of putting yourself into your appearance." She laughed. "I have too much waist for that sort of thing. I have my own game."

I seemed suddenly to want to get away to my room and think about it. I know it is absurd at my age, but I lay on the bed and cried as I hadn't since they told me my baby hadn't lived. For I knew now that all that beautiful life inside me couldn't be born either, for I was one who had to have help to be worth anything to myself, and I didn't know the game. I had never known it.

All the time I had been thinking that all I needed was to find the right person; and now I understood that, so far as anybody could guess, I wasn't the right person myself. I hadn't the art of putting myself into my appearance. I'm shy about talk, and my arms are too fat, and my skirts have a way of hanging short in front.

I've thought about it a great deal since. It doesn't seem fair. Nobody told me about it when I was a girl; I think nobody tells girls. They just have to sort of find it out; and if they don't, nobody cares. All they did tell me was about being good, and you will be happy; but it isn't so. There is a great deal more to it than that, and it seems as if people ought to know. I think we are mostly like that in Castroville: we've got powers and capacities 'way down in us, but we don't know anything about getting them out. We think it is living when we have got upholstered furniture and a top buggy. I know people who think it is worth while never to have lived in a house without a cupola. But all the time we are not in the game. We do not even know there is a game.

Sometimes I think, if it would do me any good, I could turn in and learn it now. I watched them at Fairshore, and it seemed to me it could be learned. I have wild thoughts sometimes,—such thoughts as men have when they go out and snatch things,—but it wouldn't do me any good. Henry's folks were always long-lived, and there are days when I am so down that I am glad to have even Henry. As long as people see us going about together they can't know—I'm rather looking forward to getting old now. I think perhaps I sha'n't ache so. But I *should* like to know how much Henry understands.

Willa Cather
(1873–1947)

rom childhood, Cather boldly resisted the cultural trappings and the intellectual limitations of being a girl. The eldest of seven children, she was born in Virginia, but in 1883 the family moved to the vast exposed plains of Red Cloud, Nebraska, in search of purer air, better soil, and more opportunity. For Cather, part of that opportunity lay in rejecting the limitations of the feminine role. By 1888 she had cut her long hair, dressed as a boy, and started to call herself "William Cather." At the University of Nebraska, her literary gifts were encouraged by the faculty and by professional journalists at the *Nebraska State Journal*. After her graduation in 1895, Cather moved to Pittsburgh, where she spent ten years as a journalist and editor, and then to New York, where she joined the staff of *McClure's Magazine*.

Among the seven short stories in her first book, *The Troll Garden* (1905), was "Paul's Case: A Study in Temperament," about an aesthetically minded, probably homosexual teenaged boy in Pittsburgh, who steals money and escapes for a brief but glorious fling in New York. Cather would go on to write great novels, but she would never write more memorably than in this story, where character, setting, and a vision of human existence come together.

Paul's Case: A Study in Temperament (1905)

It was Paul's afternoon to appear before the faculty of the Pittsburgh High School to account for his various misdemeanours. He had been suspended a week ago, and his father had called at the Principal's office and confessed his perplexity about his son. Paul entered the faculty room suave and smiling. His clothes were a trifle outgrown, and the tan velvet on the collar of his open overcoat was frayed and worn; but for all that there was something of the dandy about him, and he wore an opal pin in his neatly knotted black four-in-hand, and a red carnation in his buttonhole. This latter adornment the faculty somehow felt was not properly significant of the contrite spirit befitting a boy under the ban of suspension.

Paul was tall for his age and very thin, with high, cramped shoulders and a narrow chest. His eyes were remarkable for a certain hysterical brilliancy and he continually used them in a conscious, theatrical sort of way, peculiarly offensive in a boy. The pupils were abnormally large, as though he were addicted to belladonna, but there was a glassy glitter about them which that drug does not produce.

When questioned by the Principal as to why he was there, Paul stated, politely enough, that he wanted to come back to school. This was a lie, but Paul was quite accustomed to lying; found it, indeed, indispensable for overcoming friction. His teachers were asked to state their respective charges against him, which they did with such a rancour and aggrievedness as evinced that this was not a usual case. Disorder and impertinence were among the offences named, yet each of his instructors felt that it was scarcely possible to put into words the real cause of the trouble, which lay in a sort of hysterically defiant manner of the boy's; in the contempt which they all knew he felt for them, and which he seemingly made not the least effort to conceal. Once, when he had been making a synopsis of a paragraph at the blackboard, his English teacher had stepped to his side and attempted to guide his hand. Paul had started back with a shudder and thrust his hands violently behind him. The astonished woman could scarcely have been more hurt and embarrassed had he struck at her. The insult was so involuntary and definitely personal as to be unforgettable. In one way and another, he had made all his teachers, men and women alike, conscious of the same feeling of physical aversion. In one class he habitually sat with his hand shading his eyes; in another he always looked out of the window during the recitation; in another he made a running commentary on the lecture, with humorous intention.

His teachers felt this afternoon that his whole attitude was symbolized by his shrug and his flippantly red carnation flower, and they fell upon him without mercy, his English teacher leading the pack. He stood through it smiling, his pale lips parted over his white teeth. (His lips were continually twitching, and he had a habit of raising his eyebrows that was contemptuous and irritating to the last degree.) Older boys than Paul had broken down and shed tears under that baptism of fire, but his set smile did not once desert him, and his only sign of discomfort was the nervous trembling of the fingers that toyed with the buttons of his overcoat, and an occasional jerking of the other hand that held his hat. Paul was always smiling, always glancing about him, seeming to feel that people might be watching him and trying to detect something. This conscious expression, since it was as far as possible from boyish mirthfulness, was usually attributed to insolence or "smartness."

As the inquisition proceeded, one of his instructors repeated an impertinent remark of the boy's, and the Principal asked him whether he thought that a courteous speech to have made a woman. Paul shrugged his shoulders slightly and his eyebrows twitched.

"I don't know," he replied. "I didn't mean to be polite or impolite, either. I guess it's a sort of way I have of saying things regardless."

The Principal, who was a sympathetic man, asked him whether he didn't think that a way it would be well to get rid of. Paul grinned and said he guessed so. When he was told that he could go, he bowed gracefully and went out. His bow was but a repetition of the scandalous red carnation.

His teachers were in despair, and his drawing master voiced the feeling of them all when he declared there was something about the boy which none of them understood. He added: "I don't really believe that smile of his comes altogether from insolence; there's something sort of haunted about it. The boy is not strong, for one thing. I happen to know that he was born in Colorado, only a few months before his mother died out there of a long illness. There is something wrong about the fellow."

The drawing master had come to realize that, in looking at Paul, one saw only his white teeth and the forced animation of his eyes. One warm afternoon the boy had gone to sleep at his drawing-board, and his master had noted with amazement what a white, blue-veined face it was; drawn and wrinkled like an old man's about the eyes, the lips twitching even in his sleep, and stiff with a nervous tension that drew them back from his teeth.

His teachers left the building dissatisfied and unhappy; humiliated to have felt so vindictive toward a mere boy, to have uttered this feeling in cutting terms, and to have set each other on, as it were, in the gruesome game of intemperate reproach. Some of them remembered having seen a miserable street cat set at bay by a ring of tormentors.

As for Paul, he ran down the hill whistling the Soldiers' Chorus from *Faust* looking wildly behind him now and then to see whether some of his teachers were not there to writhe under his light-heartedness. As it was now late in the afternoon and Paul was on duty that evening as usher at Carnegie Hall, he decided that he would not go home to supper. When he reached the concert hall the doors were not yet open and, as it was chilly outside, he decided to go up into the picture gallery—always deserted at this hour—where there were some of Raffelli's gay studies of

Paris streets and an airy blue Venetian scene or two that always exhila-
rated him. He was delighted to find no one in the gallery but the old
guard, who sat in one corner, a newspaper on his knee, a black patch over
one eye and the other closed. Paul possessed himself of the place and
walked confidently up and down, whistling under his breath. After a
while he sat down before a blue Rico and lost himself. When he
bethought him to look at his watch, it was after seven o'clock, and he
rose with a start and ran downstairs, making a face at Augustus, peering
out from the cast-room, and an evil gesture at the Venus of Milo as he
passed her on the stairway.

When Paul reached the ushers' dressing-room half-a-dozen boys were
there already, and he began excitedly to tumble into his uniform. It was
one of the few that at all approached fitting, and Paul thought it very
becoming—though he knew that the tight, straight coat accentuated his
narrow chest, about which he was exceedingly sensitive. He was always
considerably excited while he dressed, twanging all over to the tuning of
the strings and the preliminary flourishes of the horns in the music-
room; but to-night he seemed quite beside himself, and he teased and
plagued the boys until, telling him that he was crazy, they put him down
on the floor and sat on him.

Somewhat calmed by his suppression, Paul dashed out to the front of
the house to seat the early comers. He was a model usher; gracious and
smiling he ran up and down the aisles; nothing was too much trouble for
him; he carried messages and brought programmes as though it were his
greatest pleasure in life, and all the people in his section thought him a
charming boy, feeling that he remembered and admired them. As the
house filled, he grew more and more vivacious and animated, and the
colour came to his cheeks and lips. It was very much as though this were
a great reception and Paul were the host. Just as the musicians came out
to take their places, his English teacher arrived with checks for the seats
which a prominent manufacturer had taken for the season. She betrayed
some embarrassment when she handed Paul the tickets, and a *hauteur*
which subsequently made her feel very foolish. Paul was startled for a
moment, and had the feeling of wanting to put her out; what business
had she here among all these fine people and gay colours? He looked her
over and decided that she was not appropriately dressed and must be a
fool to sit downstairs in such togs. The tickets had probably been sent her
out of kindness, he reflected as he put down a seat for her, and she had
about as much right to sit there as he had.

When the symphony began Paul sank into one of the rear seats with a long sigh of relief, and lost himself as he had done before the Rico. It was not that symphonies, as such, meant anything in particular to Paul, but the first sigh of the instruments seemed to free some hilarious and potent spirit within him; something that struggled there like the Genius in the bottle found by the Arab fisherman. He felt a sudden zest of life; the lights danced before his eyes and the concert hall blazed into unimaginable splendour. When the soprano soloist came on, Paul forgot even the nastiness of his teacher's being there and gave himself up to the peculiar stimulus such personages always had for him. The soloist chanced to be a German woman, by no means in her first youth, and the mother of many children; but she wore an elaborate gown and a tiara, and above all she had that indefinable air of achievement, that world-shine upon her, which, in Paul's eyes, made her a veritable queen of Romance.

After a concert was over Paul was always irritable and wretched until he got to sleep, and to-night he was even more than usually restless. He had the feeling of not being able to let down, of its being impossible to give up this delicious excitement which was the only thing that could be called living at all. During the last number he withdrew and, after hastily changing his clothes in the dressing-room, slipped out to the side door where the soprano's carriage stood. Here he began pacing rapidly up and down the walk, waiting to see her come out.

Over yonder, the Schenley, in its vacant stretch, loomed big and square through the fine rain, the windows of its twelve stories glowing like those of a lighted card-board house under a Christmas tree. All the actors and singers of the better class stayed there when they were in the city, and a number of the big manufacturers of the place lived there in the winter. Paul had often hung about the hotel, watching the people go in and out, longing to enter and leave schoolmasters and dull care behind him forever.

At last the singer came out, accompanied by the conductor, who helped her into her carriage and closed the door with a cordial *auf wiedersehen* which set Paul to wondering whether she were not an old sweetheart of his. Paul followed the carriage over to the hotel, walking so rapidly as not to be far from the entrance when the singer alighted and disappeared behind the swinging glass doors that were opened by a negro in a tall hat and a long coat. In the moment that the door was ajar, it seemed to Paul that he, too, entered. He seemed to feel himself go after her up the steps, into the warm, lighted building, into an exotic, tropical world of shiny, glistening surfaces and basking ease. He reflected upon the mysterious dishes that were brought into the dining-room, the green bottles in buckets of ice, as he had seen them in the supper party pictures of the *Sunday World* supplement. A quick gust of wind brought the rain down with sudden vehemence, and Paul was startled to find that he was still outside in the slush of the gravel driveway; that his boots were letting in the water and his scanty overcoat was clinging wet about him; that the lights in front of the concert hall were out, and that the rain was driving in sheets between him and the orange glow of the windows above him. There it was, what he wanted—tangibly before him, like the fairy world of a Christmas pantomime, but mocking spirits stood guard at the doors, and, as the rain beat in his face, Paul wondered whether he were destined always to shiver in the black night outside, looking up at it.

He turned and walked reluctantly toward the car tracks. The end had to come sometime; his father in his night-clothes at the top of the stairs, explanations that did not explain, hastily improvised fictions that were forever tripping him up, his upstairs room and its horrible yellow wall-paper, the creaking bureau with the greasy plush collar-box, and over his painted wooden bed the pictures of George Washington and John Calvin, and the framed motto, "Feed my Lambs," which had been worked in red worsted by his mother.

Half an hour later, Paul alighted from his car and went slowly down one of the side streets off the main thoroughfare. It was a highly respectable street, where all the houses were exactly alike, and where business men of moderate means begot and reared large families of children, all of whom went to Sabbath-school and learned the shorter catechism, and were interested in arithmetic; all of whom were as exactly alike as their homes, and of a piece with the monotony in which they lived. Paul never went up Cordelia Street without a shudder of loathing. His home was next the house of the Cumberland minister. He approached it to-night with the nerveless sense of defeat, the hopeless feeling of sinking back forever into ugliness and commonness that he had always had when he came home. The moment he turned into Cordelia Street he felt the waters close above his head. After each of these orgies of living, he experienced all the physical depression which follows a debauch; the loathing of respectable beds, of common food, of a house penetrated by kitchen odours; a shuddering repulsion for the flavourless, colourless mass of every-day existence; a morbid desire for cool things and soft lights and fresh flowers.

The nearer he approached the house, the more absolutely unequal Paul felt to the sight of it all: his ugly sleeping chamber; the cold bath-room with the grimy zinc tub, the cracked mirror, the dripping spiggots;

his father, at the top of the stairs, his hairy legs sticking out from his nightshirt, his feet thrust into carpet slippers. He was so much later than usual that there would certainly be inquiries and reproaches. Paul stopped short before the door. He felt that he could not be accosted by his father to-night; that he could not toss again on that miserable bed. He would not go in. He would tell his father that he had no car fare, and it was raining so hard he had gone home with one of the boys and stayed all night.

Meanwhile, he was wet and cold. He went around to the back of the house and tried one of the basement windows, found it open, raised it cautiously, and scrambled down the cellar wall to the floor. There he stood, holding his breath, terrified by the noise he had made, but the floor above him was silent, and there was no creak on the stairs. He found a soap-box, and carried it over to the soft ring of light that streamed from the furnace door, and sat down. He was horribly afraid of rats, so he did not try to sleep, but sat looking distrustfully at the dark, still terrified lest he might have awakened his father. In such reactions, after one of the experiences which made days and nights out of the dreary blanks of the calendar, when his senses were deadened, Paul's head was always singularly clear. Suppose his father had heard him getting in at the window and had come down and shot him for a burglar? Then, again, suppose his father had come down, pistol in hand, and he had cried out in time to save himself, and his father had been horrified to think how nearly he had killed him? Then, again, suppose a day should come when his father would remember that night, and wish there had been no warning cry to stay his hand? With this last supposition Paul entertained himself until daybreak.

The following Sunday was fine; the sodden November chill was broken by the last flash of autumnal summer. In the morning Paul had to go to church and Sabbath-school, as always. On seasonable Sunday afternoons the burghers of Cordelia Street always sat out on their front "stoops," and talked to their neighbours on the next stoop, or called to those across the street in neighbourly fashion. The men usually sat on gay cushions placed upon the steps that led down to the sidewalk, while the women, in their Sunday "waists," sat in rockers on the cramped porches, pretending to be greatly at their ease. The children played in the streets; there were so many of them that the place resembled the recreation grounds of a kindergarten. The men on the steps—all in their shirt sleeves, their vests unbuttoned—sat with their legs well apart, their stomachs comfortably protruding, and talked of the prices of things, or told anecdotes of the sagacity of their various chiefs and overlords. They occasionally looked over the multitude of squabbling children, listened affectionately to their high-pitched, nasal voices, smiling to see their own proclivities reproduced in their offspring, and interspersed their legends of the iron kings with remarks about their sons' progress at school, their grades in arithmetic, and the amounts they had saved in their toy banks.

On this last Sunday of November, Paul sat all the afternoon on the lowest step of his "stoop," staring into the street, while his sisters, in their rockers, were talking to the minister's daughters next door about how many shirt-waists they had made in the last week, and how many waffles someone had eaten at the last church supper. When the weather was warm, and his father was in a particularly jovial frame of mind, the girls made lemonade, which was always brought out in a red-glass pitcher, ornamented with forget-me-nots in blue enamel. This the girls thought very fine, and the neighbours always joked about the suspicious colour of the pitcher.

To-day Paul's father sat on the top step, talking to a young man who shifted a restless baby from knee to knee. He happened to be the young man who was daily held up to Paul as a model, and after whom it was his father's dearest hope that he would pattern. This young man was of a ruddy complexion, with a compressed, red mouth, and faded, near-sighted eyes, over which he wore thick spectacles, with gold bows that curved about his ears. He was clerk to one of the magnates of a great steel corporation, and was looked upon in Cordelia Street as a young man with a future. There was a story that, some five years ago—he was now barely twenty-six—he had been a trifle dissipated but in order to curb his appetites and save the loss of time and strength that a sowing of wild oats might have entailed, he had taken his chief's advice, oft reiterated to his employees, and at twenty-one had married the first woman whom he could persuade to share his fortunes. She happened to be an angular school-mistress, much older than he, who also wore thick glasses, and who had now borne him four children, all near-sighted, like herself.

The young man was relating how his chief, now cruising in the Mediterranean, kept in touch with all the details of the business, arranging his office hours on his yacht just as though he were at home, and "knocking off work enough to keep two stenographers busy." His father told, in turn, the plan his corporation was considering, of putting in an electric railway plant in Cairo. Paul snapped his teeth; he had an awful apprehension that they might spoil it all before he got there. Yet he rather liked to hear these legends of the iron kings, that were told and retold on Sundays and holidays; these stories of palaces in Venice, yachts on the Mediterranean, and high play at Monte Carlo appealed to his fancy, and he was interested in the triumphs of these cash boys who had become famous, though he had no mind for the cash-boy stage.

After supper was over, and he had helped to dry the dishes, Paul nervously asked his father whether he could go to George's to get some help in his geometry, and still more nervously asked for car fare. This latter request he had to repeat, as his father, on principle, did not like to hear requests for money, whether much or little. He asked Paul whether he could not go to some boy who lived nearer, and told him that he ought not to leave his school work until Sunday; but he gave him the dime. He was not a poor man, but he had a worthy ambition to come up in the world. His only reason for allowing Paul to usher was, that he thought a boy ought to be earning a little.

Paul bounded upstairs, scrubbed the greasy odour of the dish-water from his hands with the ill-smelling soap he hated, and then shook over his fingers a few drops of violet water from the bottle he kept hidden in his drawer. He left the house with his geometry conspicuously under his arm, and the moment he got out of Cordelia Street and boarded a downtown car, he shook off the lethargy of two deadening days, and began to live again.

The leading juvenile of the permanent stock company which played at one of the downtown theatres was an acquaintance of Paul's, and the boy had been invited to drop in at the Sunday-night rehearsals whenever he could. For more than a year Paul had spent every available moment loitering about Charley Edwards's dressing-room. He had won a place among Edwards's following not only because the young actor, who could not afford to employ a dresser, often found him useful, but because he recognized in Paul something akin to what churchmen term "vocation."

It was at the theatre and at Carnegie Hall that Paul really lived; the rest was but a sleep and a forgetting. This was Paul's fairy tale, and it had for him all the allurement of a secret love. The moment he inhaled the gassy, painty, dusty odour behind the scenes, he breathed like a prisoner set free, and felt within him the possibility of doing or saying splendid, brilliant, poetic things. The moment the cracked orchestra beat out the overture from *Martha*, or jerked at the serenade from *Rigoletto*, all stupid and ugly things slid from him, and his senses were deliciously, yet delicately fired.

Perhaps it was because, in Paul's world, the natural nearly always wore the guise of ugliness, that a certain element of artificiality seemed to him necessary in beauty. Perhaps it was because his experience of life elsewhere was so full of Sabbath-school picnics, petty economies, wholesome advice as to how to succeed in life, and the unescapable odours of cooking, that he found this existence so alluring, these smartly-clad men and women so attractive, that he was so moved by these starry apple orchards that bloomed perennially under the lime-light.

It would be difficult to put it strongly enough how convincingly the stage entrance of that theatre was for Paul the actual portal of Romance. Certainly none of the company ever suspected it, least of all Charley Edwards. It was very like the old stories that used to float about London of fabulously rich Jews, who had subterranean halls there, with palms, and fountains, and soft lamps and richly apparelled women who never saw the disenchanting light of London day. So, in the midst of that smoke-palled city, enamoured of figures and grimy toil, Paul had his secret temple, his wishing carpet, his bit of blue-and-white Mediterranean shore bathed in perpetual sunshine.

Several of Paul's teachers had a theory that his imagination had been perverted by garish fiction, but the truth was that he scarcely ever read at all. The books at home were not such as would either tempt or corrupt a youthful mind, and as for reading the novels that some of his friends urged upon him—well, he got what he wanted much more quickly from music; any sort of music, from an orchestra to a barrel organ. He needed only the spark, the indescribable thrill that made his imagination master of his senses, and he could make plots and pictures enough of his own. It was equally true that he was not stage struck—not, at any rate, in the usual acceptation of that expression. He had no desire to become an actor, any more than he had to become a musician. He felt no necessity to do any of these things; what he wanted was to see, to be in the atmosphere, float on the wave of it, to be carried out, blue league after blue league, away from everything.

After a night behind the scenes, Paul found the school-room more than ever repulsive; the bare floors and naked walls; the prosy men who never wore frock coats, or violets in their buttonholes; the women with their dull gowns, shrill voices, and pitiful seriousness about prepositions that govern the dative. He could not bear to have the other pupils think, for a moment, that he took these people seriously; he must convey to them that he considered it all trivial, and was there only by way of a jest, anyway. He had autographed pictures of all the members of the stock company which he showed his classmates, telling them the most incredible stories of his familiarity with these people, of his acquaintance with the soloists who came to Carnegie Hall, his suppers with them and the flowers he sent them. When these stories lost their effect, and his audience grew listless, he became desperate and would bid all the boys good-bye, announcing that he was going to travel for awhile; going to Naples, to Venice, to Egypt. Then, next Monday, he would slip back, conscious and nervously smiling; his sister was ill, and he should have to defer his voyage until spring.

Matters went steadily worse with Paul at school. In the itch to let his instructors know how heartily he despised them and their homilies, and how thoroughly he was appreciated elsewhere, he mentioned once or twice that he had no time to fool with theorems; adding—with a twitch of the eyebrows and a touch of that nervous bravado which so perplexed them—that he was helping the people down at the stock company; they were old friends of his.

The upshot of the matter was that the Principal went to Paul's father, and Paul was taken out of school and put to work. The manager at Carnegie Hall was told to get another usher in his stead; the doorkeeper at the theatre was warned not to admit him to the house; and Charley Edwards remorsefully promised the boy's father not to see him again.

The members of the stock company were vastly amused when some of Paul's stories reached them—especially the women. They were hard-working women, most of them supporting indigent husbands or brothers, and they laughed rather bitterly at having stirred the boy to such fervid and florid inventions. They agreed with the faculty and with his father that Paul's was a bad case.

The east-bound train was ploughing through a January snow-storm; the dull dawn was beginning to show grey when the engine whistled a mile out of Newark. Paul started up from the seat where he had lain curled in uneasy slumber, rubbed the breath-misted window glass with his hand, and peered out. The snow was whirling in curling eddies above the white bottom lands, and the drifts lay already deep in the fields and along the fences, while here and there the long dead grass and dried weed stalks protruded black above it. Lights shone from the scattered houses, and a gang of labourers who stood beside the track waved their lanterns.

Paul had slept very little, and he felt grimy and uncomfortable. He had made the all-night journey in a day coach, partly because he was ashamed, dressed as he was, to go into a Pullman, and partly because he was afraid of being seen there by some Pittsburgh business man, who might have noticed him in Denny & Carson's office. When the whistle awoke him, he clutched quickly at his breast pocket, glancing about him with an uncertain smile. But the little, clay-bespattered Italians were still sleeping, the slatternly women across the aisle were in open-mouthed oblivion, and even the crumby, crying babies were for the nonce stilled. Paul settled back to struggle with his impatience as best he could.

When he arrived at the Jersey City station, he hurried through his breakfast, manifestly ill at ease and keeping a sharp eye about him. After he reached the Twenty-third Street station, he consulted a cabman and had himself driven to a men's furnishings establishment that was just opening for the day. He spent upward of two hours there, buying with endless reconsidering and great care. His new street suit he put on in the fitting-room; the frock coat and dress clothes he had bundled into the cab with his linen. Then he drove to a hatter's and a shoe house. His next errand was at Tiffany's, where he selected his silver and a new scarf-pin. He would not wait to have his silver marked, he said. Lastly, he stopped at a trunk shop on Broadway, and had his purchases packed into various travelling bags.

It was a little after one o'clock when he drove up to the Waldorf, and after settling with the cabman, went into the office. He registered from Washington; said his mother and father had been abroad, and that he had come down to await the arrival of their steamer. He told his story plausibly and had no trouble, since he volunteered to pay for them in advance, in engaging his rooms; a sleeping-room, sitting-room, and bath.

Not once, but a hundred times, Paul had planned this entry into New York. He had gone over every detail of it with Charley Edwards, and in his scrap book at home there were pages of description about New York hotels, cut from the Sunday papers. When he was shown to his sitting-room on the eighth floor he saw at a glance that everything was as it should be; there was but one detail in his mental picture that the place did not realize, so he rang for the bell boy and sent him down for flowers. He moved about nervously until the boy returned, putting away his new linen and fingering it delightedly as he did so. When the flowers came he put them hastily into water, and then tumbled into a hot bath. Presently he came out of his white bath-room, resplendent in his new silk underwear, and playing with the tassels of his red robe. The snow was whirling so fiercely outside his windows that he could scarcely see across the street, but within the air was deliciously soft and fragrant. He put the violets and jonquils on the taboret beside the couch, and threw himself down, with a long sigh, covering himself with a Roman blanket. He was thoroughly tired; he had been in such haste, he had stood up to such a strain, covered so much ground in the last twenty-four hours, that he wanted to think how it had all come about. Lulled by the sound of the wind, the warm air, and the cool fragrance of the flowers, he sank into deep, drowsy retrospection.

It had been wonderfully simple; when they had shut him out of the theatre and concert hall, when they had taken away his bone, the whole thing was virtually determined. The rest was a mere matter of opportunity. The only thing that at all surprised him was his own courage—for he realized well enough that he had always been tormented by fear, a sort of apprehensive dread that, of late years, as the meshes of the lies he had told closed about him, had been pulling the muscles of his body tighter and tighter. Until now he could not remember the time when he had not been dreading something. Even when he was a little boy, it was always there—behind him, or before, or on either side. There had always been the shadowed corner, the dark place into which he dared not look, but from which something seemed always to be watching him—and Paul had done things that were not pretty to watch, he knew.

But now he had a curious sense of relief, as though he had at last thrown down the gauntlet to the thing in the corner.

Yet it was but a day since he had been sulking in the traces; but yesterday afternoon that he had been sent to the bank with Denny & Carson's deposit, as usual—but this time he was instructed to leave the book to be balanced. There was above two thousand dollars in checks, and nearly a thousand in the bank notes which he had taken from the book and quietly transferred to his pocket. At the bank he had made out a new deposit slip. His nerves had been steady enough to permit of his returning to the office, where he had finished his work and asked for a full day's holiday to-morrow, Saturday, giving a perfectly reasonable pretext. The bank book, he knew, would not be returned before Monday or Tuesday, and his father would be out of town for the next week. From the time he slipped the bank notes into his pocket until he boarded the night train for New York, he had not known a moment's hesitation. It was not the first time Paul had steered through treacherous waters.

How astonishingly easy it had all been; here he was, the thing done; and this time there would be no awakening, no figure at the top of the stairs. He watched the snow flakes whirling by his window until he fell asleep.

When he awoke, it was three o'clock in the afternoon. He bounded up with a start; half of one of his precious days gone already! He spent more than an hour in dressing, watching every stage of his toilet carefully in the mirror. Everything was quite perfect; he was exactly the kind of boy he had always wanted to be.

When he went downstairs Paul took a carriage and drove up Fifth Avenue toward the Park. The snow had somewhat abated; carriages and tradesmen's wagons were hurrying soundlessly to and fro in the winter twilight; boys in woollen mufflers were shovelling off the doorsteps; the avenue stages made fine spots of colour against the white street. Here and there on the corners were stands, with whole flower gardens blooming under glass cases, against the sides of which the snow flakes stuck and melted; violets, roses, carnations, lilies of the valley—somehow vastly more lovely and alluring that they blossomed thus unnaturally in the snow. The Park itself was a wonderful stage winter-piece.

When he returned, the pause of the twilight had ceased, and the tune of the streets had changed. The snow was falling faster, lights streamed from the hotels that reared their dozen stories fearlessly up into the storm, defying the raging Atlantic winds. A long, black stream of carriages poured down the avenue, intersected here and there by other streams, tending horizontally. There were a score of cabs about the entrance of his hotel, and his driver had to wait. Boys in livery were running in and out of the awning stretched across the sidewalk, up and down the red velvet carpet laid from the door to the street. Above, about, within it all was the rumble and roar, the hurry and toss of thousands of human beings as hot for pleasure as himself, and on every side of him towered the glaring affirmation of the omnipotence of wealth.

The boy set his teeth and drew his shoulders together in a spasm of realization; the plot of all dramas, the text of all romances, the nerve-stuff of all sensations was whirling about him like the snow flakes. He burnt like a faggot in a tempest.

When Paul went down to dinner, the music of the orchestra came floating up the elevator shaft to greet him. His head whirled as he stepped into the thronged corridor, and he sank back into one of the chairs against the wall to get his breath. The lights, the chatter, the perfumes, the bewildering medley of colour—he had, for a moment, the feeling of not being able to stand it. But only for a moment; these were his own people, he told himself. He went slowly about the corridors, through the writing-rooms, smoking-rooms, reception-rooms, as though he were exploring the chambers of an enchanted palace, built and peopled for him alone.

When he reached the dining-room he sat down at a table near a window. The flowers, the white linen, the many-coloured wine glasses, the gay toilettes of the women, the low popping of corks, the undulating repetitions of the *Blue Danube* from the orchestra, all flooded Paul's dream with bewildering radiance. When the roseate tinge of his champagne was added—that cold, precious, bubbling stuff that creamed and foamed in his glass—Paul wondered that there were honest men in the world at all. This was what all the world was fighting for, he reflected; this was what all the struggle was about. He doubted the reality of his past. Had he ever known a place called Cordelia Street, a place where fagged-looking business men got on the early car; mere rivets in a machine they seemed to Paul,—sickening men, with combings of children's hair always hanging to their coats, and the smell of cooking in their clothes. Cordelia Street—Ah! that belonged to another time and country; had he not always been thus, had he not sat here night after night, from as far back as he could remember, looking pensively over just such shimmering textures, and slowly twirling the stem of a glass like this one between his thumb and middle finger? He rather thought he had.

He was not in the least abashed or lonely. He had no especial desire to meet or to know any of these people; all he demanded was the right to look on and conjecture, to watch the pageant. The mere stage properties were all he contended for. Nor was he lonely later in the evening, in his lodge at the Metropolitan. He was now entirely rid of his nervous misgivings, of his forced aggressiveness, of the imperative desire to show himself different from his surroundings. He felt now that his surroundings explained him. Nobody questioned the purple; he had only to wear it passively. He had only to glance down at his attire to reassure himself that here it would be impossible for anyone to humiliate him.

He found it hard to leave his beautiful sitting-room to go to bed that night, and sat long watching the raging storm from his turret window. When he went to sleep it was with the lights turned on in his bedroom; partly because of his old timidity, and partly so that, if he should wake in the night, there would be no wretched moment of doubt, no horrible suspicion of yellow wall-paper, or of Washington and Calvin above his bed.

Sunday morning the city was practically snowbound. Paul breakfasted late, and in the afternoon he fell in with a wild San Francisco boy, a freshman at Yale, who said he had run down for a "little flyer" over Sunday. The young man offered to show Paul the night side of the town, and the two boys went out together after dinner, not returning to the hotel until seven o'clock the next morning. They had started out in the confiding warmth of a champagne friendship, but their parting in the elevator was singularly cool. The freshman pulled himself together to make his train, and Paul went to bed. He awoke at two o'clock in the afternoon, very thirsty and dizzy, and rang for ice-water, coffee, and the Pittsburgh papers.

On the part of the hotel management, Paul excited no suspicion. There was this to be said for him, that he wore his spoils with dignity and in no way made himself conspicuous. Even under the glow of his wine he was never boisterous, though he found the stuff like a magician's wand for wonder-building. His chief greediness lay in his ears and eyes, and his excesses were not offencive ones. His dearest pleasures were the grey winter twilights in his sitting-room; his quiet enjoyment of his flow-ers, his clothes, his wide divan, his cigarette, and his sense of power. He could not remember a time when he had felt so at peace with himself. The mere release from the necessity of petty lying, lying every day and every day, restored his self-respect. He had never lied for pleasure, even at school; but to be noticed and admired, to assert his difference from other Cordelia Street boys; and he felt a good deal more manly, more honest, even, now that he had no need for boastful pretensions, now that he could, as his actor friends used to say, "dress the part." It was characteris-tic that remorse did not occur to him. His golden days went by without a shadow, and he made each as perfect as he could.

On the eighth day after his arrival in New York he found the whole affair exploited in the Pittsburgh papers, exploited with a wealth of detail which indicated that local news of a sensational nature was at a low ebb. The firm of Denny & Carson announced that the boy's father had refunded the full amount of the theft, and that they had no intention of prosecuting. The Cumberland minister had been interviewed, and expressed his hope of yet reclaiming the motherless lad, and his Sabbath-school teacher declared that she would spare no effort to that end. The rumour had reached Pittsburgh that the boy had been seen in a New York hotel, and his father had gone East to find him and bring him home.

Paul had just come in to dress for dinner; he sank into a chair, weak to the knees, and clasped his head in his hands. It was to be worse than jail, even; the tepid waters of Cordelia Street were to close over him finally and forever. The grey monotony stretched before him in hopeless, unre-lieved years; Sabbath-school, Young People's Meeting, the yellow-papered room, the damp dish-towels; it all rushed back upon him with a sickening vividness. He had the old feeling that the orchestra had sud-denly stopped, the sinking sensation that the play was over. The sweat broke out on his face, and he sprang to his feet, looked about him with his white, conscious smile, and winked at himself in the mirror. With something of the old childish belief in miracles with which he had so often gone to class, all his lessons unlearned, Paul dressed and dashed whistling down the corridor to the elevator.

He had no sooner entered the dining-room and caught the measure of the music than his remembrance was lightened by his old elastic power of claiming the moment, mounting with it, and finding it all sufficient. The glare and glitter about him, the mere scenic accessories had again, and for the last time, their old potency. He would show himself that he was game, he would finish the thing splendidly. He doubted, more than ever, the existence of Cordelia Street, and for the first time he drank his wine recklessly. Was he not, after all, one of those fortunate beings born to the purple, was he not still himself and in his own place? He drummed a nervous accompaniment to the Pagliacci music and looked about him, telling himself over and over that it had paid.

He reflected drowsily, to the swell of the music and the chill sweetness of his wine, that he might have done it more wisely. He might have caught an outbound steamer and been well out of their clutches before now. But the other side of the world had seemed too far away and too uncertain then; he could not have waited for it; his need had been too sharp. If he had to choose over again, he would do the same thing to-morrow. He looked affectionately about the dining-room, now gilded with a soft mist. Ah, it had paid indeed!

Paul was awakened next morning by a painful throbbing in his head and feet. He had thrown himself across the bed without undressing, and had slept with his shoes on. His limbs and hands were lead heavy, and his tongue and throat were parched and burnt. There came upon him one of those fateful attacks of clear-headedness that never occurred except when he was physically exhausted and his nerves hung loose. He lay still, closed his eyes and let the tide of things wash over him.

His father was in New York; "stopping at some joint or other," he told himself. The memory of successive summers on the front stoop fell upon him like a weight of black water. He had not a hundred dollars left; and he knew now, more than ever, that money was everything, the wall that stood between all he loathed and all he wanted. The thing was winding itself up; he had thought of that on his first glorious day in New York, and had even provided a way to snap the thread. It lay on his dressing-table now; he had got it out last night when he came blindly up from dinner, but the shiny metal hurt his eyes, and he disliked the looks of it.

He rose and moved about with a painful effort, succumbing now and again to attacks of nausea. It was the old depression exaggerated; all the world had become Cordelia Street. Yet somehow he was not afraid of anything, was absolutely calm; perhaps because he had looked into the dark corner at last and knew. It was bad enough, what he saw there, but somehow not so bad as his long fear of it had been. He saw everything clearly now. He had a feeling that he had made the best of it, that he had lived the sort of life he was meant to live, and for half an hour he sat staring at the revolver. But he told himself that was not the way, so he went downstairs and took a cab to the ferry.

When Paul arrived at Newark, he got off the train and took another cab, directing the driver to follow the Pennsylvania tracks out of the town. The snow lay heavy on the roadways and had drifted deep in the open fields. Only here and there the dead grass or dried weed stalks projected, singularly black, above it. Once well into the country, Paul dismissed the carriage and walked, floundering along the tracks, his mind a medley of irrelevant things. He seemed to hold in his brain an actual picture of everything he had seen that morning. He remembered every feature of both his drivers, of the toothless old woman from whom he had bought the red flowers in his coat, the agent from whom he had got his ticket, and all of his fellow-passengers on the ferry. His mind, unable to cope with vital matters near at hand, worked feverishly and deftly at sorting and grouping these images. They made for him a part of the ugliness of the world, of the ache in his head, and the bitter burning on his tongue. He stooped and put a handful of snow into his mouth as he walked, but that, too, seemed hot. When he reached a little hillside, where the tracks ran through a cut some twenty feet below him, he stopped and sat down.

The carnations in his coat were drooping with the cold, he noticed; their red glory all over. It occurred to him that all the flowers he had seen in the glass cases that first night must have gone the same way, long before this. It was only one splendid breath they had, in spite of their brave mockery at the winter outside the glass; and it was a losing game in the end, it seemed, this revolt against the homilies by which the world is run. Paul took one of the blossoms carefully from his coat and scooped a little hole in the snow, where he covered it up. Then he dozed a while, from his weak condition, seemingly insensible to the cold.

The sound of an approaching train awoke him, and he started to his feet, remembering only his resolution, and afraid least he should be too late. He stood watching the approaching locomotive, his teeth chattering, his lips drawn away from them in a frightened smile; once or twice he glanced nervously sidewise, as though he were being watched. When the right moment came, he jumped. As he fell, the folly of his haste occurred to him with merciless clearness, the vastness of what he had left undone. There flashed through his brain, clearer than ever before, the blue of Adriatic water, the yellow of Algerian sands.

He felt something strike his chest, and that his body was being thrown swiftly through the air, on and on, immeasurably far and fast, while his limbs were gently relaxed. Then, because the picture making mechanism was crushed, the disturbing visions flashed into black, and Paul dropped back into the immense design of things.

Amy Lowell
(1874–1925)

orn into a wealthy, aristocratic, and intellectual New England family, Amy Lowell determined that poetry be her life's work. But her society background as one of the famous Boston Lowells, her forcefulness, and especially her size hindered her. In an era where the "poetess" was expected to be girlish, fragile, and slender, Lowell was fat, and cruelly mocked for it. She had a prolonged breakdown after her mother's death in 1898. Ezra Pound, whom she met in London in 1913 when she was thirty-nine, preferred dryadlike women poets like H. D.; he called Lowell the "hippopoetess." Her first book of poems, the Keatsian *A Dome of Many-Coloured Glass* (1912), was dismissed by critics. But Lowell took from Pound the ideas which shaped her subsequent bold free verse. Pound himself abandoned imagism, and Lowell became its champion, publishing a three-volume anthology called *Some Imagist Poets* (1917). In her poem "The Sisters," Lowell both saluted the women poets who came before her and declared her difference from them. In her personal life, Lowell formed a happy partnership with the actress Ada Dwyer Russell, which lasted until Lowell's early death from a stroke.

The Sisters (1925)

Taking us by and large, we're a queer lot
We women who write poetry. And when you think
How few of us there've been, it's queerer still.
I wonder what it is that makes us do it,
Singles us out to scribble down, man-wise,
The fragments of ourselves. Why are we
Already mother-creatures, double-bearing,
With matrices in body and in brain?
I rather think that there is just the reason
We are so sparse a kind of human being;
The strength of forty thousand Atlases
Is needed for our every-day concerns.

There's Sapho, now I wonder what was Sapho.
I know a single slender thing about her:
That, loving, she was like a burning birch-tree
All tall and glittering fire, and that she wrote
Like the same fire caught up to Heaven and held there,
A frozen blaze before it broke and fell.
Ah, me! I wish I could have talked to Sapho,
Surprised her reticences by flinging mine
Into the wind. This tossing off of garments
Which cloud the soul is none too easy doing
With us to-day. But still I think with Sapho
One might accomplish it, were she in the mood
To bare her loveliness of words and tell
The reasons, as she possibly conceived them,
Of why they are so lovely. Just to know
How she came at them, just to watch
The crisp sea sunshine playing on her hair,
And listen, thinking all the while 'twas she
Who spoke and that we two were sisters
Of a strange, isolated little family.
And she is Sapho—Sapho—not Miss or Mrs.,
A leaping fire we call so for convenience;
But Mrs. Browning—who would ever think
Of such presumption as to call her "Ba."
Which draws the perfect line between sea-cliffs
And a close-shuttered room in Wimpole Street.
Sapho could fly her impulses like bright
Balloons tip-tilting to a morning air
And write about it. Mrs. Browning's heart
Was squeezed in stiff conventions. So she lay
Stretched out upon a sofa, reading Greek
And speculating, as I must suppose,
In just this way on Sapho; all the need,
The huge, imperious need of loving, crushed
Within the body she believed so sick.
And it was sick, poor lady, because words
Are merely simulacra after deeds
Have wrought a pattern; when they take the place
Of actions they breed a poisonous miasma
Which, though it leave the brain, eats up the body.

So Mrs. Browning, aloof and delicate,
Lay still upon her sofa, all her strength
Going to uphold her over-topping brain.
It seems miraculous, but she escaped
To freedom and another motherhood
Than that of poems. She was a very woman
And needed both.
     If I had gone to call,
Would Wimpole Street have been the kindlier place,
Or Casa Guidi, in which to have met her?
I am a little doubtful of that meeting,
For Queen Victoria was very young and strong
And all-pervading in her apogee
At just that time. If we had stuck to poetry,
Sternly refusing to be drawn off by mesmerism
Or Roman revolutions, it might have done.
For, after all, she is another sister,
But always, I rather think, an older sister
And not herself so curious a technician
As to admit newfangled modes of writing—
"Except, of course, in Robert, and that is neither
Here nor there for Robert is a genius."
I do not like the turn this dream is taking,
Since I am very fond of Mrs. Browning
And very much indeed should like to hear her
Graciously asking me to call her "Ba."
But then the Devil of Verisimilitude
Creeps in and forces me to know she wouldn't.
Convention again, and how it chafes my nerves,
For we are such a little family
Of singing sisters, and as if I didn't know
What those years felt like tied down to the sofa.
Confound Victoria, and the slimy inhibitions
She loosed on all us Anglo-Saxon creatures!
Suppose there hadn't been a Robert Browning,
No *Sonnets from the Portuguese* would have been written.
They are the first of all her poems to be,
One might say, fertilized. For, after all,
A poet is flesh and blood as well as brain
And Mrs. Browning, as I said before,

Was very, very woman. Well, there are two
Of us, and vastly unlike that's for certain.
Unlike at least until we tear the veils
Away which commonly gird souls. I scarcely think
Mrs. Browning would have approved the process
In spite of what had surely been relief;
For speaking souls must always want to speak
Even when bat-eyed, narrow-minded Queens
Set prudishness to keep the keys of impulse.
Then do the frowning Gods invent new banes
And make the need of sofas. But Sapho was dead
And I, and others, not yet peeped above
The edge of possibility. So that's an end
To speculating over tea-time talks
Beyond the movement of pentameters
With Mrs. Browning.
            But I go dreaming on,
In love with these my spiritual relations.
I rather think I see myself walk up
A flight of wooden steps and ring a bell
And send a card in to Miss Dickinson.
Yet that's a very silly way to do.
I should have taken the dream twist-ends about
And climbed over the fence and found her deep
Engrossed in the doings of a humming-bird
Among nasturtiums. Not having expected strangers,
She might forget to think me one, and holding up
A finger say quite casually: "Take care.
Don't frighten him, he's only just begun."
"Now this," I well believe I should have thought,
"Is even better than Sapho. With Emily
You're really here, or never anywhere at all
In range of mind." Wherefore, having begun
In the strict centre, we could slowly progress
To various circumferences, as we pleased.
We could, but should we? That would quite depend
On Emily. I think she'd be exacting,
Without intention possibly, and ask
A thousand tight-rope tricks of understanding.
But, bless you, I would somersault all day

If by so doing I might stay with her.
I hardly think that we should mention souls
Although they might just round the corner from us
In some half-quizzical, half-wistful metaphor.
I'm very sure that I should never seek
To turn her parables to stated fact.
Sapho would speak, I think, quite openly,
And Mrs. Browning guard a careful silence,
But Emily would set doors ajar and slam them
And love you for your speed of observation.

Strange trio of my sisters, most diverse,
And how extraordinarily unlike
Each is to me, and which way shall I go?
Sapho spent and gained; and Mrs. Browning,
After a miser girlhood, cut the strings
Which tied her money-bags and let them run;
But Emily hoarded—hoarded—only giving
Herself to cold, white paper. Starved and tortured,
She cheated her despair with games of patience
And fooled herself by winning. Frail little elf,
The lonely brain-child of a gaunt maturity,
She hung her womanhood upon a bough
And played ball with the stars—too long—too long—
The garment of herself hung on a tree
Until at last she lost even the desire
To take it down. Whose fault? Why let us say,
To be consistent, Queen Victoria's.
But really, not to over-rate the queen,
I feel obliged to mention Martin Luther,
And behind him the long line of Church Fathers
Who draped their prurience like a dirty cloth
About the naked majesty of God.
Good-bye, my sisters, all of you are great,
And all of you are marvellously strange,
And none of you has any word for me.
I cannot write like you, I cannot think
In terms of Pagan or of Christian now.
I only hope that possibly some day
Some other woman with an itch for writing

May turn to me as I have turned to you
And chat with me a brief few minutes. How
We lie, we poets! It is three good hours
I have been dreaming. Has it seemed so long
To you? And yet I thank you for the time
Although you leave me sad and self-distrustful,
For older sisters are very sobering things.
Put on your cloaks, my dears, the motor's waiting.
No, you have not seemed strange to me, but near,
Frightfully near, and rather terrifying.
I understand you all, for in myself—
Is that presumption? Yet indeed it's true—
We are one family. And still my answer
Will not be any one of yours, I see.
Well, never mind that now. Good night! Good night!

Gertrude Stein
(1874–1946)

Often described as the mother of American modernism, Gertrude Stein was a relentlessly experimental writer, who attempted to create with words what the Cubist painters she met in Paris and whose work she collected did with paint. Stein did not use words, grammar, sentences, or paragraphs to describe reality, activities, places, or characters, as most writers of fiction attempted to do. Words, she believed, were simply a medium and material available to the literary artist. Stein was remarkably free as well from the social constraints that inhibited most American women writers. She was the youngest of five children in a Jewish family, but she did not have to conform to or rebel against parental pressure; her parents had died by the time she was seventeen, and she and her sister Bertha were raised by an aunt in Baltimore. She had inherited wealth, so she did not have to work or marry in order to support herself. She was born in time to attend Radcliffe College and went on to study medicine at Johns Hopkins University, but she decided to move to Paris with her brother Leo in 1903, where she could design her own life and career. As a lesbian in a long partnership with Alice B. Toklas, who also served as her typist, housekeeper, and hostess, she was free from domestic responsibilities but provided with love and attention.

Stein's poems, stories, plays, and essays were mainly self-published during her lifetime. By the 1920s, she had become a celebrity literary expatriate, whose salon at 27 rue de Fleurus attracted an international group of (mostly male) artists and writers. "Miss Furr and Miss Skeene" is a good introduction to Stein's techniques. It is a double "word portrait" of a lesbian couple, based on the ménage of two real Midwestern painters Stein met in Paris, Ethel Mars and Maud Hunt Squires. With its insistent repetition of the word "gay," which Stein uses over one hundred times in just a few pages, "Miss Furr and Miss Skeene" (whose names sound like fur and skin) is regarded as one of the first stories about female homosexuality. Literary scholars disagree over whether "gay" was a code word for homosexuality by the early 1920s, but certainly after Stein published this word portrait in *Vogue* it became one.

Miss Furr and Miss Skeene (1922)

Helen Furr had quite a pleasant home. Mrs. Furr was quite a pleasant woman. Mr. Furr was quite a pleasant man. Helen Furr had quite a pleasant voice a voice quite worth cultivating. She did not mind working. She worked to cultivate her voice. She did not find it gay living in the same place where she had always been living. She went to a place where some were cultivating something, voices and other things needing cultivating. She met Georgine Skeene there who was cultivating her voice which some thought was quite a pleasant one. Helen Furr and Georgine Skeene lived together then. Georgine Skeene liked travelling. Helen Furr did not care about travelling, she liked to stay in one place and be gay there. They were together then and travelled to another place and stayed there and were gay there.

They stayed there and were gay there, not very gay there, just gay there. They were both gay there, they were regularly working there both of them cultivating their voices there, they were both gay there. Georgine Skeene was gay there and she was regular, regular in being gay, regular in not being gay, regular in being a gay one who was one not being gay longer than was needed to be one being quite a gay one. They were both gay then there and both working there then.

They were in a way both gay there where there were many cultivating something. They were both regular in being gay there. Helen Furr was gay there, she was gayer and gayer there and really she was just gay there, she was gayer and gayer there, that is to say she found ways of being gay there that she was using in being gay there. She was gay there, not gayer and gayer, just gay there, that is to say she was not gayer by using the things she found there that were gay things, she was gay there, always she was gay there.

They were quite regularly gay there, Helen Furr and Georgine Skeene, they were regularly gay there where they were gay. They were very regularly gay.

To be regularly gay was to do every day the gay thing that they did every day. To be regularly gay was to end every day at the same time after they had been regularly gay. They were regularly gay. They were gay every day. They ended every day in the same way, at the same time, and they had been every day regularly gay.

The voice Helen Furr was cultivating was quite a pleasant one. The voice Georgine Skeene was cultivating was, some said, a better one. The voice Helen Furr was cultivating she cultivated and it was quite completely a pleasant enough one then, a cultivated enough one then. The voice Georgine Skeene was cultivating she did not cultivate too much. She cultivated it quite some. She cultivated and she would sometimes go on cultivating it and it was not then an unpleasant one, it would not be then an unpleasant one, it would be a quite richly enough cultivated one, it would be quite richly enough to be a pleasant enough one.

They were gay where there were many cultivating something. The two were gay there, were regularly gay there. Georgine Skeene would have liked to do more travelling. They did some travelling, not very much travelling, Georgine Skeene would have liked to do more travelling, Helen Furr did not care about doing travelling, she liked to stay in a place and be gay there.

They stayed in a place and were gay there, both of them stayed there, they stayed together there, they were gay there, they were regularly gay there.

They went quite often, not very often, but they did go back to where Helen Furr had a pleasant enough home and then Georgine Skeene went to a place where her brother had quite some distinction. They both went, every few years, went visiting to where Helen Furr had quite a pleasant home. Certainly Helen Furr would not find it gay to stay, she did not find it gay, she said she would not stay, she said she did not find it gay, she said she would not stay where she did not find it gay, she said she found it gay where she did stay and she did stay there where very many were cultivating something. She did stay there. She always did find it gay there.

She went to see them where she had always been living and where she did not find it gay. She had a pleasant home there, Mrs. Furr was a pleasant enough woman, Mr. Furr was a pleasant enough man, Helen told them and they were not worrying, that she did not find it gay living where she had always been living.

Georgine Skeene and Helen Furr were living where they were both cultivating their voices and they were gay there. They visited where Helen Furr had come from and then they went to where they were living where they were then regularly living.

There were some dark and heavy men there then. There were some who were not so heavy and some who were not so dark. Helen Furr and Georgine Skeene sat regularly with them. They sat regularly with the ones who were dark and heavy. They sat regularly with the ones who were not so dark. They sat regularly with the ones that were not so heavy. They sat with them regularly, sat with some of them. They went with them regularly went with them. They were regular then, they were gay then, they were where they wanted to be then where it was gay to be then, they were regularly gay then. There were men there then who were dark and heavy and they sat with them with Helen Furr and Georgine Skeene and they went with them with Miss Furr and Miss Skeene, and they went with the heavy and dark men Miss Furr and Miss Skeene went with them, and they sat with them, Miss Furr and Miss Skeene sat with them, and there were other men, some were not heavy men and they sat with Miss Furr and Miss Skeene and Miss Furr and Miss Skeene sat with them, and there were other men who were not dark men and they sat with Miss Furr and Miss Skeene and Miss Furr and Miss Skeene sat with them. Miss Furr and Miss Skeene went with them and they went with Miss Furr and Miss Skeene, some who were not heavy men, some who were not dark men. Miss Furr and Miss Skeene sat regularly, they sat with some men. Miss Furr and Miss Skeene went and there were some men with them. There were men and Miss Furr and Miss Skeene went with them, went somewhere with them, went with some of them.

Helen Furr and Georgine Skeene were regularly living where very many were living and cultivating in themselves something. Helen Furr and Georgine Skeene were living very regularly then, being very regular then in being gay then. They did then learn many ways to be gay and they were then being gay being quite regular in being gay, being gay and they were learning little things, little things in ways of being gay, they were very regular then, they were learning very many little things in ways of being gay, they were being gay and using these little things they were learning to have to be gay with regularly gay with then and they were gay the same amount they had been gay. They were quite gay, they were quite regular, they were learning little things, gay little things, they were gay inside them the same amount they had been gay, they were gay the same length of time they had been gay every day.

They were regular in being gay, they learned little things that are things in being gay, they learned many little things that are things in being gay, they were gay every day, they were regular, they were gay, they were gay the same length of time every day, they were gay, they were quite regularly gay.

Georgine Skeene went away to stay two months with her brother. Helen Furr did not go then to stay with her father and her mother. Helen Furr stayed there where they had been regularly living the two of them and she would then certainly not be lonesome, she would go on being gay. She did go on being gay. She was not any more gay but she was gay longer every day than they had been being gay when they were together being gay. She was gay then quite exactly the same way. She learned a few more little ways of being gay. She was quite gay and in the same way, the same way she had been gay and she was gay a little longer in the day, more of each day she was gay. She was gay longer every day than when the two of them had been being gay. She was gay quite in the way they had been gay, quite in the same way.

She was not lonesome then, she was not at all feeling any need of having Georgine Skeene. She was not astonished at this thing. She would have been a little astonished by this thing but she knew she was not astonished at anything and so she was not astonished at this thing not astonished at not feeling any need of having Georgine Skeene.

Helen Furr had quite a completely pleasant voice and it was quite well enough cultivated and she could use it and she did use it but then there was not any way of working at cultivating a completely pleasant voice when it has become a quite completely well enough cultivated one, and there was not much use in using it when one was not wanting it to be helping to make one a gay one. Helen Furr was not needing using her voice to be a gay one. She was gay then and sometimes she used her voice and she was not using it very often. It was quite completely enough cultivated and it was quite completely a pleasant one and she did not use it very often. She was then, she was quite exactly as gay as she had been, she was gay a little longer in the day than she had been.

She was gay exactly the same way. She was never tired of being gay, that way. She had learned very many little ways to use in being gay. Very many were telling about using other ways in being gay. She was gay enough, she was always gay exactly the same way, she was always learning little things to use in being gay, she was telling about using other ways in being gay, she was telling about learning other ways in being gay, she was learning other ways in being gay, she would be using other ways in being gay, she would always be gay in the same way, when Georgine Skeene was there not so long each day as when Georgine Skeene was away.

She came to using many ways in being gay, she came to use every way in being gay. She went on living where many were cultivating something and she was gay. She had used every way to be gay.

They did not live together then Helen Furr and Georgine Skeene. Helen Furr lived there the longer where they had been living regularly together. Then neither of them were living there any longer. Helen Furr was living somewhere else then and telling some about being gay and she was gay then and she was living quite regularly then. She was regularly gay then. She was quite regular in being gay then. She remembered all the little ways of being gay. She used all the little ways of being gay. She was quite regularly gay. She told many then the way of being gay, she taught very many then little ways they could use in being gay. She was living very well, she was gay then, she went on living then, she was regular in being gay, she always was living very well and was gay very well and was telling about little ways one could be learning to use in being gay, and later was telling them quite often, telling them again and again.

Alice Moore Dunbar-Nelson
(1875–1935)

lice Moore Dunbar-Nelson was a teacher and political activist for African-American rights, but her fiction and poetry were more influenced by fin de siècle aestheticism than by the tradition of black social protest. Of mixed-race ancestry and attracted to women, as well as marrying three times (her first husband was the celebrated black-dialect poet Paul Laurence Dunbar), Dunbar-Nelson did not fit comfortably into any racial or gender category except that of the New Woman. In "A Carnival Jangle," she used the metaphor of Carnival and Mardi Gras to describe the topsy-turvy New Orleans world of race and gender.

A Carnival Jangle (1895)

There is a merry jangle of bells in the air, an all-pervading sense of jester's noise, and the flaunting vividness of royal colours. The streets swarm with humanity,—humanity in all shapes, manners, forms, laughing, pushing, jostling, crowding, a mass of men and women and children, as varied and assorted in their several individual peculiarities as ever a crowd that gathered in one locality since the days of Babel.

It is Carnival in New Orleans; a brilliant Tuesday in February, when the very air gives forth an ozone intensely exhilarating, making one long to cut capers. The buildings are a blazing mass of royal purple and golden yellow, national flags, bunting, and decorations that laugh in the glint of the Midas sun. The streets are a crush of jesters and maskers, Jim Crows and clowns, ballet girls and Mephistos, Indians and monkeys; of wild and sudden flashes of music, of glittering pageants and comic ones, of befeathered and belled horses; a dream of colour and melody and fantasy gone wild in an effervescent bubble of beauty that shifts and changes and passes kaleidoscopelike before the bewildered eye.

A bevy of bright-eyed girls and boys of that uncertain age that hovers between childhood and maturity, were moving down Canal Street when there was a sudden jostle with another crowd meeting them. For a minute there was a deafening clamour of shouts and laughter, cracking of the whips, which all maskers carry, a jingle and clatter of carnival bells, and the masked and unmasked extricated themselves and moved from each other's paths. But in the confusion a tall Prince of Darkness had whispered to one of the girls in the unmasked crowd: "You'd better come with us, Flo; you're wasting time in that tame gang. Slip off, they'll never miss you; we'll get you a rig, and show you what life is."

And so it happened, when a half-hour passed, and the bright-eyed bevy missed Flo and couldn't find her, wisely giving up the search at last, she, the quietest and most bashful of the lot, was being initiated into the mysteries of "what life is."

Down Bourbon Street and on Toulouse and St. Peter Streets there are quaint little old-world places where one may be disguised effectually for a tiny consideration. Thither, guided by the shapely Mephisto and guarded by the team of jockeys and ballet girls, tripped Flo. Into one of the lowest-ceiled, dingiest, and most ancient-looking of these shops they stepped.

"A disguise for the demoiselle," announced Mephisto to the woman who met them. She was small and wizened and old, with yellow, flabby jaws, a neck like the throat of an alligator, and straight, white hair that stood from her head uncannily stiff.

"But the demoiselle wishes to appear a boy, un petit garçon?" she inquired, gazing eagerly at Flo's long, slender frame. Her voice was old and thin, like the high quavering of an imperfect tuning-fork, and her eyes were sharp as talons in their grasping glance.

"Mademoiselle does not wish such a costume," gruffly responded Mephisto.

"Ma foi, there is no other," said the ancient, shrugging her shoulders. "But one is left now; mademoiselle would make a fine troubadour."

"Flo," said Mephisto, "it's a daredevil scheme, try it; no one will ever know it but us, and we'll die before we tell. Besides, we must; it's late, and you couldn't find your crowd."

And that was why you might have seen a Mephisto and a slender troubadour of lovely form, with mandolin flung across his shoulder, followed by a bevy of jockeys and ballet girls, laughing and singing as they swept down Rampart Street.

When the flash and glare and brilliancy of Canal Street have palled upon the tired eye, when it is yet too soon to go home to such a prosaic thing as dinner, and one still wishes for novelty, then it is wise to go into the lower districts. There is fantasy and fancy and grotesqueness run wild in the costuming and the behaviour of the maskers. Such dances and whoops and leaps as these hideous Indians and devils do indulge in; such wild curvetings and long walks! In the open squares, where whole groups do congregate, it is wonderfully amusing. Then, too, there is a ball in every available hall, a delirious ball, where one may dance all day for ten cents; dance and grow mad for joy, and never know who were your companions, and be yourself unknown. And in the exhilaration of the day, one walks miles and miles, and dances and skips, and the fatigue is never felt.

In Washington Square, away down where Royal Street empties its stream of children great and small into the broad channel of Elysian Fields Avenue, there was a perfect Indian pow-wow. With a little imagination one might have willed away the vision of the surrounding houses, and fancied one's self again in the forest, where the natives were holding a sacred riot. The square was filled with spectators, masked and unmasked. It was amusing to watch these mimic Red-men, they seemed so fierce and earnest.

Suddenly one chief touched another on the elbow. "See that Mephisto and troubadour over there?" he whispered huskily.

"Yes; who are they?"

"I don't know the devil," responded the other, quietly, "but I'd know that other form anywhere. It's Leon, see? I know those white hands like a woman's and that restless head. Ha!"

"But there may be a mistake."

"No. I'd know that one anywhere; I feel it is he. I'll pay him now. Ah, sweetheart, you've waited long, but you shall feast now!" He was caressing something long and lithe and glittering beneath his blanket.

In a masked dance it is easy to give a death-blow between the shoulders. Two crowds meet and laugh and shout and mingle almost inextricably, and if a shriek of pain should arise, it is not noticed in the din, and when they part, if one should stagger and fall bleeding to the ground, can any one tell who has given the blow? There is nothing but an unknown stiletto on the ground, the crowd has dispersed, and masks tell no tales anyway. There is murder, but by whom? for what? *Quien sabe?*

And that is how it happened on Carnival night, in the last mad moments of Rex's reign, a broken-hearted mother sat gazing wide-eyed and mute at a horrible something that lay across the bed. Outside the long sweet march music of many bands floated in as if in mockery, and the flash of rockets and Bengal lights illumined the dead, white face of the girl troubadour.

Zitkala-Ša
(1876–1938)

ertrude Simmons, the daughter of a Sioux mother and a white father, was born on the Yankton Sioux reservation in South Dakota, but was rejected by members of her family who thought she had deserted her heritage by obtaining an education at a boarding school and then Earlham College. She studied music and became an accomplished violinist, and worked as a teacher at the Carlisle Indian Industrial School. She chose her Sioux literary name Zitkala-Ša, which means Red Bird, around 1900, telling stories from her Indian culture in English. She published her first book, *Old Indian Legends*, in 1901; a year later she married Raymond Bonnin, also a mixed-race Sioux, and they moved to a reservation in Utah. For the rest of her life, she continued to write, defending her people and their culture, and she campaigned actively for Indian rights.

A Warrior's Daughter (1902)

In the afternoon shadow of a large tepee, with red-painted smoke lapels, sat a warrior father with crossed shins. His head was so poised that his eye swept easily the vast level land to the eastern horizon line.

He was the chieftain's bravest warrior. He had won by heroic deeds the privilege of staking his wigwam within the great circle of tepees.

He was also one of the most generous gift givers to the toothless old people. For this he was entitled to the red-painted smoke lapels on his cone-shaped dwelling. He was proud of his honours. He never wearied of rehearsing nightly his own brave deeds. Though by wigwam fires he prated much of his high rank and widespread fame, his great joy was a wee black-eyed daughter of eight sturdy winters. Thus as he sat upon the soft grass, with his wife at his side, bent over her bead work, he was singing a dance song, and beat lightly the rhythm with his slender hands.

His shrewd eyes softened with pleasure as he watched the easy movements of the small body dancing on the green before him.

Tusee is taking her first dancing lesson. Her tightly braided hair curves over both brown ears like a pair of crooked little horns which glisten in the summer sun.

With her snugly moccasined feet close together, and a wee hand at her belt to stay the long string of beads which hang from her bare neck, she bends her knees gently to the rhythm of her father's voice.

Now she ventures upon the earnest movement, slightly upward and sidewise, in a circle. At length the song drops into a closing cadence, and the little woman, clad in beaded deerskin, sits down beside the elder one. Like her mother, she sits upon her feet. In a brief moment the warrior repeats the last refrain. Again Tusee springs to her feet and dances to the swing of the few final measures.

Just as the dance was finished, an elderly man, with short, thick hair loose about his square shoulders, rode into their presence from the rear, and leaped lightly from his pony's back. Dropping the rawhide rein to the ground, he tossed himself lazily on the grass. "Hunhe, you have returned soon," said the warrior, while extending a hand to his little daughter.

Quickly the child ran to her father's side and cuddled close to him, while he tenderly placed a strong arm about her. Both father and child, eyeing the figure on the grass, waited to hear the man's report.

"It is true," began the man, with a stranger's accent. "This is the night of the dance."

"Hunha!" muttered the warrior with some surprise.

Propping himself upon his elbows, the man raised his face. His features were of the Southern type. From an enemy's camp he was taken captive long years ago by Tusee's father. But the unusual qualities of the slave had won the Sioux warrior's heart, and for the last three winters the man had had his freedom. He was made real man again. His hair was allowed to grow. However, he himself had chosen to stay in the warrior's family.

"Hunha!" again ejaculated the warrior father. Then turning to his little daughter, he asked, "Tusee, do you hear that?"

"Yes, father, and I am going to dance tonight!"

With these words she bounded out of his arm and frolicked about in glee. Hereupon the proud mother's voice rang out in a chiding laugh.

"My child, in honour of your first dance your father must give a generous gift. His ponies are wild, and roam beyond the great hill. Pray, what has he fit to offer?" she questioned, the pair of puzzled eyes fixed upon her.

"A pony from the herd, mother, a fleet-footed pony from the herd!" Tusee shouted with sudden inspiration.

Pointing a small forefinger toward the man lying on the grass, she cried, "Uncle, you will go after the pony tomorrow!" And pleased with her solution of the problem, she skipped wildly about. Her childish faith in her elders was not conditioned by a knowledge of human limitations, but thought all things possible to grown-ups.

"Hähob!" exclaimed the mother, with a rising inflection, implying by the expletive that her child's buoyant spirit be not weighted with a denial.

Quickly to the hard request the man replied, "How! I go if Tusee tells me so!"

This delighted the little one, whose black eyes brimmed over with light. Standing in front of the strong man, she clapped her small, brown hands with joy.

"That makes me glad! My heart is good! Go, uncle, and bring a handsome pony!" she cried. In an instant she would have frisked away, but an impulse held her tilting where she stood. In the man's own tongue, for he had taught her many words and phrases, she exploded, "Thank you, good uncle, thank you!" then tore away from sheer excess of glee.

The proud warrior father, smiling and narrowing his eyes, muttered approval, "Howo! Hechetu!"

Like her mother, Tusee has finely pencilled eyebrows and slightly extended nostrils; but in her sturdiness of form she resembles her father.

A loyal daughter, she sits within her tepee making beaded deerskins for her father, while he longs to stave off her every suitor as all unworthy of his old heart's pride. But Tusee is not alone in her dwelling. Near the entrance way a young brave is half reclining on a mat. In silence he watches the petals of a wild rose growing on the soft buckskin. Quickly the young woman slips the beads on the silvery sinew thread, and works them into the pretty flower design. Finally, in a low, deep voice, the young man begins:

"The sun is far past the zenith. It is now only a man's height above the western edge of land. I hurried hither to tell you tomorrow I join the war party."

He pauses for reply, but the maid's head drops lower over her deerskin, and her lips are more firmly drawn together. He continues:

"Last night in the moonlight I met your warrior father. He seemed to know I had just stepped forth from your tepee. I fear he did not like it, for though I greeted him, he was silent. I halted in his pathway. With what boldness I dared, while my heart was beating hard and fast, I asked him for his only daughter.

"Drawing himself erect to his tallest height, and gathering his loose robe more closely about his proud figure, he flashed a pair of piercing eyes upon me.

"'Young man,' said he, with a cold, slow voice that chilled me to the marrow of my bones, 'hear me. Naught but an enemy's scalp-lock, plucked fresh with your own hand, will buy Tusee for your wife.' Then he turned on his heel and stalked away."

Tusee thrusts her work aside. With earnest eyes she scans her lover's face.

"My father's heart is really kind. He would know if you are brave and true," murmured the daughter, who wished no ill-will between her two loved ones.

Then rising to go, the youth holds out a right hand. "Grasp my hand once firmly before I go, Hoye. Pray tell me, will you wait and watch for my return?"

Tusee only nods assent, for mere words are vain.

At early dawn the round campground awakes into song. Men and women sing of bravery and of triumph. They inspire the swelling breasts of the painted warriors mounted on prancing ponies bedecked with the green branches of trees.

Riding slowly around the great ring of cone-shaped tepees, here and there, a loud-singing warrior swears to avenge a former wrong, and thrusts a bare brown arm against the purple east, calling the Great Spirit to hear his vow. All having made the circuit, the singing war-party gallops away southward.

Astride their ponies laden with food and deerskins, brave elderly women follow after their warriors. Among the foremost rides a young woman in elaborately beaded buckskin dress. Proudly mounted, she curbs with the single rawhide loop a wild-eyed pony.

It is Tusee on her father's warhorse. Thus the war-party of Indian men and their faithful women vanish beyond the southern skyline.

A day's journey brings them very near the enemy's borderland. Night-fall finds a pair of twin tepees nestled in a deep ravine. Within one lounge the painted warriors, smoking their pipes and telling weird stories by the firelight, while in the other watchful women crouch uneasily about their centre fire.

By the first grey light in the east the tepees are banished. They are gone. The warriors are in the enemy's camp, breaking dreams with their tomahawks. The women are hid away in secret places in the long thicketed ravine.

The day is far spent, the red sun is low over the west.

At length straggling warriors return, one by one, to the deep hollow. In the twilight they number their men. Three are missing. Of these absent ones two are dead; but the third one, a young man, is a captive to the foe.

"He-he!" lament the warriors, taking food in haste.

In silence each woman, with long strides, hurries to and fro, tying large bundles on her pony's back. Under cover of night the war-party must hasten homeward. Motionless, with bowed head, sits a woman in her hiding-place. She grieves for her lover.

In bitterness of spirit she hears the warriors' murmuring words. With set teeth she plans to cheat the hated enemy of their captive. In the meanwhile low signals are given, and the war-party, unaware of Tusee's absence, steal quietly away. The soft thud of pony hoofs grows fainter and fainter. The gradual hush of the empty ravine whirrs noisily in the ear of the young woman. Alert for any sound of footfalls nigh, she holds her breath to listen. Her right hand rests on a long knife in her belt. Ah, yes, she knows where her pony is hid, but not yet has she need of him. Satisfied that no danger is nigh, she prowls forth from her place of hiding. With a panther's tread and pace she climbs the high ridge beyond the low ravine. From thence she spies the enemy's campfires.

Rooted to the barren bluff the slender woman's figure stands on the pinnacle of night, outlined against a starry sky. The cool night breeze wafts to her burning ear snatches of song and drum. With desperate hate she bites her teeth.

Tusee beckons the stars to witness. With impassioned voice and uplifted face she pleads:

"Great Spirit, speed me to my lover's rescue! Give me swift cunning for a weapon this night! All-powerful Spirit, grant me my warrior-father's heart, strong to slay a foe and mighty to save a friend!"

In the midst of the enemy's campground, underneath a temporary dance-house, are men and women in gala-day dress. It is late in the night, but the merry warriors bend and bow their nude, painted bodies before a bright centre fire. To the lusty men's voices and the rhythmic throbbing drum, they leap and rebound with feathered headgears waving.

Women with red-painted cheeks and long, braided hair sit in a large half-circle against the willow railing. They, too, join in the singing, and rise to dance with their victorious warriors.

Amid this circular dance arena stands a prisoner bound to a post, haggard with shame and sorrow. He hangs his dishevelled head.

He stares with unseeing eyes upon the bare earth at his feet. With jeers and smirking faces the dancers mock the Dakota captive. Rowdy braves and small boys hoot and yell in derision.

Silent among the noisy mob, a tall woman, leaning both elbows on the round willow railing, peers into the lighted arena. The dancing centre fire shines bright into her handsome face, intensifying the night in her dark eyes. It breaks into myriad points upon her beaded dress. Unmindful of the surging throng jostling her at either side, she glares in upon the hateful, scoffing men. Suddenly she turns her head. Tittering maids whisper near her ear:

"There! There! See him now, sneering in the captive's face. 'Tis he who sprang upon the young man and dragged him by his long hair to yonder post. See! He is handsome! How gracefully he dances!"

The silent young woman looks toward the bound captive. She sees a warrior, scarce older than the captive, flourishing a tomahawk in the Dakota's face. A burning rage darts forth from her eyes and brands him for a victim of revenge. Her heart mutters within her breast, "Come, I wish to meet you, vile foe, who captured my lover and tortures him now with a living death."

Here the singers hush their voices, and the dancers scatter to their various resting-places along the willow ring. The victor gives a reluctant last twirl of his tomahawk, then, like the others, he leaves the centre ground. With head and shoulders swaying from side to side, he carries a high-pointing chin toward the willow railing. Sitting down upon the ground with crossed legs, he fans himself with an outspread turkey wing.

Now and then he stops his haughty blinking to peep out of the corners of his eyes. He hears someone clearing her throat gently. It is unmistakably for his ear. The wing-fan swings irregularly to and fro. At length he turns a proud face over a bare shoulder and beholds a handsome woman smiling.

"Ah, she would speak to a hero!" thumps his heart wildly.

The singers raise their voices in unison. The music is irresistible. Again lunges the victor into the open arena. Again he leers into the captive's face. At every interval between the songs he returns to his resting-place. Here the young woman awaits him. As he approaches she smiles boldly into his eyes. He is pleased with her face and her smile.

Waving his wing-fan spasmodically in front of his face, he sits with his ears pricked up. He catches a low whisper. A hand taps him lightly on the shoulder. The handsome woman speaks to him in his own tongue. "Come out into the night. I wish to tell you who I am."

He must know what sweet words of praise the handsome woman has for him. With both hands he spreads the meshes of the loosely woven willows, and crawls out unnoticed into the dark.

Before him stands the young woman. Beckoning him with a slender hand, she steps backward, away from the light and the restless throng of onlookers. He follows with impatient strides. She quickens her pace. He lengthens his strides. Then suddenly the woman turns from him and darts away with amazing speed. Clinching his fists and biting his lower lip, the young man runs after the fleeing woman. In his maddened pursuit he forgets the dance arena.

Beside a cluster of low bushes the woman halts. The young man, panting for breath and plunging headlong forward, whispers loud, "Pray tell me, are you a woman or an evil spirit to lure me away?"

Turning on heels firmly planted in the earth, the woman gives a wild spring forward, like a panther for its prey. In a husky voice she hisses between her teeth, "I am a Dakota woman!"

From her unerring long knife the enemy falls heavily at her feet. The Great Spirit heard Tusee's prayer on the hilltop. He gave her a warrior's strong heart to lessen the foe by one.

A bent old woman's figure, with a bundle like a grandchild slung on her back, walks round and round the dance-house. The wearied onlookers are leaving in twos and threes. The tired dancers creep out of the willow railing, and some go out at the entrance way, till the singers, too, rise from the drum and are trudging drowsily homeward. Within the arena the centre fire lies broken in red embers. The night no longer lingers about the willow railing, but, hovering into the dance-house, covers here and there a snoring man whom sleep has overpowered where he sat.

The captive in his tight-binding rawhide ropes hangs in hopeless despair. Close about him the gloom of night is slowly crouching. Yet the last red, crackling embers cast a faint light upon his long black hair, and, shining through the thick mats, caress his wan face with undying hope.

Still about the dance-house the old woman prowls. Now the embers are grey with ashes.

The old bent woman appears at the entrance way. With a cautious, groping foot she enters. Whispering between her teeth a lullaby for her sleeping child in her blanket, she searches for something forgotten.

Noisily snored the dreaming men in the darkest parts. As the lisping old woman draws nigh, the captive again opens his eyes.

A forefinger she presses to her lip. The young man arouses himself from his stupor. His senses belie him. Before his wide-open eyes the old bent figure straightens into its youthful stature. Tusee herself is beside him. With a stroke upward and downward she severs the cruel cords with her sharp blade. Dropping her blanket from her shoulders, so that it hangs from her girdled waist like a skirt, she shakes the large bundle into a light shawl for her lover. Quickly she spreads it over his bare back.

"Come!" she whispers, and turns to go; but the young man, numb and helpless, staggers nigh to falling.

The sight of his weakness makes her strong. A mighty power thrills her body. Stooping beneath his outstretched arms grasping at the air for support, Tusee lifts him upon her broad shoulders. With half-running, triumphant steps she carries him away into the open night.

Susan Glaspell
(1876–1948)

fter her graduation from Drake University in 1899, Iowa-born Glaspell worked her way from newspapers to magazines to novels, publishing her first novel in 1909. In 1915, along with her husband, George Cram Cook, she founded the influential Provincetown Players, the theatre group first produced the work of Eugene O'Neill. Glaspell wrote many plays for the group, as well as novels and short stories. "A Jury of Her Peers," now her most-read story, was based on a murder trial she had covered as a young journalist in Iowa, and dramatized fundamental issues about the differences and barriers between male law and female culture.

A Jury of Her Peers (1917)

When Martha Hale opened the storm-door and got a cut of the north wind, she ran back for her big woolen scarf. As she hurriedly wound that round her head her eye made a scandalized sweep of her kitchen. It was no ordinary thing that called her away—it was probably farther from ordinary than anything that had ever happened in Dickson County. But what her eye took in was that her kitchen was in no shape for leaving: her bread all ready for mixing, half the flour sifted and half unsifted.

She hated to see things half done; but she had been at that when the team from town stopped to get Mr. Hale, and then the sheriff came running in to say his wife wished Mrs. Hale would come too—adding, with a grin, that he guessed she was getting scarey and wanted another woman along. So she had dropped everything right where it was.

"Martha!" now came her husband's impatient voice. "Don't keep folks waiting out here in the cold."

She again opened the storm-door, and this time joined the three men and the one woman waiting for her in the big two-seated buggy.

After she had the robes tucked around her she took another look at the woman who sat beside her on the back seat. She had met Mrs. Peters the year before at the county fair, and the thing she remembered about her was that she didn't seem like a sheriff's wife. She was small and thin and didn't have a strong voice. Mrs. Gorman, sheriff's wife before Gorman went out and Peters came in, had a voice that somehow seemed to be backing up the law with every word. But if Mrs. Peters didn't look like a sheriff's wife, Peters made it up in looking like a sheriff. He was to a dot the kind of man who could get himself elected sheriff—a heavy man with a big voice, who was particularly genial with the law-abiding, as if to make it plain that he knew the difference between criminals and non-criminals. And right there it came into Mrs. Hale's mind, with a stab, that this man who was so pleasant and lively with all of them was going to the Wrights' now as a sheriff.

"The country's not very pleasant this time of year," Mrs. Peters at last ventured, as if she felt they ought to be talking as well as the men.

Mrs. Hale scarcely finished her reply, for they had gone up a little hill and could see the Wright place now, and seeing it did not make her feel like talking. It looked very lonesome this cold March morning. It had always been a lonesome-looking place. It was down in a hollow, and the poplar trees around it were lonesome-looking trees. The men were looking at it and talking about what had happened. The county attorney was bending to one side of the buggy, and kept looking steadily at the place as they drew up to it.

"I'm glad you came with me," Mrs. Peters said nervously, as the two women were about to follow the men in through the kitchen door.

Even after she had her foot on the door-step, her hand on the knob, Martha Hale had a moment of feeling she could not cross that threshold. And the reason it seemed she couldn't cross it now was simply because she hadn't crossed it before. Time and time again it had been in her mind, "I ought to go over and see Minnie Foster"—she still thought of her as Minnie Foster, though for twenty years she had been Mrs. Wright. And then there was always something to do and Minnie Foster would go from her mind. But *now* she could come.

The men went over to the stove. The women stood close together by the door. Young Henderson, the county attorney, turned around and said, "Come up to the fire, ladies."

Mrs. Peters took a step forward, then stopped. "I'm not—cold," she said.

And so the two women stood by the door, at first not even so much as looking around the kitchen.

The men talked for a minute about what a good thing it was the sheriff had sent his deputy out that morning to make a fire for them, and then

Sheriff Peters stepped back from the stove, unbuttoned his outer coat, and leaned his hands on the kitchen table in a way that seemed to mark the beginning of official business. "Now, Mr. Hale," he said in a sort of semi-official voice, "before we move things about, you tell Mr. Henderson just what it was you saw when you came here yesterday morning."

The county attorney was looking around the kitchen.

"By the way," he said, "has anything been moved?" He turned to the sheriff. "Are things just as you left them yesterday?"

Peters looked from cupboard to sink; from that to a small worn rocker a little to one side of the kitchen table.

"It's just the same."

"Somebody should have been left here yesterday," said the county attorney.

"Oh—yesterday," returned the sheriff, with a little gesture as of yesterday having been more than he could bear to think of. "When I had to send Frank to Morris Center for that man who went crazy—let me tell you. I had my hands full *yesterday*. I knew you could get back from Omaha by to-day, George, and as long as I went over everything here myself—"

"Well, Mr. Hale," said the county attorney, in a way of letting what was past and gone go, "tell just what happened when you came here yesterday morning."

Mrs. Hale, still leaning against the door, had that sinking feeling of the mother whose child is about to speak a piece. Lewis often wandered along and got things mixed up in a story. She hoped he would tell this straight and plain, and not say unnecessary things that would just make things harder for Minnie Foster. He didn't begin at once, and she noticed that he looked queer—as if standing in that kitchen and having to tell what he had seen there yesterday morning made him almost sick.

"Yes, Mr. Hale?" the county attorney reminded.

"Harry and I had started to town with a load of potatoes," Mrs. Hale's husband began.

Harry was Mrs. Hale's oldest boy. He wasn't with them now, for the very good reason that those potatoes never got to town yesterday and he was taking them this morning, so he hadn't been home when the sheriff stopped to say he wanted Mr. Hale to come over to the Wright place and tell the county attorney his story there, where he could point it all out. With all Mrs. Hale's other emotions came the fear now that maybe Harry wasn't dressed warm enough—they hadn't any of them realized how that north wind did bite.

"We come along this road," Hale was going on, with a motion of his hand to the road over which they had just come, "and as we got in sight of the house I says to Harry, 'I'm goin' to see if I can't get John Wright to take a telephone.' You see," he explained to Henderson, "unless I can get somebody to go in with me they won't come out this branch road except for a price *I* can't pay. I'd spoke to Wright about it once before; but he put me off, saying folks talked too much anyway, and all he asked was peace and quiet—guess you know about how much he talked himself. But I thought maybe if I went to the house and talked about it before his wife, and said all the women-folks liked the telephones, and that in this lonesome stretch of road it would be a good thing—well, I said to Harry that that was what I was going to say—though I said at the same time that I didn't know as what his wife wanted made much difference to John—"

Now, there he was!—saying things he didn't need to say. Mrs. Hale tried to catch her husband's eye, but fortunately the county attorney interrupted with:

"Let's talk about that a little later, Mr. Hale. I do want to talk about that, but I'm anxious now to get along to just what happened when you got here."

When he began this time, it was very deliberately and carefully:

"I didn't see or hear anything. I knocked at the door. And still it was all quiet inside. I knew they must be up—it was past eight o'clock. So I knocked again, louder, and I thought I heard somebody say, 'Come in.' I wasn't sure—I'm not sure yet. But I opened the door—this door," jerking a hand toward the door by which the two women stood, "and there, in that rocker"—pointing to it—"sat Mrs. Wright."

Every one in the kitchen looked at the rocker. It came into Mrs. Hale's mind that that rocker didn't look in the least like Minnie Foster—the Minnie Foster of twenty years before. It was a dingy red, with wooden rungs up the back, and the middle rung was gone, and the chair sagged to one side.

"How did she—look?" the county attorney was inquiring.

"Well," said Hale, "she looked—queer."

"How do you mean—queer?"

As he asked it he took out a note-book and pencil. Mrs. Hale did not like the sight of that pencil. She kept her eye fixed on her husband, as if to keep him from saying unnecessary things that would go into that note-book and make trouble.

Hale did speak guardedly, as if the pencil had affected him too.

"Well, as if she didn't know what she was going to do next. And kind of—done up."

"How did she seem to feel about your coming?"

"Why, I don't think she minded—one way or other. She didn't pay much attention. I said, 'Ho' do, Mrs. Wright? It's cold, ain't it?' And she said. 'Is it?'—and went on pleatin' at her apron.

"Well, I was surprised. She didn't ask me to come up to the stove, or to sit down, but just set there, not even lookin' at me. And so I said: 'I want to see John.'

"And then she—laughed. I guess you would call it a laugh.

"I thought of Harry and the team outside, so I said, a little sharp, 'Can I see John?' 'No,' says she—kind of dull like. 'Ain't he home?' says I. Then she looked at me. 'Yes,' says she, 'he's home.' 'Then why can't I see him?' I asked her, out of patience with her now. ''Cause he's dead,' says she, just as quiet and dull—and fell to pleatin' her apron. 'Dead?' says I, like you do when you can't take in what you've heard.

"She just nodded her head, not getting a bit excited, but rockin' back and forth.

" 'Why—where is he?' says I, not knowing *what* to say.

"She just pointed upstairs—like this"—pointing to the room above.

"I got up, with the idea of going up there myself. By this time I—didn't know what to do. I walked from there to here; then I says: 'Why, what did he die of?'

" 'He died of a rope around his neck,' says she; and just went on pleatin' at her apron."

Hale stopped speaking, and stood staring at the rocker, as if he were still seeing the woman who had sat there the morning before. Nobody spoke; it was as if every one were seeing the woman who had sat there the morning before.

"And what did you do then?" the county attorney at last broke the silence.

"I went out and called Harry. I thought I might—need help. I got Harry in, and we went upstairs." His voice fell almost to a whisper. "There he was—lying over the—"

"I think I'd rather have you go into that upstairs," the county attorney interrupted, "where you can point it all out. Just go on now with the rest of the story."

"Well, my first thought was to get that rope off. It looked—"

He stopped, his face twitching.

"But Harry, he went up to him, and he said. 'No, he's dead all right, and we'd better not touch anything.' So we went downstairs.

"She was still sitting that same way. 'Has anybody been notified?' I asked. 'No,' says she, unconcerned.

"'Who did this, Mrs. Wright?' said Harry. He said it businesslike, and she stopped pleatin' at her apron. 'I don't know,' she says. 'You don't *know*?' says Harry. 'Weren't you sleepin' in the bed with him?' 'Yes,' says she, 'but I was on the inside.' 'Somebody slipped a rope round his neck and strangled him, and you didn't wake up?' says Harry. 'I didn't wake up,' she said after him.

"We may have looked as if we didn't see how that could be, for after a minute she said, 'I sleep sound.'

"Harry was going to ask her more questions, but I said maybe that weren't our business; maybe we ought to let her tell her story first to the coroner or the sheriff. So Harry went fast as he could over to High Road—the Rivers' place, where there's a telephone."

"And what did she do when she knew you had gone for the coroner?" The attorney got his pencil in his hand all ready for writing.

"She moved from that chair to this one over here"—Hale pointed to a small chair in the corner—"and just sat there with her hands held together and looking down. I got a feeling that I ought to make some conversation, so I said I had come in to see if John wanted to put in a telephone; and at that she started to laugh, and then she stopped and looked at me—scared."

At sound of a moving pencil the man who was telling the story looked up.

"I dunno—maybe it wasn't scared," he hastened; "I wouldn't like to say it was. Soon Harry got back, and then Dr. Lloyd came, and you, Mr. Peters, and so I guess that's all I know that you don't."

He said that last with relief, and moved a little, as if relaxing. Everyone moved a little. The county attorney walked toward the stair door.

"I guess we'll go upstairs first—then out to the barn and around there."

He paused and looked around the kitchen.

"You're convinced there was nothing important here?" he asked the sheriff. "Nothing that would—point to any motive?"

The sheriff too looked all around, as if to re-convince himself.

"Nothing here but kitchen things," he said, with a little laugh for the insignificance of kitchen things.

The county attorney was looking at the cupboard—a peculiar, ungainly structure, half closet and half cupboard, the upper part of it being built in the wall, and the lower part just the old-fashioned kitchen cupboard. As if its queerness attracted him, he got a chair and opened the upper part and looked in. After a moment he drew his hand away sticky.

"Here's a nice mess," he said resentfully.

The two women had drawn nearer, and now the sheriff's wife spoke.

"Oh—her fruit," she said, looking to Mrs. Hale for sympathetic under-standing. She turned back to the county attorney and explained: "She worried about that when it turned so cold last night. She said the fire would go out and her jars might burst."

Mrs. Peters' husband broke into a laugh.

"Well, can you beat the women! Held for murder, and worrying about her preserves!"

The young attorney set his lips.

"I guess before we're through with her she may have something more serious than preserves to worry about."

"Oh, well," said Mrs. Hale's husband, with good-natured superiority, "women are used to worrying over trifles."

The two women moved a little closer together. Neither of them spoke. The county attorney seemed suddenly to remember his manners—and think of his future.

"And yet," said he, with the gallantry of a young politician, "for all their worries, what would we do without the ladies?"

The women did not speak, did not unbend. He went to the sink and began washing his hands. He turned to wipe them on the roller towel—whirled it for a cleaner place.

"Dirty towels! Not much of a housekeeper, would you say, ladies?"

He kicked his foot against some dirty pans under the sink.

"There's a great deal of work to be done on a farm," said Mrs. Hale stiffly.

"To be sure. And yet"—with a little bow to her—"I know there are some Dickson County farm-houses that do not have such roller towels." He gave it a pull to expose its full length again.

"Those towels get dirty awful quick. Men's hands aren't always as clean as they might be."

"Ah, loyal to your sex, I see," he laughed. He stopped and gave her a keen look. "But you and Mrs. Wright were neighbors. I suppose you were friends, too."

Martha Hale shook her head.

"I've seen little enough of her of late years. I've not been in this house—it's more than a year."

"And why was that? You didn't like her?"

"I liked her well enough," she replied with spirit. "Farmers' wives have their hands full, Mr. Henderson. And then—" She looked around the kitchen.

"Yes?" he encouraged.

"It never seemed a very cheerful place," said she, more to herself than to him.

"No," he agreed; "I don't think anyone would call it cheerful. I shouldn't say she had the home-making instinct."

"Well, I don't know as Wright had, either," she muttered.

"You mean they didn't get on very well?" he was quick to ask.

"No; I don't mean anything," she answered, with decision. As she turned a little away from him, she added: "But I don't think a place would be any the cheerfuler for John Wright's bein' in it."

"I'd like to talk to you about that a little later, Mrs. Hale," he said. "I'm anxious to get the lay of things upstairs now."

He moved toward the stair door, followed by the two men.

"I suppose anything Mrs. Peters does'll be all right?" the sheriff inquired. "She was to take in some clothes for her, you know—and a few little things. We left in such a hurry yesterday."

The county attorney looked at the two women they were leaving alone there among the kitchen things.

"Yes—Mrs. Peters," he said, his glance resting on the woman who was not Mrs. Peters, the big farmer woman who stood behind the sheriff's wife. "Of course Mrs. Peters is one of us," he said, in a manner of entrusting responsibility. "And keep your eye out, Mrs. Peters, for anything that might be of use. No telling; you women might come upon a clue to the motive—and that's the thing we need."

Mr. Hale rubbed his face after the fashion of a show man getting ready for a pleasantry.

"But would the women know a clue if they did come upon it?" he said; and, having delivered himself of this, he followed the others through the stair door.

The women stood motionless and silent, listening to the footsteps, first upon the stairs, then in the room above them.

Then, as if releasing herself from something strange, Mrs. Hale began to arrange the dirty pans under the sink, which the county attorney's disdainful push of the foot had deranged.

"I'd hate to have men comin' into my kitchen," she said testily—"snoopin' round and criticizin'."

"Of course it's no more than their duty," said the sheriff's wife, in her manner of timid acquiescence.

"Duty's all right," replied Mrs. Hale bluffly; "but I guess that deputy sheriff that come out to make the fire might have got a little of this on." She gave the roller towel a pull. "Wish I'd thought of that sooner! Seems mean to talk about her for not having things slicked up, when she had to come away in such a hurry."

She looked around the kitchen. Certainly it was not "slicked up." Her eye was held by a bucket of sugar on a low shelf. The cover was off the wooden bucket, and beside it was a paper bag—half full.

Mrs. Hale moved toward it.

"She was putting this in there," she said to herself—slowly.

She thought of the flour in her kitchen at home—half sifted, half not sifted. She had been interrupted, and had left things half done. What had interrupted Minnie Foster? Why had that work been left half done? She made a move as if to finish it,—unfinished things always bothered her,—and then she glanced around and saw that Mrs. Peters was watching her—and she didn't want Mrs. Peters to get that feeling she had got of work begun and then—for some reason—not finished.

"It's a shame about her fruit," she said, and walked toward the cupboard that the county attorney had opened, and got on the chair, murmuring: "I wonder if it's all gone."

It was a sorry enough looking sight, but "Here's one that's all right," she said at last. She held it toward the light. "This is cherries, too." She looked again. "I declare I believe that's the only one."

With a sigh, she got down from the chair, went to the sink, and wiped off the bottle.

"She'll feel awful bad, after all her hard work in the hot weather. I remember the afternoon I put up my cherries last summer."

She set the bottle on the table, and, with another sigh, started to sit down in the rocker. But she did not sit down. Something kept her from sitting down in that chair. She straightened—stepped back, and, half turned away, stood looking at it, seeing the woman who had sat there "pleatin' at her apron."

The thin voice of the sheriff's wife broke in upon her: "I must be getting those things from the front room closet." She opened the door into the other room, started in, stepped back. "You coming with me, Mrs. Hale?" she asked nervously. "You—you could help me get them."

They were soon back—the stark coldness of that shut-up room was not a thing to linger in.

"My!" said Mrs. Peters, dropping the things on the table and hurrying to the stove.

Mrs. Hale stood examining the clothes the woman who was being detained in town had said she wanted.

"Wright was close!" she exclaimed, holding up a shabby black skirt that bore the marks of much making over. "I think maybe that's why she kept so much to herself. I s'pose she felt she couldn't do her part; and then, you don't enjoy things when you feel shabby. She used to wear pretty clothes and be lively—when she was Minnie Foster, one of the town girls, singing in the choir. But that—oh, that was twenty years ago."

With a carefulness in which there was something tender, she folded the shabby clothes and piled them at one corner of the table. She looked up at Mrs. Peters, and there was something in the other woman's look that irritated her.

"She don't care," she said to herself. "Much difference it makes to her whether Minnie Foster had pretty clothes when she was a girl."

Then she looked again, and she wasn't so sure; in fact, she hadn't at any time been perfectly sure about Mrs. Peters. She had that shrinking manner, and yet her eyes looked as if they could see a long way into things.

"This all you was to take in?" asked Mrs. Hale.

"No," said the sheriff's wife; "she said she wanted an apron. Funny thing to want," she ventured in her nervous little way, "for there's not much to get you dirty in jail, goodness knows. But I suppose just to make her feel more natural. If you're used to wearing an apron—. She said they were in the bottom drawer of this cupboard. Yes—here they are. And then her little shawl that always hung on the stair door."

She took the small gray shawl from behind the door leading upstairs, and stood a minute looking at it.

Suddenly Mrs. Hale took a quick step toward the other woman.

"Mrs. Peters!"

"Yes, Mrs. Hale?"

"Do you think she—did it?"

A frightened look blurred the other thing in Mrs. Peters' eyes.

"Oh, I don't know," she said, in a voice that seemed to shrink away from the subject.

"Well, I don't think she did," affirmed Mrs. Hale stoutly. "Asking for an apron, and her little shawl. Worryin' about her fruit."

"Mr. Peters says—." Footsteps were heard in the room above; she stopped, looked up, then went on in a lowered voice: "Mr. Peters says—it looks bad for her. Mr. Henderson is awful sarcastic in a speech, and he's going to make fun of her saying she didn't—wake up."

For a moment Mrs. Hale had no answer. Then, "Well, I guess John Wright didn't wake up—when they was slippin' that rope under his neck," she muttered.

"No, it's *strange*," breathed Mrs. Peters. "They think it was such a— funny way to kill a man."

She began to laugh; at sound of the laugh, abruptly stopped.

"That's just what Mr. Hale said," said Mrs. Hale, in a resolutely natural voice. "There was a gun in the house. He says that's what he can't understand."

"Mr. Henderson said, coming out, that what was needed for the case was a motive. Something to show anger—or sudden feeling."

"Well, I don't see any signs of anger around here," said Mrs. Hale, "I don't—"

She stopped. It was as if her mind tripped on something. Her eye was caught by a dish-towel in the middle of the kitchen table. Slowly she moved toward the table. One half of it was wiped clean, the other half messy. Her eyes made a slow, almost unwilling turn to the bucket of sugar and the half empty bag beside it. Things begun—and not finished.

After a moment she stepped back, and said, in that manner of releasing herself:

"Wonder how they're finding things upstairs? I hope she had it a little more red up up there. You know,"—she paused, and feeling gathered,— "it seems kind of *sneaking*: locking her up in town and coming out here to get her own house to turn against her!"

"But, Mrs. Hale," said the sheriff's wife, "the law is the law."

"I s'pose 'tis," answered Mrs. Hale shortly.

She turned to the stove, saying something about that fire not being much to brag of. She worked with it a minute, and when she straightened up she said aggressively:

"The law is the law—and a bad stove is a bad stove. How'd you like to cook on this?"—pointing with the poker to the broken lining. She opened the oven door and started to express her opinion of the oven; but she was swept into her own thoughts, thinking of what it would mean, year after year, to have that stove to wrestle with. The thought of Minnie

Foster trying to bake in that oven—and the thought of her never going over to see Minnie Foster—.

She was startled by hearing Mrs. Peters say: "A person gets discouraged—and loses heart."

The sheriff's wife had looked from the stove to the sink—to the pail of water which had been carried in from outside. The two women stood there silent, above them the footsteps of the men who were looking for evidence against the woman who had worked in that kitchen. That look of seeing into things, of seeing through a thing to something else, was in the eyes of the sheriff's wife now. When Mrs. Hale next spoke to her, it was gently:

"Better loosen up your things, Mrs. Peters. We'll not feel them when we go out."

Mrs. Peters went to the back of the room to hang up the fur tippet she was wearing. A moment later she exclaimed, "Why, she was piecing a quilt," and held up a large sewing basket piled high with quilt pieces.

Mrs. Hale spread some of the blocks out on the table.

"It's log-cabin pattern," she said, putting several of them together. "Pretty, isn't it?"

They were so engaged with the quilt that they did not hear the footsteps on the stairs. Just as the stair door opened Mrs. Hale was saying:

"Do you suppose she was going to quilt it or just knot it?"

The sheriff threw up his hands.

"They wonder whether she was going to quilt it or just knot it!"

There was a laugh for the ways of women, a warming of hands over the stove, and then the county attorney said briskly:

"Well, let's go right out to the barn and get that cleared up."

"I don't see as there's anything so strange," Mrs. Hale said resentfully, after the outside door had closed on the three men—"our taking up our time with little things while we're waiting for them to get the evidence. I don't see as it's anything to laugh about."

"Of course they've got awful important things on their minds," said the sheriff's wife apologetically.

They returned to an inspection of the block for the quilt. Mrs. Hale was looking at the fine, even sewing, and preoccupied with thoughts of the woman who had done that sewing, when she heard the sheriff's wife say, in a queer tone:

"Why, look at this one."

She turned to take the block held out to her.

"The sewing," said Mrs. Peters, in a troubled way. "All the rest of them have been so nice and even—but—this one. Why, it looks as if she didn't know what she was about!"

Their eyes met—something flashed to life, passed between them; then, as if with an effort, they seemed to pull away from each other. A moment Mrs. Hale sat there, her hands folded over that sewing which was so unlike all the rest of the sewing. Then she had pulled a knot and drawn the threads.

"Oh, what are you doing, Mrs. Hale?" asked the sheriff's wife, startled.

"Just pulling out a stitch or two that's not sewed very good," said Mrs. Hale mildly.

"I don't think we ought to touch things," Mrs. Peters said, a little help-lessly.

"I'll just finish up this end," answered Mrs. Hale, still in that mild, matter-of-fact fashion.

She threaded a needle and started to replace bad sewing with good. For a little while she sewed in silence. Then, in that thin, timid voice, she heard:

"Mrs. Hale!"

"Yes, Mrs. Peters?"

"What do you suppose she was so—nervous about?"

"Oh, *I* don't know," said Mrs. Hale, as if dismissing a thing not impor-tant enough to spend much time on. "I don't know as she was—nervous. I sew awful queer sometimes when I'm just tired."

She cut a thread, and out of the corner of her eye looked up at Mrs. Peters. The small, lean face of the sheriff's wife seemed to have tightened up. Her eyes had that look of peering into something. But next moment she moved, and said in her thin, indecisive way:

"Well, I must get those clothes wrapped. They may be through sooner than we think. I wonder where I could find a piece of paper—and string."

"In that cupboard, maybe," suggested Mrs. Hale, after a glance around.

One piece of the crazy sewing remained unripped. Mrs. Peters' back turned, Martha Hale now scrutinized that piece, compared it with the dainty, accurate sewing of the other blocks. The difference was startling. Holding this block made her feel queer, as if the distracted thoughts of the woman who had perhaps turned to it to try and quiet herself were communicating themselves to her.

Mrs. Peters' voice roused her.

"Here's a bird-cage," she said. "Did she have a bird, Mrs. Hale?"

"Why, I don't know whether she did or not." She turned to look at the cage Mrs. Peters was holding up. "I've not been here in so long." She sighed. "There was a man round last year selling canaries cheap—but I don't know as she took one. Maybe she did. She used to sing real pretty herself."

Mrs. Peters looked around the kitchen.

"Seems kind of funny to think of a bird here." She half laughed—an attempt to put up a barrier. "But she must have had one—or why would she have a cage? I wonder what happened to it."

"I suppose maybe the cat got it," suggested Mrs. Hale, resuming her sewing.

"No; she didn't have a cat. She's got that feeling some people have about cats—being afraid of them. When they brought her to our house yesterday, my cat got in the room, and she was real upset and asked me to take it out."

"My sister Bessie was like that," laughed Mrs. Hale.

The sheriff's wife did not reply. The silence made Mrs. Hale turn round. Mrs. Peters was examining the bird-cage.

"Look at this door," she said slowly. "It's broke. One hinge has been pulled apart."

Mrs. Hale came nearer.

"Looks as if some one must have been—rough with it."

Again their eyes met—startled, questioning, apprehensive. For a moment neither spoke nor stirred. Then Mrs. Hale, turning away, said brusquely:

"If they're going to find any evidence, I wish they'd be about it. I don't like this place."

"But I'm awful glad you came with me, Mrs. Hale." Mrs. Peters put the bird-cage on the table and sat down. "It would be lonesome for me—sitting here alone."

"Yes, it would, wouldn't it?" agreed Mrs. Hale, a certain determined naturalness in her voice. She had picked up the sewing, but now it dropped in her lap, and she murmured in a different voice: "But I tell you what I *do* wish, Mrs. Peters. I wish I had come over sometimes when she was here. I wish—I had."

"But of course you were awful busy, Mrs. Hale. Your house—and your children."

"I could've come," retorted Mrs. Hale shortly. "I stayed away because it weren't cheerful—and that's why I ought to have come. I"—she looked around—"I've never liked this place. Maybe because it's down in a hollow and you don't see the road. I don't know what it is, but it's a lonesome place, and always was. I wish I had come over to see Minnie Foster sometimes. I can see now—" She did not put it into words.

"Well, you mustn't reproach yourself," counseled Mrs. Peters. "Somehow, we just don't see how it is with other folks till—something comes up."

"Not having children makes less work," mused Mrs. Hale, after a silence, "but it makes a quiet house—and Wright out to work all day—and no company when he did come in. Did you know John Wright, Mrs. Peters?"

"Not to know him. I've seen him in town. They say he was a good man."

"Yes—good," conceded John Wright's neighbor grimly. "He didn't drink, and kept his word as well as most, I guess, and paid his debts. But he was a hard man, Mrs. Peters. Just to pass the time of day with him—." She stopped, shivered a little. "Like a raw wind that gets to the bone." Her eye fell upon the cage on the table before her, and she added, almost bitterly: "I should think she would've wanted a bird!"

Suddenly she leaned forward, looking intently at the cage. "But what do you s'pose went wrong with it?"

"I don't know," returned Mrs. Peters; "unless it got sick and died."

But after she said it she reached over and swung the broken door. Both women watched it as if somehow held by it.

"You didn't know—her?" Mrs. Hale asked, a gentler note in her voice.

"Not till they brought her yesterday," said the sheriff's wife.

"She—come to think of it, she was kind of like a bird herself. Real sweet and pretty, but kind of timid and—fluttery. How—she—did—change."

That held her for a long time. Finally, as if struck with a happy thought and relieved to get back to everyday things, she exclaimed:

"Tell you what, Mrs. Peters, why don't you take the quilt in with you? It might take up her mind."

"Why, I think that's a real nice idea, Mrs. Hale," agreed the sheriff's wife, as if she too were glad to come into the atmosphere of a simple kindness. "There couldn't possibly be any objection to that, could there? Now, just what will I take? I wonder if her patches are in here—and her things."

They turned to the sewing basket.

"Here's some red," said Mrs. Hale, bringing out a roll of cloth. Underneath that was a box. "Here, maybe her scissors are in here—and her things." She held it up. "What a pretty box! I'll warrant that was something she had a long time ago—when she was a girl."

She held it in her hand a moment; then, with a little sigh, opened it.

Instantly her hand went to her nose.

"Why—!"

Mrs. Peters drew nearer—then turned away.

"There's something wrapped up in this piece of silk," faltered Mrs. Hale.

"This isn't her scissors," said Mrs. Peters, in a shrinking voice.

Her hand not steady, Mrs. Hale raised the piece of silk. "Oh, Mrs. Peters!" she cried. "It's—"

Mrs. Peters bent closer.

"It's the bird," she whispered.

"But, Mrs. Peters!" cried Mrs. Hale. "*Look* at it! Its *neck*—look at its neck! It's all—other side *to*."

She held the box away from her.

The sheriff's wife again bent closer.

"Somebody wrung its neck," said she, in a voice that was slow and deep.

And then again the eyes of the two women met—this time clung together in a look of dawning comprehension, of growing horror. Mrs. Peters looked from the dead bird to the broken door of the cage. Again their eyes met. And just then there was a sound at the outside door.

Mrs. Hale slipped the box under the quilt pieces in the basket, and sank into the chair before it. Mrs. Peters stood holding to the table. The county attorney and the sheriff came in from outside.

"Well, ladies," said the county attorney, as one turning from serious things to little pleasantries, "have you decided whether she was going to quilt it or knot it?"

"We think," began the sheriff's wife in a flurried voice, "that she was going to—knot it."

He was too preoccupied to notice the change that came in her voice on that last.

"Well, that's very interesting, I'm sure," he said tolerantly. He caught sight of the bird-cage. "Has the bird flown?"

"We think the cat got it," said Mrs. Hale in a voice curiously even.

He was walking up and down, as if thinking something out.

"Is there a cat?" he asked absently.

Mrs. Hale shot a look up at the sheriff's wife.

"Well, not *now*," said Mrs. Peters. "They're superstitious, you know; they leave."

She sank into her chair.

The county attorney did not heed her. "No sign at all of any one having come in from the outside," he said to Peters, in the manner of continuing an interrupted conversation. "Their own rope. Now let's go upstairs again and go over it, piece by piece. It would have to have been some one who knew just the—"

The stair door closed behind them and their voices were lost.

The two women sat motionless, not looking at each other, but as if peering into something and at the same time holding back. When they spoke now it was as if they were afraid of what they were saying, but as if they could not help saying it.

"She liked the bird," said Martha Hale, low and slowly. "She was going to bury it in that pretty box."

"When I was a girl," said Mrs. Peters, under her breath, "my kitten—there was a boy took a hatchet, and before my eyes—before I could get there—" She covered her face an instant. "If they hadn't held me back I would have"—she caught herself, looked upstairs where footsteps were heard, and finished weakly—"hurt him."

Then they sat without speaking or moving.

"I wonder how it would seem," Mrs. Hale at last began, as if feeling her way over strange ground—"never to have had any children around?" Her eyes made a slow sweep of the kitchen, as if seeing what that kitchen had meant through all the years. "No, Wright wouldn't like the bird," she said after that—"a thing that sang. She used to sing. He killed that too." Her voice tightened.

Mrs. Peters moved uneasily.

"Of course we don't know who killed the bird."

"I knew John Wright," was Mrs. Hale's answer.

"It was an awful thing was done in this house that night, Mrs. Hale," said the sheriff's wife. "Killing a man while he slept—slipping a thing round his neck that choked the life out of him."

Mrs. Hale's hand went out to the bird-cage.

"His neck. Choked the life out of him."

"We don't *know* who killed him," whispered Mrs. Peters wildly. "We don't *know*."

Mrs. Hale had not moved. "If there had been years and years of—nothing, then a bird to sing to you, it would be awful—still—after the bird was still."

It was as if something within her not herself had spoken, and it found in Mrs. Peters something she did not know as herself.

"I know what stillness is," she said, in a queer, monotonous voice. "When we homesteaded in Dakota, and my first baby died—after he was two years old—and me with no other then—"

Mrs. Hale stirred.

"How soon do you suppose they'll be through looking for the evidence?"

"I know what stillness is," repeated Mrs. Peters, in just that same way. Then she too pulled back. "The law has got to punish crime, Mrs. Hale," she said in her tight little way.

"I wish you'd seen Minnie Foster," was the answer, "when she wore a white dress with blue ribbons, and stood up there in the choir and sang."

The picture of that girl, the fact that she had lived neighbor to that girl for twenty years, and had let her die for lack of life, was suddenly more than she could bear.

"Oh, I *wish* I'd come over here once in a while!" she cried. "That was a crime! That was a crime! Who's going to punish that?"

"We mustn't take on," said Mrs. Peters, with a frightened look toward the stairs.

"I might 'a' *known* she needed help! I tell you, it's *queer*, Mrs. Peters. We live close together, and we live far apart. We all go through the same things—it's all just a different kind of the same thing! If it weren't—why do you and I *understand*? Why do we *know*—what we know this minute?"

She dashed her hand across her eyes. Then, seeing the jar of fruit on the table, she reached for it and choked out:

"If I was you I wouldn't *tell* her her fruit was gone! Tell her it *ain't*. Tell her it's all right—all of it. Here—take this in to prove it to her! She—she may never know whether it was broke or not."

She turned away.

Mrs. Peters reached out for the bottle of fruit as if she were glad to take it—as if touching a familiar thing, having something to do, could keep her from something else. She got up, looked about for something to wrap the fruit in, took a petticoat from the pile of clothes she had brought from the front room, and nervously started winding that round the bottle.

"My!" she began, in a high, false voice, "it's a good thing the men couldn't hear us! Getting all stirred up over a little thing like a—dead canary." She hurried over that. "As if that could have anything to do with—with—My, wouldn't they *laugh*?"

Footsteps were heard on the stairs.

"Maybe they would," muttered Mrs. Hale—"maybe they wouldn't."

"No, Peters," said the county attorney incisively; "it's all perfectly clear, except the reason for doing it. But you know juries when it comes to women. If there was some definite thing—something to show. Something to make a story about. A thing that would connect up with this clumsy way of doing it."

In a covert way Mrs. Hale looked at Mrs. Peters. Mrs. Peters was looking at her. Quickly they looked away from each other. The outer door opened and Mr. Hale came in.

"I've got the team round now," he said. "Pretty cold out there."

"I'm going to stay here awhile by myself," the county attorney suddenly announced. "You can send Frank out for me, can't you?" he asked the sheriff. "I want to go over everything. I'm not satisfied we can't do better."

Again, for one brief moment, the two women's eyes found one another.

The sheriff came up to the table.

"Did you want to see what Mrs. Peters was going to take in?"

The county attorney picked up the apron. He laughed.

"Oh, I guess they're not very dangerous things the ladies have picked out."

Mrs. Hale's hand was on the sewing basket in which the box was concealed. She felt that she ought to take her hand off the basket. She did not seem able to. He picked up one of the quilt blocks which she had piled on to cover the box. Her eyes felt like fire. She had a feeling that if he took up the basket she would snatch it from him.

But he did not take it up. With another little laugh, he turned away, saying:

"No; Mrs. Peters doesn't need supervising. For that matter, a sheriff's wife is married to the law. Ever think of it that way, Mrs. Peters?"

Mrs. Peters was standing beside the table. Mrs. Hale shot a look up at her; but she could not see her face. Mrs. Peters had turned away. When she spoke, her voice was muffled.

"Not—just that way," she said.

"Married to the law!" chuckled Mrs. Peters' husband. He moved toward the door into the front room, and said to the county attorney:

"I just want you to come in here a minute, George. We ought to take a look at these windows."

"Oh—windows," said the county attorney scoffingly.

"We'll be right out, Mr. Hale," said the sheriff to the farmer, who was still waiting by the door.

Hale went to look after the horses. The sheriff followed the county attorney into the other room. Again—for one final moment—the two women were alone in that kitchen.

Martha Hale sprang up, her hands tight together, looking at that other woman, with whom it rested. At first she could not see her eyes, for the sheriff's wife had not turned back since she turned away at that suggestion of being married to the law. But now Mrs. Hale made her turn back. Her eyes made her turn back. Slowly, unwillingly, Mrs. Peters turned her head until her eyes met the eyes of the other woman. There was a moment when they held each other in a steady, burning look in which there was no evasion or flinching. Then Martha Hale's eyes pointed the way to the basket in which was hidden the thing that would make certain the conviction of the other woman—that woman who was not there and yet who had been there with them all through that hour.

For a moment Mrs. Peters did not move. And then she did it. With a rush forward, she threw back the quilt pieces, got the box, tried to put it in her handbag. It was too big. Desperately she opened it, started to take the bird out. But there she broke—she could not touch the bird. She stood there helpless, foolish.

There was the sound of a knob turning in the inner door. Martha Hale snatched the box from the sheriff's wife, and got it in the pocket of her big coat just as the sheriff and the county attorney came back into the kitchen.

"Well, Henry," said the county attorney facetiously, "at least we found out that she was not going to quilt it. She was going to—what is it you call it, ladies?"

Mrs. Hale's hand was against the pocket of her coat.

"We call it—knot it, Mr. Henderson."

Dorothy Canfield Fisher
(1879–1958)

he daughter of a college professor and an artist, Dorothy Canfield grew up in the Midwest, but also traveled with her mother and lived in Paris and Spain. When her father became the chief librarian at Columbia University, she moved to New York, began writing fiction, and received a Ph.D. in French literature in 1904. She eventually spoke five languages. In 1907, she married John Redwood Fisher, a former captain of the Columbia University football team, and they settled in Arlington, Vermont, where they had two children. During the war John Fisher volunteered to serve in the American Ambulance Hospital at Neuilly, and she joined him with their children, and worked for the Red Cross, sending back articles about French life to American magazines. In Vermont, after the war, she became the family breadwinner with her popular novels, stories, and children's books. She was also an advocate of the Montessori system of early childhood education. As a member of the editorial board of the Book-of-the-Month Club from 1925 to 1951, Fisher had an important effect on American literary tastes.

The Bedquilt (1906)

Of all the Elwell family Aunt Mehetabel was certainly the most unimportant member. It was in the New England days, when an unmarried woman was an old maid at twenty, at forty was everyone's servant, and at sixty had gone through so much discipline that she could need no more in the next world. Aunt Mehetabel was sixty-eight.

She had never for a moment known the pleasure of being important to anyone. Not that she was useless in her brother's family; she was expected, as a matter of course, to take upon herself the most tedious and uninteresting part of the household labors. On Mondays she accepted as her share the washing of the men's shirts, heavy with sweat and stiff with dirt from the fields and from their own hard-working bodies. Tuesdays she never dreamed of being allowed to iron anything pretty or even interesting, like the baby's white dresses or the fancy aprons of her young lady nieces. She stood all day pressing out a tiresome monotonous succession of dish-cloths and towels and sheets.

In preserving-time she was allowed to have none of the pleasant responsibility of deciding when the fruit had cooked long enough, nor did she share in the little excitement of pouring the sweet-smelling stuff into the stone jars. She sat in a corner with the children and stoned cherries incessantly, or hulled strawberries until her fingers were dyed red to the bone.

The Elwells were not consciously unkind to their aunt, they were even in a vague way fond of her; but she was so utterly insignificant a figure in their lives that they bestowed no thought whatever on her. Aunt Mehetabel did not resent this treatment; she took it quite as unconsciously as they gave it. It was to be expected when one was an old-maid dependent in a busy family. She gathered what crumbs of comfort she could from their occasional careless kindnesses and tried to hide the hurt which even yet pierced her at her brother's rough joking. In the winter when they all sat before the big hearth, roasted apples, drank mulled cider, and teased the girls about their beaux and the boys about their sweethearts, she shrank into a dusky corner with her knitting, happy if the evening passed without her brother saying, with a crude sarcasm, "Ask your Aunt Mehetabel about the beaux that used to come a-sparkin' her!" or, "Mehetabel, how was't when you was in love with Abel Cummings." As a matter of fact, she had been the same at twenty as at sixty, a quiet, mouse-like little creature, too timid and shy for anyone to notice, or to raise her eyes for a moment and wish for a life of her own.

Her sister-in-law, a big hearty housewife, who ruled indoors with as autocratic a sway as did her husband on the farm, was rather kind in an absent, offhand way to the shrunken little old woman, and it was through her that Mehetabel was able to enjoy the one pleasure of her life. Even as a girl she had been clever with her needle in the way of patching bedquilts. More than that she could never learn to do. The garments which she made for herself were the most lamentable affairs, and she was humbly grateful for any help in the bewildering business of putting them together. But in patchwork she enjoyed a tepid importance. She could really do that as well as anyone else. During years of devotion to this one art she had accumulated a considerable store of quilting patterns. Sometimes the neighbors would send over and ask "Miss Mehetabel" for such and such a design. It was with an agreeable flutter at being able to help someone that she went to the dresser, in her bare little room under the eaves, and extracted from her crowded portfolio the pattern desired.

She never knew how her great idea came to her. Sometimes she thought she must have dreamed it, sometimes she even wondered reverently, in the phraseology of the weekly prayer-meeting, if it had not been "sent" to her. She never admitted to herself that she could have thought of it without other help; it was too great, too ambitious, too lofty a project for her humble mind to have conceived. Even when she finished drawing the design with her own fingers, she gazed at it incredulously, not daring to believe that it could indeed be her handiwork. At first it seemed to her only like a lovely but quite unreal dream. She did not think of putting it into execution—so elaborate, so complicated, so beautifully difficult a pattern could be only for the angels in heaven to quilt. But so curiously does familiarity accustom us even to very wonderful things, that as she lived with this astonishing creation of her mind, the longing grew stronger and stronger to give it material life with her nimble old fingers.

She gasped at her daring when this idea first swept over her and put it away as one does a sinfully selfish notion, but she kept coming back to it again and again. Finally she said compromisingly to herself that she would make one "square," just one part of her design, to see how it would look. Accustomed to the most complete dependence on her brother and his wife, she dared not do even this without asking Sophia's permission. With a heart full of hope and fear thumping furiously against her old ribs, she approached the mistress of the house on churning-day, knowing with the innocent guile of a child that the country woman was apt to be in a good temper while working over the fragrant butter in the cool cellar.

Sophia listened absently to her sister-in-law's halting, hesitating petition. "Why, yes, Mehetabel," she said, leaning far down into the huge churn for the last golden morsels—"why, yes, start another quilt if you want to. I've got a lot of pieces from the spring sewing that will work in real good." Mehetabel tried honestly to make her see that this would be no common quilt, but her limited vocabulary and her emotion stood between her and expression. At last Sophia said, with a kindly impatience: "Oh, there! Don't bother me. I never could keep track of your quiltin' patterns, anyhow. I don't care what pattern you go by."

With this overwhelmingly, although unconsciously, generous permission Mehetabel rushed back up the steep attic stairs to her room, and in a joyful agitation began preparations for the work of her life. It was even better than she hoped. By some heaven-sent inspiration she had invented a pattern beyond which no patchwork quilt could go.

She had but little time from her incessant round of household drudgery for this new and absorbing occupation, and she did not dare sit up late at night lest she burn too much candle. It was weeks before the little square began to take on a finished look, to show the pattern. Then Mehetabel was in a fever of impatience to bring it to completion. She was too conscientious to shirk even the smallest part of her share of the work of the house, but she rushed through it with a speed which left her panting as she climbed to the little room. This seemed like a radiant spot to her as she bent over the innumerable scraps of cloth which already in her imagination ranged themselves in the infinitely diverse pattern of her masterpiece. Finally she could wait no longer, and one evening ventured to bring her work down beside the fire where the family sat, hoping that some good fortune would give her a place near the tallow candles on the mantelpiece. She was on the last corner of the square, and her needle flew in and out with inconceivable rapidity. No one noticed her, a fact which filled her with relief, and by bedtime she had but a few more stitches to add.

As she stood up with the others, the square fluttered out of her trembling old hands and fell on the table. Sophia glanced at it carelessly. "Is that the new quilt you're beginning on?" she asked with a yawn. "It looks like a real pretty pattern. Let's see it." Up to that moment Mehetabel had labored in the purest spirit of disinterested devotion to an ideal, but as Sophia held her work toward the candle to examine it, and exclaimed in amazement and admiration, she felt an astonished joy to know that her creation would stand the test of publicity.

"Land sakes!" ejaculated her sister-in-law, looking at the many-colored square. "Why, Mehetabel Elwell, where'd you git that pattern?"

"I made it up," said Mehetabel quietly, but with unutterable pride.

"No!" exclaimed Sophia incredulously. "*Did* you! Why, I never see such a pattern in my life. Girls, come here and see what your Aunt Mehetabel is doing."

The three tall daughters turned back reluctantly from the stairs. "I don't seem to take much interest in patchwork," said one listlessly.

"No, nor I neither!" answered Sophia; "but a stone image would take an interest in this pattern. Honest, Mehetabel, did you think of it yourself? And how under the sun and stars did you ever git your courage up to start in a-making it? Land! Look at all those tiny squinchy little seams! Why the wrong side ain't a thing *but* seams!"

The girls echoed their mother's exclamations, and Mr. Elwell himself came over to see what they were discussing. "Well, I declare!" he said, looking at his sister with eyes more approving than she could ever remember. "That beats old Mis' Wightman's quilt that got the blue ribbon so many times at the county fair."

Mehetabel's heart swelled within her, and tears of joy moistened her old eyes as she lay that night in her narrow, hard bed, too proud and excited to sleep. The next day her sister-in-law amazed her by taking the huge pan of potatoes out of her lap and setting one of the younger children to peeling them. "Don't you want to go on with that quiltin' pattern?" she said; "I'd kind o' like to see how you're goin' to make the grape-vine design come out on the corner."

By the end of the summer the family interest had risen so high that Mehetabel was given a little stand in the sitting-room where she could keep her pieces, and work in odd minutes. She almost wept over such kindness, and resolved firmly not to take advantage of it by neglecting her work, which she performed with a fierce thoroughness. But the whole atmosphere of her world was changed. Things had a meaning now. Through the longest task of washing milk-pans there rose the rainbow of promise of her variegated work. She took her place by the little table and put the thimble on her knotted, hard finger with the solemnity of a priestess performing a sacred rite.

She was even able to bear with some degree of dignity the extreme honor of having the minister and the minister's wife comment admiringly on her great project. The family felt quite proud of Aunt Mehetabel as Minister Bowman had said it was work as fine as any he had ever seen, "and he didn't know but finer!" The remark was repeated verbatim to the neighbors in the following weeks when they dropped in and examined in a perverse silence some astonishingly difficult *tour de force* which Mehetabel had just finished.

The family especially plumed themselves on the slow progress of the quilt. "Mehetabel has been to work on that corner for six weeks, come Tuesday, and she ain't half done yet," they explained to visitors. They fell out of the way of always expecting her to be the one to run on errands, even for the children. "Don't bother your Aunt Mehetabel," Sophia would call. "Can't you see she's got to a ticklish place on the quilt?"

The old woman sat up straighter and looked the world in the face. She was a part of it at last. She joined in the conversation and her remarks were listened to. The children were even told to mind her when she asked them to do some service for her, although this she did but seldom, the habit of self-effacement being too strong.

One day some strangers from the next town drove up and asked if they could inspect the wonderful quilt which they had heard of, even down in their end of the valley. After that such visitations were not uncommon, making the Elwells' house a notable object. Mehetabel's quilt came to be one of the town sights, and no one was allowed to leave the town without having paid tribute to its worth. The Elwells saw to it that their aunt was better dressed than she had ever been before, and one of the girls made her a pretty little cap to wear on her thin white hair.

A year went by and a quarter of the quilt was finished; a second year passed and half was done. The third year Mehetabel had pneumonia and lay ill for weeks and weeks, overcome with terror lest she die before her work was completed. A fourth year and one could really see the grandeur of the whole design; and in September of the fifth year, the entire family watching her with eager and admiring eyes, Mehetabel quilted the last stitches in her creation. The girls held it up by the four corners, and they all looked at it in a solemn silence. Then Mr. Elwell smote one horny hand within the other and exclaimed: "By ginger! That's goin' to the county fair!" Mehetabel blushed a deep red at this. It was a thought which had occurred to her in a bold moment, but she had not dared to entertain it. The family acclaimed the idea, and one of the boys was forthwith dispatched to the house of the neighbor who was chairman of the committee for their village. He returned with radiant face, "Of course he'll take it. Like's not it may git a prize, so he says; but he's got to have it right off, because all the things are goin' to-morrow morning."

Even in her swelling pride Mehetabel felt a pang of separation as the bulky package was carried out of the house. As the days went on she felt absolutely lost without her work. For years it had been her one preoccupation, and she could not bear even to look at the little stand, now quite bare of the litter of scraps which had lain on it so long. One of the neighbors, who took the long journey to the fair, reported that the quilt was hung in a place of honor in a glass case in "Agricultural Hall." But that meant little to Mehetabel's utter ignorance of all that lay outside of her brother's home. The family noticed the old woman's depression, and one day Sophia said kindly, "You feel sort o' lost without the quilt, don't you, Mehetabel?"

"They took it away so quick!" she said wistfully; "I hadn't hardly had one real good look at it myself."

Mr. Elwell made no comment, but a day or two later he asked his sister how early she could get up in the morning.

"I dun'no'. Why?" she asked.

"Well, Thomas Ralston has got to drive clear to West Oldton to see a lawyer there, and that is four miles beyond the fair. He says if you can git up so's to leave here at four in the morning he'll drive you over to the fair, leave you there for the day, and bring you back again at night."

Mehetabel looked at him with incredulity. It was as though someone had offered her a ride in a golden chariot up to the gates of heaven. "Why, you can't *mean* it!" she cried, paling with the intensity of her emotion. Her brother laughed a little uneasily. Even to his careless indifference this joy was a revelation of the narrowness of her life in his home. "Oh, 'tain't so much to go to the fair. Yes, I mean it. Go git your things ready, for he wants to start to-morrow morning."

All that night a trembling, excited old woman lay and stared at the rafters. She, who had never been more than six miles from home in her life, was going to drive thirty miles away—it was like going to another world. She who had never seen anything more exciting than a church supper was to see the county fair. To Mehetabel it was like making the tour of the world. She had never dreamed of doing it. She could not at all imagine what it would be like.

Nor did the exhortations of the family, as they bade good-by to her, throw any light on her confusion. They had all been at least once to the scene of gayety she was to visit, and as she tried to eat her breakfast they called out conflicting advice to her till her head whirled. Sophia told her to be sure and see the display of preserves. Her brother said not to miss inspecting the stock, her nieces said the fancywork was the only thing worth looking at, and her nephews said she must bring them home an account of the races. The buggy drove up to the door, she was helped in, and her wraps tucked about her. They all stood together and waved good-by to her as she drove out of the yard. She waved back, but she scarcely saw them. On her return home that evening she was very pale, and so tired and stiff that her brother had to lift her out bodily, but her lips were set in a blissful smile. They crowded around her with thronging questions, until Sophia pushed them all aside, telling them Aunt Mehetabel was too tired to speak until she had had her supper. This was eaten in an enforced silence on the part of the children, and then the old woman was helped into an easy-chair before the fire. They gathered about her, eager for news of the great world, and Sophia said, "Now, come, Mehetabel, tell us all about it!"

Mehetabel drew a long breath. "It was just perfect!" she said; "finer even than I thought. They've got it hanging up in the very middle of a sort o' closet made of glass, and one of the lower corners is ripped and turned back so's to show the seams on the wrong side."

"What?" asked Sophia, a little blankly.

"Why, the quilt!" said Mehetabel in surprise. "There are a whole lot of other ones in that room, but not one that can hold a candle to it, if I do say it who shouldn't. I heard lots of people say the same thing. You ought to have heard what the women said about that corner, Sophia. They said—well, I'd be ashamed to *tell* you what they said. I declare if I wouldn't!"

Mr. Elwell asked, "What did you think of that big ox we've heard so much about?"

"I didn't look at the stock," returned his sister indifferently. "That set of pieces you gave me, Maria, from your red waist, come out just lovely!" she assured one of her nieces. "I heard one woman say you could 'most smell the red silk roses."

"Did any of the horses in our town race?" asked young Thomas.

"I didn't see the races."

"How about the preserves?" asked Sophia.

"I didn't see the preserves," said Mehetabel calmly.

"You see, I went right to the room where the quilt was, and then I didn't want to leave it. It had been so long since I'd seen it. I had to look at it first real good myself, and then I looked at the others to see if there was any that could come up to it. And then the people begun comin' in and I got so interested in hearin' what they had to say I couldn't think of goin' anywheres else. I ate my lunch right there too, and I'm as glad as can be I did, too; for what do you think?"—she gazed about her with kindling eyes—"while I stood there with a sandwich in one hand didn't the head of the hull concern come in and open the glass door and pin 'First Prize' right in the middle of the quilt!"

There was a stir of congratulation and proud exclamation. Then Sophia returned again to the attack. "Didn't you go to see anything else?" she queried.

"Why, no," said Mehetabel. "Only the quilt. Why should I?"

She fell into a reverie where she saw again the glorious creation of her hand and brain hanging before all the world with the mark of highest approval on it. She longed to make her listeners see the splendid vision with her. She struggled for words; she reached blindly after unknown superlatives. "I tell you it looked like——" she said, and paused, hesitating. Vague recollections of hymn-book phraseology came into her mind, the only form of literary expression she knew; but they were dismissed as being sacrilegious, and also not sufficiently forcible. Finally, "I tell you it looked real *well!*" she assured them, and sat staring into the fire, on her tired old face the supreme content of an artist who has realized his ideal.

Anne Spencer
(1882–1975)

One of the most neglected black women poets of the 1920s, Anne Spencer grew up in a racially mixed West Virginia community. Educated at the Virginia Seminary in Lynchburg, Virginia, she married at nineteen. Although she claimed to have written a thousand poems, only twenty were published in her lifetime, and only a few fragments of unpublished work remain. Nonetheless, the force of her meditation on race in "White Things," and her comments about female creative daring in "A Letter to My Sister," a poem which should be compared to Amy Lowell's "The Sisters," show a real poetic gift. She was known in Lynchburg as a fierce individualist and activist for civil rights, and was working on an epic poem about John Brown when she died at ninety-three.

White Things (1923)

Most things are colorful things-
-the sky, earth, and sea.
Black men are most men;
but the white are free!
White things are rare things;
so rare, so rare
They stole from out a silvered
world—somewhere.

Finding earth-plains fair plains,
save greenly grassed,
They strewed white feathers of
cowardice, as they passed;

The golden stars with lances fine,
The hills all red and darkened pine,
They blanched with their want of power;

And turned the blood in a ruby rose
To a poor white poppy-flower.

They pyred a race of black, black men,
And burned them to ashes white; then,
Laughing, a young one claimed a skull,
For the skull of a black is white, not dull,
But a glistening awful thing

Made, it seems, for this ghoul to swing
In the face of God with all his might,
And swear by the hell that sired him:
"Man-maker, make white!"

A Letter to My Sister (1927)

It is dangerous for a woman
to defy the gods;
To taunt them with the tongue's thin tip,
Or strut in the weakness
of mere humanity,
Or draw a line daring them to cross;
The gods own the searing lightning,
The drowning waters, tormenting fears
And anger of red sins.

Oh, but worse still if you mince timidly—
Dodge this way or that, or kneel or pray,
Be kind, or sweat agony drops
Or lay your quick body over
your feeble young;
If you have beauty or none, if celibate
Or vowed—the gods are Juggernaut,
Passing over . . . over . . .

This you may do:
Lock your heart, then, quietly,
And lest they peer within,

Light no lamp when dark comes down
Raise no shade for sun;
Breathless must your
breath come through
If you'd die and dare deny
The gods their god-like fun.

Elinor Wylie
(1885–1928)

orn into a socially and politically prominent Washington family, Elinor (Hoyt) Wylie lived a life marked by scandal. She left her first husband and their three-year-old son in 1910 to elope with Horace Wylie, a married man, whose wife would not grant him a divorce. They were legally married in 1916 but divorced in 1923, the same year Elinor married her third husband, the poet and critic William Rose Benét. Her poetry, however, was precise, traditional, and formal. Obsessed by Shelley, she wrote brittle lyrics she aimed to make "brilliant and compact." Wylie described her own poems as being "small jeweled receptacles of two or three well-polished stanzas," like an "enameled snuff box." As she writes in "Wild Peaches," winter was her favorite season, and she regarded herself as a solitary being despite her many love affairs. In an "anti-feminist letter" to her sister, published after her death, Wylie declared that she preferred playing the feminine role of victim, a role she both exploited and suffered.

Wild Peaches (1921)

I

When the world turns completely upside down
You say we'll emigrate to the Eastern Shore
Aboard a river-boat from Baltimore;
We'll live among wild peach trees, miles from town,
You'll wear a coonskin cap, and I a gown
Homespun, dyed butternut's dark gold colour.
Lost, like your lotus-eating ancestor,
We'll swim in milk and honey till we drown.

The winter will be short, the summer long,
The autumn amber-hued, sunny and hot,
Tasting of cider and of scuppernong;
All seasons sweet, but autumn best of all.

The squirrels in their silver fur will fall
Like falling leaves, like fruit, before your shot.

2

The autumn frosts will lie upon the grass
Like bloom on grapes of purple-brown and gold.
The misted early mornings will be cold;
The little puddles will be roofed with glass.
The sun, which burns from copper into brass,
Melts these at noon, and makes the boys unfold
Their knitted mufflers; full as they can hold
Fat pockets dribble chestnuts as they pass.

Peaches grow wild, and pigs can live in clover;
A barrel of salted herrings lasts a year;
The spring begins before the winter's over.
By February you may find the skins
Of garter snakes and water moccasins
Dwindled and harsh, dead-white and cloudy-clear.

3

When April pours the colours of a shell
Upon the hills, when every little creek
Is shot with silver from the Chesapeake
In shoals new-minted by the ocean swell,
When strawberries go begging, and the sleek
Blue plums lie open to the blackbird's beak,
We shall live well—we shall live very well.

The months between the cherries and the peaches
Are brimming cornucopias which spill
Fruits red and purple, sombre-bloomed and black;
Then, down rich fields and frosty river beaches
We'll trample bright persimmons, while you kill
Bronze partridge, speckled quail, and canvasback.

4

Down to the Puritan marrow of my bones
There's something in this richness that I hate.

I love the look, austere, immaculate,
Of landscapes drawn in pearly monotones.
There's something in my very blood that owns
Bare hills, cold silver on a sky of slate,
A thread of water, churned to milky spate
Streaming through slanted pastures fenced with stones.

I love those skies, thin blue or snowy gray,
Those fields sparse-planted, rendering meagre sheaves;
That spring, briefer than apple-blossom's breath,
Summer, so much too beautiful to stay,
Swift autumn, like a bonfire of leaves,
And sleepy winter, like the sleep of death.

Anti-feminist Song, for My Sister (1929)

Each of us, born every minute,
    Still wears fern-seed in her shoes;
Love of man, we always win it;
    Peace of mind, we always lose.

Drawing cheques is still our pastime;
    Paying checks our private hell;
No good swearing it's the last time
    While we know ourselves so well!

I am I, and you, my darling,
    Someone very like myself;
Hear the back-door wolf a-snarling
    For bread and cheese upon the shelf!

Well, and let him lick our platters!
    Let him drain our loving-cups!
Do we really think it matters
    Save as Cerberus his sops?

Ah, from such the rats have scampered
    Who give all, but not a damn!

How the wind remains ill-tempered
  To the thoroughly-shorn lamb!

Yes, we've had our fairly thick times
  Paying for the cakes and beers:
It's more fun to be the victims
  Than the bloody conquerors.

Anzia Yezierska
(ca. 1885–1970)

orn to poor Jewish parents in a tiny village near Warsaw,
Anzia Yezierska immigrated as a teenager to New York City,
where she worked in a sweatshop and studied English at
night. A scholarship to Columbia Teachers College allowed
Yezierska to concentrate on her education and her writing, and in 1920,
after two short marriages and giving birth to a daughter ultimately raised
by her husband, she published her first collection of short stories about
the Jewish immigrant experience. Though Samuel Goldwyn brought her
to Hollywood to make a silent movie out of her book and offered her a
lucrative screenwriting contract, Yezierska soon returned to the Lower
East Side, the place she felt was most conducive to her writing. In addi-
tion to several books of fiction, she published her work in prominent
magazines, such as *Century*, where "Wild Winter Love" appeared in 1927.
The story's relationship between a Jewish woman and a Gentile man is a
recurrent one for Yezierska, who had an affair with the philosopher John
Dewey a few years before her first book came out.

Wild Winter Love (1927)

This is a story with an unhappy ending. And I too have become Ameri-
canized enough to be terrified of unhappy endings. Yet I have to drop all
my work to write it.

Ever since I read in the papers about Ruth Raefsky, I've gone around
without a head. I can't pull myself together somehow. Her story won't
let me rest. It tears me out of my sleep at night. It leaps up at me out of
every corner where I try to hide.

And it's dumb. Dumb. Words only push back the spirit of what I feel
about her. The facts that I know so well dwindle into nothing. Only a
piece of her life here, and a piece there—the end, the middle, and the
beginning rush together in broken confusion.

The first thing that flashes to my mind is her outburst of impatience
with the monotonous theme of love in American magazines. "You pick
up one magazine after another, and it's all love-stories. Life isn't all sex.

Why are they writing only about love, as if there was nothing else real to write about?"

How much she had learned of the realness and unrealness of love before she was through!

It was in the Bronx, the up-town ghetto, that I first met her. Even before we met, her neighbor's whisperings excited my interest.

"Imagine only—such a woman—a wife of a poor tailor—a house and a baby to take care of—and such a madness in her head—goes to night-school—wants to write herself a book of her life."

Her neighbor's voice was high-pitched with indignation. "The husband sweats from early morning till late at night, stitching his life away for every penny he earns. And she is such a lady, when she goes to the market, she don't bargain herself to get things cheaper like the rest of us. She takes it wrapped up, don't even look at the change. Just like a Gentile."

I had just moved in. It was one of those newly built five-story tenements with four three-room flats on each floor. She lived in the front and I in the rear. But it was weeks before I got on friendly terms with her.

All the other women sat around together with their baby-carriages in the sun, darning and mending, discussing what was cooking in the neighbors' pots. But she and her baby-carriage were always off by themselves.

She seemed wrapped up inside herself. Not seeing, not hearing anything around her.

Sometimes she'd take up some pages and pencil from under the baby's pillow, jot down something. Then sit back very still, as if she were all alone, looking far out at the top of the world.

But when I met her in the store, or on the stairs, she looked like a neat, efficient, businesslike person with a busy concentrated expression on her face. She answered my "good morning" and "good evening" with a nod and a smile, but no more.

Gradually her life pieced itself together out of the fragments of conversation we had.

She had met Dave, her husband, in the same shop where she had worked. He was a tailor, she a finisher.

The sudden urge to write did not begin till after she was married.

"We were so happy in our little flat, all to ourselves. At first Dave wanted me to fix up a 'parlor like by other people.' But I wanted a plain living room like in the settlement.

" 'And why not?' he humored me. But I could see it wasn't because he thought the plain things I liked beautiful, but that he wanted me to have what I wanted.

"And so it was when I told him I had to write the story of my life. He hadn't much use for books. He only read the 'Vorwarts' and the 'Socialist Call.' He looked a little doubtful. But he loved me so, and he was so good and kind. He shrugged away his doubt. 'If you'll have from it pleasure, go ahead.'

"And so I began to go to night-school to learn how to write my life. But in a class of fifty, how much time can the teacher give to me?

"I didn't realize when I began how long it would take, how I'd have to tear my flesh in pieces for every little word. I am only just feeling out the beginning of my story. But now I can't stop myself."

I glanced up at her. Under that look of neat businesslike efficiency, a consuming passion flared up in her eyes. Her baby two years already. Writing every day since her marriage, and only just at the beginning.

"If I could only do it by myself! It's having to go to these teachers for help that kills me. Every evening this week they were reading in my class how Washington crossed the Delaware. Here I'm burning up with the crossing of my own Delaware. And I have to choke down my living story for a George Washington, dead a hundred years. All that waste, only to get the teacher's help for a few minutes after the class."

Her tightly clenched hands trembled with nervousness. I've seen the dumb who wanted to say something, but were too confused to know what they wanted to say. Here were brains and intelligence. Here was a woman who knew what she wanted to say, but was lost in the mazes of the new language. And more than the confusion of the new language was the realization that she was talking to strangers, to whom she always felt herself saying too much, yet not enough. To cold hard-headed Americans she was trying to make clear the feverish turmoil of the suppressed desire-driven ghetto.

One evening, several months later, I heard through the open air-shaft window loud quarreling in the Raefsky flat.

"Come to bed already. I waited up for you long enough. It's time to sleep."

"Oh, Dave! Stop bothering me. I only just got started. Why can't you go to sleep without me?"

No sound for a while.

"*Nu?* Not yet finished?"

"Let me alone, can't you? I've scrubbed and cooked and washed all day long. Only when the baby is asleep that I take to myself."

"*Gewalt!*" Dave's voice, raw with hurt, rose into a shriek. "There's an end to a man's patience. My gall is bursting. You're not a woman. I married myself to a *meshugeneh* with a book for her heart."

"God! What does that man want of me?"

"You know what I want. I want a home. I want a wife."

"Don't you have the things you like to eat? Was there ever a time that you did not have your clean shirt, your darned socks?"

"Oi-i-i! If you had flesh and blood in you, you wouldn't talk that way. What for did you marry me? So you could have a fool of a slave to give you everything, while you go on with your craziness?"

They drifted further and further apart. Whenever I entered their flat, I felt the cold chill that comes to you when you enter a house where the man and woman live under one roof yet live apart. It was only the love for their child that held them together in spite of the growing chasm between them.

As she became more and more consumed with her story, she grew impatient with the little special help she could get out of the night-school. She sought the club-leader of the settlement, a college student, the druggist on the corner, the doctor on the block. Anyone she met with a gleam of intelligence in their eyes, she would stop and make them listen to some little scene in her story that she happened to be working on. Their comments somehow helped her get a truer word, a deeper stroke in her picture.

And so the book built itself up piece by piece through the years.

I lost track of her for a long while when they moved away.

One day the club-leader of the settlement told me the exciting news that Ruth Raefsky had come through with her book, *Out of the Ghetto*.

Breathlessly I read the enthusiastic reviews of great critics who hailed Ruth Raefsky as the New Voice of the East Side.

So she got there at last! What a titanic struggle! With all her dumbness, her fearful unsureness of herself—to have pressed on and on—beaten out a voice in so much that was dumb. . . . The steerage ship on its way to America—Cherry Street. The sweat shop. The boss. The "hands." The landlord. The rag peddler. The pawnshop. The art theater. Dreams and the brutal battle for bread. Greed and self-sacrifice. The dirt and the beauty seething in the crowded ghetto—to have caught it all—framed it between the covers of a book!

How will she look released from that terrible burden? Would having reached her goal wipe away the tortured driven look on her face? What will she do with herself now? Can she pick up again the relationships she broke to pursue her dream?

I went to see her. I found her already famous. People whose names I read in the magazines were now among her guests for tea.

Success had not yet worked any miracles in her appearance. Though she was excited and elated, the tired strained expression was still on her face. Sleepless nights and tortured days still cried out of her eyes.

"How does it feel to be a famous living author?" I whispered.

"Will I ever be able to do my next thing? This is my worry now."

I wondered why she did not rejoice more in her good luck. Then Dave, grimy from his work in the shop, came in.

He tried to slip away. But Ruth pulled him forward. "Come, Dave. I want you to meet some of my friends."

He bowed awkwardly, hiding his dirty hands in his pockets. Everyone in the room felt the pain of his self-consciousness. As soon as he could, he shrank into a corner and didn't say a word till they had left.

Then he burst out: "My home is no more mine. I come tired from the shop. All I want is peace—and my house is crowded with strangers. Why didn't you tell me you'd have them here?"

"Why hide yourself from people?"

"They're not my people. But what's the difference? What do I count in this house? To a writer, what is a husband?"

"Oh, Dave!" Her voice was sharp with jangled nerves. "Don't let's go over all that again. My writing is no crime."

"Sure it's a crime," he cried, his eyes blazing. "The pleasures of writing is for millionaires. What right has a poor man's wife to give in to herself? Suppose it willed itself in me to write a book, who'd give you bread? I have to be a tailor, so you could shine in the world for a writer. Somebody's got to work for the rent."

I went away. I thought of an evening years ago, when I first knew them. Dave had come in from work, with eager shining eyes and a package in his hand. It was his wife's birthday. He had saved for months to surprise her with a Hungarian peasant shawl that he had seen her admire in a shop window. How he drank in pleasure out of his wife's delight as he wrapped the shawl around her! And now—the cold looks, the harsh voices with which they pushed one another away.

Some months later we made an appointment to meet for lunch. When the day came, I received word that she was ill. I went to see her. I found her prostrate with a headache.

She looked frightfully old. Her features stood out sharply. Her eyes seemed to have gone deep down into her head. She sat up in bed with a little jerk. Bright red spots burned on her cheeks. She barely stopped to greet me. She began talking at once, as though carrying on a conversation with herself.

"I'm a woman without a country. I'm uprooted from where I started; and I can't find roots anywhere. I've lost the religion of my fathers. I've lost the human ties that hold other women. I can only live in the world I create out of my brain. I've got so that I can't live unless I write. And I can't write. The works have stopped in me. What will be my end?"

Her reserve had unloosed through exhaustion. I never heard her talk so much. It was a torrent of high-pitched nervous words.

"My writing began with my love for Dave. But I've gone on only in my brain. I've gone too far away from life. I don't know how to get back.

"I have so much more to give out than ever before. But something has stifled this giving-out power. My terrible inadequacy is killing me. What is the agony of death to this agony I now suffer—to feel, to see, to know— and to wither in sight of it all—stifled—dumb."

Soon after this, a nervous breakdown forced her to give her daughter to board, and she went away for the first vacation in her life.

I was seeing Dave, off and on, whenever I needed my clothes to be repaired.

"How's Ruth?" I asked toward the end of the summer.

"Now she's come back with a new craziness in her head. She's got to live alone. Such selfishness—" He stopped suddenly.

I was too embarrassed to press him for details. I hurried to see her at her new address. I expected her to be in a worse mental state, now that she was living the hermit. But she was radiant. Her face, her figure, her eyes, had a verve, a sparkle, a magnetism, that I never saw in her before.

"What has happened to you?" I cried. "You look a million years younger."

A light from away inside flashed up in her face. "I'm seeing for the first time how glorious it is just to be alive. Beauty is all about us—only I was too blind to see it till now. What is that verse in the Bible—'all things work together for good to them that love God'?"

I listened in amazement. I couldn't take my eyes away from her shining face.

"Solitude has done you good."

"Solitude is only an empty cup. I have rich red wine to fill my solitude."

Now I knew what had happened to her. "Who? Who is it? You—at forty-seven, in love?"

"Yes, And with a man even older than I. What does youth know about love? What can youth bring to love, but the inexperience, the unripeness of youth?"

For a moment I looked beneath the radiance of her face into the battle-scarred, life-worn lines that the years had dug into her throat and about her eyes. In that moment she was all of her forty-seven years old. But it was only for a moment. I was caught up again by the rich warmth of her voice, the inexhaustible energy that poured out of her as she talked.

"Outwardly, my lover is one of those cold reasonable Anglo-Saxons. A lawyer. A respectable citizen. Devoted to his wife. Adores his children. We're drawn to each other by something even more compelling than the love of man for woman, and woman for man. It's that irresistible force as terrible as birth and death that sometimes flares up between Jew and Gentile."

The resonance of her own voice was like fire that fed her. She looked far out—stern forehead, exultant eyes—seeing prophecies.

"These centuries of antagonism between his race and mine have burst out in us into this transcendent love. A love that burns through the barriers of race and class and creed. . . . Since Christ was crucified, a black chasm of hate yawned between his people and mine. But now and then threads of gold have spun through the darkness—links of understanding woven by fearless souls—Gentiles and Jews—men and women who were not afraid to trust their love."

"Mad-woman—poetess!" In a kind of envy I laughed aloud. But she was too inspired to hear me.

"It's because he and I are of a different race that we can understand one another so profoundly, touch the innermost reaches of the soul, beyond the reach of those who think they know us.

"When I talk to him, it's like traveling in foreign countries. He excites my imagination and releases my imagination. . . .

"My writing is but a rushing fountain of song to him. I pour myself out at his feet, in poems of my people, their hopes, their dreams. He listens to me with the wonder of a child listening to adventure. It's all so fresh and new to him, my world, that it becomes fresh and new to me. . . .

"In some way I do not understand I've been the means of bringing release to him too. I've awakened in him a new worship of life and beauty that none of the women of his class can ever dream is in him."

She threw back her head gloriously. Her laughter was a chant of triumph. "The wonderful way that man looks at me! It's like bathing in sunshine. . . . Dave has driven into me all these years that I'm a criminal. That fire in me, that makes me what I am—a crime. And this man washes away, as in healing oil, the guilt and self-defense with which my flesh and spirit is scarred. To him I can be just as I am. He wants me as I am."

The starved tailor's wife! How it had gone to her head, the little bit of love! But what wonder? For the first time in her life, she found a lover, an inspirer, and an audience all in one—a man of brains who understood the warm rich muddle of her experience.

I was all curiosity to see the man who had so changed this lonely ghetto woman. I got to watching for them. Walking the streets where they were likely to pass. At last I saw them. It was like seeing black and white, so intense, so startling was the contrast between them. His calm Anglo-Saxon face was like a background of rock for her volatile, tempestuous, Slavic temperament.

They lit up the street with their happiness. The world seemed to sweep away before their completeness in each other. And yet, he seemed quite an old man. No different from hundreds of other plain lawyers. She, for all the fire and vivacity that lighted up her face, was unmistakably middle-aged. How could they let themselves be so wrapped up in each other? How shameless, at their age, to get so lost in their love!

But a rich power for work was that love. It put a new appeal, deeper humanity, into her writing. Her stories became the fad of the hour. Her stepping up into the world of success, while I was still low down in the struggle, gradually cut us off one from the other.

It was over three years that I had not seen her. By degrees I became aware that she appeared less and less in the public eye. I began to wonder what she was doing.

A sudden desire to see her swept me. But I pushed back the impulse. . . . What can we talk about now, when she's so happy? . . .

One morning I opened the newspaper as I sat down to breakfast. Ruth Raefsky's picture! Under it, in big letters—Suicide! I read on. But I was too shaken to take in anything. My brain was paralyzed by that one word—suicide.

Ruth Raefsky! So rich with life! So eager to live! She—of all people! I had to know the truth of what had happened. Suicide. That word meant nothing. What led to it, was her story.

I called on her relatives, her friends—on anyone who might know.

"Well, what can you expect? Left her husband, her child, for an affair with a married man," said her next-door neighbor.

And each one had something different to say.

"Such a haunted face as she had the last time I saw her! Poor thing! She looked so unhappy."

"You can't blame the man. The wife and daughters got wind of the affair. He wouldn't let them be hurt. Why should the innocent family suffer? So Ruth Raefsky had to go."

"He had a sense of duty to the community, if she didn't. I admire him for being strong enough, in the end, to do the right thing."

"How she must have suffered! She shut herself away from all of us. She wouldn't let any of us try to help her."

So their words fell about her—smug or compassionate.

How could they know the real Ruth Raefsky? Those years of toil by day and night, tearing up by the roots her starved childhood, her starved youth, trying to tell, in her personal story, the story of her people. How could they understand the all-consuming urge that drove her to voice her way across the chasm between the ghetto and America?

A lonely losing fight it was from the very beginning. Only for a moment, a hand of love stretched a magic bridge across the chasm. Inevitably the hand drew back. Inevitably the man went back to the safety of his own world.

In the fading of this dazzling mirage of friendship and love, vanished her courage, her dreams, her last illusion. And she leaped into the gulf that she could not bridge.

Hilda Doolittle
(H. D.)
(1886–1961)

ilda Doolittle's vivid and adventurous life seems almost another story than the literary career in which she produced poems, experimental fiction, and Greek translations. The daughter of a professor of math and astronomy who became director of the Observatory at the University of Pennsylvania, Doolittle attended Bryn Mawr College, but failed her English course and withdrew in her second year. In Philadelphia she had met the poet Ezra Pound, who encouraged her to write, and she moved to London to join him and other modernist expatriates who were creating new forms of art. Pound renamed her "H. D.-Imagiste," and under this signature she published her early free-verse, spare, descriptive lyrics (like "Oread") in the little magazine *Poetry*. Her life in England was tumultuous. She married the English poet Richard Aldington in 1913 and published her first volume, *Sea Garden*, in 1916.

Her brother died in World War I, she separated from her husband, had a daughter with another man, suffered serious illness, and was rescued from complete breakdown in 1919 by the wealthy writer Annie Winifred Ellerman ("Bryher"), who became first her lover and then her lifelong friend. With Bryher's support, she was able to publish her *Collected Poems* to much acclaim in 1925, and to experiment with avant-garde film and autobiography. In the 1930s she traveled to Vienna to be psychoanalyzed by Freud, about whom she later wrote. After World War II H. D. wrote a long symbolic poem, *Helen in Egypt* (1961), that attempted to see the myths of epic warfare from a female perspective, much as in "Eurydice" in which she spoke from the point of view of the woman rescued by Orpheus.

Oread (1915)

Whirl up, sea—
whirl your pointed pines,
splash your great pines

on our rocks,
hurl your green over us,
cover us with your pools of fir.

Eurydice (1917)

I

So you have swept me back,
I who could have walked with the live souls
above the earth,
I who could have slept among the live flowers
at last;

so for your arrogance
and your ruthlessness
I am swept back
where dead lichens drip
dead cinders upon moss of ash;

so for your arrogance
I am broken at last,
I who had lived unconscious,
who was almost forgot;

if you had let me wait
I had grown from listlessness
into peace,
if you had let me rest with the dead,
I had forgot you
and the past.

II

Here only flame upon flame
and black among the red sparks,
streaks of black and light
grown colourless;

why did you turn back,
that hell should be reinhabited
of myself thus
swept into nothingness?

why did you turn?
why did you glance back?
why did you hesitate for that moment?
why did you bend your face
caught with the flame of the upper earth,
above my face?

what was it that crossed my face
with the light from yours
and your glance?
what was it you saw in my face?
the light of your own face,
the fire of your own presence?

What had my face to offer
but reflex of the earth,
hyacinth colour
caught from the raw fissure in the rock
where the light struck,
and the colour of azure crocuses
and the bright surface of gold crocuses
and of the wind-flower,
swift in its veins as lightning
and as white.

III

Saffron from the fringe of the earth,
wild saffron that has bent
over the sharp edge of earth,
all the flowers that cut through the earth,
all, all the flowers are lost;

everything is lost,
everything is crossed with black,

black upon black
and worse than black,
this colourless light.

IV

Fringe upon fringe
of blue crocuses,
crocuses, walled against blue of themselves,
blue of that upper earth
blue of the depth upon depth of flowers,
lost;

flowers,
if I could have taken once my breath of them,
enough of them,
more than earth,
even than of the upper earth,
had passed with me
beneath the earth;

If I could have caught up from the earth,
the whole of the flowers of the earth,
if once I could have breathed into myself
the very golden crocuses
and the red,
and the very golden hearts of the first saffron,
the whole of the golden mass,
the whole of the great fragrance,
I could have dared the loss.

V

So for your arrogance
and your ruthlessness
I have lost the earth
and the flowers of the earth,
and the live souls above the earth,
and you who passed across the light

and reached
ruthless;

you who have your own light,
who are to yourself a presence,
who need no presence;

yet for all your arrogance
and your glance,
I tell you this:

such loss is no loss,
such terror, such coils and strands and pitfalls
of blackness,
such terror
is no loss;

hell is no worse than your earth
above the earth,
hell is no worse,
no, nor your flowers
nor your veins of light
nor your presence,
a loss;

my hell is no worse than yours
though you pass among the flowers and speak
with the spirits above the earth.

VI

Against the black
I have more fervour
than you in all the splendour of that place,
against the blackness
and the stark grey
I have more light;

and the flowers,
if I should tell you,

you would turn from your own fit paths
toward hell,
turn again and glance back
and I would sink into a place
even more terrible than this.

VII

At least I have the flowers of myself,
and my thoughts, no god
can take that;
I have the fervour of myself for a presence
and my own spirit for light;

and my spirit with its loss
knows this;
though small against the black,
small against the formless rocks,
hell must break before I am lost;

before I am lost,
hell must open like a red rose
for the dead to pass.

Marianne Moore
(1887–1972)

arianne Moore was born in Kirkwood, Missouri, but grew up in Carlisle, Pennsylvania, where her mother taught at the U.S. Indian School. In 1909 she graduated from Bryn Mawr College, and after traveling in Europe moved to New York City with her mother and brother and began to publish poems in small magazines. Two books, *Poems* (1921) and *Observations* (1924), established her reputation as a precise stylist. In 1925 she became the editor of the important modernist journal *The Dial* for four years, and for several decades wrote essays and criticism. With the publication of her *Collected Poems* (1951), which won the National Book Award and the Pulitzer Prize, Moore became a beloved American "lady poet," a kind of Grandma Moses of poetry, known for her love of baseball and for trying to name the car that became the Edsel. But her poetry is intellectual, tough, and often satirical; she invented her own complex free verse forms and used her writing to comment on the self-effacement and decorum that inhibited women writers of her generation.

Silence (1924)

My father used to say,
"Superior people never make long visits,
have to be shown Longfellow's grave
or the glass flowers at Harvard.
Self-reliant like the cat—
that takes its prey to privacy,
the mouse's limp tail hanging like a shoelace from its mouth—
they sometimes enjoy solitude,
and can be robbed of speech
by speech which has delighted them.
The deepest feeling always shows itself in silence;
not in silence, but restraint."
Nor was he insincere in saying, "Make my house your inn."
Inns are not residences.

Poetry (1935)

I, too, dislike it: there are things that are important beyond all this
              fiddle.
 Reading it, however, with a perfect contempt for it, one discovers in
 it, after all, a place for the genuine.
   Hands that can grasp, eyes
    that can dilate, hair that can rise
     if it must, these things are important not because a

high-sounding interpretation can be put upon them but because
              they are
 useful. When they become so derivative as to become
            unintelligible
 the same thing may be said for all of us, that we
   do not admire what
   we cannot understand: the bat
    holding on upside down or in quest of something to

eat, elephants pushing, a wild horse taking a roll, a tireless wolf
              under
 a tree, the immovable critic twitching his skin like a horse that
              feels a
 flea, the base-
   ball fan, the statistician—
   nor is it valid
    to discriminate against "business documents and

school-books"; all these phenomena are important. One must make
            a distinction
 however: when dragged into prominence by half poets, the
          result is not poetry,
 nor till the poets among us can be
  "literalists of
  the imagination"—above
   insolence and triviality and can present

for inspection, "imaginary gardens with real toads in them," shall
we have
it. In the meantime, if you demand on the one hand,
the raw material of poetry in
all its rawness and
that which is on the other hand
genuine, you are interested in poetry.

Katherine Anne Porter
(1890–1980)

aised by her paternal grandfather in Texas and Louisiana after the early death of her mother, Katherine Anne Porter ran away from a convent school at sixteen to marry the first of her four husbands. She participated in the bohemian life of Greenwich Village in the 1920s, lived in Mexico and Berlin in the years between the wars, and was in Washington during and after World War II. After brief forays into movies, singing, and local newspapers, she moved to Greenwich Village in 1919 and wrote short stories while supporting herself with journalism and publicity writing. One important group of stories, which she called the "Miranda cycle," appeared in *Flowering Judas and Other Stories* in 1935; they deal with female initiation into the adult world of sexuality, knowledge, and death. In "The Circus," Porter dramatized the images of freaks and femininity that had been essential to much of American women's writing since the nineteenth century.

The Circus (1944)

The long planks set on trestles rose one above the other to a monstrous height and stretched dizzyingly in a wide oval ring. They were packed with people—"lak fleas on a dog's ear," said Dicey, holding Miranda's hand firmly and looking about her with disapproval. The white billows of enormous canvas sagged overhead, held up by three poles set evenly apart down the center. The family, when seated, occupied almost a whole section on one level.

On one side of them in a long row sat Father, sister Maria, brother Paul, Grandmother; great-aunt Keziah, cousin Keziah, and second-cousin Keziah, who had just come down from Kentucky on a visit; uncle Charles Breaux, cousin Charles Breaux, and aunt Marie-Anne Breaux. On the other side sat small cousin Lucie Breaux, big cousin Paul Gay, great-aunt Sally Gay (who took snuff and was therefore a disgrace to the family); two strange, extremely handsome young men who might be cousins but who were certainly in love with cousin Miranda Gay; and cousin Miranda Gay herself, a most dashing young lady with crisp silk skirts, a half dozen of them at once, a lovely perfume and wonderful black curly hair above enormous wild gray eyes, "like a colt's," Father said. Miranda hoped to be exactly like her when she grew up. Hanging to Dicey's arm she leaned out and waved to cousin Miranda, who waved back smiling, and the strange young men waved to her also. Miranda was most fearfully excited. It was her first circus; it might also be her last because the whole family had combined to persuade Grandmother to allow her to come with them. "Very well, this once," Grandmother said, "since it's a family reunion."

This once! This once! She could not look hard enough at everything. She even peeped down between the wide crevices of the piled-up plank seats, where she was astonished to see odd-looking, roughly dressed little boys peeping up from the dust below. They were squatted in little heaps, staring up quietly. She looked squarely into the eyes of one, who returned her a look so peculiar she gazed and gazed, trying to understand it. It was a bold grinning stare without any kind of friendliness in it. He was a thin, dirty little boy with a floppy old checkerboard cap pulled over crumpled red ears and dust-colored hair. As she gazed he nudged the little boy next to him, whispered, and the second little boy caught her eye. This was too much. Miranda pulled Dicey's sleeve. "Dicey, what are those little boys doing down there?" "Down where?" asked Dicey, but she seemed to know already, for she bent over and looked through the crevice, drew her knees together and her skirts around her, and said severely: "You jus mind yo' own business and stop throwin' yo' legs around that way. Don't you pay any mind. Plenty o' monkeys right here in the show widout you studyin dat kind."

An enormous brass band seemed to explode right at Miranda's ear. She jumped, quivered, thrilled blindly and almost forgot to breathe as sound and color and smell rushed together and poured through her skin and hair and beat in her head and hands and feet and pit of her stomach. "Oh," she called out in her panic, closing her eyes and seizing Dicey's hand hard. The flaring lights burned through her lids, a roar of laughter like rage drowned out the steady raging of the drums and horns. She opened her eyes . . . A creature in a blousy white overall with ruffles at the neck and ankles, with bone-white skull and chalk-white face, with tufted eyebrows far apart in the middle of his forehead, the lids in a black sharp angle, a long scarlet mouth stretching back into sunken cheeks, turned up at the corners in a perpetual bitter grimace of pain, astonishment, not smiling, pranced along a wire stretched down the center of the ring, balancing a long thin pole with little wheels at either end. Miranda thought at first he was walking on air, or flying, and this did not surprise her; but when she saw the wire, she was terrified. High above their heads the inhuman figure pranced, spinning the little wheels. He paused, slipped, the flapping white leg waved in space; he staggered, wobbled, slipped sidewise, plunged, and caught the wire with frantic knee, hanging there upside down, the other leg waving like a feeler above his head; slipped once more, caught by one frenzied heel, and swung back and forth like a scarf . . . The crowd roared with savage delight, shrieks of dreadful laughter like devils in delicious torment . . . Miranda shrieked too, with real pain, clutching at her stomach with her knees drawn up . . . The man on the wire, hanging by his foot, turned his head like a seal from side to side and blew sneering kisses from his cruel mouth. Then Miranda covered her eyes and screamed, the tears pouring over her cheeks and chin.

"Take her home," said her father, "get her out of here at once," but the laughter was not wiped from his face. He merely glanced at her and back to the ring. "Take her away, Dicey," called the Grandmother, from under her half-raised crepe veil. Dicey, rebelliously, very slowly, without taking her gaze from the white figure swaying on the wire, rose, seized the limp, suffering bundle, prodded and lumped her way over knees and feet, through the crowd, down the levels of the scaffolding, across a space of sandy tanbark, out through a flap in the tent. Miranda was crying steadily with an occasional hiccough. A dwarf was standing in the entrance, wearing a little woolly beard, a pointed cap, tight red breeches, long shoes with turned-up toes. He carried a thin white wand. Miranda almost touched him before she saw him, her distorted face with its open mouth and glistening tears almost level with his. He leaned forward and peered at her with kind, not-human golden eyes, like a near-sighted dog: then made a horrid grimace at her, imitating her own face. Miranda struck at him in sheer ill temper, screaming. Dicey drew her away quickly, but not before Miranda had seen in his face, suddenly, a look of haughty, remote displeasure, a true grown-up look. She knew it well. It chilled her with a new kind of fear: she had not believed he was really human.

"Raincheck, get your raincheck!" said a very disagreeable looking fellow as they passed. Dicey turned toward him almost in tears herself. "Mister, caint you see I won't be able to git back? I got this young un to see to . . . What good dat lil piece of paper goin to do *me*?" All the way home she was cross, and grumbled under her breath: little ole meany . . . little ole scare-cat . . . gret big baby . . . never go nowhere . . . never see nothin . . . come on here now, hurry up—always ruinin everything for othah folks . . . won't let anybody rest a minute, won't let anybody have any good times . . . come on here now, you wanted to go home and you're going there . . . snatching Miranda along, vicious but cautious, careful not to cross the line where Miranda could say outright: "Dicey did this or said this to me . . ." Dicey was allowed a certain freedom up to a point.

The family trooped into the house just before dark and scattered out all over it. From every room came the sound of chatter and laughter. The other children told Miranda what she had missed: wonderful little ponies with plumes and bells on their bridles, ridden by darling little monkeys in velvet jackets and peaked hats . . . trained white goats that danced . . . a baby elephant that crossed his front feet and leaned against his cage and opened his mouth to be fed, *such* a baby! . . . more clowns, funnier than the first one even . . . beautiful ladies with bright yellow hair, wearing white silk tights with red satin sashes had performed on white trapezes; they also had hung by their toes, but how gracefully, like flying birds! Huge white horses had lolloped around and round the ring with men and women dancing on their backs! One man had swung by his teeth from the top of the tent and another had put his head in a lion's mouth. Ah, what she had not missed! Everybody had been enjoying themselves while she was missing her first big circus and spoiling the day for Dicey. Poor Dicey. Poor dear Dicey. The other children who hadn't thought of Dicey until that moment, mourned over her with sad mouths, their malicious eyes watching Miranda squirm. Dicey had been looking forward for weeks to this day! And then Miranda must get scared—"Can you *imagine* being afraid of that funny old clown?" each one asked the other, and then they smiled pityingly on Miranda . . .

Then too, it had been a very important occasion in another way: it was the first time Grandmother had ever allowed herself to be persuaded to go to the circus. One could not gather, from her rather generalized opinions, whether there had been no circuses when she was young, or there had been and it was not proper to see them. At any rate for her usual sound reasons, Grandmother had never approved of circuses, and though she would not deny she had been amused somewhat, still there had been sights and sounds in this one which she maintained were, to say the least, not particularly edifying to the young. Her son Harry, who came in while the children made an early supper, looked at their illuminated faces, all the brothers and sisters and visiting cousins, and said, "This basket of young doesn't seem to be much damaged." His mother said, "The fruits of their present are in a future so far off, neither of us may live to know whether harm has been done or not. That is the trouble," and she went on ladling out hot milk to pour over their buttered toast. Miranda was sitting silent, her underlip drooping. Her father smiled at her. "You missed it, Baby," he said softly, "and what good did that do you?"

Miranda burst again into tears: had to be taken away at last, and her supper was brought up to her. Dicey was exasperated and silent. Miranda could not eat. She tried, as if she were really remembering them, to think of the beautiful wild beings in white satin and spangles and red sashes who danced and frolicked on the trapezes; of the sweet little furry ponies and the lovely pet monkeys in their comical clothes. She fell asleep, and her invented memories gave way before her real ones, the bitter terrified face of the man in blowsy white falling to his death—ah, the cruel joke!—and the terrible grimace of the unsmiling dwarf. She screamed in her sleep and sat up crying for deliverance from her torments.

Dicey came, her cross, sleepy eyes half-closed, her big dark mouth pouted, thumping the floor with her thick bare feet. "I *swear*," she said, in a violent hoarse whisper. "What the matter with you? You need a good spankin, I *swear*! Wakin everybody up like this . . ."

Miranda was completely subjugated by her fears. She had a way of answering Dicey back. She would say, "Oh, hush up, Dicey." Or she would say, "I don't have to mind *you*. I don't have to mind anybody but my grandmother," which was provokingly true. And she would say, "You don't know what you're talking about." The day just past had changed that. Miranda sincerely did not want anybody, not even Dicey, to be cross with her. Ordinarily she did not care how cross she made the harassed adults around her. Now if Dicey must be cross, she still did not really care, if only Dicey might not turn out the lights and leave her to the fathomless terrors of the darkness where sleep could overtake her once more. She hugged Dicey with both arms, crying, "Don't, don't leave me. *Don't* be so angry! I c-c-can't b-bear it!"

Dicey lay down beside her with a long moaning sigh, which meant that she was collecting her patience and making up her mind to remember that she was a Christian and must bear her cross. "Now you go to sleep," she said, in her usual warm being-good voice. "Now you jes shut yo eyes and go to sleep. I ain't going to leave you. Dicey ain't mad at nobody . . . *nobody* in the whole worl' . . ."

Zora Neale Hurston
(1891–1960)

ora Neale Hurston, one of the most gifted women writers of the 1930s, was exceptional in her determination to stay free of all ideologies, parties, and narratives of victimization, whether racial, Marxist, or feminist. Her resistance to being a "Race Woman," or a proletarian writer, did not mean that she was indifferent to race or working people. Raised in the all-black community of Eatonville, Florida, where her father was the mayor, she had a direct experience of rural Southern culture. In 1917 she decided to take advantage of a Maryland Code that gave free schooling to "all colored youths between six and twenty years of age." Although she was already twenty-six, Hurston claimed to be ten years younger, and enrolled in an evening high-school program run by Morgan College (now Morgan State University) in Baltimore. After high school Hurston moved on to Howard University to study English literature. When her short story "Drenched in Light" was published in the arts journal *Opportunity* in December 1924, Hurston decided to move to Harlem in order to market her writing and earn money to complete her education.

"Sweat," published in 1926 in the only issue of an experimental Harlem literary magazine, won the attention and respect of Harlem Renaissance writers, and its discussion of the revenge of an abused wife anticipated the themes of her later fiction. Hurston had also won a scholarship to Barnard College, where she was the only black student. There she studied cultural anthropology, and with financial support from a wealthy white patron, Mrs. Osgood Mason, did graduate fieldwork in the black South, Jamaica, the Bahamas, and Haiti. Hurston's best-known novel, *Their Eyes Were Watching God* (1937), is a modernist work influenced by Katherine Mansfield as well as black folk culture, but it antagonized black male critics who accused Hurston of pandering to a white audience. Unintimidated, Hurston did not back down. In 1943 she gave an interview to the *New York World-Telegram* asserting: "I don't see life through the eyes of a Negro, but those of a person." During the last years of her life, out of favor with publishers and the public, Hurston moved from job to menial job; when she died in 1960, she was working as a maid and living in a welfare home.

Sweat (1926)

It was eleven o'clock of a Spring night in Florida. It was Sunday. Any other night, Delia Jones would have been in bed for two hours by this time. But she was a washwoman, and Monday morning meant a great deal to her. So she collected the soiled clothes on Saturday when she returned the clean things. Sunday night after church, she sorted them and put the white things to soak. It saved her almost a half day's start. A great hamper in the bedroom held the clothes that she brought home. It was so much neater than a number of bundles lying around.

She squatted in the kitchen floor beside the great pile of clothes, sorting them into small heaps according to color, and humming a song in a mournful key, but wondering through it all where Sykes, her husband, had gone with her horse and buckboard.

Just then something long, round, limp and black fell upon her shoulders and slithered to the floor beside her. A great terror took hold of her. It softened her knees and dried her mouth so that it was a full minute before she could cry out or move. Then she saw that it was the big bull whip her husband liked to carry when he drove.

She lifted her eyes to the door and saw him standing there bent over with laughter at her fright. She screamed at him.

"Sykes, what you throw dat whip on me like dat? You know it would skeer me—looks just like a snake, an' you knows how skeered Ah is of snakes."

"Course Ah knowed it! That's how come Ah done it." He slapped his leg with his hand and almost rolled on the ground in his mirth. "If you such a big fool dat you got to have a fit over a earth worm or a string, Ah don't keer how bad Ah skeer you."

"You aint got no business doing it. Gawd knows it's a sin. Some day Ah'm gointuh drop dead from some of yo' foolishness. 'Nother thing, where you been wid mah rig? Ah feeds dat pony. He aint fuh you to be drivin' wid no bull whip."

"You sho is one aggravatin' nigger woman!" he declared and stepped into the room. She resumed her work and did not answer him at once. "Ah done tole you time and again to keep them white folks' clothes outa dis house."

He picked up the whip and glared down at her. Delia went on with her work. She went out into the yard and returned with a galvanized tub and set it on the washbench. She saw that Sykes had kicked all of the clothes together again, and now stood in her way truculently, his whole manner hoping, *praying*, for an argument. But she walked calmly around him and commenced to re-sort the things.

"Next time, Ah'm gointer kick 'em outdoors," he threatened as he struck a match along the leg of his corduroy breeches.

Delia never looked up from her work, and her thin, stooped shoulders sagged further.

"Ah aint for no fuss t'night Sykes. Ah just come from taking sacrament at the church house."

He snorted scornfully. "Yeah, you just come from de church house on a Sunday night, but heah you is gone to work on them clothes. You aint nothing but a hypocrite. One of them amen-corner Christians—sing, whoop, and shout, then come home and wash white folks clothes on the Sabbath."

He stepped roughly upon the whitest pile of things, kicking them helter-skelter as he crossed the room. His wife gave a little scream of dismay, and quickly gathered them together again.

"Sykes, you quit grindin' dirt into these clothes! How can Ah git through by Sat'day if Ah don't start on Sunday?"

"Ah don't keer if you never git through. Anyhow, Ah done promised Gawd and a couple of other men, Ah aint gointer have it in mah house. Don't gimme no lip neither, else Ah'll throw 'em out and put mah fist up side yo' head to boot."

Delia's habitual meekness seemed to slip from her shoulders like a blown scarf. She was on her feet; her poor little body, her bare knuckly hands bravely defying the strapping hulk before her.

"Looka heah, Sykes, you done gone too fur. Ah been married to you fur fifteen years, and Ah been takin' in washin' fur fifteen years. Sweat, sweat, sweat! Work and sweat, cry and sweat, pray and sweat!"

"What's that got to do with me?" he asked brutally.

"What's it got to do with you, Sykes? Mah tub of suds is filled yo' belly with vittles more times than yo' hands is filled it. Mah sweat is done paid for this house and Ah reckon Ah kin keep on sweatin' in it."

She seized the iron skillet from the stove and struck a defensive pose, which act surprised him greatly, coming from her. It cowed him and he did not strike her as he usually did.

"Naw you won't," she panted, "that ole snaggle-toothed black woman you runnin' with aint comin' heah to pile up on *mah* sweat and blood. You aint paid for nothin' on this place, and Ah'm gointer stay right heah till Ah'm toted out foot foremost."

"Well, you better quit gittin' me riled up, else they'll be totin' you out sooner than you expect. Ah'm so tired of you Ah don't know whut to do. Gawd! how Ah hates skinny wimmen!"

A little awed by this new Delia, he sidled out of the door and slammed the back gate after him. He did not say where he had gone, but she knew too well. She knew very well that he would not return until nearly day-break also. Her work over, she went on to bed but not to sleep at once. Things had come to a pretty pass!

She lay awake, gazing upon the debris that cluttered their matrimonial trail. Not an image left standing along the way. Anything like flowers had long ago been drowned in the salty stream that had been pressed from her heart. Her tears, her sweat, her blood. She had brought love to the union and he had brought a longing after the flesh. Two months after the wedding, he had given her the first brutal beating. She had the memory of his numerous trips to Orlando with all of his wages when he had returned to her penniless, even before the first year had passed. She was young and soft then, but now she thought of her knotty, muscled limbs, her harsh knuckly hands, and drew herself up into an unhappy little ball in the middle of the big feather bed. Too late now to hope for love, even if it were not Bertha it would be someone else. This case dif-fered from the others only in that she was bolder than the others. Too late for everything except her little home. She had built it for her old days, and planted one by one the trees and flowers there. It was lovely to her, lovely.

Somehow, before sleep came, she found herself saying aloud: "Oh well, whatever goes over the Devil's back, is got to come under his belly. Sometime or ruther, Sykes, like everybody else, is gointer reap his sow-ing." After that she was able to build a spiritual earthworks against her husband. His shells could no longer reach her. *Amen.* She went to sleep and slept until he announced his presence in bed by kicking her feet and rudely snatching the covers away.

"Gimme some kivah heah, an' git yo' damn foots over on yo' own side! Ah oughter mash you in yo' mouf fuh drawing dat skillet on me."

Delia went clear to the rail without answering him. A triumphant indifference to all that he was or did.

The week was as full of work for Delia as all other weeks, and Saturday found her behind her little pony, collecting and delivering clothes.

It was a hot, hot day near the end of July. The village men on Joe Clarke's porch even chewed cane listlessly. They did not hurl the cane-knots as usual. They let them dribble over the edge of the porch. Even conversation had collapsed under the heat.

"Heah come Delia Jones," Jim Merchant said, as the shaggy pony came 'round the bend of the road toward them. The rusty buckboard was heaped with baskets of crisp, clean laundry.

"Yep," Joe Lindsay agreed. "Hot or col', rain or shine, jes ez reg'lar ez de weeks roll roun' Delia carries 'em an' fetches 'em on Sat'day."

"She better if she wanter eat," said Moss. "Sykes Jones aint wuth de shot an' powder hit would tek tuh kill 'em. Not to *huh* he aint."

"He sho' aint," Walter Thomas chimed in. "It's too bad, too, cause she wuz a right pritty lil trick when he got huh. Ah'd uh mah'ied huh mah-seff if he hadnter beat me to it."

Delia nodded briefly at the men as she drove past.

"Too much knockin' will ruin *any* 'oman. He done beat huh 'nough tuh kill three women, let 'lone change they looks," said Elijah Moseley. "How Sykes kin stommuck dat big black greasy Mogul he's layin' roun' wid, gits me. Ah swear dat eight-rock couldn't kiss a sardine can Ah done thowed out de back do' 'way las' yeah."

"Aw, she's fat, thass how come. He's allus been crazy 'bout fat women," put in Merchant. "He'd a' been tied up wid one long time ago if he could a' found one tuh have him. Did Ah tell yuh 'bout him come sidlin' roun' *mah* wife—bringin' her a basket uh peecans outa his yard fuh a present? Yessir, mah wife! She tol' him tuh take 'em right straight back home, cause Delia works so hard ovah dat washtub she reckon every-thing on de place taste lak sweat an' soapsuds. Ah jus' wisht Ah'd a' caught 'im 'roun' dere! Ah'd a' made his hips ketch on fiah down dat shell road."

"Ah know he done it, too. Ah sees 'im grinnin' at every 'oman dat passes," Walter Thomas said. "But even so, he useter eat some mighty big hunks uh humble pie tuh git dat lil' 'oman he got. She wuz ez pritty ez a speckled pup! Dat wuz fifteen yeahs ago. He useter be so skeered uh losin' huh, she could make him do some parts of a husband's duty. Dey never wuz de same in de mind."

"There oughter be a law about him," said Lindsay. "He aint fit tuh carry guts tuh a bear."

Clarke spoke for the first time. "Taint no law on earth dat kin make a man be decent if it aint in 'im. There's plenty men dat takes a wife lak dey do a joint uh sugar-cane. It's round, juicy an' sweet when dey gits it. But dey squeeze an' grind, squeeze an' grind an' wring tell dey wring every drop uh pleasure dat's in 'em out. When dey's satisfied dat dey is wrung dry, dey treats 'em jes lak dey do a cane-chew. Dey thows 'em away. Dey knows whut dey is doin' while dey is at it, an' hates theirselves fuh it but dey keeps on hangin' after huh tell she's empty. Den dey hates huh fuh bein' a cane-chew an' in de way."

"We oughter take Sykes an' dat stray 'oman uh his'n down in Lake Howell swamp an' lay on de rawhide till dey cain' t say Lawd a' mussy. He allus wuz uh ovahbearin' niggah, but since dat white 'oman from up north done teached 'im how to run a automobile, he done got too biggety to live—an' we oughter kill 'im," Old Man Anderson advised.

A grunt of approval went around the porch. But the heat was melting their civic virtue and Elijah Moseley began to bait Joe Clarke.

"Come on, Joe, git a melon outa dere an' slice it up for yo' customers. We'se all sufferin' wid de heat. De bear's done got *me!*"

"Thass right, Joe, a watermelon is jes' whut Ah needs tuh cure de eppizudicks," Walter Thomas joined forces with Moseley. "Come on dere, Joe. We all is steady customers an' you aint set us up in a long time. Ah chooses dat long, bowlegged Floridy favorite."

"A god, an' be dough. You all gimme twenty cents and slice way," Clarke retorted. "Ah needs a col' slice m'self. Heah, everybody chip in. Ah'll lend y'll mah meat knife."

The money was quickly subscribed and the huge melon brought forth. At that moment, Sykes and Bertha arrived. A determined silence fell on the porch and the melon was put away again.

Merchant snapped down the blade of his jackknife and moved toward the store door.

"Come on in, Joe, an' gimme a slab uh sow belly an' uh pound uh coffee—almost fuhgot 'twas Sat'day. Got to git on home." Most of the men left also.

Just then Delia drove past on her way home, as Sykes was ordering magnificently for Bertha. It pleased him for Delia to see.

"Git whutsoever yo' heart desires, Honey. Wait a minute, Joe. Give huh two botles uh strawberry soda-water, uh quart uh parched ground-peas, an' a block uh chewin' gum."

With all this they left the store, with Sykes reminding Bertha that this was his town and she could have it if she wanted it.

The men returned soon after they left, and held their watermelon feast.

"Where did Sykes Jones git da 'oman from nohow?" Lindsay asked.

"Ovah Apopka. Guess dey musta been cleanin' out de town when she lef'. She don't look lak a thing but a hunk uh liver wid hair on it."

"Well, she sho' kin squall," Dave Carter contributed. "When she gits ready tuh laff, she jes' opens huh mouf an' latches it back tuh de las' notch. No ole grandpa alligator down in Lake Bell ain't got nothin' on huh."

Bertha had been in town three months now. Sykes was still paying her room rent at Della Lewis'—the only house in town that would have taken her in. Sykes took her frequently to Winter Park to "stomps." He still assured her that he was the swellest man in the state.

"Sho' you kin have dat lil' ole house soon's Ah kin git dat 'oman outa dere. Everything b'longs tuh me an' you sho' kin have it. Ah sho' 'bominates uh skinny 'oman. Lawdy, you sho' is got one portly shape on you! You kin git *anything* you wants. Dis is *mah* town an' you sho' kin have it."

Delia's work-worn knees crawled over the earth in Gethsemane and up the rocks of Calvary many, many times during these months. She avoided the villagers and meeting places in her efforts to be blind and deaf. But Bertha nullified this to a degree, by coming to Delia's house to call Sykes out to her at the gate.

Delia and Sykes fought all the time now with no peaceful interludes. They slept and ate in silence. Two or three times Delia had attempted a timid friendliness, but she was repulsed each time. It was plain that the breaches must remain agape.

The sun had burned July to August. The heat streamed down like a million hot arrows, smiting all things living upon the earth. Grass withered, leaves browned, snakes went blind in shedding and men and dogs went mad. Dog days!

Delia came home one day and found Sykes there before her. She wondered, but started to go on into the house without speaking, even though he was standing in the kitchen door and she must either stoop under his arm or ask him to move. He made no room for her. She noticed a soap box beside the steps, but paid no particular attention to it, knowing that he must have brought it there. As she was stooping to pass under his outstretched arm, he suddenly pushed her backward, laughingly.

"Look in de box dere Delia, Ah done brung yuh somethin'!"

She nearly fell upon the box in her stumbling, and when she saw what it held, she all but fainted outright.

"Sykes! Sykes, mah Gawd! You take dat rattlesnake 'way from heah! You *gottuh*. Oh, Jesus, have mussy!"

"Ah aint gut tuh do nuthin' uh de kin'—fact is Ah aint got tuh do nothin' but die. Taint no use uh you puttin' on airs makin' out lak you skeered uh dat snake—he's gointer stay right heah tell he die. He wouldn't bite me cause Ah knows how tuh handle 'im. Nohow he wouldn't risk breakin' out his fangs 'gin yo' skinny laigs."

"Naw, now Sykes, don't keep dat thing 'roun' heah tuh skeer me tuh death. You knows Ah'm even feared uh earth worms. Thass de biggest snake Ah evah did see. Kill 'im Sykes, please."

"Doan ast me tuh do nothin' fuh yuh. Goin' 'roun' tryin' tuh be so damn asterperious. Naw, Ah aint gonna kill it. Ah think uh damn sight mo' uh him dan you! Dat's a nice snake an' anybody doan lak 'im kin jes' hit de grit."

The village soon heard that Sykes had the snake, and came to see and ask questions.

"How de hen-fire did you ketch dat six-foot rattler, Sykes?" Thomas asked.

"He's full uh frogs so he caint hardly move, thass how Ah eased up on 'm. But Ah'm a snake charmer an' knows how tuh handle 'em. Shux, dat aint nothin'. Ah could ketch one eve'y day if Ah so wanted tuh."

"Whut he needs is a heavy hick'ry club leaned real heavy on his head. Dat's de bes' way tuh charm a rattlesnake."

"Naw, Walt, y'll jes' don't understand dese diamon' backs lak Ah do," said Sykes in a superior tone of voice.

The village agreed with Walter, but the snake stayed on. His box remained by the kitchen door with its screen wire covering. Two or three days later it had digested its meal of frogs and literally came to life. It rattled at every movement in the kitchen or the yard. One day as Delia came down the kitchen steps she saw his chalky-white fangs curved like scimitars hung in the wire meshes. This time she did not run away with averted eyes as usual. She stood for a long time in the doorway in a red fury that grew bloodier for every second that she regarded the creature that was her torment.

That night she broached the subject as soon as Sykes sat down to the table.

"Sykes, Ah wants you tuh take dat snake 'way fum heah. You done starved me an' Ah put up widcher, you done beat me an Ah took dat, but you done kilt all mah insides bringin' dat varmint heah."

Sykes poured out a saucer full of coffee and drank it deliberately before he answered her.

"A whole lot Ah keer 'bout how you feels inside uh out. Dat snake aint goin' no damn wheah till Ah gits ready fuh 'im tuh go. So fur as beatin' is concerned, yuh aint took near all dat you gointer take ef yuh stay 'roun' *me*."

Delia pushed back her plate and got up from the table. "Ah hates you, Sykes," she said calmly. "Ah hates you tuh de same degree dat Ah useter love yuh. Ah done took an' took till mah belly is full up tuh mah neck. Dat's de reason Ah got mah letter fum de church an' moved mah membership tuh Woodbridge—so Ah don't haftuh take no sacrament wid yuh, Ah don't wantuh see yuh 'roun' me atall. Lay 'roun' wid dat 'oman all yuh wants tuh, but gwan 'way fum me an' mah house. Ah hates yuh lak uh suck-egg dog."

Sykes almost let the huge wad of corn bread and collard greens he was chewing fall out of his mouth in amazement. He had a hard time whipping himself up to the proper fury to try to answer Delia.

"Well, Ah'm glad you does hate me. Ah'm sho' tiahed uh you hangin' ontuh me. Ah don't want yuh. Look at yuh stringey ole neck! Yo' raw-bony laigs an' arms is enough tuh cut uh man tuh death. You looks jes' lak de devvul's doll-baby tuh *me*. You cain't hate me no worse dan Ah hates you. Ah been hatin' *you* fuh years."

"Yo' ole black hide don't look lak nothin' tuh me, but uh passle uh wrinkled up rubber, wid yo' big ole yeahs flappin' on each side lak uh paih uh buzzard wings. Don't think Ah'm gointuh be run 'way fum mah house neither. Ah'm goin' tuh de white folks bout *you*, mah young man, de very nex' time you lay yo' han's on me. Mah cup is done run ovah," Delia said this with no signs of fear and Sykes departed from the house, threatening her, but made not the slightest move to carry out any of them.

That night he did not return at all, and the next day being Sunday, Delia was glad she did not have to quarrel before she hitched up her pony and drove the four miles to Woodbridge.

She stayed to the night service—"love feast"—which was very warm and full of spirit. In the emotional winds her domestic trials were borne far and wide so that she sang as she drove homeward,

> *"Jurden water, black an' col'*
> *Chills de body, not de soul*
> *An' Ah wantah cross Jurden in uh calm time."*

She came from the barn to the kitchen door and stopped.

"Whut's de mattah, ol' satan, you aint kickin' up yo' racket?" She addressed the snake's box. Complete silence. She went on into the house with a new hope in its birth struggles. Perhaps her threat to go to the white folks had frightened Sykes! Perhaps he was sorry! Fifteen years of misery and suppression had brought Delia to the place where she would hope *anything* that looked towards a way over or through her wall of inhibitions.

She felt in the match safe behind the stove at once for a match. There was only one there.

"Dat niggah wouldn't fetch nothin' heah tuh save his rotten neck, but he kin run thew whut Ah brings quick enough. Now he done toted off nigh on tuh haff uh box uh matches. He done had dat 'oman heah in mah house, too."

Nobody but a woman could tell how she knew this even before she struck the match. But she did and it put her into a new fury.

Presently she brought in the tubs to put the white things to soak. This time she decided she need not bring the hamper out of the bedroom; she would go in there and do the sorting. She picked up the pot-bellied lamp and went in. The room was small and the hamper stood hard by the foot of the white iron bed. She could sit and reach through the bedposts—resting as she worked.

"Ah wantah cross Jurden in uh calm time." She was singing again. The mood of the "love feast" had returned. She threw back the lid of the basket almost gaily. Then, moved by both horror and terror, she sprang back toward the door. *There lay the snake in the basket!* He moved sluggishly at first, but even as she turned round and round, jumped up and down in an insanity of fear, he began to stir vigorously. She saw him pouring his awful beauty from the basket upon the bed, then she seized the lamp and ran as fast as she could to the kitchen. The wind from the open door blew out the light and the darkness added to her terror. She sped to the darkness of the yard, slamming the door after her before she thought to set down the lamp. She did not feel safe even on the ground, so she climbed up in the hay barn.

There for an hour or more she lay sprawled upon the hay a gibbering wreck.

Finally she grew quiet, and after that, coherent thought. With this, stalked through her a cold, bloody rage. Hours of this. A period of introspection, a space of retrospection, then a mixture of both. Out of this an awful calm.

"Well, Ah done de bes' Ah could. If things aint right, Gawd knows taint mah fault."

She went to sleep—a twitch sleep—and woke up to a faint gray sky. There was a loud hollow sound below. She peered out. Sykes was at the wood-pile, demolishing a wire-covered box.

He hurried to the kitchen door, but hung outside there some minutes before he entered, and stood some minutes more inside before he closed it after him.

The gray in the sky was spreading. Delia descended without fear now, and crouched beneath the low bedroom window. The drawn shade shut out the dawn, shut in the night. But the thin walls held back no sound.

"Dat ol' scratch is woke up now!" She mused at the tremendous whirr inside, which every woodsman knows, is one of the sound illusions. The rattler is a ventriloquist. His whirr sounds to the right, to the left, straight ahead, behind, close under foot—everywhere but where it is. Woe to him who guesses wrong unless he is prepared to hold up his end of the argument! Sometimes he strikes without rattling at all.

Inside, Sykes heard nothing until he knocked a pot lid off the stove while trying to reach the match safe in the dark. He had emptied his pockets at Bertha's.

The snake seemed to wake up under the stove and Sykes made a quick leap into the bedroom. In spite of the gin he had had, his head was clearing now.

"Mah Gawd!" he chattered, "ef Ah could on'y strack uh light!"

The rattling ceased for a moment as he stood paralyzed. He waited. It seemed that the snake waited also.

"Oh, fuh de light! Ah thought he'd be too sick"—Sykes was muttering to himself when the whirr began again, closer, right underfoot this time. Long before this, Sykes' ability to think had been flattened down to primitive instinct and he leaped—onto the bed.

Outside Delia heard a cry that might have come from a maddened chimpanzee, a stricken gorilla. All the terror, all the horror, all the rage that man possibly could express, without a recognizable human sound.

A tremendous stir inside there, another series of animal screams, the intermittent whirr of the reptile. The shade torn violently down from the window, letting in the red dawn, a huge brown hand seizing the window stick, great dull blows upon the wooden floor punctuating the gibberish of sound long after the rattle of the snake had abruptly subsided. All this Delia could see and hear from her place beneath the window, and it made her ill. She crept over to the four-o'clocks and stretched herself on the cool earth to recover.

She lay there. "Delia, Delia!" She could hear Sykes calling in a most despairing tone as one who expected no answer. The sun crept on up, and he called. Delia could not move—her legs were gone flabby. She never moved, he called, and the sun kept rising.

"Mah Gawd!" She heard him moan, "Mah Gawd fum Heben!" She heard him stumbling about and got up from her flower-bed. The sun was growing warm. As she approached the door she heard him call out hopefully, "Delia, is dat you Ah heah?"

She saw him on his hands and knees as soon as she reached the door. He crept an inch or two toward her—all that he was able, and she saw his horribly swollen neck and his one open eye shining with hope. A surge of pity too strong to support bore her away from that eye that must, could not, fail to see the tubs. He would see the lamp. Orlando with its doctors was too far. She could scarcely reach the Chinaberry tree, where she waited in the growing heat while inside she knew the cold river was creeping up and up to extinguish that eye which must know by now that she knew.

Edna St. Vincent Millay
(1892–1950)

dna St. Vincent Millay (1892–1950) was the most gifted, hard-working, and important woman poet of the 1920s. Millay came from a Rockland, Maine, family much like Louisa May Alcott's—an absent, improvident father; an industrious, beloved Marmee-like mother, Cora, who also wrote poetry, and had a rough edge and a bohemian streak; and two sisters, Norma and Kathleen. Edna, called "Vincent" by her sisters, was boyish, beautiful, and bisexual, as well as a precociously gifted writer. Her poem "Renascence," written when she was nineteen, won a national poetry award, and won her a scholarship to Vassar, where she was an undergraduate star. After graduation, in Greenwich Village she was a *femme fatale* with many conquests, as well as a celebrated poet. In her best-known poems, including her famous epigrams, "First Fig" and "Second Fig," and world-weary sonnets like "What Lips My Lips Have Kissed," Millay invented the image of the modern woman who is as open to sexual experience and as emotionally uninvolved as a man, yet saddened by the passage of time and the departure of unnamed young lovers.

First Fig (1920)

My candle burns at both ends;
   It will not last the night;
But ah, my foes, and oh, my friends—
   It gives a lovely light!

Second Fig (1920)

Safe upon the solid rock the ugly houses stand:
Come and see my shining palace built upon the sand!

What Lips My Lips Have Kissed (1923)

What lips my lips have kissed, and where, and why,
I have forgotten, and what arms have lain
Under my head till morning; but the rain
Is full of ghosts tonight, that tap and sigh
Upon the glass and listen for reply;
And in my heart there stirs a quiet pain
For unremembered lads that not again
Will turn to me at midnight with a cry.
Thus in the winter stands the lonely tree,
Nor knows what birds have vanished one by one,
Yet knows its boughs more silent than before:
I cannot say what loves have come and gone;
I only know that summer sang in me
A little while, that in me sings no more.

Maria Cristina Mena
(1893–1965)

aria Cristina Mena was born to Mexico City's upper classes and sent by her parents to New York City when she was fourteen years old to escape the revolution. Between 1913 and 1916, Mena became the first Mexican-American writer to be published in the prestigious *Century* magazine, where "The Vine-Leaf" appeared. But after marrying playwright and journalist Henry Kellett Chambers in 1916, Mena's publishing pace dropped dramatically, and she produced little until the 1940s, when she authored five children's books about Mexico.

The Vine-Leaf (1914)

It is a saying in the Capital of Mexico that Dr. Malsufrido carries more family secrets under his hat than any archbishop, which applies, of course, to family secrets of the rich. The poor have no family secrets, or none that Dr. Malsufrido would trouble to carry under his hat.

The doctor's hat is, appropriately enough, uncommonly capacious, rising very high, and sinking so low that it seems to be supported by his ears and eyebrows, and it has a furry look, as if it had been brushed the wrong way, which is perhaps what happens to it if it is ever brushed at all. When the doctor takes it off, the family secrets do not fly out like a flock of parrots, but remain nicely bottled up beneath a dome of old and highly polished ivory, which, with its unbroken fringe of dyed black hair, has the effect of a tonsure; and then Dr. Malsufrido looks like one of the early saints. I've forgotten which one.

So edifying is his personality that, when he marches into a sickroom, the forces of disease and infirmity march out of it, and do not dare to return until he has taken his leave. In fact, it is well known that none of his patients has ever had the bad manners to die in his presence.

If you will believe him, he is almost ninety years old, and everybody knows that he has been dosing good Mexicans for half a century. He is forgiven for being a Spaniard on account of a legend that he physicked royalty in his time, and that a certain princess—but that has nothing to do with this story.

It is sure he has a courtly way with him that captivates his female patients, of whom he speaks as his *penitentes*, insisting on confession as a prerequisite of diagnosis, and declaring that the physician who undertakes to cure a woman's body without reference to her soul is a more abominable kill-healthy than the famous *Dr. Sangrado*, who taught medicine to *Gil Blas*.

"Describe me the symptoms of your conscience, Señora," he will say. "Fix yourself that I shall forget one tenth of what you tell me."

"But what of the other nine tenths, Doctor?" the troubled lady will exclaim.

"The other nine tenths I shall take care not to believe," Dr. Malsufrido will reply, with a roar of laughter. And sometimes he will add:

"Do not confess your neighbor's sins; the doctor will have enough with your own."

When an inexperienced one fears to become a *penitente* lest that terrible old doctor betray her confidence he reassures her as to his discretion, and at the same time takes her mind off her anxieties by telling her the story of his first patient.

"Figure you my prudence, Señora," he begins, "that, although she was my patient, I did not so much as see her face."

And then, having enjoyed the startled curiosity of his hearer, he continues:

"On that day of two crosses when I first undertook the mending of mortals, she arrived to me beneath a veil as impenetrable as that of a nun, saying:

"'To you I come, Señor Doctor, because no one knows you.'

"'Who would care for fame, Señorita,' said I, 'when obscurity brings such excellent fortune?'

"And the lady, in a voice which trembled slightly, returned:

"'If your knife is as apt as your tongue, and your discretion equal to both, I shall not regret my choice of a surgeon.'

"With suitable gravity I reassured her, and inquired how I might be privileged to serve her. She replied:

"'By ridding me of a blemish, if you are skilful enough to leave no trace on the skin.'

"'Of that I will judge, with the help of God, when the señorita shall have removed her veil.'

"'No, no; you shall not see my face. Praise the saints the blemish is not there!'

"'Wherever it be,' said I, resolutely, 'my science tells me that it must be seen before it can be well removed.'

"The lady answered with great simplicity that she had no anxiety on that account, but that, as she had neither duenna nor servant with her, I must help her. I had no objection, for a surgeon must needs be something of a lady's maid. I judged from the quality of her garments that she was of an excellent family, and I was ashamed of my clumsy fingers; but she was as patient as marble, caring only to keep her face closely covered. When at last I saw the blemish she had complained of, I was astonished, and said:

"'But it seems to me a blessed stigma, Señorita, this delicate, wine-red vine-leaf, staining a surface as pure as the petal of any magnolia. With permission, I should say that the god Bacchus himself painted it here in the arch of this chaste back, where only the eyes of Cupid could find it; for it is safely below the line of the most fashionable gown.'

"But she replied:

"'I have my reasons. Fix yourself that I am superstitious.'

"I tried to reason with her on that, but she lost her patience and cried:

"'For favor, good surgeon, your knife!'

"Even in those days I had much sensibility, Señora, and I swear that my heart received more pain from the knife than did she. Neither the cutting nor the stitching brought a murmur from her. Only some strong ulterior thought could have armed a delicate woman with such valor. I beat my brains to construe the case, but without success. A caprice took me to refuse the fee she offered me.

"'No, Señorita,' I said, 'I have not seen your face, and if I were to take your money, it might pass that I should not see the face of a second patient, which would be a great misfortune. You are my first, and I am as superstitious as you.'

"I would have added that I had fallen in love with her, but I feared to appear ridiculous, having seen no more than her back.

"'You would place me under an obligation,' she said. I felt that her eyes studied me attentively through her veil. 'Very well, I can trust you the better for that. *Adiós*, Señor Surgeon.'

"She came once more to have me remove the stitches, as I had told her, and again her face was concealed, and again I refused payment; but I think she knew that the secret of the vine-leaf was buried in my heart."

"But that secret, what was it, Doctor? Did you ever see the mysterious lady again?"

"*Chist!* Little by little one arrives to the *rancho*, Señora. Five years passed, and many patients arrived to me, but, although all showed me their faces, I loved none of them better than the first one. Partly through family influence, partly through well-chosen friendships, and perhaps a little through that diligence in the art of Hippocrates for which in my old age I am favored by the most charming of Mexicans, I had prospered, and was no longer unknown.

"At a meeting of a learned society I became known to a certain *marqués* who had been a great traveler in his younger days. We had a discussion on a point of anthropology, and he invited me to his house, to see the curiosities he had collected in various countries. Most of them recalled scenes of horrors, for he had a morbid fancy.

"Having taken from my hand the sword with which he had seen five Chinese pirates sliced into small pieces, he led me toward a little door, saying:

"'Now you shall see the most mysterious and beautiful of my mementos, one which recalls a singular event in our own peaceful Madrid.'

"We entered a room lighted by a sky-light, and containing little but an easel on which rested a large canvas. The *marqués* led me where the most auspicious light fell upon it. It was a nude, beautifully painted. The model stood poised divinely, with her back to the beholder, twisting flowers in her hair before a mirror. And there, in the arch of that chaste back, staining a surface as pure as the petal of any magnolia, what did my eyes see? Can you possibly imagine, Señora?"

"*Válgame Dios!* The vine-leaf, Doctor!"

"What penetration of yours, Señora! It was veritably the vine-leaf, wine-red, as it had appeared to me before my knife barbarously extirpated it from the living flesh; but in the picture it seemed unduly conspicuous, as if Bacchus had been angry when he kissed. You may imagine how the sight startled me. But those who know Dr. Malsufrido need no assurance that even in those early days he never permitted himself one imprudent word. No, Señora; I only remarked, after praising the picture in proper terms:

"'What an interesting moon is that upon the divine creature's back!'

"'Does it not resemble a young vine-leaf in early spring?' said the *marqués*, who contemplated the picture with the ardor of a connoisseur. I agreed politely, saying:

"'Now that you suggest it, *Marqués*, it has some of the form and color of a tender vine-leaf. But I could dispense me a better vine-leaf, with many bunches of grapes, to satisfy the curiosity I have to see such a well-formed lady's face. What a misfortune that it does not appear in that mirror, as the artist doubtless intended! The picture was never finished, then?'

" 'I have reason to believe that it was finished,' he replied, 'but that the face painted in the mirror was obliterated. Observe that its surface is an opaque and disordered smudge of many pigments showing no brush-work, but only marks of a rude rubbing that in some places has over-lapped the justly painted frame of the mirror.'

" 'This promises an excellent mystery,' I commented lightly. 'Was it the artist or his model who was dissatisfied with the likeness, *Marqués*?'

" 'I suspect that the likeness was more probably too good than not good enough,' returned the *marqués*. 'Unfortunately poor Andrade is not here to tell us.'

" 'Andrade! The picture was his work?'

" 'The last his hand touched. Do you remember when he was found murdered in his studio?'

" 'With a knife sticking between his shoulders. I remember it very well.'

"The *marqués* continued:

" 'I had asked him to let me have this picture. He was then working on that rich but subdued background. The figure was finished, but there was no vine-leaf, and the mirror was empty of all but a groundwork of paint, with a mere luminous suggestion of a face.

" 'Andrade, however, refused to name me a price, and tried to put me off with excuses. His friends were jesting about the unknown model, whom no one had managed to see, and all suspected that he designed to keep the picture for himself. That made me the more determined to pos-sess it. I wished to make it a betrothal gift to the beautiful Señorita Lis-arda Monte Alegre, who had then accepted the offer of my hand, and who is now the *marquesa*. When I have a desire, Doctor, it bites me, and I make it bite others. That poor Andrade, I gave him no peace.

" 'He fell into one of his solitary fits, shutting himself in his studio, and seeing no one; but that did not prevent me from knocking at his door whenever I had nothing else to do. Well, one morning the door was open.'

" 'Yes, yes!' I exclaimed. 'I remember now, *Marqués*, that it was you who found the body.'

" 'You have said it. He was lying in front of this picture, having dragged himself across the studio. After assuring myself that he was beyond help, and while awaiting the police, I made certain observations. The first thing to strike my attention was this vine-leaf. The paint was fresh, whereas the rest of the figure was comparatively dry. Moreover, its color had not been mixed with Andrade's usual skill. Observe you, Doctor, that the blemish is not of the texture of the skin, or bathed in its admirable atmosphere. It presents itself as an excrescence. And why? Because that color had been mixed and applied with feverish haste by the hand of a dying man, whose one thought was to denounce his assassin— she who undoubtedly bore such a mark on her body, and who had left him for dead, after carefully obliterating the portrait of herself which he had painted in the mirror.'

"'*Ay Dios!* But the police, *Marqués*—they never reported these details so significant?'

"'Our admirable police are not connoisseurs of the painter's art, my friend. Moreover, I had taken the precaution to remove from the dead man's fingers the empurpled brush with which he had traced that accusing symbol.'

"'You wished to be the accomplice of an unknown assassin?'

"'Inevitably, Señor, rather than deliver that lovely body to the hands of the public executioner.'

"The *marqués* raised his lorgnette and gazed at the picture. And I—I was recovering from my agitation, Señora. I said:

"'It seems to me, *Marqués*, that if I were a woman and loved you, I should be jealous of that picture.'

"He smiled and replied:

"'It is true that the *marquesa* affects some jealousy on that account, and will not look at the picture. However, she is one who errs on the side of modesty, and prefers more austere objects of contemplation. She is excessively religious.'

"'I have been called superstitious,' pronounced a voice behind me.

"It was a voice that I had heard before. I turned, Señora, and I ask you to try to conceive whose face I now beheld."

"*Válgame la Virgin*, Dr. Malsufrido, was it not the face of the good *marquesa*, and did she not happen to have been also your first patient?"

"Again such penetration, Señora, confounds me. It was she. The *marqués* did me the honor to present me to her.

"'I have heard of your talents, Señor Surgeon,' she said.

"'And I of your beauty, *Marquesa*,' I hastened to reply; 'but that tale was not so well told.' And I added, 'If you are superstitious, I will be, too.'

"With one look from her beautiful and devout eyes she thanked me for that prudence which to this day, Señora, is at the service of my *penitentes*, little daughters of my affections and my prayers; and then she sighed and said:

" 'Can you blame me for not loving this questionable lady of the vine-leaf, of whom my husband is such a gallant accomplice?'

" 'Not for a moment,' I replied, 'for I am persuaded, *Marquesa*, that a lady of rare qualities may have power to bewitch an unfortunate man without showing him the light of her face.' "

Dorothy Parker
(1893–1967)

uring the 1920s, Dorothy Parker became an iconic figure of the clever independent woman enjoying sex and celebrity in the big city. But behind the glamorous facade, Parker lived an unhappy life. Born in New Jersey to a Jewish father and raised by a Catholic stepmother, she regarded herself as a "mongrel." When her father died in 1913, she got a job at *Vogue* and then at *Vanity Fair*, and became a member of the Algonquin Round Table of journalists and wits. In 1920, she and Robert Benchley were fired from *Vanity Fair*, and set up their own office as writers. But she had begun drinking hard and loving recklessly, and that year she had an abortion and made a failed attempt at suicide.

In her stories and verses, Parker became famous for her wry jokey tone about women living without joy or hope. Her semiautobiographical story "Big Blonde" won the O. Henry Prize in 1929. In the 1930s Parker went to Hollywood, where she had a period of fame and wealth, but her alcoholism and a wretched marriage contributed to severe writing blocks. She joined the Communist Party and was eventually blacklisted in Hollywood. In her will, however, she remained loyal to her beliefs in American equality, leaving her estate to Martin Luther King, Jr., and the NAACP.

Big Blonde (1929)

I

Hazel Morse was a large, fair woman of the type that incites some men when they use the word "blonde" to click their tongues and wag their heads roguishly. She prided herself upon her small feet and suffered for her vanity, boxing them in snub-toed, high-heeled slippers of the shortest bearable size. The curious things about her were her hands, strange terminations to the flabby white arms splattered with pale tan spots—long, quivering hands with deep and convex nails. She should not have disfigured them with little jewels.

She was not a woman given to recollections. At her middle thirties, her old days were a blurred and flickering sequence, an imperfect film, dealing with the actions of strangers.

In her twenties, after the deferred death of a hazy widowed mother, she had been employed as a model in a wholesale dress establishment— it was still the day of the big woman, and she was then prettily colored and erect and high-breasted. Her job was not onerous, and she met numbers of men and spent numbers of evenings with them, laughing at their jokes and telling them she loved their neckties. Men liked her, and she took it for granted that the liking of many men was a desirable thing. Popularity seemed to her to be worth all the work that had to be put into its achievement. Men liked you because you were fun, and when they liked you they took you out, and there you were. So, and successfully, she was fun. She was a good sport. Men liked a good sport.

No other form of diversion, simpler or more complicated, drew her attention. She never pondered if she might not be better occupied doing something else. Her ideas, or, better, her acceptances, ran right along with those of the other substantially built blondes in whom she found her friends.

When she had been working in the dress establishment some years she met Herbie Morse. He was thin, quick, attractive, with shifting lines about his shiny, brown eyes and a habit of fiercely biting at the skin around his finger nails. He drank largely; she found that entertaining. Her habitual greeting to him was an allusion to his state of the previous night.

"Oh, what a peach you had," she used to say, through her easy laugh. "I thought I'd die, the way you kept asking the waiter to dance with you."

She liked him immediately upon their meeting. She was enormously amused at his fast, slurred sentences, his interpolations of apt phrases from vaudeville acts and comic strips; she thrilled at the feel of his lean arm tucked firm beneath the sleeve of her coat; she wanted to touch the wet, flat surface of his hair. He was as promptly drawn to her. They were married six weeks after they had met.

She was delighted at the idea of being a bride; coquetted with it, played upon it. Other offers of marriage she had had, and not a few of them, but it happened that they were all from stout, serious men who had visited the dress establishment as buyers; men from Des Moines and Houston and Chicago and, in her phrase, even funnier places. There was always something immensely comic to her in the thought of living elsewhere than New York. She could not regard as serious proposals that she share a western residence.

She wanted to be married. She was nearing thirty now, and she did not take the years well. She spread and softened, and her darkening hair turned her to inexpert dabblings with peroxide. There were times when she had little flashes of fear about her job. And she had had a couple of thousand evenings of being a good sport among her male acquaintances. She had come to be more conscientious than spontaneous about it.

Herbie earned enough, and they took a little apartment far uptown. There was a Mission-furnished dining-room with a hanging central light globed in liver-colored glass; in the living-room were an "over-stuffed suite," a Boston fern, and a reproduction of the Henner "Magdalene" with the red hair and the blue draperies; the bedroom was in gray enamel and old rose, with Herbie's photograph on Hazel's dressing-table and Hazel's likeness on Herbie's chest of drawers.

She cooked—and she was a good cook—and marketed and chatted with the delivery boys and the colored laundress. She loved the flat, she loved her life, she loved Herbie. In the first months of their marriage, she gave him all the passion she was ever to know.

She had not realized how tired she was. It was a delight, a new game, a holiday, to give up being a good sport. If her head ached or her arches throbbed, she complained piteously, babyishly. If her mood was quiet, she did not talk. If tears came to her eyes, she let them fall.

She fell readily into the habit of tears during the first year of her marriage. Even in her good sport days, she had been known to weep lavishly and disinterestedly on occasion. Her behavior at the theater was a standing joke. She could weep at anything in a play—tiny garments, love both unrequited and mutual, seduction, purity, faithful servitors, wedlock, the triangle.

"There goes Haze," her friends would say, watching her. "She's off again."

Wedded and relaxed, she poured her tears freely. To her who had laughed so much, crying was delicious. All sorrows became her sorrows; she was Tenderness. She would cry long and softly over newspaper accounts of kidnapped babies, deserted wives, unemployed men, strayed cats, heroic dogs. Even when the paper was no longer before her, her mind revolved upon these things and the drops slipped rhythmically over her plump cheeks.

"Honestly," she would say to Herbie, "all the sadness there is in the world when you stop to think about it!"

"Yeah," Herbie would say.

She missed nobody. The old crowd, the people who had brought her and Herbie together, dropped from their lives, lingeringly at first. When she thought of this at all, it was only to consider it fitting. This was marriage. This was peace.

But the thing was that Herbie was not amused.

For a time, he had enjoyed being alone with her. He found the voluntary isolation novel and sweet. Then it palled with a ferocious suddenness. It was as if one night, sitting with her in the steam-heated living-room, he would ask no more; and the next night he was through and done with the whole thing.

He became annoyed by her misty melancholies. At first, when he came home to find her softly tired and moody, he kissed her neck and patted her shoulder and begged her to tell her Herbie what was wrong. She loved that. But time slid by, and he found that there was never anything really, personally, the matter.

"Ah, for God's sake," he would say. "Crabbing again. All right, sit here and crab your head off. I'm going out."

And he would slam out of the flat and come back late and drunk.

She was completely bewildered by what happened to their marriage. First they were lovers; and then, it seemed without transition, they were enemies. She never understood it.

There were longer and longer intervals between his leaving his office and his arrival at the apartment. She went through agonies of picturing him run over and bleeding, dead and covered with a sheet. Then she lost her fears for his safety and grew sullen and wounded. When a person wanted to be with a person, he came as soon as possible. She desperately wanted him to want to be with her; her own hours only marked the time till he would come. It was often nearly nine o'clock before he came home to dinner. Always he had had many drinks, and their effect would die in him, leaving him loud and querulous and bristling for affronts.

He was too nervous, he said, to sit and do nothing for an evening. He boasted, probably not in all truth, that he had never read a book in his life.

"What am I expected to do—sit around this dump on my tail all night?" he would ask, rhetorically. And again he would slam out.

She did not know what to do. She could not manage him. She could not meet him.

She fought him furiously. A terrific domesticity had come upon her, and she would bite and scratch to guard it. She wanted what she called "a nice home." She wanted a sober, tender husband, prompt at dinner, punctual at work. She wanted sweet, comforting evenings. The idea of intimacy with other men was terrible to her; the thought that Herbie might be seeking entertainment in other women set her frantic.

It seemed to her that almost everything she read—novels from the drug-store lending library, magazine stories, women's pages in the papers—dealt with wives who lost their husbands' love. She could bear those, at that, better than accounts of neat, companionable marriage and living happily ever after.

She was frightened. Several times when Herbie came home in the evening, he found her determinedly dressed—she had had to alter those of her clothes that were not new, to make them fasten—and rouged.

"Let's go wild tonight, what do you say?" she would hail him. "A person's got lots of time to hang around and do nothing when they're dead."

So they would go out, to chop houses and the less expensive cabarets. But it turned out badly. She could no longer find amusement in watching Herbie drink. She could not laugh at his whimsicalities, she was so tensely counting his indulgences. And she was unable to keep back her remonstrances—"Ah, come on, Herb, you've had enough, haven't you? You'll feel something terrible in the morning."

He would be immediately enraged. All right, crab; crab, crab, crab, crab, that was all she ever did. What a lousy sport *she* was! There would be scenes, and one or the other of them would rise and stalk out in fury.

She could not recall the definite day that she started drinking, herself. There was nothing separate about her days. Like drops upon a window-pane, they ran together and trickled away. She had been married six months; then a year; then three years.

She had never needed to drink, formerly. She could sit for most of a night at a table where the others were imbibing earnestly and never droop in looks or spirits, nor be bored by the doings of those about her. If she took a cocktail, it was so unusual as to cause twenty minutes or so of jocular comment. But now anguish was in her. Frequently, after a quarrel, Herbie would stay out for the night, and she could not learn from him where the time had been spent. Her heart felt tight and sore in her breast, and her mind turned like an electric fan.

She hated the taste of liquor. Gin, plain or in mixtures, made her promptly sick. After experiment, she found that Scotch whisky was best for her. She took it without water, because that was the quickest way to its effect.

Herbie pressed it on her. He was glad to see her drink. They both felt it might restore her high spirits, and their good times together might again be possible.

"'Atta girl," he would approve her. "Let's see you get boiled, baby."

But it brought them no nearer. When she drank with him, there would be a little while of gaiety and then, strangely without beginning, they would be in a wild quarrel. They would wake in the morning not sure what it had all been about, foggy as to what had been said and done, but each deeply injured and bitterly resentful. There would be days of vengeful silence.

There had been a time when they had made up their quarrels, usually in bed. There would be kisses and little names and assurances of fresh starts. . . ."Oh, it's going to be great now, Herb. We'll have swell times. I was a crab. I guess I must have been tired. But everything's going to be swell. You'll see."

Now there were no gentle reconciliations. They resumed friendly relations only in the brief magnanimity caused by liquor, before more liquor drew them into new battles. The scenes became more violent. There were shouted invectives and pushes, and sometimes sharp slaps. Once she had a black eye. Herbie was horrified next day at sight of it. He did not go to work; he followed her about, suggesting remedies and heaping dark blame on himself. But after they had had a few drinks "to pull themselves together"—she made so many wistful references to her bruise that he shouted at her and rushed out and was gone for two days.

Each time he left the place in a rage, he threatened never to come back. She did not believe him, nor did she consider separation. Somewhere in her head or her heart was the lazy, nebulous hope that things would change and she and Herbie settle suddenly into soothing married life. Here were her home, her furniture, her husband, her station. She summoned no alternatives.

She could no longer bustle and potter. She had no more vicarious tears; the hot drops she shed were for herself. She walked ceaselessly about the rooms, her thoughts running mechanically round and round Herbie. In those days began the hatred of being alone that she was never to overcome. You could be by yourself when things were all right, but when you were blue you got the howling horrors.

She commenced drinking alone, little, short drinks all through the day. It was only with Herbie that alcohol made her nervous and quick in offense. Alone, it blurred sharp things for her. She lived in a haze of it. Her life took on a dream-like quality. Nothing was astonishing.

A Mrs. Martin moved into the flat across the hall. She was a great blonde woman of forty, a promise in looks of what Mrs. Morse was to be. They made acquaintance, quickly became inseparable. Mrs. Morse spent her days in the opposite apartment. They drank together, to brace themselves after the drinks of the nights before.

She never confided her troubles about Herbie to Mrs. Martin. The subject was too bewildering to her to find comfort in talk. She let it be assumed that her husband's business kept him much away. It was not regarded as important; husbands, as such, played but shadowy parts in Mrs. Martin's circle.

Mrs. Martin had no visible spouse; you were left to decide for yourself whether he was or was not dead. She had an admirer, Joe, who came to see her almost nightly. Often he brought several friends with him—"The Boys," they were called. The Boys were big, red, good-humored men, perhaps forty-five, perhaps fifty. Mrs. Morse was glad of invitations to join the parties—Herbie was scarcely ever at home at night now. If he did come home, she did not visit Mrs. Martin. An evening alone with Herbie meant inevitably a quarrel, yet she would stay with him. There was always her thin and wordless idea that, maybe, this night, things would begin to be all right.

The Boys brought plenty of liquor along with them whenever they came to Mrs. Martin's. Drinking with them, Mrs. Morse became lively and good-natured and audacious. She was quickly popular. When she had drunk enough to cloud her most recent battle with Herbie, she was excited by their approbation. Crab, was she? Rotten sport, was she? Well, there were some that thought different.

Ed was one of The Boys. He lived in Utica—had "his own business" there, was the awed report—but he came to New York almost every week. He was married. He showed Mrs. Morse the then current photographs of Junior and Sister, and she praised them abundantly and sincerely. Soon it was accepted by the others that Ed was her particular friend.

He staked her when they all played poker; sat next her and occasionally rubbed his knee against hers during the game. She was rather lucky. Frequently she went home with a twenty-dollar bill or a ten-dollar bill or a handful of crumpled dollars. She was glad of them. Herbie was getting, in her words, something awful about money. To ask him for it brought an instant row.

"What the hell do you do with it?" he would say. "Shoot it all on Scotch?"

"I try to run this house half-way decent," she would retort. "Never thought of that, did you? Oh, no, his lordship couldn't be bothered with that."

Again, she could not find a definite day, to fix the beginning of Ed's proprietorship. It became his custom to kiss her on the mouth when he came in, as well as for farewell, and he gave her little quick kisses of approval all through the evening. She liked this rather more than she disliked it. She never thought of his kisses when she was not with him.

He would run his hand lingeringly over her back and shoulders.

"Some dizzy blonde, eh?" he would say. "Some doll."

One afternoon she came home from Mrs. Martin's to find Herbie in the bedroom. He had been away for several nights, evidently on a prolonged drinking bout. His face was gray, his hands jerked as if they were on wires. On the bed were two old suitcases, packed high. Only her photograph remained on his bureau, and the wide doors of his closet disclosed nothing but coat-hangers.

"I'm blowing," he said. "I'm through with the whole works. I got a job in Detroit."

She sat down on the edge of the bed. She had drunk much the night before, and the four Scotches she had had with Mrs. Martin had only increased her fogginess.

"Good job?" she said.

"Oh, yeah," he said. "Looks all right."

He closed a suitcase with difficulty, swearing at it in whispers.

"There's some dough in the bank," he said. "The bank book's in your top drawer. You can have the furniture and stuff."

He looked at her, and his forehead twitched.

"God damn it, I'm through, I'm telling you," he cried. "I'm through."

"All right, all right," she said. "I heard you, didn't I?"

She saw him as if he were at one end of a cannon and she at the other. Her head was beginning to ache bumpingly, and her voice had a dreary, tiresome tone. She could not have raised it.

"Like a drink before you go?" she asked.

Again he looked at her, and a corner of his mouth jerked up.

"Cockeyed again for a change, aren't you?" he said. "That's nice. Sure, get a couple of shots, will you?"

She went to the pantry, mixed him a stiff highball, poured herself a couple of inches of whisky and drank it. Then she gave herself another portion and brought the glasses into the bedroom. He had strapped both suitcases and had put on his hat and overcoat.

He took his highball.

"Well," he said, and he gave a sudden, uncertain laugh. "Here's mud in your eye."

"Mud in your eye," she said.

They drank. He put down his glass and took up the heavy suitcases.

"Got to get a train around six," he said.

She followed him down the hall. There was a song, a song that Mrs. Martin played doggedly on the phonograph, running loudly through her mind. She had never liked the thing.

> *"Night and daytime.*
> *Always playtime.*
> *Ain't we got fun?"*

At the door he put down the bags and faced her.

"Well," he said. "Well, take care of yourself. You'll be all right, will you?"

"Oh, sure," she said.

He opened the door, then came back to her, holding out his hand.

"'By, Haze," he said. "Good luck to you."

She took his hand and shook it.

"Pardon my wet glove," she said.

When the door had closed behind him, she went back to the pantry.

She was flushed and lively when she went in to Mrs. Martin's that evening. The Boys were there, Ed among them. He was glad to be in town, frisky and loud and full of jokes. But she spoke quietly to him for a minute.

"Herbie blew today," she said. "Going to live out west."

"That so?" he said. He looked at her and played with the fountain pen clipped to his waistcoat pocket.

"Think he's gone for good, do you?" he asked.

"Yeah," she said. "I know he is. I know. Yeah."

"You going to live on across the hall just the same?" he said. "Know what you're going to do?"

"Gee, I don't know," she said. "I don't give much of a damn. "

"Oh, come on, that's no way to talk," he told her. "What you need— you need a little snifter. How about it?"

"Yeah," she said. "Just straight."

She won forty-three dollars at poker. When the game broke up, Ed took her back to her apartment.

"Got a little kiss for me?" he asked.

He wrapped her in his big arms and kissed her violently. She was entirely passive. He held her away and looked at her.

"Little tight, honey?" he asked, anxiously. "Not going to be sick, are you?"

"Me?" she said. "I'm swell."

II

When Ed left in the morning, he took her photograph with him. He said he wanted her picture to look at, up in Utica. "You can have that one on the bureau," she said.

She put Herbie's picture in a drawer, out of her sight. When she could look at it, she meant to tear it up. She was fairly successful in keeping her mind from racing around him. Whisky slowed it for her. She was almost peaceful, in her mist.

She accepted her relationship with Ed without question or enthusiasm. When he was away, she seldom thought definitely of him. He was good to her; he gave her frequent presents and a regular allowance. She was even able to save. She did not plan ahead of any day, but her wants were few, and you might as well put money in the bank as have it lying around.

When the lease of her apartment neared its end, it was Ed who suggested moving. His friendship with Mrs. Martin and Joe had become strained over a dispute at poker; a feud was impending.

"Let's get the hell out of here," Ed said. "What I want you to have is a place near the Grand Central. Make it easier for me."

So she took a little flat in the Forties. A colored maid came in every day to clean and to make coffee for her—she was "through with that housekeeping stuff," she said, and Ed, twenty years married to a passionately domestic woman, admired this romantic uselessness and felt doubly a man of the world in abetting it.

The coffee was all she had until she went out to dinner, but alcohol kept her fat. Prohibition she regarded only as a basis for jokes. You could always get all you wanted. She was never noticeably drunk and seldom nearly sober. It required a larger daily allowance to keep her misty-minded. Too little, and she was achingly melancholy.

Ed brought her to Jimmy's. He was proud, with the pride of the transient who would be mistaken for a native, in his knowledge of small, recent restaurants occupying the lower floors of shabby brownstone houses; places where, upon mentioning the name of an habitué friend, might be obtained strange whisky and fresh gin in many of their ramifications. Jimmy's place was the favorite of his acquaintants.

There, through Ed, Mrs. Morse met many men and women, formed quick friendships. The men often took her out when Ed was in Utica. He was proud of her popularity.

She fell into the habit of going to Jimmy's alone when she had no engagement. She was certain to meet some people she knew, and join them. It was a club for her friends, both men and women.

The women at Jimmy's looked remarkably alike, and this was curious, for, through feuds, removals, and opportunities of more profitable contacts, the personnel of the group changed constantly. Yet always the newcomers resembled those whom they replaced. They were all big women and stout, broad of shoulder and abundantly breasted, with faces thickly clothed in soft, high-colored flesh. They laughed loud and often, showing opaque and lusterless teeth like squares of crockery. There was about them the health of the big, yet a slight, unwholesome suggestion of stubborn preservation. They might have been thirty-six or forty-five or anywhere between.

They composed their titles of their own first names with their husbands' surnames—Mrs. Florence Miller, Mrs. Vera Riley, Mrs. Lilian Block. This gave at the same time the solidity of marriage and the glamour of freedom. Yet only one or two were actually divorced. Most of them never referred to their dimmed spouses; some, a shorter time separated, described them in terms of great biological interest. Several were mothers, each of an only child—a boy at school somewhere, or a girl being cared for by a grandmother. Often, well on toward morning, there would be displays of Kodak portraits and of tears.

They were comfortable women, cordial and friendly and irrepressibly matronly. Theirs was the quality of ease. Become fatalistic, especially about money matters, they unworried. Whenever their funds dropped alarmingly, a new donor appeared; this had always happened. The aim of each was to have one man, permanently, to pay all her bills, in return for which she would have immediately given up other admirers and probably would have become exceedingly fond of him; for the affections of all of them were, by now, unexacting, tranquil, and easily arranged. This end, however, grew increasingly difficult yearly. Mrs. Morse was regarded as fortunate.

Ed had a good year, increased her allowance and gave her a sealskin coat. But she had to be careful of her moods with him. He insisted upon gaiety. He would not listen to admissions of aches or weariness.

"Hey, listen," he would say, "I got worries of my own, and plenty. Nobody wants to hear other people's troubles, sweetie. What you got to do, you got to be a sport and forget it. See? Well, slip us a little smile, then. That's my girl."

She never had enough interest to quarrel with him as she had with Herbie, but she wanted the privilege of occasional admitted sadness. It was strange. The other women she saw did not have to fight their moods. There was Mrs. Florence Miller who got regular crying jags, and the men sought only to cheer and comfort her. The others spent whole evenings in grieved recitals of worries and ills; their escorts paid them deep sympathy. But she was instantly undesirable when she was low in spirits. Once, at Jimmy's, when she could not make herself lively, Ed had walked out and left her.

"Why the hell don't you stay home and not go spoiling everybody's evening?" he had roared.

Even her slightest acquaintances seemed irritated if she were not conspicuously light-hearted.

"What's the matter with you, anyway?" they would say. "Be your age, why don't you? Have a little drink and snap out of it."

When her relationship with Ed had continued nearly three years, he moved to Florida to live. He hated leaving her; he gave her a large check and some shares of a sound stock, and his pale eyes were wet when he said good-by. She did not miss him. He came to New York infrequently, perhaps two or three times a year, and hurried directly from the train to see her. She was always pleased to have him come and never sorry to see him go.

Charley, an acquaintance of Ed's that she had met at Jimmy's, had long admired her. He had always made opportunities of touching her and leaning close to talk to her. He asked repeatedly of all their friends if they had ever heard such a fine laugh as she had. After Ed left, Charley became the main figure in her life. She classified him and spoke of him as "not so bad." There was nearly a year of Charley; then she divided her time between him and Sydney, another frequenter of Jimmy's; then Charley slipped away altogether.

Sydney was a little, brightly dressed, clever Jew. She was perhaps nearest contentment with him. He amused her always; her laughter was not forced.

He admired her completely. Her softness and size delighted him. And he thought she was great, he often told her, because she kept gay and lively when she was drunk.

"Once I had a gal," he said, "used to try and throw herself out of the window every time she got a can on. Jee-*zuss*," he added, feelingly.

Then Sydney married a rich and watchful bride, and then there was Billy. No—after Sydney came Fred, then Billy. In her haze, she never recalled how men entered her life and left it. There were no surprises. She had no thrill at their advent, nor woe at their departure. She seemed to be always able to attract men. There was never another as rich as Ed, but they were all generous to her, in their means.

Once she had news of Herbie. She met Mrs. Martin dining at Jimmy's, and the old friendship was vigorously renewed. The still admiring Joe, while on a business trip, had seen Herbie. He had settled in Chicago, he looked fine, he was living with some woman—seemed to be crazy about her. Mrs. Morse had been drinking vastly that day. She took the news with mild interest, as one hearing of the sex peccadilloes of somebody whose name is, after a moment's groping, familiar.

"Must be damn near seven years since I saw him," she commented. "Gee. Seven years."

More and more, her days lost their individuality. She never knew dates, nor was sure of the day of the week.

"My God, was that a year ago!" she would exclaim, when an event was recalled in conversation.

She was tired so much of the time. Tired and blue. Almost everything could give her the blues. Those old horses she saw on Sixth Avenue—struggling and slipping along the car-tracks, or standing at the curb, their heads dropped level with their worn knees. The tightly stored tears would squeeze from her eyes as she teetered past on her aching feet in the stubby, champagne-colored slippers.

The thought of death came and stayed with her and lent her a sort of drowsy cheer. It would be nice, nice and restful, to be dead.

There was no settled, shocked moment when she first thought of killing herself; it seemed to her as if the idea had always been with her. She pounced upon all the accounts of suicides in the newspapers. There was an epidemic of self-killings—or maybe it was just that she searched for the stories of them so eagerly that she found many. To read of them roused reassurance in her; she felt a cozy solidarity with the big company of the voluntary dead.

She slept, aided by whisky, till deep into the afternoons, then lay abed, a bottle and glass at her hand, until it was time to dress and go out for dinner. She was beginning to feel toward alcohol a little puzzled distrust, as toward an old friend who has refused a simple favor. Whisky could still soothe her for most of the time, but there were sudden, inexplicable moments when the cloud fell treacherously away from her, and she was sawed by the sorrow and bewilderment and nuisance of all living. She played voluptuously with the thought of cool, sleepy retreat. She had never been troubled by religious belief and no vision of an after-life intimidated her. She dreamed by day of never again putting on tight shoes, of never having to laugh and listen and admire, of never more being a good sport. Never.

But how would you do it? It made her sick to think of jumping from heights. She could not stand a gun. At the theater, if one of the actors drew a revolver, she crammed her fingers into her ears and could not even look at the stage until after the shot had been fired. There was no gas in her flat. She looked long at the bright blue veins in her slim wrists—a cut with a razor blade, and there you'd be. But it would hurt, hurt like hell, and there would be blood to see. Poison—something taste-less and quick and painless—was the thing. But they wouldn't sell it to you in drugstores, because of the law.

She had few other thoughts.

There was a new man now—Art. He was short and fat and exacting and hard on her patience when he was drunk. But there had been only occasionals for some time before him, and she was glad of a little stabil-ity. Too, Art must be away for weeks at a stretch, selling silks, and that was restful. She was convincingly gay with him, though the effort shook her.

"The best sport in the world," he would murmur, deep in her neck. "The best sport in the world."

One night, when he had taken her to Jimmy's, she went into the dressing-room with Mrs. Florence Miller. There, while designing curly mouths on their faces with lip-rouge, they compared experiences of insomnia.

"Honestly," Mrs. Morse said, "I wouldn't close an eye if I didn't go to bed full of Scotch. I lie there and toss and turn and toss and turn. Blue! Does a person get blue lying awake that way!"

"Say, listen, Hazel," Mrs. Miller said, impressively, "I'm telling you I'd be awake for a year if I didn't take veronal. That stuff makes you sleep like a fool."

"Isn't it poison, or something?" Mrs. Morse asked.

"Oh, you take too much and you're out for the count," said Mrs. Miller. "I just take five grains—they come in tablets. I'd be scared to fool around with it. But five grains, and you cork off pretty."

"Can you get it anywhere?" Mrs. Morse felt superbly Machiavellian.

"Get all you want in Jersey," said Mrs. Miller. "They won't give it to you here without you have a doctor's prescription. Finished? We'd better go back and see what the boys are doing."

That night, Art left Mrs. Morse at the door of her apartment; his mother was in town. Mrs. Morse was still sober, and it happened that there was no whisky left in her cupboard. She lay in bed, looking up at the black ceiling.

She rose early, for her, and went to New Jersey. She had never taken the tube, and did not understand it. So she went to the Pennsylvania Station and bought a railroad ticket to Newark. She thought of nothing in particular on the trip out. She looked at the uninspired hats of the women about her and gazed through the smeared window at the flat, gritty scene.

In Newark, in the first drug-store she came to, she asked for a tin of talcum powder, a nailbrush, and a box of veronal tablets. The powder and the brush were to make the hypnotic seem also a casual need. The clerk was entirely unconcerned. "We only keep them in bottles," he said, and wrapped up for her a little glass vial containing ten white tablets, stacked one on another.

She went to another drug-store and bought a face-cloth, an orange-wood stick, and a bottle of veronal tablets. The clerk was also uninterested.

"Well, I guess I got enough to kill an ox," she thought, and went back to the station.

At home, she put the little vials in the drawer of her dressing-table and stood looking at them with a dreamy tenderness.

"There they are, God bless them," she said, and she kissed her finger-tip and touched each bottle.

The colored maid was busy in the living-room.

"Hey, Nettie," Mrs. Morse called. "Be an angel, will you? Run around to Jimmy's and get me a quart of Scotch."

She hummed while she awaited the girl's return.

During the next few days, whisky ministered to her as tenderly as it had done when she first turned to its aid. Alone, she was soothed and vague, at Jimmy's she was the gayest of the groups. Art was delighted with her.

Then, one night, she had an appointment to meet Art at Jimmy's for an early dinner. He was to leave afterward on a business excursion, to be away for a week. Mrs. Morse had been drinking all the afternoon; while she dressed to go out, she felt herself rising pleasurably from drowsiness to high spirits. But as she came out into the street the effects of the whisky deserted her completely, and she was filled with a slow, grinding wretchedness so horrible that she stood swaying on the pavement, unable for a moment to move forward. It was a gray night with spurts of mean, thin snow, and the streets shone with dark ice. As she slowly crossed Sixth Avenue, consciously dragging one foot past the other, a big, scarred horse pulling a rickety express-wagon crashed to his knees before her. The driver swore and screamed and lashed the beast insanely, bringing the whip back over his shoulder for every blow, while the horse struggled to get a footing on the slippery asphalt. A group gathered and watched with interest.

Art was waiting, when Mrs. Morse reached Jimmy's.

"What's the matter with you, for God's sake?" was his greeting to her.

"I saw a horse," she said. "Gee, I—a person feels sorry for horses. I—it isn't just horses. Everything's kind of terrible, isn't it? I can't help getting sunk."

"Ah, sunk, me eye," he said. "What's the idea of all the bellyaching? What have you got to be sunk about?"

"I can't help it," she said.

"Ah, help it, me eye," he said. "Pull yourself together, will you? Come on and sit down, and take that face off you."

She drank industriously and she tried hard, but she could not overcome her melancholy. Others joined them and commented on her gloom, and she could do no more for them than smile weakly. She made little dabs at her eyes with her handkerchief, trying to time her movements so they would be unnoticed, but several times Art caught her and scowled and shifted impatiently in his chair.

When it was time for him to go to his train, she said she would leave, too, and go home.

"And not a bad idea, either," he said. "See if you can't sleep yourself out of it. I'll see you Thursday. For God's sake, try and cheer up by then, will you?"

"Yeah," she said. "I will."

In her bedroom, she undressed with a tense speed wholly unlike her usual slow uncertainty. She put on her nightgown, took off her hair-net and passed the comb quickly through her dry, vari-colored hair. Then she took the two little vials from the drawer and carried them into the bathroom. The splintering misery had gone from her, and she felt the quick excitement of one who is about to receive an anticipated gift.

She uncorked the vials, filled a glass with water and stood before the mirror, a tablet between her fingers. Suddenly she bowed graciously to her reflection, and raised the glass to it.

"Well, here's mud in your eye," she said.

The tablets were unpleasant to take, dry and powdery and sticking obstinately half-way down her throat. It took her a long time to swallow all twenty of them. She stood watching her reflection with deep, impersonal interest, studying the movements of the gulping throat. Once more she spoke aloud.

"For God's sake, try and cheer up by Thursday, will you?" she said. "Well, you know what he can do. He and the whole lot of them."

She had no idea how quickly to expect effect from the veronal. When she had taken the last tablet, she stood uncertainly, wondering, still with a courteous, vicarious interest, if death would strike her down then and there. She felt in no way strange, save for a slight stirring of sickness from the effort of swallowing the tablets, nor did her reflected face look at all different. It would not be immediate, then; it might even take an hour or so.

She stretched her arms high and gave a vast yawn.

"Guess I'll go to bed," she said. "Gee, I'm nearly dead."

That struck her as comic, and she turned out the bathroom light and went in and laid herself down in her bed, chuckling softly all the time.

"Gee, I'm nearly dead," she quoted. "That's a hot one!"

III

Nettie, the colored maid, came in late the next afternoon to clean the apartment, and found Mrs. Morse in her bed. But then, that was not unusual. Usually, though, the sounds of cleaning waked her, and she did not like to wake up. Nettie, an agreeable girl, had learned to move softly about her work.

But when she had done the living-room and stolen in to tidy the little square bedroom, she could not avoid a tiny clatter as she arranged the objects on the dressing-table. Instinctively, she glanced over her shoulder at the sleeper, and without warning a sickly uneasiness crept over her. She came to the bed and stared down at the woman lying there.

Mrs. Morse lay on her back, one flabby, white arm flung up, the wrist against her forehead. Her stiff hair hung untenderly along her face. The bed covers were pushed down, exposing a deep square of soft neck and a pink nightgown, its fabric worn uneven by many launderings; her great breasts, freed from their tight confiner, sagged beneath her arm-pits. Now and then she made knotted, snoring sounds, and from the corner of her opened mouth to the blurred turn of her jaw ran a lane of crusted spittle.

"Mis' Morse," Nettie called. "Oh, Mis' Morse! It's terrible late."

Mrs. Morse made no move.

"Mis' Morse," said Nettie. "Look, Mis' Morse. How'm I goin' get this bed made?"

Panic sprang upon the girl. She shook the woman's hot shoulder.

"Ah, wake up, will yuh?" she whined. "Ah, please wake up."

Suddenly the girl turned and ran out in the hall to the elevator door, keeping her thumb firm on the black, shiny button until the elderly car and its Negro attendant stood before her. She poured a jumble of words over the boy, and led him back to the apartment. He tiptoed creakingly in to the bedside; first gingerly, then so lustily that he left marks in the soft flesh, he prodded the unconscious woman.

"Hey, there!" he cried, and listened intently, as for an echo.

"Jeez. Out like a light," he commented.

At his interest in the spectacle, Nettie's panic left her. Importance was big in both of them. They talked in quick, unfinished whispers, and it was the boy's suggestion that he fetch the young doctor who lived on the ground floor. Nettie hurried along with him. They looked forward to the limelit moment of breaking their news of something untoward, something pleasurably unpleasant. Mrs. Morse had become the medium of drama. With no ill wish to her, they hoped that her state was serious, that she would not let them down by being awake and normal on their return. A little fear of this determined them to make the most, to the doctor, of her present condition. "Matter of life and death," returned to Nettie from her thin store of reading. She considered startling the doctor with the phrase.

The doctor was in and none too pleased at interruption. He wore a yellow and blue striped dressing-gown, and he was lying on his sofa, laughing with a dark girl, her face scaly with inexpensive powder, who perched on the arm. Half-emptied highball glasses stood beside them, and her coat and hat were neatly hung up with the comfortable implication of a long stay. Always something, the doctor grumbled. Couldn't let anybody alone after a hard day. But he put some bottles and instruments into a case, changed his dressing-gown for his coat and started out with the Negroes.

"Snap it up there, big boy," the girl called after him. "Don't be all night."

The doctor strode loudly into Mrs. Morse's flat and on to the bedroom, Nettie and the boy right behind him. Mrs. Morse had not moved; her sleep was as deep, but soundless, now. The doctor looked sharply at her, then plunged his thumbs into the lidded pits above her eyeballs and threw his weight upon them. A high, sickened cry broke from Nettie.

"Look like he tryin' to push her right on th'ough the bed," said the boy. He chuckled.

Mrs. Morse gave no sign under the pressure. Abruptly the doctor abandoned it, and with one quick movement swept the covers down to the foot of the bed. With another he flung her nightgown back and lifted the thick, white legs, cross-hatched with blocks of tiny, iris-colored veins. He pinched them repeatedly, with long, cruel nips, back of the knees. She did not awaken.

"What's she been drinking?" he asked Nettie, over his shoulder.

With the certain celerity of one who knows just where to lay hands on a thing, Nettie went into the bathroom, bound for the cupboard where Mrs. Morse kept her whisky. But she stopped at the sight of the two vials, with their red and white labels, lying before the mirror. She brought them to the doctor.

"Oh, for the Lord Almighty's sweet sake!" he said. He dropped Mrs. Morse's legs, and pushed them impatiently across the bed. "What did she want to go taking that tripe for? Rotten yellow trick, that's what a thing like that is. Now we'll have to pump her out, and all that stuff. Nuisance, a thing like that is; that's what it amounts to. Here, George, take me down in the elevator. You wait here, maid. She won't do anything."

"She won't die on me, will she?" cried Nettie.

"No," said the doctor. "God, no. You couldn't kill her with an ax."

IV

After two days, Mrs. Morse came back to consciousness, dazed at first, then with a comprehension that brought with it the slow, saturating wretchedness.

"Oh, Lord, oh, Lord," she moaned, and tears for herself and for life striped her cheeks.

Nettie came in at the sound. For two days she had done the ugly, incessant tasks in the nursing of the unconscious, for two nights she had caught broken bits of sleep on the living-room couch. She looked coldly at the big, blown woman in the bed.

"What you been tryin' to do, Mis' Morse?" she said. "What kine o' work is that, takin' all that stuff?"

"Oh, Lord," moaned Mrs. Morse, again, and she tried to cover her eyes with her arms. But the joints felt stiff and brittle, and she cried out at their ache.

"Tha's no way to ack, takin' them pills," said Nettie. "You can thank you' stars you heah at all. How you feel now?"

"Oh, I feel great," said Mrs. Morse. "Swell, I feel."

Her hot, painful tears fell as if they would never stop.

"Tha's no way to take on, cryin' like that," Nettie said. "After what you done. The doctor, he says he could have you arrested, doin' a thing like that. He was fit to be tied, here."

"Why couldn't he let me alone?" wailed Mrs. Morse. "Why the hell couldn't he have?"

"Tha's terr'ble, Mis' Morse, swearin' an' talkin' like that," said Nettie, "after what people done for you. Here I ain' had no sleep at all for two nights, an' had to give up goin' out to my other ladies!"

"Oh, I'm sorry, Nettie," she said. "You're a peach. I'm sorry I've given you so much trouble. I couldn't help it. I just got sunk. Didn't you ever feel like doing it? When everything looks just lousy to you?"

"I wouldn' think o' no such thing," declared Nettie. "You got to cheer up. Tha's what you got to do. Everybody's got their troubles."

"Yeah," said Mrs. Morse. "I know."

"Come a pretty picture card for you," Nettie said. "Maybe that will cheer you up."

She handed Mrs. Morse a post-card. Mrs. Morse had to cover one eye with her hand, in order to read the message; her eyes were not yet focusing correctly.

It was from Art. On the back of a view of the Detroit Athletic Club he had written: "Greeting and salutations. Hope you have lost that gloom. Cheer up and don't take any rubber nickels. See you on Thursday."

She dropped the card to the floor. Misery crushed her as if she were between great smooth stones. There passed before her a slow, slow pageant of days spent lying in her flat, of evenings at Jimmy's being a good sport, making herself laugh and coo at Art and other Arts; she saw a long parade of weary horses and shivering beggars and all beaten, driven, stumbling things. Her feet throbbed as if she had crammed them into the stubby champagne-colored slippers. Her heart seemed to swell and harden.

"Nettie," she cried, "for heaven's sake pour me a drink, will you?"

The maid looked doubtful.

"Now you know, Mis' Morse," she said, "you been near daid. I don' know if the doctor he let you drink nothin' yet."

"Oh, never mind him," she said. "You get me one, and bring in the bottle. Take one yourself."

"Well," said Nettie.

She poured them each a drink, deferentially leaving hers in the bathroom to be taken in solitude, and brought Mrs. Morse's glass in to her.

Mrs. Morse looked into the liquor and shuddered back from its odor. Maybe it would help. Maybe, when you had been knocked cold for a few days, your very first drink would give you a lift. Maybe whisky would be her friend again. She prayed without addressing a God, without knowing a God. Oh, please, please, let her be able to get drunk, please keep her always drunk.

She lifted the glass.

"Thanks, Nettie," she said. "Here's mud in your eye."

The maid giggled. "That's the way, Mis' Morse," she said. "You cheer up, now."

"Yeah," said Mrs. Morse. "Sure."

Genevieve Taggard
(1894–1948)

I have refused to write out of a decorative impulse," wrote Genevieve Taggard in the introduction to her *Collected Poems 1918–1938*, "because I conceive it to be the dead end of much feminine talent. . . . I hope [these poems] are not written by a poetess, but by a poet." Her 1930 critical biography of Emily Dickinson showed the poetic tradition in which she placed herself. Taggard grew up in the interracial society of Hawaii where her parents were missionaries, and taught herself enough Latin to be accepted by the University of California at Berkeley, from which she graduated in 1919. She moved to Greenwich Village, where she wrote for the *Liberator* and became a contributing editor for the Marxist journal the *New Masses*. In 1921 she married the poet Robert Wolf, gave birth to a daughter, and started her own literary journal, *Measure*. The next year she published her well-received first book of poems, *For Eager Lovers*, but in the 1930s, as she became more politically doctrinaire, Taggard repudiated the poems as too much about "love and marriage and having children." With her second husband, Kenneth Durant, she traveled to the Soviet Union and published *Calling Western Union* (1936), poems about the Depression, rural hardship, and working-class women. "Everyday Alchemy," however, which she wrote in the 1920s, shows that Taggard had found a way to negotiate the conflicts between art and politics in her lyric poems as well.

Everyday Alchemy (1922)

Men go to women mutely for their peace;
And they, who lack it most, create it when
They make—because they must, loving their men—
A solace for sad bosom-bended heads. There
Is all the meager peace men get—no otherwhere;
No mountain space, no tree with placid leaves,

Or heavy gloom beneath a young girl's hair,
No sound of valley bell on autumn air,
Or room made home with doves along the eaves,
Ever holds peace like this, poured by poor women
Out of their heart's poverty, for worn men.

Louise Bogan
(1897–1970)

ouise Bogan was born in Maine and grew up in various northeastern mill towns, attending the Boston Girls' Latin School and one year of Boston University before marrying a career army officer, Curt Alexander, in 1916. He died in 1920, and Bogan moved to New York with her daughter Maidie. She supported them by working as a film critic and reviewer, and by the end of the decade had established herself as an important lyric poet with *Body of This Death: Poems* (1923) and *Dark Summer* (1929). In 1925 she married the writer Raymond Holden. But Bogan's self-critical perfectionism, and her unease with the limitations of the woman poet's range, proved inhibiting and destructive. She had long periods of writer's block and severe depression, and was hospitalized twice. While the self-hatred expressed in "Women" persistently stalled and silenced her as a poet, Bogan was able to write more freely as a reviewer; from 1931 to 1969 she was the influential poetry editor and critic at *The New Yorker*.

Women (1923)

Women have no wilderness in them,
They are provident instead,
Content in the tight hot cell of their hearts
To eat dusty bread.

They do not see cattle cropping red winter grass,
They do not hear
Snow water going down under culverts
Shallow and clear.

They wait, when they should turn to journeys,
They stiffen, when they should bend.
They use against themselves that benevolence
To which no man is friend.

They cannot think of so many crops to a field
Or of clean wood cleft by an axe.
Their love is an eager meaninglessness
Too tense, or too lax.

They hear in every whisper that speaks to them
A shout and a cry.
As like as not, when they take life over their door-sills
They should let it go by.

Evening in the Sanitarium (1941)

The free evening fades, outside the windows fastened with decora-
    tive iron grilles.
The lamps are lighted; the shades drawn; the nurses are watching a
    little.
It is the hour of the complicated knitting on the safe bone needles;
        of the games of anagrams and bridge;
The deadly game of chess; the book held up like a mask.

The period of the wildest weeping, the fiercest delusion, is over.
The women rest their tired half-healed hearts; they are almost well.
Some of them will stay almost well always: the blunt-faced woman
        whose thinking dissolved
Under academic discipline; the manic-depressive girl
Now leveling off; one paranoiac afflicted with jealousy.
Another with persecution. Some alleviation has been possible.

O fortunate bride, who never again will become elated after child-
    birth!
O lucky older wife, who has been cured of feeling unwanted!
To the suburban railway station you will return, return,
To meet forever Jim home on the 5:35.
You will be again as normal and selfish and heartless as anybody
    else.

There is life left: the piano says it with its octave smile.
The soft carpets pad the thump and splinter of the suicide to be.

Everything will be splendid: the grandmother will not drink habitu-
ally.
The fruit salad will bloom on the plate like a bouquet
And the garden produce the blue-ribbon aquilegia.

The cats will be glad; the fathers feel justified; the mothers relieved.
The sons and husbands will no longer need to pay the bills.
Childhoods will be put away, the obscene nightmare abated.

At the ends of the corridors the baths are running.
Mrs. C. again feels the shadow of the obsessive idea.
Miss R. looks at the mantel-piece, which must mean something.

Several Voices out of a Cloud (1941)

Come, drunks and drug-takers; come perverts unnerved!
Receive the laurel, given, though late, on merit; to whom and
        wherever deserved.

Parochial punks, trimmers, nice people, joiners true-blue,
Get the hell out of the way of the laurel. It is deathless
        And it isn't for you.

Meridel Le Sueur
(1900–1996)

he daughter of socialist parents, Meridel Le Sueur grew up in the Midwest among radical farmer and labor groups. When she first moved to New York City in 1917, she lived in an anarchist commune and began an acting career, but in the 1920s she joined the Communist Party and turned to writing. Beginning with her first story, "Persephone" (published in *The Dial* magazine in 1927), Le Sueur's work was consistently political, sympathizing with the plight of Native Americans, workers, and other disadvantaged groups. "Annunciation" was written while Le Sueur was pregnant during the Depression. Though she was blacklisted during the McCarthy era, Le Sueur stored her ongoing political writing in her basement, publishing just her children's stories until the 1970s gave her freedom to publish what she wished.

Annunciation (1935)

For Rachel

Ever since I have known I was going to have a child I have kept writing things down on these little scraps of paper. There is something I want to say, something I want to make clear for myself and others. One lives all one's life in a sort of way, one is alive and that is about all that there is to say about it. Then something happens.

There is the pear tree I can see in the afternoons as I sit on this porch writing these notes. It stands for something. It has had something to do with what has happened to me. I sit here all afternoon in the autumn sun and then I begin to write something on this yellow paper; something seems to be going on like a buzzing, a flying and circling within me, and then I want to write it down in some way. I have never felt this way before, except when I was a girl and was first in love and wanted then to set things down on paper so that they would not be lost. It is something perhaps like a farmer who hears the swarming of a host of bees and goes out to catch them so that he will have honey. If he does not go out right away, they will go, and he will hear the buzzing growing more distant in the afternoon.

My sweater pocket is full of scraps of paper on which I have written. I sit here many afternoons while Karl is out looking for work, writing on pieces of paper, unfolding, reading what I have already written.

We have been here two weeks at Mrs. Mason's boarding house. The leaves are falling and there is a golden haze over everything. This is the fourth month for me and it is fall. A rich powerful haze comes down from the mountains over the city. In the afternoon I go out for a walk. There is a park just two blocks from here. Old men and tramps lie on the grass all day. It is hard to get work. Many people besides Karl are out of work. People are hungry just as I am hungry. People are ready to flower and they cannot. In the evenings we go there with a sack of old fruit we can get at the stand across the way quite cheap, bunches of grapes and old pears. At noon there is a hush in the air and at evening there are stirrings of wind coming from the sky, blowing in the fallen leaves, or perhaps there is a light rain, falling quickly on the walk. Early in the mornings the sun comes up hot in the sky and shines all day through the mist. It is strange, I notice all these things, the sun, the rain falling, the blowing of the wind. It is as if they had a meaning for me as the pear tree has come to have.

In front of Mrs. Mason's house there is a large magnolia tree with its blossoms yellow, hanging over the steps almost within reach. Its giant leaves are motionless and shining in the heat, occasionally as I am going down the steps toward the park one falls heavily on the walk.

This house is an old wooden one, that once was quite a mansion I imagine. There are glass chandeliers in the hall and fancy tile in the bathrooms. It was owned by the rich once and now the dispossessed live in it with the rats. We have a room three flights up. You go into the dark hallway and up the stairs. Broken settees and couches sit in the halls. About one o'clock the girls come down stairs to get their mail and sit on the front porch. The blinds go up in the old wooden house across the street. It is always quite hot at noon.

Next to our room lies a sick woman in what is really a kind of closet with no windows. As you pass you see her face on the pillow and a nauseating odor of sickness comes out the door. I haven't asked her what is the matter with her but everyone knows she is waiting for death. Somehow it is not easy to speak to her. No one comes to see her. She has been a housemaid all her life tending other people's children; now no one comes to see her. She gets up sometimes and drinks a little from the bottle of milk that is always sitting by her bed covered with flies.

Mrs. Mason, the landlady, is letting us stay although we have only paid a week's rent and have been here over a week without paying. But it is a bad season and we may be able to pay later. It is better perhaps for her than having an empty room. But I hate to go out and have to pass her door and I am always fearful of meeting her on the stairs. I go down as quietly as I can but it isn't easy, for the stairs creak frightfully.

The room we have on the top floor is a back room, opening out onto an old porch which seems to be actually tied to the wall of the house with bits of wire and rope. The floor of it slants downward to a rickety railing. There is a box perched on the railing that has geraniums in it. They are large, tough California geraniums. I guess nothing can kill them. I water them since I have been here and a terribly red flower has come. It is on this porch I am sitting. Just over the banisters stand the top branches of a pear tree.

Many afternoons I sit here. It has become a kind of alive place to me. The room is dark behind me, with only the huge walnut tree scraping against the one window over the kitchenette. If I go to the railing and look down I can see far below the back yard which has been made into a garden with two fruit trees and I can see where a path has gone in the summer between a small bed of flowers, now only dead stalks. The ground is bare under the walnut tree where little sun penetrates. There is a dog kennel by the round trunk but there doesn't ever seem to be a dog. An old wicker chair sits outdoors in rain or shine. A woman in an old wrapper comes out and sits there almost every afternoon. I don't know who she is, for I don't know anybody in this house, having to sneak downstairs as I do.

Karl says I am foolish to be afraid of the landlady. He comes home drunk and makes a lot of noise. He says she's lucky in these times to have anybody in her house, but I notice in the mornings he goes down the stairs quietly and often goes out the back way.

I'm alone all day so I sit on this rickety porch. Straight out from the rail so that I can almost touch it is the radiating frail top of the pear tree that has opened a door for me. If the pears were still hanging on it each would be alone and separate with a kind of bloom upon it. Such a bloom is upon me at this moment. Is it possible that everyone, Mrs. Mason who runs this boarding house, the woman next door, the girls downstairs, all in this dead wooden house have hung at one time, each separate in a mist and bloom upon some invisible tree? I wonder if it is so.

I am in luck to have this high porch to sit on and this tree swaying before me through the long afternoons and the long nights. Before we came here, after the show broke up in S.F. we were in an old hotel, a foul-smelling place with a dirty chambermaid and an old cat in the halls, and night and day we could hear the radio going in the office. We had a room with a window looking across a narrow way into another room where a lean man stood in the mornings looking across, shaving his evil face. By leaning out and looking up I could see straight up the sides of the tall building and above the smoky sky.

Most of the time I was sick from the bad food we ate. Karl and I walked the streets looking for work. Sometimes I was too sick to go. Karl would come in and there would be no money at all. He would go out again to perhaps borrow something. I know many times he begged although we never spoke of it, but I could tell by the way he looked when he came back with a begged quarter. He went in with a man selling Mexican beans but he didn't make much. I lay on the bed bad days feeling sick and hungry, sick too with the stale odor of the foul walls. I would lie there a long time listening to the clang of the city outside. I would feel thick with this child. For some reason I remember that I would sing to myself and often became happy as if mesmerized there in the foul room. It must have been because of this child. Karl would come back perhaps with a little money and we would go out to a dairy lunch and there have food I could not relish. The first alleyway I must give it up with the people all looking at me.

Karl would be angry. He would walk on down the street so people wouldn't think he was with me. Once we walked until evening down by the docks. "Why don't you take something?" he kept saying. "Then you wouldn't throw up your food like that. Get rid of it. That's what everybody does nowadays. This isn't the time to have a child. Everything is rotten. We must change it." He kept on saying, "Get rid of it. Take something why don't you?" And he got angry when I didn't say anything but just walked along beside him. He shouted so loud at me that some stevedores loading a boat for L.A. laughed at us and began kidding us, thinking perhaps we were lovers having a quarrel.

Some time later, I don't know how long it was, for I hadn't any time except the nine months I was counting off, but one evening Karl sold enough Mexican jumping beans at a carnival to pay our fare, so we got on a river boat and went up the river to a delta town. There might be a better chance of a job. On this boat you can sit up all night if you have no money to buy a berth. We walked all evening along the deck and then when it got cold we went into the saloon because we had pawned our coats. Already at that time I had got the habit of carrying slips of paper around with me and writing on them, as I am doing now. I had a feeling then that something was happening to me of some kind of loveliness I would want to preserve in some way. Perhaps that was it. At any rate I was writing things down. Perhaps it had something to do with Karl wanting me all the time to take something. "Everybody does it," he kept telling me. "It's nothing, then it's all over." I stopped talking to him much. Everything I said only made him angry. So writing was a kind of conversation I carried on with myself and with the child.

Well, on the river boat that night after we had gone into the saloon to get out of the cold, Karl went to sleep right away in a chair. But I couldn't sleep. I sat watching him. The only sound was the churning of the paddle wheel and the lap of the water. I had on then this sweater and the notes I wrote are still in the breast pocket. I would look up from writing and see Karl sleeping like a young boy.

"Tonight, the world into which you are coming"—then I was speaking to the invisible child—"is very strange and beautiful. That is, the natural world is beautiful. I don't know what you will think of man, but the dark glisten of vegetation and the blowing of the fertile land wind and the delicate strong step of the sea wind, these things are familiar to me and will be familiar to you. I hope you will be like these things. I hope you will glisten with the glisten of ancient life, the same beauty that is in a leaf or a wild rabbit, wild sweet beauty of limb and eye. I am going on a boat between dark shores, and the river and the sky are so quiet that I can hear the scurryings of tiny animals on the shores and their little breathings seem to be all around. I think of them, wild, carrying their young now, crouched in the dark underbrush with the fruit-scented land wind in their delicate nostrils, and they are looking out at the moon and the fast clouds. Silent, alive, they sit in the dark shadow of the greedy world. There is something wild about us too, something tender and wild about my having you as a child, about your crouching so secretly here. There is something very tender and wild about it. We, too, are at the mercy of many hunters. On this boat I act like the other human beings, for I do not show that I have you, but really I know we are as helpless, as wild, as at bay as some tender wild animals who might be on the ship.

"I put my hand where you lie so silently. I hope you will come glistening with life power, with it shining upon you as upon the feathers of birds. I hope you will be a warrior and fierce for change, so all can live."

Karl woke at dawn and was angry with me for sitting there looking at him. Just to look at me makes him angry now. He took me out and made me walk along the deck although it was hardly light yet. I gave him the "willies" he said, looking at him like that. We walked round and round the decks and he kept talking to me in a low voice, trying to persuade me. It was hard for me to listen. My teeth were chattering with cold, but anyway I found it hard to listen to anyone talking, especially Karl. I remember I kept thinking to myself that a child should be made by machinery now, then there would be no fuss. I kept thinking of all the places I had been with this new child, traveling with the show from Tia Juana to S.F. In trains, over mountains, through deserts, in hotels and rooming houses, and myself in a trance of wonder. There wasn't a person I could have told it to, that I was going to have a child. I didn't want to be pitied. Night after night we played in the tent and the faces were all dust to me, but traveling, through the window the many vistas of the earth meant something—the bony skeleton of the mountains, like the skeleton of the world jutting through its flowery flesh. My child too would be made of bone. There were the fields of summer, the orchards fruiting, the berry fields and the pickers stooping, the oranges and the grapes. Then the city again in September and the many streets I walk looking for work, stopping secretly in doorways to feel beneath my coat.

It is better in this small town with the windy fall days and the sudden rain falling out of a sunny sky. I can't look for work any more. Karl gets a little work washing dishes at a wienie place. I sit here on the porch as if in a deep sleep waiting for this unknown child. I keep hearing this far flight of strange birds going on in the mysterious air about me. This time has come without warning. How can it be explained? Everything is dead and closed, the world a stone, and then suddenly everything comes alive as it has for me, like an anemone on a rock, opening itself, disclosing itself, and the very stones themselves break open like bread. It has all got something to do with the pear tree too. It has come about some way as I have sat here with this child so many afternoons, with the pear tree murmuring in the air.

The pears are all gone from the tree but I imagine them hanging there, ripe curves within the many scimitar leaves, and within them many pears of the coming season. I feel like a pear. I hang secret within the curling leaves, just as the pear would be hanging on its tree. It seems possible to me that perhaps all people at some time feel this, round and full. You can tell by looking at most people that the world remains a stone to them and a closed door. I'm afraid it will become like that to me again. Perhaps after this child is born, then everything will harden and become small and mean again as it was before. Perhaps I would even have a hard time remembering this time at all and it wouldn't seem wonderful. That is why I would like to write it down.

How can it be explained? Suddenly many movements are going on within me, many things are happening, there is an almost unbearable sense of sprouting, of bursting encasements, of moving kernels, expanding flesh. Perhaps it is such an activity that makes a field come alive with millions of sprouting shoots of corn or wheat. Perhaps it is something like that that makes a new world.

I have been sitting here and it seems as if the wooden houses around me had become husks that suddenly as I watched began to swarm with livening seed. The house across becomes a fermenting seed alive with its own movements. Everything seems to be moving along a curve of creation. The alley below and all the houses are to me like an orchard abloom, shaking and trembling, moving outward with shouting. The people coming and going seem to hang on the tree of life, each blossoming from himself. I am standing here looking at the blind windows of the house next door and suddenly the walls fall away, the doors open, and within I see a young girl making a bed from which she had just risen having dreamed of a young man who became her lover . . . she stands before her looking-glass in love with herself.

I see in another room a young man sleeping, his bare arm thrown over his head. I see a woman lying on a bed after her husband has left her. There is a child looking at me. An old woman sits rocking. A boy leans over a table reading a book. A woman who has been nursing a child comes out and hangs clothes on the line, her dress in front wet with milk. A young woman comes to an open door looking up and down the street waiting for her young husband. I get up early to see this young woman come to the door in a pink wrapper and wave to her husband. They have only been married a short time, she stands waving until he is out of sight and even then she stands smiling to herself, her hand upraised.

Why should I be excited? Why should I feel this excitement, seeing a woman waving to her young husband, or a woman who has been nursing a child, or a young man sleeping? Yet I am excited. The many houses have become like an orchard blooming soundlessly. The many people have become like fruits to me, the young girl in the room alone before her mirror, the young man sleeping, the mother, all are shaking with their inward blossoming, shaken by the windy blooming, moving along a future curve.

I do not want it all to go away from me. Now many doors are opening and shutting, light is falling upon darkness, closed places are opening, still things are now moving. But there will come a time when the doors will close again, the shouting will be gone, the sprouting and the movement and the wondrous opening out of everything will be gone. I will be only myself. I will come to look like the women in this house. I try to write it down on little slips of paper, trying to preserve this time for myself so that afterwards when everything is the same again I can remember what all must have.

This is the spring there should be in the world, so I say to myself, "Lie in the sun with the child in your flesh shining like a jewel. Dream and sing, pagan, wise in your vitals. Stand still like a fat budding tree, like a stalk of corn athrob and aglisten in the heat. Lie like a mare panting with the dancing feet of colts against her sides. Sleep at night as the spring earth. Walk heavily as a wheat stalk at its full time bending toward the earth waiting for the reaper. Let your life swell downward so you become like a vase, a vessel. Let the unknown child knock and knock against you and rise like a dolphin within."

I look at myself in the mirror. My legs and head hardly make a difference, just a stem my legs. My hips are full and tight in back as if bracing themselves. I look like a pale and shining pomegranate, hard and tight, and my skin shines like crystal with the veins showing beneath blue and distended. Children are playing outside and girls are walking with young men along the walk. All that seems over for me. I am a pomegranate hanging from an invisible tree with the juice and movement of seed within my hard skin. I dress slowly. I hate the smell of clothes. I want to leave them off and just hang in the sun ripening . . . ripening.

It is hard to write it down so that it will mean anything. I've never heard anything about how a woman feels who is going to have a child, or about how a pear tree feels bearing its fruit. I would like to read these things many years from now, when I am barren and no longer trembling like this, when I get like the women in this house, or like the woman in the closed room, I can hear her breathing through the afternoon.

When Karl has no money he does not come back at night. I go out on the street walking to forget how hungry I am. This is an old town and along the streets are many old strong trees. Night leaves hang from them ready to fall, dark and swollen with their coming death. Trees, dark, separate, heavy with their down-hanging leaves, cool surfaces hanging on the dark. I put my hand among the leaf sheaves. They strike with a cool surface, their glossy surfaces surprising me in the dark. I feel like a tree swirling upwards too, muscular sap alive, with rich surfaces hanging from me, flaring outward rocket-like and falling to my roots, a rich strong power in me to break through into a new life. And dark in me as I walk the streets of this decayed town are the buds of my child. I walk alone under the dark flaring trees. There are many houses with the lights shining out but you and I walk on the skirts of the lawns amidst the down-pouring darkness. Houses are not for us. For us many kinds of hunger, for us a deep rebellion.

Trees come from a far seed walking the wind, my child too from a far seed blowing from last year's rich and revolutionary dead. My child budding secretly from far-walking seed, budding secretly and dangerously in the night.

The woman has come out and sits in the rocker, reading, her fat legs crossed. She scratches herself, cleans her nails, picks her teeth. Across the alley lying flat on the ground is a garage. People are driving in and out. But up here it is very quiet and the movement of the pear tree is the only movement and I seem to hear its delicate sound of living as it moves upon itself silently, and outward and upward.

The leaves twirl and twirl all over the tree, the delicately curving tinkling leaves. They twirl and twirl on the tree and the tree moves far inward upon its stem, moves in an invisible wind, gently swaying. Far below straight down the vertical stem like a stream, black and strong into the ground, runs the trunk; and invisible, spiraling downward and outward in powerful radiation, lie the roots. I can see it spiraling upward from below, its stem straight, and from it, spiraling the branches season by season, and from the spiraling branches moving out in quick motion, the forked stems, and from the stems twirling fragilely the tinier stems holding outward until they fall, the half-curled pear leaves.

Far below lies the yard, lying flat and black beneath the body of the upshooting tree, for the pear tree from above looks as if it had been shot instantaneously from the ground, shot upward like a rocket to break in showers of leaves and fruits twirling and falling. Its movement looks quick, sudden and rocketing. My child when grown can be looked at in this way as if it suddenly existed . . . but I know the slow time of making. The pear tree knows.

Far inside the vertical stem there must be a movement, a river of sap rising from below and radiating outward in many directions clear to the tips of the leaves. The leaves are the lips of the tree speaking in the wind or they move like many tongues. The fruit of the tree you can see has been a round speech, speaking in full tongue on the tree, hanging in ripe body, the fat curves hung within the small curves of the leaves. I imagine them there. The tree has shot up like a rocket, then stops in midair and its leaves flow out gently and its fruit curves roundly and gently in a long slow curve. All is gentle on the pear tree after its strong upward shooting movement.

I sit here all the afternoon as if in its branches, amidst the gentle and curving body of the tree. I have looked at it until it has become more familiar to me than Karl. It seems a strange thing that a tree might come to mean more to one than one's husband. It seems a shameful thing even. I am ashamed to think of it but it is so. I have sat here in the pale sun and the tree has spoken to me with its many tongued leaves, speaking through the afternoon of how to round a fruit. And I listen through the slow hours. I listen to the whispering of the pear tree, speaking to me, speaking to me. How can I describe what is said by a pear tree? Karl did not speak to me so. No one spoke to me in any good speech.

There is a woman coming up the stairs, slowly. I can hear her breathing. I can hear her behind me at the screen door.

She came out and spoke to me. I know why she was looking at me so closely. "I hear you're going to have a child," she said. "It's too bad." She is the same color as the dead leaves in the park. Was she once alive too?

I am writing on a piece of wrapping paper now. It is about ten o'clock. Karl didn't come home and I had no supper. I walked through the streets with their heavy, heavy trees bending over the walks and the lights shining from the houses and over the river the mist rising.

Before I came into this room I went out and saw the pear tree standing motionless, its leaves curled in the dark, its radiating body falling darkly, like a stream far below into the earth.

Tess Slesinger
(1905–1945)

he Jewish-American writer Tess Slesinger was born in New York, and attended Swarthmore College and the Columbia School of Journalism. After publishing her only novel, *The Unpossessed* (1934), a coruscating satirical portrait of the left-wing milieu of the New York intellectuals, and a collection of her short stories, Slesinger moved to California in 1935 with her second husband, Frank Davis, a screenwriter. There she became a screenwriter herself, with seven titles to her credit, notably *The Good Earth* (1937) and *A Tree Grows in Brooklyn* (1946). Slesinger died of cancer in 1945, however, without knowing that the latter film won an Oscar. "Missis Flinders," published in 1932 in *Story Magazine* before it became a chapter of *The Unpossessed*, is similar to Le Sueur's "Annunciation" in its feminist questioning of pregnancy and abortion during the Depression.

Missis Flinders (1932)

"Home you go!" Miss Kane, nodding, in her white nurse's dress, stood for a moment—she would catch a breath of air—in the hospital door; "and thank you again for the stockings, you needn't have bothered"— drew a sharp breath and turning, dismissed Missis Flinders from the hospital, smiling, dismissed her forever from her mind.

So Margaret Flinders stood next to her basket of fruit on the hospital steps; both of them waiting, a little shame-faced in the sudden sunshine, and in no hurry to leave the hospital—no hurry at all. It would be nicer to be alone, Margaret thought, glancing at the basket of fruit which stood respectable and a little silly on the stone step (the candy-bright apples were blushing caricatures of Miles: Miles' comfort, not hers). Flowers she could have left behind (for the nurses, in the room across the hall where they made tea at night); books she could have slipped into her suit-case; but fruit—Miles' gift, Miles' guilt, man's tribute to the Missis in the hospital—must be eaten; a half-eaten basket of fruit (she had tried to leave it: Missis Butter won't you . . . Missis Wiggam wouldn't you like . . . But Missis Butter had aplenty of her own thank you, and Missis Wiggam said she couldn't hold acids after a baby)—a half-eaten basket of fruit, in times like these, cannot be left to rot.

Down the street Miles was running, running, after a taxi. He was going after the taxi for her; it was for her sake he ran; yet this minute that his back was turned he stole for his relief and spent in running away, his shoulders crying guilt. And don't hurry, don't hurry, she said to them; I too am better off alone.

The street stretched in a long white line very finally away from the hospital, the hospital where Margaret Flinders (called there so solemnly Missis) had been lucky enough to spend only three nights. It would be four days before Missis Wiggam would be going home to Mister Wiggam with a baby; and ten possibly—the doctors were uncertain, Miss Kane prevaricated—before Missis Butter would be going home to Mister Butter without one. Zigzagging the street went the children; their cries and the sudden grinding of their skates she had listened to upstairs beside Missis Butter for three days. Some such child had she been—for the styles in children had not changed—a lean child gliding solemnly on skates and grinding them viciously at the nervous feet of grown-ups. Smile at these children she would not or could not; yet she felt on her face that smile, fixed, painful and frozen, that she had put there, on waking from ether three days back, to greet Miles. The smile spoke to the retreating shoulders of Miles: I don't need you; the smile spoke formally to life: thanks, I'm not having any. Not so the child putting the heels of his skates together Charlie Chaplin-wise and describing a scornful circle on the widest part of the sidewalk. Not so a certain little girl (twenty years back) skating past the wheels of autos, pursuing life in the form of a ball so red! so gay! better death than to turn one's back and smile over one's shoulder at life!

Upstairs Missis Butter must still be writhing with her poor caked breasts. The bed that had been hers beside Missis Butter's was empty now; Miss Kane would be stripping it and Joe would come in bringing fresh sheets. Whom would they put in beside Missis Butter, to whom would she moan and boast all night about the milk in her breasts that was turning, she said, into cheese?

Now Miles was coming back, jogging sheepishly on the running-board of a taxi, he had run away to the end of his rope and now was returning penitent, his eyes dog-like searching her out where she stood on the hospital steps (did they rest with complacence on the basket of fruit, his gift?), pleading with her, Didn't I get the taxi fast? like an anxious little boy. She stood with that smile on her face that hurt like too much ice-cream. Smile and smile; for she felt like a fool, she had walked open-eyed smiling into the trap (*Don't wriggle, Missis, I might injure you for life, Miss Kane had said cheerfully*) and felt the spring only when it was too late, when she waked from ether and knew like the thrust of a knife what she had ignored before. *Whatever did you do it for, Missis Flinders, Missis Butter was always saying; if there's nothing the matter with your insides—doesn't your husband . . . and Won't you have some fruit, Missis Butter, her calm reply: meaning, My husband gave me this fruit so what right have you to doubt that my husband . . .* Her husband who now stumbled up the steps to meet her; his eyes he had sent ahead, but something in him wanted not to come, tripped his foot as he hurried up the steps.

"Take my arm, Margaret," he said. "Walk slowly," he said. The bitter pill of taking help, of feeling weakly grateful, stuck in her throat. Miles' face behind his glasses was tense like the face of an amateur actor in the rôle of a strike-leader. That he was inadequate for the part he seemed to know. And if he felt shame, shame in his own eyes, she could forgive him; but if it was only guilt felt man-like in her presence, a guilt which he could drop off like a damp shirt, if he was putting it all off on her for being a woman! "The fruit, Miles!" she said; "you've forgotten the fruit." "The fruit can wait," he said bitterly.

He handed her into the taxi as though she were a package marked glass—something, she thought, not merely troublesomely womanly, but ladylike. "Put your legs up on the seat," he said. "I don't want to, Miles." *Goodbye Missis Butter* Put your legs up on the seat. I don't want to—*Better luck next time Missis Butter* Put your legs *I can't make out our window, Missis Butter* Put your "All right, it will be nice and uncomfortable." (She put her legs up on the seat.) *Goodbye Missis But . . .* "Nothing I say is right," he said. "It's good with the legs up," she said brightly.

Then he was up the steps agile and sure after the fruit. And down again, the basket swinging with affected carelessness, arming him, till he relinquished it modestly to her outstretched hands. Then he seated himself on the little seat, the better to watch his woman and his woman's fruit; and screwing his head round on his neck said irritably to the man who had been all his life on the wrong side of the glass pane: "Charles street!"

"Hadn't you better ask him to please drive slowly?" Margaret said.

"I was just going to," he said bitterly.

"And drive slowly," he shouted over his shoulder.

The driver's name was Carl C. Strite. She could see Carl Strite glance cannily back at the hospital: Greenway Maternity Home; pull his lever with extreme delicacy as though he were stroking the neck of a horse. There was a small roar—and the hospital glided backward: its windows ran together like the windows of a moving train; a spurt—watch out for those children on skates!—and the car was fairly started down the street.

Goodbye Missis Butter I hope you get a nice roommate in my place, I hope you won't find that Mister B let the ice-pan flow over again—and give my love to the babies when Miss Kane stops them in the door for you to wave at—goodbye Missis Butter, really goodbye.

Carl Strite (was he thinking maybe of his mother, an immigrant German woman she would have been, come over with a shawl on her head and worked herself to skin and bone so the kids could go to school and turn out good Americans—and what had it come to, here he was a taxi-driver, and what taxi-drivers didn't know! what in the course of their lackeys' lives they didn't put up with, fall in with! well there was one decent thing left in Carl Strite, he knew how to carry a woman home from a maternity hospital) drove softly along the curb . . . and the eyes of his honest puzzled gangster's snout photographed as "Your Driver" looked dimmed as though the glory of woman were too much for them, in a moment the weak cruel baby's mouth might blubber. Awful to lean forward and tell Mr Strite he was laboring under a mistake. *Missis Wiggam's freckled face when she heard that Missis Butter's roommate . . . maybe Missis Butter's baby had been born dead but anyway she had had a baby . . . whatever did you do it for Missis Flind . . .*

"Well, patient," Miles began, tentative, nervous (bored? perturbed? behind his glasses?).

"How does it feel, Maggie?" he said in a new, small voice.

Hurt and hurt this man, a feeling told her. He is a man, he could have made you a woman. "What's a D and C between friends?" she said. "Nobody at the hospital gave a damn about my little illegality."

"Well, but I do," he protested like a short man trying to be tall.

She turned on her smile; the bright silly smile that was eating up her facc.

Missis Butter would be alone now with no one to boast to about her pains except Joe who cleaned the corridors and emptied bed-pans—and thought Missis Butter was better than an angel because although she had incredible golden hair she could wise-crack like any brunette. Later in the day the eight-day mothers wobbling down the corridors for their pre-nursing constitutional would look in and talk to her; for wasn't Missis Butter their symbol and their pride, the one who had given up her baby that they might have theirs (for a little superstition is inevitable in new mothers, and it was generally felt that there must be one dead baby in a week's batch at any decent hospital) for whom they demanded homage from their visiting husbands? for whose health they asked the nurses each morning second only to asking for their own babies? That roommate of yours was a funny one, Missis Wiggam would say. Missis Wiggam was the woman who said big breasts weren't any good: here she was with a seven-pound baby and not a drop for it (here she would open the negligée Mister Wiggam had given her not to shame them before the nurses, and poke contemptuously at the floppy parts of herself within) while there was Missis Butter with no baby but a dead baby and her small breasts caking because there was so much milk in them for nothing but a . . . Yes, that Missis Flinders was sure a funny one, Missis Butter would agree.

"Funny ones," she and Miles, riding home with numb faces and a basket of fruit between them—past a park, past a museum, past elevated pillars—intellectuals they were, bastards, changelings . . . giving up a baby for economic freedom which meant that two of them would work in offices instead of one of them only, giving up a baby for intellectual freedom which meant that they smoked their cigarettes bitterly and looked out of the windows of a taxi onto streets and people and stores and hated them all. "We'd go soft," Miles had finally said, "we'd go bourgeois." Yes, with diapers drying on the radiators, bottles wrapped in flannel, the grocer getting to know one too well—yes, they would go soft, they might slump and start liking people, they might weaken and forgive stupidity, they might yawn and forget to hate. "Funny ones," class-straddlers, intellectuals, tight-rope-walking somewhere in the middle (how long could they hang on without falling to one side or the other? one more war? one more depression?); intellectuals, with habits generated from the right and tastes inclined to the left. Afraid to perpetuate themselves, were they? Afraid of anything that might loom so large in their personal lives as to outweigh other considerations? Afraid, maybe, of a personal life?

"Oh give me another cigarette," she said.

And still the taxi, with its burden of intellectuals and their inarticulate fruit-basket, its motherly, gangsterly, inarticulate driver, its license plates and its photographs all so very official, jogged on; past Harlem now; past fire-escapes loaded with flowerpots and flapping clothes; dingy windows opening to the soot-laden air blown in by the elevated roaring down its tracks. Past Harlem and through 125th street: stores and wise-cracks, Painless Dentists, cheap florists; Eighth Avenue, boarded and plastered, concealing the subway that was reaching its laborious birth beneath. But

Eighth Avenue was too jouncy for Mr Strite's precious burden of womanhood (who was reaching passionately for a cigarette); he cut through the park, and they drove past quiet walks on which the sun had brought out babies as the Fall rains give birth to worms.

"But ought you to smoke so much, so soon after—so soon?" Miles said, not liking to say so soon after what. His hand held the cigarettes out to her, back from her.

"They do say smoking's bad for child-birth," she said calmly, and with her finger-tips drew a cigarette from his reluctant hand.

And tapping down the tobacco on the handle of the fruit-basket she said, "But we've got the joke on them there, we have." (Hurt and hurt this man, her feeling told her; he is a man and could have made you a woman.)

"It was your own decision too," he said harshly, striking and striking at the box with his match.

"This damn taxi's shaking you too much," he said suddenly, bitter and contrite.

But Mr Strite was driving like an angel. He handled his car as though it were a baby-carriage. Did he think maybe it had turned out with her the way it had with Missis Butter? I could have stood it better, Missis Butter said, if they hadn't told me it was a boy. And me with my fourth little girl, Missis Wiggam had groaned (but proudly, proudly); why I didn't even want to see it when they told me. But Missis Butter stood it very well, and so did Missis Wiggam. They were a couple of good bitches; and what if Missis Butter had produced nothing but a dead baby this year, and what if Missis Wiggam would bring nothing to Mister Wiggam but a fourth little girl this year—why there was next year and the year after, there was the certain little world from grocery-store to kitchen, there were still Mister Butter and Mister Wiggam who were both (Missis Wiggam and Missis Butter vied with each other) just *crazy* about babies. Well, Mister Flinders is different, she had lain there thinking (he cares as much for his unborn gods as I for my unborn babies); and wished she could have the firm assurance they had in "husbands," coming as they did year after year away from them for a couple of weeks, just long enough to bear them babies either dead-ones or girl-ones . . . good bitches they were: there was something lustful besides smug in their pride in being "Missis." Let Missis Flinders so much as let out a groan because a sudden pain grew too big for her groins, let her so much as murmur because the sheets were hot beneath her—and Missis Butter and Missis Wiggam in the security of their maternity-fraternity exchanged glances of amusement: SHE don't know what pain is, look at what's talking about PAIN. . . .

"Mr Strite flatters us," she whispered, her eyes smiling straight and hard at Miles. (Hurt and hurt . . .)

"And why does that give you so much pleasure?" He dragged the words as though he were pounding them out with two fingers on the typewriter.

The name without the pain—she thought to say; and did not say. All at once she lost her desire to punish him; she no more wanted to "hurt this man" for he was no more man than she was woman. She would not do him the honor of hurting him. She must reduce him as she felt herself reduced. She must cut out from him what made him a man, as she had let be cut out from her what would have made her a woman. He was no man: he was a dried-up intellectual husk; he was sterile; empty and hollow as she was.

Missis Butter lying up on her pillow would count over to Missis Wiggam the fine points of her tragedy: how she had waited two days to be delivered of a dead baby; how it wouldn't have been so bad if the doctor hadn't said it was a beautiful baby with platinum-blond hair exactly like hers (and hers bleached unbelievably, but never mind, Missis Wiggam had come to believe in it like Joe and Mister Butter, another day and Missis Flinders herself, intellectual sceptic though she was, might have been convinced); and how they would pay the last instalment on— what a baby-carriage, Missis Wiggam, you'd never believe me!—and sell it second-hand for half its worth. I know when I was caught with my first, Missis Wiggam would take up the story her mouth had been open for. And that Missis Flinders was sure a funny one. . . .

But I am not such a funny one, Margaret wanted, beneath her bright and silly smile, behind her cloud of cigarette smoke (for Miles had given in; the whole package sat gloomily on Margaret's lap) to say to them; even though in my "crowd" the girls keep the names they were born with, even though some of us sleep for a little variety with one another's husbands, even though I forget as often as Miles—Mister Flinders to you—to empty the pan under the ice-box. Still I too have known my breasts to swell and harden, I too have been unable to sleep on them for their tenderness to weight and touch, I too have known what it is to undress slowly and imagine myself growing night to night . . . I knew this for two months, my dear Missis Wiggam; I had this strange joy for two months, my dear Missis Butter. But there was a night last week, my good ladies, on coming home from a party, which Mister Flinders and I spent in talk—and damn fine talk, if you want to know, talk of which I am proud, and talk not one word of which you, with your grocery-and-baby minds, could have understood; in a régime like this, Miles said, it is a terrible thing to have a baby—it means the end of independent thought and the turning of everything into a scheme for making money; and there must be institutions such as there are in Russia, I said, for taking care of the babies and their mothers; why in a time like this, we both said, to have a baby would be suicide—goodbye to our plans, goodbye to our working out schemes for each other and the world—our courage would die, our hopes concentrate on the sordid business of keeping three people alive, one of whom would be a burden and an expense for twenty years. . . . And then we grew drunk for a minute making up the silliest names that we could call it if we had it, we would call it Daniel if it were a boy, call it for my mother if it were a girl—and what a tough little thing it is, I said, look, look, how it hangs on in spite of its loving mother jumping off tables and broiling herself in hot water . . . until Miles, frightened at himself, washed his hands of it: we mustn't waste any more time, the sooner these things are done the better. And I as though the ether cap had already been clapped to my nose, agreed offhandedly. That night I did not pass my hands contentedly over my hard breasts; that night I gave no thought to the nipples grown suddenly brown and competent; I packed, instead, my suit-case: I filled it with all the white clothes I own. Why are you taking white clothes to the hospital? Miles said to me. I laughed. Why did I? White, for a bride; white, for a corpse; white, for a woman who refuses to be a woman. . . .

"Are you all right, Margaret?" (They were out now, safely out on Fifth Avenue, driving placidly past the Plaza where ancient coachmen dozed on the high seats of the last hansoms left in New York.)

"Yes, dear," she said mechanically, and forgot to turn on her smile. Pity for him sitting there in stolid New England inadequacy filled her. He was a man, and he could have made her a woman. She was a woman, and could have made him a man. He was not a man; she was not a woman. In each of them the life-stream flowed to a dead-end.

And all this time that the blood, which Missis Wiggam and Missis Butter stored up preciously in themselves every year to make a baby for their husbands, was flowing freely and wastefully out of Missis Flinders—toward what? would it pile up some day and bear a book? would it congeal within her and make a crazy woman?—all this time Mr Strite, remembering, with his pudgy face, his mother, drove his taxi softly along the curb; no weaving in and out of traffic for Mr Strite, no spurting at the corners and cheating the side-street traffic, no fine heedless rounding of rival cars for Mr Strite; he kept his car going at a slow and steady roll, its nose poked blunt ahead, following the straight and narrow—Mr Strite knew what it was to carry a woman home from the hospital.

But what in their past had warranted this? She could remember a small girl going from dolls to books, from books with colored pictures to books with frequent conversations; from such books to the books at last that one borrowed from libraries, books built up of solemn text from which you took notes; books which were gray to begin with, but which opened out to your eyes subtle layers of gently shaded colors. (And where in these texts did it say that one should turn one's back on life? Had the coolness of the stone library at college made one afraid? Had the ivy nodding in at the open dormitory windows taught one too much to curl and squat looking out?) And Miles? What book, what professor, what strange idea, had taught him to hunch his shoulders and stay indoors, had taught him to hide behind his glasses? Whence the fear that made him put, in cold block letters, implacably above his desk, the sign announcing him "Not at Home" to life?

Missis Flinders, my husband scaled the hospital wall at four o'clock in the morning, frantic I tell you. . . . But I just don't understand you, Missis Flinders (if there's really nothing the matter with your insides), do you understand her, Missis Wiggam, would your husband? . . . Why goodness, no, Mister Wiggam would sooner . . . ! And there he was, and they asked him, Shall we try an operation, Mister Butter? scaled the wall . . . shall we try an operation? (Well, you see, we are making some sort of protest, my husband Miles and I; sometimes I forget just what.) If there's any risk to Shirley, he said, there mustn't be any risk to Shirley. . . . Missis Wiggam's petulant, childish face, with its sly contentment veiled by what she must have thought a grown-up expression: Mister Wiggam bought me this negligée new, surprised me with it, you know—and generally a saving man, Mister Wiggam, not tight, but with three children—four now! Hetty, he says, I'm not going to have you disgracing us at the hospital this year, he says. Why the nurses will all remember that flannel thing you had Mabel and Suzy and Antoinette in, they'll talk about us behind our backs. (It wasn't that I couldn't make the flannel do again, Missis Butter, it wasn't that at all.) But he says, Hetty, you'll just have a new one this year, he says, and maybe it'll bring us luck, he says—you know, he was thinking maybe this time we'd have a boy. . . . Well, I just have to laugh at you, Missis Flinders, not *wanting* one, why my sister went to doctors for five years and spent her good money just *trying* to have one. . . . Well, poor Mister Wiggam, so the negligée didn't work, I brought him another little girl—but he didn't say boo to me, though I could see he was disappointed. Hetty, he says, we'll just have another try! oh I thought I'd die, with Miss Kane standing right there you know (though they do say these nurses . . .); but that's Mister Wiggam all over, he wouldn't stop a joke for a policeman. . . . No, I just can't get over you, Missis Flinders, if Gawd was willing to let you have a baby—and there really isn't anything wrong with your insides?

Miles' basket of fruit standing on the bed-table, trying its level inadequate best, poor pathetic inarticulate intellectual basket of fruit, to comfort, to bloom, to take the place of Miles himself who would come in later with Sam Butter for visiting hour. Miles' too-big basket of fruit standing there, embarrassed. Won't you have a peach, Missis Wiggam (I'm sure they have less acid)? Just try an apple, Missis Butter? Weigh Miles' basket of fruit against Mister Wiggam's negligée for luck, against Mister Butter scaling the wall at four in the morning for the mother of his dead baby. *Please* have a pear, Miss Kane; a banana, Joe? How they spat the seeds from Miles' fruit! How it hurt her when, unknowing, Missis Butter cut away the brown bruised cheek of Miles' bright-eyed, weeping apple! Miles! they scorn me, these ladies. They laugh at me, dear, almost as though I had no "husband," as though I were a "fallen woman." Miles, would you buy me a new negligée if I bore you three daughters? Miles, would you scale the wall if I bore you a dead baby? . . . Miles, I have an inferiority complex because I am an intellectual. . . . But a peach, Missis Wiggam! can't I possibly tempt you?

To be driving like this at mid-day through New York; with Miles bobbing like an empty ghost (for she could see he was unhappy, as miserable as she, he too had had an abortion) on the side-seat; with a taxi-driver, solicitous, respectful to an ideal, in front; was this the logical end of that little girl she remembered, of that girl swinging hatless across a campus as though that campus were the top of the earth? And was this all they could give birth to, she and Miles, who had closed up their books one day and kissed each other on the lips and decided to marry?

And now Mr Strite, with his hand out, was making a gentle righthand turn. Back to Fifth Avenue they would go, gently rolling, in Mr Strite's considerate charge. Down Fourteenth Street they would go, past the stores unlike any stores in the world: packed to the windows with imitation gold and imitation embroidery, with imitation men and women coming to stand in the doorways and beckon with imitation smiles; while on the sidewalks streamed the people unlike any other people in the world, drawn from every country, from every stratum, carrying babies (the real thing, with pinched anaemic faces) and parcels (imitation finery priced low in the glittering stores). There goes a woman, with a flat fat face, will produce five others just like herself, to dine off one-fifth the inadequate quantity her Mister earns today. These are the people not afraid to perpetuate themselves (forbidden to stop, indeed) and they will go on and on until the bottom of the world is filled with them; and suddenly there will be enough of them to combine their wild-eyed notions and take over the world to suit themselves. While I, while I and my Miles, with our good clear heads will one day go spinning out of the world and leave nothing behind . . . only diplomas crumbling in the museums. . . .

The mad street ended with Fifth Avenue; was left behind.

They were nearing home. Mr Strite, who had never seen them before (who would never again, in all likelihood, for his territory was far uptown) was seeing them politely to the door. As they came near home all of Margaret's fear and pain gathered in a knot in her stomach. There would be nothing new in their house; there was nothing to expect; yet she wanted to find something there that she knew she could not find, and surely the house (once so gay, with copies of old paintings, with books which lined the walls from floor to ceiling, with papers and cushions and typewriters) would be suddenly empty and dead, suddenly, for the first time, a group of rooms unalive as rooms with "For Rent" still pasted on the windows. And Miles? did he know he was coming home to a place which had suffered no change, but which would be different forever afterward? Miles had taken off his glasses; passed his hand tiredly across his eyes; was sucking now as though he expected relief, some answer, on the tortoise-shell curve which wound around his ear.

Mr Strite would not allow his cab to cease motion with a jerk. Mr Strite allowed his cab to slow down even at the corner (where was the delicatessen that sold the only loose ripe olives in the Village), so they rolled softly past No. 14; on past the tenement which would eventually be razed to give place to three-room apartments with In-a-Dor beds; then slowly, so slowly that Mr Strite must surely be an artist as well as a man who had had a mother, drew up and slid to a full stop before No. 60, where two people named Mister and Missis Flinders rented themselves a place to hide from life (both life of the Fifth Avenue variety, and life of the common, or Fourteenth Street, variety: in short, life).

So Miles, with his glasses on his nose once more, descended; held out his hand; Mr Strite held the door open and his face most modestly averted; and Margaret Flinders painfully and carefully swung her legs down again from the seat and alighted, step by step, with care and confusion. The house was before them; it must be entered. Into the house they must go, say farewell to the streets, to Mr Strite who had guided them through a tour of the city, to life itself; into the house they must go and hide. It was a fact that Mister Flinders (was he reluctant to come home?) had forgotten his key; that Missis Flinders must delve under the white clothes in her suit-case and find hers; that Mr Strite, not yet satisfied that his charges were safe, sat watchful and waiting in the front seat of his cab. Then the door gave. Then Miles, bracing it with his foot, held out his hand to Margaret. Then Mr Strite came rushing up the steps (something had told him his help would be needed again!), rushing up the steps with the basket of fruit hanging on his arm, held out from his body as though what was the likes of him doing holding a woman's basket just home from the hospital.

"You've forgotten your fruit, Missis!"

Weakly they glared at the fruit come to pursue them; come to follow them up the stairs to their empty rooms; but that was not fair: come, after all, to comfort them. "You must have a peach," Margaret said.

No, Mr Strite had never cared for peaches; the skin got in his teeth.

"You must have an apple," Margaret said.

Well, no, he must be getting on uptown. A cigarette (he waved it, deprecated the smoke it blew in the lady's face) was good enough for him.

"But a pear, just a pear," said Margaret passionately.

Mr Strite wavered, standing on one foot. "Maybe he doesn't want any fruit," said Miles harshly.

"Not want any *fruit!*" cried Margaret gayly, indignantly. Not want any fruit?—ridiculous! Not want the fruit my poor Miles bought for his wife in the hospital? Three days I spent in the hospital, in a Maternity Home, and I produced, with the help of my husband, one basket of fruit (tied with ribbon, pink—for boys). Not want any of our fruit? I couldn't bear it, I couldn't bear it. . . .

Mr Strite leaned over; put out a hand and gingerly selected a pear— "For luck," he said, managing an excellent American smile. They watched him trot down the steps to his cab, all the time holding his pear as though it were something he would put in a memory book. And still they stayed, because Margaret said foolishly, "Let's see him off"; because she was ashamed, suddenly, before Miles; as though she had cut her hair unbecomingly, as though she had wounded herself in some unsightly way—as though (summing up her thoughts as precisely, as decisively as though it had been done on an adding-machine) she had stripped and revealed herself not as a woman at all, but as a creature who would not be a woman and could not be a man. And then they turned (for there was nothing else to stay for, and on the street and in the sun before Missis Salvemini's fluttering window-curtains they were ashamed as though they had been naked or dead)—and went in the door and heard it swing to, pause on its rubbery hinge, and finally click behind them.

Ann Petry
(1908–1997)

nn Lane Petry grew up in a prosperous middle-class black family in Connecticut. She trained to become a pharmacist like her father, but after her marriage to the mystery writer George Petry, the couple moved to Harlem and she decided to become a writer herself. Petry worked for several years as a journalist and community welfare activist before winning an award for a 1943 short story, which enabled her to complete her first novel, *The Street* (1946). When it became a bestseller, the Petrys moved back to Connecticut, where she wrote two more novels, several books for young readers, and two collections of short stories. "The Migraine Workers" was first published in *Redbook* magazine in 1967.

The Migraine Workers (1967)

Pedro Gonzales was all set to go home for the night. He was sitting in the jeep with the motor running, looking idly around the gas station, telling himself that he'd left enough change for Mike, the man who worked for him, and he'd tied the dog out by the tire shed and there wasn't anything else for him to do before he took off.

He was a huge man, with hand and face darkened by the sun and from the grease and oil embedded in his skin. He knew he was too fat—his doctor and his friends were always telling him so—but he liked the feel of his own flesh, except of course in real hot weather like today around noon when he wished he was so thin he was just bone, no flesh. But now that the sun had gone down he felt fine, just fine.

He thought the station looked good, all of it—from the white one-story building that housed his office and the rest rooms and the salesroom where he sold car accessories, to the vast shed in the back where he stored truck tires and where Mike fed all the stray cats in the neighborhood. Over the years, he and Mike had made it the best-known truck stop between New York and Buffalo; it was located so the driver of a big rig could pull in right off the throughway and refuel with diesel or get a tire changed or pick up a free cup of coffee, open right around the clock, three hundred and sixty-five days a year.

While he sat there a truck came bouncing into the station—an old truck, its motor coughing and sputtering, the body rattling, bluish smoke belching out of the tail pipe. The driver pulled past the pumps and stopped off to one side with brakes squealing. Pedro wondered what the guy was carrying, because the flaps were closed in the back but every once in a while they kind of bulged out, and obviously there was something alive in there and moving around. The license plates were so covered with mud and so dented he couldn't tell what state the truck was registered in. He shook his head in disapproval, because a gypsy outfit like that could be carrying almost anything. They never had their hands on enough money to buy a new rig, had to keep spending it in driblets for gas and oil and minor repairs, and one day the truck would quit on them and they'd go pawing through junkyards trying to find spare parts or to salvage a tire or an old battery. Maybe that's why this one had come bouncing into the station—he was looking for a spare part or a tire that wasn't nailed down.

Pedro cut off the motor of the jeep. He'd wait until the gypsy left; you never knew what kind of trickery an outfit like that was up to. He'd seen many a one who gave a casual-seeming look at the tire shed, but when he or Mike said, "Shag! Guard!" and the shepherd growled a response deep in his throat, why, the gypsy would take off without a backward glance.

When Mike came out of the building, the driver got out of the truck and walked toward him. He was a black man, of medium height, not fat but fleshy, and he seemed to be asking some kind of favor of Mike because he tilted his head to one side and his manner was apologetic. Mike frowned and pointed at the ramshackle truck, and the black man kept talking and talking and gesturing, and finally Mike shrugged and pointed to the jeep, indicating that he would have to ask the boss. The driver smiled and nodded in Pedro's direction, his eyes gleaming, and Pedro, noting the layer of fat under his skin—skin so sleek it looked as though it had been oiled—thought, Bastard, pure bastard.

Mike came over to the jeep and said, "He wants to know is it all right to use the rest rooms."

"Who? Who wants to use them? Him?"

Before Mike could answer, a big rig pulled in at the diesel pumps, and Pedro said, "Go service them. Let the bastard wait. It won't hurt him."

He watched Mike at the pumps, thinking, We been in this racket close to thirty years now, so it's only to be expected we don't look the same as when we started out. Mike wasn't fat, but he had put on weight; he had kind of thickened in the middle and there was soft flesh around his jowls. Close up you could see gray in his hair and crow's-feet around his eyes.

Then he glanced at the truck again and wondered what the guy carried. Years of running a gas station had made him wary. He'd had encounters with deadbeats, thieves, punks, finks, hoods, even a murderer; everything out on rubber on the road headed for his station because it was the only one that stayed open all the time—holidays and all, day and night. So naturally he wanted to know what this black man was carrying in that broken-down truck. He could have cobras in it or boa constrictors or lions.

In the summer you never knew what would show up. Just yesterday a blonde, riding in a convertible with the top down, had stopped for gas, and when he went up to the car to see what she wanted he saw what he thought was a fur jacket lying on the seat beside her. But it turned out to be an ocelot with a black velvet ribbon around its neck and what looked like a diamond dangling from the ribbon. The beast lunged toward him, snarling, and he jumped back and tripped over his own feet and almost fell down trying to get out of the way; and the woman said, "Ooo-oooh! You looked so funny!" and laughed and laughed and laughed. He picked up a tire iron and threatened her with it, yelling, "Get out of here! Get out of here! You can't horse around here with no lion. Out!" And she drove away, cursing him, and snarling just like the beast that traveled with her.

About an hour later one of the local cops came by and asked him what happened—that's how he knew it was an ocelot and not a lion or a tiger that had lunged at him. He'd told the cop, a young fellow in a brand-new uniform with a cap too big for him—it came down over his ears and made his face look very small—that, sure he threatened the woman with a tire iron, what with the heat and the humidity and all the rat finks running over the bell, honking their horns to hurry you up, saying fill her up, wash the windshield, check the battery, can I charge it, I haven't got the toll for the bridge, I need a dime for the telephone, can I put it on my credit card, what with that and the feel of the oil and the grease on his skin, and the stink of the diesel fuel and the stink from the exhaust from the big trucks in his nose, well, with all that, why, you go up to a car and there is some grinning woman with her skirt up to her thighs and her blond hair straggling down around her shoulders and half over her face, and she laughs because the tiger on the seat with her lunges at the big slob who is working twelve hours a day, and the slob jumps back and almost falls down because his wits have been half scared out of him, why—

"All right," he'd said to the cop, and he kept talking faster and faster and his voice kept getting louder and louder, "all right. Hot as it was, what with the smell of that tiger she had with her and the look on her face when she laughed—why, if she'd stayed long enough, I would have smashed her face in with the tire iron. And if you want to make something out of it, I'll sign a statement and I'll say just that, and I'll put in what I think about all these rich kids who come in here barefoot, all of them with dirty feet, and I'll tell what I think about these women who don't wear anything but little straight pieces of cloth for dresses and have all that dirty hair hanging down their backs and they don't even bother to comb it anymore, and I'll tell you what I think about—"

The cop interrupted him. "It wasn't a tiger. It was an ocelot, and we gave her a summons for transporting an uncaged wild animal around with her. It's okay—I just wanted to hear your side of the story."

Then Mike was back beside the jeep, tapping on the side of the door. He said impatiently, "What'll I tell the man? He wants to know is it all right to use the rest rooms."

"Use the rest rooms? What's he asking that for? What's he carrying in the truck?"

"Well, they're these migraine workers."

"What's that mean?"

"It means these colored people who go from place to place to pick beans and stuff. The driver brings them from down South every year, and he's taking them upstate. He says he don't usually come through here, but he took a wrong turn somewhere."

"Are they in that truck?"

"Yeah."

"Tell him yes."

Mike nodded to the black man to indicate that the boss had approved. Pedro got out of the jeep and walked over to the truck. He was so fat that he walked with a rocking motion. He was wearing enormous dark green pants slung low, way down to his hipbones, and a voluminous dark green shirt with "Pedro's Gas Station" embroidered in red on one of the breast pockets. Both pockets bulged with papers. He wore high-laced leather shoes, bright yellow in color.

The black man opened the flaps of the truck. "Come on," he said. "Git out. Git out. All right. Now, come on, now, line up. Line up, now!"

The truck was filled with black people—men, women, children and nursing babies. They were ragged, dirty, their dark skins covered with sores, and there were burrs and straw in their matted hair.

Pedro looked at them first out of the corner of his eye, stealing glances at them, and then as he became aware that none of them was looking at him, that they kept looking down at the ground, heads down, eyes averted, he frankly stared at them.

"All right. Git in the line."

They kept coming out of the truck, blinking, stumbling, shivering a little, perhaps because of the fresh, cool air. Pedro backed away because they smelled so awful and they looked so awful, and then his curiosity made him go closer.

"Where you from?" he asked.

They did not look at him; they did not reply.

"What language do they speak?"

"Same as us," the driver said.

The last one out was an old black man, bearded, dirtier than the others, his work pants so filled with holes and torn places that he looked like a bundle of rags. After the flaps had swung back in place behind him, Pedro looked inside the truck. There was nowhere to sit except the floor. The stench made him cough, and over it was the yeasty smell of some kind of rotgut liquor. Then he moved away because there was someone lying way back in a corner—a very old woman who peered at him and then drew back in fear.

The driver of the truck was herding the people toward the rest rooms. Pedro beckoned to him and indicated that he wanted to ask him something.

"How come it's got no seats?"

"No room for seats," the driver said, smiling, his eyes gleaming, head tilted to one side. "I hauls crops so as I can pay for the gas, and if there was seats, they'd have to be nailed down and I couldn't git much of the crops in."

Pedro said, frowning, "I never seen such a sight before in my life."

"Well, folks don't usually see 'em," the driver said apologetically, head bobbing up and down in a series of small bows, smiling his ingratiating smile. "We run 'em through at night and don't stop nowhere; nobody sees 'em and nobody gets upset about 'em. But this time the truck broke down and it was morning before I could git it going, and then I took the wrong turn and that's how we come through to your place. Pure accident, boss, pure accident."

Yeah, he thought, and you're pure bastard.

"Are they hungry?"

The driver shrugged. "Well, like us, they can always eat a little. You got anything, you give it to me and I'll see they gits it further up the road where it's dark. That way nobody'll git upset about 'em."

"They'll eat it here," Pedro said. The driver couldn't get it out of their stomachs once it was inside them, and it was a sure thing they'd never see any food if the driver got his hands on it first. Pedro went inside the station and told Mike to get out the loaves of bread the baker had left—it couldn't be sold in the stores as day-old bread because the outfit that made it wouldn't permit it. He had six quarts of milk in the refrigerator and there was a crate of oranges that had bounced off the back of one of those big coast-to-coast trucks and a crate of evaporated milk and one of those big tinned hams and a case of corned beef.

Anyway, they fed everybody. They sliced up the ham and handed it out. Then he opened tin after tin of corned beef—the stuff was always falling off the back of trucks. The kids drank the fresh milk and they each ate a can of corned beef, wolfed it down, and they ate oranges. Then he and Mike opened cans of evaporated milk and mixed the stuff with water, the whole case of it, and the ragged old man poured it into paper cups and they drank it fast.

He'd never seen people eat with such haste—they put whole slices of bread in their mouths, stuffing it in, and they did the same thing with the meat. He ran out of paper cups, and the driver said, "They kin use the same ones over again, hand it to the next person," but Pedro sent Mike back into the station for more cups.

They didn't talk while they were eating, and when they got back in the truck they ducked their heads down, bowing as they went past him. The driver was annoyed and he showed it, because he said thanks in a short, sharp way and left out the obsequious ducking of his head and then herded them back into the truck, heckling them with his voice. He gave the kids a push here and a hard shove there, which they ignored, making no protest, and Pedro decided they were so accustomed to being pushed around that they accepted it as a normal part of their lives.

He watched the truck go bouncing out of the station, bluish smoke coming from the tail pipe, and thought that it carried a load of misery, pure misery, and for a long while after it left he couldn't seem to think about anything else. He felt as though he had eaten something that disagreed with him and had been left with a sour taste in his mouth.

By the next day everything was fine, just fine. The sun was out, and it was hot but not humid. The trucks came and went and the drivers drank coffee and the regular customers came in for gas and oil and there weren't any ragged, hungry people who traveled standing up in rattle-trap trucks or any blondes in convertibles with what looked like Bengal tigers on the seat beside them.

But the day after that Mike said something was snooping around the tire shed at night, knocking the garbage cans over, and that Shag went wild, barking, jumping up in the air, trying to get loose from the chain that held him. He said he ran out to the tire shed, and though he watched and waited and listened, he didn't see anything; but the dog kept hearing something or smelling something that infuriated him, making his hackles rise.

This happened three nights in a row, and on the fourth night Mike said uneasily, "I don't like it. I don't see nothing—no animal, none of those long-haired rat-fink kids that horse around here sometimes. Nothing. But Shag sees something or smells something that sets him crazy. It's spooky."

"So let the dog loose."

"No," Mike said. "Not me. That ain't right."

"That's what he's for." Until they got the German shepherd there had always been a certain amount of petty thievery. Most gas stations had the same problems—a tire or two missing, a new battery not accounted for, the Coke machine broken open for the change. After somebody pried the coin box right out of the telephone booth, Pedro figured they'd better get a guard dog, because they were open all night and they were sitting ducks for a holdup. So a couple of years ago he had bought Shag. He'd cost almost as much as a good used car, but he'd been worth it, for they hadn't had any kind of trouble since.

He told Mike to move the garbage cans right up behind the building where the office was and to turn out the lights in the back and let the dog out, and then he'd be able to catch whatever it was that was messing around with the cans.

Mike said, "I'll move the cans, but I don't want to let the dog loose."

"All right. All right. I'll come back tonight and I'll let him out."

About midnight he went back to the station and turned out the lights in the back and sat down in a straight wooden chair near the door of the room they used as a kitchen. Shag sat down beside him, leaning against him. The air coming through the screen door was balmy. There was a swamp behind the station, and honeysuckle grew there and he could smell it. He thought the night air was like some dandelion wine he'd had years ago. He could still remember the taste of it, and how at the time he drank it he'd thought the old Italian man who'd made the wine had managed to catch hold of the color of the flower and the warmth from the sun and put them in the bottle, and when he had lifted it to his mouth it was all there on the edges of his lips, on his tongue, trickling down his throat.

He could hear the hum of traffic on the turnpike and he frowned, thinking it sounded like some of the peculiar music they broadcast on those midnight-to-dawn radio programs. He sighed and shifted his weight in the hard chair. It was an uncomfortable place to sit because he was too large for the seat, yet he found himself dozing, his head nodding.

Suddenly he leaned forward and then stood up, because someone or something had lifted the cover of one of the garbage cans. It wasn't a loud noise, just a gentle telltale click of metal against metal.

Shag growled and Pedro eased the screen door open and Shag went hurtling through the air as if he'd been thrown from a catapult. Then there were screams and a man's voice saying, "Ah, down, git down, git down, git away"—a man's voice with a tremor in it.

Pedro turned on the outside lights and he saw a man standing still just beyond the door, with the dog quite close to him. Then the man tried to edge away and the dog took hold of his pants, and then as the man pulled hard, trying to run, Shag hurled his weight against him and the man went down, flat on his back. Shag stood over him, guarding him, his mouth open, the great, ravening jaws not a quarter of an inch from the man's throat.

As Pedro approached he saw that the man on the ground was an old black man. He was too frightened even to cry out; his throat quivered and his breathing made a sound like cloth being torn. Pedro bent over him and got a whiff of him and drew back; this old black man was one of those migraine workers. He was the bearded one who had poured the milk.

Mike came running out of the building. "Who is he?"

"Off the truck. He came off that broken-down truck. He's one of them migraine workers. Let him up, Shag. Let him up."

Mike helped the old man to his feet and then went through his pockets. Nothing on him—not a piece of paper, not a penny, not a cigarette or a shred of tobacco. Nothing.

They stood staring at him in a kind of wonderment and finally Pedro said, more to break the silence than anything else, "What's your name?"

"Folks calls me Ben. Yes, sir. They calls me Ben." It was impossible to imitate his speech, though Pedro found his own lips moving in a vain effort to make himself remember it; it was a soft, slurred kind of sound, difficult to understand.

"Where'd you come from?" Mike asked curiously. "Where's your home?"

"I don't know. I don't rightly know, boss." He said it apologetically.

"Where was the truck going when it left here?"

"I never did hear where driver was taking us, boss."

Pedro looked at him in amazement. He was old, emaciated, dirty, ragged. How in the name of God had he planned to live? He couldn't just eat out of garbage cans. What had made him suddenly leave the truck?

"You been up this way before?" he asked.

"Ever' year."

"How'd you come to leave the truck?"

The old man said that when they left the gas station he'd edged toward the tailgate of the truck, parted the flaps a little, and then waited for the truck to stop at a light or a stop sign. He knew he couldn't wait too long or he'd get lost and never be able to find the fat white man's place, and so finally the truck slowed a little and he jumped off and had to scramble out of the way of an oncoming car.

Mike said, "Why'd you come here?"

The old man wouldn't answer. He avoided looking at them and looked at the dog instead and said he was a mighty good dog, about the best he'd ever seen.

Mike said, "Shag, make friends."

To the old man's delight, Shag sat down and extended one of his big paws. The old man shook hands with him and began talking to him, making a soft, mumbling sound.

Pedro went back into the building to call the police and tell them to come and pick up this smelly old man. He had his hand on the telephone and was about to dial when Mike spoke, almost in his ear. He was startled because he hadn't known Mike had followed him inside.

Mike said, "Who are you calling?"

"The police."

"He ain't done nothing except try to find himself something to eat."

"Well, what am I supposed to do with him?"

"He could stay here. He could sleep in the tire shed."

"With all those cats?"

"Sure."

"And where'd he stay in the winter?"

"He could sleep here in this building."

Pedro shook his head and reached for the telephone again, and Mike's hand closed over his. Mike said, "Don't do that."

"Why not? The cops will find out where he belongs and send him back to wherever it is he came from. How else am I going to find out?"

"He don't belong nowhere. You know that. You saw them migraine workers and that stinking truck and that black bastard who was driving it. Let him stay here."

"No," Pedro said, frowning. "He can't stay here. I got all I can do to look after myself and look after you. I can't take on no old black man. Why'd he come here anyway?"

"You don't know?"

Pedro shook his head. "Of course not. And neither do you."

"Oh, yes I do. It's because you're so fat. That old man knows we got plenty of food all the time, because if we didn't have, you couldn't 'a got so fat, and you wouldn't have been giving food away if there wasn't plenty of it around. Didn't you hear him say if he hadn't jumped off the truck when he did, he couldn't 'a found the fat white man's place?" Mike said this fast, almost in one breath, and then he stopped, and when he spoke again he whispered, just as though he were telling a dirty joke he didn't want overheard. "It's because you're so fat. That's why."

"I couldn't care less," Pedro said coldly, but he felt as though he'd been betrayed by his own soft flesh, and it made him feel funny, but all he said was, "All right. All right," and he moved away from the telephone.

Elizabeth Bishop
(1911–1979)

lizabeth Bishop's father died when she was an infant, and her mother was institutionalized for mental illness. She was raised first by her maternal grandparents in Nova Scotia and then by her paternal grandparents in Worcester, Massachusetts. After graduating from Vassar College, Bishop began a lifelong friendship with the poet Marianne Moore, who published Bishop's poems in an anthology of young writers and helped her obtain a publisher for her first book, *North & South* (1946). In 1951 Bishop took a journey to Brazil where she met and settled with her lover, Lota de Macedo Soares. *A Cold Spring* (1956) and *Questions of Travel* (1965) were acclaimed as collections of exacting poems both rooted in the natural world and deeply personal. In 1966, Bishop returned to the United States to teach at several different colleges, including Harvard. Her final collection, *Geography III* (1976), won the National Book Critics Circle Award and includes some of her best poems, including her meditation on loss, "One Art." Bishop did not want to be categorized as a woman poet. In a 1977 letter to a friend she explained, "Undoubtedly gender does play an important role in the making of any art, but art is art, and to separate writings, paintings, musical compositions, etc., into two sexes is to emphasize values in them that are *not* art."

One Art (1976)

The art of losing isn't hard to master;
so many things seem filled with the intent
to be lost that their loss is no disaster.

Lose something every day. Accept the fluster
of lost door keys, the hour badly spent.
The art of losing isn't hard to master.

Then practice losing farther, losing faster:
places, and names, and where it was you meant
to travel. None of these will bring disaster.

I lost my mother's watch. And look! my last, or
next-to-last, of three loved houses went.
The art of losing isn't hard to master.

I lost two cities, lovely ones. And, vaster,
some realms I owned, two rivers, a continent.
I miss them, but it wasn't a disaster.

—Even losing you (the joking voice, a gesture
I love) I shan't have lied. It's evident
the art of losing's not too hard to master
though it may look like (*Write* it!) like disaster.

Jean Stafford
(1915–1979)

 ean Stafford grew up in Boulder, Colorado, the youngest of four children. During her years at the University of Colorado, Stafford made the most of her opportunities for bohemian experiment and intellectual development, and in 1936 went to Heidelberg to do graduate study in Anglo-Saxon and philology. In 1937 she met the young poet Robert Lowell at a writer's conference in Colorado. He courted her through letters, and in December 1938 invited her to Boston to meet his family. Taking her for a drunken drive in his father's Packard, Lowell crashed the car; Stafford sustained massive injuries to her skull, nose, and jaw that required five painful operations. Despite this warning of the ways Lowell would wreck her life, Stafford married him in 1940, shortly after she recovered from the accident. Their stormy marriage lasted eight years; she had two subsequent marriages that were happier.

Stafford's literary career started off well, with the early success of her novel *Boston Adventure* (1944), followed by *The Mountain Lion* (1947) and *The Catherine Wheel* (1952), as well as a number of short stories. "The Echo and the Nemesis," one of the earliest stories to deal with women's eating disorders, was originally published as "The Nemesis" in *The New Yorker*, December 15, 1950. But alcoholism and mental hospitalizations took a heavy toll on Stafford's writing; between 1958 and her death in 1979 she published only seven stories.

The Echo and the Nemesis (1950)

Sue Ledbetter and Ramona Dunn became friends through the commonplace accident of their sitting side by side in a philosophy lecture three afternoons a week. There were many other American students at Heidelberg University that winter—the last before the war—but neither Sue nor Ramona had taken up with them. Ramona had not because she scorned them; in her opinion, they were Philistines, concerned only with drinking beer, singing German songs, and making spectacles of themselves on their bicycles and in their little rented cars. And Sue had not because she was self-conscious and introverted and did not make friends easily. In Ramona's presence, she pretended to deplore her compatriots' escapades, which actually she envied desperately. Sometimes on Saturday nights she lay on her bed unable to read or daydream and in an agony of frustration as she listened to her fellow-lodgers at the Pension Kirchenheim laughing and teasing and sometimes bursting into song as they played bridge and Monopoly in the cozy veranda café downstairs.

Soon after the semester opened in October, the two girls fell into the habit of drinking their afternoon coffee together on the days they met in class. Neither of them especially enjoyed the other's company, but in their different ways they were lonely, and as Ramona once remarked, in her high-falutin way, "From time to time, I need a rest from the exercitation of my intellect." She was very vain of her intellect, which she had directed to the study of philology, to the exclusion of almost everything else in the world. Sue, while she had always taken her work seriously, longed also for beaux and parties, and conversation about them, and she was often bored by Ramona's talk, obscurely gossipy, of the vagaries of certain Old High Franconian verbs when they encountered the High German consonant shift, or of the variant readings of passages in Layamon's *Brut*, or the linguistic influence Eleanor of Aquitaine had exerted on the English court. But because she was well-mannered she listened politely and even appeared to follow Ramona's exuberant elucidation of Sanskrit "a"-stem declensions and her ardent plan to write a monograph on the word "ahoy." They drank their coffee in the Konditorei Luitpold, a very noisy café on a street bent like an elbow, down behind the cathedral. The din of its two small rooms was aggravated by the peripheral racket that came from the kitchen and from the outer shop, where the cakes were kept. The waiters, all of whom looked cross, hustled about at a great rate, slamming down trays and glasses and cups any which way before the many customers, who gabbled and rattled newspapers and pounded on the table for more of something. Over all the to-do was the blare of the radio, with its dial set permanently at a station that played nothing but stormy choruses from *Wilhelm Tell*. Ramona, an invincible expositor, had to shout, but shout she did as she traced words like "rope" and "calf" through dozens of languages back to their Indo-Germanic source. Sometimes Sue, somewhat befuddled by the uproar, wanted by turns to laugh and to cry with disappointment, for this was not at all the way she had imagined that she would live in Europe. Half incredulously and half irritably, she would stare at Ramona as if in some way she were to blame.

Ramona Dunn was fat to the point of parody. Her obesity fitted her badly, like extra clothing put on in the wintertime, for her embedded bones were very small and she was very short, and she had a foolish gait, which, however, was swift, as if she were a mechanical doll whose engine raced. Her face was rather pretty, but its features were so small that it was all but lost in its billowing surroundings, and covered by a thin, fair skin that was subject to disfiguring affections, now hives, now eczema, now impetigo, and the whole was framed by fine, pale hair that was abused once a week by a *Friseur* who baked it with an iron into dozens of horrid little snails. She habitually wore a crimson tam-o'-shanter with a sportive spray of artificial edelweiss pinned to the very top of it. For so determined a bluestocking, her eccentric and extensive wardrobe was a surprise; nothing was ever completely clean or completely whole, and nothing ever matched anything else, but it was apparent that all these odd and often ugly clothes had been expensive. She had a long, fur-lined cape, and men's tweed jackets with leather patches on the elbows, and flannel shirts designed for hunters in the State of Maine, and high-necked jerseys, and a waistcoat made of unborn gazelle, dyed Kelly green. She attended particularly to the dressing of her tiny hands and feet, and she had gloves and mittens of every color and every material, and innumerable pairs of extraordinary shoes, made for her by a Roman bootmaker. She always carried a pair of field glasses, in a brassbound leather case that hung over her shoulder by a plaited strap of rawhide; she looked through the wrong end of them, liking, for some reason that she did not disclose, to diminish the world she surveyed. Wherever she went, she took a locked pigskin satchel, in which she carried her grammars and lexicons and the many drafts of the many articles she was writing in the hope that they would be published in learned journals. One day in the café, soon after the girls became acquainted, she opened up the satchel, and Sue was shocked at the helter-skelter arrangement of the papers, all mussed and frayed, and stained with coffee and ink. But, even more, she was dumfounded to see a clear-green all-day sucker stuck like a bookmark between the pages of a glossary to "Beowulf."

Sue knew that Ramona was rich, and that for the last ten years her family had lived in Italy, and that before that they had lived in New York. But this was all she knew about her friend; she did not even know where she lived in Heidelberg. She believed that Ramona, in her boundless erudition, was truly consecrated to her studies and that she truly had no other desire than to impress the subscribers to *Speculum* and the *Publications of the Modern Language Association*. She was the sort of person who seemed, at twenty-one, to have fought all her battles and survived to enjoy the quiet of her unendangered ivory tower. She did not seem to mind at all that she was so absurd to look at, and Sue, who was afire with ambitions and sick with conflict, admired her arrogant self-possession.

The two girls had been going to the Konditorei Luitpold three times a week for a month or more, and all these meetings had been alike; Ramona had talked and Sue had contributed expressions of surprise (who would have dreamed that "bolster" and "poltroon" derived from the same parent?), or murmurs of acquiescence (she agreed there might be something in the discreet rumor that the Gothic language had been made up by nineteenth-century scholars to answer riddles that could not otherwise be solved), or laughter, when it seemed becoming. The meetings were neither rewarding nor entirely uninteresting to Sue, and she came to look upon them as a part of the week's schedule, like the philosophy lectures and the seminar in Schiller.

And then, one afternoon, just as the weary, mean-mouthed waiter set their cake down before them, the radio departed from its custom and over it came the "Minuet in G," so neat and winning and surprising that for a moment there was a general lull in the café, and even the misanthropic waiter paid the girls the honor, in his short-lived delight, of not slopping their coffee. As if they all shared the same memories that the little sentimental piece of music awoke in her, Sue glanced around smiling at her fellows and tried to believe that all of them—even the old men with Hindenburg mustaches and palsied wattles, and even the Brown Shirts fiercely playing chess—had been children like herself and had stumbled in buckled pumps through the simple steps of the minuet at the military command of a dancing teacher, Miss Conklin, who had bared her sinewy legs to the thigh. In some public presentation of Miss Conklin's class, Sue had worn a yellow bodice with a lacing of black velvet ribbon, a bouffant skirt of chintz covered all with daffodils, and a cotton-batting wig that smelled of stale talcum powder. Even though her partner had been a sissy boy with nastily damp hands and white eyelashes, and though she had been grave with stage-fright, she had had moments of most thrilling expectation, as if this were only the dress rehearsal of the grown-up ball to come.

If she had expected all the strangers in the café to be transported by the "Minuet" to a sweet and distant time, she had not expected Ramona Dunn to be, and she was astonished and oddly frightened to see the fat girl gazing with a sad, reflective smile into her water glass. When the music stopped and the familiar hullabaloo was re-established in the room, Ramona said, "Oh, I don't know of anything that makes me more nostalgic than that tinny little tune! It makes me think of Valentine parties before my sister Martha died."

It took Sue a minute to rearrange her family portrait of the Dunns, which heretofore had included, besides Ramona, only a mother and a father and three brothers. Because this was by far the simplest way, she had seen them in her mind's eye as five stout, scholarly extensions of Ramona, grouped together against the background of Vesuvius. She had imagined that they spent their time examining papyri and writing Latin verses, and she regretted admitting sorrow into their lives, as she had to do when she saw Ramona's eyes grow vague and saw her, quite unlike her naturally greedy self, push her cake aside, untouched. For a moment or two, the fat girl was still and blank, as if she were waiting for a pain to go away, and then she poured the milk into her coffee, replaced her cake, and began to talk about her family, who, it seemed, were not in the least as Sue had pictured them.

Ramona said that she alone of them was fat and ill-favored, and the worst of it was that Martha, the most beautiful girl who ever lived, had been her twin. Sue could not imagine, she declared, how frightfully good-looking all the Dunns were—except herself, of course: tall and dark-eyed and oval-faced, and tanned from the hours they spent on their father's boat, the San Filippo. And they were terribly gay and venturesome; they were the despair of the croupiers at the tables on the Riviera, the envy of the skiers at San Bernardino and of the yachtsmen on the Mediterranean. Their balls and their musicales and their dinner parties were famous. All the brothers had unusual artistic gifts, and there was so much money in the family that they did not have to do anything but work for their own pleasure in their studios. They were forever involved in scandals with their mistresses, who were either married noblewomen or notorious dancing girls, and forever turning over a new leaf and getting themselves engaged to lovely, convent-bred princesses, whom, however, they did not marry; the young ladies were too submissively Catholic, or too stupid, or their taste in painting was vulgar.

Of all this charming, carefree brood, Martha, five years dead, had been the most splendid, Ramona said, a creature so slight and delicate that one wanted to put her under a glass bell to protect her. Painters were captivated by the elegant shape of her head, around which she wore her chestnut hair in a coronet, and there were a dozen portraits of her, and hundreds of drawings hanging in the big bedroom where she had died and which now had been made into a sort of shrine for her. If the Dunns were odd in any way, it was in this devotion to their dead darling; twice a year Mrs. Dunn changed the nibs in Martha's pens, and in one garden there grew nothing but anemones, Martha's favorite flower. She had ailed from birth, pursued malevolently by the disease that had melted her away to the wick finally when she was sixteen. The family had come to Italy in the beginning of her mortal languor in the hope that the warmth and novelty would revive her, and for a while it did, but the wasting poison continued to devour her slowly, and for years she lay, a touching invalid, on a balcony overlooking the Bay of Naples. She lay on a blond satin chaise longue, in a quaint peignoir made of leaf-green velvet, and sometimes, as she regarded her prospect of sloops and valiant skiffs on the turbulent waves, the cypress trees, white villas in the midst of olive groves, and the intransigent smoldering of Vesuvius, she sang old English airs and Irish songs as she accompanied herself on a lute. If, in the erratic course of her illness, she got a little stronger, she asked for extra cushions at her back and half sat up at a small easel to paint in water colors, liking the volcano as a subject, trite as it was, and the comic tourist boats that romped over the bay from Naples to Capri. If she was very unwell, she simply lay smiling while her parents and her sister and her brothers attended her, trying to seduce her back to health with their futile offerings of plums and tangerines and gilt-stemmed glasses of Rhine wine and nosegays bought from the urchins who bargained on the carriage roads.

When Martha died, Ramona's own grief was despair, because the death of a twin is a foretaste of one's own death, and for months she had been harried with premonitions and prophetic dreams, and often she awoke to find that she had strayed from her bed, for what awful purpose she did not know, and was walking barefoot, like a pilgrim, down the pitch-black road. But the acute phase of her mourning had passed, and now, although sorrow was always with her, like an alter ego, she had got over the worst of it.

She paused in her narrative and unexpectedly laughed. "What a gloom I'm being!" she said, and resumed her monologue at once but in a lighter tone, this time to recount the drubbing her brother Justin had given someone when he was defending the honor of a dishonorable soprano, and to suggest, in tantalizing innuendoes, that her parents were not faithful to each other.

Sue, whose dead father had been an upright, pessimistic clergyman and whose mother had never given voice to an impure thought, was bewitched by every word Ramona said. It occurred to her once to wonder why Ramona so frowned upon the frolics of the other American students when her beloved relatives were so worldly, but then she realized that the manners of the *haut monde* were one thing and those of undergraduates another. How queer, Sue thought, must seem this freakish bookworm in the midst of it all! And yet such was the ease with which Ramona talked, so exquisitely placed were her fillips of French, so intimate and casual her allusions to the rich and celebrated figures of international society, that Ramona changed before Sue's eyes; from the envelope of fat emerged a personality as *spirituelle* and knowing as any practicing sophisticate's. When, in the course of describing a distiller from Milan who was probably her mother's lover, she broke off and pressingly issued Sue an invitation to go with her a month from then, at the Christmas holiday, to San Bernardino to meet her brothers for a fortnight of skiing, Sue accepted immediately, not stopping to think, in the heady pleasure of the moment, that the proposal was unduly sudden, considering the sketchy nature of their friendship. "My brothers will adore you," she said, giving Sue a look of calm appraisal. "They are eclectic and they'll find your red hair and brown eyes irresistibly naive." As if the plan had long been in her mind, Ramona named the date they would leave Heidelberg; she begged permission, in the most gracious and the subtlest possible way, to let Sue be her guest, even to the extent of supplying her with ski equipment. When the details were settled—a little urgently, she made Sue promise "on her word of honor" that she would not default—she again took up her report on Signor da Gama, the distiller, who was related by blood to the Pope and had other distinctions of breeding as well to recommend him to her mother, who was, she confessed, something of a snob. "Mama," she said, accenting the ultima, "thinks it is unnecessary for anyone to be badly born."

The Konditorei Luitpold was frequented by teachers from the Translators' Institute, and usually Ramona rejoiced in listening to them chattering and expostulating, in half a dozen European languages, for she prided herself on her gift of tongues. But today her heart was in Sorrento, and she paid no attention to them, not even to two vociferous young Russians at a table nearby. She disposed of the roué from Milan (Sue had read Catullus? Signor da Gama had a cottage at Sirmio not far from his reputed grave) and seemed to be on the point of disclosing her father's delinquencies when she was checked by a new mood, which made her lower her head, flush, and, through a long moment of silence, study the greasy hoops the rancid milk had made on the surface of her coffee.

Sue felt as if she had inadvertently stumbled upon a scene of deepest privacy, which, if she were not careful, she would violate, and, pretending that she had not observed the hiatus at all, she asked, conversationally, the names of Ramona's brothers besides Justin.

The two others were called Daniel and Robert, but it was not of them, or of her parents, or of Martha, that Ramona now wanted to speak but of herself, and haltingly she said that the "Minuet in G" had deranged her poise because it had made her think of the days of her childhood in New York, when she had been no bigger than her twin and they had danced the minuet together, Ramona taking the dandy's part. A friend of the family had predicted that though they were then almost identical, Ramona was going to be the prettier of the two. Now Sue was shocked, for she had thought that Ramona must always have been fat, and she was nearly moved to tears to know that the poor girl had been changed from a swan into an ugly duckling and that it was improbable, from the looks of her, that she would ever be changed back again. But Sue was so young and so badly equipped to console someone so beset that she could not utter a word, and she wished she could go home.

Ramona summoned the waiter and ordered her third piece of cake, saying nervously, after she had done so, "I'm sorry. When I get upset, I have to eat to calm myself. I'm awful! I ought to kill myself for eating so much." She began to devour the cake obsessively, and when she had finished it down to the last crumb and the last fragment of frosting, she said, with shimmering eyes, "Please let me tell you what it is that makes me the unhappiest girl in the world, and maybe you can help me." Did Sue have any idea what it was like to be ruled by food and half driven out of one's mind until one dreamed of it and had at last no other ambition but to eat incessantly with an appetite that grew and grew until one saw oneself, in nightmares, as nothing but an enormous mouth and a tongue, trembling lasciviously? Did she know the terror and the remorse that followed on the heels of it when one slyly sneaked the lion's share of buttered toast at tea? Had she ever desired the whole of a pudding meant for twelve and hated with all her heart the others at the dinner table? Sue could not hide her blushing face or put her fingers in her ears or close her eyes against the tortured countenance of that wretched butterball, who declared that she had often come within an ace of doing away with herself because she was so fat.

Leaning across the table, almost whispering, Ramona went on, "I didn't come to Heidelberg for its philologists—they don't know any more than I do. I have exiled myself. I would not any longer offend that long-suffering family of mine with the sight of me." It had been her aim to fast throughout this year, she continued, and return to them transformed, and she had hoped to be thinner by many pounds when she joined her brothers at Christmastime. But she had at once run into difficulties, because, since she was not altogether well (she did not specify her illness and Sue would not have asked its name for anything), she had to be under the supervision of a doctor. And the doctor in Heidelberg, like the doctor in Naples, would not take her seriously when she said her fatness was ruining her life; they had both gone so far as to say that she was *meant* to be like this and that it would be imprudent of her to diet. Who was bold enough to fly in the face of medical authority? Not she, certainly.

It appeared, did it not, to be a dilemma past solution, Ramona asked. And yet this afternoon she had begun to see a way out, if Sue would pledge herself to help. Sue did not reply at once, sensing an involvement, but then she thought of Ramona's brothers, whom she was going to please, and she said she would do what she could.

"You're not just saying that? You are my friend? You know, of course, that you'll be repaid a hundredfold." Ramona subjected Sue's sincerity to some minutes of investigation and then outlined her plan, which seemed very tame to Sue after all these preparations, for it consisted only of Ramona's defying Dr. Freudenburg and of Sue's becoming a sort of unofficial censor and confessor. Sue was to have lunch with her each day, at Ramona's expense, and was to remind her, by a nudge or a word now and again, not to eat more than was really necessary to keep alive. If at any time Sue suspected that she was eating between meals or late at night, she was to come out flatly with an accusation and so shame Ramona that it would never happen again. The weekends were particularly difficult, since there were no lectures to go to and it was tempting not to stir out of her room at all but to gorge throughout the day on delicacies out of tins and boxes that she had sent to herself from shops in Strasbourg and Berlin. And since, in addition to fasting, she needed exercise, she hoped that Sue would agree to go walking with her on Saturdays and Sundays, a routine that could be varied from time to time by a weekend trip to some neighboring town of interest.

When Sue protested mildly that Ramona had contradicted her earlier assertion that she would not dare dispute her doctor's word, Ramona grinned roguishly and said only, "Don't be nosy."

Ramona had found an old ladies' home, called the Gerstnerheim, which, being always in need of funds, welcomed paying guests at the midday meal, whom they fed for an unimaginably low price. Ramona did not patronize it out of miserliness, however, but because the food was nearly inedible. And it was here that the girls daily took their Spartan lunch. It was quite the worst that Sue had ever eaten anywhere, for it was cooked to pallor and flaccidity and then was seasoned with unheard-of condiments, which sometimes made her sick. The bread was sour and the soup was full of pasty clots; the potatoes were waterlogged and the old red cabbage was boiled until it was blue. The dessert was always a basin of molded farina with a sauce of gray jelly that had a gray taste. The aged ladies sat at one enormously long table, preserving an institutional silence until the farina was handed around, and, as if this were an alarm, all the withered lips began to move simultaneously and from them issued high squawks of protest against the dreary lot of being old and homeless and underfed. Sue could not help admiring Ramona, who ate her plate of eel and celeriac as if she really preferred it to tuna roasted with black olives and who talked all the while of things quite other than food—of Walther von der Vogelweide's eccentric syntax, of a new French novel that had come in the mail that morning, and of their trip to Switzerland.

Justin and Daniel and Robert were delighted that Sue was coming, Ramona said, and arrangements were being made in a voluminous correspondence through the air over the Alps. Sue had never been on skis in her life, but she did not allow this to deflate her high hopes. She thought only of evenings of lieder (needless to say, the accomplished Dunns sang splendidly) and hot spiced wine before a dancing fire, of late breakfasts in the white sun and brilliant conversation. And of what was coming afterward! The later holidays (Ramona called them *villeggiatura*), spent in Sorrento! The countesses' garden parties in Amalfi and the cruises on the Aegean Sea, the visits to Greece, the balls in the princely houses of Naples! Ramona could not decide which of her brothers Sue would elect to marry. Probably Robert, she thought, since he was the youngest and the most affectionate.

It was true that Sue did not quite believe all she was told, but she knew that the ways of the rich are strange, and while she did not allow her fantasies to invade the hours assigned to classes and study, she did not rebuff them when they came at moments of leisure. From time to time, she suddenly remembered that she was required to give something in return for Ramona's largess, and then she would say how proud she was of her friend's self-discipline or would ask her, like a frank and compassionate doctor, if she had strayed at all from her intention (she always had; she always immediately admitted it and Sue always put on a show of disappointment), and once in a while she said that Ramona was looking much thinner, although this was absolutely untrue. Sometimes they took the electric tram to Neckargemünd, where they split a bottle of sweet Greek wine. Occasionally they went to Mannheim, to the opera, but they never stayed for a full performance; Ramona said that later in the year Signor da Gama would invite them to his house in Milan and then they could go to the Scala every night. Once they went for a weekend to Rothenburg, where Ramona, in an uncontrollable holiday mood, ate twelve cherry tarts in a single day. She was tearful for a week afterward, and to show Sue how sorry she was, she ground out a cigarette on one of her downy wrists. This dreadful incident took place in the Luitpold and was witnessed by several patrons, who could not conceal their alarm. Sue thought to herself, Maybe she's cuckoo, and while she did not relinquish any of her daydreams of the festivities in Italy, she began to observe Ramona more closely.

She could feel the turmoil in her when they went past bakeshop windows full of cream puffs and cheesecake and petits fours. Ramona, furtively glancing at the goodies out of the corner of her eye, would begin a passionate and long-winded speech on the present-day use of Latin in Iceland. When, on a special occasion, they dined together at the Ritterhalle, she did not even look at the menu but lionheartedly ordered a single dropped egg and a cup of tea and resolutely kept her eyes away from Sue's boiled beef and fritters. When drinking cocktails in the American bar at the Europäischer Hof, she shook her head as the waiter passed a tray of canapés made of caviar, anchovy, lobster, foie gras, and Camembert, ranged fanwise around a little bowl of ivory almonds. But sometimes she did capitulate, with a piteous rationalization—that she had not eaten any breakfast or that she had barely touched her soup at the Gerstnerheim and that therefore there would be nothing wrong in her having two or perhaps three or four of these tiny little sandwiches. One time Sue saw her take several more than she had said she would and hide them under the rim of her plate.

As the date set for their departure for Switzerland drew nearer, Ramona grew unaccountable. Several times she failed to appear at lunch, and when Sue, in a friendly way, asked for an explanation, she snapped, "None of your business. What do you think you are? My nurse?" She was full of peevishness, complaining of the smell of senility in the Gerstnerheim, of students who sucked the shells of pistachio nuts in the library, of her landlady's young son, who she was sure rummaged through her bureau drawers when she was not at home. Once she and Sue had a fearful row when Sue, keeping up her end of the bargain, although she really did not care a pin, told her not to buy a bag of chestnuts from a vendor on a street corner. Ramona shouted, for all the world to hear, "You are sadly mistaken, Miss Ledbetter, if you think you know more than Dr. Augustus Freudenburg, of the Otto-Ludwigs Clinic!" And a little after that she acquired the notion that people were staring at her, and she carried an umbrella, rain or shine, to hide herself from them. But, oddest of all, when the skis and boots and poles that she had ordered for Sue arrived, and Sue thanked her for them, she said, "I can't think what use they'll be. Obviously there never is any snow in this ghastly, godforsaken place."

There was an awful afternoon when Ramona was convinced that the waiter at the Luitpold had impugned her German, and Sue found herself in the unhappy role of intermediary in a preposterous altercation so bitter that it stopped just short of a bodily engagement. When the girls left the café—at the insistence of the management—they were silent all the way to the cathedral, which was the place where they usually took leave of each other to go their separate ways home. They paused a moment there in the growing dark, and suddenly Ramona said, "Look at me!" Sue looked at her. "I say!" said Ramona. "In this light you look exactly like my sister. How astonishing! Turn a little to the left, there's a dear." And when Sue had turned as she directed, a whole minute—but it seemed an hour to Sue—passed before Ramona broke from her trance to cry, "How blind I've been! My brothers would be shocked to death if they should see you. It would kill them!"

She put out her hands, on which she wore white leather mittens, and held Sue's face between them and studied it, half closing her eyes and murmuring her amazement, her delight, her perplexity at her failure until now to see this marvelous resemblance. Once, as her brown eyes nimbly catechized the face before her, she took off her right mitten and ran her index finger down Sue's nose, as if she had even learned her sister's bones by heart, while Sue, unable to speak, could only think in panic, What does she mean *if* they should see me?

Ramona carried on as if she were moon-struck, making fresh discoveries until not only were Sue's and Martha's faces identical but so were their voices and their carriage and the shape of their hands and feet. She said, "You must come to my room and see a picture of Martha right now. It's desperately weird."

Fascinated, Sue nodded, and they moved on through the quiet street. Ramona paused to look at her each time they went under a street light, touched her hair, begged leave to take her arm, and called her Martha, Sister, Twin, and sometimes caught her breath in an abortive sob. They went past the lighted windows of the *Bierstuben*, where the shadows of young men loomed and waved, and then turned at the Kornmarkt and began to climb the steep, moss slick steps that led to the castle garden. As they went through the avenue of trees that lay between the casino and the castle, Ramona, peering at Sue through the spooky mist, said, "They would have been much quicker to see it than I," so Sue knew, miserably and for sure, that something had gone wrong with their plans to go to San Bernardino. And then Ramona laughed and broke away and took off her tam-o'-shanter, which she hurled toward the hedge of yew, where it rested tipsily.

"I could vomit," she said, standing absolutely still.

There was a long pause. Finally, Sue could no longer bear the suspense, and she asked Ramona if her brothers knew that she and Ramona were not coming.

"Of course they know. They've known for two weeks, but you're crazy if you think the reason we're not going is that you look like Martha. How beastly vain you are!" She was so angry and she trembled so with her rage that Sue did not dare say another word. "It was Freudenburg who said I couldn't go," she howled. "He has found out that I have lost ten pounds."

Sue had no conscious motive in asking her, idly and not really caring, where Dr. Freudenburg's office was; she had meant the guileless question to be no more than a show of noncommittal and courteous interest, and she was badly frightened when, in reply, Ramona turned on her and slapped her hard on either cheek, and then opened her mouth to emit one hideous, protracted scream. Sue started instinctively to run away, but Ramona seized and held her arms, and began to talk in a lunatic, fast monotone, threatening her with lawsuits and public exposure if she ever mentioned the name Freudenburg again *or* her brothers *or* her mother and father *or* Martha, that ghastly, puling, pampered hypochondriac who had totally wrecked her life.

Sue felt that the racket of her heart and her hot, prancing brain would drown out Ramona's voice, but it did nothing of the kind, and they stood there, rocking in their absurd attitude, while the fit continued. Sue was sure that the police and the townsfolk would come running at any moment and an alarm would be sounded and they would be arrested for disturbing the peace. But if anyone heard them, it was only the shades of the princes in the castle.

It was difficult for Sue to sort out the heroes and the villains in this dia-tribe. Sometimes it appeared that Ramona's brothers and her parents hated her, sometimes she thought they had been glad when Martha died; sometimes Dr. Freudenburg seemed to be the cause of everything. She had the impression that he was an alienist, and she wondered if now he would send his patient to an institution; at other times she thought the Doctor did not exist at all. She did not know whom to hate or whom to trust, for the characters in this *Walpurgisnacht* changed shape by the minute and not a one was left out—not Signor da Gama or the ballet girls in Naples or the old ladies at the Gerstnerheim or the prehistoric fig-ures of a sadistic nurse, a base German governess, and a nefarious boy cousin who had invited Ramona to misbehave when she was barely eight years old. Once she said that to escape Dr. Freudenburg she meant to order her father to take her cruising on the San Filippo; a minute later she said that that loathsome fool Justin had wrecked the boat on the coast of Yugoslavia. She would go home to the villa in Sorrento and be comforted by her brothers, who had always preferred her to everyone else in the world—except that they hadn't! They had always despised her. Freuden-burg would write to her father and he would come to fetch her back to that vulgar, parvenu house, and there, in spite of all her efforts to outwit them, they would make her eat and eat until she was the laughing stock of the entire world. What *were* they after? Did they want to indenture her to a sideshow?

She stopped, trailed off, turned loose Sue's arm, and stood crestfallen, like a child who realizes that no one is listening to his tantrum. Tears, ter-ribly silent, streamed down her round cheeks.

Then, "It isn't true, you know. They aren't like that, they're good and kind. The only thing that's true is that I eat all the time," and softly, to herself, she repeated, "All the time." In a mixture of self-hatred and abstracted bravado, she said that she had supplemented all her lunches at the Gerstnerheim and had nibbled constantly, alone in her room; that Dr. Freudenburg's recommendation had been just the opposite of what she had been saying all along.

Unconsolable, Ramona moved on along the path, and Sue followed, honoring her tragedy but struck dumb by it. On the way through the courtyard and down the street, Ramona told her, in a restrained and rational voice, that her father was coming the next day to take her back to Italy, since the experiment of her being here alone had not worked.

Her parents, at the counsel of Dr. Freudenburg, were prepared to take drastic measures, involving, if need be, a hospital, the very thought of which made her blood run cold. "Forgive me for that scene back there," she said. "You grow wild in loneliness like mine. It would have been lovely if it had all worked out the way I wanted and we had gone to Switzerland."

"Oh, that's all right," said Sue, whose heart was broken. "I don't know how to ski anyway."

"Really? What crust! I'd never have bought you all that gear if I had known." Ramona laughed lightly. They approached the garden gate of a tall yellow house, and she said, "This is where I live. Want to come in and have a glass of kirsch?"

Sue did not want the kirsch and she knew she should be on her way home if she were to get anything hot for supper, but she was curious to see the photograph of Martha, and since Ramona seemed herself again, she followed her down the path. Ramona had two little rooms, as clean and orderly as cells. In the one where she studied, there was no furniture except a long desk with deep drawers and a straight varnished chair and a listing bookcase. She had very few books, really, for one so learned—not more than fifty altogether—and every one of them was dull: grammars, dictionaries, readers, monographs reprinted from scholarly journals, and treatises on semantics, etymology, and phonetics. Her pens and pencils lay straight in a lacquered tray, and a pile of notebooks sat neatly at the right of the blotter, and at the left there was a book open to a homily in Anglo-Saxon which, evidently, she had been translating. As soon as they had taken off their coats, Ramona went into the bedroom and closed the door; from beyond it Sue could hear drawers being opened and quickly closed, metal clashing, and paper rustling, and she imagined that the bureaus were stocked with contraband—with sweets and sausages and cheese. For the last time, she thought of Daniel and Justin and Robert, of whom she was to be forever deprived because their sister could not curb her brutish appetite.

She wandered around the room and presently her eye fell on a photograph in a silver frame standing in a half-empty shelf of the bookcase. It could only be Martha. The dead girl did not look in the least like Sue but was certainly as pretty as she had been described, and as Sue looked at the pensive eyes and the thoughtful lips, she was visited by a fugitive feeling that this was really Ramona's face at which she looked and that it had been refined and made immaculate by an artful photographer who did not scruple to help his clients deceive themselves. For Martha wore a look of lovely wonder and remoteness, as if she were all disconnected spirit, and it was the same as a look that sometimes came to Ramona's eyes and lips just as she lifted her binoculars to contemplate the world through the belittling lenses.

Sue turned the photograph around, and on the back she read the penned inscription "Martha Ramona Dunn at sixteen, Sorrento." She looked at that ethereal face again, and this time had no doubt that it had once belonged to Ramona. No wonder the loss of it had left her heart-broken! She sighed to think of her friend's desperate fabrication. In a sense, she supposed the Martha side of Ramona Dunn *was* dead, dead and buried under layers and layers of fat. Just as she guiltily returned the picture to its place, the door to the bedroom opened and Ramona, grandly gesturing toward her dressing table, cried, "Come in! Come in! Enter the banquet hall!" She had emptied the drawers of all their forbidden fruits, and arrayed on the dressing table, in front of her bottles of cologne and medicine, were cheeses and tinned fish and pickles and pressed meat and cakes, candies, nuts, olives, sausages, buns, apples, raisins, figs, prunes, dates, and jars of pâté and glasses of jelly and little pots of caviar, as black as ink. "Don't stint!" she shouted, and she bounded forward and began to eat as if she had not had a meal in weeks.

"All evidence must be removed by morning! What a close shave! What if my father had come without telling me and had found it all!" Shamelessly, she ranged up and down the table, cropping and lowing like a cow in a pasture. There were droplets of sweat on her forehead and her hands were shaking, but nothing else about her showed that she had gone to pieces earlier or that she was deep, deeper by far than anyone else Sue had ever known.

Sucking a rind of citron, Ramona said, "You must realize that our friendship is over, but not through any fault of yours. When I went off and turned on you that way, it had nothing to do with you at all, for of course you don't look any more like Martha than the man in the moon."

"It's all right, Ramona," said Sue politely. She stayed close to the door, although the food looked very good. "I'll still be your friend."

"Oh, no, no, there would be nothing in it for you," Ramona said, and her eyes narrowed ever so slightly. "Thank you just the same. I am exceptionally ill." She spoke with pride, as if she were really saying "I am exceptionally talented" or "I am exceptionally attractive."

"I didn't know you were," said Sue. "I'm sorry."

"*I'm* not sorry. It is for yourself that you should be sorry. You have such a trivial little life, poor girl. It's not your fault. Most people do."

"I'd better go," said Sue.

"Go! Go!" cried Ramona, with a gesture of grand benediction. "I weep not."

Sue's hand was on the knob of the outer door, but she hesitated to leave a scene so inconclusive. Ramona watched her as she lingered; her mouth was so full that her cheeks were stretched out as if in mumps, and through the food and through a devilish, mad grin she said, "Of *course* you could never know the divine joy of being twins, provincial one! Do you know what he said the last night when my name was Martha? The night he came into that room where the anemones were? He pretended that he was looking for a sheet of music. Specifically for a sonata for the harpsichord by Wilhelm Friedrich Bach."

But Sue did not wait to hear what he, whoever he was, had said; she ran down the brown-smelling stairs and out into the cold street with the feeling that Ramona was still standing there before the food, as if she were serving herself at an altar, still talking, though there was no one to listen. She wondered if she ought to summon Dr. Freudenburg, and then decided that, in the end, it was none of her business. She caught a trolley that took her near her pension, and was just in time to get some hot soup and a plate of cold meats and salad before the kitchen closed. But when the food came, she found that she had no appetite at all. "What's the matter?" asked Herr Sachs, the fresh young waiter. "Are you afraid to get fat?" And he looked absolutely flabbergasted when, at this, she fled from the café without a word.

James Tiptree, Jr.
(*Alice Bradley Sheldon*)
(*1915–1987*)

lice Bradley Sheldon was one of the few American women writers who successfully used a male pseudonym; and surprisingly, she wrote in the 1960s and 1970s, rather than in the eighteenth or nineteenth centuries. Her father was a lawyer and explorer; her mother was a fiction and travel writer. They lived in Chicago but traveled widely and had taken Alice to the Belgian Congo on safari when she was only six, as well as India, China, and Japan. She attended a Swiss boarding school, attended Sarah Lawrence College, and made her debut in blue taffeta at a Chicago tea party in December 1934. But nine days after the party, desperate to escape from her fashionable life, she impulsively eloped with a Princeton student she had only known for a few days. The stormy marriage lasted until 1941; then Alice joined the Women's Army Auxiliary Corps, and worked in air intelligence. After the war she moved to Washington and worked for the CIA; in the 1950s and 60s she returned to college to complete her B.A., and went on to earn a Ph.D. in experimental psychology. Meanwhile she had married Huntington "Ting" Sheldon, a divorced intelligence analyst who also worked for the CIA.

Sheldon had long been interested in writing, and had published some short stories in *The New Yorker* in the 1940s. But she also found "in all the writings of women, a strange muffled quality, as if the living word, as it left the lips, had been hastily suppressed and another substituted." In 1967, when she set out to write science fiction, she decided to conceal her identity under a male signature, "James Tiptree, Jr." Conducting all her literary business through the mail, Sheldon absolutely convinced her editors, readers, and fellow science fiction writers that she was a man. Her military, scientific, and CIA experience, plus her long life of travel and adventure, seemed absolute proof of her manhood. But by the mid-1970s, Tiptree/Sheldon was outed by a suspicious reader. Although she continued to write as a woman, she never had the same success or critical acclaim. In 1987, in a long-planned suicide pact, she killed her husband, who had Alzheimer's disease, and took her own life.

The Last Flight of Doctor Ain (1969)

Doctor Ain was recognized on the Omaha–Chicago flight. A biologist colleague from Pasadena came out of the toilet and saw Ain in an aisle seat. Five years before, this man had been jealous of Ain's huge grants. Now he nodded coldly and was surprised at the intensity of Ain's response. He almost turned back to speak, but he felt too tired; like nearly everyone, he was fighting the flu.

The stewardess handing out coats after they landed remembered Ain too: a tall thin nondescript man with rusty hair. He held up the line staring at her; since he already had his raincoat with him she decided it was some kooky kind of pass and waved him on.

She saw Ain shamble off into the airport smog, apparently alone. Despite the big Civil Defense signs, O'Hare was late getting underground. No one noticed the woman.

The wounded, dying woman.

Ain was not identified en route to New York, but a 2:40 jet carried an "Ames" on the checklist, which was thought to be a misspelling of Ain. It was. The plane had circled for an hour while Ain watched the smoky seaboard monotonously tilt, straighten, and tilt again.

The woman was weaker now. She coughed, picking weakly at the scabs on her face half-hidden behind her long hair. Her hair, Ain saw, that great mane which had been so splendid, was drabbed and thinning now. He looked to seaward, willing himself to think of cold, clean breakers. On the horizon he saw a vast black rug: somewhere a tanker had opened its vents. The woman coughed again. Ain closed his eyes. Smog shrouded the plane.

He was picked up next while checking in for the BOAC flight to Glasgow. Kennedy Underground was a boiling stew of people, the air system unequal to the hot September afternoon. The check-in line swayed and sweated, staring dully at the newscast. SAVE THE LAST GREEN MANSIONS—a conservation group was protesting the defoliation and drainage of the Amazon basin. Several people recalled the beautifully colored shots of the new clean bomb. The line squeezed together to let a band of uniformed men go by. They were wearing buttons inscribed: WHO'S AFRAID?

That was when a woman noticed Ain. He was holding a newssheet, and she heard it rattling in his hand. Her family hadn't caught the flu, so she looked at him sharply. Sure enough, his forehead was sweaty. She herded her kids to the side away from Ain.

He was using *Instac* throat spray, she remembered. She didn't think much of *Instac*; her family used *Kleer*. While she was looking at him, Ain suddenly turned his head and stared into her face, with the spray still floating down. Such inconsiderateness! She turned her back. She didn't recall him talking to any woman, but she perked up her ears when the clerk read off Ain's destination. Moscow!

The clerk recalled that too, with disapproval. Ain checked in alone, he reported. No woman had been ticketed for Moscow, but it would have been easy enough to split up her tickets. (By that time they were sure she was with him.)

Ain's flight went via Iceland with an hour's delay at Keflavik. Ain walked over to the airport park, gratefully breathing the sea-filled air. Every few breaths he shuddered. Under the whine of bulldozers the sea could be heard running its huge paws up and down the keyboard of the land. The little park had a grove of yellowed birches and a flock of wheatears foraged by the path. Next month they would be in North Africa, Ain thought. Two thousand miles of tiny wing-beats. He threw them some crumbs from a packet in his pocket.

The woman seemed stronger here. She was panting in the sea wind, her eyes fixed on Ain. Above her the birches were as gold as those where he had first seen her, the day his life began . . . Squatting under a stump to watch a shrewmouse he had been, when he caught a falling ripple of green and recognized the shocking girl-flesh, creamy, pink-tipped—coming toward him among the golden bracken! Young Ain held his breath, his nose in the sweet moss and his heart going *crash—crash*. And then he was staring at the outrageous fall of that hair down her narrow back, watching it dance around her heart-shaped buttocks, while the shrewmouse ran over his paralyzed hand. The lake was utterly still, dusty silver under the misty sky, and she made no more than a muskrat's ripple to rock the floating golden leaves. The silence closed back, the trees like torches where the naked girl had walked the wild wood, reflected in Ain's shining eyes. For a time he believed he had seen an oread.

Ain was last on board for the Glasgow leg. The stewardess recalled dimly that he seemed restless. She could not identify the woman. There were a lot of women on board, and babies. Her passenger list had several errors.

At Glasgow airport a waiter remembered that a man like Ain had called for Scottish oatmeal, and eaten two bowls, although of course it wasn't really oatmeal. A young mother with a pram saw him tossing crumbs to the birds.

When he checked in at the BOAC desk, he was hailed by a Glasgow professor who was going to the same conference in Moscow. This man had been one of Ain's teachers. (It was now known that Ain had done his postgraduate work in Europe.) They chatted all the way across the North Sea.

"I wondered about that," the professor said later. "Why have you come round about? I asked him. He told me the direct flights were booked up." (This was found to be untrue: Ain had apparently avoided the Moscow jet hoping to escape attention.)

The professor spoke with relish of Ain's work.

"Brilliant? Oh, aye. And stubborn, too; very very stubborn. It was as though a concept—often the simplest relation, mind you—would stop him in his tracks, and fascinate him. He would hunt all round it instead of going on to the next thing as a more docile mind would. Truthfully, I wondered at first if he could be just a bit thick. But you recall who it was said that the capacity for wonder at matters of common acceptance occurs in the superior mind? And, of course, so it proved when he shook us all up over that enzyme conversion business. A pity your government took him away from his line, there. No, he said nothing of this, I say it to you, young man. We spoke in fact largely of my work. I was surprised to find he'd kept up. He asked me what my *sentiments* about it were, which surprised me again. Now, understand, I'd not seen the man for five years, but he seemed—well, perhaps just tired, as who is not? I'm sure he was glad to have a change; he jumped out for a legstretch wherever we came down. At Oslo, even Bonn. Oh, yes, he did feed the birds, but that was nothing new for Ain. His social life when I knew him? Radical causes? Young man, I've said what I've said because of who it was that introduced you, but I'll have you know it is an impertinence in you to think ill of Charles Ain, or that he could do a harmful deed. Good evening."

The professor said nothing of the woman in Ain's life.

Nor could he have, although Ain had been intimately with her in the university time. He had let no one see how he was obsessed with her, with the miracle, the wealth of her body, her inexhaustibility. They met at his every spare moment; sometimes in public pretending to be casual strangers under his friends' noses, pointing out a pleasing view to each other with grave formality. And later in their privacies—what doubled intensity of love! He reveled in her, possessed her, allowed her no secrets. His dreams were of her sweet springs and shadowed places and her white rounded glory in the moonlight, finding always more, always new dimensions of his joy.

The danger of her frailty was far off then in the rush of birdsong and the springing leverets of the meadow. On dark days she might cough a bit, but so did he . . . In those years he had had no thought to the urgent study of disease.

At the Moscow conference nearly everyone noticed Ain at some point or another, which was to be expected in view of his professional stature. It was a small, high-caliber meeting. Ain was late in; a day's reports were over, and his was to be on the third and last.

Many people spoke with Ain, and several sat with him at meals. No one was surprised that he spoke little; he was a retiring man except on a few memorable occasions of argument. He did strike some of his friends as a bit tired and jerky.

An Indian molecular engineer who saw him with the throat spray kidded him about bringing over Asian flu. A Swedish colleague recalled that Ain had been called away to the transatlantic phone at lunch; and when he returned Ain volunteered the information that something had turned up missing in his home lab. There was another joke, and Ain said cheerfully, "Oh yes, quite active."

At that point one of the Chicom biologists swung into his daily propaganda chores about bacteriological warfare and accused Ain of manufacturing biotic weapons. Ain took the wind out of his sails by saying: "You're perfectly right." By tacit consent, there was very little talk about military applications, industrial dusting, or subjects of that type. And nobody recalled seeing Ain with any woman other than old Madame Vialche, who could scarcely have subverted anyone from her wheelchair.

Ain's one speech was bad, even for him. He always had a poor public voice, but his ideas were usually expressed with the lucidity so typical of the first-rate mind. This time he seemed muddled, with little new to say. His audience excused this as the muffling effects of security. Ain then got into a tangled point about the course of evolution in which he seemed to be trying to show that something was very wrong indeed. When he wound up with a reference to Hudson's bellbird "singing for a later race," several listeners wondered if he could be drunk.

The big security break came right at the end, when he suddenly began to describe the methods he had used to mutate and redesign a leukemia virus. He explained the procedure with admirable clarity in four sentences and paused. Then gave a terse description of the effects of the mutated strain, which were maximal only in the higher primates. Recovery rate among the lower mammals and other orders was close to ninety percent. As to vectors, he went on, any warm-blooded animal served. In addition, the virus retained its viability in most environmental media and performed very well airborne. Contagion rate was extremely high. Almost offhand, Ain added that no test primate or accidentally exposed human had survived beyond the twenty-second day.

These words fell into a silence broken only by the running feet of the Egyptian delegate making for the door. Then a gilt chair went over as an American bolted after him.

Ain seemed unaware that his audience was in a state of unbelieving paralysis. It had all come so fast: a man who had been blowing his nose was staring pop-eyed around his handkerchief. Another who had been lighting a pipe grunted as his fingers singed. Two men chatting by the door missed his words entirely, and their laughter chimed into a dead silence in which echoed Ain's words: "—really no point in attempting."

Later they found he had been explaining that the virus utilized the body's own immunomechanisms, and so defense was by definition hopeless.

That was all. Ain looked around vaguely for questions and then started down the aisle. By the time he got to the door, people were swarming after him. He wheeled about and said rather crossly, "Yes, of course it is very wrong. I told you that. We are all wrong. Now it's over."

An hour later they found he had gone, having apparently reserved a Sinair flight to Karachi.

The security men caught up with him at Hong Kong. By then he seemed really very ill, and went with them peacefully. They started back to the States via Hawaii.

His captors were civilized types; they saw he was gentle and treated him accordingly. He had no weapons or drugs on him. They took him out handcuffed for a stroll at Osaka, let him feed his crumbs to the birds, and they listened with interest to his account of the migration routes of the common brown sandpiper. He was very hoarse. At that point, he was wanted only for the security thing. There was no question of a woman at all.

He dozed most of the way to the islands, but when they came in sight he pressed to the window and began to mutter. The security man behind him got the first inkling that there was a woman in it, and turned on his recorder.

". . . Blue, blue and green until you see the wounds. O my girl, O beautiful, you won't die. I won't let you die. I tell you girl, it's over. . . . Lustrous eyes, look at me, let me see you now alive! Great queen, my sweet body, my girl, have I saved you? . . . O terrible to know, and noble,

Chaos's child green-robed in blue and golden light . . . the thrown and spinning ball of life alone in space . . . Have I saved you?"

On the last leg, he was obviously feverish.

"She may have tricked me, you know," he said confidentially to the government man. "You have to be prepared for that, of course. I know her!" He chuckled confidentially. "She's no small thing. But wring your heart out—"

Coming over San Francisco he was merry. "Don't you know the otters will go back in there? I'm certain of it. That fill won't last; there'll be a bay there again."

They got him on a stretcher at Hamilton Air Base, and he went unconscious shortly after takeoff. Before he collapsed, he'd insisted on throwing the last of his birdseed on the field.

"Birds are, you know, warm-blooded," he confided to the agent who was handcuffing him to the stretcher. Then Ain smiled gently and lapsed into inertness. He stayed that way almost all the remaining ten days of his life. By then, of course, no one really cared. Both the government men had died quite early, after they finished analyzing the birdseed and throat spray. The woman at Kennedy had just started feeling sick.

The tape recorder they put by his bed functioned right on through, but if anybody had been around to replay it they would have found little but babbling. "Gaea Gloriatrix," he crooned, "Gaea girl, queen . . ." At times he was grandiose and tormented. "Our life, your death!" he yelled. "Our death would have been your death too, no need for that, no need."

At other times he was accusing. "What did you do about the dinosaurs?" he demanded. "Did they annoy you? How did you fix *them*? Cold. Queen, you're too cold! You came close to it this time, my girl," he raved. And then he wept and caressed the bedclothes and was maudlin.

Only at the end, lying in his filth and thirst, still chained where they had forgotten him, he was suddenly coherent. In the light clear voice of a lover planning a summer picnic he asked the recorder happily:

"Have you ever thought about bears? They have so much . . . funny they never came along further. By any chance were you saving them, girl?" And he chuckled in his ruined throat, and later died.

Shirley Jackson
(1916–1965)

ne of the most important American writers of the mid-twentieth century, Shirley Jackson had two very different literary personae. On one side, she wrote cheery domestic fiction for women's magazines, which were collected in popular books about being a wife and mother raising four children in rural Vermont. On the other side, she told terrifyingly perceptive stories in the genre of female gothic, which uses the female body, the haunted house, the rural community, and the mother-daughter relationship to explore the dark mysteries of the psyche. In the novels *Hangsamen* (1951), *The Bird's Nest* (1954), *The Haunting of Hill House* (1959), and her masterpiece, *We Have Always Lived in the Castle* (1962), Jackson dramatized female anger, aggression, sexuality, and creativity. Her most celebrated publication, however, was the unforgettable and subversive short story, "The Lottery," published in *The New Yorker* on June 26, 1948. At the editors' behest, Jackson had changed the date of the lottery in the story to June 27, to emphasize its contemporary shock and relevance. She received stacks of letters from defensive readers, who argued that the story's allegorical representation of evil, scapegoating, and communal violence lurking in daily American life after the war could not be true; and other readers who wanted to know where they could go to watch the next lottery.

The Lottery (1948)

The morning of June 27th was clear and sunny, with the fresh warmth of a full-summer day; the flowers were blossoming profusely and the grass was richly green. The people of the village began to gather in the square, between the post office and the bank, around ten o'clock; in some towns there were so many people that the lottery took two days and had to be started on June 26th, but in this village, where there were only about three hundred people, the whole lottery took less than two hours, so it could begin at ten o'clock in the morning and still be through in time to allow the villagers to get home for noon dinner.

The children assembled first, of course. School was recently over for the summer, and the feeling of liberty sat uneasily on most of them; they tended to gather together quietly for a while before they broke into boisterous play, and their talk was still of the classroom and the teacher, of books and reprimands. Bobby Martin had already stuffed his pockets full of stones, and the other boys soon followed his example, selecting the smoothest and roundest stones; Bobby and Harry Jones and Dickie Delacroix—the villagers pronounced this name "Dellacroy"—eventually made a great pile of stones in one corner of the square and guarded it against the raids of the other boys. The girls stood aside, talking among themselves, looking over their shoulders at the boys, and the very small children rolled in the dust or clung to the hands of their older brothers or sisters.

Soon the men began to gather, surveying their own children, speaking of planting and rain, tractors and taxes. They stood together, away from the pile of stones in the corner, and their jokes were quiet and they smiled rather than laughed. The women, wearing faded house dresses and sweaters, came shortly after their menfolk. They greeted one another and exchanged bits of gossip as they went to join their husbands. Soon the women, standing by their husbands, began to call to their children, and the children came reluctantly, having to be called four or five times. Bobby Martin ducked under his mother's grasping hand and ran, laughing, back to the pile of stones. His father spoke up sharply, and Bobby came quickly and took his place between his father and his oldest brother.

The lottery was conducted—as were the square dances, the teen-age club, the Halloween program—by Mr. Summers, who had time and energy to devote to civic activities. He was a round-faced, jovial man and he ran the coal business, and people were sorry for him, because he had no children and his wife was a scold. When he arrived in the square, carrying the black wooden box, there was a murmur of conversation among the villagers, and he waved and called, "Little late today, folks." The postmaster, Mr. Graves, followed him, carrying a three-legged stool, and the stool was put in the center of the square and Mr. Summers set the black box down on it. The villagers kept their distance, leaving a space between themselves and the stool, and when Mr. Summers said, "Some of you fellows want to give me a hand?" there was a hesitation before two men, Mr. Martin and his oldest son, Baxter, came forward to hold the box steady on the stool while Mr. Summers stirred up the papers inside it.

The original paraphernalia for the lottery had been lost long ago, and the black box now resting on the stool had been put into use even before Old Man Warner, the oldest man in town, was born. Mr. Summers spoke frequently to the villagers about making a new box, but no one liked to upset even as much tradition as was represented by the black box. There was a story that the present box had been made with some pieces of the box that had preceded it, the one that had been constructed when the first people settled down to make a village here. Every year, after the lottery, Mr. Summers began talking again about a new box, but every year the subject was allowed to fade off without anything's being done. The black box grew shabbier each year; by now it was no longer completely black but splintered badly along one side to show the original wood color, and in some places faded or stained.

Mr. Martin and his oldest son, Baxter, held the black box securely on the stool until Mr. Summers had stirred the papers thoroughly with his hand. Because so much of the ritual had been forgotten or discarded, Mr. Summers had been successful in having slips of paper substituted for the chips of wood that had been used for generations. Chips of wood, Mr. Summers had argued, had been all very well when the village was tiny, but now that the population was more than three hundred and likely to keep on growing, it was necessary to use something that would fit more easily into the black box. The night before the lottery, Mr. Summers and Mr. Graves made up the slips of paper and put them in the box, and it was then taken to the safe of Mr. Summers's coal company and locked up until Mr. Summers was ready to take it to the square next morning. The rest of the year, the box was put away, sometimes one place, sometimes another; it had spent one year in Mr. Graves's barn and another year underfoot in the post office, and sometimes it was set on a shelf in the Martin grocery and left there.

There was a great deal of fussing to be done before Mr. Summers declared the lottery open. There were the lists to make up—of heads of families, heads of households in each family, members of each household in each family. There was the proper swearing-in of Mr. Summers by the postmaster, as the official of the lottery; at one time, some people remembered, there had been a recital of some sort, performed by the official of the lottery, a perfunctory, tuneless chant that had been rattled off duly each year; some people believed that the official of the lottery used to stand just so when he said or sang it, others believed that he was supposed to walk among the people, but years and years ago this part of the ritual had been allowed to lapse. There had been, also, a ritual salute, which the official of the lottery had had to use in addressing each person who came up to draw from the box, but this also had changed with time, until now it was felt necessary only for the official to speak to each person approaching. Mr. Summers was very good at all this; in his clean white shirt and blue jeans, with one hand resting carelessly on the black box, he seemed very proper and important as he talked interminably to Mr. Graves and the Martins.

Just as Mr. Summers finally left off talking and turned to the assembled villagers, Mrs. Hutchinson came hurriedly along the path to the square, her sweater thrown over her shoulders, and slid into place in the back of the crowd. "Clean forgot what day it was," she said to Mrs. Delacroix, who stood next to her, and they both laughed softly. "Thought my old man was out back stacking wood," Mrs. Hutchinson went on, "and then I looked out the window and the kids was gone, and then I remembered it was the twenty-seventh and came a-running." She dried her hands on her apron, and Mrs. Delacroix said, "You're in time, though. They're still talking away up there."

Mrs. Hutchinson craned her neck to see through the crowd and found her husband and children standing near the front. She tapped Mrs. Delacroix on the arm as a farewell and began to make her way through the crowd. The people separated good-humoredly to let her through; two or three people said, in voices just loud enough to be heard across the crowd, "Here comes your Missus, Hutchinson," and "Bill, she made it after all." Mrs. Hutchinson reached her husband, and Mr. Summers, who had been waiting, said cheerfully, "Thought we were going to have to get on without you, Tessie." Mrs. Hutchinson said, grinning, "Wouldn't have me leave m'dishes in the sink, now, would you, Joe?," and soft laughter ran through the crowd as the people stirred back into position after Mrs. Hutchinson's arrival.

"Well, now," Mr. Summers said soberly, "guess we better get started, get this over with, so's we can go back to work. Anybody ain't here?"

"Dunbar," several people said. "Dunbar, Dunbar."

Mr. Summers consulted his list. "Clyde Dunbar," he said. "That's right. He's broke his leg, hasn't he? Who's drawing for him?"

"Me, I guess," a woman said, and Mr. Summers turned to look at her. "Wife draws for her husband," Mr. Summers said. "Don't you have a grown boy to do it for you, Janey?" Although Mr. Summers and everyone else in the village knew the answer perfectly well, it was the business of the official of the lottery to ask such questions formally. Mr. Summers waited with an expression of polite interest while Mrs. Dunbar answered.

"Horace's not but sixteen yet," Mrs. Dunbar said regretfully. "Guess I gotta fill in for the old man this year."

"Right," Mr. Summers said. He made a note on the list he was holding. Then he asked, "Watson boy drawing this year?"

A tall boy in the crowd raised his hand. "Here," he said. "I'm drawing for m'mother and me." He blinked his eyes nervously and ducked his head as several voices in the crowd said things like "Good fellow, Jack," and "Glad to see your mother's got a man to do it."

"Well," Mr. Summers said, "guess that's everyone. Old Man Warner make it?"

"Here," a voice said, and Mr. Summers nodded.

A sudden hush fell on the crowd as Mr. Summers cleared his throat and looked at the list. "All ready?" he called. "Now, I'll read the names—heads of families first—and the men come up and take a paper out of the box. Keep the paper folded in your hand without looking at it until everyone has had a turn. Everything clear?"

The people had done it so many times that they only half listened to the directions; most of them were quiet, wetting their lips, not looking around. Then Mr. Summers raised one hand high and said, "Adams." A man disengaged himself from the crowd and came forward. "Hi, Steve," Mr. Summers said, and Mr. Adams said, "Hi, Joe." They grinned at one another humorlessly and nervously. Then Mr. Adams reached into the black box and took out a folded paper. He held it firmly by one corner as he turned and went hastily back to his place in the crowd where he stood a little apart from his family, not looking down at his hand.

"Allen," Mr. Summers said. "Anderson. . . . Bentham."

"Seems like there's no time at all between lotteries any more," Mrs. Delacroix said to Mrs. Graves in the back row. "Seems like we got through with the last one only last week."

"Time sure goes fast," Mrs. Graves said.

"Clark. . . . Delacroix."

"There goes my old man," Mrs. Delacroix said. She held her breath while her husband went forward.

"Dunbar," Mr. Summers said, and Mrs. Dunbar went steadily to the box while one of the women said, "Go on, Janey," and another said, "There she goes."

"We're next," Mrs. Graves said. She watched while Mr. Graves came around from the side of the box, greeted Mr. Summers gravely and selected a slip of paper from the box. By now, all through the crowd there were men holding the small folded papers in their large hands, turning them over and over nervously. Mrs. Dunbar and her two sons stood together, Mrs. Dunbar holding the slip of paper.

"Harburt. . . . Hutchinson."

"Get up there, Bill," Mrs. Hutchinson said, and the people near her laughed.

"Jones."

"They do say," Mr. Adams said to Old Man Warner, who stood next to him, "that over in the north village they're talking of giving up the lottery."

Old Man Warner snorted. "Pack of crazy fools," he said. "Listening to the young folks, nothing's good enough for *them*. Next thing you know, they'll be wanting to go back to living in caves, nobody work any more, live *that* way for a while. Used to be a saying about 'Lottery in June, corn be heavy soon.' First thing you know, we'd all be eating stewed chickweed and acorns. There's *always* been a lottery," he added petulantly. "Bad enough to see young Joe Summers up there joking with everybody."

"Some places have already quit lotteries," Mrs. Adams said.

"Nothing but trouble in *that*," Old Man Warner said stoutly. "Pack of young fools."

"Martin." And Bobby Martin watched his father go forward. "Overdyke. . . . Percy."

"I wish they'd hurry," Mrs. Dunbar said to her older son. "I wish they'd hurry."

"They're almost through," her son said.

"You get ready to run tell Dad," Mrs. Dunbar said.

Mr. Summers called his own name and then stepped forward precisely and selected a slip from the box. Then he called, "Warner."

"Seventy-seventh year I been in the lottery," Old Man Warner said as he went through the crowd. "Seventy-seventh time."

"Watson." The tall boy came awkwardly through the crowd. Someone said, "Don't be nervous, Jack," and Mr. Summers said, "Take your time, son."

"Zanini."

After that, there was a long pause, a breathless pause, until Mr. Summers, holding his slip of paper in the air, said, "All right, fellows." For a minute, no one moved, and then all the slips of paper were opened. Suddenly, all the women began to speak at once, saying, "Who is it?," "Who's got it?," "Is it the Dunbars?," "Is it the Watsons?" Then the voices began to say, "It's Hutchinson. It's Bill," "Bill Hutchinson's got it."

"Go tell your father," Mrs. Dunbar said to her older son.

People began to look around to see the Hutchinsons. Bill Hutchinson was standing quiet, staring down at the paper in his hand. Suddenly, Tessie Hutchinson shouted to Mr. Summers. "You didn't give him time enough to take any paper he wanted. I saw you. It wasn't fair!"

"Be a good sport, Tessie." Mrs. Delacroix called, and Mrs. Graves said, "All of us took the same chance."

"Shut up, Tessie," Bill Hutchinson said.

"Well, everyone," Mr. Summers said, "that was done pretty fast, and now we've got to be hurrying a little more to get done in time." He consulted his next list. "Bill," he said, "you draw for the Hutchinson family. You got any other households in the Hutchinsons?"

"There's Don and Eva," Mrs. Hutchinson yelled. "Make *them* take their chance!"

"Daughters draw with their husbands' families, Tessie," Mr. Summers said gently. "You know that as well as anyone else."

"It wasn't *fair*," Tessie said.

"I guess not, Joe," Bill Hutchinson said regretfully. "My daughter draws with her husband's family, that's only fair. And I've got no other family except the kids."

"Then, as far as drawing for families is concerned, it's you," Mr. Summers said in explanation, "and as far as drawing for households is concerned, that's you, too. Right?"

"Right," Bill Hutchinson said.

"How many kids, Bill?" Mr. Summers asked formally.

"Three," Bill Hutchinson said. "There's Bill, Jr., and Nancy, and little Dave. And Tessie and me."

"All right, then," Mr. Summers said. "Harry, you got their tickets back?"

Mr. Graves nodded and held up the slips of paper. "Put them in the box, then," Mr. Summers directed. "Take Bill's and put it in."

"I think we ought to start over," Mrs. Hutchinson said, as quietly as she could. "I tell you it wasn't *fair*. You didn't give him time enough to choose. *Every*body saw that."

Mr. Graves had selected the five slips and put them in the box, and he dropped all the papers but those onto the ground, where the breeze caught them and lifted them off.

"Listen, everybody," Mrs. Hutchinson was saying to the people around her.

"Ready, Bill?" Mr. Summers asked, and Bill Hutchinson, with one quick glance around at his wife and children, nodded.

"Remember," Mr. Summers said, "take the slips and keep them folded until each person has taken one. Harry, you help little Dave." Mr. Graves took the hand of the little boy, who came willingly with him up to the box. "Take a paper out of the box, Davy," Mr. Summers said. Davy put his hand into the box and laughed. "Take just *one* paper," Mr. Summers said. "Harry, you hold it for him." Mr. Graves took the child's hand and removed the folded paper from the tight fist and held it while little Dave stood next to him and looked up at him wonderingly.

"Nancy next," Mr. Summers said. Nancy was twelve, and her school friends breathed heavily as she went forward, switching her skirt, and took a slip daintily from the box. "Bill, Jr.," Mr. Summers said, and Billy, his face red and his feet overlarge, nearly knocked the box over as he got a paper out. "Tessie," Mr. Summers said. She hesitated for a minute, looking around defiantly, and then set her lips and went up to the box. She snatched a paper out and held it behind her.

"Bill," Mr. Summers said, and Bill Hutchinson reached into the box and felt around, bringing his hand out at last with the slip of paper in it.

The crowd was quiet. A girl whispered, "I hope it's not Nancy," and the sound of the whisper reached the edges of the crowd.

"It's not the way it used to be," Old Man Warner said clearly. "People ain't the way they used to be."

"All right," Mr. Summers said. "Open the papers. Harry, you open little Dave's."

Mr. Graves opened the slip of paper and there was a general sigh through the crowd as he held it up and everyone could see that it was blank. Nancy and Bill, Jr., opened theirs at the same time, and both beamed and laughed, turning around to the crowd and holding their slips of paper above their heads.

"Tessie," Mr. Summers said. There was a pause, and then Mr. Summers looked at Bill Hutchinson, and Bill unfolded his paper and showed it. It was blank.

"It's Tessie," Mr. Summers said, and his voice was hushed. "Show us her paper, Bill."

Bill Hutchinson went over to his wife and forced the slip of paper out of her hand. It had a black spot on it, the black spot Mr. Summers had made the night before with the heavy pencil in the coal-company office. Bill Hutchinson held it up, and there was a stir in the crowd.

"All right, folks," Mr. Summers said. "Let's finish quickly."

Although the villagers had forgotten the ritual and lost the original black box, they still remembered to use stones. The pile of stones the boys had made earlier was ready; there were stones on the ground with the blowing scraps of paper that had come out of the box. Mrs. Delacroix selected a stone so large she had to pick it up with both hands and turned to Mrs. Dunbar. "Come on," she said. "Hurry up."

Mrs. Dunbar had small stones in both hands, and she said, gasping for breath, "I can't run at all. You'll have to go ahead and I'll catch up with you."

The children had stones already, and someone gave little Davy Hutchinson a few pebbles.

Tessie Hutchinson was in the center of a cleared space by now, and she held her hands out desperately as the villagers moved in on her. "It isn't fair," she said. A stone hit her on the side of the head.

Old Man Warner was saying, "Come on, come on, everyone." Steve Adams was in the front of the crowd of villagers, with Mrs. Graves beside him.

"It isn't fair, it isn't right," Mrs. Hutchinson screamed, and then they were upon her.

Gwendolyn Brooks
(1917–2000)

wendolyn Brooks was born in Topeka, Kansas, but grew up in a poor black neighborhood on the South Side of Chicago. In the 1940s she attended a poetry workshop and discovered her vocation. From her first collection, *A Street in Bronzeville* (1945), Brooks drew on her experience of everyday life as an African American and as a woman. Her poetry collection *Annie Allen* (1949) won the Pulitzer Prize, making her the first black woman so honored. Later works like *In the Mecca* (1968), *Riot* (1970), and *Primer for Blacks* (1981) showed her increasing interest in the civil rights movement. Unlike many twentieth-century poets, Brooks often used traditional devices of rhyme and fixed stanza form.

Maud Martha (1953), her only novel, followed the story of a poor black Chicago housewife, in a form like that of Virginia Woolf's *Mrs. Dalloway*, but in a voice suffused with anger against racism, war, and the daily small tragedies of women's lives. Told in thirty-four short sections, some almost vignettes, the novel takes Maud Martha Brown Phillips from the age of seven to her forties. Maud Martha has no great ambitions for herself; she "did not want to be a 'star.' To create—a role, a poem, picture, music, a rapture in stone: great. But not for her." In her autobiography, Brooks acknowledged that "much in the story was taken out of my own life, and twisted, highlighted, or dulled, dressed up or dressed down." In 1955 she published a more feminist story called "The Rise of Maud Martha," which she intended to be the first chapter of a sequel to the novel. Like Kate Chopin's "Story of an Hour," it reveals the heroine's feelings of liberation when her husband dies.

The Rise of Maud Martha (1955)

The pastor stood in the small areaway, his coat on, and looked after the ladies carrying flowers and at the speeding casket (whose lid had been closed as quietly as possible, to avoid jarring the family), his hands together, closing and unclosing behind him. It was impossible to tell just what he was thinking. It could have been about the look of the deceased, or the quality of the casket, or death itself, or strawberries.

Maud Martha, the children, Mama—and *his* mama—sat in the first car, the longest and shiny-blackest of the long black cars. They waited. Eventually, the assistant at the funeral parlor came to the end of his lists, all the doors were shut as if forever, the motors made their little noise, and the funeral procession began.

Maud Martha had not seen him in the casket. No one had. For the casket was sealed beforehand. Banked upon it were flowers, fresh and barely fresh, and in front of it were wreaths, big and little and few.

What the fire had done to the little man Paul. Exhaled at him. Teased him, touched him, pleaded with him, put its swelling arms around him. It ate what it desired. Of him and 30-odd. It was strange to think of—that streetcar (the new green model with the sealed windows—the "Green Hornet") after the collision with the gas truck (INFLAMMABLE—in big white letters) standing there, patiently, while the invader ate at the flesh of 30-odd. It almost seemed as tho the streetcar might have done something, something to help itself and its little faint charges.

The women in the street. Would she ever forget the women? To think that women could turn into ripped-open wounds, and into sores that cankered before the eyes. Pretty women, begrimed, with stretching slits for mouths. Ugly women, grown almost beautiful in their grief. Herself. Herself, with nothing to feel but surprise.

This was what gripped her still. That, at that moment, thru the sick smoke, the boiling air above it, the strict stench, when the policeman lifted up the grimmest piece of cloth she had even seen and exposed her husband—black with a more "dreadful" blackness than that which he had ever known and despised—hairless, eroded chin outthrust, and with never one more dream of sophistication remaining, all she could feel was a big surprise that this was happening to her.

A high-school girl with glossy braids behind her ears and pretty clothes to sweeten the half-charm of her face, and books in one arm and a boyfriend in the other, was standing just inside the curb, searching her eyes. The girl had been positively fascinated. Enjoying herself. Seeing Life. At school the next day: There was this hag. You should've seen her bending over what was left of her man. Maud Martha had thought, as she turned her gaze from the sight beneath her: Why should I envy her, that little girl. Her time is coming. There isn't a woman alive can hope to escape a something bad.

"He was sure a good boy," suddenly choked Paul's mother, "that he was, and whoever says no is a liar." She looked at Maud Martha, who looked straight ahead at the mole on the neck of the driver.

"Always a-laughin', and a-jokin', and a-makin' you feel good, that's what he was always a-doin'," went on Mrs. Phillips, "and when I think of him on that streetcar, screamin', and tryin' to dodge the fire, and burnin' up alive, I could just—oh, I could just—"

Here, what Mrs. Phillips could just do, she did, and with such energy that the man with the mole jumped, and for a moment the car slowed down. Mrs. Phillips reached over and, wiping her wet face with one hand, patted Maud Martha's knee with the other. "Nobody can say you didn't do pretty good by my boy," she declared. "You didn't fix him hot meals all the time. They should be hot enough so that the steam rises up thru his nostrils. That's what makes for a healthy man. And I always thought it wouldn't have hurt you to get a little job, to help out, and left them little ones with Paulette, wouldn't have hurt her to miss a year or two out of school—"

"Paulette being ten," interrupted Maud Martha, "the Board of Education mightn't have liked it."

"But take her all in all, Mrs. Brown," went on Mrs. Phillips, directing her eye-swords at Maud Martha's mother, "she did about as well as most of these young gals." Belva Brown said nothing. She did part her lips. But she snapped them shut again.

"Now, Maudie," said Mrs. Phillips, "now, Maudie, you know I want to see those children. They're mine just as much as they're your mother's. I want you to bring them to see their grandmother every few days. Do you understand?"

"I understand," said Maud Martha.

But she was listening only a little, because there was something else she was about to begin to understand. It was fuzzy, she could not yet see it properly, or properly finger it. But a hint nudged her, promised her that very soon a reality more horrible than that fact of her first surprise would establish itself, would command her recognition.

The hint got larger, louder, more palpable. By the time they stood beside the grave, she had it by the hand and it talked to her. It was willing to tell her what was cold and rude.

It told her this: When you love a man, he becomes more than a body. His physical limits expand, and his outlines recede, vanish. Suddenly he has no bowels, his eliminatory functions seem unimportant or beautiful: He is rich and sweet and right. He is part of the world, the atmosphere, the blue sky and the blue water. If he happens to be dead, he is still what you love; and your big pity is for yourself, not for him.

It told her this—that for her now, none of this was true.

At what point it had all stopped being true she did not know. Perhaps when vicissitudes were no longer adventures but only vicissitudes. Perhaps when he had made her feel like a pumpkin for the least little minute too long. She could not locate that little minute. She had been feeling like a pumpkin for a very long time.

Her pity was all for him. He, who had so loved physical beauty, in the end a fire-used, repulsive thing.

But for herself (she did not think of groceries, she did not think, as yet, a certain, old, child-helplessness of the eyes)—why, she could actually feel herself rising. She felt higher and more like a citizen of—what?

A road was again clean before her. She held the destinies of herself and of her children in her individual power—all was up to her.

Down and down they sent her Paul. The relatives, for some time worried, looked on her with approval at last. For she was crying.

Crying because she could not stop herself from thinking about the after-funeral white cake that waited in her mother's home.

The Bean Eaters (1960)

They eat beans mostly, this old yellow pair.
Dinner is a casual affair.
Plain chipware on a plain and creaking wood,
Tin flatware.

Two who are Mostly Good.
Two who have lived their day,
But keep on putting on their clothes
And putting things away.

And remembering . . .
Remembering, with twinklings and twinges,
As they lean over the beans in their rented back room that
    is full of beads and receipts and dolls and cloths,
        tobacco crumbs, vases and fringes.

We Real Cool (1960)

THE POOL PLAYERS.
SEVEN AT THE GOLDEN SHOVEL.

We real cool. We
Left school. We

Lurk late. We
Strike straight. We

Sing sin. We
Thin gin. We

Jazz June. We
Die soon.

Hisaye Yamamoto
(1921–)

orn in California to Japanese parents, Hisaye Yamamoto was imprisoned along with her family in an American internment camp in Arizona during World War II. She started writing as a reporter and columnist for the camp's newspaper and, after her 1945 release, moved to Los Angeles and wrote for a small African-American weekly newspaper. In 1949 "Seventeen Syllables" appeared in the *Partisan Review*. As one of the first Asian Americans to gain national literary recognition, Yamamoto wrote numerous stories about the cultural and personal challenges of Japanese and Japanese-American women during the next few years, but soon refocused on her new marriage and growing family.

Seventeen Syllables (1949)

The first Rosie knew that her mother had taken to writing poems was one evening when she finished one and read it aloud for her daughter's approval. It was about cats, and Rosie pretended to understand it thoroughly and appreciate it no end, partly because she hesitated to disillusion her mother about the quantity and quality of Japanese she had learned in all the years now that she had been going to Japanese school every Saturday (and Wednesday, too, in the summer). Even so, her mother must have been skeptical about the depth of Rosie's understanding, because she explained afterwards about the kind of poem she was trying to write.

See, Rosie, she said, it was a *haiku*, a poem in which she must pack all her meaning into seventeen syllables only, which were divided into three lines of five, seven, and five syllables. In the one she had just read, she had tried to capture the charm of a kitten, as well as comment on the superstition that owning a cat of three colors meant good luck.

"Yes, yes, I understand. How utterly lovely," Rosie said, and her mother, either satisfied or seeing through the deception and resigned, went back to composing.

The truth was that Rosie was lazy; English lay ready on the tongue but

Japanese had to be searched for and examined, and even then put forth
tentatively (probably to meet with laughter). It was so much easier to say
yes, yes, even when one meant no, no. Besides, this was what was in her
mind to say: I was looking through one of your magazines from Japan
last night, Mother, and towards the back I found some *haiku* in English
that delighted me. There was one that made me giggle off and on until I
fell asleep—

> *It is morning, and lo!*
> *I lie awake, comme il faut,*
> *sighing for some dough.*

Now, how to reach her mother, how to communicate the melancholy
song? Rosie knew formal Japanese by fits and starts, her mother had even
less English, no French. It was much more possible to say yes, yes.

It developed that her mother was writing the *haiku* for a daily newspaper,
the *Mainichi Shimbun*, that was published in San Francisco. Los Angeles,
to be sure, was closer to the farming community in which the Hayashi
family lived and several Japanese vernaculars were printed there, but
Rosie's parents said they preferred the tone of the northern paper. Once
a week, the *Mainichi* would have a section devoted to *haiku*, and her
mother became an extravagant contributor, taking for herself the blos-
soming pen name, Ume Hanazono.

So Rosie and her father lived for awhile with two women, her mother
and Ume Hanazono. Her mother (Tome Hayashi by name) kept house,
cooked, washed, and, along with her husband and the Carrascos, the
Mexican family hired for the harvest, did her ample share of picking
tomatoes out in the sweltering fields and boxing them in tidy strata in the
cool packing shed. Ume Hanazono, who came to life after the dinner
dishes were done, was an earnest, muttering stranger who often neg-
lected speaking when spoken to and stayed busy at the parlor table as late
as midnight scribbling with pencil on scratch paper or carefully copying
characters on good paper with her fat, pale green Parker.

The new interest had some repercussions on the household routine.
Before, Rosie had been accustomed to her parents and herself taking
their hot baths early and going to bed almost immediately afterwards,
unless her parents challenged each other to a game of flower cards or
unless company dropped in. Now if her father wanted to play cards, he
had to resort to solitaire (at which he always cheated fearlessly), and if a

group of friends came over, it was bound to contain someone who was also writing *haiku*, and the small assemblage would be split in two, her father entertaining the non-literary members and her mother comparing ecstatic notes with the visiting poet.

If they went out, it was more of the same thing. But Ume Hanazono's life span, even for a poet's, was very brief—perhaps three months at most.

One night they went over to see the Hayano family in the neighboring town to the west, an adventure both painful and attractive to Rosie. It was attractive because there were four Hayano girls, all lovely and each one named after a season of the year (Haru, Natsu, Aki, Fuyu), painful because something had been wrong with Mrs. Hayano ever since the birth of her first child. Rosie would sometimes watch Mrs. Hayano, reputed to have been the belle of her native village, making her way about a room, stooped, slowly shuffling, violently trembling (*always* trembling), and she would be reminded that this woman, in this same condition, had carried and given issue to three babies. She would look wonderingly at Mr. Hayano, handsome, tall, and strong, and she would look at her four pretty friends. But it was not a matter she could come to any decision about.

On this visit, however, Mrs. Hayano sat all evening in the rocker, as motionless and unobtrusive as it was possible for her to be, and Rosie found the greater part of the evening practically anaesthetic. Too, Rosie spent most of it in the girls' room, because Haru, the garrulous one, said almost as soon as the bows and other greetings were over, "Oh, you must see my new coat!"

It was a pale plaid of grey, sand, and blue, with an enormous collar, and Rosie, seeing nothing special in it, said, "Gee, how nice."

"Nice?" said Haru, indignantly. "Is that all you can say about it? It's gorgeous! And so cheap, too. Only seventeen-ninety-eight, because it was a sale. The saleslady said it was twenty-five dollars regular."

"Gee," said Rosie. Natsu, who never said much and when she said anything said it shyly, fingered the coat covetously and Haru pulled it away.

"Mine," she said, putting it on. She minced in the aisle between the two large beds and smiled happily. "Let's see how your mother likes it."

She broke into the front room and the adult conversation and went to stand in front of Rosie's mother, while the rest watched from the door. Rosie's mother was properly envious. "May I inherit it when you're through with it?"

Haru, pleased, giggled and said yes, she could, but Natsu reminded gravely from the door, "You promised me, Haru."

Everyone laughed but Natsu, who shamefacedly retreated into the bedroom. Haru came in laughing, taking off the coat. "We were only kidding, Natsu," she said. "Here, you try it on now."

After Natsu buttoned herself into the coat, inspected herself solemnly in the bureau mirror, and reluctantly shed it, Rosie, Aki, and Fuyu got their turns, and Fuyu, who was eight, drowned in it while her sisters and Rosie doubled up in amusement. They all went into the front room later, because Haru's mother quaveringly called to her to fix the tea and rice cakes and open a can of sliced peaches for everybody. Rosie noticed that her mother and Mr. Hayano were talking together at the little table—they were discussing a *haiku* that Mr. Hayano was planning to send to the *Mainichi*, while her father was sitting at one end of the sofa looking through a copy of *Life*, the new picture magazine. Occasionally, her father would comment on a photograph, holding it toward Mrs. Hayano and speaking to her as he always did—loudly, as though he thought someone such as she must surely be at least a trifle deaf also.

The five girls had their refreshments at the kitchen table, and it was while Rosie was showing the sisters her trick of swallowing peach slices without chewing (she chased each slippery crescent down with a swig of tea) that her father brought his empty teacup and untouched saucer to the sink and said, "Come on, Rosie, we're going home now."

"Already?" asked Rosie.

"Work tomorrow," he said.

He sounded irritated, and Rosie, puzzled, gulped one last yellow slice and stood up to go, while the sisters began protesting, as was their wont.

"We have to get up at five-thirty," he told them, going into the front room quickly, so that they did not have their usual chance to hang onto his hands and plead for an extension of time.

Rosie, following, saw that her mother and Mr. Hayano were sipping tea and still talking together, while Mrs. Hayano concentrated, quivering, on raising the handleless Japanese cup to her lips with both her hands and lowering it back to her lap. Her father, saying nothing, went out the door, onto the bright porch, and down the steps. Her mother looked up and asked, "Where is he going?"

"Where is he going?" Rosie said. "He said we were going home now."

"Going home?" Her mother looked with embarrassment at Mr. Hayano and his absorbed wife and then forced a smile. "He must be tired," she said.

Haru was not giving up yet. "May Rosie stay overnight?" she asked, and Natsu, Aki, and Fuyu came to reinforce their sister's plea by helping her make a circle around Rosie's mother. Rosie, for once having no desire to stay, was relieved when her mother, apologizing to the perturbed Mr. and Mrs. Hayano for her father's abruptness at the same time, managed to shake her head no at the quartet, kindly but adamant, so that they broke their circle and let her go.

Rosie's father looked ahead into the windshield as the two joined him. "I'm sorry," her mother said. "You must be tired." Her father, stepping on the starter, said nothing. "You know how I get when it's *haiku*," she continued, "I forget what time it is." He only grunted.

As they rode homeward silently, Rosie, sitting between, felt a rush of hate for both—for her mother for begging, for her father for denying her mother. I wish this old Ford would crash, right now, she thought, then immediately, no, no, I wish my father would laugh, but it was too late: already the vision had passed through her mind of the green pick-up crumpled in the dark against one of the mighty eucalyptus trees they were just riding past, of the three contorted, bleeding bodies, one of them hers.

Rosie ran between two patches of tomatoes, her heart working more rambunctiously than she had ever known it to. How lucky it was that Aunt Taka and Uncle Gimpachi had come tonight, though, how very lucky. Otherwise she might not have really kept her half-promise to meet Jesus Carrasco. Jesus was going to be a senior in September at the same school she went to, and his parents were the ones helping with the tomatoes this year. She and Jesus, who hardly remembered seeing each other at Cleveland High where there were so many other people and two whole grades between them, had become great friends this summer—he always had a joke for her when he periodically drove the loaded pick-up up from the fields to the shed where she was usually sorting while her mother and father did the packing, and they laughed a great deal together over infinitesimal repartee during the afternoon break for chilled watermelon or ice cream in the shade of the shed.

What she enjoyed most was racing him to see which could finish picking a double row first. He, who could work faster, would tease her by slowing down until she thought she would surely pass him this time, then speeding up furiously to leave her several sprawling vines behind. Once he had made her screech hideously by crossing over, while her back was turned, to place atop the tomatoes in her green-stained bucket a truly monstrous, pale green worm (it had looked more like an infant snake). And it was when they had finished a contest this morning, after she had pantingly pointed a green finger at the immature tomatoes evident in the lugs at the end of his row and he had returned the accusation (with justice), that he had startlingly brought up the matter of their possibly meeting outside the range of both their parents' dubious eyes.

"What for?" she had asked.

"I've got a secret I want to tell you," he said.

"Tell me now," she demanded.

"It won't be ready till tonight," he said.

She laughed. "Tell me tomorrow then."

"It'll be gone tomorrow," he threatened.

"Well, for seven hakes, what is it?" she had asked, more than twice, and when he had suggested that the packing shed would be an appropriate place to find out, she had cautiously answered maybe. She had not been certain she was going to keep the appointment until the arrival of mother's sister and her husband. Their coming seemed a sort of signal of permission, of grace, and she had definitely made up her mind to lie and leave as she was bowing them welcome.

So as soon as everyone appeared settled back for the evening, she announced loudly that she was going to the privy outside, "I'm going to the *benjo!*" and slipped out the door. And now that she was actually on her way, her heart pumped in such an undisciplined way that she could hear it with her ears. It's because I'm running, she told herself, slowing to a walk. The shed was up ahead, one more patch away, in the middle of the fields. Its bulk, looming in the dimness, took on a sinisterness that was funny when Rosie reminded herself that it was only a wooden frame with a canvas roof and three canvas walls that made a slapping noise on breezy days.

Jesus was sitting on the narrow plank that was the sorting platform and she went around to the other side and jumped backwards to seat herself on the rim of a packing stand. "Well, tell me," she said without greeting, thinking her voice sounded reassuringly familiar.

"I saw you coming out the door," Jesus said. "I heard you running part of the way, too."

"Uh-huh," Rosie said. "Now tell me the secret."

"I was afraid you wouldn't come," he said.

Rosie delved around on the chicken-wire bottom of the stall for number two tomatoes, ripe, which she was sitting beside, and came up with a left-over that felt edible. She bit into it and began sucking out the pulp and seeds. "I'm here," she pointed out.

"Rosie, are you sorry you came?"

"Sorry? What for?" she said. "You said you were going to tell me something."

"I will, I will," Jesus said, but his voice contained disappointment, and Rosie fleetingly felt the older of the two, realizing a brand-new power which vanished without category under her recognition.

"I have to go back in a minute," she said. "My aunt and uncle are here from Wintersburg. I told them I was going to the privy."

Jesus laughed. "You funny thing," he said. "You slay me!"

"Just because you have a bathroom *inside*," Rosie said. "Come on, tell me."

Chuckling, Jesus came around to lean on the stand facing her. They still could not see each other very clearly, but Rosie noticed that Jesus became very sober again as he took the hollow tomato from her hand and dropped it back into the stall. When he took hold of her empty hand, she could find no words to protest; her vocabulary had become distressingly constricted and she thought desperately that all that remained intact now was yes and no and oh, and even these few sounds would not easily come out. Thus, kissed by Jesus, Rosie fell for the first time entirely victim to a helplessness delectable beyond speech. But the terrible, beautiful sensation lasted no more than a second, and the reality of Jesus' lips and tongue and teeth and hands made her pull away with such strength that she nearly tumbled.

Rosie stopped running as she approached the lights from the windows of home. How long since she had left? She could not guess, but gasping yet, she went to the privy in back and locked herself in. Her own breathing deafened her in the dark, close space, and she sat and waited until she could hear at last the nightly calling of the frogs and crickets. Even then, all she could think to say was oh, my, and the pressure of Jesus' face against her face would not leave.

No one had missed her in the parlor, however, and Rosie walked in and through quickly, announcing that she was next going to take a bath. "Your father's in the bathhouse," her mother said, and Rosie, in her room, recalled that she had not seen him when she entered. There had been only Aunt Taka and Uncle Gimpachi with her mother at the table, drinking tea. She got her robe and straw sandals and crossed the parlor again to go outside. Her mother was telling them about the *haiku* competition in the *Mainichi* and the poem she had entered.

Rosie met her father coming out of the bathhouse. "Are you through, Father?" she asked. "I was going to ask you to scrub my back."

"Scrub your own back," he said shortly, going toward the main house.

"What have I done now?" she yelled after him. She suddenly felt like doing a lot of yelling. But he did not answer, and she went into the bathhouse. Turning on the dangling light, she removed her denims and T-shirt and threw them in the big carton for dirty clothes standing next to the washing machine. Her other things she took with her into the bath compartment to wash after her bath. After she had scooped a basin of hot water from the square wooden tub, she sat on the grey cement of the floor and soaped herself at exaggerated leisure, singing "Red Sails in the Sunset" at the top of her voice and using da-da-da where she suspected her words. Then, standing up, still singing, for she was possessed by the notion that any attempt now to analyze would result in spoilage and she believed that the larger her volume the less she would be able to hear herself think, she obtained more hot water and poured it on until she was free of lather. Only then did she allow herself to step into the steaming vat, one leg first, then the remainder of her body inch by inch until the water no longer stung and she could move around at will.

She took a long time soaking, afterwards remembering to go around outside to stoke the embers of the tin-lined fireplace beneath the tub and to throw on a few more sticks so that the water might keep its heat for her mother, and when she finally returned to the parlor, she found her mother still talking *haiku* with her aunt and uncle, the three of them on another round of tea. Her father was nowhere in sight.

At Japanese school the next day (Wednesday, it was), Rosie was grave and giddy by turns. Preoccupied at her desk in the row for students on Book Eight, she made up for it at recess by performing wild mimicry for the benefit of her friend Chizuko. She held her nose and whined a witticism or two in what she considered was the manner of Fred Allen; she assumed intoxication and a British accent to go over the climax of the Rudy Vallee recording of the pub conversation about William Ewart Gladstone; she was the child Shirley Temple piping, "On the Good Ship Lollipop"; she was the gentleman soprano of the Four Inkspots trilling, "If I Didn't Care." And she felt reasonably satisfied when Chizuko wept and gasped, "Oh, Rosie, you ought to be in the movies!"

Her father came after her at noon, bringing her sandwiches of minced ham and two nectarines to eat while she rode, so that she could pitch right into the sorting when they got home. The lugs were piling up, he said, and the ripe tomatoes in them would probably have to be taken to the cannery tomorrow if they were not ready for the produce haulers tonight. "This heat's not doing them any good. And we've got no time for a break today."

It *was* hot, probably the hottest day of the year, and Rosie's blouse stuck damply to her back even under the protection of the canvas. But she worked as efficiently as a flawless machine and kept the stalls heaped, with one part of her mind listening in to the parental murmuring about the heat and the tomatoes and with another part planning the exact words she would say to Jesus when he drove up with the first load of the afternoon. But when at last she saw that the pick-up was coming, her hands went berserk and the tomatoes started falling in the wrong stalls, and her father said, "Hey, hey! Rosie, watch what you're doing!"

"Well, I have to go to the *benjo*," she said, hiding panic.

"Go in the weeds over there," he said, only half-joking.

"Oh, Father!" she protested.

"Oh, go on home," her mother said. "We'll make out for awhile."

In the privy Rosie peered through a knothole toward the fields, watching as much as she could of Jesus. Happily she thought she saw him look in the direction of the house from time to time before he finished unloading and went back toward the patch where his mother and father worked. As she was heading for the shed, a very presentable black car purred up the dirt driveway to the house and its driver motioned to her. Was this the Hayashi home, he wanted to know. She nodded. Was she a Hayashi? Yes, she said, thinking that he was a good-looking man. He got out of the car with a huge, flat package and she saw that he warmly wore a business suit. "I have something here for your mother then," he said, in a more elegant Japanese than she was used to.

She told him where her mother was and he came along with her, patting his face with an immaculate white handkerchief and saying something about the coolness of San Francisco. To her surprised mother and father, he bowed and introduced himself as, among other things, the *haiku* editor of the *Mainichi Shimbun*, saying that since he had been coming as far as Los Angeles anyway, he had decided to bring her the first prize she had won in the recent contest.

"First prize?" her mother echoed, believing and not believing, pleased and overwhelmed. Handed the package with a bow, she bobbed her head up and down numerous times to express her utter gratitude.

"It is nothing much," he added, "but I hope it will serve as a token of our great appreciation for your contributions and our great admiration of your considerable talent."

"I am not worthy," she said, falling easily into his style. "It is I who should make some sign of my humble thanks for being permitted to contribute."

"No, no, to the contrary," he said, bowing again.

But Rosie's mother insisted, and then saying that she knew she was being unorthodox, she asked if she might open the package because her curiosity was so great. Certainly she might. In fact, he would like her reaction to it, for personally, it was one of his favorite *Hiroshiges*.

Rosie thought it was a pleasant picture, which looked to have been sketched with delicate quickness. There were pink clouds, containing some graceful calligraphy, and a sea that was a pale blue except at the edges, containing four sampans with indications of people in them. Pines edged the water and on the far-off beach there was a cluster of thatched huts towered over by pine-dotted mountains of grey and blue. The frame was scalloped and gilt.

After Rosie's mother pronounced it without peer and somewhat prodded her father into nodding agreement, she said Mr. Kuroda must at least have a cup of tea after coming all this way, and although Mr. Kuroda did not want to impose, he soon agreed that a cup of tea would be refreshing and went along with her to the house, carrying the picture for her.

"Ha, your mother's crazy!" Rosie's father said, and Rosie laughed uneasily as she resumed judgment on the tomatoes. She had emptied six lugs when he broke into an imaginary conversation with Jesus to tell her to go and remind her mother of the tomatoes, and she went slowly.

Mr. Kuroda was in his shirtsleeves expounding some *haiku* theory as he munched a rice cake, and her mother was rapt. Abashed in the great man's presence, Rosie stood next to her mother's chair until her mother looked up inquiringly, and then she started to whisper the message, but her mother pushed her gently away and reproached, "You are not being very polite to our guest."

"Father says the tomatoes . . ." Rosie said aloud, smiling foolishly.

"Tell him I shall only be a minute," her mother said, speaking the language of Mr. Kuroda.

When Rosie carried the reply to her father, he did not seem to hear and she said again, "Mother says she'll be back in a minute."

"All right, all right," he nodded, and they worked again in silence. But suddenly, her father uttered an incredible noise, exactly like the cork of a bottle popping, and the next Rosie knew, he was stalking angrily toward the house, almost running in fact, and she chased after him crying, "Father! Father! What are you going to do?"

He stopped long enough to order her back to the shed. "Never mind!" he shouted. "Get on with the sorting!"

And from the place in the fields where she stood, frightened and vacillating, Rosie saw her father enter the house. Soon Mr. Kuroda came out alone, putting on his coat. Mr. Kuroda got into his car and backed out down the driveway onto the highway. Next her father emerged, also alone, something in his arms (it was the picture, she realized), and, going over to the bathhouse woodpile, he threw the picture on the ground and picked up the axe. Smashing the picture, glass and all (she heard the explosion faintly), he reached over for the kerosene that was used to encourage the bath fire and poured it over the wreckage. I am dreaming, Rosie said to herself, I am dreaming, but her father, having made sure that his act of cremation was irrevocable, was even then returning to the fields.

Rosie ran past him and toward the house. What had become of her mother? She burst into the parlor and found her mother at the back window watching the dying fire. They watched together until there remained only a feeble smoke under the blazing sun. Her mother was very calm.

"Do you know why I married your father?" she said without turning.

"No," said Rosie. It was the most frightening question she had ever been called upon to answer. Don't tell me now, she wanted to say, tell me tomorrow, tell me next week, don't tell me today. But she knew she would be told now, that the telling would combine with the other violence of the hot afternoon to level her life, her world to the very ground.

It was like a story out of the magazines illustrated in sepia, which she had consumed so greedily for a period until the information had somehow reached her that those wretchedly unhappy autobiographies, offered to her as the testimonials of living men and women, were largely inventions: Her mother, at nineteen, had come to America and married her father as an alternative to suicide.

At eighteen she had been in love with the first son of one of the well-to-do families in her village. The two had met whenever and wherever they could, secretly, because it would not have done for his family to see him favor her—her father had no money; he was a drunkard and a gambler besides. She had learned she was with child; an excellent match had already been arranged for her lover. Despised by her family, she had given premature birth to a stillborn son, who would be seventeen now. Her family did not turn her out, but she could no longer project herself in any direction without refreshing in them the memory of her indiscretion. She wrote to Aunt Taka, her favorite sister in America, threatening to kill herself if Aunt Taka would not send for her. Aunt Taka hastily arranged a marriage with a young man of whom she knew, but lately arrived from Japan, a young man of simple mind, it was said, but of kindly heart. The young man was never told why his unseen betrothed was so eager to hasten the day of meeting.

The story was told perfectly, with neither groping for words nor untoward passion. It was as though her mother had memorized it by heart, reciting it to herself so many times over that its nagging vileness had long since gone.

"I had a brother then?" Rosie asked, for this was what seemed to matter now; she would think about the other later, she assured herself, pushing back the illumination which threatened all that darkness that had hitherto been merely mysterious or even glamorous. "A half-brother?"

"Yes."

"I would have liked a brother," she said.

Suddenly, her mother knelt on the floor and took her by the wrists. "Rosie," she said urgently, "Promise me you will never marry!" Shocked more by the request than the revelation, Rosie stared at her mother's face. Jesus, Jesus, she called silently, not certain whether she was invoking the help of the son of the Carrascos or of God, until there returned sweetly the memory of Jesus' hand, how it had touched her and where. Still her mother waited for an answer, holding her wrists so tightly that her hands were going numb. She tried to pull free. Promise, her mother whispered fiercely, promise. Yes, yes, I promise, Rosie said. But for an instant she turned away, and her mother, hearing the familiar glib agreement, released her. Oh, you, you, you, her eyes and twisted mouth said, you fool. Rosie, covering her face, began at last to cry, and the embrace and consoling hand came much later than she expected.

Flannery O'Connor
(1925–1964)

orn in Savannah, Georgia, to middle-class Catholic parents, Southern Gothic writer Flannery O'Connor had scarcely begun her career before she was diagnosed in 1950 with lupus, the blood disease that had killed her father less than a decade earlier. Determined to continue writing, she returned to live with her mother in Milledgeville, Georgia, where she completed two novels and thirty-two short stories before her death in 1964. O'Connor's biographers disagree about whether to present her as a vivacious woman with a great capacity for friendship and experience whose life was tragically abbreviated by a terrible disease, or as a writer who was singular, isolated, dedicated to her art, and rejecting of ordinary life. Although she studied at the prestigious Iowa Writers' Workshop and spent many months at Yaddo, the writers' colony in New York, O'Connor was always resistant to the demands of sexuality and adulthood: "When I was twelve," she recalled, "I made up my mind absolutely that I would not get any older." By the time she arrived at Iowa, she "knew she was a great writer," one of her friends reported, and she had arranged her life to give writing absolute priority, alongside an increasingly arcane and philosophical Catholic faith.

In 1955, O'Connor wrote to a friend, "If I were to live long enough and develop as an artist to the proper extent, I would like to write a comic novel about a woman—and what is more comic and terrible than the angular intellectual proud woman approaching God inch by inch with gritted teeth?" "Revelation," published in the *Sewanee Review* in 1964, can be seen as a savagely comic story about an intellectual girl and a racist Southern woman—the dyad that O'Connor formed with her devoted but conventional mother—that ends with a spiritual and compassionate, although brutally ironic, view of the universe.

Revelation (1964)

The doctor's waiting room, which was very small, was almost full when the Turpins entered and Mrs. Turpin, who was very large, made it look

even smaller by her presence. She stood looming at the head of the mag-
azine table set in the center of it, a living demonstration that the room
was inadequate and ridiculous. Her little bright black eyes took in all the
patients as she sized up the seating situation. There was one vacant chair
and a place on the sofa occupied by a blond child in a dirty blue romper
who should have been told to move over and make room for the lady. He
was five or six, but Mrs. Turpin saw at once that no one was going to tell
him to move over. He was slumped down in the seat, his arms idle at his
sides and his eyes idle in his head; his nose ran unchecked.

Mrs. Turpin put a firm hand on Claud's shoulder and said in a voice
that included anyone who wanted to listen, "Claud, you sit in that chair
there," and gave him a push down into the vacant one. Claud was florid
and bald and sturdy, somewhat shorter than Mrs. Turpin, but he sat
down as if he were accustomed to doing what she told him to.

Mrs. Turpin remained standing. The only man in the room besides
Claud was a lean stringy old fellow with a rusty hand spread out on each
knee, whose eyes were closed as if he were asleep or dead or pretending
to be so as not to get up and offer her his seat. Her gaze settled agreeably
on a well-dressed gray-haired lady whose eyes met hers and whose
expression said: if that child belonged to me, he would have some man-
ners and move over—there's plenty of room there for you and him too.

Claud looked up with a sigh and made as if to rise.

"Sit down," Mrs. Turpin said. "You know you're not supposed to stand
on that leg. He has an ulcer on his leg," she explained.

Claud lifted his foot onto the magazine table and rolled his trouser leg
up to reveal a purple swelling on a plump marble-white calf.

"My!" the pleasant lady said. "How did you do that?"

"A cow kicked him," Mrs. Turpin said.

"Goodness!" said the lady.

Claud rolled his trouser leg down.

"Maybe the little boy would move over," the lady suggested, but the
child did not stir.

"Somebody will be leaving in a minute," Mrs. Turpin said. She could
not understand why a doctor—with as much money as they made charg-
ing five dollars a day to just stick their head in the hospital door and look
at you—couldn't afford a decent-sized waiting room. This one was
hardly bigger than a garage. The table was cluttered with limp-looking
magazines and at one end of it there was a big green glass ash tray full of
cigarette butts and cotton wads with little blood spots on them. If she
had had anything to do with the running of the place, that would have

been emptied every so often. There were no chairs against the wall at the head of the room. It had a rectangular-shaped panel in it that permitted a view of the office where the nurse came and went and the secretary listened to the radio. A plastic fern in a gold pot sat in the opening and trailed its fronds down almost to the floor. The radio was softly playing gospel music.

Just then the inner door opened and a nurse with the highest stack of yellow hair Mrs. Turpin had ever seen put her face in the crack and called for the next patient. The woman sitting beside Claud grasped the two arms of her chair and hoisted herself up; she pulled her dress free from her legs and lumbered through the door where the nurse had disappeared.

Mrs. Turpin eased into the vacant chair, which held her tight as a corset. "I wish I could reduce," she said, and rolled her eyes and gave a comic sigh.

"Oh, *you* aren't fat," the stylish lady said.

"Ooooo I am too," Mrs. Turpin said. "Claud he eats all he wants to and never weighs over one hundred and seventy-five pounds, but me I just look at something good to eat and I gain some weight," and her stomach and shoulders shook with laughter. "You can eat all you want to, can't you, Claud?" she asked, turning to him.

Claud only grinned.

"Well, as long as you have such a good disposition," the stylish lady said, "I don't think it makes a bit of difference what size you are. You just can't beat a good disposition."

Next to her was a fat girl of eighteen or nineteen, scowling into a thick blue book which Mrs. Turpin saw was entitled *Human Development*. The girl raised her head and directed her scowl at Mrs. Turpin as if she did not like her looks. She appeared annoyed that anyone should speak while she tried to read. The poor girl's face was blue with acne and Mrs. Turpin thought how pitiful it was to have a face like that at that age. She gave the girl a friendly smile but the girl only scowled the harder. Mrs. Turpin herself was fat but she had always had good skin, and, though she was forty-seven years old, there was not a wrinkle in her face except around her eyes from laughing too much.

Next to the ugly girl was the child, still in exactly the same position, and next to him was a thin leathery old woman in a cotton print dress. She and Claud had three sacks of chicken feed in their pump house that was in the same print. She had seen from the first that the child belonged with the old woman. She could tell by the way they sat—kind of vacant and white-trashy, as if they would sit there until Doomsday if nobody called and told them to get up. And at right angles but next to the well-dressed pleasant lady was a lank-faced woman who was certainly the child's mother. She had on a yellow sweat shirt and wine-colored slacks, both gritty-looking, and the rims of her lips were stained with snuff. Her dirty yellow hair was tied behind with a little piece of red paper ribbon. Worse than niggers any day, Mrs. Turpin thought.

The gospel hymn playing was, "When I looked up and He looked down," and Mrs. Turpin, who knew it, supplied the last line mentally, "And wona these days I know I'll we-ear a crown."

Without appearing to, Mrs. Turpin always noticed people's feet. The well-dressed lady had on red and gray suede shoes to match her dress. Mrs. Turpin had on her good black patent leather pumps. The ugly girl had on Girl Scout shoes and heavy socks. The old woman had on tennis shoes and the white-trashy mother had on what appeared to be bedroom slippers, black straw with gold braid threaded through them—exactly what you would have expected her to have on.

Sometimes at night when she couldn't go to sleep, Mrs. Turpin would occupy herself with the question of who she would have chosen to be if she couldn't have been herself. If Jesus had said to her before he made her, "There's only two places available for you. You can either be a nigger or white-trash," what would she have said? "Please, Jesus, please," she would have said, "just let me wait until there's another place available," and he would have said, "No, you have to go right now and I have only those two places so make up your mind." She would have wiggled and squirmed and begged and pleaded but it would have been no use and finally she would have said, "All right, make me a nigger then—but that don't mean a trashy one." And he would have made her a neat clean respectable Negro woman, herself but black.

Next to the child's mother was a red-headed youngish woman, reading one of the magazines and working a piece of chewing gum, hell for leather, as Claud would say. Mrs. Turpin could not see the woman's feet. She was not white-trash, just common. Sometimes Mrs. Turpin occupied herself at night naming the classes of people. On the bottom of the heap were most colored people, not the kind she would have been if she had been one, but most of them; then next to them—not above, just away from—were the white-trash; then above them were the home-owners, and above them the home-and-land owners, to which she and Claud belonged. Above she and Claud were people with a lot of money and much bigger houses and much more land. But here the complexity of it would begin to bear in on her, for some of the people with a lot of money were common and ought to be below she and Claud and some of the people who had good blood had lost their money and had to rent and then there were colored people who owned their homes and land as well. There was a colored dentist in town who had two red Lincolns and a swimming pool and a farm with registered white-face cattle on it. Usually by the time she had fallen asleep all the classes of people were moiling and roiling around in her head, and she would dream they were all crammed in together in a box car, being ridden off to be put in a gas oven.

"That's a beautiful clock," she said and nodded to her right. It was a big wall clock, the face encased in a brass sunburst.

"Yes, it's very pretty," the stylish lady said agreeably. "And right on the dot too," she added, glancing at her watch.

The ugly girl beside her cast an eye upward at the clock, smirked, then looked directly at Mrs. Turpin and smirked again. Then she returned her eyes to her book. She was obviously the lady's daughter because, although they didn't look anything alike as to disposition, they both had the same shape of face and the same blue eyes. On the lady they sparkled pleasantly but in the girl's seared face they appeared alternately to smolder and to blaze.

What if Jesus had said, "All right, you can be white-trash or a nigger or ugly"!

Mrs. Turpin felt an awful pity for the girl, though she thought it was one thing to be ugly and another to act ugly.

The woman with the snuff-stained lips turned around in her chair and looked up at the clock. Then she turned back and appeared to look a little to the side of Mrs. Turpin. There was a cast in one of her eyes. "You want to know wher you can get you one of themther clocks?" she asked in a loud voice.

"No, I already have a nice clock," Mrs. Turpin said. Once somebody like her got a leg in the conversation, she would be all over it.

"You can get you one with green stamps," the woman said. "That's most likely wher he got hisn. Save you up enough, you can get you most anythang. I got me some joo'ry."

Ought to have got you a wash rag and some soap, Mrs. Turpin thought.

"I get contour sheets with mine," the pleasant lady said.

The daughter slammed her book shut. She looked straight in front of her, directly through Mrs. Turpin and on through the yellow curtain and the plate glass window which made the wall behind her. The girl's eyes seemed lit all of a sudden with a peculiar light, an unnatural light like night road signs give. Mrs. Turpin turned her head to see if there was anything going on outside that she should see, but she could not see anything. Figures passing cast only a pale shadow through the curtain. There was no reason the girl should single her out for her ugly looks.

"Miss Finley," the nurse said, cracking the door. The gum-chewing woman got up and passed in front of her and Claud and went into the office. She had on red high-heeled shoes.

Directly across the table, the ugly girl's eyes were fixed on Mrs. Turpin as if she had some very special reason for disliking her.

"This is wonderful weather, isn't it?" the girl's mother said.

"It's good weather for cotton if you can get the niggers to pick it," Mrs. Turpin said, "but niggers don't want to pick cotton any more. You can't get the white folks to pick it and now you can't get the niggers— because they got to be right up there with the white folks."

"They gonna *try* anyways," the white-trash woman said, leaning forward.

"Do you have one of those cotton-picking machines?" the pleasant lady asked.

"No," Mrs. Turpin said, "they leave half the cotton in the field. We don't have much cotton anyway. If you want to make it farming now, you have to have a little of everything. We got a couple of acres of cotton and a few hogs and chickens and just enough white-face that Claud can look after them himself."

"One thang I don't want," the white-trash woman said, wiping her mouth with the back of her hand. "Hogs. Nasty stinking things, a-gruntin and a-rootin all over the place."

Mrs. Turpin gave her the merest edge of her attention. "Our hogs are not dirty and they don't stink," she said. "They're cleaner than some children I've seen. Their feet never touch the ground. We have a pig-parlor— that's where you raise them on concrete," she explained to the pleasant lady, "and Claud scoots them down with the hose every afternoon and washes off the floor." Cleaner by far than that child right there, she thought. Poor nasty little thing. He had not moved except to put the thumb of his dirty hand into his mouth.

The woman turned her face away from Mrs. Turpin. "I know I wouldn't scoot down no hog with no hose," she said to the wall.

You wouldn't have no hog to scoot down, Mrs. Turpin said to herself.

"A-gruntin and a-rootin and a-groanin," the woman muttered.

"We got a little of everything," Mrs. Turpin said to the pleasant lady. "It's no use in having more than you can handle yourself with help like it is. We found enough niggers to pick our cotton this year but Claud he has to go after them and take them home again in the evening. They can't walk that half a mile. No they can't. I tell you," she said and laughed merrily, "I sure am tired of buttering up niggers, but you got to love em if you want em to work for you. When they come in the morning, I run out and I say, 'Hi yawl this morning?' and when Claud drives them off to the field I just wave to beat the band and they just wave back." And she waved her hand rapidly to illustrate.

"Like you read out of the same book," the lady said, showing she understood perfectly.

"Child, yes," Mrs. Turpin said. "And when they come in from the field, I run out with a bucket of icewater. That's the way it's going to be from now on," she said. "You may as well face it."

"One thang I know," the white-trash woman said. "Two thangs I ain't going to do: love no niggers or scoot down no hog with no hose." And she let out a bark of contempt.

The look that Mrs. Turpin and the pleasant lady exchanged indicated they both understood that you had to *have* certain things before you could *know* certain things. But every time Mrs. Turpin exchanged a look with the lady, she was aware that the ugly girl's peculiar eyes were still on her, and she had trouble bringing her attention back to the conversation.

"When you got something," she said, "you got to look after it." And when you ain't got a thing but breath and britches, she added to herself, you can afford to come to town every morning and just sit on the Court House coping and spit.

A grotesque revolving shadow passed across the curtain behind her and was thrown palely on the opposite wall. Then a bicycle clattered down against the outside of the building. The door opened and a colored boy glided in with a tray from the drugstore. It had two large red and white paper cups on it with tops on them. He was a tall, very black boy in discolored white pants and a green nylon shirt. He was chewing gum slowly, as if to music. He set the tray down in the office opening next to the fern and stuck his head through to look for the secretary. She was not in there. He rested his arms on the ledge and waited, his narrow bottom stuck out, swaying to the left and right. He raised a hand over his head and scratched the base of his skull.

"You see that button there, boy?" Mrs. Turpin said. "You can punch that and she'll come. She's probably in the back somewhere."

"Is that right?" the boy said agreeably, as if he had never seen the button before. He leaned to the right and put his finger on it. "She sometime out," he said and twisted around to face his audience, his elbows behind him on the counter. The nurse appeared and he twisted back again. She handed him a dollar and he rooted in his pocket and made the change and counted it out to her. She gave him fifteen cents for a tip and he went out with the empty tray. The heavy door swung to slowly and closed at length with the sound of suction. For a moment no one spoke.

"They ought to send all them niggers back to Africa," the white-trash woman said. "That's wher they come from in the first place."

"Oh, I couldn't do without my good colored friends," the pleasant lady said.

"There's a heap of things worse than a nigger," Mrs. Turpin agreed. "It's all kinds of them just like it's all kinds of us."

"Yes, and it takes all kinds to make the world go round," the lady said in her musical voice.

As she said it, the raw-complexioned girl snapped her teeth together. Her lower lip turned downwards and inside out, revealing the pale pink inside of her mouth. After a second it rolled back up. It was the ugliest face Mrs. Turpin had ever seen anyone make and for a moment she was certain that the girl had made it at her. She was looking at her as if she had known and disliked her all her life—all of Mrs. Turpin's life, it seemed too, not just all the girl's life. Why, girl, I don't even know you, Mrs. Turpin said silently.

She forced her attention back to the discussion. "It wouldn't be practical to send them back to Africa," she said. "They wouldn't want to go. They got it too good here."

"Wouldn't be what they wanted—if I had anythang to do with it," the woman said.

"It wouldn't be a way in the world you could get all the niggers back over there," Mrs. Turpin said. "They'd be hiding out and lying down and turning sick on you and wailing and hollering and raring and pitching. It wouldn't be a way in the world to get them over there."

"They got over here," the trashy woman said. "Get back like they got over."

"It wasn't so many of them then," Mrs. Turpin explained.

The woman looked at Mrs. Turpin as if here was an idiot indeed but Mrs. Turpin was not bothered by the look, considering where it came from.

"Nooo," she said, "they're going to stay here where they can go to

New York and marry white folks and improve their color. That's what they all want to do, every one of them, improve their color."

"You know what comes of that, don't you?" Claud asked.

"No, Claud, what?" Mrs. Turpin said.

Claud's eyes twinkled. "White-faced niggers," he said with never a smile.

Everybody in the office laughed except the white-trash and the ugly girl. The girl gripped the book in her lap with white fingers. The trashy woman looked around her from face to face as if she thought they were all idiots. The old woman in the feed sack dress continued to gaze expressionless across the floor at the high-top shoes of the man opposite her, the one who had been pretending to be asleep when the Turpins came in. He was laughing heartily, his hands still spread out on his knees. The child had fallen to the side and was lying now almost face down in the old woman's lap.

While they recovered from their laughter, the nasal chorus on the radio kept the room from silence.

> *"You go to blank blank*
> *And I'll go to mine*
> *But we'll all blank along*
> *To-geth-ther,*
> *And all along the blank*
> *We'll hep eachother out*
> *Smile-ling in any kind of Weath-ther!"*

Mrs. Turpin didn't catch every word but she caught enough to agree with the spirit of the song and it turned her thoughts sober. To help anybody out that needed it was her philosophy of life. She never spared herself when she found somebody in need, whether they were white or black, trash or decent. And of all she had to be thankful for, she was most thankful that this was so. If Jesus had said, "You can be high society and have all the money you want and be thin and svelte-like, but you can't be a good woman with it," she would have had to say, "Well don't make me that then. Make me a good woman and it don't matter what else, how fat or how ugly or how poor!" Her heart rose. He had not made her a nigger or white-trash or ugly! He had made her herself and given her a little of everything. Jesus, thank you! she said. Thank you thank you thank you! Whenever she counted her blessings she felt as buoyant as if she weighed one hundred and twenty-five pounds instead of one hundred and eighty.

"What's wrong with your little boy?" the pleasant lady asked the white-trashy woman.

"He has a ulcer," the woman said proudly. "He ain't give me a minute's peace since he was born. Him and her are just alike," she said, nodding at the old woman, who was running her leathery fingers through the child's pale hair. "Look like I can't get nothing down them two but Co' Cola and candy."

That's all you try to get down em, Mrs. Turpin said to herself. Too lazy to light the fire. There was nothing you could tell her about people like them that she didn't know already. And it was not just that they didn't have anything. Because if you gave them everything, in two weeks it would all be broken or filthy or they would have chopped it up for lightwood. She knew all this from her own experience. Help them you must, but help them you couldn't.

All at once the ugly girl turned her lips inside out again. Her eyes fixed like two drills on Mrs. Turpin. This time there was no mistaking that there was something urgent behind them.

Girl, Mrs. Turpin exclaimed silently, I haven't done a thing to you! The girl might be confusing her with somebody else. There was no need to sit by and let herself be intimidated. "You must be in college," she said boldly, looking directly at the girl. "I see you reading a book there."

The girl continued to stare and pointedly did not answer.

Her mother blushed at this rudeness. "The lady asked you a question, Mary Grace," she said under her breath.

"I have ears," Mary Grace said.

The poor mother blushed again. "Mary Grace goes to Wellesley College," she explained. She twisted one of the buttons on her dress. "In Massachusetts," she added with a grimace. "And in the summer she just keeps right on studying. Just reads all the time, a real book worm. She's done real well at Wellesley; she's taking English and Math and History and Psychology and Social Studies," she rattled on, "and I think it's too much. I think she ought to get out and have fun."

The girl looked as if she would like to hurl them all through the plate glass window.

"Way up north," Mrs. Turpin murmured and thought, well, it hasn't done much for her manners.

"I'd almost rather to have him sick," the white-trash woman said, wrenching the attention back to herself. "He's so mean when he ain't. Look like some children just take natural to meanness. It's some gets bad when they get sick but he was the opposite. Took sick and turned good.

He don't give me no trouble now. It's me waitin to see the doctor," she said.

If I was going to send anybody back to Africa, Mrs. Turpin thought, it would be your kind, woman. "Yes, indeed," she said aloud, but looking up at the ceiling, "it's a heap of things worse than a nigger." And dirtier than a hog, she added to herself.

"I think people with bad dispositions are more to be pitied than any-one on earth," the pleasant lady said in a voice that was decidedly thin.

"I thank the Lord he has blessed me with a good one," Mrs. Turpin said. "The day has never dawned that I couldn't find something to laugh at."

"Not since she married me anyways," Claud said with a comical straight face.

Everybody laughed except the girl and the white-trash.

Mrs. Turpin's stomach shook. "He's such a caution," she said, "that I can't help but laugh at him."

The girl made a loud ugly noise through her teeth.

Her mother's mouth grew thin and tight. "I think the worst thing in the world," she said, "is an ungrateful person. To have everything and not appreciate it. I know a girl," she said, "who has parents who would give her anything, a little brother who loves her dearly, who is getting a good education, who wears the best clothes, but who can never say a kind word to anyone, who never smiles, who just criticizes and com-plains all day long."

"Is she too old to paddle?" Claud asked.

The girl's face was almost purple.

"Yes," the lady said, "I'm afraid there's nothing to do but leave her to her folly. Some day she'll wake up and it'll be too late."

"It never hurt anyone to smile," Mrs. Turpin said. "It just makes you feel better all over."

"Of course," the lady said sadly, "but there are just some people you can't tell anything to. They can't take criticism."

"If it's one thing I am," Mrs. Turpin said with feeling, "it's grateful. When I think who all I could have been besides myself and what all I got, a little of everything, and a good disposition besides, I just feel like shout-ing, 'Thank you, Jesus, for making everything the way it is!' It could have been different!" For one thing, somebody else could have got Claud. At the thought of this, she was flooded with gratitude and a terrible pang of joy ran through her. "Oh thank you, Jesus, Jesus, thank you!" she cried aloud.

The book struck her directly over her left eye. It struck almost at the same instant that she realized the girl was about to hurl it. Before she could utter a sound, the raw face came crashing across the table toward her, howling. The girl's fingers sank like clamps into the soft flesh of her neck. She heard the mother cry out and Claud shout, "Whoa!" There was an instant when she was certain that she was about to be in an earthquake.

All at once her vision narrowed and she saw everything as if it were happening in a small room far away, or as if she were looking at it through the wrong end of a telescope. Claud's face crumpled and fell out of sight. The nurse ran in, then out, then in again. Then the gangling figure of the doctor rushed out of the inner door. Magazines flew this way and that as the table turned over. The girl fell with a thud and Mrs. Turpin's vision suddenly reversed itself and she saw everything large instead of small. The eyes of the white-trashy woman were staring hugely at the floor. There the girl, held down on one side by the nurse and on the other by her mother, was wrenching and turning in their grasp. The doctor was kneeling astride her, trying to hold her arm down. He managed after a second to sink a long needle into it.

Mrs. Turpin felt entirely hollow except for her heart which swung from side to side as if it were agitated in a great empty drum of flesh.

"Somebody that's not busy call for the ambulance," the doctor said in the off-hand voice young doctors adopt for terrible occasions.

Mrs. Turpin could not have moved a finger. The old man who had been sitting next to her skipped nimbly into the office and made the call, for the secretary still seemed to be gone.

"Claud!" Mrs. Turpin called.

He was not in his chair. She knew she must jump up and find him but she felt like some one trying to catch a train in a dream, when everything moves in slow motion and the faster you try to run the slower you go.

"Here I am," a suffocated voice, very unlike Claud's, said.

He was doubled up in the corner on the floor, pale as paper, holding his leg. She wanted to get up and go to him but she could not move. Instead, her gaze was drawn slowly downward to the churning face on the floor, which she could see over the doctor's shoulder.

The girl's eyes stopped rolling and focused on her. They seemed a much lighter blue than before, as if a door that had been tightly closed behind them was now open to admit light and air.

Mrs. Turpin's head cleared and her power of motion returned. She leaned forward until she was looking directly into the fierce brilliant eyes.

There was no doubt in her mind that the girl did know her, knew her in some intense and personal way, beyond time and place and condition. "What you got to say to me?" she asked hoarsely and held her breath, waiting, as for a revelation.

The girl raised her head. Her gaze locked with Mrs. Turpin's. "Go back to hell where you came from, you old wart hog," she whispered. Her voice was low but clear. Her eyes burned for a moment as if she saw with pleasure that her message had struck its target.

Mrs. Turpin sank back in her chair.

After a moment the girl's eyes closed and she turned her head wearily to the side.

The doctor rose and handed the nurse the empty syringe. He leaned over and put both hands for a moment on the mother's shoulders, which were shaking. She was sitting on the floor, her lips pressed together, holding Mary Grace's hand in her lap. The girl's fingers were gripped like a baby's around her thumb. "Go on to the hospital," he said. "I'll call and make the arrangements."

"Now let's see that neck," he said in a jovial voice to Mrs. Turpin.

He began to inspect her neck with his first two fingers. Two little moon-shaped lines like pink fish bones were indented over her windpipe. There was the beginning of an angry red swelling above her eye. His fingers passed over this also.

"Lea' me be," she said thickly and shook him off. "See about Claud. She kicked him."

"I'll see about him in a minute," he said and felt her pulse. He was a thin gray-haired man, given to pleasantries. "Go home and have yourself a vacation the rest of the day," he said and patted her on the shoulder.

Quit your pattin me, Mrs. Turpin growled to herself.

"And put an ice pack over that eye," he said. Then he went and squatted down beside Claud and looked at his leg. After a moment he pulled him up and Claud limped after him into the office.

Until the ambulance came, the only sounds in the room were the tremulous moans of the girl's mother, who continued to sit on the floor. The white-trash woman did not take her eyes off the girl. Mrs. Turpin looked straight ahead at nothing. Presently the ambulance drew up, a long dark shadow, behind the curtain. The attendants came in and set the stretcher down beside the girl and lifted her expertly onto it and carried her out. The nurse helped the mother gather up her things. The shadow of the ambulance moved silently away and the nurse came back in the office.

"That ther girl is going to be a lunatic, ain't she?" the white-trash woman asked the nurse, but the nurse kept on to the back and never answered her.

"Yes, she's going to be a lunatic," the white-trash woman said to the rest of them.

"Po' critter," the old woman murmured. The child's face was still in her lap. His eyes looked idly out over her knees. He had not moved during the disturbance except to draw one leg up under him.

"I thank Gawd," the white-trash woman said fervently, "I ain't a lunatic."

Claud came limping out and the Turpins went home.

As their pick-up truck turned into their own dirt road and made the crest of the hill, Mrs. Turpin gripped the window ledge and looked out suspiciously. The land sloped gracefully down through a field dotted with lavender weeds and at the start of the rise their small yellow frame house, with its little flower beds spread out around it like a fancy apron, sat primly in its accustomed place between two giant hickory trees. She would not have been startled to see a burnt wound between two blackened chimneys.

Neither of them felt like eating so they put on their house clothes and lowered the shade in the bedroom and lay down, Claud with his leg on a pillow and herself with a damp washcloth over her eye. The instant she was flat on her back, the image of a razor-backed hog with warts on its face and horns coming out behind its ears snorted into her head. She moaned, a low quiet moan.

"I am not," she said tearfully, "a wart hog. From hell." But the denial had no force. The girl's eyes and her words, even the tone of her voice, low but clear, directed only to her, brooked no repudiation. She had been singled out for the message, though there was trash in the room to whom it might justly have been applied. The full force of this fact struck her only now. There was a woman there who was neglecting her own child but she had been overlooked. The message had been given to Ruby Turpin, a respectable, hard-working, church-going woman. The tears dried. Her eyes began to burn instead with wrath.

She rose on her elbow and the washcloth fell into her hand. Claud was lying on his back, snoring. She wanted to tell him what the girl had said. At the same time, she did not wish to put the image of herself as a wart hog from hell into his mind.

"Hey, Claud," she muttered and pushed his shoulder.

Claud opened one pale baby blue eye.

She looked into it warily. He did not think about anything. He just went his way.

"Wha, whasit?" he said and closed the eye again.

"Nothing," she said. "Does your leg pain you?"

"Hurts like hell," Claud said.

"It'll quit derreckly," she said and lay back down. In a moment Claud was snoring again. For the rest of the afternoon they lay there. Claud slept. She scowled at the ceiling. Occasionally she raised her fist and made a small stabbing motion over her chest as if she was defending her innocence to invisible guests who were like the comforters of Job, reasonable-seeming but wrong.

About five-thirty Claud stirred. "Got to go after those niggers," he sighed, not moving.

She was looking straight up as if there were unintelligible handwriting on the ceiling. The protuberance over her eye had turned a greenish-blue. "Listen here," she said.

"What?"

"Kiss me."

Claud leaned over and kissed her loudly on the mouth. He pinched her side and their hands interlocked. Her expression of ferocious concentration did not change. Claud got up, groaning and growling, and limped off. She continued to study the ceiling.

She did not get up until she heard the pick-up truck coming back with the Negroes. Then she rose and thrust her feet in her brown oxfords, which she did not bother to lace, and stumped out onto the back porch and got her red plastic bucket. She emptied a tray of ice cubes into it and filled it half full of water and went out into the back yard. Every afternoon after Claud brought the hands in, one of the boys helped him put out hay and the rest waited in the back of the truck until he was ready to take them home. The truck was parked in the shade under one of the hickory trees.

"Hi yawl this evening?" Mrs Turpin asked grimly, appearing with the bucket and the dipper. There were three women and a boy in the truck.

"Us doin nicely," the oldest woman said. "Hi you doin?" and her gaze stuck immediately on the dark lump on Mrs. Turpin's forehead. "You done fell down, ain't you?" she asked in a solicitous voice. The old woman was dark and almost toothless. She had on an old felt hat of Claud's set back on her head. The other two women were younger and lighter and they both had new bright green sunhats. One of them had hers on her head; the other had taken hers off and the boy was grinning beneath it.

Mrs. Turpin set the bucket down on the floor of the truck. "Yawl hep yourselves," she said. She looked around to make sure Claud had gone. "No, I didn't fall down," she said, folding her arms. "It was something worse than that."

"Ain't nothing bad happen to you!" the old woman said. She said it as if they all knew that Mrs. Turpin was protected in some special way by Divine Providence. "You just had you a little fall."

"We were in town at the doctor's office for where the cow kicked Mr. Turpin," Mrs. Turpin said in a flat tone that indicated they could leave off their foolishness. "And there was this girl there. A big fat girl with her face all broke out. I could look at that girl and tell she was peculiar but I couldn't tell how. And me and her mama was just talking and going along and all of a sudden WHAM! She throws this big book she was read-ing at me and . . ."

"Naw!" the old woman cried out.

"And then she jumps over the table and commences to choke me."

"Naw!" they all exclaimed, "naw!"

"Hi come she do that?" the old woman asked. "What ail her?"

Mrs. Turpin only glared in front of her.

"Somethin ail her," the old woman said.

"They carried her off in an ambulance," Mrs. Turpin continued, "but before she went she was rolling on the floor and they were trying to hold her down to give her a shot and she said something to me." She paused. "You know what she said to me?"

"What she say?" they asked.

"She said," Mrs. Turpin began, and stopped, her face very dark and heavy. The sun was getting whiter and whiter, blanching the sky over-head so that the leaves of the hickory tree were black in the face of it. She could not bring forth the words. "Something real ugly," she muttered.

"She sho shouldn't said nothin ugly to you," the old woman said. "You so sweet. You the sweetest lady I know."

"She pretty too," the one with the hat on said.

"And stout," the other one said. "I never knowed no sweeter white lady."

"That's the truth befo' Jesus," the old woman said. "Amen! You des as sweet and pretty as you can be."

Mrs. Turpin knew exactly how much Negro flattery was worth and it added to her rage. "She said," she began again and finished this time with a fierce rush of breath, "that I was an old wart hog from hell."

There was an astounded silence.

"Where she at?" the youngest woman cried in a piercing voice.

"Lemme see her. I'll kill her!"

"I'll kill her with you!" the other one cried.

"She b'long in the sylum," the old woman said emphatically. "You the sweetest white lady I know."

"She pretty too," the other two said. "Stout as she can be and sweet. Jesus satisfied with her!"

"Deed he is," the old woman declared.

Idiots! Mrs. Turpin growled to herself. You could never say anything intelligent to a nigger. You could talk at them but not with them. "Yawl ain't drunk your water," she said shortly. "Leave the bucket in the truck when you're finished with it. I got more to do than just stand around and pass the time of day," and she moved off and into the house.

She stood for a moment in the middle of the kitchen. The dark protuberance over her eye looked like a miniature tornado cloud which might any moment sweep across the horizon of her brow. Her lower lip protruded dangerously. She squared her massive shoulders. Then she marched into the front of the house and out the side door and started down the road to the pig parlor. She had the look of a woman going single-handed, weaponless, into battle.

The sun was a deep yellow now like a harvest moon and was riding westward very fast over the far tree line as if it meant to reach the hogs before she did. The road was rutted and she kicked several good-sized stones out of her path as she strode along. The pig parlor was on a little knoll at the end of a lane that ran off from the side of the barn. It was a square of concrete as large as a small room, with a board fence about four feet high around it. The concrete floor sloped slightly so that the hog wash could drain off into a trench where it was carried to the field for fertilizer. Claud was standing on the outside, on the edge of the concrete, hanging onto the top board, hosing down the floor inside. The hose was connected to the faucet of a water trough nearby.

Mrs. Turpin climbed up beside him and glowered down at the hogs inside. There were seven long-snouted bristly shoats in it—tan with liver-colored spots—and an old sow a few weeks off from farrowing. She was lying on her side grunting. The shoats were running about shaking themselves like idiot children, their little slit pig eyes searching the floor for anything left. She had read that pigs were the most intelligent animal. She doubted it. They were supposed to be smarter than dogs. There had even been a pig astronaut. He had performed his assignment perfectly but died of a heart attack afterwards because they left him in his electric suit, sitting upright throughout his examination when naturally a hog should be on all fours.

A-gruntin and a-rootin and a-groanin.

"Gimme that hose," she said, yanking it away from Claud. "Go on and carry them niggers home and then get off that leg."

"You look like you might have swallowed a mad dog," Claud observed, but he got down and limped off. He paid no attention to her humors.

Until he was out of earshot, Mrs. Turpin stood on the side of the pen, holding the hose and pointing the stream of water at the hind quarters of any shoat that looked as if it might try to lie down. When he had had time to get over the hill, she turned her head slightly and her wrathful eyes scanned the path. He was nowhere in sight. She turned back again and seemed to gather herself up. Her shoulders rose and she drew in her breath.

"What do you send me a message like that for?" she said in a low fierce voice, barely above a whisper but with the force of a shout in its concentrated fury. "How am I a hog and me both? How am I saved and from hell too?" Her free fist was knotted and with the other she gripped the hose, blindly pointing the stream of water in and out of the eye of the old sow whose outraged squeal she did not hear.

The pig parlor commanded a view of the back pasture where their twenty beef cows were gathered around the hay-bales Claud and the boy had put out. The freshly cut pasture sloped down to the highway. Across it was their cotton field and beyond that a dark green dusty wood which they owned as well. The sun was behind the wood, very red, looking over the paling of trees like a farmer inspecting his own hogs.

"Why me?" she rumbled. "It's no trash around here, black or white, that I haven't given to. And break my back to the bone every day working. And do for the church."

She appeared to be the right size woman to command the arena before her. "How am I a hog?" she demanded. "Exactly how am I like them?" and she jabbed the stream of water at the shoats. "There was plenty of trash there. It didn't have to be me."

"If you like trash better, go get yourself some trash then," she railed. "You could have made me trash. Or a nigger. If trash is what you wanted why didn't you make me trash?" She shook her fist with the hose in it and a watery snake appeared momentarily in the air. "I could quit working and take it easy and be filthy," she growled. "Lounge about the sidewalks all day drinking root beer. Dip snuff and spit in every puddle and have it all over my face. I could be nasty.

"Or you could have made me a nigger. It's too late for me to be a nigger," she said with deep sarcasm, "but I could act like one. Lay down in the middle of the road and stop traffic. Roll on the ground."

In the deepening light everything was taking on a mysterious hue. The pasture was growing a peculiar glassy green and the streak of highway had turned lavender. She braced herself for a final assault and this time her voice rolled out over the pasture. "Go on," she yelled, "call me a hog! Call me a hog again. From hell. Call me a wart hog from hell. Put that bottom rail on top. There'll still be a top and bottom!"

A garbled echo returned to her.

A final surge of fury shook her and she roared, "Who do you think you are?"

The color of everything, field and crimson sky, burned for a moment with a transparent intensity. The question carried over the pasture and across the highway and the cotton field and returned to her clearly like an answer from beyond the wood.

She opened her mouth but no sound came out of it.

A tiny truck, Claud's, appeared on the highway, heading rapidly out of sight. Its gears scraped thinly. It looked like a child's toy. At any moment a bigger truck might smash into it and scatter Claud's and the niggers' brains all over the road.

Mrs. Turpin stood there, her gaze fixed on the highway, all her muscles rigid, until in five or six minutes the truck reappeared, returning. She waited until it had had time to turn into their own road. Then like a monumental statue coming to life, she bent her head slowly and gazed, as if through the very heart of mystery, down into the pig parlor at the hogs. They had settled all in one corner around the old sow who was grunting softly. A red glow suffused them. They appeared to pant with a secret life.

Until the sun slipped finally behind the tree line, Mrs. Turpin remained there with her gaze bent to them as if she were absorbing some abysmal life-giving knowledge. At last she lifted her head. There was only a purple streak in the sky, cutting through a field of crimson and leading, like an extension of the highway, into the descending dusk. She raised her hands from the side of the pen in a gesture hieratic and profound. A visionary light settled in her eyes. She saw the streak as a vast swinging bridge extending upward from the earth through a field of living fire. Upon it a vast horde of souls were rumbling toward heaven. There were whole companies of white-trash, clean for the first time in their lives, and bands of black niggers in white robes, and battalions of freaks and lunatics shouting and clapping and leaping like frogs. And bringing up the end of the procession was a tribe of people whom she recognized at once as those who, like herself and Claud, had always had a little of everything and the God-given wit to use it right. She leaned forward to observe them closer. They were marching behind the others with great dignity, accountable as they had always been for good order and common sense and respectable behavior. They alone were on key. Yet she could see by their shocked and altered faces that even their virtues were being burned away. She lowered her hands and gripped the rail of the hog pen, her eyes small but fixed unblinkingly on what lay ahead. In a moment the vision faded but she remained where she was, immobile.

At length she got down and turned off the faucet and made her slow way on the darkening path to the house. In the woods around her the invisible cricket choruses had struck up, but what she heard were the voices of the souls climbing upward into the starry field and shouting hallelujah.

Anne Sexton
(1928–1974)

aving eloped at nineteen and given birth to two daughters in the suburbs, Massachusetts-born Anne Sexton did not start writing poetry until the mid-1950s. At a writing workshop at Boston University, Sexton met fellow poet Maxine Kumin, who became a close friend and writing partner. Later they participated along with Sylvia Plath and George Starbuck in a poetry workshop led by Robert Lowell. Sexton's technically deft, confessional poetry gained quick recognition, starting with her first volume *To Bedlam and Part Way Back* (1960). Winning most major poetry prizes, Sexton continued to write about her sexuality, depression, and experience as a woman in *All My Pretty Ones* (1962), *Live or Die* (1966), and *Love Poems* (1969). "Her Kind," with its chilling references to the woman poet as witch, was Sexton's signature poem. She used it to introduce her dramatic poetry readings, in which she smoked, wore clinging gowns, and sometimes was backed up by a rock band. "Housewife," which suggests that women marry houses, is both Freudian in its imagery of the female body, the house, and the mother, and an acid comment on the confining domesticity of American women in the 1950s. While Sexton enjoyed her fame and celebrity, depression was always her enemy. In 1974 she committed suicide.

Her Kind (1960)

I have gone out, a possessed witch,
haunting the black air, braver at night;
dreaming evil, I have done my hitch
over the plain houses, light by light:
lonely thing, twelve-fingered, out of mind.
A woman like that is not a woman, quite.
I have been her kind.

I have found the warm caves in the woods,
filled them with skillets, carvings, shelves,

closets, silks, innumerable goods;
fixed the suppers for the worms and the elves:
whining, rearranging the disaligned.
A woman like that is misunderstood.
I have been her kind.

I have ridden in your cart, driver,
waved my nude arms at villages going by,
learning the last bright routes, survivor
where your flames still bite my thigh
and my ribs crack where your wheels wind.
A woman like that is not ashamed to die.
I have been her kind.

Housewife (1962)

Some women marry houses.
It's another kind of skin; it has a heart,
a mouth, a liver, and bowel movements.
The walls are permanent and pink.
See how she sits on her knees all day,
faithfully washing herself down.
Men enter by force, drawn back like Jonah
into their fleshy mothers.
A woman is her mother.
That's the main thing.

Cynthia Ozick

(1928–)

ynthia Ozick was born in New York City, the daughter of Russian-Jewish immigrants, and received a B.A. from New York University in 1949 and an M.A. from Ohio State University in 1950. Beginning with a novel *Trust* (1966), she has gone on to publish essays, plays, stories, and novels, including *The Pagan Rabbi and Other Stories* (1971), *The Cannibal Galaxy* (1983), *The Messiah of Stockholm* (1987), *The Shawl* (1989), *The Puttermesser Papers* (1997), *Heir to the Glimmering World* (2004), *Dictation: A Quartet* (2008), and *Foreign Bodies* (2010). In 1972, Ozick published "We Are the Crazy Lady and Other Feisty Feminist Fables" in *Ms.* magazine. These witty autobiographical parables about intellectual women, very much in the tradition of Edith Wharton's "The Valley of Childish Things," are as relevant today as they were then. But Ozick has scrupulously corrected a phrase in "Section VI: Ambition": "Polemics are nearly always a bit skewed away from truth-telling, and here I have had a serious life-lesson. . . . I'm afraid I inserted a bit of imaginary history-that-never-was, in order to heighten an argument. No relative, or anyone else, ever charged me with being 'a childless housewife, a failed woman.' Alas, I invented these nasty phrases. . . . I have vowed, though perhaps too late, to confine make-believe to stories and novels."

We Are the Crazy Lady and Other Feisty Feminist Fables (1972)

I: The Crazy Lady Double

A long, long time ago, in another century—1951, in fact—when you, dear younger readers, were most likely still in your nuclear-family playpen (where, if female, you cuddled a rag-baby to your potential titties, or, if male, let down virile drool over your plastic bulldozer), Lionel Trilling told me never, never to use a parenthesis in the very first sentence. This was in a graduate English seminar at Columbia University. To get into this seminar, you had to submit to a grilling wherein you renounced all former allegiance to the then-current literary religion, New Criticism, which considered that only the text existed, not the world. I passed the interview by lying, cunningly, and against any real convictions. I said that probably the world *did* exist—and walked triumphantly into the seminar room.

There were four big tables arranged in a square, with everyone's feet sticking out into the open middle of the square. You could tell who was nervous, and how much, by watching the pairs of feet twist around each other. Professor Trilling presided awesomely from the high bar of the square. His head was a majestic granite-gray, like a centurion in command; he *looked* famous. His clean shoes twitched only slightly, and only when he was angry.

It turned out he was angry at me a lot of the time. He was angry because he thought me a disrupter, a rioter, a provocateur, and a fool; also crazy. And this was twenty years ago, before these things were *de rigueur* in the universities. Everything was very quiet in those days. There were only the Cold War and Korea and Joe McCarthy and the Old Old Nixon, and the only revolutionaries around were in Henry James's *The Princess Casamassima*.

Habit governed the seminar. Where you sat the first day was where you settled forever. So, to avoid the stigmatization of the ghetto, I was careful not to sit next to the other woman in the class: the Crazy Lady.

At first the Crazy Lady appeared to be remarkably intelligent. She was older than the rest of us, somewhere in her thirties (which was why we thought of her as a Lady), with wild tan hair, a noticeably breathing bosom, eccentric gold-rimmed old-pensioner glasses, and a tooth-crowded wild mouth that seemed to get wilder the more she talked. She talked like a motorcycle, fast and urgent. Everything she said was almost brilliant, only not actually on point, and frenetic with hostility. She was tough and negative. She volunteered a lot and she stood up and wobbled with rage, pulling at her hair and mouth. She fought Trilling point for point, piecemeal and wholesale, mixing up queerly angled literary insights with all sorts of private and public fury. After the first meetings, he was fed up with her. The rest of us accepted that she probably wasn't all there, but in a room where everyone was on the make for recognition—you talked to save your life, and the only way to save your life was to be the smartest one that day—she was a nuisance, a distraction, a pain in the ass. The class became a bunch of Good Germans, determinedly indifferent onlookers to a vindictive match between Trilling and the Crazy Lady, until finally he subdued her by shutting his eyes, and, when that didn't always work, by cutting her dead and lecturing right across the sound of her strong, strange voice.

All this was before R. D. Laing had invented the superiority of madness, of course, and, cowards all, no one liked the thought of being tarred with the Crazy Lady's brush. Ignored by the boss, in the middle of everything she would suddenly begin to mutter to herself. She mentioned certain institutions she'd been in, and said we all belonged there. The people who sat on either side of her shifted chairs. If the Great Man ostracized the Crazy Lady, we had to do it too. But one day the Crazy Lady came in late and sat down in the seat next to mine, and stayed there the rest of the semester.

Then an odd thing happened. There, right next to me, was the noisy Crazy Lady, tall, with that sticking-out sighing chest of hers, orangey curls dripping over her nose, snuffling furiously for attention. And there was I, a brownish runt, a dozen years younger and flatter and shyer than the Crazy Lady, in no way her twin, physically or psychologically. In those days I was bone-skinny, small, sallow and myopic, and so scared I could trigger diarrhea at one glance from the Great Man. All this stress on looks is important. The Crazy Lady and I had our separate bodies, our separate brains. We handed in our separate papers.

But the Great Man never turned toward me, never at all, and if ambition broke feverishly through shyness so that I dared to push an idea audibly out of me, he shut his eyes when I put up my hand. This went on for a long time. I never got to speak, and I began to have the depressing feeling that Lionel Trilling hated me. It was no small thing to be hated by the man who had written "Wordsworth and the Rabbis" and *Matthew Arnold*, after all. What in hell was going on? I was in trouble, because, like everyone else in that demented contest, I wanted to excel. Then, one slow afternoon, wearily, the Great Man let his eyes fall on me. He called me by name, but it was not my name—it was the Crazy Lady's. The next week the papers came back—and there, right at the top of mine, in the Great Man's own handwriting, was a rebuke to the Crazy Lady for starting an essay with a parenthesis in the first sentence, a habit he took to be a continuing sign of that unruly and unfocused mentality so often exhibited in class. And then a Singular Revelation crept coldly through me. Because the Crazy Lady and I sat side by side, because we were a connected blur of Woman, Lionel Trilling, master of ultimate distinctions, couldn't tell us apart. The Crazy Lady and I! He couldn't tell us apart! It didn't matter that the Crazy Lady was crazy! *He couldn't tell us apart!*

Moral 1: All cats are gray at night, all darkies look alike.

Moral 2: Even among intellectual humanists, every woman has a *Doppelgänger*—every other woman.

II: The Lecture, 1

I was invited by a women's group to be guest speaker at a Book-Author Luncheon. The women themselves had not really chosen me: the speaker had been selected by a male leader and imposed on them. The plan was that I would autograph copies of my book, eat a good meal and then lecture. The woman in charge of the programming phoned to ask me what my topic would be. This was a matter of some concern, since they had never had a woman author before, and no one knew how the idea would be received. I offered as my subject "The Contemporary Poem."

When the day came, everything went as scheduled—the autographing, the food, the welcoming addresses. Then it was time to go to the lectern. I aimed at the microphone and began to speak of poetry. A peculiar rustling sound flew up from the audience. All the women were lifting their programs to the light, like hundreds of wings. Confused murmurs ran along the walls. I began to feel very uncomfortable. Then I too took up the program. It read, "Topic: The Contemporary Home."

Moral: Even our ears practice the caste system.

III: The Lecture, 2

I was in another country, the only woman at a philosophical seminar lasting three days. On the third day, I was to read a paper. I had accepted the invitation with a certain foreknowledge. I knew, for instance, that I could not dare to be the equal of any other speaker. To be an equal would be to be less. I understood that mine had to be the most original and powerful paper of all. I had no choice; I had to toil beyond my most extreme possibilities. This was not ambition, but only fear of disgrace.

For the first two days, I was invisible. When I spoke, people tapped impatiently, waiting for the interruption to be over with. No one took either my presence or my words seriously. At meals, I sat with my colleagues' wives.

The third day arrived, and I read my paper. It was successful beyond my remotest imaginings. I was interviewed, and my remarks appeared in newspapers in a language I could not understand. The Foreign Minister invited me to his home. I hobnobbed with famous poets.

Now my colleagues noticed me. But they did not notice me as a colleague. They teased and kissed me. I had become their mascot.

Moral: There is no route out of caste which does not instantly lead back into it.

IV: Propaganda

For many years, I had noticed that no book of poetry by a woman was ever reviewed without reference to the poet's sex. The curious thing was that, in the two decades of my scrutiny, there were *no* exceptions whatever. It did not matter whether the reviewer was a man or woman: in every case the question of the "feminine sensibility" of the poet was at the center of the reviewer's response. The maleness of male poets, on the other hand, hardly ever seemed to matter.

Determined to ridicule this convention, I wrote a tract, a piece of purely tendentious mockery, in the form of a short story. I called it "Virility."

The plot was, briefly, as follows: A very bad poet, lustful for fame, is despised for his pitiful lucubrations and remains unpublished. But luckily, he comes into possession of a cache of letters written by his elderly spinster aunt, who lives an obscure and secluded working-class life in a remote corner of England. The letters contain a large number of remarkable poems; the aunt, it turns out, is a genius. The bad poet publishes his find under his own name, and instantly attains worldwide adulation. Under the title *Virility*, the poems become immediate classics. They are translated into dozens of languages and are praised and revered for their unmistakably masculine qualities: their strength, passion, wisdom, energy, boldness, brutality, worldliness, robustness, authenticity, sensuality, compassion. A big, handsome, sweating man, the poet swaggers from country to country, courted everywhere, pursued by admirers, yet respected by the most demanding critics.

Meanwhile, the old aunt dies. The supply of genius runs out. Bravely and contritely the poor poet confesses his ruse, and, in a burst of honesty, publishes the last batch under the real poet's name. The book is entitled *Flowers from Liverpool*. But the poems are at once found negligible and dismissed: "Thin feminine art," say the reviews, "a lovely girlish voice." Also: "Choked with female inwardness," and "The fine womanly intuition of a competent poetess." The poems are utterly forgotten.

I included this fable in a collection of short stories. In every review, the salvo went unnoticed. Not one reviewer recognized that the story was a sly tract. Not one reviewer saw the smirk or the point. There was one delicious comment, though. "I have some reservations," a man in Washington, D.C., wrote, "about the credibility of some of her male characters when they are chosen as narrators."

Moral: In saying what is obvious, never choose cunning. Yelling works better.

V: Hormones

During a certain period of my life, I was reading all the time, and fairly obsessively. Sometimes, though, sunk in a book of criticism or philosophy, I would be brought up short. Consider: here is a paragraph that excites the intellect. Inwardly, one assents passionately to its premises; the writer's idea is an exact diagram of one's own deepest psychology or conviction; one feels oneself seized as for a portrait. Then the disclaimer: "It is, however, otherwise with the female sex . . ." A rebuke from the World of Thinking, *I didn't mean you, lady*. In the instant one is in possession of one's humanity most intensely, it is ripped away.

These moments I discounted. What is wrong—intrinsically, psychologically, culturally, morally—can be dismissed.

But to dismiss in this manner is to falsify one's most genuine actuality. A Jew reading of the aesthetic glories of European civilization without taking notice of his victimization during, say, the era of the building of the great cathedrals, is self-forgetful in the most dangerous way. So would be a black who read of King Cotton with an economist's objectivity.

I am not offering any strict analogy between the situation of women and the history of Jews or colonialized blacks, as many politically radical women do (though the analogy with blacks is much the more frequent one). It seems to me to be abusive of language in the extreme when some women speak, in the generation after Auschwitz, in the very hour of the Bengali horror, of the "oppression" of women. Language makes culture, and we make a rotten culture when we abuse words. We raise up rotten heroines. I use "rotten" with particular attention to its precise meanings: foul, putrid, tainted, stinking. I am thinking now especially of a radical women's publication, *Off Our Backs*, which not long ago presented Leila Khaled, terrorist and foiled murderer, as a model for the political conduct of women.

But if I would not support the extreme analogy (and am never surprised when black women, who have a more historical comprehension of actual, not figurative, oppression, refuse to support the analogy), it is anyhow curious to see what happens to the general culture when any enforced class in any historical or social condition is compelled to doubt its own self-understanding, when identity is extremely defined, when individual humanity is called into question as being different from "standard" humanity. What happens is that the general culture, along with the object of its debasement, is also debased. If you laugh at women, you play Beethoven in vain. If you laugh at women, your laboratory will lie.

We can read in Charlotte Perkins Gilman's 1912 essay, "Are Women Human Beings?", an account of an opinion current sixty years ago. Women, said one scientist, are not only "not the human race—they are not even half the human race, but a sub-species set apart for purposes of reproduction merely."

Though we are accustomed to the idea of "progress" in science, if not in civilization generally, the fact is that more information has led to something very like regression.

I talked with an intelligent physician, the Commissioner of Health of a middle-sized city in Connecticut, a man who sees medicine not discretely but as part of the social complex. He treated me to a long list of all the objective differences between men and women, including particularly an account of current endocrinal studies relating to female hormones. Aren't all of these facts? he asked. How can you distrust facts? Very good, I said, I'm willing to take your medically educated word for it. I'm not afraid of facts, I welcome facts—*but a congeries of facts is not equivalent to an idea.* This is the essential fallacy of the so-called "scientific" mind. People who mistake facts for ideas are incomplete thinkers; they are gossips.

You tell me, I said, that my sense of my own humanity as being "standard" humanity—which is, after all, a subjective idea—is refuted by hormonal research. My psychology, you tell me, which in your view is the source of my ideas, is the result of my physiology. It is not I who express myself, it is my hormones which express me. A part is equal to the whole, you say. Worse yet, the whole is simply the issue of the part: my "I" is a flash of chemicals. You are willing to define all my humanity by hormonal investigation under a microscope. This you call "objective irrefutable fact," as if tissue-culture were equivalent to culture. But each scientist can assemble his own (subjective) constellation of "objective irrefutable fact," just as each social thinker can assemble his own (subjective) selection of traits that define "humanity." Who can prove what is "standard" humanity, and which sex, class, or race is to be exempted from whole participation in it? On what basis do you regard female hormones as causing a modification from normative humanity? And what better right do you have to define normative humanity by what males have traditionally apperceived than by what females have traditionally apperceived—assuming (as I, lacking presumptuousness, do not) that their apperceptions have not been the same? Only Tiresias—that mythological character who was both man and woman consecutively—is in a position to make the comparison and present the proof. And then not even Tiresias, because to be a hermaphrodite is to be a monster, and not human.

"Why are you so emotional about all this?" said the Commissioner of Health. "You see how it is? Those are your female hormones working on you right now."

Moral: Defamation is only applied research.

VI: Ambition

After thirteen years, I at last finished a novel. The first seven years were spent in a kind of apprenticeship—the book that came out of that time was abandoned without much regret. A second one was finished in six weeks and buried. It took six years to write the third novel, and this one was finally published.

How I lived through those years is impossible to recount in a short space. I was a recluse, a priest of Art. I read seas of books. I believed in the idea of masterpieces. I was scornful of the world of journalism, jobs, everydayness. I did not live like any woman I knew. I lived like some men I had read about—Flaubert, or Proust, or James—the subjects of those literary biographies I endlessly drank in. I did not think of them as men, but as writers. I read the diaries of Virginia Woolf, and biographies of George Eliot, but I did not think of them as women. I thought of them as writers. I thought of myself as a writer.

It goes without saying that all this time my relatives regarded me as abnormal. I accepted this. It seemed to me, from what I had read, that most writers were abnormal. Yet on the surface, I could easily have passed for normal. The husband goes to work, the wife stays home—that is what is normal. Well, I was married. My husband went to his job every day. His job paid the rent and bought the groceries. I stayed home, reading and writing, and felt myself to be an economic parasite. To cover guilt, I joked that I had been given a grant from a very private, very poor, foundation—my husband.

But my relatives never thought of me as a parasite. The very thing I was doubtful about—my economic dependence—they considered my due as a woman. They saw me not as a failed writer without an income, but as a childless housewife, a failed woman. They did not think me abnormal because I was a writer, but because I was not properly living my life as a woman. In one respect we were in agreement utterly—my life was failing terribly, terribly. For me it was because, already deep into my thirties, I had not yet published a book. For them, it was because I had not yet borne a child.

I was a pariah, not only because I was a deviant, but because I was not recognized as the kind of deviant I meant to be. A failed woman is not the same as a failed writer. Even as a pariah I was the wrong kind of pariah.

Still, relations are only relations. What I aspired to, what I was in thrall to, was Art, was Literature, not familial contentment. I knew how to distinguish the trivial from the sublime. In Literature and in Art, I saw, my notions were not pariah notions. There, I inhabited the mainstream. So I went on reading and writing. I went on believing in Art, and my intention was to write a masterpiece. Not a saucer of well-polished craft (the sort of thing "women writers" are always accused of being accomplished at), but something huge, contemplative, Tolstoyan. My ambition was a craw.

I called the book *Trust*. I began it in the summer of 1957 and finished it in November of 1963, on the day President John Kennedy was assassinated. In manuscript, it was 801 pages divided into four parts: "America," "Europe," "Birth," and "Death." The title was meant to be ironic. In reality, it was about distrust. It seemed to me I had touched on distrust in every order or form of civilization. It seemed to me I had left nothing out. It was (though I did not know this then) a very hating book. What it hated above all was the whole—the whole—of Western Civilization. It told how America had withered into another Europe. It dreamed dark and murderous pagan dreams, and hated what it dreamed.

In style, the book was what has come to be called "mandarin": a difficult, aristocratic, unrelenting virtuoso prose. It was, in short, unreadable. I think I knew this. I was sardonic enough to say, echoing Joyce about *Finnegan's Wake*, "I expect you to spend your life at this." In any case, I had spent a decade-and-a-half of my own life at it. Though I did not imagine the world would fall asunder at its appearance, I thought—at the very least—the ambition, the all-swallowingness, the wild insatiability of the writer would be plain to everyone who read it. I had, after all, taken History for my subject: not merely History as an aggregate of events, but History as a judgment on events. No one could say my theme was flighty. Of all the novelists I read (and in those days I read them all, broiling in the envy of the unpublished, which is like no envy on earth), who else had dared so vastly?

During that period, Françoise Sagan's first novel was published. I held the thin little thing and laughed. Women's pulp!

My own novel, I believed, contained everything—the whole world.

But there was one element I had consciously left out. Though on principle I did not like to characterize it or think about it much, the truth is I was thinking about it all the time. It was only a fiction-technicality, but I was considerably afraid of it. It was the question of the narrator's "sensibility." The narrator, as it happened, was a young woman; I had chosen her to be the eye—and the "I"—of the novel because all the other characters in some way focused on her. She was the one most useful to my scheme. Nevertheless, I wanted her not to live. Everything I was reading in reviews of other people's books made me fearful: I would have to be very cautious; I would have to drain my narrator of emotive value of any kind, because I was afraid to be pegged as having written a "woman's" novel. Nothing was more certain to lead to that than a point-of-view seemingly lodged in a woman, and no one takes a woman's novel seriously. I was in terror, above all, of sentiment and feelings, those telltale taints. I kept the fury and the passion for other, safer, characters.

So what I left out of my narrator entirely, sweepingly, with exquisite consciousness of what exactly I *was* leaving out, was any shred of "sensibility." I stripped her of everything, even a name. I crafted and carpentered her. She was for me a bloodless device, fulcrum or pivot, a recording voice, a language-machine. She confronted moment or event, took it in, gave it out. And what to me was all the more wonderful about this nameless fiction-machine I had invented was that the machine itself, though never alive, was a character in the story, without ever influencing the story. My machine-narrator was there for efficiency only, for flexibility, for craftiness, for subtlety, but never, never, as a "woman." I wiped the "woman" out of her. And I did it out of fear, out of vicarious vindictive critical imagination, out of the terror of my ambition, out of, maybe, paranoia. I meant my novel to be taken for what it really was. I meant to make it impossible for it to be mistaken for something else.

Publication. Review in *The New York Times* Sunday Book Review.

Review is accompanied by a picture of a naked woman seen from the back. Her bottom is covered by some sort of drapery.

Title of review: "Daughter's Reprieve."

Excerpts from review: "These events, interesting in themselves, exist to reveal the sensibility of the narrator." "She longs to play some easy feminine role." "She has been unable to define herself as a woman." "The main body of the novel, then, is a revelation of the narrator's inner, turbulent, psychic drama."

O rabid, rotten Western Civilization, where are you? O judging History, O foul Trust and fouler Distrust, where?

O Soap Opera, where did you come from?

(Meanwhile the review in *Time* was calling me a "housewife.")

Pause.

All right, let us take up the rebuttals.

Q. Maybe you *did* write a soap opera without knowing it. Maybe you only *thought* you were writing about Western Civilization when you were really only rewriting Stella Dallas.

A. A writer may be unsure of everything—trust the tale not the teller is a good rule—but not of his obsessions; of these he is certain. If I were rewriting Stella Dallas, I would turn her into the Second Crusade and demobilize her.

Q. Maybe you're like the blind Jew who wants to be a pilot, and when they won't give him the job he says they're anti-Semitic. Look, the book was lousy, you deserved a lousy review.

A. You mistake me, I never said it was a bad review. It was in fact an extremely favorable review, full of gratifying adjectives.

Q. Then what's eating you?

A. I don't know. Maybe the question of language. By language I mean literacy. See the next section, please.

Q. No Moral for *this* section?

A. Of course. If you look for it, there will always be a decent solution for female ambition. For instance, it is still not too late to enroll in a good secretarial school.

Q. Bitter, bitter! You mean your novel failed?

A. Perished, is dead and buried. I sometimes see it exhumed on the shelf in the public library. It's always there. No one ever borrows it.

Q. Dummy! You should've written a soap opera. Women are good at that.

A. Thank you. You almost remind me of a Second Moral: In conceptual life, junk prevails. Even if you do not produce junk, it will be taken for junk.

Q. What does that have to do with women?

A. The products of women are frequently taken for junk.

Q. And if a woman *does* produce junk . . . ?

A. Glory—they will treat her almost like a man who produces junk. They will say her name on television. Do please go on to the next section. Thank you.

VII: Conclusion, and a Peek

Actually I had two more stories to tell you. One was about Mr. Machismo, a very angry, well-groomed, *clean man* (what a pity he isn't a woman—ah, deprived of vaginal spray) who defines as irresponsible all those who do not obey him, especially his mother and sister. A highly morbid and titillating Gothic tale. The other story was about Mr. Littletable, the Petty Politician, at the Bankers' Feast—how he gathered up the wives in a pretty garland, threw them a topic to chatter over. A Bronx neighborhood where you can buy good lox, I think it was. Having set them all up so nicely, he went off to lick the nearest Vice-President-of-Morgan-Guaranty.

But these are long stories, Ladies and Gentlemen. No room up there for another Woman's Novel.

Ursula K. Le Guin
(1929–)

orn in Berkeley, California, to an anthropologist father and writer mother, Ursula K. Le Guin is known for her brilliant science fiction and feminist fantasy stories. Since the 1960s, when she began publishing her many novels and short stories, Le Guin created alternate worlds and filled them with variants of gender and social organization. "She Unnames Them" (published in *The New Yorker* in 1985) is a retelling of the Garden of Eden story in which Eve rejects Adamic definitions and fashions her own language, unnaming all of creation and finally herself, in a language of fresh metaphor which signifies a new realm of writing.

She Unnames Them (1985)

Most of them accepted namelessness with the perfect indifference with which they had so long accepted and ignored their names. Whales and dolphins, seals and sea otters consented with particular grace and alacrity, sliding into anonymity as into their element. A faction of yaks, however, protested. They said that "yak" sounded right, and that almost everyone who knew they existed called them that. Unlike the ubiquitous creatures such as rats and fleas, who had been called by hundreds or thousands of different names since Babel, the yaks could truly say, they said, that they had *a name*. They discussed the matter all summer. The councils of elderly females finally agreed that though the name might be useful to others, it was so redundant from the yak point of view that they never spoke it themselves, and hence might as well dispense with it. After they presented the argument in this light to their bulls, a full consensus was delayed only by the onset of severe early blizzards. Soon after the beginning of the thaw their agreement was reached and the designation "yak" was returned to the donor.

Among the domestic animals, few horses had cared what anybody called them since the failure of Dean Swift's attempt to name them from their own vocabulary. Cattle, sheep, swine, asses, mules, and goats, along with chickens, geese, and turkeys, all agreed enthusiastically to give their names back to the people to whom—as they put it—they belonged.

A couple of problems did come up with pets. The cats, of course, steadfastly denied ever having had any name other than those self-given, unspoken, ineffably personal names which, as the poet named Eliot said, they spend long hours daily contemplating—though none of the contemplators has ever admitted that what they contemplate is in fact their name, and some onlookers have wondered if the object of that meditative gaze might not in fact be the Perfect, or Platonic, Mouse. In any case, it is a moot point now. It was with the dogs, and with some parrots, lovebirds, ravens, and mynahs, that the trouble arose. These verbally talented individuals insisted that their names were important to them, and flatly refused to part with them. But as soon as they understood that the issue was precisely one of individual choice, and that anybody who wanted to be called Rover, or Froufrou, or Polly, or even Birdie in the personal sense, was perfectly free to do so, not one of them had the least objection to parting with the lowercase (or, as regards German creatures, uppercase) generic appellations poodle, parrot, dog, or bird, and all the Linnaean qualifiers that had trailed along behind them for two hundred years like tin cans tied to a tail.

The insects parted with their names in vast clouds and swarms of ephemeral syllables buzzing and stinging and humming and flitting and crawling and tunneling away.

As for the fish of the sea, their names dispersed from them in silence throughout the oceans like faint, dark blurs of cuttlefish ink, and drifted off on the currents without a trace.

None were left now to unname, and yet how close I felt to them when I saw one of them swim or fly or trot or crawl across my way or over my skin, or stalk me in the night, or go along beside me for a while in the day. They seemed far closer than when their names had stood between myself and them like a clear barrier: so close that my fear of them and their fear of me became one same fear. And the attraction that many of us felt, the desire to smell one another's smells, feel or rub or caress one another's scales or skin or feathers or fur, taste one another's blood or flesh, keep one another warm,—that attraction was now all one with the fear, and the hunter could not be told from the hunted, nor the eater from the food.

This was more or less the effect I had been after. It was somewhat more powerful than I had anticipated, but I could not now, in all conscience, make an exception for myself. I resolutely put anxiety away, went to Adam, and said, "You and your father lent me this—gave it to me, actually. It's been really useful, but it doesn't exactly seem to fit very well lately. But thanks very much! It's really been very useful."

It is hard to give back a gift without sounding peevish or ungrateful, and I did not want to leave him with that impression of me. He was not paying much attention, as it happened, and said only, "Put it down over there, OK?" and went on with what he was doing.

One of my reasons for doing what I did was that talk was getting us nowhere; but all the same I felt a little let down. I had been prepared to defend my decision. And I thought that perhaps when he did notice he might be upset and want to talk. I put some things away and fiddled around a little, but he continued to do what he was doing and to take no notice of anything else. At last I said, "Well, goodbye, dear. I hope the garden key turns up."

He was fitting parts together, and said without looking around, "OK, fine, dear. When's dinner?"

"I'm not sure," I said. "I'm going now. With the—" I hesitated, and finally said, "With them, you know," and went on out. In fact I had only just then realized how hard it would have been to explain myself. I could not chatter away as I used to do, taking it all for granted. My words now must be as slow, as new, as single, as tentative as the steps I took going down the path away from the house, between the dark-branched, tall dancers motionless against the winter shining.

Adrienne Rich
(1929–)

Winner of the Yale Younger Poets Prize in 1951, the year she graduated from Radcliffe, Adrienne Rich began her writing career as a formalist poet who pleased and impressed her male predecessors and judges. But with her third book, *Snapshots of a Daughter-in-Law* (1963), Rich broke explosively free of these paternal influences with a more personal and angry collection of poems. By the 1970s Rich had become an iconic figure of the American women's movement, whose books pushed the boundaries of political, personal, and aesthetic traditions. "Power" (1978) both mourns the death of Marie Curie and challenges the illusions of female power in male-dominated society. In addition to her many poetry collections, Rich has written several books of essays, and has maintained a decades-long involvement with progressive political causes.

Power (1978)

Living   in the earth-deposits   of our history

Today a backhoe divulged   out of a crumbling flank of earth
one bottle   amber   perfect   a hundred-year-old
cure for fever   or melancholy   a tonic
for living on this earth   in the winters of this climate.

Today I was reading about Marie Curie:
she must have known she suffered   from radiation sickness
her body bombarded for years   by the element
she had purified
It seems she denied to the end
the source of the cataracts on her eyes

the cracked and suppurating skin   of her finger-ends
till she could no longer hold   a test-tube or a pencil

She died   a famous woman   denying
her wounds
denying
her wounds   came   from the same source as her power

Sylvia Plath
(1932–1963)

ylvia Plath committed suicide at the age of thirty, but since her death, she has become the iconic figure of the American woman poet in the twentieth century. A brilliant student, who started publishing poetry and fiction in her teens, Plath grew up in Wellesley, Massachusetts, and graduated summa cum laude from Smith College in 1955. In the summer of her junior year she had attempted suicide, been hospitalized for several months, and received electroshock treatments for depression. But she seemed fully recovered when she went to Cambridge to study English literature on a Fulbright fellowship. There she met the magnetic English poet Ted Hughes, whom she married, and bore two children. In their marriage, Plath felt overshadowed by his professional success and isolated by his decision that they should live in a rural village. Her first book of poems, *The Colossus* (1960), was well received but regarded as conventional. When she discovered in October 1962 that Hughes was having an affair, she moved to London with the children and went through a period of both despair and raging creativity, writing poems that she herself knew would make her reputation. In the early winter of 1963 Plath's semiautobiographical novel *The Bell Jar* was published in Britain under the pseudonym "Victoria Lucas." But her depression worsened, and she killed herself in February 1963.

Toward the end of her life, Plath and Hughes had been keeping bees at their home in the country. "Stings" and "Wintering" were part of a sequence called "The Bee Poems" written between October 3 and 9, 1962, during Plath's month of almost manic creativity. These poems use the imagery of bees and flowers characteristic of American women's poetry in the nineteenth century, but reverse it to make the queen bee and her maidens symbols of female creative power, independence, and regeneration.

Stings (1962)

Bare-handed, I hand the combs.
The man in white smiles, bare-handed,
Our cheesecloth gauntlets neat and sweet,
The throats of our wrists brave lilies.
He and I

Have a thousand clean cells between us,
Eight combs of yellow cups,
And the hive itself a teacup,
White with pink flowers on it,
With excessive love I enameled it

Thinking "Sweetness, sweetness."
Brood cells gray as the fossils of shells
Terrify me, they seem so old.
What am I buying, wormy mahogany?
Is there any queen at all in it?

If there is, she is old,
Her wings torn shawls, her long body
Rubbed of its plush——
Poor and bare and unqueenly and even shameful.
I stand in a column

Of winged, unmiraculous women,
Honey-drudgers.
I am no drudge
Though for years I have eaten dust
And dried plates with my dense hair.

And seen my strangeness evaporate,
Blue dew from dangerous skin.
Will they hate me,
These women who only scurry,
Whose news is the open cherry, the open clover?

It is almost over.
I am in control.
Here is my honey-machine,
It will work without thinking,
Opening, in spring, like an industrious virgin

To scour the creaming crests
As the moon, for its ivory powders, scours the sea.
A third person is watching.
He has nothing to do with the bee-seller or with me.
Now he is gone

In eight great bounds, a great scapegoat.
Here is his slipper, here is another,
And here the square of white linen
He wore instead of a hat.
He was sweet,

The sweat of his efforts a rain
Tugging the world to fruit.
The bees found him out,
Molding onto his lips like lies,
Complicating his features.

They thought death was worth it, but I
Have a self to recover, a queen.
Is she dead, is she sleeping?
Where has she been,
With her lion-red body, her wings of glass?

Now she is flying
More terrible than she ever was, red
Scar in the sky, red comet
Over the engine that killed her——
The mausoleum, the wax house.

Wintering (1962)

This is the easy time, there is nothing doing.
I have whirled the midwife's extractor,
I have my honey,
Six jars of it,
Six cat's eyes in the wine cellar,

Wintering in a dark without window
At the heart of the house
Next to the last tenant's rancid jam
and the bottles of empty glitters——
Sir So-and-so's gin.

This is the room I have never been in.
This is the room I could never breathe in.
The black bunched in there like a bat,
No light
But the torch and its faint

Chinese yellow on appalling objects——
Black asininity. Decay.
Possession.
It is they who own me.
Neither cruel nor indifferent,

Only ignorant.
This is the time of hanging on for the bees—the bees
So slow I hardly know them,
Filing like soldiers
To the syrup tin

To make up for the honey I've taken.
Tate and Lyle keeps them going,
The refined snow.
It is Tate and Lyle they live on, instead of flowers.
They take it. The cold sets in.

Now they ball in a mass,
Black
Mind against all that white.
The smile of the snow is white.
It spreads itself out, a mile-long body of Meissen,

Into which, on warm days,
They can only carry their dead.
The bees are all women,
Maids and the long royal lady.
They have got rid of the men,

The blunt, clumsy stumblers, the boors.
Winter is for women——
The woman, still at her knitting,
At the cradle of Spanish walnut,
Her body a bulb in the cold and too dumb to think.

Will the hive survive, will the gladiolas
Succeed in banking their fires
To enter another year?
What will they taste of, the Christmas roses?
The bees are flying. They taste the spring.

Annie Proulx
(1935–)

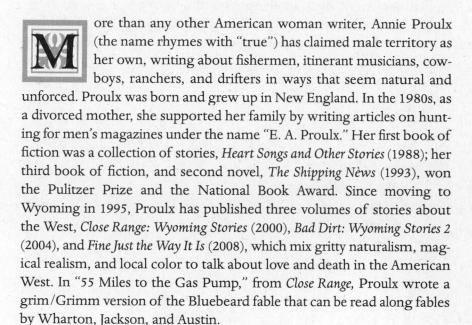

More than any other American woman writer, Annie Proulx (the name rhymes with "true") has claimed male territory as her own, writing about fishermen, itinerant musicians, cowboys, ranchers, and drifters in ways that seem natural and unforced. Proulx was born and grew up in New England. In the 1980s, as a divorced mother, she supported her family by writing articles on hunting for men's magazines under the name "E. A. Proulx." Her first book of fiction was a collection of stories, *Heart Songs and Other Stories* (1988); her third book of fiction, and second novel, *The Shipping Nèws* (1993), won the Pulitzer Prize and the National Book Award. Since moving to Wyoming in 1995, Proulx has published three volumes of stories about the West, *Close Range: Wyoming Stories* (2000), *Bad Dirt: Wyoming Stories 2* (2004), and *Fine Just the Way It Is* (2008), which mix gritty naturalism, magical realism, and local color to talk about love and death in the American West. In "55 Miles to the Gas Pump," from *Close Range,* Proulx wrote a grim/Grimm version of the Bluebeard fable that can be read along fables by Wharton, Jackson, and Austin.

55 Miles to the Gas Pump (2000)

Rancher Croom in handmade boots and filthy hat, that walleyed cattleman, stray hairs like curling fiddle string ends, that warm-handed, quick-foot dancer on splintery boards or down the cellar stairs to a rack of bottles of his own strange beer, yeasty, cloudy, bursting out in garlands of foam, Rancher Croom at night galloping drunk over the dark plain, turning off at a place he knows to arrive at a canyon brink where he dismounts and looks down on tumbled rock, waits, then steps out, parting the air with his last roar, sleeves surging up windmill arms, jeans riding over boot tops, but before he hits he rises again to the top of the cliff like a cork in a bucket of milk.

Mrs. Croom on the roof with a saw cutting a hole into the attic where she has not been for twelve years thanks to old Croom's padlocks and warnings, whets to her desire, and the sweat flies as she exchanges the saw for a chisel and hammer until a ragged slab of peak is free and she can see inside: just as she thought: the corpses of Mr. Croom's paramours—she recognizes them from their photographs in the paper: MISS-ING WOMAN—some desiccated as jerky and much the same color, some moldy from lying beneath roofleaks, and all of them used hard, covered with tarry handprints, the marks of boot heels, some bright blue with the remnants of paint used on the shutters years ago, one wrapped in newspaper nipple to knee.

When you live a long way out you make your own fun.

Joyce Carol Oates

(1938–)

n astoundingly prolific, disciplined, and versatile writer, Joyce Carol Oates has published over a hundred books including novels, short stories, plays, poems, and critical essays. Growing up on a farm in upstate New York, Oates excelled, and was the 1960 valedictorian at Syracuse University. She earned her MFA from the University of Wisconsin in 1961. While teaching in Detroit, Michigan, and then Ontario, Canada, during the tumultuous 1960s and 1970s, Oates recorded the social turmoil around her in her many popular books, winning the 1970 National Book Award for her novel *them*. In 1978, she moved to Princeton University, where she is the Roger S. Berlind Professor of the Humanities in the Creative Writing Program.

From the beginning of her writing career, Oates has chosen to write about men as well as women, and about male as well as female consciousness, especially men facing violent conflict whether random or ritualized, as in boxing. "Golden Gloves," like her essays on Mike Tyson and her book *On Boxing* (1987), sees boxing as a masculine rite of passage, with parallels to childbirth for women.

Golden Gloves (1985)

He was a premature baby, seven months old, born with deformed feet: the tiny arches twisted, the toes turned inward like fleshly claws. He didn't learn to walk until the age of three; then he tottered and lurched from side to side, his small face contorted with an adult rage, a rim of white showing above the irises of his eyes. His parents watched him in pity and despair—his father with a kind of embarrassment as well. Even at that age he hated to be helped to walk. Sometimes he hated to be touched.

Until the age of eight, when both his feet were finally operated on, he was always stumbling, falling, hurting himself, but he was accustomed to pain, he rarely cried. He wasn't like other children! At school, on the playground, out on the street, the cruelest children mocked him, called him names—Cripple, Freak—sometimes they even tripped him—but as he got older and stronger they learned to keep their distance. If he could grab them he'd hurt them with his hard pummeling fists, he'd make them cry. And even with his handicap he was quick: quick and clever and sinewy as a snake.

After the operation on his feet his father began to take him to boxing matches downtown in the old sports arena. He will remember all his life the excitement of his first Golden Gloves tournament, some of the boxers as young as fifteen, ribs showing, backs raw with acne, hard tight muscles, tiny glinting gold crosses on chains around their necks. He remembers the brick-red leather gloves that looked as if they must be soft to the touch, the bodies hotly gleaming with sweat, white boys, black boys, their amazing agility, the quickness of their feet and hands, high-laced shoes and ribbed socks halfway to their knees. They wore trunks like swimming trunks, they wore robes like bathrobes, and all with such nonchalance, in public. He remembers the dazzling lights focused upon the elevated ring, the shouts of the crowd that came in waves, the warm rippling applause when one boy of a pair was declared the winner of his match, his arm held aloft by the referee. What must it be, to be that boy!—to stand in his place!

He was seated in a child's wheelchair in the aisle, close beside his father's seat. Both legs encased in plaster from hip to toe: and him trapped inside. He was a quiet child, a friendly child, uncomplaining and perhaps even shy, showing none of the emotion that welled up in him—hurt, anger, shame—when people stared. They were curious, mainly—didn't mean to be insulting. Just ignore them, honey, his mother always said. But when he was alone with his father and people looked at him a little too long his father bristled with irritation. If anyone dared ask what had happened to him his father would say, Who wants to know? in a certain voice. And the subject was quickly dropped.

To him his father said, Let the sons of bitches mind their own business and we'll mind ours. Right?

The operation had lasted nine hours but he remembered little of it afterward except the needle going into his arm, into a vein, the careening lights, then waking alone and frightened in a room so cold his teeth began to chatter. Such cold, and such silence: he thought he must have died. Then the pain began and he knew he was alive, he cried in short breathless incredulous sobs until the first shock was past. A nurse stood over him telling him he'd be all right. He'd been a brave, brave little boy, she said.

The promise all along had been: he'd be able to walk now like any other boy. As soon as the casts were removed.

And: he'd be able to run. (Until now he'd crawled on his hands and knees faster than he'd been able to walk, like something scuttling along a beach.)

In his wheelchair at the Golden Gloves tournament he told himself he would be a boxer: he told himself at the conclusion of the first three-round match when a panting grinning boy was declared the winner of his match, on points, his arm held high, the gleaming brick-red glove raised for all to see. And the applause!—immediate, familial, rising and swelling like a heartbeat gone wild. The boy's father was in the ring with him, other boys who might have been his brothers or cousins—they were hugging one another in their happiness at the victory. Then the ring was emptied except for the referee, and the next young boxers and their seconds appeared.

He knew: he would be up there in the ring one day in the lights, rows of people watching. He would be there in the lighted ring, not in a wheelchair. Not in the audience at all.

After the casts were removed he had to learn to walk again.

They stood him carefully against a wall like a small child and encouraged him, Don't be afraid, take a step, take another step, come to them as best he could. They told him it wouldn't hurt and though it did hurt he didn't care, he plunged out lurching, swaying, falling panicked into his mother's arms. Yes, said his mother. Like that. Come *on*, said his father. Try again.

It was a year before he could walk inside the house without limping or turning his left foot helplessly inward. It was another year before he could run in the yard or in the school playground. By then his father had bought him a pair of child's boxing gloves, soft simulated dark brown leather. The gloves were the size of melons and so beautiful his eyes filled with tears when he first saw them. He would remember their sharp pungent smell through his life.

His father laced on the gloves, crouched to spar with him, taught him a few basic principles—how to hold his guard, how to stand at an angle with his chin tucked against his shoulder (Joe Louis style), how to jab, how to keep moving—later arranged for him to take boxing lessons at the YMCA. His father had wanted to be a boxer himself when he was a boy, he'd fought in a few three-round matches at a local club but had won only the first match; his reflexes, he said, were just slightly off: when his opponent's jab got to him he forgot everything he knew and wanted to slug it out. He'd known enough to quit before he got hurt. Either you have the talent or you don't, his father said. It can't be faked.

He began to train at the Y, he worked out every day after school and on Saturday mornings; by the age of sixteen he'd brought his weight up to 130 pounds standing five foot six, he could run ten, twelve, as many as fifteen miles without tiring. He was quick, light, shrewd, he was good at boxing and he knew he was good, everyone acknowledged it, everyone watched him with interest. When he wasn't at the gym—when he had to be in school, or in church, or at home, even in bed—he was thinking about the gym, the ring, himself in his boxing trunks and leather gloves, Vaseline smeared on his face and his headgear on his head, he was in his crouch but getting ready to move, his knees bent, his hands closed into fists. He was ready! He couldn't be taken unawares! He couldn't be stopped! He became obsessed with some of the boys and young men he knew at the gym, their weights, their heights, the reach of their arms, could they knock him out if he fought them, could he knock them out? What did they think about *him*? There were weeks when he was infatuated with one or another boy who might be a year or two older than he, a better boxer, until it was revealed that he wasn't a better boxer after all: he had his weaknesses, his bad habits, his limitations. He concentrated a good deal on the feel of his own body, building up his muscles, strengthening his stomach, his neck, learning not to wince at pain—not to show pain at all. He loved the sinewy springiness of his legs and feet, the tension in his shoulders; he loved the way his body came to life, moving, it seemed, of its own will, knowing by instinct how to strike his opponent how to get through his opponent's guard, how to hurt him and hurt him again and make it last. His clenched fists inside the shining gloves. His teeth in the mouthpiece. Eyes narrowed and shifting behind the hot lids as if they weren't his own eyes merely but those belonging to someone he didn't yet know, an adult man, a man for whom all things were possible.

Sometimes on Saturday afternoons the boys were shown film clips and documentaries of the great fighters. Jack Dempsey—Gene Tunney— Benny Leonard—Joe Louis—Billy Conn—Archie Moore—Sandy Saddler—Carmen Basilio—Sugar Ray Robinson—Jersey Joe Walcott— Rocky Marciano. He watched entranced, staring at the flickering images on the screen; some of the films were aged and poorly preserved, the blinds at the windows fitted loosely so that the room wasn't completely darkened, and the boxers took on an odd ghostly insubstantial look as they crouched and darted and lunged at one another. Feinting, clinching, backing off, then the flurry of gloves so swift the eye couldn't follow, one man suddenly down and the other in a neutral corner, the announcer's voice rising in excitement as if it were all happening now right now and not decades ago. More astonishing than the powerful blows dealt were the blows taken, the punishment absorbed as if really finally one could not be hurt by an opponent, only stopped by one's own failure of nerve or judgment. If you're hurt you deserve to be hurt! If you're hurt badly you deserve to be hurt badly! Turning to the referee to protest a low blow, his guard momentarily lowered—there was Jack Sharkey knocked out by Jack Dempsey with a fast left hook. Like that! And the fight was over. And there was aging Archie Moore knocked down repeatedly, savagely, by young Yvon Durrelle, staggering on his feet part-conscious but indomitable—how had he come back to win? how had he done it?—boasting he wasn't tired afterward, he could fight the fight all over again. Young Joe Louis baffled and outboxed by stylish Billy Conn for twelve rounds, then suddenly as Conn swarmed all over him trying to knock him out Louis came alive, turned into a machine for hitting, combinations so rapid the eye couldn't follow, left hooks, right crosses, uppercuts, a dozen punches within seconds and Conn was finished—that was the great Joe Louis in his prime. And here, Jersey Joe Walcott outboxing Rocky Marciano until suddenly Marciano connected with his right, that terrible incalculably powerful right. Let's see the knockout in slow motion, the announcer said, and you could see this time how it happened, Walcott hit so hard his face so stunned so distorted it was no longer a human face, no longer recognizable. And Rocky Marciano and Ezzard Charles fighting for Marciano's heavyweight title in 1954—after fifteen rounds both men covered in blood from cuts and gashes in their faces but embracing each other like brothers, smiling, laughing it seemed, in mutual respect and admiration and it didn't—almost—seem to matter that one man had to lose and the other had to win: they'd fought one of the great fights of the century and everyone knew it.

And *he* knew he was of their company. If only he might be allowed to show it.

He was sixteen years old, he was seventeen years old, boxing in local matches, working his way steadily up into state competitions, finally into the Golden Gloves Tri-State tournament. He had a good trainer, his father had seen to that. He had trophies, plaques, photographs taken at ringside, part of the living room was given over to his boxing as to a shrine. What do your friends think about your boxing? his relatives asked. Isn't it a dangerous sport? But he hadn't any friends that mattered and if his classmates had any opinion about him he couldn't have guessed what it might be, or cared. And, no, it wasn't a dangerous sport. It was only dangerous if you made mistakes.

It was said frequently at the gym that he was "coming along." The sportswriter for the local newspaper did a brief piece on him and a few other "promising" amateurs. He was quick and clever and intuitive, he knew to let a blow slide by his shoulder then to get his own in then to retreat, never to panic, never to shut his eyes, never to breathe through his mouth, it was all a matter of breath you might say, a matter of the most exquisite tuning, momentum, a dancer's intelligence in his legs, the instinct to hit, to hit hard, and to hit again. He was a young Sandy Saddler they said—but he didn't fight dirty! No, he was a young Sugar Ray. Styled a bit on that brilliant new heavyweight Cassius Clay, who'd surprised the boxing world by knocking out Sonny Liston. He hadn't a really hard punch but he was working on it, working constantly, in any case he was winning all his matches or fighting to a draw, there's nothing wrong in fighting to a draw his father told him, though he could see his father was disappointed sometimes, there were fights he should have won but just didn't—couldn't. The best times were when he won a match by a knock-out, his opponent suddenly falling, and down, not knocked out really, just sitting there on the canvas dazed and frightened, blinking, looking as if he were about to cry but no one ever cried, that never happened.

You have real talent, he was told. Told repeatedly.

You have a future!

The promise was—he seemed to know—that he couldn't lose. He'd understood that years before, watching one or another of the films, young Dempsey fierce as a tiger against the giant Jess Willard, twenty-year-old Joe Louis in action, Sugar Ray Robinson who'd once killed an opponent in the ring with the force of his blows: he was of their company and he knew it and he knew he couldn't lose, he couldn't even be seriously hurt, that seemed to be part of the promise. But sometimes he woke in the night in his bed not knowing at first where he was, was he in the gym, in the ring, staring panicked across the wide lighted canvas to his opponent shadowy in the opposite corner, he lay shivering, his heart racing, the bedclothes damp with sweat. He liked to sweat most of the time, he liked the rank smell of his own body, but this was not one of those times. His fists when he woke would be clenched so hard his fingernails would be cutting into his palms, his toes curled in tight and cramped as if still deformed, secretly deformed. Cripple! Freak! The blow you can't see coming is the blow that knocks you out—the blow out of nowhere. How can you protect yourself against a blow out of nowhere? How can you stop it from happening again? He'd been surprised like that only a few times, sparring, not in real fights. But the surprise had stayed with him.

Yet there was a promise. Going back to when he was very small, before the operation.

And his father adored him, his father was so happy for him, placing bets on him, not telling him until afterward—after he'd won. Just small bets. Just for fun. His father said, I don't want you to feel any pressure, it's just for fun.

Then of course he was stopped and his "career" ended abruptly and unromantically. As he should have foreseen. Just a few weeks before his eighteenth birthday.

It happened midway in the first round of a Golden Gloves semifinal lightweight match in Buffalo, New York, when a stocky black boy from Trenton, New Jersey, came bounding at him like a killer, pushing and crowding and bulling him back into the ropes, forcing him backward as he'd never been forced; the boy brushed aside his jabs and ignored his feints, popped him with a hard left then landed a blow to his exposed mouth that drove his upper front teeth back through his slack lower lip but somehow at the same time smashed the teeth upward into his palate. He'd lost his mouthpiece in the confusion, he'd never seen the punch coming, he was told afterward it had been a hard straight right like no amateur punch anyone could recall.

He fell dazed into the ropes, he fell to the canvas, he hid his bleeding face with his gloves, gravity pulled him down and his instinct was to submit to curl up into a tight ball to lie very still maybe he wouldn't be hit again maybe it was all over.

And so it happened.

That was his career as an amateur boxer. Twenty or so serious matches: that was it.

Never again, he told himself. That *was* it.

(The black boy from New Jersey—Roland Bush Jr.—was eighteen years old at the time of the fight but had the face of a mature man, heavy-lidded eyes, broad flat nose, scars in his forehead and fanning his eyes. An inch shorter than his white opponent but his shoulder and leg muscles rippled with high-strung nervous strength, he'd thickened his neck muscles to withstand all blows, he was ready, he was hot, he couldn't be stopped. His skin was very dark and the whites of his eyes were an eerie bluish-white, luminous, threaded almost invisibly with blood. He weighed no more than his opponent but he had a skull and a body built to absorb punishment, he was solid, hard, relentless, taking no joy in his performance just doing it, doing it superbly, getting it done, he went on to win the Golden Gloves title in his division with another spectacular knockout and a few months later turned professional and was advanced swiftly through the lightweight ranks then into the junior welterweights where he was ranked number fourteen by *Ring* magazine at the time of his death—he died aged twenty of a cerebral hemorrhage following a ten-round fight in Houston, Texas, which he'd lost in the ninth round by a technical knockout.)

The fight was stopped, the career of "promise" was stopped, now he is thirty-four years old and it seems to him his life is passing swiftly. But at a distance. It doesn't seem in fact to belong to him, it might be anybody's life.

In his professional career, in his social life, he is successful, no doubt enviable, but he finds himself dreaming frequently these days of the boy with the crippled feet. Suppose he'd never had the operation: what then! He sees the creature on its hands and knees crawling crablike along the ground, there is a jeering circle of boys, now the terrible blinding lights of the operating room snuff him out and he's gone. And now seated in his aluminum wheelchair staring down helplessly at the white plaster casts: his punishment. Hips to toes, toes to hips. His punishment.

The adults of the world conspire in lies leaning over him smiling into his face. He will be able to walk he will be able to run he won't feel any pain he won't be hurt again doesn't he want to believe?—and of course he does. He does. His wife's name is Annemarie, a name melodic and lovely he sometimes shapes with his lips, in silence: an incantation.

He had fallen in love with Annemarie seeing her for the first time amid a large noisy gathering of relatives and friends. When they were introduced and he was told her name he thought extravagantly, Annemarie, yes—she's the one!

From the first she inspired him to such extravagant fancies, such violations of his own self. Which is why he loves her desperately.

Annemarie is twenty-nine years old but has the lithe small-boned features of a girl. Her hair is light brown, wavy, silvery in sunshine, her eyes wide-set and intelligent, watchful. Most of the time she appears to be wonderfully assured, her center of gravity well inside her, yet in the early weeks of the pregnancy she cried often and asked him half angrily, Do you love me? And he told her, Yes, of course. Of course I love you. But shortly afterward she asked him again, as if she hadn't believed him, Do you love me—*really*? More than before, or less? and he laughed as if she were joking, as if it were one of her jokes, closing his arms around her to comfort her. This was Annemarie's second pregnancy after all: the first had ended in a miscarriage.

Don't be absurd, Annemarie, he tells her.

Most of the time, of course, she is good-natured, sunny, uncomplaining; she loves being pregnant and she is eager to have the baby. She chooses her maternity outfits with care and humor: flowing waistless dresses in colorful fabrics, blouses with foppish ties, shawls, Indian beads, cloth flowers in her hair. Some of the outfits are from secondhand shops in the city, costumes from the forties and fifties, long skirts, culottes, silk pants suits, a straw boater with clusters of artificial berries on the rim: to divert the eye from her prominent belly, she says. But the childlike pleasure Annemarie takes in dressing is genuine and her husband is charmed by it, he adores her for all that is herself, yes, he'd fight to the death to protect her he'd die in her place if required.

Odd how, from the start, she has had the power to inspire him to such melodramatic extravagant claims.

The miscarriage took place in the fifth month of the first pregnancy. One night Annemarie woke with mock-labor pains and began to bleed, she bled until nothing remained in her womb of what was to have been their son. And they were helpless, helpless to stop it.

They'd known for weeks that the fetus was impaired, the pregnancy might not go to term; still, the premature labor and the premature death were blows from which each was slow to recover. Annemarie wept in his arms and, he thought, in his place: her angry childish mourning helped purge his soul. And Annemarie was the first to recover from the loss for after all—as her doctor insisted—it wasn't anything personal, *it's just physical*. The second pregnancy has nothing at all to do with the first.

So we'll try again, Annemarie said reasonably.

And he hesitated saying, Not now. Saying, Isn't it too soon? You aren't recovered.

And she said, Of course I'm recovered.

And he said, But I think we should wait.

And she said, chiding, *Now*. When if not *now*?

(Twenty-nine years old isn't young, in fact it is "elderly" in medical terms for a woman pregnant with her first child. And they want more than one child, after all. They want a family.)

So they made love. And they made love. And he gave himself up to her in love, in love, in a drowning despairing hope, it's just physical after all it doesn't mean anything. Such failures of the physical life don't mean anything. You take the blow then get on with living isn't that the history of the world? Of course it is.

He's an adult man now, not a boy any longer. He knows.

He cradles his wife's belly in his hands. Stroking her gently. Kissing her. Fiercely attentive to the baby's secret life, that mysterious interior throb, that ghostly just-perceptible kick. Through the doctor's stethoscope each listened to the baby's heartbeat, a rapid feverish-sounding beat, *I am, I am, I am*. This pregnancy, unlike the first, has been diagnosed as "normal." This fetus unlike the first has been promised as "normal."

Approximately fifteen days yet to go: the baby has begun its descent head first into the pelvic cavity and Annemarie has begun, oddly, to feel more comfortable than she has felt in months. She assures him she is excited—not frightened—and he remembers the excitement of boxing, the excitement of climbing through the ropes knowing he couldn't turn back. Elation or panic? euphoria or terror?—that heartbeat beating everywhere in his body.

For months they have attended natural childbirth classes together and he oversees, genially but scrupulously, her exercises at home: he will be in the delivery room with her, he'll be there all the while.

This time, like last time, the fetus is male, and again they have drawn up a list of names. But the names are entirely different from the first list, Patrick, William, Alan, Seth, Sean, Raymond; sometimes Annemarie favors one and sometimes another but she doesn't want to choose a name until the baby is born. Safely born.

Why hasn't he ever told Annemarie about his amateur boxing, his "career" in the Golden Gloves?—he has told her virtually everything else about his life. But it is a matter of deep shame to him, recalling not only the evening of his public defeat but his hope, his near-lunatic hope that he would be a hero, a star! a great champion! He has told her he'd been a premature baby, born with a "slight deformity" of one foot which was corrected by surgery immediately after his birth: this is as near to the truth as he can manage.

Which foot was it? Annemarie asks sympathetically.

He tells her he doesn't remember which foot, it isn't important.

But one night he asks her to caress his feet. They are in bed, he is feeling melancholy, worried, not wholly himself. He has begun to profoundly dislike his work in proportion to his success at it and this is a secret he can't share with Annemarie; there are other secrets too he can't share, won't share, he fears her ready sympathy, the generosity of her spirit. At such times he feels himself vulnerable to memory, in danger of reliving that last fight, experiencing moments he hadn't in a sense experienced at the time—it had all happened too swiftly. Roland Bush Jr. pressing through his defense, jabbing him with precise machinelike blows, that gleaming black face those narrowed eyes seeking him out. White boy! White boy who are *you*! Bush was the true fighter stalking his prey. Bush was the one.

He hadn't been a fighter at all, merely a victim.

He asks Annemarie to caress his feet. Would she hold them? Warm them? Would she . . . ? It would mean so much, he can't explain.

Perhaps he is jealous of their son so cozy and tight upside down beneath his wife's heart but this is a thought he doesn't quite think.

Of course Annemarie is delighted to massage his feet, it's the sort of impulsive whimsical thing she loves to do, no need for logic, no need for explanations, she has wanted all along to nourish the playful side of his personality. So she takes his feet between her small dry warm hands and gently massages them. She brings to the intimate task a frowning concentration that flatters him, fills him with love. What is she thinking? he wonders. Then suddenly he is apprehensive: What does she know of me? What can she guess? Annemarie says, smiling, Your feet are so terribly cold! But I'll make them warm.

The incident is brief, silly, loving, quickly forgotten. One of those moments between a husband and a wife not meant to be analyzed, or even remembered. It never occurs a second time, never again does Annemarie offer to caress his feet and out of pride and shame he certainly isn't going to ask.

The days pass, the baby is due in less than a week, he keeps thinking, dreaming, of that blow to his mouth: the terrible power of the punch out of nowhere. His skull shook with a fierce reverberation that ran through his entire body and he'd known then that no one had ever hit him before.

It was his own death that had crashed into him—yet no more than he deserved. He was hit as one is hit only once in a lifetime. He was hit and time stopped. He was hit in the second minute of the first round of a long-forgotten amateur boxing match in Buffalo, New York; he was hit and he died and they carried him along a corridor of blinding lights, strapped to a stretcher, drooling blood and saliva, eyes turned up in his head. Something opened, lifted, a space of some kind clearing for him to enter, his own death but he hadn't had the courage to step forward.

Someone whose face he couldn't see was sinking a needle deep into his forearm, into the fleshy part of his forearm, afterward they spoke calmly and reassuringly saying it isn't really serious, a mild concussion not a serious fracture, his nose wasn't broken, only his mouth and teeth injured, that could be fixed. He flinched remembering the blow flying at him out of nowhere. He flinched, remembering. It happens once in a lifetime after that you're dead white boy but you pick yourself up and keep going.

There followed then the long period—months, years—when his father shrank from looking him fully in the face. Sometimes, however, his father examined his mouth, wasn't entirely pleased with the plastic surgeon's work. It had cost so damned much after all. But the false teeth were lifelike, wonderfully convincing, some consolation at least. Expensive too but everyone in the family was impressed with the white perfect teeth affixed to their lightweight aluminum plate.

All that the old tales of pregnancy promise of a female beauty luminous and dewy, lit from within, was true: here is Annemarie with eyes moist and bright as he'd rarely seen them, a skin with a faint rosy bloom, feverish to the touch. Here is the joy of the body as he had known it long ago and had forgotten.

There were days, weeks, when she felt slightly unwell yet the bloom of pregnancy had held and deepened month following month. A woman fully absorbed in herself, suffused with light, heat, radiance, entranced by the plunge into darkness she is to take. Pain—the promised pain of childbirth—frightens yet fascinates her: she means to be equal to it. She doesn't shrink from hearing the most alarming stories, labors of many hours without anesthetic, cesarean deliveries where natural childbirth had been expected, sudden losses of blood. She means to triumph.

Within the family they joke—it's the father-to-be, not Annemarie, who is having difficulty sleeping these past few weeks. But that too is natural, isn't it?

One night very late in her term Annemarie stares down at herself as if she'd never seen herself before—the enormous swollen belly, the blue-veined stretched skin with its uncanny luminous pallor—and because she has been feeling melancholy for days, because she is fatigued, suddenly doubting, not altogether herself, she exclaims with a harsh little laugh, God look at me, at this, how can you love anything like—*this*!

His nerves are torn like silk. He knows she isn't serious, he knows it is the lateness of the hour and the strain of waiting, it can't be Annemarie herself speaking. Quickly he says, Don't be absurd.

But that night as he falls slowly asleep he hears himself explaining to Annemarie in a calm measured voice that she will be risking something few men can risk, she should know herself exalted, privileged, in a way invulnerable to hurt even if she is very badly hurt, she'll be risking something he himself cannot risk again in his life. And maybe he never risked it at all.

You'll be going to a place I can't reach, he says.

He would touch her, in wonder, in dread, he would caress her, but his body is heavy with sleep, growing distant from him. He says softly, I'm not sure I'll be here when you come back.

But by now Annemarie's breathing is so deep and rhythmic she must be asleep. In any case she gives no sign of having heard.

Maxine Hong Kingston
(1940–)

Born to Chinese immigrants in Stockton, California, Maxine Hong graduated in 1962 from the University of California at Berkeley where she now teaches creative writing. A teacher in California and Hawaii schools for more than a decade, Kingston found sudden literary acclaim with the publication of two critically praised books, *The Woman Warrior: Memoirs of a Girlhood among Ghosts* (1976) and *China Men* (1980), mixtures of memoir, myth, and fiction about her Chinese-American upbringing and Chinese ancestors, from which "On Discovery" is taken. Her other books include a novel, *Tripmaster Monkey: His Fake Book* (1989), and *The Fifth Book of Peace* (2003), a memoir of her antiwar activism, and a reimagining of the novel's sequel, which was destroyed in a fire.

On Discovery (1980)

Once upon a time, a man, named Tang Ao, looking for the Gold Mountain, crossed an ocean, and came upon the Land of Women. The women immediately captured him, not on guard against ladies. When they asked Tang Ao to come along, he followed; if he had had male companions, he would've winked over his shoulder.

"We have to prepare you to meet the queen," the women said. They locked him in a canopied apartment equipped with pots of makeup, mirrors, and a woman's clothes. "Let us help you off with your armor and boots," said the women. They slipped his coat off his shoulders, pulled it down his arms, and shackled his wrists behind him. The women who kneeled to take off his shoes chained his ankles together.

A door opened, and he expected to meet his match, but it was only two old women with sewing boxes in their hands. "The less you struggle, the less it'll hurt," one said, squinting a bright eye as she threaded her needle. Two captors sat on him while another held his head. He felt an old woman's dry fingers trace his ear; the long nail on her little finger scraped his neck. "What are you doing?" he asked. "Sewing your lips together," she joked, blackening needles in a candle flame. The ones who sat on him bounced with laughter. But the old women did not sew his lips together. They pulled his earlobes taut and jabbed a needle through each of them. They had to poke and probe before puncturing the layers of skin correctly, the hole in the front of the lobe in line with the one in back, the layers of skin sliding about so. They worked the needle through—a last jerk for the needle's wide eye ("needle's nose" in Chinese). They strung his raw flesh with silk threads; he could feel the fibers.

The women who sat on him turned to direct their attention to his feet. They bent his toes so far backward that his arched foot cracked. The old ladies squeezed each foot and broke many tiny bones along the sides. They gathered his toes, toes over and under one another like a knot of ginger root. Tang Ao wept with pain. As they wound the bandages tight and tighter around his feet, the women sang footbinding songs to distract him: "Use aloe for binding feet and not for scholars."

During the months of a season, they fed him on women's food: the tea was thick with white chrysanthemums and stirred the cool female winds inside his body; chicken wings made his hair shine; vinegar soup improved his womb. They drew the loops of thread through the scabs that grew daily over the holes in his earlobes. One day they inserted gold hoops. Every night they unbound his feet, but his veins had shrunk, and the blood pumping through them hurt so much, he begged to have his feet rewrapped tight. They forced him to wash his used bandages, which were embroidered with flowers and smelled of rot and cheese. He hung the bandages up to dry, streamers that drooped and draped wall to wall. He felt embarrassed; the wrappings were like underwear, and they were his.

One day his attendants changed his gold hoops to jade studs and strapped his feet to shoes that curved like bridges. They plucked out each hair on his face, powdered him white, painted his eyebrows like a moth's wings, painted his cheeks and lips red. He served a meal at the queen's court. His hips swayed and his shoulders swiveled because of his shaped feet. "She's pretty, don't you agree?" the diners said, smacking their lips at his dainty feet as he bent to put dishes before them.

In the Women's Land there are no taxes and no wars. Some scholars say that that country was discovered during the reign of Empress Wu (A.D. 694–705), and some say earlier than that, A.D. 441, and it was in North America.

She may have been unusually beloved, the precious only daughter, spoiled and mirror gazing because of the affection the family lavished on her. When her husband left, they welcomed the chance to take her back from the in-laws; she could live like the little daughter for just a while longer. There are stories that my grandfather was different from other people, "crazy ever since the little Jap bayoneted him in the head." He used to put his naked penis on the dinner table, laughing. And one day he brought home a baby girl, wrapped up inside his brown western-style greatcoat. He had traded one of his sons, probably my father, the youngest, for her. My grandmother made him trade back. When he finally got a daughter of his own, he doted on her. They must have all loved her, except perhaps my father, the only brother who never went back to China, having once been traded for a girl.

Brothers and sisters, newly men and women, had to efface their sexual color and present plain miens. Disturbing hair and eyes, a smile like no other, threatened the ideal of five generations living under one roof. To focus blurs, people shouted face to face and yelled from room to room. The immigrants I know have loud voices, unmodulated to American tones even after years away from the village where they called their friendships out across the fields. I have not been able to stop my mother's screams in public libraries or over telephones. Walking erect (knees straight, toes pointed forward, not pigeon-toed, which is Chinese-feminine) and speaking in an inaudible voice, I have tried to turn myself American-feminine. Chinese communication was loud, public. Only sick people had to whisper. But at the dinner table, where the family members came nearest one another, no one could talk, not the outcasts nor any eaters. Every word that falls from the mouth is a coin lost. Silently they gave and accepted food with both hands. A preoccupied child who took his bowl with one hand got a sideways glare. A complete moment of total attention is due everyone alike. Children and lovers have no singularity here, but my aunt used a secret voice, a separate-attentiveness.

Amy Tan
(1952–)

he daughter of Chinese immigrants, Amy Tan grew up in California, but was also educated in Europe after the death of her father and older brother from brain cancer. Her mother had insisted on taking Amy and her younger brother abroad to find the best possible education. The determination and tenacity of her mother's ambitions created intense conflicts for Tan as a girl and young woman, and she defied her mother's hopes that she would become a concert pianist, first to study for a Ph.D. (never completed) in linguistics at Berkeley, and then to become a writer. Tan's first novel, *The Joy Luck Club* (1989), sixteen interrelated stories about four Chinese-American mothers and their American-born daughters, became a best-seller, and then a hit film, for which Tan herself wrote the screenplay. The autobiographical vignette, "Two Kinds," is taken from the novel. Tan has also published *The Bonesetter's Daughter* (2001) and *The Opposite of Fate* (2003), which retells the mother-daughter story.

Two Kinds (1989)

My mother believed you could be anything you wanted to be in America. You could open a restaurant. You could work for the government and get good retirement. You could buy a house with almost no money down. You could become rich. You could become instantly famous.

"Of course, you can be a prodigy, too," my mother told me when I was nine. "You can be best anything. What does Auntie Lindo know? Her daughter, she is only best tricky."

America was where all my mother's hopes lay. She had come to San Francisco in 1949 after losing everything in China: her mother and father, her family home, her first husband, and two daughters, twin baby girls. But she never looked back with regret. There were so many ways for things to get better.

We didn't immediately pick the right kind of prodigy. At first my mother thought I could be a Chinese Shirley Temple. We'd watch Shirley's old movies on TV as though they were training films. My mother would poke my arm and say, "*Ni kan*"—You watch. And I would see Shirley tapping her feet, or singing a sailor song, or pursing her lips into a very round O while saying, "Oh my goodness."

"*Ni kan,*" said my mother as Shirley's eyes flooded with tears. "You already know how. Don't need talent for crying!"

Soon after my mother got this idea about Shirley Temple, she took me to a beauty training school in the Mission district and put me in the hands of a student who could barely hold the scissors without shaking. Instead of getting big fat curls, I emerged with an uneven mass of crinkly black fuzz. My mother dragged me off to the bathroom and tried to wet down my hair.

"You look like a Negro Chinese," she lamented, as if I had done this on purpose.

The instructor of the beauty training school had to lop off these soggy clumps to make my hair even again. "Peter Pan is very popular these days," the instructor assured my mother. I now had hair the length of a boy's, with straight-across bangs that hung at a slant two inches above my eyebrows. I liked the haircut and it made me actually look forward to my future fame.

In fact, in the beginning, I was just as excited as my mother, maybe even more so. I pictured this prodigy part of me as many different images, trying each one on for size. I was a dainty ballerina girl standing by the curtains, waiting to hear the music that would send me floating on my tiptoes. I was like the Christ child lifted out of the straw manger, crying with holy indignity. I was Cinderella stepping from her pumpkin carriage with sparkly cartoon music filling the air.

In all of my imaginings, I was filled with a sense that I would soon become *perfect*. My mother and father would adore me. I would be beyond reproach. I would never feel the need to sulk for anything.

But sometimes the prodigy in me became impatient. "If you don't hurry up and get me out of here, I'm disappearing for good," it warned. "And then you'll always be nothing."

Every night after dinner, my mother and I would sit at the Formica kitchen table. She would present new tests, taking her examples from stories of amazing children that she read in *Ripley's Believe It or Not,* or *Good Housekeeping, Reader's Digest*, and a dozen other magazines she kept in a pile in our bathroom. My mother got these magazines from people whose houses she cleaned. And since she cleaned many houses each week, we had a great assortment. She would look through them all, searching for stories about remarkable children.

The first night she brought out a story about a three-year-old boy who knew the capitals of all the states and even most of the European countries. A teacher was quoted as saying the little boy could also pronounce the names of the foreign cities correctly.

"What's the capital of Finland?" my mother asked me, looking at the magazine story.

All I knew was the capital of California, because Sacramento was the name of the street we lived on in Chinatown. "Nairobi!" I guessed, saying the most foreign word I could think of. She checked to see if that was possibly one way to pronounce "Helsinki" before showing me the answer.

The tests got harder—multiplying numbers in my head, finding the queen of hearts in a deck of cards, trying to stand on my head without using my hands, predicting the daily temperatures in Los Angeles, New York, and London.

One night I had to look at a page from the Bible for three minutes and then report everything I could remember. "Now Jehoshaphat had riches and honor in abundance and . . . that's all I remember, Ma," I said.

And after seeing my mother's disappointed face once again, something inside of me began to die. I hated the tests, the raised hopes and failed expectations. Before going to bed that night, I looked in the mirror above the bathroom sink and when I saw only my face staring back—and that it would always be this ordinary face—I began to cry. Such a sad, ugly girl! I made high-pitched noises like a crazed animal, trying to scratch out the face in the mirror.

And then I saw what seemed to be the prodigy side of me—because I had never seen that face before. I looked at my reflection, blinking so I could see more clearly. The girl staring back at me was angry, powerful. This girl and I were the same. I had new thoughts, willful thoughts, or rather thoughts filled with lots of won'ts. I won't let her change me, I promised myself. I won't be what I'm not.

So now on nights when my mother presented her tests, I performed listlessly, my head propped on one arm. I pretended to be bored. And I was. I got so bored that I started counting the bellows of the foghorns out on the bay while my mother drilled me in other areas. The sound was comforting and reminded me of the cow jumping over the moon. And the next day, I played a game with myself, seeing if my mother would give up on me before eight bellows. After a while I usually counted only one bellow, maybe two bellows at most. At last she was beginning to give up hope.

Two or three months went by without any mention of my being a prodigy again. And then one day my mother was watching *The Ed Sullivan Show* on TV. The TV was old and the sound kept shorting out. Every time my mother got halfway up from the sofa to adjust the set, the sound would come back on and Ed would be talking. As soon as she sat down, Ed would go silent again. She got up, the TV broke into loud piano music. She sat down. Silence. Up and down, back and forth, quiet and loud. It was like a stiff embraceless dance between her and the TV set. Finally she stood by the set with her hand on the sound dial.

She seemed entranced by the music, a frenzied little piano piece with a mesmerizing quality, sort of quick passages and then teasing lilting ones before it returned to the quick playful parts.

"*Ni kan,*" my mother said, calling me over with hurried hand gestures. "Look here."

I could see why my mother was fascinated by the music. It was being pounded out by a little Chinese girl, about nine years old, with a Peter Pan haircut. The girl had the sauciness of a Shirley Temple. She was proudly modest like a proper Chinese child. And she also did a fancy sweep of a curtsy, so that the fluffy skirt of her white dress cascaded slowly to the floor like petals of a large carnation.

In spite of these warning signs, I wasn't worried. Our family had no piano and we couldn't afford to buy one, let alone reams of sheet music and piano lessons. So I could be generous in my comments when my mother bad-mouthed the little girl on TV.

"Play note right, but doesn't sound good! No singing sound," complained my mother.

"What are you picking on her for?" I said carelessly. "She's pretty good. Maybe she's not the best, but she's trying hard." I knew almost immediately I would be sorry I said that.

"Just like you," she said. "Not the best. Because you not trying." She gave a little huff as she let go of the sound dial and sat down on the sofa.

The little Chinese girl sat down also to play an encore of "Anitra's Dance" by Grieg. I remember the song, because later on I had to learn how to play it.

Three days after watching *The Ed Sullivan Show*, my mother told me what my schedule would be for piano lessons and piano practice. She had talked to Mr. Chong, who lived on the first floor of our apartment building. Mr. Chong was a retired piano teacher and my mother had traded housecleaning services for weekly lessons and a piano for me to practice on every day, two hours a day, from four until six.

When my mother told me this, I felt as though I had been sent to hell. I whined and then kicked my foot a little when I couldn't stand it anymore.

"Why don't you like me the way I am? I'm *not* a genius! I can't play the piano. And even if I could, I wouldn't go on TV if you paid me a million dollars!" I cried.

My mother slapped me. "Who ask you to be genius?" she shouted. "Only ask you be your best. For you sake. You think I want you to be genius? Hnnh! What for! Who ask you!"

"So ungrateful," I heard her mutter in Chinese. "If she had as much talent as she has temper, she'd be famous now."

Mr. Chong, whom I secretly nicknamed Old Chong, was very strange, always tapping his fingers to the silent music of an invisible orchestra. He looked ancient in my eyes. He had lost most of the hair on top of his head and he wore thick glasses and had eyes that always looked tired and sleepy. But he must have been younger than I thought, since he lived with his mother and was not yet married.

I met Old Lady Chong once and that was enough. She had a peculiar smell like a baby that had done something in its pants. And her fingers felt like a dead person's, like an old peach I once found in the back of the refrigerator; the skin just slid off the meat when I picked it up.

I soon found out why Old Chong had retired from teaching piano. He was deaf. "Like Beethoven!" he shouted to me. "We're both listening only in our head!" And he would start to conduct his frantic silent sonatas.

Our lessons went like this. He would open the book and point to different things, explaining their purpose: "Key! Treble! Bass! No sharps or flats! So this is C major! Listen now and play after me!"

And then he would play the C scale a few times, a simple chord, and then, as if inspired by an old, unreachable itch, he gradually added more notes and running trills and a pounding bass until the music was really something quite grand.

I would play after him, the simple scale, the simple chord, and then I just played some nonsense that sounded like a cat running up and down on top of garbage cans. Old Chong smiled and applauded and then said, "Very good! But now you must learn to keep time!"

So that's how I discovered that Old Chong's eyes were too slow to keep up with the wrong notes I was playing. He went through the motions in half-time. To help me keep rhythm, he stood behind me, pushing down on my right shoulder for every beat. He balanced pennies on top of my wrists so I would keep them still as I slowly played scales and arpeggios. He had me curve my hand around an apple and keep that shape when playing chords. He marched stiffly to show me how to make each finger dance up and down, staccato like an obedient little soldier.

He taught me all these things, and that was how I also learned I could be lazy and get away with mistakes, lots of mistakes. If I hit the wrong notes because I hadn't practiced enough, I never corrected myself. I just kept playing in rhythm. And Old Chong kept conducting his own private reverie.

So maybe I never really gave myself a fair chance. I did pick up the basics pretty quickly, and I might have become a good pianist at that young age. But I was so determined not to try, not to be anybody different that I learned to play only the most ear-splitting preludes, the most discordant hymns.

Over the next year, I practiced like this, dutifully in my own way. And then one day I heard my mother and her friend Lindo Jong both talking in a loud bragging tone of voice so others could hear. It was after church, and I was leaning against the brick wall wearing a dress with stiff white petticoats. Auntie Lindo's daughter, Waverly, who was about my age, was standing farther down the wall about five feet away. We had grown up together and shared all the closeness of two sisters squabbling over crayons and dolls. In other words, for the most part, we hated each other. I thought she was snotty. Waverly Jong had gained a certain amount of fame as "Chinatown's Littlest Chinese Chess Champion."

"She bring home too many trophy," Auntie Lindo lamented that Sunday. "All day she play chess. All day I have no time do nothing but dust off her winnings." She threw a scolding look at Waverly, who pretended not to see her.

"You lucky you don't have this problem," said Auntie Lindo with a sigh to my mother.

And my mother squared her shoulders and bragged: "Our problem worser than yours. If we ask Jing-mei wash dish, she hear nothing but music. It's like you can't stop this natural talent."

And right then, I was determined to put a stop to her foolish pride.

A few weeks later Old Chong and my mother conspired to have me play in a talent show which would be held in the church hall. By then, my parents had saved up enough to buy me a secondhand piano, a black Wurlitzer spinet with a scarred bench. It was the showpiece of our living room.

For the talent show, I was to play a piece called "Pleading Child" from Schumann's *Scenes From Childhood*. It was a simple, moody piece that sounded more difficult than it was. I was supposed to memorize the whole thing, playing the repeat parts twice to make the piece sound longer. But I dawdled over it, playing a few bars and then cheating, looking up to see what notes followed. I never really listened to what I was playing. I daydreamed about being somewhere else, about being someone else.

The part I liked to practice best was the fancy curtsy: right foot out, touch the rose on the carpet with a pointed foot, sweep to the side, left leg bends, look up and smile.

My parents invited all the couples from the Joy Luck Club to witness my debut. Auntie Lindo and Uncle Tin were there. Waverly and her two older brothers had also come. The first two rows were filled with children both younger and older than I was. The littlest ones got to go first. They recited simple nursery rhymes, squawked out tunes on miniature violins, twirled Hula Hoops, pranced in pink ballet tutus, and when they bowed or curtsied, the audience would sigh in unison, "Awww," and then clap enthusiastically.

When my turn came, I was very confident. I remember my childish excitement. It was as if I knew, without a doubt, that the prodigy side of me really did exist. I had no fear whatsoever, no nervousness. I remember thinking to myself, This is it! This is it! I looked out over the audience, at my mother's blank face, my father's yawn, Auntie Lindo's stiff-lipped smile, Waverly's sulky expression. I had on a white dress layered with sheets of lace, and a pink bow in my Peter Pan haircut. As I sat down I envisioned people jumping to their feet and Ed Sullivan rushing up to introduce me to everyone on TV.

And I started to play. It was so beautiful. I was so caught up in how lovely I looked that at first I didn't worry about how I would sound. So it was a surprise to me when I hit the first wrong note and I realized something didn't sound quite right. And then I hit another and another followed that. A chill started at the top of my head and began to trickle down. Yet I couldn't stop playing, as though my hands were bewitched. I kept thinking my fingers would adjust themselves back, like a train switching to the right track. I played this strange jumble through two repeats, the sour notes staying with me all the way to the end.

When I stood up, I discovered my legs were shaking. Maybe I had just been nervous and the audience, like Old Chong, had seen me go through the right motions and had not heard anything wrong at all. I swept my right foot out, went down on my knee, looked up and smiled. The room was quiet, except for Old Chong, who was beaming and shouting "Bravo! Bravo! Well done!" But then I saw my mother's face, her stricken face. The audience clapped weakly, and as I walked back to my chair, with my whole face quivering as I tried not to cry, I heard a little boy whisper loudly to his mother, "That was awful," and the mother whispered, "Well, she certainly tried."

And now I realized how many people were in the audience, the whole world it seemed. I was aware of eyes burning into my back. I felt the shame of my mother and father as they sat stiffly through the rest of the show.

We could have escaped during intermission. Pride and some strange sense of honor must have anchored my parents to their chairs. And so we watched it all: the eighteen-year-old boy with a fake mustache who did a magic show and juggled flaming hoops while riding a unicycle. The breasted girl with white makeup who sang from *Madame Butterfly* and got honorable mention. And the eleven-year-old boy who won first prize playing a tricky violin song that sounded like a busy bee.

After the show the Hsus, the Jongs, and the St. Clairs from the Joy Luck Club came up to my mother and father.

"Lots of talented kids," Auntie Lindo said vaguely, smiling broadly.

"That was somethin' else," my father said, and I wondered if he was referring to me in a humorous way, or whether he even remembered what I had done.

Waverly looked at me and shrugged her shoulders. "You aren't a genius like me," she said matter-of-factly. And if I hadn't felt so bad, I would have pulled her braids and punched her stomach.

But my mother's expression was what devastated me: a quiet, blank look that said she had lost everything. I felt the same way, and it seemed as if everybody were now coming up, like gawkers at the scene of an accident, to see what parts were actually missing. When we got on the bus to go home, my father was humming the busy-bee tune and my mother was silent. I kept thinking she wanted to wait until we got home before shouting at me. But when my father unlocked the door to our apartment, my mother walked in and then went to the back, into the bedroom. No accusations. No blame. And in a way, I felt disappointed. I had been waiting for her to start shouting, so that I could shout back and cry and blame her for all my misery.

I assumed my talent-show fiasco meant I never had to play the piano again. But two days later, after school, my mother came out of the kitchen and saw me watching TV.

"Four clock," she reminded me as if it were any other day. I was stunned, as though she were asking me to go through the talent-show torture again. I wedged myself more tightly in front of the TV.

"Turn off TV," she called from the kitchen five minutes later.

I didn't budge. And then I decided. I didn't have to do what my mother said anymore. I wasn't her slave. This wasn't China. I had listened to her before and look what happened. She was the stupid one.

She came out from the kitchen and stood in the arched entryway of the living room. "Four clock," she said once again, louder.

"I'm not going to play anymore," I said nonchalantly. "Why should I? I'm not a genius."

She walked over and stood in front of the TV. I saw her chest was heaving up and down in an angry way.

"No!" I said, and I now felt stronger, as if my true self had finally emerged. So this was what had been inside me all along.

"No! I won't!" I screamed.

She yanked me by the arm, pulled me off the floor, snapped off the TV. She was frighteningly strong, half pulling, half carrying me toward the piano as I kicked the throw rugs under my feet. She lifted me up onto the hard bench. I was sobbing by now, looking at her bitterly. Her chest was heaving even more and her mouth was open, smiling crazily as if she were pleased that I was crying.

"You want me to be something that I'm not!" I sobbed. "I'll never be the kind of daughter you want me to be!"

"Only two kinds of daughters," she shouted in Chinese. "Those who are obedient and those who follow their own mind! Only one kind of daughter can live in this house. Obedient daughter!"

"Then I wish I wasn't your daughter. I wish you weren't my mother," I shouted. As I said these things I got scared. I felt like worms and toads and slimy things were crawling out of my chest, but it also felt good, as if this awful side of me had surfaced, at last.

"Too late to change this," my mother said shrilly.

And I could sense her anger rising to its breaking point. I wanted to see it spill over. And that's when I remembered the babies she had lost in China, the ones we never talked about. "Then I wish I'd never been born!" I shouted. "I wish I were dead! Like them."

It was as if I had said magic words. Alakazam!—and her face went blank, her mouth closed, her arms went slack, and she backed out of the room, stunned, as if she were blowing away like a small brown leaf, thin, brittle, lifeless.

It was not the only disappointment my mother felt in me. In the years that followed, I failed her so many times, each time asserting my will, my right to fall short of expectations. I didn't get straight As. I didn't become class president. I didn't get into Stanford. I dropped out of college.

For unlike my mother, I did not believe I could be anything I wanted to be. I could only be me.

And for all those years, we never talked about the disaster at the recital or my terrible accusations afterward at the piano bench. All that remained unchecked, like a betrayal that was now unspeakable. So I never found a way to ask her why she had hoped for something so large that failure was inevitable.

And even worse, I never asked her what frightened me the most: Why had she given up hope?

For after our struggle at the piano, she never mentioned my playing again. The lessons stopped, the lid to the piano was closed, shutting out the dust, my misery, and her dreams.

So she surprised me. A few years ago, she offered to give me the piano, for my thirtieth birthday. I had not played in all those years. I saw the offer as a sign of forgiveness, a tremendous burden removed.

"Are you sure?" I asked shyly. "I mean, won't you and Dad miss it?"

"No, this your piano," she said firmly. "Always your piano. You only one can play."

"Well, I probably can't play anymore," I said. "It's been years."

"You pick up fast," said my mother, as if she knew this was certain. "You have natural talent. You could been genius if you want to."

"No I couldn't."

"You just not trying," said my mother. And she was neither angry nor sad. She said it as if announcing a fact that could never be disproved. "Take it," she said.

But I didn't at first. It was enough that she had offered it to me. And after that, every time I saw it in my parents' living room, standing in front of the bay window, it made me feel proud, as if it were a shiny trophy I had won back.

Last week I sent a tuner over to my parents' apartment and had the piano reconditioned, for purely sentimental reasons. My mother had died a few months before and I had been getting things in order for my father, a little bit at a time. I put the jewelry in special silk pouches. The sweaters she had knitted in yellow, pink, bright orange—all the colors I hated—I put those in moth-proof boxes. I found some old Chinese silk dresses, the kind with little slits up the sides. I rubbed the old silk against my skin, then wrapped them in tissue and decided to take them home with me.

After I had the piano tuned, I opened the lid and touched the keys. It sounded even richer than I remembered. Really, it was a very good piano. Inside the bench were the same exercise notes with handwritten scales, the same secondhand music books with their covers held together with yellow tape.

I opened up the Schumann book to the dark little piece I had played at the recital. It was on the left-hand side of the page, "Pleading Child." It looked more difficult than I remembered. I played a few bars, surprised at how easily the notes came back to me.

And for the first time, or so it seemed, I noticed the piece on the right-hand side. It was called "Perfectly Contented." I tried to play this one as well. It had a lighter melody but with the same flowing rhythm and turned out to be quite easy. "Pleading Child" was shorter but slower; "Perfectly Contented" was longer but faster. And after I played them both a few times, I realized they were two halves of the same song.

Jhumpa Lahiri
(1967–)

Lahiri's Bengali parents moved to Rhode Island when she was a baby. She graduated from Barnard College and received a Ph.D. in Renaissance Studies from Boston University. *Interpreter of Maladies*, in which "A Temporary Matter" is the first (and saddest) story, came out in 1999 and received the Pulitzer Prize. Her first novel, *The Namesake* (2003), was made into a movie directed by Mira Nair. In 2008 her collection of stories, *Unaccustomed Earth*, told the stories of second- and third-generation hybrid Indian Americans.

A Temporary Matter (1998)

The notice informed them that it was a temporary matter: for five days their electricity would be cut off for one hour, beginning at eight p.m. A line had gone down in the last snowstorm, and the repairmen were going to take advantage of the milder evenings to set it right. The work would affect only the houses on the quiet tree-lined street, within walking distance of a row of brick-faced stores and a trolley stop, where Shoba and Shukumar had lived for three years.

"It's good of them to warn us," Shoba conceded after reading the notice aloud, more for her own benefit than Shukumar's. She let the strap of her leather satchel, plump with files, slip from her shoulders, and left it in the hallway as she walked into the kitchen. She wore a navy blue poplin raincoat over grey sweatpants and white sneakers, looking, at thirty-three, like the type of woman she'd once claimed she would never resemble.

She'd come from the gym. Her cranberry lipstick was visible only on the outer reaches of her mouth, and her eyeliner had left charcoal patches beneath her lower lashes. She used to look this way sometimes, Shukumar thought, on mornings after a party or a night at a bar, when she'd been too lazy to wash her face, too eager to collapse into his arms. She dropped a sheaf of mail on the table without a glance. Her eyes were still fixed on the notice in her other hand. "But they should do this sort of thing during the day."

"When I'm here, you mean," Shukumar said. He put a glass lid on a pot of lamb, adjusting it so only the slightest bit of steam could escape. Since January he'd been working at home, trying to complete the final chapters of his dissertation on agrarian revolts in India. "When do the repairs start?"

"It says March nineteenth. Is today the nineteenth?" Shoba walked over to the framed corkboard that hung on the wall by the fridge, bare except for a calendar of William Morris wallpaper patterns. She looked at it as if for the first time, studying the wallpaper pattern carefully on the top half before allowing her eyes to fall to the numbered grid on the bottom. A friend had sent the calendar in the mail as a Christmas gift, even though Shoba and Shukumar hadn't celebrated Christmas that year.

"Today then," Shoba announced. "You have a dentist appointment next Friday, by the way."

He ran his tongue over the tops of his teeth; he'd forgotten to brush them that morning. It wasn't the first time. He hadn't left the house at all that day, or the day before. The more Shoba stayed out, the more she began putting in extra hours at work and taking on additional projects, the more he wanted to stay in, not even leaving to get the mail, or to buy fruit or wine at the stores by the trolley stop.

Six months ago, in September, Shukumar was at an academic conference in Baltimore when Shoba went into labor, three weeks before her due date. He hadn't wanted to go to the conference, but she had insisted; it was important to make contacts, and he would be entering the job market next year. She told him that she had his number at the hotel, and a copy of his schedule and flight numbers, and she had arranged with her friend Gillian for a ride to the hospital in the event of an emergency. When the cab pulled away that morning for the airport, Shoba stood waving goodbye in her robe, with one arm resting on the mound of her belly as if it were a perfectly natural part of her body.

Each time he thought of that moment, the last moment he saw Shoba pregnant, it was the cab he remembered most, a station wagon, painted red with blue lettering. It was cavernous compared to their own car. Although Shukumar was six feet tall, with hands too big ever to rest comfortably in the pockets of his jeans, he felt dwarfed in the back seat. As the cab sped down Beacon Street, he imagined a day when he and Shoba might need to buy a station wagon of their own, to cart their children back and forth from music lessons and dentist appointments. He imagined himself gripping the wheel, as Shoba turned around to hand the children juice boxes. Once, these images of parenthood had troubled

Shukumar, adding to his anxiety that he was still a student at thirty-five. But that early autumn morning, the trees still heavy with bronze leaves, he welcomed the image for the first time.

A member of the staff had found him somehow among the identical convention rooms and handed him a stiff square of stationery. It was only a telephone number, but Shukumar knew it was the hospital. When he returned to Boston it was over. The baby had been born dead. Shoba was lying on a bed, asleep, in a private room so small there was barely enough space to stand beside her, in a wing of the hospital they hadn't been to on the tour for expectant parents. Her placenta had weakened and she'd had a cesarean, though not quickly enough. The doctor explained that these things happen. He smiled in the kindest way it was possible to smile at people known only professionally. Shoba would be back on her feet in a few weeks. There was nothing to indicate that she would not be able to have children in the future.

These days Shoba was always gone by the time Shukumar woke up. He would open his eyes and see the long black hairs she shed on her pillow and think of her, dressed, sipping her third cup of coffee already, in her office downtown, where she searched for typographical errors in textbooks and marked them, in a code she had once explained to him, with an assortment of colored pencils. She would do the same for his dissertation, she promised, when it was ready. He envied her the specificity of her task, so unlike the elusive nature of his. He was a mediocre student who had a facility for absorbing details without curiosity. Until September he had been diligent if not dedicated, summarizing chapters, outlining arguments on pads of yellow lined paper. But now he would lie in their bed until he grew bored, gazing at his side of the closet which Shoba always left partly open, at the row of the tweed jackets and corduroy trousers he would not have to choose from to teach his classes that semester. After the baby died it was too late to withdraw from his teaching duties. But his adviser had arranged things so that he had the spring semester to himself. Shukumar was in his sixth year of graduate school. "That and the summer should give you a good push," his adviser had said. "You should be able to wrap things up by next September."

But nothing was pushing Shukumar. Instead he thought of how he and Shoba had become experts at avoiding each other in their three-bedroom house, spending as much time on separate floors as possible. He thought of how he no longer looked forward to weekends, when she sat for hours on the sofa with her colored pencils and her files, so that he feared that putting on a record in his own house might be rude. He thought of how long it had been since she looked into his eyes and smiled, or whispered his name on those rare occasions they still reached for each other's bodies before sleeping.

In the beginning he had believed that it would pass, that he and Shoba would get through it all somehow. She was only thirty-three. She was strong, on her feet again. But it wasn't a consolation. It was often nearly lunchtime when Shukumar would finally pull himself out of bed and head downstairs to the coffeepot, pouring out the extra bit Shoba left for him, along with an empty mug, on the countertop.

Shukumar gathered onion skins in his hands and let them drop into the garbage pail, on top of the ribbons of fat he'd trimmed from the lamb. He ran the water in the sink, soaking the knife and the cutting board, and rubbed a lemon half along his fingertips to get rid of the garlic smell, a trick he'd learned from Shoba. It was seven-thirty. Through the window he saw the sky, like soft black pitch. Uneven banks of snow still lined the sidewalks, though it was warm enough for people to walk about without hats or gloves. Nearly three feet had fallen in the last storm, so that for a week people had to walk single file, in narrow trenches. For a week that was Shukumar's excuse for not leaving the house. But now the trenches were widening, and water drained steadily into grates in the pavement.

"The lamb won't be done by eight," Shukumar said. "We may have to eat in the dark."

"We can light candles," Shoba suggested. She unclipped her hair, coiled neatly at her nape during the days, and pried the sneakers from her feet without untying them. "I'm going to shower before the lights go," she said, heading for the staircase. "I'll be down."

Shukumar moved her satchel and her sneakers to the side of the fridge. She wasn't this way before. She used to put her coat on a hanger, her sneakers in the closet, and she paid bills as soon as they came. But now she treated the house as if it were a hotel. The fact that the yellow chintz armchair in the living room clashed with the blue-and-maroon Turkish carpet no longer bothered her. On the enclosed porch at the back of the house, a crisp white bag still sat on the wicker chaise, filled with lace she had once planned to turn into curtains.

While Shoba showered, Shukumar went into the downstairs bathroom and found a new toothbrush in its box beneath the sink. The cheap, stiff bristles hurt his gums, and he spit some blood into the basin. The spare brush was one of many stored in a metal basket. Shoba had bought them once when they were on sale, in the event that a visitor decided, at the last minute, to spend the night.

It was typical of her. She was the type to prepare for surprises, good and bad. If she found a skirt or a purse she liked she bought two. She kept the bonuses from her job in a separate bank account in her name. It hadn't bothered him. His own mother had fallen to pieces when his father died, abandoning the house he grew up in and moving back to Calcutta, leaving Shukumar to settle it all. He liked that Shoba was different. It astonished him, her capacity to think ahead. When she used to do the shopping, the pantry was always stocked with extra bottles of olive and corn oil, depending on whether they were cooking Italian or Indian. There were endless boxes of pasta in all shapes and colors, zippered sacks of basmati rice, whole sides of lambs and goats from the Muslim butchers at Haymarket, chopped up and frozen in endless plastic bags. Every other Saturday they wound through the maze of stalls Shukumar eventually knew by heart. He watched in disbelief as she bought more food, trailing behind her with canvas bags as she pushed through the crowd, arguing under the morning sun with boys too young to shave but already missing teeth, who twisted up brown paper bags of artichokes, plums, gingerroot, and yams, and dropped them on their scales, and tossed them to Shoba one by one. She didn't mind being jostled, even when she was pregnant. She was tall, and broad-shouldered, with hips that her obstetrician assured her were made for childbearing. During the drive back home, as the car curved along the Charles, they invariably marveled at how much food they'd bought.

It never went to waste. When friends dropped by, Shoba would throw together meals that appeared to have taken half a day to prepare, from things she had frozen and bottled, not cheap things in tins but peppers she had marinated herself with rosemary; and chutneys that she cooked on Sundays, stirring boiling pots of tomatoes and prunes. Her labeled mason jars lined the shelves of the kitchen, in endless sealed pyramids, enough, they'd agreed, to last for their grandchildren to taste. They'd eaten it all by now. Shukumar had been going through their supplies steadily, preparing meals for the two of them, measuring out cupfuls of rice, defrosting bags of meat day after day. He combed through her cookbooks every afternoon, following her penciled instructions to use two teaspoons of ground coriander seeds instead of one, or red lentils instead of yellow. Each of the recipes was dated, telling the first time they had eaten the dish together. April 2, cauliflower with fennel. January 14, chicken with almonds and sultanas. He had no memory of eating those meals, and yet there they were, recorded in her neat proofreader's hand. Shukumar enjoyed cooking now. It was the one thing that made him feel productive. If it weren't for him, he knew, Shoba would eat a bowl of cereal for her dinner.

Tonight, with no lights, they would have to eat together. For months now they'd served themselves from the stove, and he'd taken his plate into his study, letting the meal grow cold on his desk before shoving it into his mouth without pause, while Shoba took her plate to the living room and watched game shows, or proofread files with her arsenal of colored pencils at hand.

At some point in the evening she visited him. When he heard her approach he would put away his novel and begin typing sentences. She would rest her hands on his shoulders and stare with him into the blue glow of the computer screen. "Don't work too hard," she would say after a minute or two, and head off to bed. It was the one time in the day she sought him out, and yet he'd come to dread it. He knew it was something she forced herself to do. She would look around the walls of the room, which they had decorated together last summer with a border of march- ing ducks and rabbits playing trumpets and drums. By the end of August there was a cherry crib under the window, a white changing table with mint-green knobs, and a rocking chair with checkered cushions. Shuku- mar had disassembled it all before bringing Shoba back from the hospi- tal, scraping off the rabbits and ducks with a spatula. For some reason the room did not haunt him the way it haunted Shoba. In January, when he stopped working at his carrel in the library, he set up his desk there deliberately, partly because the room soothed him, and partly because it was a place Shoba avoided.

Shukumar returned to the kitchen and began to open drawers. He tried to locate a candle among the scissors, the eggbeaters and whisks, the mortar and pestle she'd bought in a bazaar in Calcutta, and used to pound garlic cloves and cardamom pods, back when she used to cook. He found a flashlight, but no batteries, and a half-empty box of birthday candles. Shoba had thrown him a surprise birthday party last May. One hundred and twenty people had crammed into the house—all the friends and the friends of friends they now systematically avoided. Bottles of vinho verde had nested in a bed of ice in the bathtub. Shoba was in her fifth month, drinking ginger ale from a martini glass. She had made a vanilla cream cake with custard and spun sugar. All night she kept Shukumar's long fin- gers linked with hers as they walked among the guests at the party.

Since September their only guest had been Shoba's mother. She came from Arizona and stayed with them for two months after Shoba returned from the hospital. She cooked dinner every night, drove herself to the supermarket, washed their clothes, put them away. She was a religious woman. She set up a small shrine, a framed picture of a lavender-faced goddess and a plate of marigold petals, on the bedside table in the guest room, and prayed twice a day for healthy grandchildren in the future. She was polite to Shukumar without being friendly. She folded his sweaters with an expertise she had learned from her job in a department store. She replaced a missing button on his winter coat and knit him a beige and brown scarf, presenting it to him without the least bit of ceremony, as if he had only dropped it and hadn't noticed. She never talked to him about Shoba; once, when he mentioned the baby's death, she looked up from her knitting, and said, "But you weren't even there."

It struck him as odd that there were no real candles in the house. That Shoba hadn't prepared for such an ordinary emergency. He looked now for something to put the birthday candles in and settled on the soil of a potted ivy that normally sat on the windowsill over the sink. Even though the plant was inches from the tap, the soil was so dry that he had to water it first before the candles would stand straight. He pushed aside the things on the kitchen table, the piles of mail, the unread library books. He remembered their first meals there, when they were so thrilled to be married, to be living together in the same house at last, that they would just reach for each other foolishly, more eager to make love than to eat. He put down two embroidered place mats, a wedding gift from an uncle in Lucknow, and set out the plates and wineglasses they usually saved for guests. He put the ivy in the middle, the white-edged, star-shaped leaves girded by ten little candles. He switched on the digital clock radio and tuned it to a jazz station.

"What's all this?" Shoba said when she came downstairs. Her hair was wrapped in a thick white towel. She undid the towel and draped it over a chair, allowing her hair, damp and dark, to fall across her back. As she walked absently toward the stove she took out a few tangles with her fingers. She wore a clean pair of sweatpants, a T-shirt, an old flannel robe. Her stomach was flat again, her waist narrow before the flare of her hips, the belt of the robe tied in a floppy knot.

It was nearly eight. Shukumar put the rice on the table and the lentils from the night before into the microwave oven, punching the numbers on the timer.

"You made *rogan josh*," Shoba observed, looking through the glass lid at the bright paprika stew.

Shukumar took out a piece of lamb, pinching it quickly between his fingers so as not to scald himself. He prodded a larger piece with a serving spoon to make sure the meat slipped easily from the bone. "It's ready," he announced.

The microwave had just beeped when the lights went out, and the music disappeared.

"Perfect timing," Shoba said.

"All I could find were birthday candles." He lit up the ivy, keeping the rest of the candles and a book of matches by his plate.

"It doesn't matter," she said, running a finger along the stem of her wineglass. "It looks lovely."

In the dimness, he knew how she sat, a bit forward in her chair, ankles crossed against the lowest rung, left elbow on the table. During his search for the candles, Shukumar had found a bottle of wine in a crate he had thought was empty. He clamped the bottle between his knees while he turned in the corkscrew. He worried about spilling, and so he picked up the glasses and held them close to his lap while he filled them. They served themselves, stirring the rice with their forks, squinting as they extracted bay leaves and cloves from the stew. Every few minutes Shukumar lit a few more birthday candles and drove them into the soil of the pot.

"It's like India," Shoba said, watching him tend his makeshift candelabra. "Sometimes the current disappears for hours at a stretch. I once had to attend an entire rice ceremony in the dark. The baby just cried and cried. It must have been so hot."

Their baby had never cried, Shukumar considered. Their baby would never have a rice ceremony, even though Shoba had already made the guest list, and decided on which of her three brothers she was going to ask to feed the child its first taste of solid food, at six months if it was a boy, seven if it was a girl.

"Are you hot?" he asked her. He pushed the blazing ivy pot to the other end of the table, closer to the piles of books and mail, making it even more difficult for them to see each other. He was suddenly irritated that he couldn't go upstairs and sit in front of the computer.

"No. It's delicious," she said, tapping her plate with her fork. "It really is."

He refilled the wine in her glass. She thanked him.

They weren't like this before. Now he had to struggle to say something that interested her, something that made her look up from her plate, or from her proofreading files. Eventually he gave up trying to amuse her. He learned not to mind the silences.

"I remember during power failures at my grandmother's house, we all had to say something," Shoba continued. He could barely see her face, but from her tone he knew her eyes were narrowed, as if trying to focus on a distant object. It was a habit of hers.

"Like what?"

"I don't know. A little poem. A joke. A fact about the world. For some reason my relatives always wanted me to tell them the names of my friends in America. I don't know why the information was so interesting to them. The last time I saw my aunt she asked after four girls I went to elementary school with in Tucson. I barely remember them now."

Shukumar hadn't spent as much time in India as Shoba had. His parents, who settled in New Hampshire, used to go back without him. The first time he'd gone as an infant he'd nearly died of amoebic dysentery. His father, a nervous type, was afraid to take him again, in case something were to happen, and left him with his aunt and uncle in Concord. As a teenager he preferred sailing camp or scooping ice cream during the summers to going to Calcutta. It wasn't until after his father died, in his last year of college, that the country began to interest him, and he studied its history from course books as if it were any other subject. He wished now that he had his own childhood story of India.

"Let's do that," she said suddenly.

"Do what?"

"Say something to each other in the dark."

"Like what? I don't know any jokes."

"No, no jokes." She thought for a minute. "How about telling each other something we've never told before."

"I used to play this game in high school," Shukumar recalled. "When I got drunk."

"You're thinking of truth or dare. This is different. Okay, I'll start." She took a sip of wine. "The first time I was alone in your apartment, I looked in your address book to see if you'd written me in. I think we'd known each other two weeks."

"Where was I?"

"You went to answer the telephone in the other room. It was your mother, and I figured it would be a long call. I wanted to know if you'd promoted me from the margins of your newspaper."

"Had I?"

"No. But I didn't give up on you. Now it's your turn."

He couldn't think of anything, but Shoba was waiting for him to speak. She hadn't appeared so determined in months. What was there left to say to her? He thought back to their first meeting, four years earlier at a lecture hall in Cambridge, where a group of Bengali poets were giving a recital. They'd ended up side by side, on folding wooden chairs. Shukumar was soon bored; he was unable to decipher the literary diction, and couldn't join the rest of the audience as they sighed and nodded solemnly after certain phrases. Peering at the newspaper folded in his lap, he studied the temperatures of cities around the world. Ninety-one degrees in Singapore yesterday, fifty-one in Stockholm. When he turned his head to the left, he saw a woman next to him making a grocery list on the back of a folder, and was startled to find that she was beautiful.

"Okay," he said, remembering. "The first time we went out to dinner, to the Portuguese place, I forgot to tip the waiter. I went back the next morning, found out his name, left money with the manager."

"You went all the way back to Somerville just to tip a waiter?"

"I took a cab."

"Why did you forget to tip the waiter?"

The birthday candles had burned out, but he pictured her face clearly in the dark, the wide tilting eyes, the full grape-toned lips, the fall at age two from her high chair still visible as a comma on her chin. Each day, Shukumar noticed, her beauty, which had once overwhelmed him, seemed to fade. The cosmetics that had seemed superfluous were necessary now, not to improve her but to define her somehow.

"By the end of the meal I had a funny feeling that I might marry you," he said, admitting it to himself as well as to her for the first time. "It must have distracted me."

The next night Shoba came home earlier than usual. There was lamb left over from the evening before, and Shukumar heated it up so that they were able to eat by seven. He'd gone out that day, through the melting snow, and bought a packet of taper candles from the corner store, and batteries to fit the flashlight. He had the candles ready on the countertop, standing in brass holders shaped like lotuses, but they ate under the glow of the copper-shaded ceiling lamp that hung over the table.

When they had finished eating, Shukumar was surprised to see that Shoba was stacking her plate on top of his, and then carrying them over to the sink. He had assumed she would retreat to the living room, behind her barricade of files.

"Don't worry about the dishes," he said, taking them from her hands.

"It seems silly not to," she replied, pouring a drop of detergent onto a sponge. "It's nearly eight o'clock."

His heart quickened. All day Shukumar had looked forward to the lights going out. He thought about what Shoba had said the night before, about looking in his address book. It felt good to remember her as she was then, how bold yet nervous she'd been when they first met, how hopeful. They stood side by side at the sink, their reflections fitting together in the frame of the window. It made him shy, the way he felt the first time they stood together in a mirror. He couldn't recall the last time they'd been photographed. They had stopped attending parties, went nowhere together. The film in his camera still contained pictures of Shoba, in the yard, when she was pregnant.

After finishing the dishes, they leaned against the counter, drying their hands on either end of a towel. At eight o'clock the house went black. Shukumar lit the wicks of the candles, impressed by their long, steady flames.

"Let's sit outside," Shoba said. "I think it's warm still."

They each took a candle and sat down on the steps. It seemed strange to be sitting outside with patches of snow still on the ground. But everyone was out of their houses tonight, the air fresh enough to make people restless. Screen doors opened and closed. A small parade of neighbors passed by with flashlights.

"We're going to the bookstore to browse," a silver-haired man called out. He was walking with his wife, a thin woman in a windbreaker, and holding a dog on a leash. They were the Bradfords, and they had tucked a sympathy card into Shoba and Shukumar's mailbox back in September. "I hear they've got their power."

"They'd better," Shukumar said. "Or you'll be browsing in the dark."

The woman laughed, slipping her arm through the crook of her husband's elbow. "Want to join us?"

"No thanks," Shoba and Shukumar called out together. It surprised Shukumar that his words matched hers.

He wondered what Shoba would tell him in the dark. The worst possibilities had already run through his head. That she'd had an affair. That she didn't respect him for being thirty-five and still a student. That she blamed him for being in Baltimore the way her mother did. But he knew those things weren't true. She'd been faithful, as had he. She believed in him. It was she who had insisted he go to Baltimore. What didn't they know about each other? He knew she curled her fingers tightly when she slept, that her body twitched during bad dreams. He knew it was honey-dew she favoured over cantaloupe. He knew that when they returned from the hospital the first thing she did when she walked into the house was pick out objects of theirs and toss them into a pile in the hallway: books from the shelves, plants from the windowsills, paintings from walls, photos from tables, pots and pans that hung from the hooks over the stove. Shukumar had stepped out of her way, watching as she moved methodically from room to room. When she was satisfied, she stood there staring at the pile she'd made, her lips drawn back in such distaste that Shukumar had thought she would spit. Then she'd started to cry.

He began to feel cold as he sat there on the steps. He felt that he needed her to talk first, in order to reciprocate.

"That time when your mother came to visit us," she said finally. "When I said one night that I had to stay late at work, I went out with Gillian and had a martini."

He looked at her profile, the slender nose, the slightly masculine set of her jaw. He remembered that night well; eating with his mother, tired from teaching two classes back to back, wishing Shoba were there to say more of the right things because he came up with only the wrong ones. It had been twelve years since his father had died, and his mother had come to spend two weeks with him and Shoba, so they could honour his father's memory together. Each night his mother cooked something his father had liked, but she was too upset to eat the dishes herself; and her eyes would well up as Shoba stroked her hand. "It's so touching," Shoba had said to him at the time. Now he pictured Shoba with Gillian, in a bar with striped velvet sofas, the one they used to go to after the movies, making sure she got her extra olive, asking Gillian for a cigarette. He imagined her complaining, and Gillian sympathizing about visits from in-laws. It was Gillian who had driven Shoba to the hospital.

"Your turn," she said, stopping his thoughts.

At the end of their street Shukumar heard sounds of a drill and the electricians shouting over it. He looked at the darkened façades of the houses lining the street. Candles glowed in the windows of one. In spite of the warmth, smoke rose from the chimney.

"I cheated on my Oriental Civilization exam in college," he said. "It was my last semester, my last set of exams. My father had died a few months before. I could see the blue book of the guy next to me. He was an American guy, a maniac. He knew Urdu and Sanskrit. I couldn't remember if the verse we had to identify was an example of a *ghazal* or not. I looked at his answer and copied it down."

It had happened over fifteen years ago. He felt relief now, having told her.

She turned to him, looking not at his face, but at his shoes—old moccasins he wore as if they were slippers, the leather at the back permanently flattened. He wondered if it bothered her, what he'd said. She took his hand and pressed it. "You didn't have to tell me why you did it," she said, moving closer to him.

They sat together until nine o'clock, when the lights came on. They heard some people across the street clapping from their porch, and televisions being turned on. The Bradfords walked back down the street, eating ice-cream cones and waving. Shoba and Shukumar waved back. Then they stood up, his hand still in hers, and went inside.

Somehow, without saying anything, it had turned into this. Into an exchange of confessions—the little ways they'd hurt or disappointed each other, and themselves. The following day Shukumar thought for hours about what to say to her. He was torn between admitting that he once ripped out a photo of a woman in one of the fashion magazines she used to subscribe to and carried it in his books for a week, or saying that he really hadn't lost the sweater-vest she bought him for their third wedding anniversary but had exchanged it for cash at Filene's, and that he had gotten drunk alone in the middle of the day at a hotel bar. For their first anniversary, Shoba had cooked a ten-course dinner just for him. The vest depressed him. "My wife gave me a sweater-vest for our anniversary," he complained to the bartender, his head heavy with cognac. "What do you expect?" the bartender had replied. "You're married."

As for the picture of the woman, he didn't know why he'd ripped it out. She wasn't as pretty as Shoba. She wore a white sequinned dress, and had a sullen face and lean, mannish legs. Her bare arms were raised, her fists around her head, as if she were about to punch herself in the ears. It was an advertisement for stockings. Shoba had been pregnant at the time, her stomach suddenly immense, to the point where Shukumar no longer wanted to touch her. The first time he saw the picture he was lying in bed next to her, watching her as she read. When he noticed the magazine in the recycling pile he found the woman and tore out the page as carefully as he could. For about a week he allowed himself a glimpse each day. He felt an intense desire for the woman, but it was a desire that turned to disgust after a minute or two. It was the closest he'd come to infidelity.

He told Shoba about the sweater on the third night, the picture on the fourth. She said nothing as he spoke, expressed no protest or reproach. She simply listened, and then she took his hand, pressing it as she had before. On the third night, she told him that once after a lecture they'd attended, she let him speak to the chairman of his department without telling him that he had a dab of pâté on his chin. She'd been irritated with him for some reason, and so she'd let him go on and on, about securing his fellowship for the following semester, without putting a finger to her own chin as a signal. The fourth night, she said that she never liked the one poem he'd ever published in his life, in a literary magazine in Utah. He'd written the poem after meeting Shoba. She added that she found the poem sentimental.

Something happened when the house was dark. They were able to talk to each other again. The third night after supper they'd sat together on the sofa, and once it was dark he began kissing her awkwardly on her forehead and her face, and though it was dark he closed his eyes, and knew that she did, too. The fourth night they walked carefully upstairs, to bed, feeling together for the final step with their feet before the landing, and making love with a desperation they had forgotten. She wept without sound, and whispered his name, and traced his eyebrows with her finger in the dark. As he made love to her he wondered what he would say to her the next night, and what she would say, the thought of it exciting him. "Hold me," he said, "hold me in your arms." By the time the lights came back on downstairs, they'd fallen asleep.

The morning of the fifth night Shukumar found another notice from the electric company in the mailbox. The line had been repaired ahead of schedule, it said. He was disappointed. He had planned on making shrimp *malai* for Shoba, but when he arrived at the store he didn't feel like cooking anymore. It wasn't the same, he thought, knowing that the lights wouldn't go out. In the store the shrimp looked grey and thin. The coconut milk tin was dusty and overpriced. Still, he bought them, along with a beeswax candle and two bottles of wine.

She came home at seven-thirty. "I suppose this is the end of our game," he said when he saw her reading the notice.

She looked at him. "You can still light candles if you want." She hadn't been to the gym tonight. She wore a suit beneath the raincoat. Her makeup had been retouched recently.

When she went upstairs to change, Shukumar poured himself some wine and put on a record, a Thelonius Monk album he knew she liked.

When she came downstairs they ate together. She didn't thank him or compliment him. They simply ate in a darkened room, in the glow of a beeswax candle. They had survived a difficult time. They finished off the shrimp. They finished off the first bottle of wine and moved on to the second. They sat together until the candle had nearly burned away. She shifted in her chair, and Shukumar thought that she was about to say something. But instead she blew out the candle, stood up, turned on the light switch, and sat down again.

"Shouldn't we keep the lights off?" Shukumar asked.

She set her plate aside and clasped her hands on the table. "I want you to see my face when I tell you this," she said gently.

His heart began to pound. The day she told him she was pregnant, she had used the very same words, saying them in the same gentle way, turning off the basketball game he'd been watching on television. He hadn't been prepared then. Now he was.

Only he didn't want her to be pregnant again. He didn't want to have to pretend to be happy.

"I've been looking for an apartment and I've found one," she said, narrowing her eyes on something, it seemed, behind his left shoulder. It was nobody's fault, she continued. They'd been through enough. She needed some time alone. She had money saved up for a security deposit. The apartment was on Beacon Hill, so she could walk to work. She had signed the lease that night before coming home.

She wouldn't look at him, but he stared at her. It was obvious that she'd rehearsed the lines. All this time she'd been looking for an apartment, testing the water pressure, asking a Realtor if heat and hot water were included in the rent. It sickened Shukumar, knowing that she had spent these past evenings preparing for a life without him. He was relieved and yet he was sickened. This was what she'd been trying to tell him for the past four evenings. This was the point of her game.

Now it was his turn to speak. There was something he'd sworn he would never tell her, and for six months he had done his best to block it from his mind. Before the ultrasound she had asked the doctor not to tell her the sex of their child, and Shukumar had agreed. She had wanted it to be a surprise.

Later, those few times they talked about what had happened, she said at least they'd been spared that knowledge. In a way she almost took pride in her decision, for it enabled her to seek refuge in a mystery. He knew that she assumed it was a mystery for him, too. He'd arrived too late from Baltimore—when it was all over and she was lying on the hospital bed. But he hadn't. He'd arrived early enough to see their baby, and to hold him before they cremated him. At first he had recoiled at the suggestion, but the doctor said holding the baby might help him with the process of grieving. Shoba was asleep. The baby had been cleaned off, his bulbous lids shut tight to the world.

"Our baby was a boy," he said. "His skin was more red than brown. He had black hair on his head. He weighed almost five pounds. His fingers were curled shut, just like yours in the night."

Shoba looked at him now, her face contorted with sorrow. He had cheated on a college exam, ripped a picture of a woman out of a magazine. He had returned a sweater and got drunk in the middle of the day instead. These were the things he had told her. He had held his son, who had known life only within her, against his chest in a darkened room in an unknown wing of the hospital. He had held him until a nurse knocked and took him away, and he promised himself that day that he would never tell Shoba, because he still loved her then, and it was the one thing in her life that she had wanted to be a surprise.

Shukumar stood up and stacked his plate on top of hers. He carried the plates to the sink, but instead of running the tap he looked out the window. Outside the evening was still warm, and the Bradfords were walking arm in arm. As he watched the couple the room went dark, and he spun around. Shoba had turned the lights off. She came back to the table and sat down, and after a moment Shukumar joined her. They wept together, for the things they now knew.

Acknowledgments

This anthology has undergone many changes since I first began to think about it in 2003, and I am grateful to a number of people who helped me in the early, middle, and late stages. Briallen Hopper and Jules Hurtado helped me track down texts in the Princeton University Library in 2003–2004; Adena Spingarn researched the writers and drafted versions of the headnotes in 2004–2005; and English Showalter took up the task of digitizing the texts, editing the headnotes, and helping with permissions up to the end. LuAnn Walther at Knopf envisioned it first as a companion to *A Jury of Her Peers* and encouraged me to prepare it. Diana Secker Tesdell, my editor at Vintage, was resourceful, tireless, practical, and endlessly supportive. Many thanks to all.

Permissions Acknowledgments

Elizabeth Bishop: "One Art" from *The Complete Poems 1927–1979* by Elizabeth Bishop, copyright © 1979, 1983 by Alice Helen Methfessel. Reprinted by permission of Farrar, Straus and Giroux, LLC.

Louise Bogan: "Evening in the Sanitarium," "Several Voices out of a Cloud," and "Women" from *The Blue Estuaries* by Louise Bogan, copyright © 1968 by Louise Bogan, copyright renewed 1996 by Ruth Limmer. Reprinted by permission of Farrar, Straus and Giroux, LLC.

Gwendolyn Brooks: "The Rise of Maud Martha," "The Bean Eaters," and "We Real Cool" by Gwendolyn Brooks. Reprinted by permission of Brooks Permissions.

Shirley Jackson: "The Lottery" from *The Lottery* by Shirley Jackson, copyright © 1948, 1949 by Shirley Jackson, copyright renewed 1976, 1977 by Laurence Hyman, Barry Hyman, Mrs. Sarah Webster and Mrs. Joanne Schnurer. Reprinted by permission of Farrar, Straus and Giroux, LLC.

Maxine Hong Kingston: "On Discovery" from *China Men* by Maxine Hong Kingston, copyright © 1977, 1978, 1979, 1980 by Maxine Hong Kingston. Reprinted by permission of Alfred A. Knopf, a division of Random House, Inc.

Jhumpa Lahiri: "A Temporary Matter" from *Interpreter of Maladies* by Jhumpa Lahiri, copyright © 1999 by Jhumpa Lahiri. All rights reserved. Reprinted by permission of Houghton Mifflin Harcourt Publishing Company.

Genevieve Taggard: "Everyday Alchemy" from *Collected Poems, 1918–1938* by Genevieve Taggard (Harper & Row, 1938). Reprinted by permission of Judith Benet Richardson.

Amy Tan: "Two Kinds" from *The Joy Luck Club* by Amy Tan, copyright © 1989 by Amy Tan. Reprinted by permission of G. P. Putnam's Sons, a division of Penguin Group (USA) Inc.

James Tiptree, Jr.: "The Last Flight of Dr. Ain," copyright © 1969, copyright renewed 1997 by James Tiptree, Jr., from *Her Smoke Rose Up Forever* by James Tiptree, Jr. Reprinted by permission of the author's estate and the estate's agents, the Virginia Kidd Agency, Inc.

Elinor Wylie: "Anti-feminist Song, for My Sister" from *Selected Works of Elinor Wylie* by Elinor Wylie, copyright © 2005 by Kent State University Press, Ohio.

Hisaye Yamamoto: "Seventeen Syllables" from *Seventeen Syllables* by Hisaye Yamamoto, copyright © 1998 by Rutgers, the State University. Reprinted by permission of Rutgers University Press.

Anzia Yezierska: "Wild Winter Love" from *How I Found America* by Anzia Yezierska, copyright © 1985, 1991 by Louise Levitas Henriksen. Reprinted by permission of Persea Books, Inc., New York.

ALSO BY ELAINE SHOWALTER

"*A work of astonishing vision, breadth, intelligence, and audacity. . . .*
Sure to be required reading for all who have an interest in
American literary history."
—Joyce Carol Oates

A JURY OF HER PEERS

Celebrating American Women Writers
from Anne Bradstreet to Annie Proulx

An unprecedented literary landmark: the first comprehensive history of
American women writers from 1650 to the present. In a narrative of
immense scope and fascination, here are more than 250 female writers,
including the famous—Harriet Beecher Stowe, Dorothy Parker, Flannery
O'Connor, and Toni Morrison, among others—and the little known,
from the early American bestselling novelist Catharine Sedgwick to the
Pulitzer Prize–winning playwright Susan Glaspell. Showalter integrates
women's contributions into our nation's literary heritage with brilliance
and flair, making the case for the unfairly overlooked and putting the
overrated firmly in their place.

Literary Criticism/978-1-4000-3442-0

VINTAGE BOOKS
Available from your local bookstore, or visit
www.randomhouse.com